Encyclopedia of
the Literature of Empire

MARY ELLEN SNODGRASS

Facts On File
An imprint of Infobase Publishing

ENCYCLOPEDIA OF THE LITERATURE OF EMPIRE

Facts On File, Inc.
An imprint of Infobase Publishing
132 West 31st Street
New York NY 10001

Library of Congress Cataloging-in-Publication Data

Snodgrass, Mary Ellen.
Encyclopedia of the literature of empire / Mary Ellen Snodgrass.
p.   cm.
Includes bibliographical references and index.
ISBN 978-0-8160-7524-9 (hc : alk. paper)
1. Imperialism in literature—Encyclopedias. 2. Colonies in literature—
Encyclopedias. 3. Power (Social sciences) in literature—Encyclopedias.
4. Politics in literature—Encyclopedias. 5. Slavery in literature—
Encyclopedias. I. Title. II. Title: Literature of empire.
PN56.I465.S66 2009
809'.933581—dc22
2008047154

You can find Facts On File on the World Wide Web at
http://www.factsonfile.com

Text design by Joan M. McEvoy
Cover design by Takeshi Takahashi

Printed in the United States of America

VB KT 10 9 8 7 6 5 4 3 2 1

This book is printed on acid-free paper
and contains 30 percent postconsumer recycled content.

He that ruleth over men must be just,
ruling in the fear of God.

—David, 2 Samuel 23:3

The silent pirates of the shore
Eat and sleep soft, and pocket more . . .
Here is the key to right and wrong:
Steal little but steal all day long.

**—Robert Louis Stevenson, "Robin and Ben"
in Moral Emblems and Other Poems (1921)**

Our right is to live and be free;
Freedom will not come from outside.
It is only in ourselves united.

—Filipino fishermen's song

CONTENTS

Acknowledgments

Barry and Diana Norman, Writers
Stevenage, England

Hannah Owen, Deputy Director
Mary Sizemore, Director
Patrick Beaver Library
Hickory, North Carolina

Wanda Rozzelle, Reference Librarian
Catawba County Library
Newton, North Carolina

Mark Schumacher, Reference Librarian
Jackson Library, University of North Carolina–
    Greensboro
Greensboro, North Carolina

I am especially grateful to Stephen Rhind-Tutt and Eileen Lawrence, president and vice president, respectively, of Alexander Street Press, Alexandria, Virginia, for providing primary sources. Additional thanks go to my publicist, Joan Lail, whose advice dissuades me from folly.

INTRODUCTION

A SURVEY OF THE LITERATURE OF EMPIRE

From Ur to Judah, from Ireland to the Gilbert Islands, the dominion of one nation over others has been cyclical throughout history. Strong nations take advantage of weaker ones, sometimes cloaking their aggression within altruistic or religious causes. Imperialists have found means to rationalize outright conquest as exemplified by the crusader lore of Geoffrey de Villehardouin and Chrétien de Troyes, Anna Comnena's *Alexiad*, Gabriele D'Annunzio's *Poems on Naval Deeds*, and Snorri Sturluson's Icelandic *Prose Edda*. The condition of the dominated, however, has also managed to find expression—for example, the Sufist prayers of Rumi; the Hebrew epic Exodus; the heroic tales from Firdawsi's *Book of Kings*; and the beast fables of Aesop, Marie de France, and Vishnu Sarma's *Panchatantra*. The causes of freedom and individualism enliven and inform wisdom literature and Scripture, such as in the Vedas and the Koran. Unrepressed, the outrage of subject peoples in world literature is voiced through meditations on kingship and admonitions to monarchs to satisfy the needs and demands of the conquered, such as in Herodotus's *Histories, El Cid*, and Miguel de Cervantes's *Don Quixote*. In retaliation for hurt and loss, threnody, satire, and invective express the grievances of the intimidated, dispossessed, enslaved, and imprisoned, particularly in works by Anna Akhmatova, Yevgeny Yevtushenko, and Jonathan Swift. Short stories, novels, and dramas capture the predicament of the civil servant, the go-betweens, as examined by (among others) Biragio Diop, George Orwell, Ruth Prawer Jhabvala, Rudyard Kipling, Peter Carey, and Yi Kwangsu, whose works decry the subjugation of the oppressed. Lyrics, psalms, and vignettes allow the vassal's temporary escape from harsh reality, giving rise to romantic illusions, fantasies, and nature pastorals, such as in the writing of Yamanoue no Okura, Johann Wolfgang von Goethe, and Li Bo.

The longest-lived empires generated thought-provoking narratives on the human condition, as evidenced by the *I Ching*, the *Epic of Gilgamesh*, the Avesta, the Bhagavad Gita, and the *Popul Vuh*. A variety of literature was influenced by the downfall of such empires as those of the Mayans and Persians and the demise of the Roman Republic. Julius Caesar's assassination precipitated 17 years of political chaos resulting in the gestation and birth of the Imperium Romanum. Upheaval and insecurity demonstrated a historical truism—that unsettled times produce great literature. During the Augustan era of senatorial purges, death lists, and reformulation of the national credo, Horace produced satires, belles lettres, epodes, and a miniature version of his own exile in the beast fable "The City Mouse and the Country Mouse." Virgil completed 10 pastorals for his *Eclogues* as well as the *Aeneid*, a propaganda epic validating Rome's self-image.

After the Roman Empire settled into peace and prosperity, an abundance of classics exemplified the nation's literary achievements, from the letters of Pliny the Younger to Suetonius's *Lives of the Caesars* and Flavius Josephus's *History of the Jewish War*. Literary reflection on past traditions and on emerging customs and mores reflected both hope and unease with the violent process that had wrenched Rome from its conservative republican moorings. In the silver age (A.D. first century), reaction to corruption in the imperial families led to a moral renaissance. Flagrant immoral public and private behavior inspired Roman writers to urge dignity, fortitude, self-restraint, and respect for God and nation, the lapsed values on which the republic had once prided itself. The theme of *prisca virtus* (old-fashioned values) returned in the works of Tertullian and Plutarch, who advocated gravitas and concern for spirituality, marriage, and future generations. Unlike the evolving Christian theory of virtue as goodness or righteousness by Paul of Tarsus among others, the Roman concept of *virtus* (strength) in period writings reverted to the original implications of the root word *vir* (man) to imply "all that becomes a man."

Throughout the world, religious and secular authors struggled to sustain endangered beliefs and ideals. The key writers—such as Augustine, Du Fu, and al-Jahiz—encouraged flagging spirits to throw off oppression. Marco Polo's account of his travels, Ibn Battuta's *On the Curiosities of Cities and the Wonders of Travel*, Alfred the Great's *Anglo-Saxon Chronicle*, and Niccolò Machiavelli's *The Prince* lauded human will and achievement. At a starting point for feminist literature, women seized opportunities to voice their perspectives, the focus of *The Thousand and One Nights*, the Japanese court diaries of Izumi Shikibu and Murasaki Shikibu, and Christine de Pisan's *Hymn to Joan of Arc*.

From the late 16th century into modern times, the possibilities of compromise, reconciliation, and peace imbued William Shakespeare's *The Merchant of Venice* and *The Tempest*; Voltaire's *Candide*; and *The White Roots of Peace*, a social philosophy and guide to Native American governance practiced by the Iroquois. While France, Great Britain, and Spain vied for control of the New World, the vicious extremes of conquest and slavery sharpened Bartolomé de Las Casas's *History of the Indies*, Garcilaso de la Vega's *The Florida of the Inca*, *The Interesting Narrative of the Life of Olaudah Equiano*, Alexandre Dumas's *The Count of Monte Cristo*, and Matthew Gregory Lewis's "The Anaconda." Women held fast to their points of view, expressed in Aphra Behn's *Oroonoko*; Maria Edgeworth's *Castle Rackrent*; Anzia Yezierska's *Salome of the Tenements*; and *The History of Mary Prince, a West Indian Slave*. The intellectual curiosity of such women as the traveler Isabella Bird, the writer Pauline Johnson, the governess Anna Leonowens, and the pioneer Catherine Parr Traill led to journeys to remote outposts. Humanitarian writings expressed a joy in travel and frontier living tinged with regret for damaged nature and the sufferings of the subjugated.

In the late 19th and early 20th centuries, the slow collapse of imperialism in Europe, South and central Africa, the Caribbean, Korea, and Russia and Siberia inspired subjective appraisals of oppression and crushed hopes. Loss and regret invigorated the poems of Saint-John Perse; the Mexican *corridos*; the novels of Charles Dickens and William Makepeace Thackeray; the fables of Ivan Andreyevich Krylov; the reportage of Nellie Bly; and the allegories of Honoré de Balzac, Franz Kafka, and Isak Dinesen (Karen Blixen). The proponents of anti-imperialism produced masterworks such as Nikolay Gogol's *Taras Bulba*, Robert Louis Stevenson's *Treasure Island*, Leo Tolstoy's *War and Peace*, W. W. Jacobs's "The Monkey's Paw," Rudyard Kipling's *The Man Who Would Be King*, Joseph Conrad's *Heart of Darkness*, and E. M. Forster's *A Passage to India*, with warnings of the two-way corruption of the colonized and the colonizer. The writings of T. E. Lawrence, the speeches of Emma Goldman, the mythography of David Kalakaua, folk verse of Henry Lawson and A. B. Paterson, novels of Fyodor Dostoyevsky and Chinua Achebe, the short stories of Katherine Mansfield, autobiographical musings of Queen Liliuokalani, and the protest writings of Anne-Louise-Germaine de Staël reminded readers of the damage inflicted on tradition by the breakup of native power bases. Through worldwide publication, their works presaged devastation and upheaval, especially that wrought by World War I.

The rise of Adolf Hitler and his allies Benito Mussolini and Hideki Tojo, produced so unimaginable a fusion of intolerance and perverted science that writers merged realism with gothic convention. Documenting the horrors of genocide were the phantasms of Mervyn Peake, interviews of John Hersey, the memoirs of Elie Wiesel, the diary of Anne Frank, the futurism of Filippo Tommaso Marinetti, and the folk writings of Isaac Bashevis Singer, all of which contrasted with the posturing of Hitler's *Mein Kampf*, a pinnacle of paranoia and demonic rationalization. Balancing an era of global madness with humanism, the stories of Rabindranath Tagore and Primo Levi, the novels of Graham Greene, verse by José Martí, and the sermons of Dietrich Bonhoeffer held fast to visions of balance and sanity. During this era, admiration for the intellectual community resulted in Nobel awards to writers of the literature of empire—Joseph Brodsky (1907), Pearl S. Buck (1938), Nadine Gordimer (1991), Seamus Heaney (1995), V. S. Naipaul (2001), Boris Pasternak (1958), Aleksandr Solzhenitsyn (1970), Sigrid Undset (1928), and Elie Wiesel (1986). In the aftermath, popular writers such as Maryse Condé, Jamaica Kincaid, Adeline Yen Mah, and Amy Tan have heightened readers' awareness of vestiges of the colonial past still evident in postmodern nightmares.

ABOUT THIS BOOK

Encyclopedia of the Literature of Empire invites the student, teacher, librarian, feminist, writer, literary historian, researcher, and reader to sample a wide range of fiction and nonfiction by writers from around the world. The text offers easy-to-use information arranged alphabetically into 201 entries. Discussions of themes and genres summarize the style and focus of writings about empires and subject nations. Featured authors, titles, and topics draw from world literature, women's studies, and the social issues curricula of colleges and universities across the English-speaking world. The selection of authors and works reflects the tables of contents of textbooks, supplemental reading lists, and writing and discussion projects and seminars that have brought together teachers, students, writers, historians, and analysts of colonial and postcolonial concerns.

Enhancing the reader's understanding, lengthy essays on the hero; women's journals, diaries, and letters; visionary literature; autobiography; and biography discuss the implications of imperialism within a wide literary field. Numerous citations highlight authors' perspectives on such topics as creation and godhood, military service, coercion, and combat. Discussion of recurrent censorship

illustrates the struggle of forthright observers of oppression, such as the Roman fabulist Phaedrus and the Nigerian prison memoirist Wole Soyinka to publicize the truth. The development of such genres as children's, frontier, and apocalyptic literature and discussions of feminism, epithalamiums, and erotic literature personalize issues of powerlessness and human potential. Individual entries on writers (Sir William Schwenck Gilbert, Mariama Bâ), eyewitnesses (Mary Jane Seacole, Amos Tutuola), major works (*Kim, Ramayana, Kalevala*), sources (Greek drama, koan, tantras), literary history (African epic, Napoleonic literature, literature on the Aztec), motifs (goddess lore, violence, prison literature), conventions (prophecy, gothic literature), style (storytelling, travelogue, Book of the Dead), and political and social issues (slavery, protest literature, feminism) broaden awareness of the impact of empire building on life and art. Rounding out the text are entries that particularize the lives of less familiar writers such as Eduard Douwes Dekker and Buchi Emecheta, as well as details of translation, particularly the King James Bible, the Persian poetry of Edward FitzGerald, and Japanese gothic rendered by Lafcadio Hearn.

Research materials include various sources, beginning with a lengthy list of primary materials—for example, *The Lusiads, Dhammapada, Dream of the Red Chamber*, the book of Genesis, the Dead Sea Scrolls, and Confucius's *Analects*. Of particular assistance were major works on world literature: J. M. Coetzee's *Giving Offense: Essays on Censorship*; Nawal El Saadawi's *The Hidden Face of Eve: Women in the Arab World*; Thomas Fleming's *The Morality of Everyday Life*; Patrick Colm Hogan's *Empire and Poetic Voice: Cognitive and Cultural Studies of Literary Tradition and Colonialism*; Larry May's *War Crimes and Just War*; Jacqueline McLeod's *Crossing Boundaries: Comparative History of Black People in Diaspora*; Philip D. Morgan and Sean Hawkins's *Black Experience and the Empire*; Catherine Osborne's *Dumb Beasts and Dead Philosophers: Humanity and the Humane in Ancient Philosophy and Literature*; Edward Said's *Orientalism*; Eric Sundquist's *Empire and Slavery in American Literature, 1820–1865*; Sue Vice's *Holocaust Fiction*; Gillian Whitlock's *The Intimate Empire: Reading Women's Autobiography*; Julia M. Wright's *Ireland, India, and Nationalism in*

Nineteenth-Century Literature; and two of my own works, *Encyclopedia of Satire and Encyclopedia of World Scripture*. Appendixes include alphabetic listings of major titles and authors and the empires they represent, a time line of literature by empire and country, an overview of 213 cinematic versions of literary works, and separate bibliographies of primary and secondary sources. A thorough index covers people, places, sources, motifs, literary terms, titles, issues, and rulers of empires.

Abu Tamman   See HAMASA.

Achebe, Chinua (Albert Chinualumogu Achebe) (1930–   ) *Nigerian ethnographer and novelist*

In his peasant fiction, the writer and freedom fighter Albert Chinualumogu "Chinua" Achebe captures the wrenching shift in outlook between traditional and modern West African values. Born to Protestant parents in Ogidi, Nigeria, 30 years before his country obtained independence from the British Empire, Achebe learned word games and STORYTELLING from his mother Janet and sister Zinobia. He later exalted CREATION LORE and beast FABLEs about tortoise, the trickster, as "the very center, the very heart of our civilization and culture" for the way they interwove the foundations of stability and change with admonitions of danger and endurance (Achebe and Lindfors 1997, 80).

When Christian missionaries first arrived in Ogidi, Achebe's great-grandfather tossed them out of his compound because their hymns were too depressing. Years later, at a turning point in Nigerian history, Achebe observed in his family a fusion of beliefs among proselytized natives of the Niger delta. His uncle maintained reverence for Igbo animism while receiving instruction from Western missionaries and, as Achebe wrote in his AUTO-BIOGRAPHY, *Home and Exile* (2000), "considered it safe to install his heathen shrine of Ikenga (village) and other household divinities in the piazza" (Achebe 2000, 9). The duality of beliefs confused the author, who received lumps on the head from a primary schoolteacher who punished any mention of Igbo ritual. According to Achebe, "You can't fool around with children—you have to be honest with language: cleverness won't do" (83).

Achebe realized that his people had a natural talent for right thinking, but that colonialism and its material boost to villagers promoted exhibitionism, pride, and envy. In *The Trouble with Nigeria* (1998), he stated his fear that his country would turn into "one huge, helpless electoral dupe" (52). At age 24, he wrote and performed radio programs for the Nigerian Broadcasting Corporation while also working as a freelancer, providing short sketches for the *University Herald* and *The Bug*. Settled in Lagos, he established his career as a writer of short fiction, children's books, and African folklore that tend toward motifs of culture clash as it impacts the Igbo village.

In defense of ancestral forms of organization, Achebe honored the village assembly, which tolerated no monarch and linked all people with spirits, the dead, and future generations into a single social system based on equality. In 1972, he taught university courses and toured campuses in Great Britain and the United States to refute misconceptions about Nigerian people, such as their inability to value the individual, to govern by popular assembly, or to appreciate traditional lore as WISDOM LITERATURE. He charged the literature of earlier years with exonerating white Europeans for barbaric practices during the slave era, including concubinage and the marketing of children.

1

The targets of his spite were two esteemed novels: Anglo-Polish writer JOSEPH CONRAD's HEART OF DARKNESS (1902) and Irish author Joyce Cary's *Mister Johnson* (1939), both of which depict Nigerians as incapable of fending for themselves. In "An Image of Africa: Racism in Conrad's 'Heart of Darkness'" (1975), a Chancellor's Lecture delivered on February 18, 1975, at the University of Massachusetts, Achebe accused Conrad of racism, for depriving black characters of language, expression, and humanity.

Paganism v. Christianity

When it was published in 1958, Achebe's classic pro-African tragedy *Things Fall Apart* reset standards of European thought about Africans. The narrative depicts the dilemma of Okonkwo, a superstitious tribal bully who falls victim to Western rationalism. During the reign of Queen Victoria, the intrusion of British imperialists and missionaries in the tribal affairs of Umuofia, Nigeria, destroys a society dating to 4000 B.C. One method of reshaping thought and worship is the renaming of converts with Hebrew first names. Okonkwo's son Nwoye undermines paternal control by shucking off paganism and taking the name Isaac, son of Abraham, a monotheistic patriarch. The Hebrew name means "laughter" but holds no mirth for Achebe or his antihero. Okonkwo survives exile and redeems himself through industry and planning rather than propitiation of gods, but he returns to an old order subverted by new beliefs.

In their pristine state, the Igbo value agriculture and revere conversation. The wise stress that "Proverbs are the palm-oil with which words are eaten" (Achebe 2005, 10). Through metaphor, the village sage Obierika summarizes the trickery of Mr. Brown, the white missionary: "We were amused at his foolishness and allowed him to stay. . . . He has put a knife on the things that held us together and we have fallen apart" (162). Angered by his powerlessness against evangelists and colonizers, Okonkwo, the conservative villager, lashes out at change and expresses outrage by beheading a court messenger. His suicide portrays not only despair but also a violation of natural order. In the final sentence, Achebe creates irony out of a paragraph in *The Pacification of the Primitive Tribes of the Lower Niger*, a book by the arrogant district commissioner. A faceless bureaucrat who devalues Africans, he dismisses the downfall of the people under his control as insignificant.

Tradition v. Oppression

Suspicion fell on Achebe during the political instability that preceded the military coups of 1966 and the creation of the short-lived Republic of Biafra on May 30, 1967. Undaunted by warlords' menace, he delved further into issues of tradition and coercion in the victim story "Civil Peace" (1971), told in dialect, and the novels *No Longer at Ease* (1960); *Arrow of God* (1964); and *A Man of the People* (1966), a postcolonial SATIRE on guile and political fraud. In the latter work, Achebe highlights the citizens' criticism of the murderous Chief Koko, which comes too late: "Overnight everyone began to shake their heads at the excesses of the last regime, at its graft, oppression and corrupt government: newspapers, the radio, the hitherto silent intellectuals and civil servants—everybody said what a terrible lot" (1988, 149). The pause for consensus illustrates Achebe's strongest charge against Nigerians: that they lack spunk and leadership.

Amid threats to his life, including the firebombing of his house and library in September 1968, Achebe turned to verse to capture the tensions of struggle. Collected in *Beware, Soul Brother* (1971), the poems honor the courage of families and their losses due to a brutal military junta. For the sake of future Nigerians, in the title poem, he urges, "Pray / protect this patrimony to which / you must return when the song is finished" (1997, 569).

In 1988, Achebe wrote *Anthills of the Savannah*, a postcolonial allegory of the military coups that paralyzed Nigeria. At a high point in the author's survey of changes in the imperial order, he celebrated Britain's loss of Southern Rhodesia (now Zimbabwe) in 1980. In place of fears of the mother country, he raised new specters, "that fat, adolescent and delinquent millionaire, America" and puppet despots like Idi Amin of Uganda (1988, 52). Because of Achebe's demands for courage and truth, admirers named him the father of modern African fiction. In 2008 on the 50th anniversary of *Things Fall Apart*, scholars worldwide celebrated the novel for its revelations on imperialism.

Sources

Achebe, Chinua. *Anthills of the Savannah*. New York: Heinemann, 1988.

———. "Beware, Soul Brother." In *Divine Inspiration: The Life of Jesus in World Poetry*, edited by Robert Atwan, George Dardess, and Peggy Rosenthal, p. Oxford: Oxford University Press, 1997.

———. *Home and Exile*. Oxford: Oxford University Press, 2000.

———. "An Image of Africa: Racism in Conrad's 'Heart of Darkness.'" In *The Norton Anthology of Theory and Criticism*, edited by Vincent B. Leitch, et al., New York: Norton, 2001.

———. *A Man of the People*. New York: Anchor, 1988.

———. *Things Fall Apart*. New York: Macmillan, 2005.

———. *The Trouble with Nigeria*. New York: Heinemann, 1998.

———, and Bernth Lindfors. *Conversations with Chinua Achebe*. Jackson: University Press of Mississippi, 1997.

Adi Granth   See GRANTH.

Aeneid (Virgil) (19 B.C.)

A description of the foundation of the Roman Empire, the *Aeneid* effectively praises the emperor Caesar Augustus (63 B.C.–A.D. 14). Following the epic style of Homer's *Iliad* and *Odyssey*, the iambic hexameter narrative, composed by the poet VIRGIL (70–19 B.C.), tells of the Trojan prince Aeneas, a valiant 12th-century B.C. warrior, rescuer of the gods and traditions of his fallen country, and national HERO. The poet's love of balance marks the opening phrase—*Arma virumque cano* (I sing of arms and the man)—with a paean contrasting views of the hero's military acumen and his humanity. The epic statement concludes with a PROPHECY that from Aeneas's voyage toward the mythic Hesperia come political realities—the conquest of Latium, the homeland called Alba Longa, and the eventual ramparts of Rome. For justification, Virgil reminds the reader that Juno, queen of the gods, hates the future city-state because it is destined to obliterate Carthage, her pet kingdom. This long-range view of Roman history attests to ill fate and state enemies as unavoidable risks during the rise of empires.

The wanderings of Homer's Odysseus form a pattern for events in Aeneas's protracted voyage from the Troad on the northwestern coast of Turkey to Latium, a semibarbaric nation on the Tiber River on the west-central coast of Italy. Beginning in Homeric style in medias res (in the middle of things), the poet depicts Aeneas and his lieutenant Achates at a nadir after Aeolus, king of the winds, wrecks their fleet near Carthage, a Libyan kingdom on the northern shore of Africa. Grasping for comfort for his mariners, Aeneas speaks a mellifluous human truth: "We must not forget what we have suffered before— and there has been worse, but the Gods will grant sometime an end to it" (Virgil 1961, 12). Virgil halts his concern for the peripatetic Trojans long enough to recount the foundations of the Carthaginian Empire, which the Phoenicians established in 814 B.C. and which spread to Syracusa, Sardinia, Corsica, the Balearic Islands, southern Spain, Gibraltar, and northern Morocco until Rome defeated Carthage in the Third Punic War (146 B.C.).

Virgil crafted his epic to stress Roman virtues. Despite the allure and wealth of Dido, widowed queen of the Carthaginians, Aeneas clings to *pietas*, the Roman concept of responsibility and devotion to duty that motivates the voyager away from temporal pleasures and toward his divine destiny. In book four at an ominous moment in his romance with Dido, a dismal EPITHALAMIUM marks their ill-fated sexual encounter in the forest. In a dramatic turnabout, the shimmering aura of Venus, Aeneas's mother and the ancestor of Julius Caesar, foreshadows godly endorsement of a mission that nature and heavenly antipathies have seriously compromised. The outcome as Virgil describes in book six during Aeneas's sojourn in the underworld projects a boundless empire for Rome, exempt from borders and a defined time span.

From Troy to Hesperia

In Book II, the Homeric convention that gave Odysseus an opportunity to describe his past sufferings allows Virgil's Aeneas to recap the fall of Troy, a conquest scenario that dominates much of the sculpture, art, dance, drama, and mythos of the Mediterranean world. Gothic details—a child-crushing sea monster, the disbelieved prophetess Cassandra, and a night vision of Hector's ghost—intensify Aeneas's narrative. He describes the presentation to Trojans of a wooden horse that Odysseus designed to trick the unwary into letting down their guard. During the resulting conflict, the Greek warriors who poured out of a trapdoor in the horse and opened the city gates initiated a GENOCIDE that sapped the Trojans' royal line. The "dark wing of shadowy night . . . the holocaust" foretold death for the elderly King Priam, whom Pyrrhus slaughtered on the altar, and the end for his citadel and dynasty (39). More drama in the form of thunder and a comet led Aeneas to try to escape from Troy with his wife Creusa, son Iulus (also called Ascanius), and father Anchises, though in the confusion he became separated from Creusa. With this departure amid calamity, Virgil stresses the basis for Roman mores—the crucial role of the nuclear family to the imperial state. Implicit in the loss and death of Creusa in Troy is the centrality of males to imperial dynasty. Creusa was expendable because she had completed her job as mother to Iulus, the progenitor of the Julian line.

Virgil opens Book III on another Roman value, the regard for wise elders and their advice in the midst of catastrophe. At a refuge in Thrace, while Aeneas's followers construct a fleet of ships, Anchises directs them toward a new Troy, a pivotal moment in nation building involving three patriarchal generations—grandfather, father, and son. The departing company leaves behind heaps of corpses, barren fields, withered grass, and flaming battlements. Troy's royal family is put to the sword, hurled over the battlements, or allotted to Greek warriors as combat prizes. Unruffled in the face of grim phantasms—harpies, Scylla and Charybdis, Cyclopes, and a volcano—Aeneas relies on his father's guidance until the old man dies. The dutiful son mourns this passage of wisdom as "my last disaster" (74). The loss parallels the death of Julius Caesar centuries later and the leadership of the neophyte Octavian through Rome's 10 years of revolution, proscription and execution of aristocrats, and the birth of the empire under a young, untried ruler. At a theatrical point in the narration, Aeneas ends his saga and faces a hushed audience.

Aeneas the Patriarch

Book IV enlarges on the leader's humanity. Picturing Aeneas as a widower tempted by Queen Dido and her prosperous North African realm, Virgil engineers a sinister forest mockery of a sexual union between man and woman, serenaded by ululating wood sprites, which Dido decides constitutes a wedding. The epic contrasts the unsanctified union with the summons of Mercury, the winged messenger of the Gods who reminds the voyager that transporting the dynasty of Teucer, Troy's founder, to a new landfall outweighs the physical charms of Dido, ruler of Carthage. Aeneas therefore leaves, and Dido climbs a funeral pyre and stabs herself to death. A dire spectacle—Aeneas's disembarkation from the harbor under the smoke generated by Dido's funeral pyre—reminds readers that empire building exacts a human price as well as ongoing struggle toward a national aim. The allusion to Carthaginian enmity summons a vision of the Punic Wars (264–146 B.C.), a costly hiatus in Rome's rise to greatness.

Virgil inserts order into the lives of the wearied refugees. The zigzag course that Aeneas follows makes landfall at Sicily, where tradition obligates him to honor his father Anchises with Homeric accolades to manhood—the traditional postfuneral athletic contests and appropriate titles and prizes to the winners. The poet takes a bizarre turn in Book V when Trojan women go mad with grief and light a sacred fire that spreads to the fleet. A pair of prophecies from the Trojan elder Nautes and from the disembodied Anchises convinces Aeneas to take new directions and sail on with only the hardiest of the Trojan voyagers. The winnowing out of the weak presages Charles Darwin's theory of survival of the fittest as an assurance of genus survival. One near miss—a brush with the Sirens' rocks—repositions Palinurus, who is at the pilot's wheel to guide Troy's brightest and best from Sicily east to Latium on the Italian mainland. His valor and sacrifice after he tumbles into the sea can be interpreted as a reflection on past Roman heroes who arose at a crucial moment to decide the nation's fate by giving their lives for their country.

Virgil constantly emphasizes the fate of the fallen. In Book VI, Aeneas makes his way to Hades to glimpse Rome's future. The ancient literary traditions of Charon, ferryman over the River Styx, retain their terrors as the hero ventures among hordes of wraiths; these include the voiceless spirits of warriors and citizens slain, trampled, or burned in the fall of Troy, an overwhelming proof of the mortal cost of founding Rome. This backdrop contrasts with the Elysian Fields, home of the blessed, where Anchises enumerates for his son Rome's seven kings; patriots Brutus and the Gracchi (Tiberius and Gaius Gracchus); warriors Scipio and Julius Caesar; and the pinnacle of greatness, Augustus Caesar, whom Virgil extols with his epic. To exalt history over myth, the poet proclaims, "Not even Hercules covered so much of the world" (143). Virgil halts long enough to toss a second sop to the emperor—an encomium to Marcus Claudius Marcellus, Augustus's heir, who sickened and died in 23 B.C. at age 19. The text links Marcellus and Aeneas in their reverence for old-style morality: "Oh weep for his piety! His faith like the faith of old! His invincible valor!" (145). The passage anticipates the opening of the Theater of Marcellus, which neared completion in Virgil's last year.

A Battle for Conquest

With Book VII, Virgil looks toward the ideal, an eternal nation wreathed in honor. He builds suspense with a grand invocation to Erato, muse of lyric poetry: "Goddess, O guide me, Goddess, O guide your poet! I shall tell of a grim war, of battlelines, of kings whose courage drove them deathward" (147). Again, the action focuses on male concerns—a battle of monarchs for control of the realm. Virgil foretells the history of the Latins and their dynastic union with the Trojans through the Princess Lavinia's marriage to Aeneas. At the acme of exaltation for Imperial Rome, Virgil anticipates a leader who "shall bear our name to the stars, and our descendants rule all the peoples of the turning world from sunrise to sunset" (149), an overstatement of Rome's centrality to world history. Meanwhile, Aeneas arrives in Latium and sketches an outline of conquest in the dirt, the epitome of humble beginnings for human dreams.

The union of dynasties preceding a universal golden age requires a mustering of warriors in book

VIII for an epic battle, which draws heavily on Homeric posturing and conflict and, in Book X, on the intrusion of the gods of Mount Olympus. With Juno sowing discord throughout the faceoff in Book IX, the fight for Lavinia—a female war prize—boils down to a duel in Book XII, an evocation of Achilles's battle with the Trojan Hector in the *Iliad*. Destiny tips in favor of the Trojan refugees with the thrust of Aeneas's spear through the thigh of his rival Turnus. The last five lines savor the coup de grâce to Turnus's heart and the flight of his groaning, sighing spirit to Hades. Aeneas's victory ends a spiritual journey that began in arson and genocide and concluded with single combat. The restoration of order in Latium suits Virgil's lofty celebration of national character and of the peace that Augustus brought to the Roman Empire.

During the era of CRUSADER LORE, the German knight-poet Heinrich von Veldeke turned the Norman *Aeneas* story *Roman d'Eneas* (ca. 1160) into a chivalric romance in *Eneit* (ca. 1186). In 1428, Italian poet Maffeo Vegio wrote a supplement to the *Aeneid* that summarizes Aeneas's marriage to Lavinia. The Portuguese epic *Os Lusíadas* (*The Lusiads*; 1572), by Luís Vaz de Camões, emulates Virgil's rhythm and elevated tone. The story recurs in the writings of WILLIAM SHAKESPEARE, the operas by Hector Berlioz and Henry Purcell, and Ursula Le Guin's feminist novel *Lavinia* (2008).

Sources

Adler, Eve. *Vergil's Empire: Political Thought in the Aeneid.* Lanham, Md.: Rowman and Littlefield, 2003.
Virgil. *The Aeneid.* Translated by Patric Dickinson. New York: Mentor, 1961.

Aeschylus   See GREEK DRAMA.

Aesop (ca. 620–560 B.C.) *Greek fabulist*
The Thracian slave Aesop of Mesembria, a mystic figure during a period of Greek conquest and colonizing, created a prototype for astute ethical tales that dominated the FABLE genre in Western literature. Allegedly, following the Homeric period, Aesop accepted a commission by the Delphic

god Apollo to equip humankind with illustrative axioms. Rather than ponderous, violence-prone epics, however, the storyteller chose 350 brief nuggets of truth.

Prototypes of fables existed in Eastern Mediterranean oral lore, including the admonitory tale of "The Rich Man and the Poor Man's Lamb" (ca. 950 B.C.), which the Israelite priest Nathan used to humble King David for wife stealing. A fable by the Greek moralist and mythographer Hesiod, "The Hawk and the Nightingale" from *Works and Days* (ca. 700 B.C.), took a pragmatic stance concerning the vulnerable in the talons of the mighty, who can easily subdue the weak. According to the surviving lines of "The Fox and Hedgehog" (650 B.C.), the soldier-poet Archilochus of Paros turned similar advice about power mongering into verse fable: "The fox knows many things, the hedgehog one great thing" (Archilochus 1992, 202).

These focused pairings—rich man/poor man, hawk/nightingale, fox/hedgehog—foretokened Aesop's motifs, but not his rhetorical gift. Proclaimed the father of the Western fable, he earned the respect of the historian HERODOTUS, who identified Aesop as a story maker rather than a story collector. In 1711, Joseph Addison, an essayist for the neoclassic age London newspaper the *Spectator*, wrote that Aesop was the world's first wit and a literary touchstone to more civilized ages.

The famed eastern Mediterranean storyteller created a model for one of the most enduring literary genres. Drawing on oral narrative for his style, he effectively created the model for the apologue, a refined animal or beast fable that serves as a brain teaser, like the Buddhist KOAN, or a source of *agon*, or competition story, like those of the Spanish scholar TOMÁS DE IRIARTE. Succinct and insightful, each of Aesop's fables concludes with a quippy, nature-based *epimythium*, or self-evident moral. His most finely honed include "Look before you leap," "Deceit and wisdom can be stronger than force," "One trickster may trick another," "No act of kindness is ever wasted," and "No one can serve two masters." For visual impact, he created emblematic fables about animals stereotyped by their behavior, such as the strength of the ox, the mindless chatter of the magpie, and the vainglory of the lion.

Advice to Rulers

After his second master, Xanthus of Samos, freed Aesop, the fabulist appears to have counseled the Lydian king Croesus and served as an emissary to courts at Corinth, Egypt, and Sardis. At a difficult pass in Athenian politics, he urged restraint against the tyrant Peisistratus with the story "The Frogs Who Desired a King." The moral warns peasants not to venture into kingmaking lest they create a monster. Of the uneven distribution of blessings, Aesop provided salient counsel: "There is always somebody worse off than you," "Don't dismiss the ordinary," and "The coveter loses all." Of the overdressed social climber, he remarked, "Fine feathers don't make fine birds." To the would-be conqueror, he warned, "Pride precedes a fall" and "Danger comes from where you least expect it." To dictators, Aesop hinted, "Evil will not last forever"; he also spoke of "Strength in numbers," a veiled reference to the massing of the weak to overthrow suppressors. He may have met his death at Delphi for telling saucy stories with indiscreet morals. According to the fable "The Eagle and the Beetle" in *The Birds* (414 B.C.) by comic playwright Aristophanes, the Delphians seized Aesop from the shrine of the Muses and murdered him.

Aesop's original stories influenced fabulists in subsequent eras, notably Socrates in his prison cell at the base of the Acropolis in Athens. According to Plato's *Phaedo* (ca. 345 B.C.), the doomed philosopher translated into poetry the Aesopian fables that he had memorized in prose. The translations, which occurred on Socrates's last days in 399 B.C., during the short-term rise of Sparta to empire status, relieved him of thoughts of suicide. He imagined Aesop allying abstract pleasure with pain in an allegory "about God trying to reconcile their strife, and when he could not, he fastened their heads together" (Plato 1875, 48). While Socrates awaited a state executioner bearing a cup of poison hemlock, his sentence for the crime of impiety, the fables helped the philosopher interpret troubling dreams and engaged his intellect in shaping the curt closing lines for which Aesop was famous.

Other admirers and emulators of Aesop's fables include subsequent fabulists, such as the Greek philosopher Aristotle, who warned of catastrophes in two *pourquoi* ("why") stories: "Aesop at the

Shipyards," a segment of *Meteorologica* (ca. 335 B.C.), and "The Lions and the Hares" in *Politica* (ca. 335 B.C.). In the next millennium, Rabbi Joshua ben Hananiah of Jerusalem narrated Aesop's "The Crane and Lion" (ca. A.D. 120) during a heated exchange between Jews and the agents of the Emperor Hadrian, who refused to restore Jerusalem's temple after its destruction by Roman soldiers. Some three decades later, the orator Aelius Aristides of Hadriani, Mysia (present-day Turkey), honed the two-animal confrontation in "The Mouse and the Oyster" (150 B.C.), a cautionary tale warning of political situations that entrap or slaughter the unwary caught between dangerous allies. Later fabulists imitated Aesop's succinct wit, including the Middle Eastern poet Valerius Babrius, a Greco-Roman author living in Christianized Syria around A.D. 235.

Aesop imitators tended to be scholars and polemists. At the height of classicism in medieval Japan, court councilor Minamoto Takakuni emulated Aesop with his collection *Konjaku Monogatari* (Tales, ancient and modern, 1075). In "The Monkey's Gratitude," a complex two-stage animal tale, Minamoto describes the battle of two dissimilar beasts when a monkey kidnaps a baby to protect it from the talons of an eagle. In Constantinople (present-day Istanbul, Turkey) around 1290 during the Byzantine Empire, the Greek monk and editor Maximus Planudes published critical revisions of original Aesopic fables. Western Europeans read Aesopic stories by the Anglo-Norman poet MARIE DE FRANCE; by the Parisian fabulist JEAN DE LA FONTAINE; and, during the 18th century, by the ethicist Gotthold Ephraim Lessing of Saxony and JOHANN WOLFGANG VON GOETHE, who predicted the rise of Napoleon I in the bestiary *Reineke Fuchs* (*Reynard the Fox*; 1794). The Senegalese storyteller BIRAGO DIOP produced his own Aesopic twists in riddles, adages, and beast fables from West Africa.

Sources

Aesop. *Aesop's Fables with a Life of Aesop*. Translated by John E. Keller and L. Clark Keating. Lexington: University Press of Kentucky, 1993.

Archilochus. "The Fox and the Hedgehog." In *Early Greek Poetry,* translated by David D. Mulroy, Ann Arbor: University of Michigan Press, 1992.

Babrius. *Babrius and Phaedrus*. Translated by Ben Edwin Perry. Cambridge, Mass.: Loeb Classical Library, 1990.

Plato. *Plato's Phaedo.* Translated by E. M. Cope. Cambridge, U.K.: University Press, 1875.

Aidoo, Ama Ata (Christina Ama Ata Aidoo) (1942–) *Ghanian fiction writer, poet, and dramatist*

A native of Abeadzi Kyiakor, Gold Coast (present-day Ghana), and expert in Fanti drama, Christina Ama Ata Aidoo grew up during a time of strained relations between black Africans and Great Britain. Colonizers tortured her grandfather to death and threatened the position of her father, Yaw Fama, a tribal chief and village educator. Her mother, Maame Abba, influenced Aidoo's incipient political views with womanly talk-stories. Aidoo was 15 years old when the militaristic Ashanti Empire, Gold Coast, and part of Togoland merged into Ghana, the first sub-Saharan nation to free itself from British imperialism. Under the influence of Ghanian concepts of liberty, she became a pacesetter during her years at the University of Ghana, where she majored in English and drama and studied African fiction, notably the affirmation of native identity in Nigerian novelist CHINUA ACHEBE's *Things Fall Apart* (1958). She began submitting verse and vignettes to *Black Orpheus* and the *Okyeame* literary magazine. After her appointment to the ministry of education, in support of pan-Africanism, she directed her literary projects toward the relief of ignorance and the empowerment of rural women, particularly widows and working mothers who were raising fatherless children.

After settling in Harare Zimbabwe in 1983, Ama Ata Aidoo battled the diminution of women, a pervasive element of Victorian ideologies and a residue of slavery. She stimulated audiences with her witty social drama *The Dilemma of a Ghost* (1965), a rescue plot that features a traditional mother's salvation of her son, Ato Yawson, after he returns to West Africa with a college degree and citified wife from the United States. A matrifocal anthology, *No Sweetness Here* (1970), surveys the domestic upheavals in women's lives following Ghana's emergence as a model of black

African independence, a scenario that dominates the novels of Nigerian author BUCHI EMECHETA. In the story "Everything Counts," Aidoo mocks Westernized natives "scrambling to pay exorbitant prices for second-hand clothes from America" (Aidoo 1995, 1). In "For Whom Things Did Not Change," she turns a rotted yam into a symbol of the oversized promise of nationhood and the morning-after disillusion when it arrives. The song-play *Anowa* (1970), enriched with Ashanti proverbs and Africanisms, challenges mid-19th century feudal wedlock on the Guinea coast by turning the title character into a liberated woman and symbol of the motherland. Cultural dissonance and discontent remained at the core of Aidoo's verse and epistolary novel *Our Sister Killjoy; or, Reflections from a Black-Eyed Squint* (1977), a feminist revelation of postcolonial bigotry. The novel won the author a fellowship to Stanford University.

Aidoo's contributions to global feminism earned her the support of the nonprofit publisher the Feminist Press. The prize-winning social SATIRE *Changes: A Love Story* (1991) moved more boldly into women's issues with the recoil of a career woman, Esi Sekyi, from spousal abuse, polygamy, and patriarchal despotism, the themes of contemporary Senegalese author MARIAMA BÂ. Aidoo bases the examination of male-female relationships on such outdated wisdom as the belief that "It's not safe to show a woman you love her . . . not too much anyway" (Aidoo 1993, 7). She parallels male insecurities with the admonitions of Esi's pragmatic grandmother Nana, the epitome of the female enforcer of tradition and good sense. Out of outrage at Esi's demand for affection, Nana warns, "Love? . . . Love? . . . Love is not safe, my lady Silk, love is dangerous" (42). Esi's breach of Ghanian morality by carrying on an affair with Ali, a married Muslim, proves counterproductive. With a poet's grace, Aidoo speaks the unease of adultery: "Guilt is born in the same hour with pleasure, / like anything in this universe and its enemy" (69). By renegotiating the conjugal alternatives of the past, Esi relives the female struggles that endure from prehistory. Aidoo's teaching career has taken her to England, Germany, and the United States, where she teaches at Brown University.

Sources

Aidoo, Ama Ata. *Changes: A Love Story.* New York: Feminist Press, 1993.
———. *The Dilemma of a Ghost and Anowa: Two Plays.* Harlow, U.K.: Longman, 1987.
———. *No Sweetness Here and Other Stories.* New York: Feminist Press, 1995.
Killam, G. D. *Literature of Africa.* Westport, Conn.: Greenwood, 2004.

Akhmatova, Anna (Anna Andreyevna Gorenko) (1889–1966) *Russo-Ukrainian critic and poet*

Through anguished verse, the feminist poet and translator Anna Akhmatova distilled the fall of the last Romanov czar, Stalinist purges, and the quashing of dissent in Soviet Russia. Born Anna Andreyevna Gorenko in Bolshoy Fontan near Odessa on the Black Sea, she came of age outside the royal enclave at St. Petersburg and attended the Kiev College for Women. Anna rejected her father's insistence that she establish a law career. Instead, influenced by the works of VIRGIL, Dante, WILLIAM SHAKESPEARE, FYODOR DOSTOYEVSKY, and ALEKSANDR PUSHKIN, she opened a literary salon in St. Petersburg. Under a surname honoring Akhmat Khan, a 15th-century Tatar rebel against Czar Ivan III the Great, she submitted poems to the journal *Sirius*. She married the poet Nikolay Gumilyov in 1910 (they later separated) and gave birth to their son Lev two years later. Akhmatova's best-selling anthology *Evening* (1912) and *At the Edge of the Sea* (1915), a long elegy reflecting the uncertainties preceding World War I, introduced readers to her lyricism and moral authority, two qualities her work shared with fellow experimentalist BORIS PASTERNAK.

In 1917, the year of the Russian Revolution, Akhmatova wrote of PROPHECY fulfilled and the coming of turmoil and starvation. She completed *White Flock*, a collection of poems on czarist Russia's transformation that she recited to receptive audiences. In the poem "Petrograd, 1919," she anticipated with regret the savage future that awaited Peter's holy city. By 1921, the same year her former husband was executed, terror at Josef Stalin's control of the Red Army had come to dominate the tone and atmosphere of Akhmatova's poems. Like the Czech poet Rainer Maria Rilke, she wrote of the spirit withering without joy or hope. Her popularity among libertarians resulted in the banning of her works from 1925 to 1940; she earned her living during this time through translating work and publishing essays.

In *Requiem* (written 1935–40; published 1963), Akhmatova accused Stalin of lawlessness and exposed the loss of Russian civil rights during his tyranny. She criticized the Soviet alliance with Nazi Germany in the poem "In 1940," which derives its fervor from the Luftwaffe's bombardment of London and the German occupation of Paris, where she had spent her month-long honeymoon in 1911. The Soviet press branded her a traitor; communist authorities censored her work and sentenced her son, ethnographer Lev Nikolaevich Gumilev, to hard labor mining copper and nickel at the Norilsk gulag in northern Siberia from 1938 to 1956.

Anna under Siege

Akhmatova married twice more after Nikolai Gumilyov was executed. She never stopped writing, even when her works were banned before and after World War II. Speaking for the people, she denounced Russia's humiliation during the war. By commiserating with the Egyptian queen in "Cleopatra" (1940), the poet dramatized the enslavement of the Egyptian royal children and the title figure's impotence before Octavian, the future first emperor of Rome, whom heralds announce with screaming trumpets and eagle standards. The backdrop mimics the bravado of Hitler's public speeches in Berlin's city center. Before her evacuation from Leningrad in 1941, Akhmatova cheered terrified citizens over the radio. Her play *Prologue: A Dream within a Dream* (1942) reprised the bleakness of the public tribunal in the Czech-German novelist Franz Kafka's *The Trial* (1925). She filled her verse collections *Poem without a Hero* (1943) and *Winds of War* (1946) with images of walls, chains, prisons, guards, tombs, shadows, and a dark wing obscuring the light, a symbol of Soviet paranoia and secrecy. Upon return to Leningrad in 1944, she found the city reduced to a ghost of its former glory. Fans of her silenced verse resorted to *samizdat* (private publication) by memorizing, hand-copying, or typing forbidden poems for clandestine circulation.

Banishment from print raised Akhmatova's esteem among Russians. Ousted from the writer's guild, she served as godmother to a generation of post-Stalin libertarian writers and continued to earn her living by translating the works of others. In 1950, she wrote a series of sham propaganda pieces in the monthly journal *Ogonek* (Cedilla) that praised Stalin with clichés. When Premier Nikita Khrushchev introduced a thaw in Soviet rigidity in 1953, public acclaim welcomed her keen observations, but her painful fawning failed to release her son Lev from prison for three more years. Furthermore, her third husband, Nikolai Punin, died in a Siberian gulag in 1953.

Akhmatova's stature as a preeminent Russian poet grew, and in 1964, new collections of her verses preceded celebration of her 75th birthday. The following year, she received an honorary doctorate from Oxford University. She died in Leningrad on March 5, 1966, and was interred in Komarovo Cemetery. Many of her great works, such as *Poema bez geroya* (*Poem without a Hero*), reached print after her death. The poets JOSEPH BRODSKY and YEVGENY YEVTUSHENKO as well as literary historians exalted her as one of the greatest female lyricists of all time.

Sources

Akhmatova, Anna. *The Complete Poems of Anna Akhmatova*. Brookline, Mass.: Zephyr Press, 1998.
———. *Selected Poems of Anna Akhmatova*. Brookline, Mass.: Zephyr Press, 2000.
Amert, Susan. *In a Shattered Mirror: The Later Poetry of Anna Akhmatova*. Palo Alto, Calif.: Stanford University Press, 1992.

Alexiad   See ANNA COMNENA.

Alfred the Great (Ælfred) (849–899) *Anglo-Saxon king, lawgiver, and sage*

Under threat from Norse conquerors, the Anglo-Saxon monarch Alfred the Great defended the southern kingdom of Wessex from invasion. He was the youngest of five sons. Three of his brothers succeeded their father Aethelwulf as king, two for only short periods, before Alfred succeeded to the throne in 871. According to Alfred's biography, *Vita Alfredi* (*Life of Alfred*, 893), by the Welsh monk Asser, the newly crowned king garrisoned towns against the incursions of the Danish king Guthrum but failed to retrieve the kingdom of Mercia from Nordic marauders. However, Alfred won three more campaigns and captured London in 886. His construction of a network of forts and a fleet of ships thwarted the Danes' attempt to add Wessex to its empire. Peace produced a cultural renaissance featuring learning centers, a manuscript archive at Winchester, and the king's handbook of laws called the *Doom Book* (ca. 900), the basis of English common law and jurisprudence and the unifier of Anglo-Saxon kingdoms into one nation.

In 891, Alfred commissioned the *Anglo-Saxon Chronicle*, an accomplishment that earned him the title of father of English prose. The text describes the size and settlement of Britannia before delineating a pattern of rule and conquest, era by era. A modest summation of Alfred's military victory in 871 notes the constant skirmishing in nine battles, proof of his long years in the saddle ahead of soldiers and guerrilla forces. By summer 875, Alfred had launched England's first navy and captured one of seven Viking rovers, the longboats that enabled Norse predators to strike rapidly, loot, murder, and slip away. Entries for the mid-890s attest to the unceasing job of warding off the Danish plunderers.

Updates of the *Anglo-Saxon Chronicle* continued until 1154. According to the commentary on Alfred's death, his subjects considered him king of all the English. A posthumous manuscript of WISDOM LITERATURE, *The Proverbs of Alfred* (ca. 1251), reflects in alliterative verse that he was "king ant cleric, / ful wel he louede godis werc. / He was wis on his word" (king and religious leader who loved godly work. He spoke wise words; 1908, 1–2).

Sources

Alfred the Great. *The Proverbs of Alfred.* Translated by Edvard Borgström. Stockholm: Hakan Ohlsson, 1908.

Smyth, Alfred P. *King Alfred the Great.* New York: Oxford University Press, 1996.

Analects (*Analects of Confucius, Lun Yu, The Sayings of Confucius*) Confucius (Kongfuzi, K'ung Fu Tzu) (ca. 210 B.C.)

The WISDOM LITERATURE of Confucius (551–479 B.C.) represents the acme of humanity, learning, and cultural reform in early China. Known by the honorific Kongfuzi (K'ung Fu-tsu [Grand Master]), Confucius was a wandering philosopher and political theorist who taught his disciples to trust humankind and behave respectfully to all while anticipating no reward or divine salvation. Born in Qufu (Ch'ü-fu), Lu Province (present-day Shandong) of the Chu kingdom during the Zhou (Chou) dynasty, he lived during a feudal time known as the Spring and Autumn Period (770–481 B.C.), named after the *Spring and Autumn Annals,* which he is credited for compiling. This was also the time of the Hundred Schools of Thought (770–221 B.C.), an era of great intellectual and philosophical growth in China—as well as tremendous chaos and strife among the feudal nobility.

Confucius studied at the Grand Temple of the Duke of Zhou and with state philosopher and antiquarian Laozi (Lao Tsu), the formulator of Daoism (Taoism; see DAODEJING). He became a high minister in Lu Province but resigned in 497 B.C. because he disapproved of the Duke of Lu's behavior. Thereafter, he became an itinerant adviser and teacher to promising young males from all social and economic classes. Around 530 B.C., he began teaching in the household of Baron Qi (Chi). Wherever Confucius went, he expounded democratic ideals. Throughout his life, he urged China's unification under a benevolent emperor, an outcome that was later achieved when Qin Shi Huangdi founded the Qin dynasty in 221 B.C., marking the end of the violent time known as the Warring States Period.

In his teachings, to prepare the whole man, Confucius devised a curriculum ranging from classical Chinese literature and history to ritual and ethics, archery, charioteering, calligraphy, music, and math. In 501 B.C., he launched a crusade to revive the nonmaterialistic values of home and community from China's agrarian past. For models, he pictured an androcentric world with the sovereign as a father and the subjects as sons. About 488 B.C., the philosopher became China's first professional ethicist by authoring the *Tuan Quan* (*T'uan Chuan* [Commentary on the decision]), an application of the *I Ching* (*The Book of Changes*, 1144 B.C.–206 B.C.) to morality. One adherent predicted, "The Empire has long been lying in evil ways, but now God is going to make Confucius his herald to rouse the land" (Confucius 1910, 118). His lectures, drawing on such works as the *Daodejing* (*Tao-te Ching* [Classic of the way of power, 300 B.C.]) of Laozi, denounced arrogance, bias, and the vainglory of the political hierarchy.

In retirement, Confucius edited 305 aphorisms, verses, and hymns in *The Book of Songs* (ca. 480 B.C.), which introduced the utopian concept of the Dao (Tao [the Way]), a path to serenity. Following his death a year later, his concepts started to influence childhood education through student memorization of wise sayings. His long-lasting philosophy is known as Confucianism.

Editions of Confucius's Sayings

Confucius's anthologized writings, like those of the Buddha, Jesus, Muhammad, and Socrates, were the collections of disciples. In the decade preceding the rise of imperial China, the sage Mencius (also Mengzi or Meng Tzu, 372–289 B.C.) compiled 497 aphorisms into Chinese scripture known as the *Analects of Confucius*, a series of teacher-student discussions. In Mencius's version, the master's advice is direct, a style later popularized by the Roman emperor Marcus Aurelius: "Promote the deserving and instruct those who fall short, and they will be encouraged to follow the path of virtue" (40). Of public affairs, the master urges "scrupulous attention to business, honesty, economy, charity, and the employment of the people at the proper season" (39). Additional aphorisms warn of petty criticisms, wasted funds, ruthless authorities, and the devaluation of the citizen's toil. Mencius's representation of Confucianism anticipates an ideal sovereignty based on right thinking and the generosity of ordinary citizens. One metaphor depicts the philosopher-king as wind and his people as grass: "For it is the nature of grass to bend when the wind blows upon it" (42). Through core beliefs in human rights, the *Analects* denounce the ruling class for indulgence and exonerate rebels for overthrowing corrupt regimes.

In the eastern state of Qi (Ch'i), Xunzi (Xun zi, or Hsün-tzu, ca. 312–230 B.C.), an intellectual from Chi-Hsia, shaped the simplistic Confucian doctrines into a pragmatic text of social and political behavior governed by balance and acquired learning. Other first- and second-generation disciples of Confucius enlarged and amended the *Analects* over time, making it a collective work rather than the work of Confucius himself. The book's final editors were probably disciples of the Confucian Zengzi (Tsengtzu, 505–436 B.C.). By 136 B.C., the emperor Wudi (Wu Ti) (140 B.C.–87 B.C.), fifth ruler of the Han dynasty, had legitimized Confucianism as the state cult and the *Analects* as a standard text of Confucian-trained civil servants. By A.D. 58, Confucianism was serving China as the imperial ideology.

The version of the *Analects* known today was compiled by Zhang Yu, a teacher of Emperor Cheng (51–7 B.C.), during the late Han dynasty. Zhang Yu combined previous versions known as the *Lu* and *Qi Analects* but retained the number of chapters in the *Lu Analects*. The 501 short chapters (none longer than 15 lines) are organized into 20 books. One of the Four Books of Confucianism (the others are the *Mengzi* [*Book of Mencius*], *Zhongyong* [*Doctrine of the Mean*], and *Daxue* [*The Great Learning*]), the *Analects* is also one of the cornerstones of Confucianism, a moral code that not only played an important role in the unification of China but continued to resonate through the ages.

Confucianism and its disciples spread from China to distant nations. Among the devout Chinese Confucians was poet-historian DU FU of Shaoling. In the Nara period in eighth-century Japan, poet YAMANOUE NO OKURA incorporated Confucian morality in his altruistic verse. The novelist Cao Xueqin, author of DREAM OF THE RED CHAMBER (1791), illustrated the value of Confucius's philosophy to subsequent generations by depicting the success of the scholarly protagonist Chia Pao-yu at studying the original texts and placing seventh on state exams. American novelists PEARL S. BUCK and AMY TAN attacked the patriarchy of Confucius's writings in feminist novels depicting the lives of silenced and overworked peasant women in the final decades of imperial China.

Sources

Clements Jonathan. *Confucius: A Biography*. Charleston, S.C.: History Press, 2005.

Confucius. *The Book of Songs: The Ancient Chinese Classic of Poetry*. Translated by Arthur Waley. New York: Grove, 1996.

———. *The Sayings of Confucius*. Translated by Lionel Giles. New York: E. P. Dutton, 1910.

Androcles and the Lion (Apion) (ca. A.D. first century)

A classical FABLE that has flourished in multiple forms, *Androcles and the Lion* derives its power from the first glimmers of mass savagery in the Roman Empire. The story was anthologized in *Aegyptiaca* (ca. A.D. 40) by the Greco-Libyan ambassador Apion of Alexandria, Egypt, and reprised in "De beneficiis" ("On Benefits," A.D. 56) by the essayist SENECA. It suited a perilous era in the early empire during the notorious reigns of the Julio-Claudian emperors Tiberius (A.D. 14–37), Caligula (37–41), and Claudius (41–54). Rhetorician Aulus Gellius's version of the fable, anthologized in his 20-volume *Noctes Atticae* (*Attic Nights*, ca. A.D. 180), uses the animal motif for a tale of confrontation between the mighty and the weak, which the author claimed to have witnessed.

The story centers on Androcles, an escaped Carthaginian slave who encounters a wounded lion. He removes a thorn from the lion's paw, treats the infection, and bandages the wound, resulting in friendship between man and animal. Years later, Androcles is captured as a fugitive slave and condemned to be devoured by wild animals in Rome's Circus Maximus. But the ferocious beast that enters the arena proves to be his old lion friend, and the two have a jubilant reunion. Recognizing a unique relationship, the unnamed emperor frees Androcles, and amid a shower of blossoms from onlookers, the fable concludes, "This is the lion who was a man's friend! This is the man who was the lion's physician" (Aulus Gellius 1795, 1:321).

The narrative also appears in volume 7 of Claudius Aelian's 17-book bestiary *De natura animalium* (On the nature of animals, ca. A.D. 230), in which the wound escalates to a sharp stake through the paw. In the "Romulus" collection of an elegiac poet possibly named Romulus, the story appears under the title "The Lion and the Shepherd" (ca. 950). In whatever version it appears, the story contrasts the benevolence of Androcles and the lion with the faceless inhumanity of imperial Rome.

During the time of the British Empire, Dublin-born playwright George Bernard Shaw (1856–1950) recast the Roman fable as *Androcles and the Lion: A Fable Play* (1912). The two-act stage SATIRE of ethnic and religious persecution and decadence in the Roman Empire premiered at St. James's Theatre, London, on September 1, 1913. In a famous preface appended in 1915, Shaw declares that "Christ is not the lifeless harmless image he has hitherto been to you, but a rallying centre for revolutionary influences," a salute to the philosophical uprising begun in imperial Rome demanding human liberty and equality (Shaw 1916, 66). The playwright examines the play's premises as they apply to the governance of a round-the-globe empire, particularly Ireland. He reminds the reader that "Jesus certainly did not consider the overthrow of the Roman empire or the substitution of a new ecclesiastical organization for the Jewish Church or for the priesthood of the Roman Gods as part of his program. He said that God was better than Mammon; but he never said that Tweedledum was better than Tweedledee" (126–127).

Using grim comedy, Shaw's play examines the cultism, elitism, and barbarity that belie Jesus's unorthodox social doctrines. One of the targets of the farce is the militarism of the hymn "Onward, Christian Soldiers" (1864), with lyrics by the English hagiographer Sabine Baring-Gould that composer Sir Arthur Sullivan set to a march tune in 1871. The popular hymn validated British imperialism with an implied connection to evangelistic zeal. In Shaw's drama, the Roman Captain states, "This [hymn] may be sung, except when marching through the forum or within hearing of the Emperor's palace; but the words must be altered to 'Throw them to the Lions'" (Shaw 1916, 10). Shaw's drollery implies that Christian militarism during the Crusades and in British colonies varied little from Roman persecution.

The 1952 film version of *Androcles and the Lion* featured Jean Simmons as a Christian captive, Victor Mature as a Roman legion captain, and Alan Young as Androcles.

Sources

Aelian. *On the Characteristics of Animals.* Translated by Alwyn Faber Scholfield. Cambridge, Mass.: Harvard University Press, 1958.

Aulus Gellius. *The Attic Nights of Aulus Gellius.* 3 vols. Translated by William Beloe. London: J. Johnson, 1795.

Holford-Strevens, Leofranc, and Amiel D. Vardi. *The Worlds of Aulus Gellius.* Oxford: Oxford University Press, 2004.

Osborne, Catherine. *Dumb Beasts and Dead Philosophers: Humanity and the Humane in Ancient Philosophy and Literature.* Oxford: Oxford University Press, 2007.

Shaw, George Bernard. *Androcles and the Lion; Overruled; Pygmalion.* New York: Brentano's, 1916.

Wheatley, Edward. *Mastering Aesop: Medieval Education, Chaucer and His Followers.* Gainesville: University Press of Florida, 2000.

Anna Comnena (Anna Komnene)
(1083–1153) *Byzantine historian*

Anna Comnena, the world's first acknowledged female historian, produced a classic examination of the Byzantine Empire. The first of nine children born to Emperor Alexius I Comnenus, she was trained from girlhood for service to the realm and expected to become empress. Born "in the purple" (porphyra) on December 1, 1083, she was the *porphyrogenita,* or first princess. Renouncing girlish amusements she grew up intellectually sophisticated but sheltered and protected from the sexual libertinism expressed in ancient verse. In a household dominated by assertive females, she gained respect for bold women from the wisdom of her paternal grandmother, Anna Dalassena, a widow who administered the state while her son Alexius conducted wars.

After studying astronomy, geography, geometry, history, Homer's epics, math, medicine, and philosophy, in her mid-teens, Anna Comnena organized her father's hospital, refugee center, and foundling home. In 1097, during the First Crusade (1096–1099), at age 14, she wed Caesar Nicephorus Bryennius, a general and statesman 21 years older than she. She subsequently connived with her mother, Empress Irene Dukaina, to replace Anna's brother, John Comnenius, who was four years her junior, because Alexius named him heir to the throne of the Eastern Empire. When the emperor died on August 15, 1118, the 35-year-old princess championed her husband's claim to the position of *basileus* (king). She lost land and her title by attempting to poison her brother, who became Emperor John II Comnenius.

Following the failure of her plot, Anna Comnena retreated with her mother and younger sister Eudocia to the Convent of the Mother of God Kecharitomene (Full of Grace), which Empress Irene had founded in Constantinople. In solitude, Anna wrote medical texts and family history. Meanwhile, Nicephorus Bryennius, who had not cooperated with her plot, continued to act as a royal adviser to Emperor John. He had also begun work on an essay on the reign of Alexius I Comnenus. After he died in 1137, Anna Comnena assumed the completion of her husband's work, researching the imperial archives, combat data, foreign dispatches, and a history written by John, archdeacon of Bari. Influenced by the style of Greek historians Polybius, THUCYDIDES, and XENOPHON, she thus began an 11-year project, compiling in Greek a major work of CRUSADER LORE: the *Alexiad,* or *Alexias* (ca. 1148), a chronicle of Byzantine events from her father's crowning in 1081 to his death in 1118. In 15 books, she presented political and cultural events of the First Crusade (1095–96), when Robert Guiscard and his son Bohemund of Taranto led Norman warriors southeast to recover the Holy Lands from the Saracens. In addition to a biography of the Emperor Alexius I, she reported on etiquette and protocol, disease and healing, field strategy, fire ships, siege machinery and weaponry, learning and divination, state finances, character profiles, and court intrigues of the High Middle Ages.

The *Alexiad*

The first major history to arise from the medieval Greek renaissance, the *Alexiad* contrasts the cultures that warred over Constantinople during and after the First Crusade. In mature, focused prose phrased in high literary style, Anna Comnena introduces a dilemma: the two-pronged intrusions of Turks to the east and Norman Franks to the west. She states in Book 4, "Turkish infiltration had scattered the eastern armies in all directions and the Turks were in almost complete control of all the districts between the Black Sea and the Hellespont" (Anna Comnena 2004, 38). At the height of danger, she pictures Alexius as man of the hour, the only savior shrewd and experienced enough to rescue the Eastern Empire. He is paired with the author's grandmother, Anna Dalassena, and the two governors manage a situation that threatens chaos equal to the sacking of Rome by the Visigoths. The author remarks that her grandmother understood "motives, ultimate consequences, interrelations good and bad of various courses of action, penetrating quickly to the right solution, adroitly and safely carrying it out" (119).

Although secluded in a convent, Anna Comnena kept herself informed. She admired her mother in Book 14 for accompanying Alexius on his campaigns and lauded Sichelgaita of Salerno, an Amazonian Lombard called "Gaita" who married Robert Guiscard and followed him into battle against the infidels. According to Anna Comnena, Gaita was "another Pallas, if not a second Athena" (147). The author turned Gaita's courage into high drama. Prefiguring Joan of Arc, Gaita raises the fighting spirit of men by dressing in armor and brandishing a spear while riding at full gallop ahead of the Norman phalanx. Questioning the manhood of deserters, she yells in Homeric style, "How far will ye run? Halt! Be men!" The image, grandly pictorial, preserves for history one of the stunning female warriors of the Middle Ages.

Critics admire Anna Comnena's eloquence, scope, and command of geography, combat tactics, and psychology. Composing in her early sixties, she excelled at characterizing enemies in brief, describing Robert Guiscard as nourished on evil, Bohemond as a streaking thunderbolt, and Gregory VII as a prelate unworthy of the position of high priest. Contemporaries who doubted the authorship offered a left-handed compliment in claiming that so excellent a history could not be the work of a mere woman. The stream of praise to Alexius raises questions of author objectivity, beginning in Book 1, when the text describes Bryennius's failure to murder the emperor as the hand of God preserving Alexius for a great destiny. More favorable critiques value Anna Comnena for detailing the personalities of significant figures—Tancred, Malik

Shah, Hugh of Vermandois, Marianus, Kilij Arslan, Henry IV, Godfrey de Bouillon, and Michael VII. Like Greek tragedy, the text winds down from the burning of Basil the Bogomil at the stake in the Hippodrome to Alexius's death, perhaps the most significant moment in the author's life. Like epic, the history preserves Alexius's deeds and statecraft as turning points in the survival of the Byzantine Empire. The high points of Alexius's reign colored an anonymous Bavarian hero tale, *König Rother* (King Rother, ca. 1150), a crusader adventure from the Lombard Cycle.

Sources

Anna Comnena. *Alexias*. Translated by E. R. A. Sewter. London: Penguin, 2004.

Edgington, Susan, and Sarah Lambert. *Gendering the Crusades*. New York: Columbia University Press, 2002.

Gouma-Peterson, Thalia, ed. *Anna Komnene and Her Times*. New York: Routledge, 2000.

Antin, Mary   See AUTOBIOGRAPHY.

apocalypse

A mystic literature of disclosure, apocalypse ranges beyond PROPHECY and VISIONARY LITERATURE to allegorical visions of the end of time. Dramatizations of the earth's annihilation often employ imaginative beasts and supernatural forces, elements of the Hindu WISDOM LITERATURE in the BHAGAVAD GITA (ca. 200 B.C.) and of The War of the Sons of Light against the Sons of Darkness and The Vision of Michael, two of the DEAD SEA SCROLLS completed in an Essene enclave in Palestine in 27 B.C. Another surge of last days occurs in LEO TOLSTOY's WAR AND PEACE (1869), which satirizes Russian peasants for declaring Napoleon Bonaparte to be the Antichrist.

Biblical Apocalypse

The New Testament book of Revelation (A.D. 95), also called the Apocalypse of John, thunders with wrath and condemnation and tells of celestial justice and recompense for victims. The subjects are probably defiant Christians persecuted by the

Roman Empire and forced into worship of the emperors Tiberius between A.D. 14 and 37, Caligula for the next four years, Claudius until 54, and Nero until 68. A new round of torments under Septimius Severus aroused the wrathful prophecy of the Carthaginian essayist TERTULLIAN, author of *Apologeticus* (*The Apology,* ca. A.D. 198). His pro-Christian polemics picture the Roman Empire as the beast known as the Antichrist.

Scriptural interpreters surmise that the book of Revelation, full of futuristic phantasms, is also an ecstatic form of PRISON LITERATURE written during the reign of Domitian. The putative author is John the Divine, an inmate of a penal colony on Patmos island, southwest of Ephesus. Based on Old Testament prophecy, the vision dramatizes a battle between good and evil after the descent of a glorious messiah. Superstition links seven candles, candleholders, lamps, and stars to the light shed by the first Christian churches at Ephesus, Laodicea, Pergamum, Philadelphia, Sardis, Smyrna, and Thyatira. Orchestrating thunder, lightning, hail, and an earthquake, John sweeps into a resounding doxology: "Holy, holy, holy, Lord God Almighty, which was, and is, and is to come" (Revelation 4:8). In anticipation of the second coming of Christ, John links the Messiah to the Israelite empire and the Davidic line, which claims the truest light, "the bright and morning star" (Revelation 22:16).

Islamic Apocalypse

In the KORAN (A.D. 633), the holy book of the Islamic Empire (622–1258), no sinner escapes punishment in the afterlife. A surreal vision of the earth's demise and the opening of graves dominates Surah 100. The return of the dead to sit under Allah's judgment takes on terrifying extremes of galloping horses and eternal damnation for materialists. A promised requital to lovers of luxury pictures a cluster of moths, a metaphor for a fluttering emptiness. In Surah 7, believers refuse even the comfort of water to apostates, an image typical of desert literature.

Like the underworld tribunal in the Egyptian BOOK OF THE DEAD (ca. 1240 B.C.), Muslims anticipate the weighing of their sins on Allah's scales of justice and the condemnation of the corrupt to a fiery abyss. In Surah 21, the prophet Muhammad states, "We shall set up just scales on the Day of Resurrection, so that no man shall in the least be wronged. Actions as small as a grain of mustard seed shall be weighed out" (Koran 21:47). The second surah asserts, "God has set a seal upon their hearts and ears; their sight is dimmed and grievous punishment awaits them" (Koran 2:5). In the next surah, the text warns that apostates "shall become the fuel of the Fire" (Koran 3:10). By the time that Muslims possessed a standardized text, the Koran served as a spiritual guide to late seventh-century proselytizing in Persia, Turkey, and North Africa.

Sources

The Koran. Translated by N. J. Dawood. London: Penguin Classics, 2004.
Revelation. In the Holy Bible. Iowa Falls, Iowa: World Bible Publishers, 1986.

Arabian Nights, The   See THOUSAND AND ONE NIGHTS, THE.

Aristophanes   See GREEK DRAMA.

Augustine, Saint **(Aurelius Augustinus, St. Augustine of Hippo)** (354–430) *Numidian philosopher and theologian*

Three years after the sack of Rome by the Visigoths in A.D. 410, a priestly visionary and student of Latin philosophy, Aurelius Augustinus of Tagaste, Numidia (present-day Algeria), looked beyond the failures of Rome's 69 emperors to a celestial utopia. The son of Monica, a Christian, and of Patricius, a Roman civil servant, St. Augustine of Hippo, as he was later called, studied at a Numidian school in Madaurus (present-day M'Daourouch, Algeria). At age 15, he completed a self-study of Cicero's writings and speeches. In A.D. 371, a benefactor paid for Augustine's tuition to an academy of rhetoric at Carthage in Tunisia. After teaching in Rome and Milan, he began questioning his own licentious behavior, a process he later related in an AUTOBIOGRAPHY, *Confessiones* (*Confessions,* A.D. 398). This classic personal narrative outlines his atonement, search for salvation, and conversion to Christianity. During the last decades of Roman imperialism, Augustine admits, "I was storm-tossed by a confused mixture . . . swept over the precipices of desire and thrust into the whirlpools of vice" (Augustine 2001, 25–26). The prayerful tone of his self-castigation served anti-Roman pietists as a model of contrition.

As the Roman world collapsed, Augustine sided with Christianity, and he rose to the ecclesiastical position of bishop of Hippo (present-day Bone, Algeria) in 396. He admired the movement that replaced Roman arrogance and soullessness with the charity and otherworldliness embodied in the life of Jesus and championed by the evangelist PAUL of Tarsus. In *De civitate dei contra paganos* (*Concerning the City of God against the Pagans*, A.D. 426), Augustine refutes a pervasive fear that the collapse of the Roman hegemony would precipitate an end to the world. In chapter 9 of the first book, he consoles the faithful, "In this universal catastrophe, the sufferings of Christians have tended to their moral improvement, because they viewed them with the eyes of faith" (Augustine 1984, 14). In his critique of imperialism, the Eternal City of Rome gave the impression of solidarity, but the Christian City of God repudiated earthly glory and conquest with a truly unending paradise.

Augustine maintained equanimity in his view of imperialism. In chapter 12 of Book 5, he declares that "the true God deigned to help the Romans in the extension of their empire; for in his control are all the kingdoms of the earth" (196). He summarizes the passage of power from Julius Caesar to Augustus through Nero, Vespasian, Titus, Domitian, and Julian. Of the divine blessing on Constantine, the first Christian emperor, the text assures readers that God directed Rome's advance from paganism to righteousness. Augustine concludes his spiritual guidebook with a description of God as a giver of the elements, nature, and human life and a bestower of divine right to govern: "Among those gifts is dominion . . . and this God bestowed in accordance with his government of temporal affairs" (223). In the philosopher's perspective, the spiritual vacuum that marked Rome's last centuries provided a suitable milieu for the rise of God's utopia.

Sources

Augustine. *Concerning the City of God against the Pagans.* Translated by Henry Bettenson. London: Penguin, 1984.

———. *The Confessions of St. Augustine.* Translated by Rex Warner. New York: Signet, 2001.

Mitchell, Stephen. *A History of the Later Roman Empire,* A.D. *284–641: The Transformation of the Ancient World.* London: Blackwell, 2006.

autobiography

As a source on the establishment and growth of empires, autobiography offers eyewitness accounts of the fate of nations. Examples range from the even-tempered musings in *Travels of Marco Polo* (1298) and in the globe-trotter IBN BATTUTA's *On the Curiosities of Cities and the Wonders of Travel* (1354) to the apologia for Arab sovereignty in THOMAS EDWARD LAWRENCE's *Seven Pillars of Wisdom* (1922); JOSEPH BRODSKY's reminiscences on imprisonment and censorship in *So Forth* (1996); and Marjane Satrapi's children's tale *Persepolis* (2002), Iran's first graphic novel. Nonwhite memoirists set standards of multicultural commentary on empires, notably in the combat reportage of Scots-Jamaican herbalist MARY JANE SEACOLE's *Wonderful Adventures of Mrs. Seacole in Many Lands* (1857) and Mohandas Gandhi's advice to passive resisters in *An Autobiography: The Story of My Experiments with Truth* (1927–29).

The novelist George Sand (1804–76), a notoriously self-centered author and socialite, turned philosophical in *Histoire de Ma Vie* (*Story of My Life*, 1855) by compiling her observations about the Napoleonic Empire. She viewed all centralized powers as an "eternal secret society," a danger to the peasantry and to democracy (Sand 1991, 342). Like a couturier critiquing costume, she accused the government of overdressing in its self-important title of empire. Of Napoleon's fall, she warned of a perilous interim when his subjects "were going to perish by the thousands for his glory, and the reign of the courtiers was going to flourish anew, more brilliantly and more insolently than under the former monarchy" (178). In a shot at Bonapartist imperialism, Sand dismissed the emperor for "his fundamental flaw—the profound aristocratic vanity of the parvenu" (526).

In the last years of the Hawaiian kingdom, the text of *Hawaii's Story by Hawaii's Queen, Liliuokalani* (1898) surveyed the excellent administration of the autobiographer and her brother. David Kalakaua (1836–91), the island chain's last king, was both a journalist and a mythographer of Polynesian stories anthologized as *The Legends and Myths of Hawaii: The Fables and Folklore of a Strange People* (1888). Liliuokalani (1838–1917) followed his scholarly example with a translated account of the history of the archipelagos, the *Kumulipo* (The beginning, 1897), a chant that moves from the creation story to her family's genealogy. Like VIRGIL's AENEID (17 B.C.), the text has propaganda value for Liliuokalani's validation of Hawaii's dynasty. However, her autobiography, *Hawaii's Story,* is more explicit on issues of imperialism. In chapter 29, the memoir summarizes the faults of John L. Stevens, the American minister to the islands who, in 1895, imprisoned Liliuokalani at Iolani Palace for 10 months and deposed her for an alleged rebellion. The queen charges the ambassador with outright piracy: "As they became wealthy and acquired lands through the simplicity of our people and their ignorance of values and of the new land laws, their greed and their love of power proportionately increased" (Liliuokalani 1898, 177), an accusation also supported by the outcome of American dealings with Indians.

In the patriotic style of the Byzantine chronicler ANNA COMNENA and Russian novelist LEO TOLSTOY, Liliuokalani takes the measure of vying parties and exposes the rapacity that brought down Hawaii's native Polynesian rule. She mourns, "My kingdom was but the assured prey of these 'conquistadores'" (234), a verbal connection of Hawaii's fate with that of the Aztec Empire of Montezuma. In her reflection over imperialism, she complains of personal humiliation, the treachery of American investors, and the devaluation of her native culture, which white interlopers mocked and reviled. She refers to a sentiment of WILLIAM SHAKESPEARE in her declaration that "it is excellent to have a giant's strength, but it is tyrannous to use it like a giant" (370). She left her people a legacy:

land for an orphanage and some 150 songs in *The Queen's Songbook* (1973), a posthumous collection of Polynesian originals containing her most famous lyric, "Aloha Oe."

The Immigrant's Memoir

Books by newcomers to North America, such as the Polish immigrant ANZIA YEZIERSKA, author of *Bread Givers* (1925), and ADELINE YEN MAH (b. 1937), author of *Falling Leaves: The True Story of an Unwanted Chinese Daughter* (1997), also document, with hindsight, prejudice and turmoil left behind in their home countries when realms collapse. The classic immigrant autobiography *The Promised Land* (1912), by journalist Mary Antin (1881–1949), opens on childhood memories of life "Within the Pale," her term for Jewish ghetto life on the Polish border in Polotzk, Russia (present-day Belarus). Of the purpose of autobiography, she exults, "I take the hint from the Ancient Mariner, who told his tale in order to be rid of it. I will write a bold 'Finis' at the end, and shut the book with a bang!" (Antin 1912, xv). From a child's perspective, she visualizes imperial power: "Why, in Russia lived the Czar, and a great many cruel people; and in Russia were the dreadful prisons from which people never came back" (3), a situation that developed into the post–World War II gulag system of Joseph Stalin. To her bemusement, her father, the scholar Isaiah Antin, posted in their home the obligatory portrait of Czar Alexander III, "a Titus, a Haman, a sworn foe of all Jews" (18). Forced fealty required peasants to pawn their goods to buy flags to fly for the ruler's birthday, a cruel hypocrisy that drove some Jews into penury.

From toddlerhood, Antin learned that she belonged to an outcast race. Russian Jews suffered pogroms, confiscation of goods, child kidnap, and military impressment. More common hardships involved capricious arrest, taxation, and extortion by gentile police, who thrust the offenders behind the fence around Polotzk that segregated Jews from gentile Russians. More fearful to Antin were processions of Catholics and priests, who "might baptize me. That would be worse than death by torture" (9). Rather than accept a triune god, Antin preferred to "be seized with the plague, and be eaten up by vermin" (9). In so fearful a Russian Orthodox and czarist milieu, Jewish children "with old, old faces and eyes glazed with secrets" learned to "dodge and cringe and dissemble" (26). The toughening of youngsters growing up "hungry-minded and empty-hearted" instilled pride in her people's religious integrity, which they refused to water down or compromise (228).

After settling in Boston at age 13, Antin published her first poem in the *Boston Herald* only two years later. She subsequently moved to New York, where she married Amadeus Grabau, a professor at Columbia University, and attended Barnard College. After publishing *The Promised Land*, she produced *They Who Knock at Our Gates: A Complete Gospel of Immigration* (1914), a stirring treatise on civil liberties. Fervid with American nationalism, the text salutes Russian revolutionaries for plotting "under the very nose of the Czar" against "the benighted condition of the Russian masses" (Antin 1914, 41). The publication preceded by three years the successful Russian Revolution and the assassination of the last Romanov emperor, Nicholas II.

Empire Seen from the Air

A heroic chronicler of the French empire in Africa, Antoine de Saint-Exupéry (1900–44) of Lyon observed a borderless earth from the cockpit of a single-engine plane. He won a wide audience for his pilot's memoir *Terre des hommes*, published in English as *Wind, Sand, and Stars* (1939). The author's philosophy of global cooperation presaged the air age. Comparing the establishment of airlines to the founding of empires, he stated, "For the colonial soldier who founds an empire, the meaning of life is conquest. He despises the colonist" (Saint-Exupéry 2002, 46). He warned that forcing people to serve technology created an advanced form of imperialism until "little by little the machine will become part of humanity" (46).

While pioneering long-distance commercial flights that preceded the establishment of Aéropostale, the first French aviation corporation, the author observed changes in the world preceding World War II, particularly the intoxicating egotism of pan-Germanism, the philosophy underlying the Nazi empire. In his final collection, *Ecrits de guerre* (*Wartime Writings*, 1938–44), he stated, "There

are forty million people over there in France who must endure their slavery," a reference to the fearful appetite of the Nazi regime for expansion and for exterminating French gypsies and Jews (Saint-Exupéry 1982, 91). He declared that "war ceased to be a glorious outing" when Europe became one vast mortuary (48). Outraged at the carnage, he called for an end to imperialists' game playing and an end to territorial conquest and GENOCIDE.

A contemporary of Saint-Exupéry and fellow commercial pilot, Beryl Markham (1902–86) lived a multicultural existence in the far reaches of the British Empire. She captured the atmosphere of British East Africa (present-day Kenya) in a best-selling memoir, *West with the Night* (1942), which the National Geographic Society chose as one of the 100 best adventure books of all time. Her oneness with a colonial homeland derived from personal liberty on an unconquerable veld: "Competitors in conquest have overlooked the vital soul of Africa herself, from which emanates the true resistance to conquest" (Markham 1942, 7). Born in Rutland, England, she came to Africa as a toddler and grew up on a farm in the Great Rift Valley at Njoro, 70 miles northwest of Nairobi. In acknowledgement of Nairobi's centrality to world commerce, she called it "a counting house in the wilderness—a place of shillings and pounds and land sales and trade, extraordinary successes and extraordinary failures" (6). While apprenticing at her father's horse-breeding trade, she played Kenyan board games; memorized stories and African march rhythms; wrestled in the style of the Nandi tribe; and rode her horse, Wee MacGregor, at Elkington Farm near the Kikuyu Reserve. In addition to bow hunting and surviving in the wild, she mastered Swahili from Bishon Singh, a Sikh stableman, and spoke the African dialects of the Kikuyu, Kipsigis, Luo, and Nandi.

After learning to pilot a Gypsy Moth bush plane in 1931, Markham completed a 23-day solo flight from Nairobi to Juba, Sudan, up the Nile to Cairo, and across Europe to London's Heston Airport. She balanced adventuring as an aerial safari scout and relay ambulance pilot with writing short stories, including "Praise God for the Blood of the Bull" (1942), an account of the Masai blood cult and spear-hunting warthogs on the Molo

River. In her autobiography, she thought back on the illusion of total freedom in Kenya, when her friend Kibii warned, "What a child does not know and does not want to know of race and colour and class, he learns soon enough as he grows to see each man flipped inexorably into some predestined groove like a penny or a sovereign in a banker's rack" (1942, 149). During World War II, she wrote of international plotting to seize African assets. Of Kenya's fate, she called European invasion a "foothold" secured by "endless dispute and bloodshed . . . and the noisy drum-rolling of bickering empires" (1942, 7, 8). Upon retirement to postcolonial Kenya, the author turned an early chapter of her memoir into a children's story, *The Good Lion* (1983), her first-person encounter with a pet lion named Paddy. In the film *Out of Africa* (1985), the character Felicity portrays Markham and her relationship with fabulist and memoirist ISAK DINESEN (Karen Blixen) and hunter Denys Finch-Hatton. A biopic, *Beryl Markham: Shadow on the Sun* (1988), features Stefanie Powers as Markham.

See also EQUIANO, OLAUDAH; NAPOLEONIC LITERATURE; POLO, MARCO; PRINCE, MARY; PRINCE, NANCY GARDNER; PRISON LITERATURE; WOMEN'S JOURNALS, DIARIES, AND LETTERS.

Sources

Antin, Mary. *The Promised Land*. Boston: Houghton Mifflin, 1912.

———. *They Who Knock at Our Gates: A Complete Gospel of Immigration*. Boston: Houghton Mifflin, 1914.

Liliuokalani. *Hawaii's Story by Hawaii's Queen, Liliuokalani*. Boston: Lothrop, Lee & Shepard, 1898.

———. *The Kumulipo: An Hawaiian Creation Myth*. Honolulu: Pueo Press, 1978.

———. *The Queen's Songbook*. Edited by Dorothy K. Gillett and Barbara B. Smith. Honolulu: Hui Hanai, 1999.

Markham, Beryl. *The Good Lion*. Boston: Houghton Mifflin, 1983.

———. *The Splendid Outcast: Beryl Markham's African Stories*. San Francisco, Calif.: North Point, 1987.

———. *West with the Night*. Berkeley, Calif.: North Point Press, 1942.

McCay, Mary A. "Beyond Femaleness: Beryl Markham, Africa's Adopted Daughter in *West with the Wind*." In *Nwanyibu: Womanbeing & African Literature*, edited by Phanuel Akubueze Egejuru and Ketu H. Katrak. New Orleans, La.: Africa World Press, 1997.

Saint-Exupéry, Antoine de. *Wartime Writings*. Translated by Lewis Galantière. Fort Washington, Pa.: Harvest, 1982.

———. *Wind, Sand, and Stars*. Translated by Lewis Galantière. Fort Washington, Pa.: Harvest, 2002.

Sand, George. *Story of My Life: The Autobiography of George Sand*. Edited by Thelma Jurgrau. New York: State University of New York Press, 1991.

Silva, Noenoe K. *Aloha Betrayed: Native Hawaiian Resistance to American Colonialism*. Durham, N.C.: Duke University Press, 2004.

Avesta (ca. 530)

A collection of scripture, hymns, and Zoroastrian doctrines, the Avesta ("Praise of God") preserves libertarian wisdom from the last years of the Achaemenid-Persian Empire (550–330 B.C.) and the beginnings of the Sassanian dynasty (A.D. 224–651). A member of a pastoral tribe at Rhages, outside Tehran, near the juncture of the current borders of Afghanistan, Iran, and Turkmenistan, the monotheist Zarathustra (628–551 B.C.) served as a priest-diviner of the creator-god Ahura Mazda. Around 600–590 B.C., a vision of light, omniscience, power, virtue, charity, and immortality led Zarathustra to spread a felicitous Middle Eastern faith. Like the Chinese Buddhist DAODEJING (*Tao-te Ching* [Classic of the way of power, 300 B.C.]) and the *Meditations* (ca. A.D. 180) of the Roman emperor MARCUS AURELIUS, Zarathustra's works advocated a well-ordered life dedicated to justice, thrift, neighborliness, and compassion. His writings comprised the first ancient scripture based on the universality of all races and cultures, male and female, slave and free. By compiling oral traditions from the previous millennium, he assimilated Iranian poetry and theology in 2 million verses that anticipated the monotheism of Judaism, Christianity, and Islam. Central to the prophet's thinking were images of the character of God and of Satan, the resurrection of the dead, and an eternal struggle between *asha* and *druj* (truth and lies), a yin-yang duality underlying the human condition. Against centuries of tribalism and vengeance, his sermons looked ahead to a messiah and an era of peace.

Zoroastrianism emerged from central Asia during the advance of rootless people from nomadism to agrarianism. When Cyrus II the Great of Persia (r. ca. 550–529 B.C.) seized Media in 549 B.C., the disciple Vishtaspa secured the first texts of the Avesta in a settlement that became Persepolis, Iran. He stored a second copy in the safe at a fire temple in Samarkand, Uzbekistan. After Zarathustra introduced the emperor Cyrus and his family and court to Zoroastrianism in 588 B.C., the priest promoted ethical ideals as a goal higher than tribal feuds, hatred, banditry, ruin, and waste. Ironically, tribalism ended the prophet's life. During a ritual service at the Temple of the Sacred Fire, nomadic Hyaona (Bactrian) insurgents stabbed the 77-year-old Zarathustra, slew his priests, and burned the Avesta. To survivors, the rainbow became a symbol of the founder's guardianship in the afterlife, but life on earth reduced worshippers to decades of war and conquest as the Persian Empire became the mightiest in human history.

Imperiled Scripture

While the boundaries of Persia expanded from the Mediterranean Sea south to Egypt and East to India, Zoroastrians clung to the spirit of peace and brotherhood. They venerated their martyred priest and kept alive the 21-word Ahuna Vairya, the sect's simplest and most sacred prayer, or hymn, the first that children memorized and recited. Under the Persian king Darius I (r. 522–486 B.C.), Zoroastrianism briefly syncretized with polytheism, then restored Ahura Mazda to primacy at Naqsh-i-Rustam, a cube-shaped tower near Persepolis in south-central Iran. Under emperors Artaxerxes II (r. 404–358 B.C.) and Artaxerxes III (r. 358–338 B.C.), the monotheism of Ahura Mazda developed into a trinity with Anahita and Mithra. To foster Hellenism, Alexander the Great (356–323 B.C.; r. 336–323 B.C.) threatened the survival of the Avesta by murdering temple keepers and torching Persepolis in 330 B.C., reducing 12,000 inscribed cowhides to 3,000 manuscripts covering creation, law, ritual, prayers, and wisdom.

The Sassanian dynasty, led by Ardashir I (ruled ca. A.D. 206–241) the great unifier of Persia, coaxed a flicker of Zoroastrianism back to life by restoring ceremonial fire altars, the heart of reverence for Ahura Mazda. During the Roman emperor Alexander Severus's invasion of Persia in A.D. 232, the theologian Tansar rescued holy writings by compiling Zarathustra's remaining holy texts, which his son, the high priest Kirder, expanded with new writings anthologized as the Khurda Avesta (younger Avesta), a compendium of prayers, chants, and rituals composed for specific occasions. In the Khurda Avesta, Kirder stressed the danger of conquest to Zoroastrianism and wrote, "Strip ye the wicked of all power. Absolute in power may the holy be" (Avesta, 2004, 10). In place of imperial control, Kirder pled for Ahura to empower the poor to alleviate their misery. To a nation long suppressed, the text called for liberty, healing, and an end to imperial materialism. Devotees reverenced the text until the mid-seventh century, when Islam supplanted Zoroastrianism as the state religion of Iran and the Koran superseded the Avesta.

A Canon of Old and New

The completed Avesta, written in Zend and Aramaic, represents a shift from barbarity to civilized urbanism. The text opens with the 72-part Yasna (worship), a life-affirming liturgy devoid of the wine drinking of Greek worship of Dionysus and the animal sacrifice of the Hebrews to Yahweh. Symbolizing regeneration, fire ritual incorporated recitations of holy vows, prayers, litanies, a creed, propitiation of the day, hymns to Ahura Mazda, and blessings. The core of the Avesta venerates good thoughts, good words, and good deeds as antidotes to evil. The text includes the Zoroastrian creed, a first-person declaration of allegiance to goodness and of defiance of wrongdoing. Lyric poems give thanks for the liberty to build a home and raise livestock, a statement that disavows nomadism and semicivilized lifestyles based on hit-and-run thievery, "whom wide-hoofed horses carry against havocking hosts, against enemies coming in battle array, in the strife of conflicting nations" (Avesta 2004, 65).

A more sacred section, the Gathas, consists of ancient songs akin to the Indian Vedas and the biblical PSALMS of David. They preserve in Gatha-Avestan dialect the allusive chants, PROPHECY, revelations, and meditations of Zarathustra himself. Theological sections portray God as a parent reassuring a child: "My name is the protector, my name is the well-wisher; my name is the creator, my name is the keeper, my name is the maintainer" (24). Graced with metaphysical and transcendent elements, the lines exhort the devout to embrace the universe in its tangible and mystical forms, including marriage and family, righteousness, and an afterlife in the "House of Song." Verses demand an end to religious persecution of pacifists.

Imagery of light anchors Zoroastrian holy writ. For guidance, the worshipper cries out like the Hebrew poet David to Yahweh, "Give me, O Fire, . . . the best world of the righteous, the shining, the all-happy, so that it may fulfill my wish, now and for ever, so as to attain to good reward, and to good renown, and to long happiness of my soul!" (21). On earth, a holy idyll foresees wide pastures for the peasant stockman and offers "homage to the sun, the swift-horsed," a metaphor that suggests the Greek myth of Helios and his chariot of the sun (12). In anticipation of eternal bliss, one gatha pictures the soul crossing the bridge into immortality and wishes that the spirit "may be released from hell and may . . . pass over to the best existence of the holy, the bright" (16). Sonorous praise pictures God as "radiant, glorious, omniscient, maker, lord of lords, king over all kings, watchful, creator of the universe, giver of daily bread, powerful, strong, eternal, forgiver, merciful, loving, mighty, wise, holy, and nourisher" (12).

The humanity of the Avesta addresses the needs and questions of Middle Easterners of all castes. In the Vendidad (protection), composed in Parthian between 141 B.C. and A.D. 224, ancient mantras against terror calm frightened chanters during the night. Imagery parallels Hebrew mythology of Noah and the flood, Levitican laws and purification rites, and formulaic healing. The Yashts (anthems), written in Aryan, the ancient Persian language, muse on adversity and destruction and on the joys of peace in limitless nature.

The concepts of Zoroastrianism survived in the naming of the hero Sorastro in Wolfgang Amadeus Mozart's opera *The Magic Flute* (1791) and in German philosopher Friedrich Wilhelm Nietzsche's *Also Sprach Zarathustra* (*Thus Spake Zarathustra*, 1883–85), an anti-Judaeo-Christian treatise on willpower and self-mastery from the Austro-Hungarian Empire that influenced Adolf Hitler's manifesto MEIN KAMPF (1925–26), the wellspring of Nazism.

Sources

Avesta Khorda Avesta: Book of Common Prayer. Translated by James Darmesteter. Whitefish, Mont.: Kessenger, 2004.

Moulton, James Hope. *Early Religious Poetry of Persia.* Boston: Adamant Media, 2005.

Aztec, literature on the

Pre-Columbian Indian lore and the downfall of the Aztec Empire (1375–1521) of central Mexico at the hands of Spanish conquistadores inspired dramatic, often contradictory Nahuatl codices and Spanish chronicles. The narratives, recorded in pictographs and words on cloth, hide, and paper, contain CREATION myths, ritual calendars, astral and geological marvels, PROPHECY, herbalism, trades and artistry, dynastic and military biography, and tactical and diplomatic details. In the pre-Columbian decades, Nezahualcoyotl (1402–72), a poet-sage and ruler of Texcoco, spoke from an existentialist point of view the brevity and fragility of life. He encouraged monotheism through gifts of incense and garlands to Moyocoyatia, the creator and supreme being. One of his hymns, "Flowers Have Come" (ca. 1460), speaks humbly of borrowing "your flowered drum, / your bells, / your song" as elements of peaceful worship (Roberts 1991, 302). The gentle verse refutes claims of the brutal Aztecs reported by travelers from Spain.

In 1568, the soldier of fortune Bernal Díaz del Castillo (1496–1584) of Medina del Campo, Spain, corrected mistaken or false accounts with *Historia verdaera de la conquista de la Nueva España* (*The True History of the Conquest of New Spain*), a military account of Hernán Cortés's crushing of the Aztec realm (1519–21). Written with a veteran's swagger, the text employs the lingua franca of the conquistador in terms of safe harborage, substantial rations, and the occasional comely female. During a one-sided battle at a low point during their conquest, Díaz regrets losing female servants, equipment, cannon, and men drowned and slain by Indians; he and other warriors cry to the Virgin Mary and to Santiago de Compostella, Spain's patron saint. Díaz, like WILLIAM SHAKESPEARE's Falstaff, speaks the survivor's wisdom: "That man would, indeed, have been a fool who had thought of anything else but of his own safety!" (Díaz 1844, 350). In Díaz's account, even Cortés runs for his life.

Writing Imperial History

While Díaz was reliving his expeditionary glories and brushes with death in the New World, Dominican monk and translator Diego Durán (ca. 1537–88) took a chronicler's view of the fall of the Aztec Empire. Published in 1867 as *Historia de las Indias de Nueva-España* (*The History of the Indies of New Spain*), the Aubin Codex is a history of the Aztecs in text and pictures, as overseen by Durán. Begun in 1576, it outlines royal genealogies and ritual and is substantiated in part by the Dominican historian BARTOLOMÉ DE LAS CASAS's *Brevísima relación de la destrucción de las Indias* (*A Short Account of the Destruction of the Indies*, 1542). Written during the golden age of Mexican historiography, the codex predicts disaster for the highland Mexica at the hands of Spain, a muscular, enterprising empire in the first decades of its powers.

Durán's lethal vision accounts for the collapse of the Aztec civilization. In April 1520, during the Feast of Huitzilopochtli, some 600 Aztec citizens drummed and danced naked at the sacred Patio of the Gods when 50 Spanish soldiers, led by Lieutenant Pedro de Alvarado, closed three gates and, amid wails of trapped celebrants, cut down 200 Indian nobles with sword slashes. The narrative reports: "Everywhere were intestines, severed heads, hands and feet. Some men walked around with their entrails hanging out due to knife and lance thrusts" (Durán 1994, 537). Durán supplied an Aztec account of the death of 54-year-old Montezuma II on La Noche Triste (the night of sorrows)—June 30, 1520—in the 18th year of his reign at the Temple of Tenochtitlan (present-day Mexico City). (Many Spanish accounts say Montezuma was killed by his own people. Indigenous accounts blame the Spanish, and one reports Cortés pouring molten gold down the emperor's throat.) The codex blames the emperor for a fatal error in allying with Cortés, whom the Aztec considered a double dealer. A subsequent Nahuatl publication,

Anales de Tlatelolco (Annals of Tlatelolco, 1528), assembles anonymous Aztec reflections on the state of the traumatized nation following conquest.

Polished Chronicles

More thorough reportage appeared in the latter portion of the 16th century. Bernardino de Sahagún (1499–1590), a Franciscan Latin grammarian, dictionary compiler, and mendicant friar from León, Spain, earned the title of father of modern ethnography and became the world's first anthropologist for his detailed study of Mesoamerican aborigines. He excelled at recording and analyzing Mesoamerican speech, the most researched language indigenous to the Western Hemisphere. From Nahua elders, he collected elements of native culture and religion for his *Florentine Codex,* a 12-volume encyclopedia completed in Nahuatl and Spanish and illustrated between 1547 and 1569. Among his contributions to the literature of empire is a floor plan of the Temple of Tenochtitlan and a description of the Aztec refusal to claim Emperor Montezuma's remains. Before Cortés breached the inner sanctum, prophets warned the emperor, "His power and his pride are coming to an end" (Sahagún 1979, 33). A frequently quoted addendum from 1585 reports a more insidious onslaught, the plague of 1576, when tongues turned black and eyes yellow, boils arose behind the ears, and lips and genitalia developed gangrene. Sahagún himself saw thousands of victims die in an advanced state of putrefaction. Until 1979, the Catholic church suppressed uncensored sections of the work, later known as the *Historia General de las cosas de Nueva España* (A general history of things in New Spain).

Recovered literature from the preconquest era introduced Europeans to the authentic Aztec philosophy of life. A song collection by native scribes for a Catholic missionary, the *Cantares Mexicanos* (Mexican songs, ca. 1590), contains 91 of some 175 known Nahuatl verses and music representative of an oral culture. Included in the text are variations of the *Romances de los señores de Nueva España* (*Ballads of the Lords of New Spain,* 1582), collected by historian Juan Bautista Pomar (ca. 1535–90) of Texcoco, Mexico, a bilingual mestizo who investigated preconquest customs by interviewing elderly

Aztec. The collection, like the extant Anglo-Saxon epic *Beowulf,* reflects monotheistic teachings obviously interpolated by Pomar. Universal in scope, like the Hebrew singer David's Psalm 8 (see PSALMS), the Nahua poetry captures the blaze of the quetzal's feathers, blossom songs, and the intimate joys of weddings as well as questions of life's meaning and the mysteries of death. The bard proclaims, "The Giver of Life makes us live, he knows, he decides, how we men will die. Nobody, nobody, nobody, truly lives on earth" (quoted in Portilla and Shorris 2002, 79). Of the spiritual comfort of prayer, a verse states, "Where the smoke is rising, I shall go there, I shall go, I shall go to lose myself, I shall lie down on the mat of precious feathers" a source of comfort combining the softness and brilliant colors of the quetzal, the Aztec holy bird. From these sources, William Hickling Prescott compiled his three-volume *History of the Conquest of Mexico* (1843).

Sources

Boone, Elizabeth Hill. *Cycles of Time and Meaning in the Mexican Books of Fate.* Austin: University of Texas Press, 2007.

Cantares Mexicanos: Songs of the Aztecs. Translated by John Bierhorst. Stanford, Calif.: Stanford University Press, 1985.

Díaz del Castillo, Bernal. *The Memoirs of the Conquistador Bernal Díaz del Castillo: Containing a True and Full Account of the Discovery and Conquest of Mexico and New Spain.* Translated by John Ingram Lockhart. London: J. Hatchard and Son, 1844.

———. *The True History of the Conquest of New Spain.* 5 vols. Edited by Genaro García. Translated by Alfred Percival Maudslay. London: Hakluyt Society, 1908–16.

Durán, Diego. *The History of the Indies of New Spain.* Translated by Doris Heyden. Norman: University of Oklahoma Press, 1994.

Las Casas, Bartolomé de. *A Short Account of the Destruction of the Indies.* Edited and translated by Nigel Griffin. London and New York: Penguin, 1992.

Portilla, Miguel León. *Bernardino de Sahagún, First Anthropologist.* Translated by Mauricio J. Mixco. Norman: University of Oklahoma Press, 2002.

———, and Earl Shorris. *In the Language of Kings: An Anthology of Mesoamerican Literature—Pre-Columbian to the Present.* New York: W. W. Norton, 2002.

Roberts, Elizabeth, and Elias Amidon, eds. *Earth Prayers from around the World.* San Francisco: Harper San Francisco, 1991.

Sahagún, Bernardino de. *Florentine Codex.* Translated by Charles E. Dibble and Arthur J. Anderson. Santa Fe: Monographs of the School of American Research and Museum of New Mexico, 1979.

Todorov, Tzvetan. *The Morals of History.* Translated by Alyson Waters. Minneapolis: University of Minnesota Press, 1995.

B

Bâ, Mariama (1929–1981) *Senegalese journalist and novelist*

West African feminist orator and writer Mariama Bâ promoted the empowerment of black women through affirmation and self-assertion. Born in French-controlled Dakar, Senegal, to a prominent family, she lived with maternal grandparents, Muslims who favored education for males only. Though indoctrinated with recitations of the KORAN, she began writing prose in French while enrolled at L'École Normale for girls at Rufisque. Her essays rejected assimilation, perceiving it as a slow death for African culture and language. At her father's insistence, she completed a degree in education during a period of dissolution of the European colonial empire. In 1960, Senegal threw off French imperialism, combating chauvinistic colonialism. She married Member of Parliament Obèye Diop and bore nine children. After the collapse of her marriage, she taught primary grades while serving the district as educational inspector and supporting a family of 10. A lengthy bout with cancer ended her life at age 52.

Bâ wrote of the disillusion of women with the coming of independence favoring men only. Critics praised Bâ for her epistolary novella *Une si longue lettre* (*So Long a Letter*, 1979), a semiautobiographical hymn to woman-to-woman friendship and support. Dedicated to "all women and to men of good will," the narrative adopts the style of a female griot (storyteller). Bâ encourages black females to demand civil rights and to maintain their femaleness rather than imitate Western superficiality and materialism (Bâ 1981, i). Set in modern Dakar, the first-person story dramatizes the misgivings of Ramatoulaye Fall, a widowed teacher who was married to Modou Fall, a technical consultant at the Ministry of Public Works. As though desperate for affection, she calls "My friend, my friend, my friend" to Aissatou, an immigrant to America, in a missive that is a "diary, my prop in my distress" (1). Because Aissatou abandoned a polygamous marriage to Mawdo, she is the only acquaintance who will listen without judging. Without self-pity, Ramatoulaye expresses her disillusion during an African Islamic funeral and a 40-day mourning period, a period of reflection of a 30-year marriage and 12 pregnancies: "If over the years ... dreams die, I still keep intact my memories, the salt of remembrance" (1).

Bâ's sympathetic novel spills the hidden shame of Islamic polygamy. Ramatoulaye regrets Modou's choice of another wife, Binetou, a contemporary of his daughter Daba. To justify his betrayal of Ramatoulaya, he claims that Allah wills that their home support two wives. Temporary solace, the womanly unbraiding of the widow's hair and settling her in a red mourning tent, is the work of sisters-in-law. To oust evil spirits, the women toss a fistful of coins on the tent's canopy. Contributing to Ramatoulaye's humiliation is the repossession of her worldly goods by Modou's family. She resents having to "[give] up her personality, her dignity, becoming a thing in the service of the man who has married her, his grandfather, his grandmother, his father, his mother, his brother, his sister, his uncle, his aunt, his male and female cousins, his friends" (4). After escapist trips to the cinema, she retreats into religious faith.

Bâ espoused sisterhood as a way to unify and strengthen West African women, whom she honored as social pillars and victims of patriarchy and cultural imperialism. Her journalistic pieces advocated the expunging of colonial subjugation through "archaic practices, traditions, and customs that are not a real part of our precious cultural heritage" (Bâ 1989, i). A posthumous novel, *Un chant écarlate* (*Scarlet Song*, 1981), dramatizes a bicultural union that precipitates the madness and abandonment of Mireille, the white Parisian wife of Ousmane, a traditional African male. Bâ expanded on spousal infidelity to include the French exploitation of its African colonies and the African politicians who succeeded them. "Noble sentiments have forsaken the African soul. Look how many of our African leaders, who were in the vanguard of the movements for national liberation, are unrecognisable now that they have their feet in the stirrups of power. Now they censure the very things they used to preach" (Bâ, 1995, 45–46). She concludes that men are incapable of fidelity.

Sources

Ba, Mariama. *Scarlet Song*. Translated by Dorothy S. Blair. London: Longman, 1995.
———. *So Long a Letter*. Translated by Modupé Bodé-Thomas. Heinemann, 1989.
Ibnlfassi, Laila, and Nicki Hitchcott. *African Francophone Writing: A Critical Introduction*. Oxford: Berg, 1996.

Baillie, Joanna   See FEMINISM.

Balzac, Honoré de   See NAPOLEONIC LITERATURE.

Behn, Aphra (1640–1689) *English playwright and fiction writer*

England's first abolitionist author, Aphra Behn (born Aphra Johnson) wrote feminist, anti-imperialist fiction during the English Restoration that depicted women compromised by sexism, SLAVERY, and racism. At some point in her life, either in her childhood with her parents or as an adult about 1663 (sources vary), she traveled to the Suriname River in eastern Venezuela, the source of her interest in bicultural relations in South America and the West Indies. At home at a sugar colony on St. John's Hill, Suriname, she kept a journal and educated herself through reading. In the mid-1660s, she began writing under the pseudonym Astraea. She married Johan Behn, a Dutch or German merchant, in England in 1664, though some scholars doubt whether she married at all. In 1668, after spying for Charles II in Antwerp, Belgium, during the Second Anglo-Dutch War (1665–67) and failing to be reimbursed for her expenses, she spent a short time in debtors' prison.

To clear herself of debt, Behn began writing for the stage. One tragedy based on the Othello myth, *Abdelazar; or, The Moor's Revenge* (1671), features a vengeance plot and themes of slavery and racism during the Hapsburg rule of Spain. Like a Moroccan Moses, the title character, a black-skinned prince rescued during the sack of Fez, serves the Spanish as a general but dies in ignominy in prison after a lifetime of nurturing hatred for the Spanish conquerors of the Moroccan royal family. In reference to his misery living at the royal court of a European empire enslaved as the lover of Queen Isabella, he complains, "I cannot ride through the Castilian streets, / But a thousand eyes / Throw killing looks at me" (Behn 2004, 5). He later explains the contretemps generated by the seizure of a black nation by Hispanic forces when King Philip stole the crown of King Abdela of Fez. The fifth act closes on a familiar racist stereotype, the defense of white womanhood by male family members.

With the rapid development of the trans-Atlantic slave trade from West Africa, Behn produced a tragic novella, *Oroonoko, or The Royal Slave* (1688). This elegiac work centers on humanist outrage at the Dutch flesh trade and the loss of love, dynasty, and home in the deaths of Oroonoko, his lover Imoinda, and their unborn child, a symbol of promise for the black race. Behn replaces the title character's negroid traits with European features and expressions. Christian posturing becomes the pretense by which enslavers trick black captives and force them to work on the sugarcane plantation of Lord Willoughby of Parham. Alternatives for the more rebellious heathens range from imprisonment to shackling, lashing, torture, and execution. The fate of those who escape and the deception of tribal blacks into bondage merge in a critical speech in which the hero, the nobleman called Caesar, denounces imperial degeneracy. He demands, "And why my dear friends and fellow-sufferers, should we be slaves to an unknown people. . . . We are bought and sold like apes or monkeys, to be the sport of women, fools and cowards" (Behn 1994, 61). The romance influenced Behn's contemporary, the playwright Thomas Southerne, as well as the Hispano-Cuban writer Gertrudis Gómez de Avellaneda, author of *Sab* (1841), an antislavery drama.

Sources

Behn, Aphra. *Abdelazar; or, The Moor's Revenge.* Whitefish, Mont.: Kessinger, 2004.

———. *Oroonoko and Other Writings.* Oxford: Oxford University Press, 1994.

Brown, Laura. *Ends of Empire: Women and Ideology in Early Eighteenth-Century English Literature.* Ithaca, N.Y.: Cornell University Press, 1993.

Bhagavad Gita (Song of God) (ca. 200 B.C.)

The Bhagavad Gita (Song of God) has long been the treasured scripture of devout Hindus. A moral guidebook known simply as the Gita, the Sanskrit narrative is the sixth volume of the *Mahabharata*, the epic of the Bharata dynasty and the world's longest poem, attributed to Vyasa; earliest known references to the *Mahabharata* are around the fourth century B.C. In 700 verses, the Gita echoes the moral thinking of northern Indian Brahminism, a monotheism espoused by a brotherhood of disciples of Vishnu, the supreme god. As tribes migrated across the Indian subcontinent, they spread the influence of the Gita to the Maurya Empire, an amalgamation of petty kingdoms. Like the Greek and Roman stoics, Hindus chose forbearance over anguish at ongoing power struggles and personal calamities. Devotees of the Gita gained serenity of body and spirit by contemplating the soul's release from its cyclical reincarnation into the pain and uncertainty of the material world, an action it shares with the Akkadian-Sumerian epic of GILGAMESH (ca. 1800 B.C.) and the samurai tales of Japan.

The Elements of Conquest

The Gita centers on a conversation between Arjuna, one of the Pandava brothers, and his friend and charioteer, Lord Krishna, prior to a major battle. Prince Duryodhana has seized territory from the Pandava princes, initiating the standard taking of sides through a series of alliances among lesser rulers across India. In the first stave, Arjuna, the mighty archer, captains his followers with the help of Krishna, who steers while the bowman aims and shoots. As the two advance toward their enemy on the plain of Kurukshetra in northern India, they reach a site of past struggles of over-confident conquerors. Arjuna regrets the cost of territoriality in bodies strewn across the battlefield. Many of his army are friends and relatives, notably, Karna, his enemy and half brother, whom Arjuna beheads in the Mahabharata. Arjuna admits, "I can find no means to drive away this grief. . . . I will not be able to dispel it even if I win a prosperous, unrivaled kingdom on earth with sovereignty like the demigods in heaven" (Bhagavad Gita 1989, 76). A model of the neophyte warrior-king, he begs his mentor, Krishna, for perspective on power gained through slaughter.

Like Moses in the Hebrew epic Exodus or like Phoenix, the wise Myrmidon adviser of Achilles in Homer's *Iliad*, Krishna establishes his role as the politico-religious sage of India. Before the battle begins, the mentor differentiates between material goals and the imperishability of the soul. He insists that a noble leader must think of war as a duty rather than as the source of glory or conquest. The driver reveals that he is really Vishnu in human form—the "friend of the distressed and the source of creation" (2). Through measured advice, he weans Arjuna away from terror and despair by declaring fate as the master of human affairs and death as the ultimate end for all living things. The godly voice exhorts the commander to carry out his destiny to restore order among his people. Similar in tone to the apocalyptic The War of the Sons of Light against the Sons of Darkness in the DEAD SEA SCROLLS (27 B.C.), the Hindu motif of the battle of good versus evil covers 18 days of combat before the Pandavans defeat Prince Duryodhana.

Touching the Sublime

Krishna's outline of spirituality in chapter six of the Gita transcends earthly desire by directing the spirit toward a form of detachment or selflessness called *yoga* (yoking). He urges daily meditation, a cessation of yearning, a silent contemplation of God, an embrace of serenity, a life of balanced diet and rest, and self-control based on spiritual merger with holiness. Krishna alerts the warrior to worldly delusions, a common strand in literatures of empire that feature commanders and conquerors inflamed by greed and self-aggrandizement—for example, in WILLIAM SHAKESPEARE's tragedy *Julius Caesar* (1599) and in William Beckford's *Vathek, an Arabian Tale* (1782). In place of temporal desire, Krishna recommends meditation on the all-encompassing energy that fuels the world, a mysticism that Hindus share with animists, Buddhists, Christians, Jews, Muslims, and Zoroastrians. Arjuna prays for enlightenment, "O Lord of lords . . . I want to know about You" (509).

The focus of godhood steadies the neophyte charioteer. With a simplicity replicated by Allah's revelation of godhood to Muhammad and by Yahweh's confrontation of Moses at the burning bush, Krishna reduces the nature of divinity to two words: "I am" (510). By reassuring Arjuna that he can never be separated from God, Krishna strips away the commander's fears: "Wherever there is Krishna . . . there will also certainly be opulence, victory, extraordinary power, and morality" (761). The covenant with Vishnu echoes the formulaic "last words of David," which links rule with justice: "He that ruleth over man must be just, ruling in the fear of God" (2 Samuel 23:3).

The recounting of the Gita in subsequent literature and art includes the 1977 film *Daana Veera Soora Karna*, filmed in Hyderabad, India, which dramatizes Karna's relationship with Arjuna.

Sources

The Bhagavad Gita As It Is. Translated by A. C. Bhaktivedanta Swami Prabhupada. Los Angeles: Bhaktivedanta Book Trust, 1989.

Chatterjee, Suhas. *Indian Civilization and Culture.* New Delhi: M. D. Publications, 1998.

2 Samuel. In the *Holy Bible.* Iowa Falls, Iowa: World Bible Publishers, 1986.

Bible See APOCALYPSE; BIOGRAPHY; EPITHALAMIUM; EXODUS; GENESIS; TRANSLATION; WISDOM LITERATURE.

biography

Useful to historians and archaeologists, the life stories of victims of subjugation and oppression preserve social and political motivation as well as details of empire. The importance of biography in illuminating struggles for power survives in the Welsh monk Asser's *Life of King Alfred* (893), the feminist poet Christine de Pisan's *Hymn to Joan of Arc* (1429), and the Indian journalist Nayantara Sahgal's *Indira Gandhi: Her Road to Power* (1982). An Old Testament study of wise and unwise rule occurs in 2 Samuel with the emergence of David, shepherd poet and first to unify desert tribes into a Hebrew state. Mentored by Jonathan, King Saul's son, around 980 B.C., David epitomized the physical hardening of the professional warrior. According to the anonymous biographer, "They were swifter than eagles, they were stronger than lions" (2 Samuel 1:23). The narrative, possibly written by the priest Abiathar, balances King David's political promise with his arrogance in stealing Bathsheba, another soldier's wife.

The biblical text illustrates the power of the Middle Eastern sage over monarchy through a FABLE told by the priest Nathan to David. With an allegory about the rich man's theft of the poor man's pet lamb, Nathan charges David with despoiling Bathsheba and concealing her pregnancy by having her husband, Uriah the Hittite, abandoned in battle against the Ammonites (2 Samuel 12:1–15). The rhetorical mousetrap so shatters the king's composure that he confesses to Nathan in a scenario that survives in art, drama, and film. Actors vied for the parts of king and prophet—Gregory Peck and Raymond Massey in *David and Bathsheba* (1951), Richard Gere and Niall Buggy in *King David* (1985), and Nathaniel Parker and Franco Nero in *David* (1997).

Nathan's PROPHECY of ongoing strife within the Davidic dynasty holds true through much of the king's reign, when he struggles for political accord. After David's son Absalom rebels and falls to the spears of Captain Joab's men, the abject father keens with the loss of his treacherous child: "O my son Absalom, my son, my son Absalom! would God I had died for thee, O Absalom, my son, my son!" (2 Samuel 18:33). Five chapters later, the biographer restores the king's dignity by recording the last words of David, an idealized portrait of the perfect ruler: "He that ruleth over men must be just, ruling in the fear of God. And he shall be as the light of the morning, when the sun riseth" (2 Samuel 23:3–4). The emerging star of Israel, David's son Solomon, restores justice by dispensing wisdom that turned the adjective *Solomonic* into a standard descriptor of judicious emperors as far east as Malaysia.

The Life of Jesus

Three New Testament texts—the gospels of Mark (ca. A.D. 70), Matthew (ca. A.D. 80), and Luke (ca. A.D. 90)—portray the execution of Jesus as an example of Roman retribution against outside agitators who threaten the status quo. According to the 16 chapters that John Mark (Saint Mark the Evangelist), a disciple of St. Peter, composed in koine (Greek dialect), the Hebrew prophet and teacher Jesus was born in the last years of Emperor Augustus's reign and came of age during the early years of the Julio-Claudian dynasty. Looking back some four decades, the biographer, a congregant of Jerusalem's first Christian church living in Rome, begins with the Messiah's baptism in the Jordan River and reproduces verbatim the pronouncements of Jesus in the original Aramaic. As a collection of WISDOM LITERATURE, the narrative amasses three agrarian parables—about the sower, the wheat and tares, and the mustard seed—alongside prophecies and confrontational episodes preceding Jesus's crucifixion around A.D. 36. At a high point in gospel advice, Mark records a challenge to skeptics: "For what shall it profit a man, if he shall gain the whole world, and lose his own soul! Or what shall a man give in exchange for his soul" (Mark 8:36–37). The rhetorical question bears implications for the Roman Empire and its minions, who disenfranchised Middle Easterners through four centuries of suppression and slaughter.

A cornerstone of the New Testament, the Aramaic summation of Jesus's birth and ministry is the work of tax accountant Matthew, a putative Galilean whom the bureaucracy of Herod Antipas

posted to Capharnaum on the Damascus highway. The biography excels at accuracy and thorough coverage. Beginning with a lengthy genealogy dating to the Abrahamic and Davidic dynasties, the life story pulls details from Isaiah's prophecy and from Mark's gospel and includes aphorisms and the Sermon on the Mount, the core oration of Christian philosophy. Matthew constructs his biography chronologically, from the arrival of unnamed magi from the East to honor the Christ Child to King Herod's paranoid infanticide of Hebrew boys to subvert the messianic prediction. The legend took on more detail in the account provided in MARCO POLO's *The Travels of Marco Polo* (1298), which identifies the magi as Caspar, Melchior, and Balthasar.

Skipping Jesus's coming of age, Matthew's narrative depicts the Messiah as an evangelist. At the height of the Sermon on the Mount, he comforts a fringe people of the Roman Empire: "Blessed are ye, when men shall revile you, and persecute you and shall say all manner of evil against you falsely for my sake" (Matthew 5:11). The imagery of the commoner honors Christians from two perspectives—as "the salt of the earth" and as "the light of the world" (Matthew 5:13, 14). The metaphor of illumination is common to such ancient writings as the Sumerian GODDESS LORE in the EPITHALAMIUM "The Courtship of Inanna and Dumuzi" (ca. 2800 B.C.), the HERO stories in the Sanskrit BHAGAVAD GITA (Song of God, ca. 200 B.C.), and the AVESTA (ca. A.D. 530), the holy writ of Zoroastrianism.

Like the Chinese philosophers Laozi (Laotze) and Confucius (see ANALECTS), the Frankish emperor CHARLEMAGNE, and the Mohawk prophet Deganawida, founder of the Iroquois Confederacy (see WHITE ROOTS OF PEACE, THE), Jesus became a force for good in troubled times. He advocated peace and forbearance at a time when Roman legionaries trampled the civil and property rights of eastern Mediterranean citizens. In terms of world VISIONARY LITERATURE, a model invocation known as the Lord's Prayer (Matthew 6:9–13) describes anticipation of a celestial kingdom for the faithful. With a benevolent touch, Jesus chides his followers for dividing their loyalties between worldly and spiritual rewards: "For where your treasure is, there will your heart be also" (Matthew 6:21).

Matthew depicts Jesus as a man of action and of heart. The VIOLENCE of Herod's decapitation of John the Baptist precedes a view of the gracious suffering servant after Jesus turns two fish and five loaves into enough food for a crowd of 4,000. Matthew provides evidence of Jesus' counsel, healing, resurrecting the dead, and working of wonders as prefaces to a more humane version of Mosaic law, a legalistic treatise lacking compassion and forgiveness. In place of the proscriptions on behavior found in the Ten Commandments laid out in EXODUS, Jesus uses a personal approach to the gospel of love: "Thou shalt love thy neighbour as thyself" (Matthew 19:19). The subsequent clash with the Roman governor Pontius Pilate, the prefect of Judaea, foretokens beatings, scourging, mockery, and Jesus' execution in the Roman style, the inevitable demise of a troublemaking seer claiming to be divine. To heighten the pathos of a lingering torment, Matthew quotes a last outcry: "My God, my God, why hast thou forsaken me?" (Matthew 27:46), a dramatic humanization of the Messiah.

A Populist View

The most beloved Christian biography, the gospel of Luke, a Gentile physician from Antioch (present-day Antakya, Turkey), fleshes out Matthew's account with stories of Jesus' birth and boyhood, written primarily in refined Greek. Less judgmental of women and the poor than previous Hebrew scriptures, the biography sets the prototype of Mariology (study of the Virgin Mary) by depicting Jesus' modest mother as a vessel of godhood. Luke characterizes the magnificat, or Song of Mary, as a reply to her exaltation by God: "For he hath regarded the low estate of his handmaiden. . . . He hath put down the mighty from their seats, and exalted them of low degree" (Luke 1:48, 52). From her miraculous pregnancy comes the Prince of Peace. For the occasion of Jesus' birth, Luke composed an epiphanic welcome to shepherds sung by a host of angels: "Glory to God in the highest, and on earth peace, good will toward men" (Luke 2:14)—a source for art, film, theater, literature, and music, from the Middle Ages to the present.

Luke's populist text honors the peasantry by picturing Jesus' recruitment of disciples from Galilean fishermen and his healing of lepers, the untouch-

ables of ancient European and Mediterranean societies. Similarly compassionate are the classic parables found only in Luke's gospel, those of the good Samaritan and the prodigal son, both models of forgiveness and redemption. The latter teaching text concludes with a family celebration of unity when the wanderer returns: "It was meet that we should make merry, and be glad: for this thy brother was dead, and is alive again; and was lost, and is found" (Luke 15:32).

A statement of the power of the individual conscience served LEO TOLSTOY as the title of a pacifist treatise, *The Kingdom of God Is Within You* (1894), taken from Jesus' words recorded in Luke 17:21. As a token of hope, the biography concludes Jesus' background with death, resurrection, and ascension to heaven. Blended with the writings of Mark and Matthew into the synoptic, or combined, gospels, Luke's biography of Jesus formed the basis of enduring Hollywood epics, including *The Robe* (1953), *Ben-Hur* (1959), *The Greatest Story Ever Told* (1965), *The Last Temptation of Christ* (1988), *The Passion of the Christ* (2004), and *The Nativity Story* (2006).

The Life of Buddha

Messianic biography spread reverence for the Buddha much as it did for David and Jesus. Around A.D. 100, the Brahmin poet, playwright, and philosopher Ashvaghosa (ca. 80–ca. 150) of Saketa in northern India summarized in Sanskrit the acts of the Buddha in the epic *Buddhacarita* (*The Life of the Buddha*). As an expert in Buddhist teachings, Ashvaghosa served the Kushanite emperor Kanishka as an adviser on affairs in northern India, Kashmir, and present-day Afghanistan. His biography of Gautama Buddha balances admiration for the master without exaggerating his miracles. To dignify the subject, Ashvaghosa rid his collection of outlandish tales that had marred the sacred history with magic and showmanship. A classic scriptural poem, the completed 28-chapter narrative is on a par with the sanctity of the Christian New Testament. The text flourished in Dharmaraksa's Chinese translation in 420 and in Tibetan versions produced in the late 600s.

The life events that distinguish the Buddha begin with purification of Queen Maya's womb by a white elephant and the miraculous conception of a prince, Siddhartha Gautama. The narrative depicts a birthing "for the welfare of the world, without pain and without illness" (Ashvaghosa 1969, 10). At his arrival in Lumbini, Nepal, the brightness of the child's physiognomy compares with Matthew's revelation of a rare star marking Jesus' birth. (Accounts of illumination have produced centuries of lustrous drawings and statuary.) The gods themselves pay homage to the royal child with blessings on his wisdom; the heavens release a shower of lotus and waterlillies scented with sandalwood, an olfactory motif that permeates the entire biography. Ashvaghosa records a prophecy of the prince's aid to a suffering world, a vision similar to the predictions of the Old Testament seer Isaiah about Jesus' peace mission and to European legends of King Arthur's civilizing powers. The anticipation of Buddha's gentleness, moral laws, deliverance of earth from sorrow, and release of all people from yearning and delusions takes palpable form in the Buddha's travels on a "noble path" (18).

Ashvaghosa carries his narrative to the acme of the lord's earthly accomplishment. A lengthy study of the Buddha's asceticism, meditation, temptation, and search for truth results in the *bodhi* (enlightenment) and the anticipation of thousands of incarnations that refine his capacity for compassion. In the last book, Ashvaghosa pictures the Buddha surrounded by beggars and hermits and lodging in forests, caves, mountains, and on the banks of the Ganges River. Integral to his ministry is his comfort to "the blind, the humpbacked, the lame, the insane, the maimed as well as the destitute," the sufferers of India's lowest caste (200–201).

Biographic Integrity

The composition of authentic life histories forces the biographer to make decisions about difficult truths, such as the Roman historian SUETONIUS's survey of the first century of the Roman Empire in *De vita Caesarum* (*Lives of the Caesars*, ca. A.D. 121), the imperial adviser Einhard's scrupulous objectivity about CHARLEMAGNE's empire building in *Vita Caroli Magni* (*The Life of Charlemagne*, ca. 830), and Bishop Asser's attempt to honor the feats of a living legend in *Life of King Alfred* (893) without sounding like a sycophant. Later models struggle

with historical conflict, as in Alexandre Dumas's *Napoleon* (1855), with its survey of megalomania; *Hawaii's Story by Hawaii's Queen, Liliuokalani* (1898), depicting the American usurpation of a Polynesian king's realm; Elizabeth Berryhill's summation of Dietrich Bonhoeffer's wartime resistance spying and attempted assassination in *The Cup of Trembling* (1962); and MARYSE CONDÉ's reprise of American colonial female persecution in *I, Tituba, Black Witch of Salem* (1986).

On more tenuous grounds, the intellectual author and literary theorist YI KWANGSU attempted to appease Japanese invaders in his native Korea by collaborating with the enemy. After the occupation of Korea in 1910, Yi continued his steady output of historical fiction and nonfiction, often concealing his defense of home through nationalistic allegory. In 1929, he depicted the life of a 15th-century boy-king during the Joseon dynasty in *Tanjong Aesa* (*The Tragic History of King Tanjong* 1929), a tale of a prince who died in 1455 at age 14 at the hands of King Sejo. Three years later, Yi maintained his covert patriotism by honoring a naval commander, the title figure in the semihistorical biography *Yi Sun-sin* (1932), who defeated the Sui invasion of Korea in 1592. By exalting past Korean heroes, Yi realized his intent to rebuild national spirit and image through literature.

See also AUTOBIOGRAPHY.

Sources
Ashvaghosa. *The Buddha-Karita of Asvaghosha* in *Buddhist Mahayana Texts.* Translated by E. B. Cowell. New York: Dover, 1969.
Holy Bible. Iowa Falls: World Bible Publishers, 1986.
Lee, Ann Sung-Hi. *Yi Kwang-su and Modern Korean Literature.* New York: Columbia University East Asia Program, 2005.

Bird, Isabella Lucy   See WOMEN'S JOURNALS, DIARIES, AND LETTERS.

Blixen, Karen, Baroness   See DINESEN, ISAK.

Bly, Nellie   See TRAVELOGUE.

Bonhoeffer, Dietrich (1906–1945) *German theologian and diarist*

A Lutheran pastor from Breslau, Silesia (modern Wroclaw, Poland), Dietrich Bonhoeffer courted martyrdom for Christian activism. He was born on February 4, 1906, to Karl and Paula Bonhoeffer; his father was a prominent Berlin psychiatrist. An older brother, Walter Bonhoeffer, died in combat during World War I. Dietrich Bonhoeffer prepared for the pulpit with degrees from Tübingen and Berlin universities and from Union Theological Seminary in New York City. On November 6, 1932, he espoused anti-Hitler policies in a sermon to members of the Confessing Church, a Protestant religious movement that opposed the perverted nationalism of the rising Nazi Party. He lectured students at the University of Berlin in *Creation and Fall: A Theological Exposition of Genesis 1–3* (his lectures were published in 1933) on the necessity of returning to the Bible for guidance and strength during the political unrest following the collapse of the Weimar Republic in 1933. After spending two years in London as the pastor of two churches (1933–35), he went to India, where he studied nonviolent resistance with Mohandas Gandhi before returning to Germany and becoming a leader of the Confessing Church. His masterwork, *The Cost of Discipleship* (1937), introduced the world to his belief that struggle is the price of Christian salvation.

In his 1936 pastoral report to the Lutheran synod, Bonhoeffer compiled the pervasive despair generated by Nazi dictatorship and looming disaster. He asserted, "We all know the distress, the inner contradiction, the sloth which seek to hold us back. . . . We still have enough time and warning" (quoted in Bethge 2000, 561). Idealistic in a time of peril, he considered threat to be a gift from god. He preached that faith requires obedience and action, the focus of *Life Together* (1939), a polemic on Christian cooperation reflecting the solidarity of the first disciples. His writings stressed that Christian tenets "affect civil life and, indeed, the entire earthly existence of people" (Bonhoeffer 2003, 4–5). He and others in the Confessing Church channeled humanitarian energies toward the revolutionary concepts of Jesus's Sermon on the Mount concerning persecution and rescue of the innocent.

Bonhoeffer preached and taught with the intention of shocking German Christians into revolt against Nazi barbarities targeting Jews, gypsies, homosexuals, dissidents, and the elderly and handicapped. Because of his activities, the Gestapo banned Bonhoeffer from teaching, oratory, and evangelizing. In 1939, he joined a group of army officers seeking an end to Hitler's power. For his role in financing the escape of Jews to Switzerland, he was jailed in April 1943. After the discovery of his association with the conspirators who tried to kill Hitler in July 1944, he was again jailed and subsequently executed on April 9, 1945. His grisly death entailed being hanged from a meat hook in a piano wire noose at the Tegel prison camp for criminals in Flossenbürg, Bavaria.

Bonhoeffer's courageous letters, his prison diary, and essays inspired several books, both fiction and nonfiction; an opera; and the films *The Restless Conscience* (1991), *Hanged on a Twisted Cross* (1996), and *Bonhoeffer—Agent of Grace* (2000). Author Elizabeth Berryhill dramatized his costly resistance in the two-act play *The Cup of Trembling* (1962). In 2005, the film *Bonhoeffer* summarized the pastor's risk in defying the spread of fascism.

Sources

Berryhill, Elizabeth. *The Cup of Trembling—A Play in Two Acts Derived from the Life of Dietrich Bonhoeffer.* New York: Seabury, 1962.

Bethge, Eberhard. *Dietrich Bonhoeffer: A Biography.* Minneapolis: Augsburg Fortress, 2000.

Bethge, Renate. *Dietrich Bonhoeffer: A Brief Life.* Translated by K. C. Hanson. Minneapolis: Augsburg Fortress, 2004.

Bonhoeffer, Dietrich. *Discipleship.* Translated by John D. Godsey. Minneapolis: Fortress Press, 2003.

———. *A Testament to Freedom: The Essential Writings of Dietrich Bonhoeffer.* New York: HarperCollins, 1995.

Book of the Dead

The concept of a guide book for corpses aided the priestly ministrations to congregants in Egypt, Ethiopia, and Tibet.

The funerary writings of the Egyptian Empire (1550–1070 B.C.), the Egyptian Book of the Dead (ca. 1240 B.C.) anthologizes some 200 chants or charms to the Sun Father to protect the deceased from monsters and terrors of the land of the dead (in Roberts 1991, 159). The magic spells shield the soul from attack on its way to the netherworld, a dark underground realm that presages the Roman concept of Hades, the Jewish Sheol, and the Christian Hell. Written in the style of quest lore, the formulaic liturgy that priests recite over corpses appeases the goddess Isis, an archetypal wife and mother figure, and names the beneficent monarchs whom Egyptians revered like divinities.

Egyptian liturgy clings to earthly life as the height of being. A lyric chant to the divine Shu, god of the air, declares, "My soul is God, my soul is eternity." Responses assert the survival of the deceased: "I shall possess my flesh for ever and ever, I shall not decay, I shall not crumble away, I shall not wither away, I shall not become corruption" (Egyptian, Book of the Dead, 1898, 50, 52). In a moment of exultation, the deceased realizes his preservation in human form: "I exist, I exist, I live, I live, I germinate, I germinate" (52). Blameless spirits acquire privileges after proper preparation of the corpse and after the soul's recitation of secret formulas at stopping places on the way to the gods' courtroom. For its democratized view of humankind, the anthology became a stabilizing social force guaranteeing eternal life to any Egyptian with a clear conscience.

An early scroll from the 18th dynasty, the Book of What Is in the Netherworld (ca. 1554 B.C.), uses metaphors of light and dark to dramatize the conflict between good and evil, a standard struggle in world religion. In chapter 125, to avoid a second death and permanent eradication, upon arrival at the Hall of the Two Truths, or Hall of Double Justice, the deceased must settle accounts before a tribunal of 42 provincial judges, representing the districts of the Egyptian empire. The spirit confesses wrongdoing, proclaims a lifetime of obedience to the king, and requests the right to mercy and *ma'at* (justice). Of the centrality of the conscience, the seeker cries out, "My heart my mother, my heart my mother, my heart my coming into being!" (140). Coffin inscriptions and pyramid texts describe the critical point—the weighing of the heart, restoration of breath to the righteous, and the soul's union with the sun god Re, who steers a boat that

traverses the waters of the underworld. In the next chapter, the anointed soul passes through portals to the presence of northern and southern kings, with whom he remains for eternity.

The Ethiopian Afterlife

Another version of northeastern African funerary lore, the Ethiopian Book of the Dead (A.D. 400), is an anonymous folk anthology composed in Ethiopic and Amharic at the beginning of the Aksumite empire (ca. fourth century B.C.–ca. A.D. 950). Like Arabs, Celts, Copts, Egyptians, and Hebrews, the people of Abyssinia (present-day Ethiopia), inscribed various divine names and traits on stones and charms to ward off suffering and despair. The manuscript reprises Egyptian burial chants, verse amulets, and Christian monotheism introduced to ancient Abyssinia by Saint Frumentius, an evangelist shipwrecked at Aksum in A.D. 316. He converted to Christianity the pagan queen Sofya and her son, the future Emperor Ezana, who founded Abyssinian trade with Egypt. The immediate cultural response—the Egyptian superstitions of three millennia and the Christian faith that began to encroach on ancient customs—straddled two empires.

The Ethiopian Book of the Dead consists of spells, conjurations, and alternative names for divinities—for example, the Merciful, Dominant, Creator, Protector, Knower, and Restrainer, a series similar to godly honorifics in the Arabic KORAN. In Ethiopian theology, exact recitation of the mystic Ethiopian burial liturgy, comprised of 141 secret names for God, shielded the soul from demons and served as a token of passage through after-death obstacles, mutilation, and torture. The syncretic Ethiopian text comforts the deceased and, like the Egyptian Book of the Dead, reanimates them through repetitions of cross symbols and magic geometric shapes as well as incantations pleading for mercy. Mixed into animistic ritual are the prayers of St. Athanasius, St. Peter, and the Virgin Mary and a funeral homily by St. Frumentius.

The Tibetan Afterlife

A much later collection, the Tibetan Book of the Dead (ca. A.D. 775), composed in Sanskrit by the wandering mystic Padmasambhava in the second century of the Tibetan Empire, incorporates strands of Buddhism from China and Nepal. After Sambhava began serving King Trisong Detsen at Samye, Tibet, as prophet and exorcist, he converted the court to Buddhism. As a conservator of scripture at the royal monastery he built in A.D. 749, he translated 65 volumes of the TANTRAS from Sanskrit to Tibetan and composed his Tibetan Book of the Dead, a compendium on mortal faults and perpetual change. The collection of pragmatic incantations sung by the lama serves the dying as a guide to self-purification and a preparation for the soul's issuance into a higher state of consciousness. At the subject's last breath, the lama calls the dying individual from a permanent sleep. The mind clears as the soul seeks oneness with God. Priestly chanting or whispering steadies the expiring individual and bolsters the next of kin with compassion and acceptance of the inevitable.

The Tibetan text assuages sorrow by offering enlightenment or salvation to the departed and comfort to the living. If the corpse is destroyed, lost, or missing, the lama addresses a photograph or a personal belonging of the deceased, reciting step-by-step directions for the after-death journey. Over 49 days, during six stages of consciousness, the liturgist's voice exhorts the soul to liberate itself from evil and desire. The liturgy begins with the moribund state. The spirit acknowledges that death "is dawning upon me—after having given up indolence, since there is no time to waste in life—may I undistractedly enter the path of listening, reflecting, and meditating" (Tibetan, Book of the Dead 2000, lxi). At first, the departed struggles against inattention and enjoys seven peaceful days. Mourners hear advice on avoiding phobias, faults, and illusions, an instruction that prepares the next generation for death and reincarnation. In a painless existence, earthly life gives place to "the very Reality, the All-Good," which takes the form of "the Great Body of Radiance . . . the immutable Light" (xxxix). In the final 30 days, the spirit rids itself of destructive habits for a return to earth and rebirth as a better person.

Sources

Assmann, Jan. *Death and Salvation in Ancient Egypt.* Ithaca, N.Y.: Cornell University Press, 2005.

The Egyptian Book of the Dead: The Chapters of Coming Forth by Day. Translated by E. A. Wallis Budge. London: Kegan Paul, Trench, Trübner, & Co., 1898.

An Ethiopian Book of the Dead: The Bandlet of Righteousness. Translated by E. A. Wallis Budge. London: Kegan Paul International, 2002.

Roberts, Elizabeth, and Elias Amidon, eds. *Earth Prayers from around the World.* San Francisco: HarperSanFrancisco, 1991.

The Tibetan Book of the Dead. Translated by W. Y. Evans-Wentz. Oxford: Oxford University Press, 2000.

Brodsky, Joseph (1940–1996) *Russian-Jewish poet and essayist*

A disciple of anti-Stalinist Russian poet ANNA AKHMATOVA, Joseph Brodsky wove images of his nation's disgrace into existential lyrics and essays about nature, love, change, and moral convictions. Born into a Jewish family on May 24, 1940, he was a toddler at the time of the 900-day German siege of Leningrad (1941–43), his hometown. In boyhood, he absorbed the atheism espoused in Soviet schools. He applied to a submariner academy, which rejected him for his ethnicity, and developed into a drifter and street fighter. Eschewing a professional career, he operated milling equipment at an arms factory and, over 13 short-term jobs, found work at a prison mortuary, hospital, boiler room, and crystallography lab. In his free time, he read FYODOR DOSTOYEVSKY's *Notes from the Underground* (1864) and the verse of Polish poet Czeslaw Milosz, and he dabbled in translations of British, Serbo-Croatian, and Spanish poetry. In 1961, he moved next door to Akhmatova's cottage to begin a daily education in writing and analyzing verse. By age 24, he was on the run from official denunciation and censorship.

The official censure of Brodsky epitomized the heavy-handed authoritarianism of the Soviet regime. In 1964, Brodsky became the first poet stigmatized by the Nikita Khrushchev administration. The Soviet KGB whisked the poet away from a city street and impounded his library and manuscripts. An accusation of "social parasitism" stemmed from writings that influenced citizens to think for themselves and to control their own culture. In *So Forth* (1996), in which he tells of his trial before a female judge on February 14, 1964, he forgave witnesses the "petty, twenty-odd-year-old secrets of purblind [nearly blind] hearts obsessed with a silly quest for power" (Brodsky 1998, 8). Authorities incarcerated him, first at the Kashchenko insane asylum in Moscow and later at Kresty Prison in Leningrad. In "New Stanzas to Augusta" (1982) and "Autumn in Norenskaia" (1965), he claimed that starved, bored inmates felt buried alive. For 18 months, he was imprisoned at Archangelsk on an inlet of the White Sea, and made to chop wood, load grain and stone, and muck out horse stalls. In 1965, as Leonid Brezhnev's regime was beginning, pressure from the poets Akhmatova and Yevgeny Yevtushenko as well as other literary figures resulted in Brodsky's release. He was expelled from the Soviet Union in 1972. His work remained officially suppressed in Russia but circulated in *samizdat* (underground) publications that assembled his 2,000-page canon poem by poem, in defiance of official CENSORSHIP.

Depicting a Life Struggle

To Brodsky, language threw a lifeline, enabling him to objectify experience by estranging himself from the moment. During his imprisonment, two volumes of his works reached the Western world. Of their reception, he declared, "If there's any deity to me, it's language" (Brodsky and Haven 2003, cover). At age 32, he went into exile minus his wife and four-year-old son Andrei and parted forever from his parents. Rejecting resettlement in Israel, he emigrated via Vienna and London to Ann Arbor, Michigan, from where he defied the Soviet attempt to belittle and discredit him. Under the sponsorship of his traveling companion, poet W. H. Auden, Brodsky prospered. He lectured at the University of Michigan and other universities, gained American citizenship in 1977, and submitted his hypnotic, colloquial verse to the *New York Review of Books, Partisan Review,* and *Times Literary Supplement.* Years later, he wrote "Infinitive" (1996), a retrospective poem on the events of his life. He concluded that Americans view him as an anomaly, "an island within an island" (Brodsky 1998, 3). Yet as he lived effectively isolated in America, his Russian editors incurred arrest, gulags, and banishment.

Using imaginative rhythm and literary conceits, Brodsky's poetry scorned imperialism. Two poems, "On the Death of Zhukov" (1974) and "Lullaby of Cape Cod" (1975), picture the malaise and darkness that follow war and regimentation. Publication of *Less Than One* (1986), a collection of essays, revealed unbearable conditions under the Soviet regime, particularly in the autobiographical vignette "In a Room and a Half," which echoes the spiritual ennui of the Swedish author August Strindberg's *The Red Room* (1879). Writing of cramped, dehumanizing living conditions, Brodsky charged, "There is something tribal about this dimly lit cave, something primordial—evolutionary" (Brodsky 1998, 455). The anthology preceded his receipt of the Nobel Prize for literature in 1987 and selection as the U.S. poet laureate in 1991 for the clarity and intensity of his verse.

In English and Russian, Brodsky's skill at historical nostalgia relied on detail and atmosphere. He shaped history into a warning to the West that dictators like Lenin and Stalin begin as the people's gods. In "Elegy" (1985) and "I Sit by the Window" (1971), he describes a battleground, memories of traitors and of commanders extolled in cast iron monuments, and the mediocrity of the Soviet Union's tattered Iron Curtain. In "May 24, 1980," regret over his expulsion from Russia summons visions of the motherland in the time of the Huns and the czars. In 1995, the publication of *On Grief and Reason* disclosed Brodsky's emotional tie with the American poet Robert Frost. Beneath the pastoral grace of Frost's poems, the Russian successor unearthed an inner suffering that intellect alone could not mask. Brodsky died on January 28, 1996, in New York City and was buried in the Isola di San Michele cemetery in Venice, Italy.

Sources

Brodsky, Joseph. *Joseph Brodsky: Selected Poems.* Translated by George I. Kline. New York: Harper & Row, 1974.

———. *Joseph Brodsky: Conversations.* Edited by Cynthia L. Haven. Jackson: University Press of Mississippi, 2003.

———. *Less Than One.* New York: Farrar, Straus and Giroux, 1986.

———. *So Forth.* New York: Farrar, Straus and Giroux, 1998.

Lincoln, Bruce. *Sunlight at Midnight: St. Petersburg and the Rise of Modern Russia.* New York: Basic Books, 2002.

Buck, Pearl S. (Pearl Comfort Sydenstricker Buck) (1892–1973) *American novelist*

In her fiction, Nobel laureate Pearl S. Buck depicted the inequities of peasant life in feudal China. Born Pearl Sydenstricker on June 26, 1892, in Hillsboro, West Virginia, she grew up in east central China, where her parents operated a Presbyterian mission and where she became bilingual. Like the journalist and novelist JOHN HERSEY, also raised in China, she viewed native life like a native. Her nurse Alma introduced her to Chinese theater and bargaining at the market; a tutor, Mr. Kung, increased her awareness of human issues while teaching her Confucius's philosophy and literary classics (see ANALECTS). When the Empress Dowager Cixi (Tzu Hsi) encouraged the slaughter of whites in China during the Boxer Rebellion of 1900, eight-year-old Pearl joined her family in hiding in Shanghai. In July 1901, the Sydenstrickers went to San Francisco, but they returned to China the following year. In 1910, Pearl went back to the United States for her higher education.

With a degree from Randolph-Macon Woman's College, Pearl returned to China in 1914 to teach English literature at Chung Yang, Nanjing, and Southeastern universities. She married John Lossing Buck, a missionary, in May 1917. As the nation began to modernize, she observed threats to Chinese sovereignty from Britain, Germany, Japan, Russia, and the United States, all poised to dominate the emerging giant. At age 31, she began submitting stories to American magazines and writing longer works of fiction based on the socioeconomic impact of political change. Another dangerous period during the Chinese Civil War in March 1927 forced her, her husband, children, and widowed father to flee the Chinese Nationalists at Nanjing and seek shelter in the hut of a domestic, Mrs. Lu, until American warships could transport them to safety in Japan.

By 1935, Buck had published several works, including (in 1931) her Pulitzer Prize–winning novel *The Good Earth*. That year, she divorced John Buck and married her publisher, Richard Walsh, moving with him to Bucks County, Pennsylvania. There she wrote more novels, short stories, and works of nonfiction, while also becoming a champion of human rights. In 1949, she founded Welcome House, an adoption service for outcast Chinese children sired by black American soldiers, which she supported for the rest of her life, in addition to raising humanitarian aid for postwar orphans.

Unrest and Upheaval

Buck applied an insider's knowledge of feudal China to *The Good Earth* (1931), the first of a three-volume saga—*The House of Earth*—on peasant survival in Anhui Province, a land dominated by a propertied oligarchy. (The other two volumes are *Sons* [1932] and *A House Divided* [1935]) Set late in the 19th century during the decline of the Manchu dynasty, the story of farmer Wang Lung begins on his wedding day, when he buys O-lan, a homely kitchen drudge in the House of Hwang, for his bride. For contrast, Buck allows the protagonist a tiptoe through the feudal manor and a peek at the indolence, whoring, and opium use that characterized China's wealthiest 15 percent. As the couple begin their life together, Buck sets the tone of her canon with an adage: "Each had his turn at this earth," reminding the reader of individual opportunities and mortality (Buck 1931, 33). Because of his bride's initiative and thrift, Wang compares her to his faithful ox, a commentary on males devaluation of females to the level of serviceable livestock. Wang's family thrives during drought, famine, riot, and looting in Jiangsu Province and war in Nanjing. Through a contemplative cottager, Buck describes the predictable rise of unrest among the poor when the socioeconomic system favors aristocrats: "There is a way when the rich are too rich" (85).

The overturn of fortunes, a focus of *The Good Earth*, illustrates how the destabilization of traditional power structures leaves a vacuum open to lawlessness and predations against the vulnerable. The tide of violence, derived from the author's childhood memories, spreads without predictable aim or direction. Of opportunist bandits in his own family, Wang regrets that "many houses had they burned and women they had carried away, and good farmers they had bound with ropes . . . and men found them there next day, raving mad if they lived and burnt and crisp as roasted meat if they were dead" (165–166). At a turning point in China's fortunes, the arrival of a nephew from a southern city brings a horde of uncouth soldiers to Wang's compound. Their swaggering impresses the couple's son Nung Wen, who dreams of the glory of combat: "There is to be a war such as we have not heard of—there is to be a revolution and fighting and war such as never was, and our land is to be free!" (245). His naïveté terrifies Wang Lung, who knows firsthand the sufferings of war.

Buck modeled her trilogy of dynastic rot on Cao Xueqin's classic Qing dynasty novel DREAM OF THE RED CHAMBER (1791). During the Chinese Civil War (1927–37), her masterwork and its sequels, *Sons* and *A House Divided*, pursue the issue of militarism. In the later novel Wang's grandson, Wang Yuan, flaunts his uniform to the agrarian elders. To the disapproval of the landed gentry, the youth takes comfort in "the hardness he had learned in the school of war" (Buck 1984, 2) and envisions the unseating of the weak emperor and his warlords for the good of an unspecified peasant uprising.

In the midst of writing about the house of Wang, Buck pursued feminist issues in *The Mother* (1934), a lyric portrait on the pragmatism of a nameless abandoned wife and her duty to a blind daughter and an elderly mother-in-law. In old age, the mother reflects on a life of struggle and admits "how little there had been of any good to lay hold on in her years," a bleak summation of the destiny of female peasants in the Chinese empire (Buck 1971, 300).

Public acclaim for the author's humanism won her the 1938 Nobel Prize in literature, a first for an American woman. In 1941, she examined war-torn Asia in the historical novel *China Sky*, a story of a Chinese doctor colluding with a Japanese prisoner in an American hospital compound during the Japanese invasion. *Imperial Woman* (1956), a fictional biography of Cixi, the imperial concubine and last Chinese empress, and *The Living Reed* (1963), an overview of Korean power mongering, reprise Buck's themes of the endurance of the lowly through courage and persistence. In *Imperial Woman*, she defends the tenacity of Empress Dowager Cixi, who rules from the Forbidden City during China's critical transition to Westernization. *The Living Reed* depicts the agony of Korea's occupation by the Japanese until liberation in 1945 through the Kim clan's losses and sacrifices.

Pearl Buck died in Danby, Vermont, on March 6, 1973, and was buried on her farm in Pennsylvania. Her tombstone bears the name Pearl Sydenstricker in Chinese characters.

Sources

Buck, Pearl S. *The Good Earth*. New York: Pocket Books, 1931.

———. *A House Divided*. Berkeley, Calif.: Moyer Bell, 1984.

———. *The Mother*. New York: HarperCollins, 1971.

Conn, Peter. *Pearl S. Buck: A Cultural Biography*. Cambridge: Cambridge University Press, 1998.

C

Camões, Luís Vaz de (Luís Vaz de Camoëns)
(ca. 1524–1580) *Portuguese poet*

The epic poet of Renaissance Portugal, Luís Vaz de Camões (or Luís Vaz de Camoëns) exalted the nation's Golden Age of dominion over the seas and over Muslims, whom he dismissed as degenerate and small-minded. Born in Coimbra or Lisbon in the second century of the Portuguese Empire (1415–1999), he grew to maturity during explorer Pedro Álvares Cabral's discovery of Brazil. After the death of his father, Captain Simon Vaz de Camões, while adventuring in Goa, India, Camões lived in Chaves outside Galicia with his widowed mother, Anne de Macedo of Santarem. Following a preliminary education under the tutelage of Dominicans and Jesuits, he studied classical literature, Latin, and modern European languages at the University of Coimbra under the patronage of an uncle, Abbé Bento de Camões, the university chancellor.

Camões nurtured ideals and ambitions beyond his rank. In spring 1548, he escaped the death penalty for a perceived insult against the royal family. Instead, he was exiled from the capital for his courtship of a royal lady-in-waiting, Catherina de Athaide, and also of the Princess Maria, sister of King João III. With sympathetic friends, he secluded himself in Ribatejo in central Portugal. The next fall, he accompanied the militia to Ceuta, Morocco, where cannon shrapnel blinded his right eye during a battle against Moors. While adjusting to monocular vision, he wrote Petrarchan sonnets, dramas, and songs and began the 20-year task of writing a national epic.

Camões settled in Lisbon in 1551, and a year later, at age 32, he attacked one of the royal grooms, Gaspar Borges. Camões's three-stage punishment began with imprisonment. He paid a fine of 4,000 réis and, in March 1553, began a three-year probation in the Asian militia at Goa on India's Malabar Coast. After exploring the Red Sea, Arabia, and East Africa and surviving combat in India and Egypt, he took a treasury clerkship in Macao, an island in the South China Sea that Portugal annexed in 1557.

Camões became the first European poet to cross the equator and see firsthand remote world wonders and threats to Christian hegemony. Drawing on his views of Portugal's declining national vision, compromised integrity, and precarious grasp on world power, he composed the epic poem *Os Lusíadas* (1572), also called *The Lusiads* or *The Sons of Lusus,* the founder of Lusitania, an ancient Roman province dating before 500 B.C. In a shipwreck off Cambodia's Mekong Delta, he salvaged the manuscript from seawater that drowned his Chinese wife, Ti-Na-Men. In Mozambique, he languished in penury and filth. Repatriated at age 46, he lived the remaining decade in Lisbon on a legionary's pension. Wracked with grief for his country's military disaster after Sultan Abd al-Malik and his brother Ahmad killed King Sebastian I on August 4, 1578, at the battle of Alcácer Quibir during a Portuguese invasion of Morocco, Camões died on June 10, 1580.

The Portuguese Epic

Out of patriotism and Catholic fervor, Camões used verse to glorify the Portuguese; demonize the Moors as part of the Islamic war machine; slander Hindus as a wicked people governed by Satan's laws; and honor commerce and Roman Catholicism, Portugal's state religion. He dedicated *The Lusiads* to the boy-king Sebastian I, who had colonized Angola, Macao, Malacca, and Mozambique, a place the poet denigrated as a fount of "treachery and bad faith" (Camões 1997, 114). For style, Camões echoed the natural Portuguese cadence in ottava rima, which he adapted from the Latin iambic hexameter of VIRGIL's AENEID (17 B.C.). In canto 3, Camões pleads with the muse Calliope to empower his accuracy and gravity: "Inspire living song and a godlike voice in this mortal" (48). His humility adds gravitas to a nationalistic endeavor.

A salute to the age of discovery, the poet's 10 cantos survey the Portuguese Empire during the discoveries of the explorer Vasco da Gama, a family relative who chose a life of challenge "from motives of pride and honor" (11). Camões states the nation's ambition in the opening lines: "We look to yoke and humble Arabia's wild horsemen, infidel Turks, and India's sons and daughters" (4). In place of Virgil's pagan and mythic symbols of Roman imperialism, the poet merges the Christian cross with the astrolabe, a historical union of the guidance system of the Iberian navigator with the Catholic mission to proselytize and rescue pagans from eternal damnation, a period rationalization for invasion and conquest. Canto 6 declares "heaven was fully resolved to make of Lisbon a second Rome" (120), an affirmation of Portuguese tactics to secure their celestial destiny. Camões later boasts that "even the vanquished will feel no disgrace, having been overcome by such a race" (150). In the midst of grand predictions of a Portuguese triumph over its enemies, the poet intersperses moral aphorisms as warnings to vainglorious pirates. Of greed, he warns, "Gold conquers the strongest citizens, turns friends into traitors and liars, ... blinding discernment and impartial thought" (176).

Camões emulates Virgil's beginning in medias res (in the middle of things) and reprises prophecies of victory, merciless storms, and metaphysical forces in nature and the heavens. The narrative provides contrast to da Gama's hardships by reflecting on empires established by Alexander the Great, the Romans, the Queen of Sheba, and CHARLEMAGNE, the warrior-king of the Frankish Empire. In imitation of the Trojan Aeneas's sojourn with Queen Dido of Carthage, canto 9 includes a visit to paradise on the Island of Love and the reliance of the hero on Venus, Aeneas's mother. Through the logic of association, Camões honors her as a patroness of Portugal because of "her love of the Roman virtue she saw resurrected in them" (9). His amorous lines reflect the style and tone of 13th-century troubadour verse to the Virgin Mary, a form of GODDESS LORE that Alfonso X El Sabio (The Wise), king of Castile-Leon, compiled in *Cantigas de Santa María* (Songs to the Virgin Mary, ca. 1283). For theme, the poet pursues a traditional view of fate: "That no human resistance can prevail against such forces, for man is powerless before destiny" (150). The statement thus exonerates Vasco da Gama's militarism on the African coast, his bombardment of the port of Calicut, India, in 1502, and the piracy of Arab merchant vessels as a worthy modus operandi blessed by God.

Less subtle and more romantic than Virgil, Camões's panegyric elaborates on scene and character. His Venus becomes a sensual coquette and Jupiter a blatant despoiler of females, even goddesses. Applying verbal high relief, the poet contrasts glory with barbarity and enslavement. As "Capitad" da Gama sails his three caravels along the African shoreline during his first voyage to and from Calicut in 1497–98, Camões heightens the actions with the sounds and sights of battles, the glamour of dinner at Neptune's palace, and threats from the sea ogre Adamastor, a composite of the forces of nature that lurk off the Cape of Good Hope. While da Gama walks the decks and stares up at an occluded sky, the monster "materialized in the night air, grotesque and of enormous stature, with heavy jowls and an unkempt beard ... its complexion earthy and pale, its hair grizzled and matted with clay, its mouth coal black, teeth yellow with decay" (105). In contrast, during the battle off the coast of Ormuz on the

Persian Gulf, Camões blesses a propitious wind that generates poetic justice by redirecting Arab arrows against the bowmen who shot them. The poet applies an epic boast to da Gama that he "will try his hand at ruling the empire, when at his sight the Red Sea will turn yellow in sheer fright' (209). The hyperbole illustrates how far the author strays from the controlled Roman model to achieve historic stature.

The Lusiads was very influential on world literature. Its style inspired a legend of the Brazilian empire—the epic *Caramuru* (1781), a conquest story of the Tupinamba Indians by Santa Rita Durao—and appealed to the authors Herman Melville and Edgar Allan Poe as well as poets such as Elizabeth Barrett Browning, Henry Wadsworth Longfellow, and Ezra Pound. A romantic scenario influenced the German-Jewish composer Giacomo Meyerbeer to reset a section of the narrative in his opera *L'Africaine* (produced posthumously, 1865), a musical fantasy of Vasco da Gama's troubled infatuation with the beautiful Inèz of Lisbon.

Sources

Camões, Luís Vaz de. *The Lusiads.* Translated by Landeg White. 1997. Reprint, Oxford and New York: Oxford University Press, 2002.

Nicolopulos, James. *The Poetics of Empire in the Indies: Prophecy and Imitation in La Araucana and Os Lusiadas.* Philadelphia: Pennsylvania State University Press, 2000.

Candide   See VOLTAIRE.

Cao Xueqin   See *DREAM OF THE RED CHAMBER.*

Carey, Peter (Peter Philip Carey) (1943–)
Australian novelist

A prize-winning fiction writer and storyteller, Peter Carey has captured the imperial elitism that marked Australia's settlement by Europeans, most from Great Britain. Born Peter Philip Carey in Bacchus Marsh, Victoria, he began taking courses in chemistry and zoology at Monash University in 1961. He left at the end of the first semester the following year and started work in advertising in Melbourne,

lasting four years until readings of JAMES JOYCE's fiction and the dark PROPHECY of Franz Kafka turned him to literature and travel. Carey journeyed through the Middle East and Europe, writing visually engrossing fiction and working in advertising in London before returning to Australia in 1970. In 1980, he opened an advertising firm in Sydney, though he continued to produce fiction and developed an inventive writing style that sampled FABLE, FRONTIER LITERATURE, magical realism, grotesquerie, and the absurd. Like ISAAC BASHEVIS SINGER's memories of Poland and JAMAICA KINCAID's defense of the West Indies, Carey's visions of Australia elicited controversy as well as praise.

In the year celebrating the bicentennial of Australia's settlement, Carey won the first of his two Booker Prizes for fiction and the second of his three Miles Franklin Awards after publishing *Oscar and Lucinda* (1988), an allegorical epic of British presumption, racism, and religious superiority in the mid-1860s in its Pacific colonies. The pioneer romance features Anglican priest Oscar Hopkins and glass manufacturer Lucinda Leplastrier in a doomed effort to import religious mores and architecture to outback settlers at Bellingen in northern New South Wales. The two eccentrics outrage fastidious Sydney society by high-stakes gambling that becomes folly in an expedition into the interior with a prefabricated glass church, the epitome of one-size-fits-all colonialism. Their ambivalent love match, disguised as philanthropy, takes an ironic form—a grand, but impractical see-through structure that can be dismantled, moved, and reassembled. Carey idealizes the church as "a knife of an idea, but also one of great beauty, silvery, curved, dancing with light" (Carey 1988, 383), a visual hint at the couple's ill-defined and distorted view of human love and sexuality.

A tale of troubled consciences and realization of the casual slaughter of Australian aborigines, *Oscar and Lucinda* builds on paradox. The theme of fragile, transparent intent implies the unsuitability of the phobic, ghost-ridden cleric Dennis Hasset, himself agnostic in matters of orthodoxy, for counseling and proselytizing islanders and first nations. The native observer, the storyteller Kumbaingiri Billy, states the obvious and the allusive about a glass structure: "It cuts. Cuts trees. Cuts the skin of the tribes" (469). The slicing image highlights the ruination of aborigines, whom England will chop away from their earth moorings and from possession of traditional lands and mythology. Oscar's passion for Lucinda remains unrequited, though they are friends; his wife finds satisfaction in her rearing of an illegitimate child, the offspring of stodgy England and the rapacious bush country. Ralph Fiennes and Cate Blanchett starred in the 1997 film version, which closes on the surreal drowning of the priest in a floating glass-and-iron chapel, "a miracle, a spider web, a broken thing, a tragedy, a dream like something constructed for George III" (420).

Carey ventured further into historical fiction with a frame narrative, *True History of the Kelly Gang* (2000), for which he won his second Booker Prize and the Commonwealth Writers Prize. The juxtaposition of Irish colonials with the mythic wilderness substantiates Australia's 19th-century reputation for breeding squatters, transported criminals, fallen women, and raffish outlaws. By humanizing a bushranger, ostensibly in his own semiliterate language, Carey validates the obsession of Australians with shedding the exaggerations and falsehoods that cloud the nation's struggle with illegitimacy and dispossession. Ned Kelly recognizes his ilk as "left alone ignorant as tadpoles spawned in puddles on the moon" (Carey 2001, 278). He speaks for himself and other gallows birds when he voices his frustration with the hypocrisy of respectability: "I wished only to be a citizen I had tried to speak but the mongrels stole my tongue when I asked for justice they give me none" (328). Ned's saga identifies global silencing and slandering of the semicivilized as justification for his recovered history of a colonial class dismissed as Irish lowlifes.

Sources

Carey, Peter. *Oscar and Lucinda*. Brisbane: University of Queensland Press, 1988.

———. *True History of the Kelly Gang: A Novel*. New York: Vintage, 2001.

Gaile, Andreas. *Fabulating Beauty: Perspectives on the Fiction of Peter Carey*. Amsterdam: Rodopi, 2005.

censorship

Suppression of truth is a common event in the literary history of empires. In the literary theory of the Polish–South African author John Maxwell Coetzee, censorship arises directly from the insecurity and paranoia of tyrants: "It is precisely at the point at which an intention to offend is detected behind every action giving offense that the gates of paranoia are opened" (Coetzee 1997, 20). Using the Stalinist regime in the Soviet Union as a model, he describes the effects on the populace of the state's perverse rationalization for suppression. Authorities encourage citizens to spy on dissidents and to report suspicious words and deeds, particularly artistic expression, a situation Coetzee characterized in his allegory *Waiting for the Barbarians* (1980). He explains that control renders "society fragmented into tens of millions of individuals living on individual islets of mutual suspicions" (1997, 34).

During the consolidation of the Roman Empire, storytellers faced a wall of official menace. The slave fabulist PHAEDRUS annoyed Sejanus, the palace prefect of Emperor Tiberius, and stood trial for ridiculing the regime. Out of spite, Tiberius shelved the satiric quips in the storyteller's *Fabulae Aesopiae* (Aesopic fables, ca. A.D. 31).

The audacity of the Kurdish poet-theologian Ahmed-i Hani turned MEM-U ZIN (Mem and Zin, 1695) into a popular oral text for the stateless tribes of Kurdistan by bypassing literary Persian and the Arabic of Islam. The text remained unprinted until its appearance in Istanbul in 1919.

Russian fabulist IVAN ANDREYEVICH KRYLOV had similar problems issuing cutting SATIREs of Catherine II the Great and the ruling class. After imperial police rifled his print shop, he retreated to Latvia for 12 years to tutor at Riga. Only after his death did government officials embrace his witty beast stories as vernacular treasures. Similarly ostracized, ALEKSANDR PUSHKIN endured exile to Odessa in 1826. LEO TOLSTOY suffered the suppression of his pacifist treatise *The Kingdom of God Is within You* (1894) and antiwar novel *Hadji Murád* (1904). Even worse, he witnessed the rewriting of a vignette, "Sevastopol in May" (1855), into pro-war propaganda for dissemination in the September issue of Pushkin's magazine *Sovremennik* (The Contemporary). Ukrainian author NIKOLAY GOGOL required the intervention of Czar Nicholas I in the staging of *The Government Inspector* (1836), a three-act send-up of government corruption on the Russian frontier that reached print in a second edition in 1842. A less damaging suppression of Gogol's picaresque novel *Dead Souls* (1842) required a lessening of impact by changing the title to *The Adventures of Chichikov; or, Dead Souls*.

Suppressed publication in world empires epitomizes disregard for civil rights, the extenuation of SLAVERY, and capricious jailing and torture of freedom fighters, the subject of the French author VOLTAIRE's satire *Candide* (1759) and the Nigerian writer Wole Soyinka's prison memoir *The Man Died: Prison Notes of Wole Soyinka* (1973). In Cuba, the melodramatic novella *Sab* (1841), the tragic romance of a mulatto slave in love with his white master's daughter Carlota, created a backlash against its author, Gertrudis Gómez de Avellaneda. In Spain, miscegenation so outraged readers that censorship denied the novel publication until 1914. In 1957, the smuggling of BORIS PASTERNAK's anti-Soviet saga *Doctor Zhivago* (1956) brought to worldwide acclaim a novel that infuriated Kremlin censors for its honest depiction of a family man and his mistress. Another quandary, the negative response of Polish Catholics to Polish-American novelist Jerzy Kosinski's surreal fairy tale *The Painted Bird* (1965), derives from the book's anti-peasant subtext that charges ostensibly charitable families with sadism, sexual deviance, and ongoing torment of a lone boy fleeing the chaos of the Holocaust. Clouding the issue of blame is the obscurity of time, place, and the boy's ethnic identity, whom some consider a Jewish stray and others a gypsy bastard. Polish authorities suppressed the book until 1989, when it emerged to controversy and mixed charges of plagiarism and lies. In South Africa, humanist author NADINE GORDIMER met similar opposition to her antiapartheid views in *The Late Bourgeois World* (1976), *Burger's Daughter* (1979), and *July's People* (1981).

Limiting Russian Readership

Post-czarist Russia resulted in one of the most repressive regimes in terms of literature, especially for freethinkers, libertarians, and anti-Marxists. The Sherlock Holmes mystery "The Adventure of the Sussex Vampire" (1924), which builds tension with cannibalistic behaviors and poisoned darts, brought about the banning of all of Sir ARTHUR CONAN DOYLE's stories in Russia. Another

unusual candidate for suppression, SIGRID UNDSET's *Tillbake til Fremtiden* (*Return to the Future*, 1942), a wartime memoir, angered Joseph Stalin by depicting Siberians forced into beggary, starvation, and imprisonment. During the Stalinist tyranny, the poet ANNA AKHMATOVA's *Requiem* (written 1935–40) charged the dictator with lawlessness and the truncation of Russian civil rights, particularly as they applied to the arts. With "In 1940," she denounced the Soviet alliance with Nazi Germany and lamented the Luftwaffe's bombardment of London and the occupation of Paris by the German SS. Labeled a traitor in the Soviet media, she realized her work was one of the reasons her son, Lev Gumilev, served a term at hard labor in a northern gulag. Fans of her verse resorted to *samizdat* (private publication) by memorizing, hand-copying, or typing forbidden poems for clandestine circulation.

Akhmatova's disciple, Russian-Jewish poet JOSEPH BRODSKY, fought the censorship of Nikita Khrushchev's administration. In an action that was all too common at the time, the secret police kidnapped the poet from the street and seized his writings and books. In *So Forth* (1996), he recounts his testimony before a female judge on February 14, 1964, and subsequent jailing at the Kashchenko insane asylum in Moscow and later at Kresty Prison in Leningrad as well as hard labor in Archangelsk on an inlet of the White Sea. The protests of Akhmatova and the poet YEVGENY YEVTUSHENKO persuaded General Secretary Leonid Brezhnev to free Brodsky, but his canon remained impounded. Without the *samizdat*, readers would have missed his collected works until their publication in the United States after he emigrated to Ann Arbor, Michigan.

Another victim of Soviet censorship, Nina Lugovskaya (1918–93) suffered the seizure of her diary by the Soviet secret police in 1937. She, her mother, and her sisters faced sentences of five years' hard labor. Her journal was published in 2006 as *I Want to Live: The Diary of a Young Girl in Stalin's Russia*. Similar in measured style and desperation to Holocaust victim Anne Frank's *The Diary of a Young Girl* (1947) (see CHILDREN'S LITERATURE), Lugovskaya's work offers a damning view of Communist repression of eyewitness accounts detailing unforeseen arrest, interrogation, and jailing, as well as the imperial paranoia, sadism, and hypocrisy taking place from 1932 to 1937. Labeled counterrevolutionary, the diary concludes with Lugovskaya's confinement in the Kolyma gulag, the beginning of 12 years in exile.

Sources

Coetzee, J. M. *Giving Offense: Essays on Censorship.* Chicago: University of Chicago Press, 1997.

Lugovskaya, Nina. *I Want to Live: The Diary of a Young Girl in Stalin's Russia.* New York: Houghton Mifflin, 2006.

Cervantes, Miguel de (Miguel de Cervantes Saavedra) (1547–1616)
Spanish novelist and poet

A failure at drama and verse, Miguel de Cervantes nonetheless provided Spain with a poignant burlesque epic at the height of the Renaissance. Born at Alcalá de Henares, he grew up on the outskirts of Madrid in a family with impoverished aristocratic connections. During his education at a Jesuit academy and the University of Salamanca, he spent his teens exploring verse and absorbing the Christian dogma that gave strength to the Spanish Empire. A short-lived secretarial post at the Vatican to Cardinal Nuncio Acquavita was followed by fighting as an infantryman at Genoa, Naples, Sardinia, Sicily, and Tunis. At age 24, he was aboard the galley *Marquesa* at the Battle of Lepanto (1571), his left hand paralyzed from a bullet wound. His adventures in early manhood included six months of hospital rehabilitation and kidnap by Mediterranean buccaneers in 1575. In an Algerian slave pen, his struggles to free himself and 60 bondsmen won the admiration of Dey Hassan Pasha. Ransomed in 1580 and returned to genteel poverty, Cervantes wed for money and began a writing career. The failure of his marriage and his arrest and jailing for embezzlement as a purchasing agent for the Spanish Armada produced the ideal setting for writing an anti-epic and parody of knight errantry.

From his cell in Seville, Cervantes wrote *El ingenioso hidalgo Don Quijote de la Mancha* (*Don Quixote of La Mancha*, first part composed in 1605, second part in 1615), a best-selling collection of tales containing observations and commentary on rakes, rogues, peasant herders, and an antihero from Spain's Golden Age. Don Quixote's farcical exploits derive from his delusions promoted through readings of Garci Rodríguez de Montalvo's Portuguese chivalric tale *Amadis of Gaul* (1508) and other CRUSADER LORE. An episodic quest story replete with axioms, irony, symbolism, puns, mythological and biblical allusions, and interpolated romances, Cervantes's work elevates an eccentric 50-year-old dreamer into a champion of justice. Throughout his interaction with duplicitous innkeepers, barmaids, picaros, and con artists, the don clings to his vision of the unreachable Dulcinea, a paragon of beauty and grace to uplift and inspire him. His dependence on the worn-out nag Rocinante epitomizes his tendency to rationalize, for he insists that "neither the Bucephalus of Alexander nor the CID's Babieca could be compared with [his horse]" (Cervantes 1957, 17). Cervantes' mockery of past examples of heroism suggests his intent to infuse Spain with a new, more sensible expectation.

Cervantes interweaves his quest story with examples of state cruelty and vengeance in the Ottoman Empire, Spain's prime opponent of her sovereignty and religion. Of the establishment of a Christian empire, Don Quixote lectures his squire, Sancho Panza, on elements of governance suggesting NICCOLÒ MACHIAVELLI's pragmatic views on revolution and spite. For example, the Christian apostate Uchalin spends 14 years rowing a galley for the Grand Turk and abandons his faith to reconcile himself to shipboard brutality. Once Uchalin ascends the throne of Algiers, his experiences cause him to extend benevolence and humanity to prisoners of war. Don Quixote's solution to retribution is to adopt moral principles—benevolence and a love of citizenship and freedom. Of the latter, he exclaims, "There is on earth . . . no contentment that can equal that of regaining liberty" (39). By surrounding the spirit with a sweet serenity, the avenger ceases wanting to retaliate for past injustices, even forced labor as a galley slave. Some literary critics suspect the author of purposefully undermining Spain's lust for empire and wealth in the Western Hemisphere by instilling virtue in its citizens and discouraging the need for conquest and plunder.

Other works by Cervantes include *La Galatea* (1585), a pastoral romance; *Novelas ejemplares* (*Exemplary Novels*, 1613), a collection of short stories; the novel *Los trabajos de Persiles y Sigismunda* (*Travels of Persiles and Sigismunda*, 1617; published posthumously); and unsuccessful attempts at drama and poetry. He died in Madrid on April 22, 1616, and was buried on April 23, the same day that WILLIAM SHAKESPEARE died. UNESCO therefore established April 23 as the International Day of the Book.

Sources

Cervantes, Miguel de. *Don Quixote of La Mancha.* Translated by Walter Starkie. New York: New American Library, 1957.

Higuera, Henry. *Eros and Empire: Politics and Christianity in Don Quixote.* Lanham, Md.: Rowman & Littlefield, 1995.

Charlemagne (Charles the Great, Charles I)
(742–814) *Emperor of the Franks*

The Frankish warrior king Charlemagne, or Charles the Great, furthered Western Christendom by creating the Frankish Empire out of much of central and western Europe, a realm that rivaled the Byzantine Empire. He was the son of the Frankish king Pépin (or Pippin) the Short and grandson of the great Frankish ruler Charles Martel. After Pépin's death in 768, Charlemagne became co-ruler with his brother, Carloman I, succeeding to sole kingship after Carloman's death in 771.

In an era of growing pan-Europeanism, Charlemagne's imperial boundaries reached from southern Bavaria and Thuringia in central Germany to northern Holland, and from the Pyrenees to northern Italy. A forerunner of the chivalric knight, he combined the strengths of a professional soldier, governor, educator, translator, and evangelist. More than three and a half centuries before the First Crusade (1095–99), he launched a campaign to proselytize the Lombards and Saxons. In 778, he attempted to secure Spain from the Moors. His empire building spread Frankish influence from Bohemia in 788 to the Danube in 796. On December 25, 800, Pope Leo III crowned Charlemagne the first Holy Roman Emperor. A thousand years later, the French Bonapartists extolled Napoleon Bonaparte for resurrecting Charlemagne's vision of a Gallic empire.

Around 830, Einhard, Charlemagne's adviser and emissary, became the emperor's biographer. The publication of *Vita Caroli Magni* (*The Life of Charlemagne*) introduced a model of the literary BIOGRAPHY, a succinct yet thorough accounting scrupulous in its objectivity. Patterned on the Roman historian SUETONIUS's *De vita Caesarum* (*Lives of the Caesars*, ca. A.D. 121), the life story written by Einhard pictures Charlemagne in public and private but offers no citations of the emperor's own words or reenactments of his conversations or speeches. Of Charlemagne's campaign skills, Einhard admires his persistence: "With no small perseverance and continued effort, he brought to complete fruition what he was striving to achieve" (Einhard 1969, 59). Attesting to the significance of the emperor's passing, the biographer retreats to the style of the Greek historiographer HERODOTUS and connects Charlemagne's failing health in the last three years to eclipses of the moon and sun and a black spot on the sun.

A Rebirth of the Arts

During the Carolingian Renaissance (late eighth and ninth centuries), the Charlemagne years saw the flowering of architecture, the arts, and literature; and the scholarship of the educator and royal councilor Alcuin, the epic poet Angilbert, the historian and fabulist Paul the Deacon, and the Carolingian poet laureate Theodulph of Orléans. Legends picture the emperor in battle against Saracens and as the leader of paladins commanded by Roland, hero of the *Chanson de Roland* (*Song of Roland*, ca. 1080), the oldest French text and a touchstone of CRUSADER LORE. The emperor served as the model monarch in courtly literature and a cycle of anonymous *chansons de geste* (songs of deeds) developed from peasant tales—for example, a SATIRE of chivalric feats in the Holy Lands in *Le Pèlerinage de Charlemagne* (*The Pilgrimage of Charlemagne*, ca. 1140); the emperor's exploits in company with his 12 retainers in *The Sowdone of Babylone* (*The Sultan of Babylon*, ca. 1250); and the emperor's journey to Constantinople in *Roland and Vernagu* (ca. 1325), which concludes with a duel in Galicia, Spain.

Around 1262, with the waning of Provençal lyric poetry, the Genoese ambassador and troubadour Luchetto Gattilusio (fl. 1248–1307), honored Charlemagne in passing. In the song "D'un Sirventes M'es Granz," Luchetto notes that Charles of Anjou deserves respect just for bearing the same name as the Carolingian king. Less specific are images of Charlemagne as commander in chief in a conversion-by-combat story of a Saracen knight in Spain in *Otuel* (ca. 1325), the glorification of the French king and his knights in *The Sege of Melayne* (*The Siege of Milan*, ca. 1350), and the reconquest of Spain in *Sir Ferumbras* (ca. 1375) and *Duke Rowlande and Sir Ottuell of Spayne* (ca. 1390s). An endearing Scots fable, the rags-to-riches story of a sturdy French yeoman meeting the king incognito in *The Taill of Rauf Coilyear* (*The Tale of Ralph the Collier*, ca. 1475), exemplifies a Renaissance shift in emphasis from feudal hierarchy to respect for the individual. In 1995, the French actor Christian Brendel recreated early episodes from the emperor's life in the film *Charlemagne*.

Sources

Einhard. *Two Lives of Charlemagne*. Translated by Lewis Thorpe. Harmondsworth, U.K.: Penguin, 1969.

The English Charlemagne Romances: Sir Ferumbras. Boston: Adamant Media, 2001.

Oelsner, Herman. *History of Italian Literature to the Death of Dante*. Translated by Adolf Gaspary. London: George Bell & Sons, 1901.

children's literature

As with adult literature of empire, children's chronicles tend to feature the tensions and conflicts of imperialism and can overlap with other genres, such as FRONTIER LITERATURE. CATHERINE PARR TRAILL produced two titles for youth—*Canadian Crusoes: A Tale of the Rice Lake Plains* (1852) and *Lady Mary and Her Nurse: or, a Peep into the Canadian Forest* (1856)—that provide stories of courage and endurance. Fiction classics such as ROBERT LOUIS STEVENSON's *TREASURE ISLAND* (1883) and RUDYARD KIPLING's *KIM* (1901) present young people with difficult, complex predicaments requiring pluck and determination to solve, such as the theft of a pirate vessel or a holy Hindu quest.

In 1901, four years before the dissolution of the Swedish union with Norway, the Swedish National Teachers Association hired Selma Lagerlöf, a former teacher and Nobel laureate from Värmland, to write a primary reader devoid of the dry pedagogy of standard textbooks. Drawing on the suspense and whimsy of Stevenson's masterworks, she composed *Nils Holgerssons underbara resa* (*The Wonderful Adventures of Nils*, 1906–07) as a boost to the national self-image and to an understanding of Scandinavian mythos, topography, flora, and fauna. Borrowing a writer's trick from Kipling, she depicted the progression of chapters as the view of wild geese in flight as they gaze down on Sweden, province by province. In 1955, a Soviet film studio adapted the text as *The Enchanted Boy*, an animated feature about a flight across Lapland.

Children's works do not preclude realism from their profiles of courage. A nonfiction landmark, *The Diary of a Young Girl* (1947), recounts the brief life of the German-Jewish teenager Anne Frank, who succumbed to typhus at the Nazis' Bergen-Belsen concentration camp in Saxony. From 1942 to 1944, she kept a journal, written from the perspective of a girl hidden in an *achterhuis* (secret annex) on the upper floor of an Amsterdam office building during the Nazi occupation of Holland. She recorded her fears and the inevitable tensions resulting from living with others in crowded quarters. In the process, she recorded experiences of gross anti-Semitism as well as yearnings for freedom. Her emotional outpourings offer readers and historians an eyewitness account of the plight of the individual at a moment in imperial history when GENOCIDE threatened the survival of European Jews.

Although limited in scope and maturity, Anne Frank's observations give her a voice in a time of repression and provide catharsis for the suffering that reduces her nuclear family from four members to a single HOLOCAUST survivor: her father, Otto Frank. The poignant text was adapted as a play, *The Diary of Anne Frank* (1955), and a film version was made in 1959, starring Millie Perkins, Shelley Winters, and Diane Baker. In 1995, Kenneth Branagh, Joely Richardson, and Glenn Close narrated a documentary of the diary, *Anne Frank Remembered*. In 2006, publication of Nina Lugovskaya's *I Want to Live: The Diary of a Young Girl in Stalin's Russia* replicated the measured style and desperation of Anne Frank's journal. The suppressed work, which the KGB (Russian secret police) labeled counterrevolutionary, covers capricious incarcerations and imperial paranoia, injustice, and hypocrisy from 1932 to 1937, when the author entered the Kolyma gulag, the beginning of 12 years of imprisonment and exile. (See CENSORSHIP.)

Youth's Dilemmas

The struggle of girls like Anne and Nina inspired children's writers to set fictional characters in wrenching political dilemmas, often demanding valor and discretion, two qualities not common to the immature. In 1942, Marie McSwigan (1907–62), an editor for the *Pittsburgh Express*, extracted from wire service news the elements of a plot about youthful nationalism and daring. A combination of wartime fact and McSwigan's own imagination resulted in *Snow Treasure*, a historical novel featuring the theme of self-help and a motif of deception by the Norwegian underground. Set on the Arctic Circle at Riswyk at the time of the Nazi invasion of Norway on April 8, 1940, the action places 12-year-old Peter Lundstrom in the role of hero for smuggling the nation's gold past German occupation troops.

In the novel, McSwigen captures her audience with suspense. Bar by bar, teams of sledders cross mountains and deposit the gold under snowmen in reach of the crew of a freighter, the *Bomma*, captained by Peter's uncle Victor. Central to the gripping story is the transformation of child fantasy and play into necessary cunning to save the country's treasury. According to national legend, Norwegian fishermen carried a total of $9 million in bullion to safety in the United States. In 1968, the narrative supplied filmdom with an adventure starring James Franciscus and featuring Paul Austad as Peter.

McSwigan subsequently wrote of other protagonists who display vulnerability and resistance to tyranny. These include the two ham radio transmitters who are threatened by torture in *Juan of Manila* (1947), a story of brotherly solidarity for the Philippine underground during Japanese insurgency. In *All Aboard for Freedom* (1954), the Czechoslovakian orphans escape communist oppressors in 1951 by heisting a train, locking switches, and driving it into West Germany.

Stark Imperialism

The late 20th-century trend toward multiculturalism and realism in children's works inspired Asian-American writers to inform young readers about aspects of World War II in Pacific rim countries that are often glossed over by standard textbooks. Linda Sue Park's *When My Name Was Keoko* (2002) offers a child's view of Japanese occupation and the identity crisis foisted on Koreans stripped of birth names and assigned a Japanese name. Contributing to the unrest is the title character's loss of a brother, Tae-yul, a teenage pilot for the Youth Air Corps who disappears into the ranks of the kamikazes. The narrative explores mixed feelings in wartime: the family's receipt of extra rations as an honorarium for producing a pilot, the death letter that fliers post to their parents before departing on a suicide mission, and Tae-yul's joy in attaining his ambition to fly airplanes. During indoctrination, he is wise enough to recognize Japanese propaganda, "the usual speech about the divinity of the Emperor and the glory of his Empire" (Park 2002, 128). The resolution leaves loose emotional ends, the type of anguish that assails a people long oppressed, culturally deprived, and separated from friends, relatives, and nationhood.

From the Middle East, Marjane Satrapi, an emigré from Iran to France, recapped the history of her noble family in *Persepolis: The Story of a Childhood* (2002). A graphic autobiographical novel adapted as an animated film in 2007, *Persepolis*'s story connects a stateless humanist to her family's role in the shaping of the Persian empire into modern Iran. By explaining the nation's lack of education, she accounts for a shift in rule in 1896 after the death of Great-Grandfather Nasser al-Din Shah in 1896, the seizure of Azerbaijan by the Russian Empire in 1920, the downfall of Shah Reza Pahlavi in 1979, and the creation of a repressive Islamic state under the Ayatollah Khomeini. Through family storytelling from her parents and Uncle Anoosh, she learns that Iran's history has been one oppressive regime after another, punctuated by invasions by Arabs and Mongols and by exploiters from Great Britain and the United States.

Sources

Davé, Shilpa, et al., eds. *East Main Street: Asian American Popular Culture.* New York: New York University Press, 2005.

Frank, Anne. *The Diary of a Young Girl: The Definitive Edition.* Edited by Otto H. Frank and Mirjam Pressler. Translated by Susan Massotty. New York: Bantam, 1997.

Grice, Helena. *Negotiating Identities: An Introduction to Asian American Women's Writing.* Manchester, U.K.: Manchester University Press, 2002.

Huang, Guiyou. *Asian American Autobiographers: A Bio-Bibliographical Critical Sourcebook.* Westport, Conn.: Greenwood, 2001.

Lugovskaya, Nina. *I Want to Live: The Diary of Young Girl in Stalin's Russia.* Translated by Andrew Bronfield. Boston: Houghton Mifflin, 2006.

McSwigan, Marie. *Snow Treasure.* New York: E. P. Dutton, 1942.

Park, Linda Sue. *When My Name Was Keoko.* New York: Random House, 2002.

Satrapi, Marjane. *Persepolis: The Story of a Childhood.* Paris: L'Association, 2003.

Schiwy, Marlene A. *Voice of Her Own: Women and the Journal Writing Journey.* New York: Fireside, 1996.

Christine de Pisan   See FEMINISM.

Chrétien de Troyes   See CRUSADER LORE.

Cid, El (Cantar de mio Cid, El poema del Cid, Song of My Cid)

A puzzle for medievalists, the anonymous Spanish epic *Cantar de mio Cid* (*Song of My Cid*), also called *El poema del Cid* (*The Poem of the Cid*), transforms popular Castilian and Valencian legend into a literary tale of clashing empires. The text lionizes Rodrigo (also Ruy) Díaz de Vivar (ca. 1043–99), called El Campeador (the champion) for his skill at hand-to-hand combat. The feats of El Cid ("the Lord" or "the Master," from the elision of the Arabic *al-Sayyid*) carry the Christian warrior from his home north of Burgos, the capital of Castille, to his death and cult veneration in Valencia on Spain's east central coast. During his coming of age at the palace of Ferdinand I, the Cid became fast friends with the future king, Sancho II. At age 22, the Cid rode as commander of the royal vanguard. Two years later, he won battlefield acclaim for best-

ing the Moors at Zaragoza and for reducing the Islamic king al-Muqtadir to a vassal. Sancho's war against his brother, Alfonso VI, king of León, ended in death for Sancho and alienation for the Cid at court, even after his marriage to the king's cousin, Jimena of Oviedo.

Various folk treatments of the Cid's unenviable political position picture him as a master of psychological tactics, especially for asking advice from his military staff and for doing the unthinkable. In 1079, he trounced an insidious enemy, Count García Ordóñez, during the Granadine invasion of Cabra outside Sevilla. At age 47, when he authorized a raid on the Moors at Toledo, envious courtiers convinced Alfonso to banish the Cid for overreaching his authority by launching an attack without royal approval. At Zaragoza, while learning Mozarabic customs, law, and government, the Cid hired out as a mercenary leader for Yusuf al-Mutamin, the founder of Morocco. Victories at Barcelona earned the knight a fortune. When the Berbers from the Almoravid empire in Northwestern Africa invaded Iberia on October 23, 1086, the Cid once more abandoned his Castilian allegiance to besiege Valencia, which he maintained from December 1093 to May 1094. As the ruler of both Islamic and Christian citizens, he allied his family by marriage with the dynasties of Aragon and Navarre.

According to the 3,700-verse epic *Cantar de mio Cid*, by Spanish author Ramón Menéndez Pidal, the charismatic adventurer holds credit for unifying the splintered Iberian Peninsula. At the time of *la reconquista* (the reconquest), native Iberians fought off Islam while battling among themselves for realms and thrones. Unlike the heroism in VIRGIL's AENEID, the subtext of the Cid's renown lies in triumph and opportunism, not piety, royal bloodline, or ethnic superiority. The anonymous narrative, composed by a lawgiver familiar with Burgos, preserves romantic strands from ballad and legend that include the Cid's admiration for his warhorse Babieca; dependence on his sword Tizona, a steel weapon captured from a Moorish paladin; and love for Jimena, their two daughters, and a son who later dies in combat. At a turning point in the knight's loyalties, the angel Gabriel appears in a vision urging him to take advantage of "so propitious a moment; as long as you live that which is yours will prosper" (*Poem of the Cid* 1959, 65). Without qualm, the Cid rides out the next day at the head of 300 lancers, each bearing a pennon. His courage later infused Spain's epic antihero, Don Quixote, the creation of MIGUEL DE CERVANTES.

Missing from the text of *El Cid* are conventional elements of magic, divine intervention, and the crusader's zeal. In place of idealized heroic traits, the poet provides raw hand-to-hand combat that describes close ups of a broken buckler and girth, a lance strike through two of three layers of chain mail, and a flow of blood from a combatant's mouth as he tumbles over his horse's crupper. When unengaged, the Cid also maintains a husband's loyalty to his wife and children, an open mind toward religious and military pluralism, and a realistic appreciation of plunder. At a high point of gallantry, the knight defends his daughters, Doña Elvira and Doña Sol, from disgrace by caddish mates, two princes of Carrión, and assures the girls' happiness as the respected wives of Iberian princes. A formal reunion depicts the Cid at a gallop: "It was a wonder to watch. When he had ridden one round everyone marveled; from that day Babieca was famous through all Spain" (155). He leaps to the ground to embrace his wife and daughters and weeps with joy before dedicating to them the captured city of Valencia.

In 1961, the screen version of *El Cid* featured Charlton Heston and Sophia Loren as the chivalric husband and his wife Chimene.

Sources

Barton, Simon, and Richard Fletcher, anno. and trans. *The World of El Cid: Chronicles of the Spanish Reconquest.* Manchester, U.K.: Manchester University Press, 2000.

The Poem of the Cid. Translated by W. S. Merwin. New York: New American Library 1959.

Condé, Maryse (Maryse Boucolon Condé)
(1937–) *Guadeloupian critic, playwright, and historical novelist*

Through feminist, egalitarian fiction, Maryse Condé writes of the evil and sorrow of the black African diaspora. Called the grande dame of French Caribbean literature, she pioneered the self-analysis of French West Indians and explored the connections between the New England colonies and the Caribbean. Born Maryse Boucolon to a teacher and a business executive in Pointe-à-Pitre, Guadeloupe, she and her seven younger siblings were reared like French bourgeois. In her mid-teens, while she earned degrees in English and comparative literature at the Lycée Fénélon and the Sorbonne in Paris, she experienced discrimination because of her race and dialect speech. She befriended fellow expatriates from the French Antilles and fostered a creative outlook based on *métissage* (hybridization). She married the African actor Mamadou Condé in 1958 (they divorced in 1981) and took up teaching positions in the language arts at schools in Guinea, Ghana, the Ivory Coast, and Senegal. At age 31, she produced media programming at the BBC office in London before resuming classroom work in Jussieu and Nanterre, France, and at the Sorbonne Nouvelle, the University of California at Berkeley, and Columbia University.

Condé began her writing career with stage plays and two anticolonial novels, *Hérémakhonon* (1976) and *Une saison à Rihata* (*A Season in Rihata,* 1981), a fictional study of political chaos under an African dictator. To recreate the transatlantic slave trade to Brazil and the Caribbean, she depicted captives from the Bambaran Empire of Ségou (present-day Mali) in a two-part African saga, *Ségou: Les murailles de terre* (*Segu: The Children of Segu,* 1984) and *Ségou: La terre en miettes* (*Segu: The Earth in Pieces,* 1985), both best sellers. Returning to black beginnings in the style of Alex Haley's *Roots* saga, Condé's text opens in the kingdom of Segu in the heart of the Bambaran empire, which lies under threat from the Fulani of the Songhay kingdom of Gao. She explores the political dominance of Segu, stretching from Jenne on the Bani River to the desert enclave at Timbuktu.

The novelist makes the most of humankind's age-old foibles. Naive characters marvel at the approach of a Caucasian, a "white man, white, with two red ears like embers," a source of terror presaging waves of Dutch, English, French, and Portuguese invasions in the time of King Guezo of Dahomey, the heyday of the global slave trade (Condé *Segu* 1998, 9). The author inserts an ironic song honoring the Islamic concept of jihad (holy war): "War is good because it makes our kings rich. / Wives, slaves, cattle—it brings them all these" (481). In the end, as the new king supports Fulani battalions in a battle against the Muslim El-Hadj Omar, the wisdom of peasants informs a rhetorical question: "Don't kings ever learn?" (483). Anticipating a massacre, Condé compares the fate of Segu to a woman with smallpox—before the pustules appear on her face, "death is at work within her" (484).

Condé and the Black Diaspora

Condé earned the Grand Prix Littéraire de la Femme for *Moi, Tituba, sorcière noire Salem* (*I, Tituba, Black Witch of Salem*, 1986), which she researched at Occidental College in Los Angeles on a Fulbright scholarship. A dramatization of black runaways, the novel associates the real, historical figure of Tituba with Condé as though they were contemporaries. The fictional biography of the Anglo-Ashanti martyr begins with her conception during the passage from West Africa to North America aboard the slave galley *Christ the King*, as a result of her mother Abena's rape by an English sailor. Tituba describes herself from a colonial perspective as "born from this act of aggression. From this act of hatred and contempt" (Condé 1994, 3). After entering domestic bondage in Barbados, Tituba is shuffled north to colonial New England to scrub and clean for Susanna Endicott, a supercilious white in Salem, Massachusetts, who sneers, "I cannot bear to have you niggers touching my food" (21). The jibe creates a self-SATIRE of a woman who expects a black domestic to perform the most intimate of household chores, yet cringes at the blackness of her hands.

African traditions prove Tituba's undoing among callous, stiff-necked Puritans. Alienated, abused, and helpless, she prays supine on the ground and receives a visitation from her grandmother Mama Yaya and mother Abena. In 1692, as punishment for telling the fortunes of supposedly innocent Christian girls, a skill based on nature lore that she learned from Mama Yaya, Tituba stands branded a sorceror. Remanded to Barbados to serve as midwife and herbalist to plantation blacks, she is pregnant when she goes to the gallows for practicing sorcery there. She looks forward to the afterlife as a reprieve from bondage and accession to "a kingdom where the light of truth burns bright and unrelenting" (172).

In subsequent bicultural storytelling, Condé has depicted more elements of the nightmarish existence of women victimized by empire's misogyny and cruelty. Through the voices of Mabo Sandrine, Sanjita the Housekeeper, and Sanjita's daughter Etiennise, the author narrated *La migration des coeurs* (*Windward Heights*, 1995). The novella restructures Emily Brontë's feminist *Wuthering Heights* (1847) by casting Razyé, a swarthy foundling, as the passionate Heathcliff. A Byronic hero of unknown parentage, he pursues a doomed love for Catherine Gagneur, his foster sister. Against the backdrop of the racism and social stratification of Cuba and Guadeloupe, the action depicts a merging of cultures through islanders' participation in African tradition and Santeria, a form of obeah. Etiennise's lapse into the female fantasy of rescue by a strong male foreshadows a universal misadventure—the role of ignorance and naïveté in a continuation of parental faults.

Sources

Condé, Maryse. *I, Tituba, Black Witch of Salem.* Translated by Richard Philcox. New York: Ballantine, 1994.
———. *Segu.* Translated by Barbara Bray. New York: Penguin, 1998.
———. *Windward Heights.* Translated by Richard Philcox. New York: Soho, 1998.
Hargreaves, Alec G. *Memory, Empire, and Postcolonialism: Legacies of French Colonialism.* Lanham, Md.: Lexington Books, 2005.

Confucius   See ANALECTS.

Conrad, Joseph (Józef Teodor Konrad Korzeniowski) (1857–1924) *Polish-British fiction writer*

In the last years of the Victorian era (1837–1901) and the beginning of the Edwardian era (1901–10), Joseph Conrad branded imperial racism and exploitation as corrosive evils. Born Józef Teodor Konrad Korzeniowski in Berdichev, Ukraine, he was the son of Apollo Korzeniowski, a Polish poet and freedom fighter in a period when Russian expansionism threatened Poles in the territory. During his family's exile to Vologda in northeast Russia in 1862, the seven-year-old Joseph first became aware of the shadow of the Russian Empire, an oppression that fostered factional hatred. He lost his mother to tuberculosis contracted during the prison sentence for sedition she voluntarily shared with her husband. Father and son returned to Poland in 1868, shortly before Apollo Korzeniowski's death, and young Joseph became the ward of his uncle in Krakow.

At age 16, to avoid being drafted into the Russian army, Conrad moved to Marseilles and went to sea at a time when the British ruled almost two-thirds of the global land mass. In travels to Venezuela, the West Indies, and the French Antilles, he became involved in gun smuggling on behalf of the Spanish royal family. Burdened by debt, a failed romance, and melancholy, he took passage as a steward on a British freighter to Constantinople (present-day Istanbul, Turkey). He mastered English as his third language and collected wisps of pidgin dialect from the nomads who scoured the world's ports for livelihood and company.

In 1886, at age 29, Conrad rose to the rank of master mariner in the British merchant navy, altered his name, and gained British citizenship. While sailing to colonial berths in Java, Borneo, Australia, Hong Kong, Singapore, and Siam, he wrote up his travels and composed his first story, "The Black Mate" (1884), a tale of treachery published in *London Magazine* in April 1908. Conrad's posting in 1889 to Kinshasa in the Belgian Congo (present-day Zaire), exposed him to the beatings of servants and bearers, some of whom were young boys. His experience ended in frustration, fever, and near drowning, but his Congo diary gave him material for his masterwork, HEART OF DARKNESS (1899), an antiheroic classic. The diary reveals an epiphany—that the darkness of Africa radiated from the conqueror, not the conquered. The novel's title reflects a grim perspective on foreign dominion and the beginning of globalization.

Unlike RUDYARD KIPLING, who distinguished between his understanding of nationalism and imperialism, Conrad critiqued the macho posturing and amorality of the frontiersman. He rejected imperial assumptions about ethnicity, entitlement, and European-based civilization, which Kipling described as the "white man's burden" in his poem published the same year as Conrad's novel.

At age 40, Conrad retired from the sea to treat gout and depression. At his home outside Canterbury, Kent, he supported his wife, Jessie George Conrad, and sons John and Borys by writing stories and serializing novels in *Blackwood's, Cornhill, Cosmopolis, Harper's*, the *Illustrated London News, Pall Mall Magazine*, and *T. P.'s Weekly*. In a literary manifesto in the preface to *The Nigger of the Narcissus* (1897), he claimed to empower the written word with hearing, feeling, and visualization. He prospered as a writer until his death from heart failure on August 3, 1924. He was buried in Canterbury, England, under his birth name.

Conrad and Imperialism

Conrad's first novel, *Almayer's Folly: A Story of an Eastern River* (1895), set a pattern of motifs and themes that dominated his works—the battles with conscience and circumstance that demoralize colonial settlers. The book is a character study of a Dutch merchant, Kaspar Almayer, at an isolated trading post in Borneo, where he expends his energies and his humanity on dreams of wealth. Ostensibly, he, like other imperialists, rules in the tropics, but he soon finds himself devoured by isolation and betrayed by a "vision of a great and splendid reward" (Conrad 1904, 10). Conrad's familiar symbol of a pier and lone residence built by a languid river reminds the reader that the passage of life is ever in motion, propelling opportunities out of Almayer's reach toward the sea. At a distance, his nation profits by colonizing the Dutch East Indies; up close, the one-on-one cost of maintaining the ledgers of commerce is loss of soul and a defeat for Western ideals. As events unfold among shadowy trees and tangled creepers, he longs for peace, "that inanimate thing now growing small and indistinct in the deepening darkness" (11). At the nadir of his fantasies, he looks toward a grinning monkey and exclaims, "Eternity!"—an enigmatic response to disillusion and terror (244).

The author ventured into more complex moral study with *Lord Jim* (1900), a historical novel based on the abandonment of 800 Muslim pilgrims by the British officers of a transport vessel. Scandal dogs the title character, a British water clerk who has traveled the Asian ports and trading centers of the British Empire. As a scapegoat for the abandonment of the SS *Patna* in Indonesian waters, he is stripped of his certification for dereliction of duty. The narrator remarks on Jim's self-torment: "He made so much of his disgrace while it is the guilt alone that matters," a reference to his leaving trusting passengers to drown (Conrad 1920, 177). Conrad describes Jim's martyrdom as the appropriate retribution for moral weakness, also the theme of the short story "The Lagoon" (1897), an Indonesian love story, and of the novels *Nostromo, a Tale of the Seaboard* (1904), set amid revolutionary upheaval in fictional Costaguana, South America; and *Under Western Eyes* (1911), an antihero study of betrayal and guilt during Russia's czarist regime.

Lauded by giants of the era—Arnold Bennett, Stephen Crane, John Galsworthy, Henry James, and James Joyce—and emulated by the Bengali novelist ANITA MAZUMDAR DESAI, the German-born writer RUTH PRAWER JHABVALA, and the Trinidadian-British writer V. S. NAIPAUL, Conrad remained a pivotal figure in the literature of empire until Nigerian author CHINUA ACHEBE's essay "An Image of Africa: Racism in Conrad's 'Heart of Darkness'" (1975) reevaluated Conrad's perception of colonialism. Two films brought new audiences to Conrad's works: *Lord Jim* (1964), featuring Peter O'Toole, James Mason, Eli Wallach, Curt Jurgens, and Jack Hawkins; and *Apocalypse Now* (1979), with Martin Sheen and Marlon Brando in an adaptation of *Heart of Darkness* set during the Vietnam War.

Sources

Achebe, Chinua. "An Image of Africa: Racism in Conrad's 'Heart of Darkness.'" In *The Norton Anthology of Theory and Criticism*, edited by Vincent B. Leitch, et al., 782–794. New York: Norton, 2001.

Ash, Beth Sharon. *Writing in Between: Modernity and Psychosocial Dilemma in the Novels of Joseph Conrad*. London: Macmillan, 1999.

Conrad, Joseph. *Almayer's Folly: A Story of an Eastern River*. London: Eveleigh Nash, 1904.

———. *Heart of Darkness and The Secret Sharer.* New York: Signet, 1983.

———. *Lord Jim.* Garden City, N.Y.: Doubleday, Doran, 1920.

corrido

A form of oral journalism, a *corrido* is a narrative in song that usually commences with a prologue, tells the central story, and concludes with a moral. The popular ballads of northern Mexico broadcast the outrage of working-class Mexicans at their abasement and exploitation by foreigners. *Corridos* included crime alerts, propaganda, and border PRO-TESTS from the 1820s onward. Sensational, earthy, passionate, and violent, the usually anonymous folk form suited a simple tune that troubadours strummed on a guitar or played on the accordion to a polka beat. Octosyllabic lines rhyming *abcb* and stories of men of action saluted their defiance of polite society, clergy, and officials. Such songs as of "El corrido de Kiansis" ("The Ballad of Kansas," ca. 1860) placed *dueños vaqueros* (Tex-Mex cowboys), Southwest American rough riders, and herders alongside popular heroes, freedom fighters, womanizers, and Robin Hoods, protagonists of broadsides and Spanish-language theater productions in Mexico, Texas, and California.

Whether humorous, satiric, or blood-curdling, *corridos* dramatized conflict and VIOLENCE. During the Mexican War of Independence (1810–21) singers provided news of Apache and Yaqui raids, banditry and bank holdups, rustlers, lynch mobs, railroad camps, and rabble rousing for national independence. Amid the protagonists of *corrido* verse, the noble victim stood at the center of sagas of daring and treachery. The stanzas of "Corrido de los oprimidos" ("Ballad of the Oppressed," 1821), reflect the perspective of Mexican Indians on racial prejudice. In "El corrido de Gregorio Cortez" ("The Ballad of Gregorio Cortez," ca. 1890), a rebel *"con su pistola en la mano"* (with a pistol in his hand) resists Anglo-American incursions and racism (Sundquist 2006, 55). In a concluding boast, the man-on-the-run smirks at his notoriety among so large a posse: "Ah, so many mounted Rangers / Just to take one Mexican!" (quoted in Paredes 1958, 3). The 10-line "El corrido de los

Franceses" (The Ballad of the French, ca. 1860s) and "El corrido de Ignacio Zaragoza" (The Ballad of Ignacio Zaragoza, 1867) reprise the events of May 5, 1862, when Mexico defeated a French invasion at Puebla and chose Cinco de Mayo as a day of celebration. The 19th-century guitarist Onofre Cárdenas popularized "A Zaragoza" (To Zaragoza, 1867), a heroic song commemorating a native son of the border. In this same period, folk ballads about Juan Nepomuceno Cortina, fomenter of the First Cortina War in Brownsville, Texas, in 1859, remembers the gunfight between Marshal Robert Shears and Cortina, the leader of a band of irregulars. The defeat and execution of Emperor Maximilian I in 1867 resulted in the Los Franceses cycle, a loose repertory of gibes at the Austrian-born ruler, such as "Corrido del tiro de gracia" ("Ballad of the Coup de Grâce," 1867), which pictures Maximilian as he crumbles before a firing squad.

The *corrido* survived into the 20th century in hybrid verses dealing with urban crime against the people and touting effective means of subverting anglocentrism. Similar sloganeering honored Che Guevara for resisting the dictator Fulgencio Batista's dominion in Cuba and César Chávez for fighting for the economic rights of Chicano laborers in California. In 1958, the musicologist and folklorist Américo Paredes of Brownsville, Texas, introduced Chicano folklore scholarship in *With His Pistol in His Hand: A Border Ballad and Its Hero*, a survey of the colonial romance and songs of machismo. The evolution of the *corrido* as a countercultural protest song includes "Los deportados" (The deported), "La discriminación," "Los enganchados" (Press gangs), and *narcocorridos*, drug ballads glorifying *narcotraficantes* (drug dealers).

Sources

Frazer, Chris. *Bandit Nation: A History of Outlaws and Cultural Struggle in Mexico, 1810–1920*. Lincoln: University of Nebraska Press, 2006.

Paredes, Américo. *With His Pistol in His Hand: A Border Ballad and Its Hero*. Austin: University of Texas Press, 1958.

Sundquist, Eric J. *Empire and Slavery in American Literature, 1820–1865*. Jackson: University Press of Mississippi, 2006.

creation lore

Throughout world literature, creation lore elicits questions about the divine right of sovereignty. Cosmogony, or origin theory and myth, takes many forms: verse, epics, dialogues, narratives, PSALMS, and mystic chants, all attempting to explain the creation of matter from nothing. From oral traditions of a supreme being or creator come scriptures, doctrines, liturgies, and philosophies of reality, the focus of the Genesis Apocryphon in the DEAD SEA SCROLLS (130–27 B.C.); AZTEC codices; YEHUDA HALEVI's pietist philosophy in *Kuzari* (ca. 1125); the Finnish book of folklore, KALEVALA (1836); Hawaiian queen Liliuokalani's *Kumulipo* (The beginning, 1897), a sourcebook of Hawaiian cosmogony (see AUTOBIOGRAPHY); and the Martinican author Aimé Césaire's *A Tempest* (1969), a stagy resurgence of Nigerian spirits evoked to cleanse the French Antilles of imperialism. In a translation of Valmiki's Hindu *Ramayana* (ca. 400 B.C.), King Rama I, founder of the Chakri dynasty, added creation myth to produce a Thai version, the *Ramakien* (1797). The interpolation of Thai origination stories turned the Hindu original into a unique epic.

The style of the creation myth veers away from dominance toward wonder and mystery, as in Pharaoh Akhenaten's "Hymn to the Sun" in the Egyptian BOOK OF THE DEAD (ca. 1240 B.C.). The text, composed by Egypt's ruler, marvels at the power of the divine over all life: "You give breath to all your creation, / Opening the mouth of the newborn / And giving him nourishment" (quoted in Roberts 1991, 141). The compilation of verses by the Punjabi guru known as Arjan Dev in the GRANTH (1604), the Sikh holy book, expresses similar elation in the strength of the Almighty. Among his most inspired verses are creation praises that look beyond earthly empires to the universe: "Many times the expanse of the world was spread out. Many worlds of many kinds were made. From the Lord they emanated and in the Lord they are absorbed" (*Adi Granth* 1877, c). The author expresses the whole-heartedness of the man of God: "Into whose heart thou givest thy name, they are made pure" (138).

The earliest models of cosmogony, the Egyptian *Creating the World and Defeating Apophis* (2000 B.C.), and the Babylonian agon, or contest story, "Nisaba and Wheat" (ca. 1900 B.C.), imagine struggle as the source of being, a concept characterized in 1864 by the naturalist Charles Darwin as "survival of the fittest." To the Egyptian priests at Heliopolis, the contest pitted the sun god Ra in a sea fight against the underworld water serpent Apophis, an emblem of dark anarchy and strangulation. From their struggle emerged the universal elements of land, sky, water, and wind. Central to creation mythology is the naming of phenomena, an act of identifying and classifying that initiated the literary and artistic depiction of the world.

Like the prophetic poem *Voluspa* in SNORRI STURLUSON's Icelandic *Prose Edda* (1225), the Indian Rig Veda (ca. 1200 B.C.), the original Hindu scripture, ranges from nature imagery to metaphysical or abstract ideas of unimanifested power and being. The narrative legitimizes numerous myths of creation, including a cosmic conflict and a divine separation of earth from heaven by the All-Maker. The compiler describes the acts of the sages as a straining of the word, the equivalent of bakers forcing flour through a sieve. The "Hymn of Man" pictures humankind as a cosmic creation, "the ruler of immortality" who "spread out in all directions, into that which eats and that which does not eat" (Rig Veda 1981, 30). The text concludes with the anointing of Man for the altar, a sacrifice motif common to world mythography. From the fat exuding from man's immolation arise birds and herds of cows, goats, horses, and sheep, which become food for the earth's carnivores.

Mythic Beginnings of Power

Source material for creation varies within cultures. The *DAODEJING* (*Tao-Te Ching* [Classic of the way of power, 300 B.C.]) of the Chinese philosopher Laozi (Lao Tsu) pictures the shaping of the universe as ineffable, the ultimate enigma that transcends power and materials as rivers and streams flow back into the sea. He attributes the emergence of empires to self-serving human ambitions that view the universe superficially as plunder. The wise individual, who is only a guest in the world, seeks tranquility by valuing the earth not as a source of personal wealth but as a nourishing mother. In a similar vein, Islamic tradition envisions the gift of life as a form of divine grace—a gift that human-

kind does not have to deserve. According to the KORAN (A.D. 633), the first acts of Allah involved the regulation of nature: "He gave all plants their male and female parts and drew the veil of night over the day" (Koran 13:3). The abundance of foodstuffs applies to the fauna and flora of Muslim countries in the declaration, "He brings forth corn and olives, dates and grapes and fruits of every kind" (Koran 16:10). The somber paean to the almighty influenced the Persian poet FIRDAWSI's epic *Shahnameh* (*The Book of Kings*, ca. 1010). He opens his dynastic list with the omnipotent maker of life, "Who gives the sun and moon and Venus light, / Above all name and thought, exceeding all / Of his creation, and unknowable" (Firdawsi 2006, xiv). Firdawsi's epic belittles the vainglorious attempts of humankind to build their empires and imitate the control of God over Earth.

Often initiated by a sky god, the act of creating is a deliberate ordering of chaos by one deity, as demonstrated by the lyric beginning of the Hebrew book of GENESIS (ca. 500 B.C.) and the Mayan *POPUL VUH* (A.D. 1558). The *Enuma Elish* (ca. 1700 B.C.), the Babylonian creation myth, comprises oral myths dating to the beginning of the Babylonian empire. Written in Akkadian and recorded on clay tablets in Ashurbanipal (present-day Mosul, Iraq), it summarizes in 1,000 lines the birth and godhood of Marduk, the deity controlling the supernatural, water, plants, and wisdom. The energy for creation derives from the Almighty, expressed as emanations of light from the divine Marduk, the supervisor of 50 lesser divinities. The narration looks back on nothingness when "no field was formed, no marsh was to be seen; when of the gods none had been called into being, and none bore a name, and no destinies were ordained" (*Enuma Elish* 2004, 2). Marduk uses his own bone and blood to fashion humans to rule over other living beings. Like the Greek Zeus, Marduk overcomes prehistoric divinities and grasps the Tablets of Destiny, the source of primacy over all creation.

Gods and Emperors

Associating the cosmic order with the imperial order links the emperor to God and allows him to impose his will on his subject people. Anthologized during Japan's Nara period (710–784), the *Kojiki* (*Records of Ancient Matters*, A.D.712) was written by the scribe O no Yasumaro, based on the oral storytelling of the bard Hieda no Are. Like Virgil's *Aeneid* (17 B.C.) and Garcilaso de la Vega's *Royal Commentaries of the Incas and General History of Peru* (1617), O no Yasumaro's lush passages validate the Japanese empire as the gods' will. Beginning with the scriptural compilations of Emperor Temmu in A.D. 681, five- and seven-line poems composed orally as early as A.D. 400 stripped Japanese creation concepts of corruption from Chinese and Korean sources. In pure Japanese philosophy, the verses honor the Yamato dynasty as a source of order. Combined with the 30-volume *Nihon Shoki* (Chronicle of Japan, A.D. 720), compiled by Emperor Sodoujinkei, the narrative begins with universal chaos in the "age of the gods" when "Heaven and Earth were not yet separated and [yin and yang] not yet divided" (*Nihongi* 2006, 1). The text synchronizes Japanese genealogy, nature myth, love lyrics, and dream cycles into a unified history concluding around A.D. 600 during the reign of Empress Suiko. In justification of empire, the narrative states, "The previous emperors therefore established an illustrious designation and handed down a vast fame: in magnanimity they were a match with Heaven and Earth: in glory they resembled the sun and moon" (29). The events and their "mollifying influence" formed the foundation of Shintoism, Japan's earliest formal religion.

The mythic ordering of life on earth incorporates natural wonder tales with violence and blood sacrifice on a par with the sufferings of the Egyptian Osiris and the Greek Prometheus. In Japanese lore, the divine couple, Izanagi and Izanami, who are sibling mates like the Greek Zeus and Hera, lean from a heavenly floating bridge to stir up eight islands with a swirl of a spear in the primordial soup "till it went curdle-curdle" (*Kojiki* 2005, 22). After Izanami's death in childbirth, Izanagi, like the Greek Orpheus mourning his dead bride Eurydice, traverses the underworld to find her. He discovers that Izanami, like the Greek Persephone, has eaten the food of Hades, which binds her to death: "Maggots were swarming, and she was rotting" (42). The creator's breach of the divide between life and death releases evil on humanity in the same way that the Greek Pandora unsealed the jar of evil and the Hebrew

Eve disobeyed Yahweh and tasted the fruit of the Tree of Knowledge. To prepare himself once more for his tasks, Izanagi introduces purification rites that permeate national customs and ritual. Book II connects prehistory to history with the rule of Jimmu (660–585 B.C.) and concludes with Emperor Ojin in the early A.D. third century.

Sources

The Adi Granth, or, The Holy Scriptures of the Sikhs. Translated by Ernst Trumpp. London: Great Britain India Office, 1877.

Brownlee, John S. *Political Thought in Japanese Historical Writing: From Kojiki (712) to Tokushi Yoron (1712).* Waterloo, Ont.: Wilfrid Laurier University Press, 1991.

Enuma Elish: The Epic of Creation. Translated by L. W. King. Whitefish, Mont.: Kessinger, 2004.

Firdawsi. *Shahnameh: The Persian Book of Kings.* Translated by Dick Davis. New York: Viking, 2006.

The Kojiki: Records of Ancient Matters. Translated by Basil Hall Chamberlain. North Clarendon, Vt.: Tuttle, 2005.

The Koran. Translated by N. J. Dawood. London: Penguin Classics, 2004.

Nihongi: Chronicles of Japan from the Earliest Times to A.D. 697. Translated by W. G. Aston. New York: Cosimo Classics, 2006.

The Rig Veda. Translated and edited by Wendy Doniger. Harmondsworth, U.K.: Penguin Classics, 1981.

Roberts, Elizabeth, and Elias Amidon, eds. *Earth Prayers from around the World.* San Francisco: HarperSanFrancisco, 1991.

crusader lore

Overlapping the output of the Angevin empire (12th and early 13th centuries), and covering lands from Ireland to the Pyrenees, the literature generated by two centuries of Christian crusades to the Holy Lands displays a unique aura of medieval grandeur, mission, and self-sacrifice. When, on November 27, 1095, Pope Urban II began the quest to capture Jerusalem from Muslim forces, his religious and political aim targeted the advance of the Seljuk Empire—a realm reaching from Turkey to the Punjab and south to Arabia—into the Levant (present-day Turkey) and, potentially, northwest into Europe. The pope exonerated and blessed Christian warriors for proselytizing Muslims by the sword and for reclaiming from the infidels the burial place of Christ in Jerusalem, or Zion, two place names that dominate crusader verse. The collision of cultures required that both sides promote the "big lie"—in this case, the demonization of both Muslims and Christians as godless imperialists. To unify troops from varied states, the Catholic Church promoted the use of the Christian cross and the pilgrim's insignia in place of national banners and combat badges. The pope promised reception into paradise as an everlasting reward to volunteers risking bankruptcy, exhaustion, pestilence, capture, torture, and death.

Crusader literature drew on a noble model. From the age of CHARLEMAGNE, the warrior-king of the Frankish Empire, the *Chanson de Roland* (*Song of Roland*, ca. 1080), the oldest French text, stood out as a pinnacle of the medieval chanson de geste (song of deeds). Set in the Spanish sector of the Islamic Empire, the epic gained renown as well as imitators for its depiction of a Saracen attack on the Franks at Roncevaux Pass in the Pyrenees on August 15, 778. The blowing of bugles to summon the French leader invigorates the climax: "The pagans say: 'The emperor is returning. Hear how the men of France sound their bugles; if Charles comes, we shall have great losses. Our war will begin afresh, if Roland is alive; we have lost Spain'" (*Song of Roland*, 96). The emperor's blessing of his forces and his prostration before God enhanced the concept of the divine right of kings, a justification for Frankish hegemony. The tragic clash ennobled the ideals of knighthood and mercy and anticipated by over three centuries the Christian campaign against Islam in the Middle East. Norman soldiers under William the Conqueror sang of Roland at the Battle of Hastings on October 14, 1066, as they assaulted the forces of Harold of England. By the end of the First Crusade in 1099, hagiography, epic poetry, memoir, song, and the chivalric verse of MARIE DE FRANCE were finding eager audiences.

War and Sanctity

In all, there were eight crusades: 1096–99, 1147–49, 1189–92, 1201–04, 1218–21, 1228–29, 1248–54, and 1270. Under the aegis of religious leaders, the exotic elements of holy war underpin generations of crusader balladry, romantic and penitential poems, sermons, legendary genealogy, folklore, FABLES, and chansons de geste. In the Middle East, crusader lore influenced the historian ANNA COMNENA's *Alexiad* (1148), a chronicle of Byzantium up to the death of her father, Alexius I Comnenius, emperor of Constantinople. During the struggle in Iberia to oust Muslims from southwestern Europe, an anonymous author compiled French conventions and motifs into the Portuguese *Demanda do Santo Graal* (Quest for the Holy Grail, ca. 1400). The 70-volume chivalric cycle of the deeds of Lancelot and his son Galahad remained in manuscript form until editor Augusto Magne first published it in 1944 in Rio de Janeiro, Brazil.

The soldier Charles the Good of Flanders (1084–1127; First Crusade) and Louis IX of France (1214–70), the spearheads of the Seventh and Eighth Crusades, dominated the lore of saints admired for battlefield feats. Geoffrey de Villehardouin (ca. 1160–ca. 1212), a knight-poet from Champagne, France, immortalized the French king Philip II in *Conquête de Constantinople* (*The Conquest of Constantinople*, 1207). In the style of the Greek historian THUCYDIDES, Villehardouin accounted for the numbers of ships, war steeds, squires, knights, and infantrymen involved in the Fourth Crusade. The chronicler perpetuated the folk belief in God's favor by promising warriors, "If God permits you to restore his inheritance to him, he will place his whole empire under the authority of Rome" (Joinville and Villehardouin, 1963, 50). A century later, Jean de Joinville (ca. 1224–1317), the famous chronicler of medieval France, described Louis's military feats in the *Memoirs of the Lord of Joinville* (1309), a recap of the Seventh Crusade.

The Grail Quest

From 1180 to 1240, grail romances—stories focused on the quest for the Holy Grail—flourished by grafting onto adventure and HERO tales the elements of religious dedication, celibacy, reverence for the Virgin Mary, and asceticism espoused by the papacy. Following an era of theocratic dominance, grail lore introduced a departure from feudal fealty to kings, focusing instead on the high-mindedness of individual knights who operated outside royal courts and religious institutions. Medieval entertainers called jongleurs performed the narratives to stir audience interest and portray Christian heroes as invincible. The chivalric notion of the Holy Grail, the chalice that Jesus consecrated to distribute the Eucharist to his disciples at the Last Supper, dominated a medieval cycle containing the Percival (or Perceval) idylls, a subset of Arthurian lore. Gradually, the self-denial and mysticism of early medieval literature gave place to crusader sagas with robust religious fervor and feats of daring and romance.

The first star trouvère (troubadour), Chrétien de Troyes (ca. 1150–ca. 1190), of Champagne, France, advanced grail literature and *frauenlieder* (women's songs) by combining the vigor of Celtic mythology and the elegance of the Roman poet OVID's *Metamorphosis* (Transformations A.D. 8) with Arthurian romances. Funded by Philip of Flanders, a noble of the Holy Roman Empire, Chrétien's chivalric songs *Erec et Enide* (*Erec and Enide*, ca. 1170) and *Cligès* (ca. 1176), a tale of imperial power in Constantinople and Greece, set the tone and atmosphere of his later works. Chrétien developed concepts of courage and self-denial in *Yvain, le chevalier au lion* (*Yvain, the Knight of the Lion*, ca. 1177) and *Lancelot, ou le chevalier de la charrette* (*Lancelot, or the Knight of the Cart*, ca. 1181), a metrical verse cycle based on courtly love and completed by Godefroi de Leigny, Chrétien's colleague.

Chrétien achieved lasting fame with *Perceval, ou le conte du Graal* (*Percival, or the Account of the Grail*, ca. 1182), a popular spiritual quest that he left unfinished. The bildungsroman (coming-of-age tale) follows the neophyte warrior from naïveté and folly to sophistication and insight. The author's vision of knightly character as both deadly and righteous emphasizes the contradictions of crusader traits. The militarism of the Christian mercenary imbues the knight Gawain, whose support includes "knights with first-rate shields and lances, helmets and swords," evidence of the "arts of battle" that crusader lore idealized (Chrétien de Troyes 1999, 152, 47).

In search of the cup in which Joseph of Arimathea reputedly collected Christ's blood after the Crucifixion, Chrétien's campaigners ride into danger while the women left behind, claw their faces in grief, swoon from a welter of emotion, and sob over the risk to young manhood from alien forces. In an idealized depiction of crusading, the symbolic quest story dispatches the hero Perceval alone to battle evil on symbolic terrain. The narrative pictures him in a castle, where a wounded king guards the Christian treasure. A handmaiden presents Perceval with a series of mysterious gifts—Longinus's bloody lance, a silver salver that once held the Paschal lamb, and the jewel-crusted grail. This tableau is a transcendent moment that lifts crusader lore from ordinary combat literature to the sublime.

The Chivalric Motif

Chrétien's *Perceval* characterized a verse genre featuring crusaders who live pure, devout lives and who devote themselves to a 12th-century concept of holy endeavor—the recovery of the Holy Grail. In France a three-part cycle of chansons de geste celebrated the First Crusade. Composed in Picardy, the cycle began with the Old French epic *Chanson d'Antioche* (Song of Antioch, ca. 1130), an introduction to the original Christian campaign to reclaim the holy land. Tradition names its author as Graindor de Douai, an obscure Flemish writer or redactor who supposedly based events on the eyewitness account of Richard the Pilgrim, who accompanied Godfrey de Bouillon to Palestine and died before crusaders captured Jerusalem. The text claims that God selected French champions to establish a Christian dominance in the Middle East, challenging the Islamic Empire.

In Homeric style, the narrative covers the organization of forces, the march to Constantinople, and the triumph of crusaders at Antioch following a nine-month siege from October 21, 1097, to June 2, 1098. The boasts of a single slice of the French sword through a Saracen's chain mail attest to the divine empowerment of Christian arms with superhuman strength. Dialogue features the exhortatory speeches of leaders who detect occasions when crusader enthusiasm lags and who revive esprit de corps by stimulating soldiers' pride in family and ancestry. The story seethes with sexual implications—in the proposed French emasculation of Saracens by shaving their beards and in the Saracen threats to rape French wives. As a change from male superiority, the chanson depicts women forming a female battalion to aid their crusader husbands by bearing water and hurling stones at enemy ramparts. At a dramatic point, the warrior Robert II of Flanders sets an example of selfless valor by volunteering to lead invaders up a ladder and over the walls of Antioch. Literary historians surmise that performances of the epic entertained and inspired men and women who gathered at postwar feasts to honor martyrs and to commend veterans of the First Crusade.

The last two parts of the cycle, the *Chanson de Jérusalem* (Song of Jerusalem, ca. 1150) and the *Chanson des Chétiffs* (Song of the captives, ca. 1150) furthered the theme of character enhancement through service to the faith. The two verse sagas systematized and embellished adventure stories of a Christian knight, Godfrey de Bouillon (1058–1100), duke of Lower Lorraine, a Belgian descendent of Charlemagne. Under the command of Emperor Alexius Comnenus of Constantinople, Godfrey de Bouillon led the first expedition of 70,000 French and German troops through Hungary to seize Jerusalem from the pagans. In 1099, he became the first Latin ruler of Palestine. His followers reflected his zeal by accepting a military pilgrimage as an opportunity to commune with saints at holy shrines. Prior to the pilgrimage, the bishop of Martirano directed campaigners to depart shoeless and in humble shirts. For the warriors' willingness to abandon greed and glory, he blessed their efforts. The poems follow their historic combat, including the capture of stragglers from Peter the Hermit's armies and the seizure of Jerusalem in 1099. The height of the march, entering the Holy Sepulchre, served as reward for sacrifice and hardship.

Literary historians surmise that the three-stage Old French Crusade Cycle had a propagandist purpose—to recruit men and donors for the Third Crusade, which began in 1189.

German Minnesingers

In the decades after the French chivalric surge, the *Spielleute* (wandering minstrels) turned the campaign stories and prowess of German crusaders into entertainment. Unlike the poets of earlier propagandist verse, German epicists focused on dilemma and discomforts of life in the field. The most successful, the Bavarian hero tale *König*

Rother (King Rother, ca. 1150), an adventure from the Teutonic combat tales of the Lombard Cycle, involves the king of Rome and his 12 cohorts in disguise. The action features storytelling, rescue, and bride abduction from the court of King Constantine of Constantinople. Later writers evolved a poetry of disenchantment with religious crusading and expressed doubts about risking life and health in a land dominated by Saracens. Friedrich von Hausen (ca. 1150–90), of Mainz, Swabia, a casualty of the Third Crusade who died at the battle of Philomelium near Antioch, was perhaps the earliest Rhineland minnesinger (songwriter). In ambiguous reflections on a military career, Hausen wrote courtly love plaints that stressed the absence of sweethearts, a pervasive theme in war literature. His imagery in "Civil War" epitomizes a dissociative state—a body in Christian battle against the infidels and a heart at home with his ladylove. In the poem "Home Thoughts," he regrets that he is not "somewhere by the Rhine" (quoted in Nicholson 1907, 2). In "Scala Amoris" (Stairs of love), the speaker confesses a human failing common to young men—that earthly love outweighs the crusader's pledge to God: "This is my wrong, to have forgotten God so long" (19). The candor of his plaint suggests that skepticism lurks in the spirit of the common foot soldier.

A decade after Hausen, the second of the major German poet-knights, Hartmann von Aue (ca. 1160–ca. 1215) of Swabia, steeped himself in the French verse of Chrétien de Troyes. When Hartmann began writing his own court epics at age 20, he published crusader lore in *Der Arme Heinrich* (Poor Henry, 1195) and introduced into German literature two Arthurian romances, *Erec* (ca. 1190s) and *Iwein* (1203). He composed anti-Catholic, anticrusade scenarios in *Gregorius* (1195), a religious study of double incest and penance by a knight whose guilt condemns him to chains and near starvation. After Hartmann's departure on a year's crusade in 1197 for Holy Roman Emperor Henry VI, the poet's love lyrics spoke more vividly of the individual. He identified with the young knight's struggle to remain chaste while on campaign in the Middle East. In "Dejection," the soldier regrets the daily yearning for his lover, which interferes with his attempt to focus on religious devotion through his feats in battle. In "The Journey," Hartmann mentions the enemy Saladin by name. The text describes warring for Jerusalem as a quid pro quo with the almighty: "If I by this crusade can bring him any aid, I'll yield him half the store. May I see him in heaven once more!" (quoted in Nicholson 1907, 63). Unlike earlier ecstatic crusader verse, Hartmann's lines exonerated the troubled warrior for remaining fiscally earthbound.

In a retreat to original themes and tone, the epic poet Wolfram von Eschenbach (ca. 1170–ca. 1220) from Ober-Eschenbach, Bavaria, produced two outstanding works in Middle High German. Through the patronage of Hermann I of Thuringia, Wolfram wrote *Parzival* (ca. 1210) and began an unfinished tragic warrior epic, *Willehalm* (ca. 1217). *Parzival* clarifies the ideal of the courageous crusader as the "highest man, so proven in loyalty, devoid of all falsity" (Wolfram 2006, 145). In token of devotion to the task of reclaiming Jerusalem from the Muslims for Christianity, Wolfram carries religious obsession to the extremes of human expectation: "I will say no word of joy until I have first seen the Grail, whether the time till then be short or long. That is the end to which my thoughts hunt me" (139). The knight's fixation on the relic reflects the fanatic religiosity that fueled crusader zeal to achieve an unlikely victory for Christianity in Islamic territory, where European knights were seriously outnumbered. The fervor and fluidity of the minnesingers' work influenced the literary development of Danish-Norwegian author SIGRID UNDSET, recipient of the 1928 Nobel Prize in literature, who favored the perspective of Hartmann's clear-eyed fighters to Wolfram's dreamers.

Post-Crusade Literature

The worldliness of the Renaissance supplanted otherworldly grail lore, which in the 19th century returned to splendor in the paintings of the Pre-Raphaelite brotherhood; Alfred, Lord Tennyson's cycle *Idylls of the King* (1869); Richard Wagner's music spectacle *Parsifal* (1882); and T. S. Eliot's apocryphal poem *The Waste Land* (1922), a resetting of crusader lore in the post–World War I era. In the 1930s, the Nazi paramilitary brotherhood fed on the fanatic crusader mentality and the cult of the man of destiny, a description fitting Adolf Hitler. Of great interest to the Nazis were tales of the Holy Grail; the Roman soldier Longinus's spear, which pierced the side of the crucified Christ; the Far Eastern empire of the Christian king Prester John; and the loss of the True Cross to the Saracens on July 4, 1187, at the battle of Hattin, the height of despair for a doomed cause.

When World War II and the cold war threatened Western confidence, writer T. H. White, born in Bombay during the British Raj in India, reprised crusader lore in *The Once and Future King,* composed in four installments: *The Sword in the Stone* (1938), *The Queen of Air and Darkness* (1939), *The Ill-Made Knight* (1940), and *The Candle in the Wind* (1958). A stream of films captured elements of crusader lore: *The Knights of the Round Table* (1953), Walt Disney's animated movie *The Sword in the Stone* (1963), the film version of the Broadway musical *Camelot* (1967), *Robin Hood: Prince of Thieves* (1991), *First Knight* (1995), and *King Arthur* (2004).

Crusader lore took a new twist in 2003 with the publication of the thriller-detective novel *The Da Vinci Code,* by Dan Brown, the source of a film three years later featuring Tom Hanks in a tangle of crusades symbology in modern Europe. The legends of Christ's marriage to Mary Magdalene and the crusaders' protection of their offspring generated a cottage industry of reviving fantasies and mysteries that have been common knowledge since the 13th century. Buoying the mystique of Knights Templar secrets from the Holy Lands, Brown laced his text with secret societies, puns, cryptograms, alchemic code, mazes, anagrams, and puzzles. A feminist parallel, Kathleen McGowan's *The Expected One* (2006), redirects androcentric warrior lore to the writings of a fictional Mary Magdalene, who summarized the story of her marriage and widowhood after the crucifixion and the salvation of her child and subsequent generations by crusaders.

Sources

Chrétien de Troyes. *Perceval: The Story of the Grail.* Translated by Burton Raffel. Hartford, Conn.: Yale University Press, 1999.

Edgington, Susan, and Sarah Lambert. *Gendering the Crusades.* New York: Columbia University Press, 2002.

Hartmann von Aue. *Arthurian Romances, Tales, and Lyric Poetry: The Complete Works of Hartmann von Aue.* Translated by Frank Tobin, Kim Vivian, and Richard H. Lawson. Philadelphia: Pennsylvania State University Press, 2001.

Hindman, Sandra. *Sealed in Parchment: Rereadings of Knighthod in the Illuminated Manuscripts of Chrétien de Troyes.* Chicago: University of Chicago Press, 1994.

Jackson, William E. *Ardent Complaints and Equivocal Pietry: The Portrayal of the Crusader in Medieval German Poetry.* Lanham, Md.: University Press of America, 2003.

Joinville, Jean de, and Geoffrey de Villehardouin. *Chronicles of the Crusades.* Translated by Margaret R. B. Shaw. London: Penguin, 1963.

Nelson, Jan, ed. *La Chanson d'Antioche.* Tuscaloosa: University of Alabama Press, 2003.

Nicholson, Frank Carr, trans. *Old German Love Songs.* Chicago: University of Chicago Press, 1907.

The Song of Roland. Translated by Glyn S. Burgess. London: Penguin, 1990.

Wolfram von Eschenbach. *Parzival and Titurel.* Translated by Cyril Edwards. Oxford: Oxford University Press, 2006.

D

D'Annunzio, Gabriele (1863–1938) *Italian poet, dramatist, journalist and fiction writer*

A dashing freedom fighter during the Italian Empire (1885–1943), Gabriele D'Annunzio entwined vulnerability and love in the tentacles of cruelty and death through his journalism and fiction. To the world canon, he contributed operatic-style prose and verse featuring the amoral Nietzschean superman amid European decadence. His themes ennobled those who snatched pleasure under the shadow of destruction.

D'Annunzio was born in Pescara, Italy, and educated at the Liceo Cicognini in Prato, Tuscany. He was only 16 and still a student when he published his first volume of poetry, *Primo vere* (Spring 1879). Two years later, he entered the University of Rome, La Sapienza, where he continued to write poetry and began his journalistic career, writing articles and criticism for local newspapers. He subsequently joined the staff of the *Tribuna*, producing some great journalistic articles while also writing poetry, short stories, and novels. Later in life, he turned his hand to writing plays.

In his first best seller, the novel *Il trionfo della morte* (*The Triumph of Death*, 1894), D'Annunzio explored the negating forces that destroyed Ysolde, lover of Tristan, at the crest of passion. The author pictured her obsessed with "a homicidal mania . . . a hostile instinct of existence, a need of dissolution, of annihilation" (D'Annunzio 1896, 366). His next flight of imagination, *I sogni della stagioni* (Dreams of the seasons, 1898), dramatizes a young woman's long night caressing the chilled corpse of her lover,

who lies murdered at her breast. At dawn, she sinks into madness, a symbolic state that turns unrequited desire into a fatal disorientation.

At the height of his career, D'Annunzio developed a morbid interest in love sickness and crime into static tableaux intended to shock and bemuse. His incomplete five-book verse collection *Laudi del cielo, del mare, della terra e degli eroi* (In praise of sky, sea, earth, and heroes, 1899), an international success, demonstrates his command of mystic lyricism. In *Canzoni della gesta d'oltremare* (Poems on naval deeds, 1912), he served as state bard by celebrating the Italian invasion of Libya on October 5, 1911. He conducted a dizzying affair with the actress Eleanora Duse, for whom he wrote an erotic novel, *Il fuoco* (*The Flame of Life*, 1900) and two tragedies, *La Gioconda* (1899) and *Francesca da Rimini* (1901). The latter, based on the 13th-century scandal involving Paolo Malatesta, his brave but deformed brother Giovanni, and Paolo's love for Giovanni's wife Francesca, incurred censorship because of its sensuality and indiscretion. At a climactic point in the love triangle, the title figure summarizes for her sister Samaritana the ruins of illicit love: "What have I seen? It is life runs away, runs away like a river, ravening, and yet cannot find its sea" (D'Annunzio 2005, 63). The line captures the poet's vision of love as a yearning that goads the loins and heart to destructive extremes.

Italy's founding of an African empire in Libya and Abyssinia stirred D'Annunzio's nationalist pride and fervor and gave shape to his philosophy of *machtpolitik* (power politics), which he voiced in war odes for the newspaper *Corriere della Sera* (Evening courier). He wrote of a new world order, the basis of his PROPHECY and his idealistic ardor for grandeur and for creative and spiritual renewal. During World War I, he lost the sight in his right eye while serving as a fighter pilot and distributor of airborne propaganda. A year after the Treaty of Versailles of 1918, D'Annunzio tried to rescue Fiume, Dalmatia (present-day Rijeka, Croatia), from a territorial shuffle by ruling it himself as a sovereign state. Preceding World War II, he gave up writing for politics. His defiance of Allied powers later influenced Fascist dictator Benito Mussolini, whom D'Annunzio admired as a model imperialist, to cultivate drama and ritual in Italian politics to recoup the glory of imperial Rome and Renaissance Italy. Croats of Fiume so despised the author that they ripped his plays from the public library and burned them in the town square.

Sources

D'Annunzio, Gabriele. *The Flame of Life.* Translated by
    Kassandra Vivaria. Boston: L. C. Page, 1900.
———. *Francesca da Rimini.* Translated by Arthur
    Symons. Whitefish, Mont.: Kessinger, 2005.
———. *The Triumph of Death.* Translated by Arthur
    Hornblow. New York: George H. Richmond, 1896.
Gonadeo, Alfredo. *D'Annunzio and the Great War.*
    Madison, N.J.: Fairleigh Dickinson University
    Press, 1995.
Woodhouse, John. *Gabriele D'Annunzio: Defiant
    Archangel.* Oxford: Oxford University Press, 2001.

Daodejing Laozi (*Tao-te Ching, Tao Te Ching*) (ca. 500 B.C.)

A stimulus to meditation and serenity, the *Daodejing* (*Tao-te Ching* [Classic of the way of power]) guides seekers of the idealized Dao (Tao [way]) to wisdom and harmony. Described in scripture as holy, silent, and permanent, the Dao is the source of sacred power over life. A compilation of folk wisdom traced back to the Chinese emperor Huangdi around 2500 B.C., the canon claims as one of its authors Laozi (Lao Tzu, fl. 500 B.C.), a diviner and court librarian at Lo-yang (present-day Luoyang in the west-central Chinese province of Henan). He began distilling aphorisms on two parchment scrolls, which he completed in three days. The final version took shape during a time of military upheaval, when ordinary Chinese longed for peace and stability and foresaw the overthrow of corrupt evildoers. In the opening stave, the text—like the *Zohar,* the mystical text of Hebrew school of Kabbalah—depicts the Dao as a mystery of all mysteries and a door to wonders, a sentiment shared by the Indian tantrists, Japanese Buddhists, and Hebrew psalmists.

The *Daodejing* applies the simplest of metaphors to explain the functionality of the "way," from the spokes that extend a hub into a wheel, and clay that enfolds empty space to make a pitcher, to the opening of a room to the outside world with the addition of doors and windows. Specific comments on the Dao describe it as a great unity—"Silent and void, it stands alone and does not change, goes round and does not weary" (stave 25:56). Just as the Hebrew PSALMS urge "Be still and know that I am God" (Psalms 46:10), in stave 16, Laozi suggests stilling the mind to await the secrets of eternity. In contrast to the inexhaustible and ever-faithful Dao, in stave 38, the text describes the decline of civilization as the collapse of virtue, charity, righteousness, and courtesy. As religion loses its sincerity, Laozi characterizes ritual as a dry husk of spirituality and a preface to social chaos. His austere advice served not only his own time but future adherents he could not have imagined. In translation into Japanese and English, the enigmatic *Daodejing* has calmed and reassured readers in subsequent phases of global unrest.

Laozi's mystic aphorisms have yielded thousands of tomes of commentary. Chief among the contrasts with Confucius's ANALECTS (ca. 210 B.C.) is the Dao's emphasis on inclusion. Similar in beneficence to the *Meditations* (ca. A.D. 180) of the Roman emperor MARCUS AURELIUS and the Zoroastrian or Mazdan doctrines in the AVESTA (ca. 530 B.C.), the Dao acknowledges female intellect and accords honor to the lowest in society. Like his Chinese predecessors, Laozi embraces the concept of yin and yang, particularly in the matter of gender, in stave 42. Of Earth's beginning, in stave 52, he credits a world mother, a divine nourisher who protects humanity with maternal regard. Stave 28 advises the blending of the male and female aspects of personality into an androgynous whole. As a display of strength, he exhorts the individual "to hold fast to the submissive" (stave 52:119). The author admires villagers who content themselves with home and who avoid materialism, arrogance, and artificial mannerisms. Prefiguring the tone of TAO QIAN's *Poems* (ca. A.D. 420), the philosopher's wise words encourage humility, self-denial, and silent contemplation, whether in the farmer or the emperor.

Displays of power, which Laozi addresses in stave 30, result in the constant commissioning of soldiers to battlefields. He views short-term combat as a waste of troop power and a destruction of fields, which grow thick with thorn and thistle that compromise earth's motherhood. For the plotter and schemer, wise observations urge pacifism rather than ambition and promote compromise over imperial striving and military confrontation. Of the insatiable lust for control, Laozi explains, "Know when to stop and you will meet with no danger" (stave 44:100).

The success of the *Daodejing* as a handbook to rulers earned godhood for Laozi in A.D. 165, when Emperor Huan established four shrines for the philosopher's veneration. During the Tang dynasty, his text carved in stone offered scriptural advice in every provincial capital. In the Qing dynasty, the autobiographical novelist Cao Xueqin and his successor, Gao E, applied Daoist principles to China's most famous novel, DREAM OF THE RED CHAMBER (1791), the story of the collapse of feudalism.

Sources

Laozi. *Tao Te Ching.* Translated by Aleister Crowley. New York: Weiser, 1995.

Mair, Victor H. *The Columbia History of Chinese Literature.* New York: Columbia University Press, 2001.

Dead Sea Scrolls (130–27 B.C.)

A collection of writings long concealed by semi-monastic Jewish ascetics, the Dead Sea Scrolls preserve the library of a fringe cult forced into hiding due to oppression by the Romans during a civil uprising. At a cliff complex of 11 caves, a mystical brotherhood called the Essenes established their headquarters far from Herodean control and temple turf wars. In accordance with Isaiah's PROPHECY, they took shelter in the desert to await the coming of a messiah. In the meantime, laymen of the sect organized a religious academy comprised of discussion rooms, a priestly burial site, and a scriptorium and archive of works dating to 200 B.C. The hideaway flourished from 130 to 27 B.C., when Roman rule weakened the power of orthodox Jewry.

The desert librarians compiled myriad sectarian perspectives on shifting territorial control. One scroll, the Habakkuk Commentary (ca. 5 B.C.), dates to the first decades of the Roman Empire, when greed whetted appetites for power and wealth across the Middle East and North Africa. The Nahum Commentary notes that "God did not permit the city (Jerusalem) to be delivered into the hands of the king of Syria, from the time of Antiochus Epiphanes until the coming of the Kittim (the Romans)" (*Dead Sea Scrolls* 2005, 4Q169), but the author correctly anticipates that Roman conquerors will devour the Hasmonean dynasty, who descended from the Maccabees, a Hebraic dynasty of heroes. The Manual of Discipline, the brotherhood's handbook, notes the coming of a prophet, Yohanan the Baptizer (John the Baptist), who, around A.D. 25, cleanses sinners with purifying water. Because of the frequent appearance and discreditation of such prophets, Yohanan receives limited attention.

Too late, the Essenes spread the alarm that the "sons of darkness" may destroy Jerusalem and crush hopes for a resurgence of the Davidic kingdom, which date to 1005 B.C. A scroll of Psalms warns of "pangs of travail that rock the world's great womb" (11Q). Although the library depicts the Jewish ascetics as victims, the Roman chronicler TACITUS declared in book 5 of his *Histories* (A.D. 107) that the Jews were the aggressors. In A.D. 39, an envoy from Caligula raised a statue to the emperor of Jerusalem in the temple to proclaim his divinity. His successor, the emperor Nero, so outraged the righteous that they created a code term labeling him the Nebuchadnezzar of Babylon. After the emperor Vespasian's son Titus razed the temple at Jerusalem in April A.D. 70, the desert academy appears to have fallen to a legionary invasion and arson, events corroborated by the Judaeo-Roman historian FLAVIUS JOSEPHUS in *History of the Jewish*

War (A.D. 75). In Jerusalem, according to the Copper Scroll, from A.D. 70 to 90, temple priests continued to collect tithes and fees for performing sacrifices, but they escrowed the money until it was safe to practice their faith in the open.

Recovery of the Scrolls

There are approximately 900 texts among the Dead Sea Scrolls, the first of which a Bedouin goatherd or shepherd found in early 1947. Scroll discoveries continued, all from caverns at Wadi Qumran, the desert frontier near Jericho. The weathered leather, papyrus, and copper manuscripts in Aramaic, Greek, and Hebrew are still informing archivists and scriptural scholars about the rule of a Jewish rabbinate and the emergence of Christianity. The seven linen-wrapped scrolls and fragments comprise a library of texts in a variety of genres, including psalteries; daily PRAYERs; and The Songs of the Sabbath Sacrifice and the Hymns of Thanksgiving, which extol the rise of David from shepherd to king of Judah. The scrolls include BIOGRAPHY in the Book of Noah and the Letter of Jeremiah; Pesharim (Commentaries) on Genesis, 2 Samuel, Psalms, and the minor prophets; the prophecy of Isaiah in The Messianic Leader and of Abraham's dynasty in the Book of Jubilees; sermons in the Testaments of the Twelve Patriarchs; WISDOM LITERATURE in Tobit; 45 Psalms of Joshua; allegory in The Heavenly Prince Melchizedek; VISIONARY LITERATURE by Daniel and Ezekiel; a priestly handbook, the Book of Ordinances; a FABLE, the Tree of Evil; and examples of APOCALYPSE LITERATURE: The War of the Sons of Light against the Sons of Darkness, The Resurrection Fragment, The Angels of Mastemoth and the Rule of Belial, I Enoch, and the Apocalypse of Lamech. A surprising addition to scripture includes a paean to Sarah's beauty and wisdom in the Genesis Apocryphon, a compendium of CREATION LORE and patriarchal lore describing Abraham, Noah, Lamech, and Enoch. In one of the fragments of Psalms, a scrap of exultation injects hope into the fall of nations: "Kings of great armies flee; even the housewife shares the spoil" (1Q16:3).

Sources

The Dead Sea Scrolls: A New Translation Rev. ed. Translated by Michael O. Wise, Martin G. Abegg, and Edward M. Cook. San Francisco: HarperSanFrancisco, 2005.

Thiede, Carsten Peter. *The Dead Sea Scrolls and the Jewish Origins of Christianity.* New York: Macmillan, 2003.

Dekker, Eduard Douwes (Multatuli)
(1820–1887) *Dutch satirist*

Anticolonial iconoclast Eduard Douwes Dekker used literature to fight imperial abuses in Indonesia. A native of Amsterdam, Holland, he sailed on his father's trading vessel to the Dutch Indies at age 18 but chose not to become a sea captain. Over the next 18 years, he witnessed the dehumanizing aspects of colonialism on the island of Java, where he worked for the Dutch government's accounting office in Batavia (present-day Jakarta). He advanced to a civil clerkship in Ambon, the Moluccas, and resisted despotism over the Muslim Javanese until he was forced to resign a powerful position as assistant magistrate and provincial commissioner at Lebak. Under the pen name Multatuli, Latin for "I have borne much," he denounced petty profiteering and press labor gangs through published tracts, journalism, and stage drama.

During the rise of Dutch colonial literature, Dekker impoverished himself to become a reformer and crusader for humanism. He is best known for the didactic classic *Max Havelaar: or, The Coffee Auctions of the Dutch Trading Company* (1860). For its romantic subplot "Saïdjah and Adinda," the novel earned the sobriquet "the Dutch Uncle Tom's Cabin." Describing the reactions of mercenary Dutch coffee merchants to the revelation of corruption contained in manuscripts written by the title character, Dekker appeals to the conscience of William III, the autocratic king of Holland. The message is painfully direct: "13,000,000 of your subjects are being maltreated and sucked dry in your name" (quoted in Leipoldt 1903, 442). As PROPHECY, Dekker's vision of revolt came true with the Aceh rebellion against Dutch sovereignty, a costly guerrilla conflict in North Sumatra that raged from 1873 to 1904. After some 100,000 deaths and 10 times that many wounded, the Aceh capitulated to the Dutch forces.

Dekker's writings made explicit charges against loss of civil rights for natives under their Dutch rulers, the sexual concubinage of Javanese women by Dutch men, and racism against the "liplap" (half-caste) offspring. The authorities offered him a new post in the East Indian Civil Service to dissuade him from writing antigovernment diatribes calling Holland a pirate state. He refused the bribe and lived as an expatriate in Antwerp and Brussels, Belgium, while exposing the venality and corruption in Dutch Pacific colonies. The saucily titled SATIRE *Minnebrieven* (Love letters, 1861) outlines his grievances against the Dutch military through a fictitious romantic correspondence with his wife Fancy. One of his parables, "Life in the Heights," pictures a butterfly's choice of a milieu high in the hill country of the Dutch East Indies, far from the dismaying scandal, graft, and exploitation of the lowlands.

For his spirited devotion to social truth in the midst of protestant hypocrisy and inflexible social hierarchy, Dekker earned the titles of the Dutch Aesop and father of contemporary Dutch literature. He died in Nieder Ingelheim, Germany, on February 19, 1887.

Sources

Leipoldt, C. Louis. "Multatuli and the 'Max Havelaar.'" *Westminster Review* 160, no. 10 (October 1903): 438–447.

Multatuli. *The Oyster and the Eagle: Selected Aphorisms & Parables of Multatuli.* Translated by E. M. Beekman. Amherst: University of Massachusetts Press, 1974.

Desai, Anita Mazumdar (1937–) *Bengali writer and journalist*

Feminist author, essayist, and scholar, Anita Desai applies realism and irony to her views of the postcolonial Indian subcontinent. Born Anita Mazumdar of German-Bengali parentage in Mussoorie, India, she grew up in Delhi during World War II, when her mother feared for her safety and abandoned ties to her homeland. Desai's childhood was a blend of fierce Delhi heat on lazy afternoons in the garden, Muslim festivals, and her mother's German lullabies and the piano solos of Franz Schubert. Desai spoke Hindustani in public and German at home, but she chose the British English she learned in school as a literary vehicle. From the oral tradition of Bengali FABLEs and ghost stories, CREATION LORE, recitations of the BHAGAVAD GITA, and Grimms' fairy tales (see GRIMM, JACOB, AND GRIMM, WELHELM), she mastered the art of STORYTELLING. When she was 10 years old, India obtained its freedom, a liberation that deeply affected women's lives. After attending Queen Mary's Higher Secondary School and then graduating from Miranda House, Delhi University in 1957, she married Ashvin Desai, a businessman, in 1958; they had four children. Anita Desai had begun writing even before her marriage, and in 1963 she made her debut as a novelist with *Cry, the Peacock.*

In addition to lecturing on English literature and creative writing at Cambridge University, Smith College, Mt. Holyoke College, and the Massachusetts Institute of Technology, Desai writes Indo-Anglian adult and children's lore, essays, and book reviews for the *New York Times Magazine, New York Times Book Review,* and *Washington Post.* In her work, she focuses on exploring social and spiritual disharmony and despair. Like the themes and motifs of the Antiguan author JAMAICA KINCAID and the Nigerian novelist CHINUA ACHEBE, Desai examines imperialist dilemmas from multiple perspectives. In *Voices in the City* (1965), she reflects on the complexity and anarchy of Calcutta, the third-largest metropolis in India. Of the restlessness of youthful urbanites in the early 1960s, she later regretted that "nothing had come of it, only violence, and the streets were littered with its casualties, the city itself almost perpetually in darkness . . . the graveyard of the ideals and dreams of an independent and renewed India" (Dutta and Desai 2003, x).

Desai has attacked both colonialism and Indian nationalism for silencing women and for limiting their horizons to traditional boundaries, two subjects of *Cry, the Peacock* and of the award-winning *Fire on the Mountain* (1977), a study of female disillusion. Her perusal of Hindu atavism in *Baumgartner's Bombay* (1988) echoes the pathos of RUDYARD KIPLING's peasant society in *KIM* (1901) and the colonial barbarities of JOSEPH CONRAD's *HEART OF DARKNESS* (1899) with visions of "an ancient and backward land . . . the land of snakes and fakirs" (Desai 1989, 53). The layered cultures of Bombay predictably startle the newcomer Hugo, an aged German-Jewish exile: "India flashed the mirror in your face. . . . You could be blinded by it" (85). In 1993, Merchant Ivory Productions filmed *In Custody* (1984), a comic lamentation for the demise of Urdu as the intellectual and court language of nawabs and moghul emperors. The book on which it was based was shortlisted for the Booker Prize.

Sources

Desai, Anita. *Baumgartner's Bombay.* New York: Knopf, 1989.
———. *In Custody.* New York: Harper & Row, 1984.
———. *Voices in the City.* New Delhi: Orient Paperbacks, 1965.
Dutta, Krishna, and Anita Desai. *Calcutta: A Cultural and Literary History.* Oxford: Signal Books, 2003.
Hogan, Patrick Colm. *Empire and Poetic Voice: Cognitive and Cultural Studies of Literary Tradition and Colonialism.* New York: State University of New York Press, 2004.

Dhammapada (The Way of Truth)
Siddhartha Gautama (ca. 50 B.C.)

A treasure of world scripture, the *Dhammapada* (*The Way of Truth*) is a 423-verse collection of Buddhist aphorisms that is revered by Southeast Asians. A store of holy writings, the text consists of three segments and 26 chapters composed in Pali, the west Indian dialect of the Buddha. The source is the WISDOM lore of Siddhartha Gautama (Gautama Buddha, 563–483 B.C.), a Hindu aristocrat born to a royal household in Lumbini in present-day Nepal. Prince Gautama withdrew into asceticism and meditation and became the founder of Buddhism. Like Jesus, he left no written record—only the oral tradition of his disciples and biographers.

Gautama Buddha rejected the idea of creating an earthly kingdom. He turned his attention from dominion and personal gain to a passionlessness and a heavenly state he called nirvana, which is Sanskrit for "letting go." After study with mystics and sages, he developed a four-part life strategy based on the acceptance of impermanence and the renunciation of yearning, the source of all suffering. Of the sacred life, he warned men to avoid sensual women and declared, "He who wants nothing of either this world or the next, who is desire-free and emancipat-

ed—him do I call a holy man" (*Dhammapada* 1985, 121). His choice of serenity over aggression ruled out argument and punishments as well as killings. During the 41-year reign of the peacemaker Ashoka the Great (273–232 B.C.), a Mauryan emperor of lands stretching from Iran and Afghanistan to Pakistan, Bengal, and Assam, Siddhartha Gautama's teaching spread over southern Asia.

Like Confucius's ANALECTS (ca. 210 B.C.) and the *Meditations* (ca. A.D. 180) of the Roman emperor-philosopher MARCUS AURELIUS, the *Dhammapada* contrasts the conquest of the self with the lordship of empires. The text exhorts the seeker to strip away delusion, folly, and lies about success and prosperity and to seek blamelessness and inner control. In the first lesson, a peasant image expresses the danger of unclean thoughts: "If with an impure mind a person speaks or acts, suffering follows him like the wheel that follows the foot of the ox," a cyclical image of inescapable pain (21). Gautama issued 10 commandments that forbid killing, stealing, adultery, lying, alcoholic indulgence, and the luxuries of evening meals, amusements, perfumes, jewelry, and sleeping in a bed. His warnings against *mara* (temptation) employ a martial motif: "Realizing that this body is as fragile as a clay pot, and fortifying this mind like a well-fortified city, fight out Mara with the sword of wisdom" (30). By appropriating war imagery, he energizes his alert to battles of the inner self.

Sources

The Dhammapada: The Buddha's Path to Freedom, trans. Acharya Buddharakkhita. Kandy, Sri Lanka: Buddhist Publication Society, 1985.
Snodgrass, Mary Ellen. *Encyclopedia of World Scripture.* Jefferson, N.C.: McFarland, 2001.

Dickens, Charles (Charles John Huffam Dickens) (1812–1870) *English social novelist*

Like other observers of his day, the writer Charles Dickens noted the impact of the British Empire on England's social and economic values. He was born in Portsmouth, England, on February 7, 1812, to a navy pay clerk. He came of age at the height of underworld melodrama, ghost tales, picaresque novels, and episodic crime thrillers

or vehement writing against inhuman-
ickens earned a major place among world
s. Queen Victoria and gothic masters Edgar
Poe and Wilkie Collins were among his
is of readers; his concern for the underdog
iced the peasant stories of the Nigerian
r CHINUA ACHEBE and the postcolonial fic-
of RUTH PRAWER JHABVALA, a survivor of
olocaust. Hollywood increased Dickens's fan
In 1946, director David Lean featured Finlay
e as the convict Magwitch in a film version
at Expectations. Subsequent remakes starred
Mason as Magwitch in 1974, Anthony
ins 1989, and Robert De Niro in 1998. In
the satirist Evelyn Waugh assembled strands
ckens's gothic plots for a short story, "The
Who Liked Dickens," set in the Amazonian
e of Brazil.

es

ns, Charles. *American Notes for General
Circulation.* Boston: Ticknor and Fields, 1867.
-. *The Annotated Dickens.* 2 vols. Edited by Edward
Guiliano and Philip Collins. New York: Clarkson
N. Potter, 1986.
e, Grace. *Dickens and Empire: Discourses of Class,
Race, and Colonialism in the Works of Charles
Dickens.* Aldershot, U.K.: Ashgate, 2004.

**sen, Isak (Karen Christence Dinesen,
ness Karen Blixen, Baroness Blixen-
cke, Pierne Andrézel)** (1885–1962)
ish storyteller and memoirist

artime memoirist and doyenne of FABLE,
sy, and horror tales, Isak Dinesen surveyed
cultural upheaval before, during, and after
d War I. Born Karen Christence Dinesen
ungsted, Denmark, to Ingeborg Westenholz
Wilhelm Dinesen, she was schooled at home
e enrolling at Miss Sode's Art School and the
l Academy of Art in Copenhagen. On the eve
bal conflict, she married, at age 29, a Swedish
e, Baron Bror von Blixen-Finecke. The couple
hased a 6,000-acre coffee plantation in British
Africa (present-day Kenya) at the base of the
ng hills outside Nairobi, but they separated in
and divorced in 1925. Dinesen survived the

divorce and the exigencies of colonial life—vener-
al disease, border wars and the postwar foundering
of the coffee market—with an altruistic attitude
toward the shuffling of small nations among pow-
ermongers and profiteers.

To the delight of native audiences, Dinesen
was a teller of tales in the folkloric tradition, and
she mastered oral fiction and popular GOTHIC
conventions in English and Swahili. On her return
to Denmark in 1931, financially ruined, she wrote
the best-selling allegorical collection *Seven Gothic
Tales* (1934), which she developed in Kenya and
published under the male pseudonym of Isak
Dinesen. In "The Monkey," a prioress's swap
of her soul to a demon taps a common motif in
the literature of empire—the representation of
colonial bestiality in animal form, a motif that
can also be found in the writings of Sir ARTHUR
CONAN DOYLE, W. W. JACOBS, RUDYARD KIPLING,
and ROBERT LOUIS STEVENSON. Dinesen followed
with two more collections, *Winter's Tales* (1942)
and *Last Tales* (1957). In her memoir *Out of Africa*
(1937), describing rural life in Kenya from 1917 to
1931, the author observed the slide of European
imperialism into world war. The narrative depicts
her farm outside Nairobi as a fragile Eden, a utopian coexistence with nature and with the pastoral
Kikuyu tribespeople, whose survival depended
on the British creation of the Kikuyu Reserve.
Dinesen's romanticized view of serene cultural
relations derived from residence on her farm of the
Somali Muslim majordomo Farah Aden, the Kikuyu
cook-trainee Kamante Gatura, the Danish storyteller old Knudsen, and the Kashmiri blacksmith
Pooran Singh. Like Rudyard Kipling in India and
the Welsh educator ANNA LEONOWENS in Siam,
Dinesen felt welcome in the African environment
but ambivalent toward the proposed colonization
of the indigenous Kikuyu and Masai and toward
the professional big-game hunting popularized in
the adventure fiction of H. RIDER HAGGARD. She
treated local tribespeople with motherly medical
care and defended blacks against British racism,
particularly the impressment of Kenyans for the
Carrier Corps, porters for the army. Critics vary in
their interpretations of Dinesen's relationship with
Africans. The most damning refer to her benevolence as a benign feudalism, an issue that Indian

featuring murderers, scoundrels, highwaymen, and procurers. Poverty ended his education at age 12, when he began supporting his family with a factory job pasting labels on bottles of shoe blacking. For professional on-the-job training as a writer, he collected court, jail, and gallows news for the London *Morning Chronicle.* In freelanced articles, he pictured the moral decline of the world's major trading nation in terms of the miscarriages of justice resulting in alienation and human misery. Later, his novels appeared initially as serials in newspapers, beginning with *The Pickwick Papers* in 1836–37.

Hardship sharpened the author's investigation of England's underclass. As models of venality, he populated his novels with child enslavers, grifters, misers, and grotesque orphan tenders, stepparents, and foster parents flourishing in London, which he considered the empire's heart. By serializing vignettes, stories, and potboilers in weekly journals, he amassed a huge following of readers. Like Sir ARTHUR CONAN DOYLE in his popular Sherlock Holmes detective stories, Dickens tinged his didactic fiction with a dark tone, disturbing atmosphere, and GOTHIC glimpses of the colonies as sources of villainy, profiteering, and escape, such as slave trafficking in Brazil and Cuba in *The Pickwick Papers* and the escape of the bankrupt Micawbers and of Mr. Peggoty and Little Em'ly to a new life in Australia in *David Copperfield* (1849–50). In *Pickwick,* Dickens draws SATIRE out of the misguided intentions of missionaries "for providing the infant negroes in the West Indies with flannel waistcoats and moral pocket handkerchiefs" (Dickens 1986, 1:256). Of the contrast of human fortunes at home and in the colonies, chapter 57 of *David Copperfield* tells of the upbeat departure to Australia of "crowded groups of people, making new friendships, taking leave of one another, talking, laughing, crying, eating and drinking, some, already settled down into the possession of their few feet of space" (Dickens 1986, 2:535). Subsequent generations enjoyed the 1969 and 1999 film versions of the emigrants' embarking.

The Empire's Failures
Dickens doubted the attainment of lasting world peace through Britain's infliction of war, diplomacy, and law on dependent nations. His distaste for colonial excesses cropped up in unforeseen

places—for example, in chapter
Notes for General Circulation (18
tion of the Southern plantation sy
warns of future imperialism in t
with the enslavement of "human
1867, 115). He referred to imperia
empire's destruction of social inst
Chuzzlewit (1844) and promote
domesticity over imperial treasur
of Edwin Drood, left incomplete a
in 1870. In *Bleak House* (1853),
Mr. Baguet's purchase of a brac
imperial luxury. In a speech in Lo
on May 20, 1865, he warned of t
empire in which the press has
However, in his summation for
the British past, *A Child's History*
he lessened charges against the
ing events and concluding with a
Victoria for her benevolence.

In his most enduring works
into particulars of malfeasance
including administrative corrupti
the transportation of felons to alle
prisons. In *A Tale of Two Cities* (18
doppelgänger motif to contrast th
Sydney Carton with his lookalike
and condemned Bastille prisoner
Carton takes the place of Darn
tine as a victim of the French R
executed Louis XVI and Marie
ended the king's rapacious, self
Great Expectations (1860–61), a
man, idealizes New South Wale
second chance for Abel Magwitc
thwarted father. While England
in the mid-1800s on investments
ings, Dickens shamed the explo
for accumulated human failings
degrading effects of a fleet of de
out as floating prisons. Like Alice
returned from transportation in
(1846–48), the escaped convict
to London after making his fortu
sheep market. He conveniently
land of colonial contamination
monia after a self-sacrificing feat
Compeyson, a more virulent crim

journalist SANTHA RAMA RAU covers in "The Trial of Jomo Kenyatta" (1976).

Civil Rights at Issue

Like OLIVE SCHREINER's *The Story of an African Farm* (1883) and G. B. Lancaster's *A Spur to Smite* (1906), Dinesen's memoir *Out of Africa* reveals her distaste for European condescension and her advocacy for local civil rights, including the right to purchase land. Because of the British fear of armed uprising, tribe members lost the right to bear arms, even to hunt for food or to protect themselves from snakes and predatory animals. Dinesen states that the bumbling of white outsiders proves the racial superiority of Kenyans, and she asserts, "It is more than their land that you take away from the people, whose Native land you take. It is their past as well, their roots and their identity" (Dinesen 1985, 359). English locals ostracize her for promoting education and a tribal court system and for siding with natives against police. The Kikuyu honor her as an incarnation of the earth mother for allowing black squatters to live free on her acreage. In deference to their traditional homeland, she considers herself the head squatter. The critic Susan R. Horton typifies the farm project as "living on the slash" that separates black/white, African/European, and male/female (quoted in Brantly 2002, 92). Dinesen's dispossession prefatory to returning to Denmark increases her sympathies with blacks ousted from their homelands by European opportunists.

In 1985, Robert Redford and Meryl Streep played hunter and safari guide Denys Finch-Hatton and farm manager Karen Blixen in the film *Out of Africa,* which revived interest in the author's storytelling and memoirs. A third character, Felicity, represents the author and pilot Beryl Markham, a resident of British East Africa, author of the memoir *West with the Night* (1942), and friend to Dinesen (see AUTOBIOGRAPHY).

Dinesen picked up the strand of *Out of Africa* in *Shadows on the Grass* (1960), a collection of vignettes. Nostalgically, she remarks on departing for British East Africa before World War I "where the Highlands were still in very truth the happy hunting grounds, and while the white pioneers lived in guileless harmony with the children of the

land" (Dinesen 1985, 414). She describes white pioneers as "country-bred and open-air people" who enjoy roughing it in the wild (415). She characterizes the white-black friendships as a "Hawkeye-Chingachgook fellowship" (415), a reference to James Fennimore Cooper's Leatherstocking Tales, an American frontier cycle describing the annihilation of forest Indian tribes by colonials invading the northeastern United States. She regrets that, after World War I, officers received plots of Kenyan land that ill-suit their lifestyles. Another setback, the German occupation of Denmark in April 1940, ends her communication with friends in Africa. She refers to the persecution of Danish Jews and the rescue of many by Swedes. At the withdrawal of Nazi troops in May 1945, she declares, "We all began to rise from our sham graves" (491).

Fairy Tale and Fable

During the Nazi occupation of Denmark, under the pseudonym Pierre Andrézel, Dinesen wrote an anti-Nazi thriller, *The Angelic Avengers* (1944), which she tinged with fairy-tale touches of blasphemy, silencing, starvation, hexes, diabolism, slavery, cellar vaults, hangings, and cannibalism. She smuggled the manuscript out of German-occupied territory for publication and had it translated into English in 1946. A surprisingly popular allegory chosen by the Book-of-the-Month Club, the tale excoriates the Nazi empire as indecent for its atrocities against innocents, symbolized by the orphaned characters Lucan Bellenden and Zosine Tabbernor. In the words of the villain, Reverend Pennhallow, "The evil of this world is mighty, an abyss, a deep sea that cannot be emptied with a spoon, or by any human acts or measures" (Dinesen 1946, 262). By depicting the girls, one bourgeois and one an aristocrat, as bonding to defeat the corrupt Pennhallow, their common adversary, Dinesen proposes unity among Europeans of all classes to defeat Hitler's scheme of a world empire.

Three years before her death from arsenic treatments for syphilis, Dinesen composed an allegorical fable, *Babette's Feast* (1959). Set at a Norwegian fjord, during the Second French Empire under Napoleon III, when Norway was a protectorate of Sweden, the tale features the graciousness of a female exile who wins the French lottery. The story depicts displacement and redemption through cooking and feasting, a symbolic eucharist. A displaced person set adrift amid Lutheran cant and local disgruntlement, Babette makes the most of her individualism, an assuagement to the rootless exile. To questions of her ultimate pennilessness, she remarks, "Poor? . . . No, I shall never be poor. I told you that I am a great artist. A great artist, Mesdames, is never poor. We have something, Mesdames, of which other people know nothing" (Dinesen 1953, 47). In 1988, the film version of the fable, starring Stephane Audran in the title role, won an Oscar and a BAFTA award for best foreign-language film as well as much acclaim for how it depicted the unification of a community with a splendid meal.

Dinesen also examined empire in works published posthumously. In "Oration at a Bonfire, Fourteen Years Late," collected in *Daguerreotypes and Other Essays* (1984), she salutes female imperialists—Maria Theresa, Elizabeth I, and Queen Victoria—for expanding their holdings and for imprinting their respective historical epochs with a woman's name. Feminism aside, she admits the irreversible wrongs of colonizing. In the essay "Letters from a Land at War," she regrets the change in German East Africa (present-day Tanzania) after World War I: "Much water has gone over the dam and much blood into the earth since then, and those times have not returned" (Dinesen 1984, 92).

See also FRONTIER LITERATURE.

Sources

Brantly, Susan. *Understanding Isak Dinesen*. Columbia: University of South Carolina Press, 2002.

Dinesen, Isak. *Anecdotes of Destiny*. London: Michael Joseph, 1958.

———. *The Angelic Avengers*. London: Putnam, 1946.

———. *Babette's Feast and Other Anecdotes of Destiny*. New York: Vintage Books, 1953.

———. *Daguerreotypes and Other Essays*. Chicago: University of Chicago Press, 1984.

———. *Out of Africa and Shadows on the Grass*. New York: Vintage, 1985.

Hansen, Frantz Leander. *The Aristocratic Universe of Karen Blitzen: Destiny and the Denial of Fate*. Eastbourne, U.K.: Sussex Academic Press, 2003.

Diop, Birago (Birago Ishmael Diop)
(1906–1989) *Senegalese storyteller and poet*

Through verse, drama, and fables and cautionary tales of the Wolof people, diplomat and ethnographer Birago Diop epitomized the resilience of the West African colonial. Born in Ouakam outside Dakar, Senegal, a French colony on the western horn of Africa, he acquired from his grandmother the oral skills of a village griot (storyteller). In libraries, he discovered the works of the French romanticists Charles Baudelaire (1821–67) and Victor Hugo (1802–85). After an early education in a Muslim academy, Diop began writing verse at age 15 while enrolled at the Lycée Faidherbe in Saint-Louis (at that time Senegal's capital). During an obligatory stint in the Senegalese army, he joined the medical corps.

At the École Nationale Vétérinaire of the University of Toulouse in France, Diop earned a veterinary degree while supporting the Négritude political and literary movement, which began during the 1930s. He, Martinican author Aimé Césaire, and other students from the French colonies, the Antilles, Guadeloupe, Guyana, and Madagascar affirmed black pride by submitting poems to the Parisian newspaper *L'Etudiant noir* (the black student). One of Diop's animistic poems, "Breaths," characterizes the West African terrain as the living repository of black ancestry and of the maternalism of nature. The verse implies not only immortality of the soul but the timelessness of culture, which survives the invasions of European outsiders. A more acerbic line from the story "Sarzan" (1960) declares that "The Toubabs, the Whites, wore masks for amusement and not to teach their children the rudiments of the wisdom of the ancients," evidence of European devaluation and desecration of Senegalese customs (as translated in Sana, 2002, 113). Diop's amalgamation of rhythm, chant, and call and response earned the respect of the French critic Jean-Paul Sartre, who praised the Senegalese poet for his overlay of tension with calm, the controlling element of African survival.

Diop was 28 when he completed his postdoctoral training at the Institut de Médecine Vétérinaire Exotique and École Française des Cuirs et Peaux. He left Paris for Senegal, but he returned to France during World War II. Because of travel restrictions following the Nazi occupation of Paris in June 1940, he dispelled homesickness for his seaside residence for two years by reciting Wolof folklore for friends and by transcribing it into French for publication. He returned to West Africa to inspect cattle and treat sick animals in French Sudan (present-day Mali), the Ivory Coast, Mauritania, Niger, and Upper Volta (present-day Burkina Faso). Traveling by canoe, horseback, car, and foot, he encountered bush people and absorbed peasant entertainments, indigenous tunes, and chants. In his late 50s, he served as Senegal's ambassador to Tunisia (1960–64). During this fertile period of his dual career, Diop published authentic Senegalese lore in *Les contes d'Amadou Koumba* (*Tales of Amadou Koumba*, 1947), *Les nouveaux contes d'Amadou Koumba* (New tales of Amadou Koumba, 1958), verse written between 1924 and 1945 in *Leurres et lueurs* (Lures and glimmers, 1960), and WISDOM LITERATURE in *Contes et lavanes* (Stories and commentaries, 1963). In old age, he completed an autobiography, *La plume raboutée* (The spliced pen, 1978), and a sequel, *A Rebrousse-Temps* (Backward time, 1982).

Critics admired Diop's ability to translate ancient oral style, repetition, and wordcraft onto the printed page. His poem "Viaticum" (1960) praises oral tradition as the *souffle des ancêtres* (breath of ancestors) that protects him from "men with black hearts," an allusion to French imperialists. His trickster tales and allegories, like those of the Greek slave AESOP and the French fabulist JEAN DE LA FONTAINE, laud the cunning survivor for depending on wit rather than brawn. A standard feature of cautionary tales, the protection of the weak—Civet-cat, Leuk the hare, Palm-squirrel, Rat, Skunk—from the strong but simple-witted hyena, dominates Diop's "Mother Crocodile," an anthropomorphic depiction of the European usurpation of West Africa. Demand for his nativist stories resulted in publication of translator Rosa Guy's English version as a children's picture FABLE, *Maman caiman* (*Mother Crocodile*, 1981), winner of a 1982 Coretta Scott King Award.

Sources

Camara Sana. "Birago Diop's Poetic Contribution to the Ideology of Negritude." *Research in African Literatures* 33, no. 4 (January 2002): 101–123.

Diop, Birago. *Mother Crocodile.* Translated by Rosa Guy. New York: Delacorte, 1981.

Djangrang, Nimrod Bena. "Africa: The Breath of Life." *UNESCO Courier* 51, no. 3 (March 1998): 6–9.

Roberts, Elizabeth, and Elias Amidon, eds. *Earth Prayers from around the World.* San Francisco: HarperSanFrancisco, 1991.

Don Quixote of La Mancha   See CERVANTES, MIGUEL DE.

Dostoyevsky, Fyodor Mikhaylovich
(1821–1881) *Russian novelist*

During the golden age of the Russian novel, Fyodor Dostoyevsky composed psychological works reflecting the inhumanity of the Russian Empire. A Muscovite born to a military surgeon and a cultured mother, the author understood the effects of poverty and the value of piety to a stable character. He read European romances and GOTHIC fiction, sources of his rebellion against his father's demand that he serve the army as an engineer. The popular success of his first publication, the epistolary novel *Poor Folk* (1846), derives from its 55 letters outlining the despair of Mákar Djevuschkin, an underpaid copyist. The protagonist attempts to soothe with words his correspondent Varvara Alexeyevna, the concubine of Squire Bykov, an aristocrat who forces her into wedlock. Dostoyevsky depicts the terror of a debauched girl on her honeymoon departure to the steppes with Bykov, a bored landowner who "amused himself hunting hares" (Dostoyevsky 1894, 171), a parallel to the rabbit-like demeanor of Varvara. The narrative establishes a sympathy with the underdog that underlies the author's humanism, a quality he shares with the French social novelist Victor Hugo and the English author CHARLES DICKENS. In Dostoyevsky's *Pages from the Journal of an Author* (1864), he spells out his hatred of opportunism, "an abstract sorrow for slavery in mankind: it must not be, it is uncivilised" (Dostoyevsky 1916, 88).

At age 26, Dostoyevsky anticipated the collapse of the Russian Empire and entered a period of meditation on undeserved suffering and indignities. He debated utopianism with intellectuals in the Petrashevsky Circle and associated with propagandists and radicals. In 1849, during the extensive spying and informing system formed by Czar Nicholas I, agents arrested Dostoyevsky for conspiracy. He served an eight-month prison sentence in solitary confinement at Peter Paul Fortress in St. Petersburg. His incarceration concluded on December 22, 1847, before a fake firing squad in Semyonovsky Square. This trauma triggered a return of the epilepsy he suffered throughout his life. After four years in a Siberian gulag and five years as an army conscript in the Imperial Russian Army, he wrote *The House of the Dead* (1862), the origin of Russian PRISON LITERATURE. In that novel, the sadism of the guards and the torment of children generates humiliation and indecency among inmates.

With the existential novella *Notes from the Underground* (1864), Dostoyevsky stated his doctrinal differences with revolutionaries and liberals. The popularity of his *Notes* extended through France, Germany, Great Britain, and North America and influenced the 20th-century Russian prison exposés of Aleksandr Solzhenitsyn and the concept of the "underground man" in psychological novels by Anton Chekhov, Ralph Ellison, William Faulkner, and Joseph Heller.

Crime Literature

The author's terror at his mock execution inspired *Crime and Punishment* (1866), perhaps the most celebrated novel of conscience in Western literature. Its popularity boosted the schizoid student Rodion Romanovich Raskolnikov to a prototype of morbid bestiality, a doomed serial killer whose experience parallels the panic disorder of the dreamer Yevgeny in ALEKSANDR PUSHKIN's *The Bronze Horseman* (1833). Through perverted rationalism, Raskolnikov wars against conventionality by hacking an elderly female pawnbroker to death. The ax murderer's tortured psyche contrasts with the alcoholic delusions of Semyon Marmeladov, the hallucinations of the morally destitute sensualist Arkady Svidrigailov, and the Christian goodness of Sonya Marmeladov, Raskolnikov's rescuer.

With *The Possessed* (1872), Dostoyevsky developed his belief in civil liberties and in the spirituality of Russian laborers. In 1881, he published *The Brothers Karamazov*, which expanded his musings on wickedness, faith, human suffering, and liberty. His psychological study of intelligence and conscience later influenced Solzhenitsyn; the South African libertarian NADINE GORDIMER; and the writers Aldous Huxley, GEORGE ORWELL, and Yevgeny Zamyatin.

In 1881, Dostoyevsky published *Buried Alive; or, Ten Years of Penal Servitude in Siberia*, a fictionalized memoir of his incarceration. He described the perversity of prison jailers who "fly into a rage because their victim would not scream or ask for mercy, thereby infringing an ancient custom, which demands that every culprit who is being whipped should scream as loud as he can, and ask for mercy" (Dostoyevsky 1881, 255). The punishment for failure to beg is lashing, 50 strokes above the official number, an almost certain death from trauma, shock, and blood loss. For the author's realism and integrity, he won the regard of the psychologists Alfred Adler and Sigmund Freud; of the Russian poets ANNA AKHMATOVA and JOSEPH BRODSKY; and of the novelists Albert Camus, Hermann Hesse, Franz Kafka, Thomas Mann, Jean-Paul Sartre, ISAAC BASHEVIS SINGER, and IVAN TURGENEV. Dostoyevsky's fiction flourishes in the films *The Possessed* (1970), *Notes from the Underground* (1995), and *Crime and Punishment* (1998, 2002). A 1958 adaptation of *The Brothers Karamazov* features the actors Yul Brynner, Maria Schell, Claire Bloom, Lee J. Cobb, and Richard Basehart.

Sources

Dostoyevsky, Fyodor. *Buried Alive; or, Ten Years of Penal Servitude in Siberia.* Translated by Marie von Thilo. London: Longmans, Green, & Co., 1881.

———. *Notes from the Underground.* Translated by Jane Kentish. Oxford: Oxford University Press, 1999.

———. *Pages from the Journal of an Author.* Translated by S. Koteliansky and J. Middleton Murry. Boston: John W. Luce, 1916.

———. *Poor Folk.* Translated by Lena Milman. London: Elkin Matthews and John Lane, 1894.

Frank, Joseph. *Dostoevsky: The Stir of Liberation, 1860–1865.* Princeton, N.J.: Princeton University Press, 1988.

Doyle, Sir Arthur Conan (1859–1930)
Scottish novelist, short story writer, and memoirist

Eclipsed in fame by his fictional detective, Sherlock Holmes, Sir Arthur Ignatius Conan Doyle incorporated the menace of colonialism in stories of crime and ingenious sleuthing. Born in Edinburgh and educated by Jesuits at Stonyhurst College and the University of Edinburgh, he completed specialized training in ophthalmology in Vienna. Simultaneously, he developed detective stories for a male audience, primarily fans of railroad fiction, the escapist short reads favored by business travelers. Already well-known for his short works in *Chambers's Edinburgh Journal, Beeton's Christmas Annual, McClure's, Lippincott's,* and *Strand Magazine,* he treated combat wounds during the Second Boer War (1899–1902) and received a knighthood for medical contributions at field dressing stations. At the war's end, he published *The War in South Africa: Its Cause and Conduct* (1902), an apologia for the British military presence.

Seven years later, Doyle shifted positions on colonialism. He championed human rights with a humanitarian pamphlet, *The Crime of the Congo* (1909), an exposé of the private reserve of Leopold II of Belgium at Ikoko, where Congolese peasants lived in the bush like prehistoric cave dwellers and died of exposure and starvation because rules forbade making fires. Punishment for infractions was 25 lashes with the chicotte, a whip made of dried hippopotamus hide curled into a spiral. Doyle proposed that France, Germany, and the United States intervene in a humanitarian crisis, but he felt that "Great Britain, whose responsibilities of empire are already too vast, might well play the most self-denying part" (Doyle 1909, 124). He accused Belgian usurpers of "an odious pretence of philanthropy" and concluded with a call to conscience, stating that "there should be some punishment for those who by their injustice and violence have dragged Christianity and civilization in the dirt" (126).

Colonial Menace

As Wilkie Collins had done in his GOTHIC novel *The Moonstone* (1868), Doyle's literary response to imperialism demonstrated his skepticism and anxiety toward colonial influence on the United Kingdom. In "A Study in Scarlet" (1887), the first of 56 short stories featuring Sherlock Holmes, Doyle sets an accusatory tone by characterizing London as "that great cesspool into which all the loungers and idlers of the Empire are irresistably drained" (Doyle 1960, 3). His next forays into colonial symbolism, the novels *The Mystery of Cloomber* (1889) and *The Sign of Four* (1890), depict superstitions and crime on the Indian subcontinent. He turned a swamp adder, India's most venomous reptile, into an instrument of death in "The Adventures of the Speckled Band" (1892). At a climactic revelation, Holmes sermonizes, "Violence does, in truth, recoil upon the violent, and the schemer falls into the pit which he digs for another," an intertextual message to British imperialists (272).

Doyle spread colonial doubts to settings in the Western Hemisphere. One of his four Holmes novels, *The Hound of the Baskervilles* (1902), imagines a phantom dog with macabre phosphorescent teeth as a test for Holmes's forensic skills. He connects strands of evidence to the villain Stapleton's sojourn in South America, where he devised an extortion plot. In "The Adventure of the Sussex Vampire" (1924), the detective analyzes the apparently cannibalistic behavior of Robert Ferguson's Peruvian wife, a devotee of an alien religion who appears to suck blood from her infant son. To ensure objectivity, Holmes compartmentalizes logic from feeling and discloses that the Fergusons' 15-year-old son, Master Jacky, has been shooting poisoned darts at the baby and that Mrs. Ferguson rescues the infant by sucking out the toxin. Because of Doyle's suggestions of occultism, censors banned Sherlock Holmes stories from Russia in 1929.

It is obvious to most Holmes fans, however, that Doyle leaned more to realism than occultism. Sherlockiana juxtaposes imperial decadence with native diseases, madness, and poisons in a variety of places, primarily the British Isles but also with references to Afghanistan, Bohemia, Canada, China, Egypt, India, Italy, Japan, Poland, Napoleonic France, Russia, and Sumatra. Against a panoply of psychoses and opium dens in London, the Holmes-Watson investigations allude to enteritis in India, opium addiction in the Punjab and Malaya, curare poisoning in South America, a jungle malaise in the Andaman Islands, yellow fever in Central America, and leprosy in South Africa. In *The Sign of Four*, the detective discourses on the miseries of Agra, India, with a recitation of ills from a 20-year prison sentence. The inmate survives incarceration "in a fever-ridden swamp, all day at work under the mangrove-tree, all night chained up in the filthy convict-huts, bitten by mosquitoes, racked with ague, bullied by every black-faced policeman who loved to take it out of a white man" (144). A gibe at colonial Dutch insensitivity in "His Last Bow" (1894) describes "a coolie disease from Sumatra—a thing that the Dutch know more about than we, though they have made little of it up to date" (933). In "The Dying Detective" (1894), Doyle enlarges on Tapanuli fever (septicemic melioidosis), one of the mysterious diseases of Formosa that cause "many problems of disease, many strange pathological possibilities," a suggestion of the unknowable pathogens of distant places (934).

For Doyle, a more insidious threat than contagion was spiritual corruption. In "The Reigate Puzzle" (1894), Dr. Watson introduces his partner Holmes's interest in the backwash caused by "The Netherland-Sumatra Company and the colossal schemes of Baron Maupertuis" (398), a covert hint at the author's distaste for the East India Company's sullied dealings and trade monopolies. "The Bascombe Valley Mystery" (1891) presents an Australian gang, led by Black Jack of Ballarat, as an unsubtle linkage between the colony of Victoria and rampant stickups and convoy robberies. Black Jack exults, "We got away with the gold, became wealthy men, and made our way to England without being suspected" (216), a condemnation of the English for harboring colonial criminals and exploiters. In perhaps Doyle's most damning moment, in "The 'Gloria Scott'" (1894), he summarizes the profiteering of the British in Australian goldfields, where justice is lax or nonexistent: "We prospered, we travelled, we came back as rich colonials to England, and we bought country houses" (385).

Sources

Arata, Stephen. *Fictions of Loss in the Victorian Fin de Siècle: Identity and Empire.* Cambridge: Cambridge University Press, 1996.

Doyle, Arthur Conan. *The Complete Sherlock Holmes.* New York: Bantam, 1960.

———. *The Crime of the Congo.* New York: Doubleday, Page & Co., 1909.

Harlow, Barbara, and Mia Carter, eds. *Archives of Empire: The Scramble for Africa.* Durham, N.C.: Duke University Press, 2004.

Wynne, Catherine. *The Colonial Conan Doyle: British Imperialism, Irish Nationalism, and the Gothic.* Westport, Conn.: Greenwood, 2004.

Dream of the Red Chamber (A Dream of Red Mansions) Cao Xueqin (1791)

China's most famous novel, *Dream of the Red Chamber* reveals in a three-volume allegory the individual and clan faults that destroy two imperial families. By presenting the tragic life of a brash, immature prince, Jia Baoyu (Chia Pao-yu), Beijing-born novelist Cao Xueqin (Ts'ao Hsueh-ch'in, ca. 1724–ca. 1763) and Gao E (Kao Ngo, who apparently finished the novel at the time of its publication) recreated the disorder of the Qing dynasty (1644–1912). Similar in narration to MURASAKI SHIKIBU's Japanese court novel *The Tale of Genji* (1019) and PEARL S. BUCK's House of Wang trilogy—*The Good Earth* (1931), *Sons* (1932), and *A House Divided* (1935)—*Dream of the Red Chamber* follows the fortunes of four noble Manchu households: the Jia (Chia), Xue (Hsueh), Shi, and Wang. The four families form a microcosm of China. Cao bases the story in PROPHECY and legend by depicting the birth of Jia Baoyu with pure translucent jade in his mouth, a symbol of oral truth. A dream in chapter 5 places him under the power of the goddess of disillusionment, whose appearance sets his destiny to be an eccentric reformer.

In the decline of feudalism, fiscal corruption and bankruptcy haunt landowners and their peasant tenants. The novel is set in Grand View Garden, a land grant plot bestowed by the emperor. The 400 characters include political enemies, hermits, scholars, servants, concubines, reprobates, madmen, seers, suicides, and libertines. The theme of progressivism versus traditional patriarchy requires vernacular language and an ironic tone to express the author's distaste for indolence, elitism, and waste. Wise old retainers mutter to themselves that aristocratic children grow up to be devious, impudent, and profligate. The promotion of an inept aristocrat to authority further destabilizes the wobbly social hierarchy. Although the novel ends with amnesty for the emperor's exiled successors and honor for Jia Baoyu's piety, the shambles that underlie the empire bode ill for the future of the Qing dynasty and for China.

Based on the principles of Laozi's WISDOM text, the *DAODEJING* (*Tao-Te Ching* [Classic of the way of power], 300 B.C.), the semiautobiographical novel appears to reflect vicissitudes in Cao's own clan. In a world segregated by gender, women living in the red chamber live according to the whims of male authority figures, who debauch females at will. Firstborn males such as Jia Baoyu claim the privilege of a classical Chinese education introduced by Confucius's ANALECTS (ca. 210 B.C.). The author explains that the pampering of males results in self-indulgence: "Girls are made of water while men are made of clay" (Cao, 1958, 22). Because of a romantic heartbreak, Jia Baoyu's decision to become a religious scholar subverts his training in patriarchy and encourages his sympathy with women's diminution to feudal pawns, trophy wives, and bedroom slaves. Upon his disappearance from society, his page offers a philosophic salute to the former master: "An Elevated Man could not be lost, since his name would be heralded throughout the Empire" (326). The novel's classic ideals influenced Korean freedom fighter and poet HAN YONG-UN.

Sources

Cao Xueqin. *Dream of the Red Chamber.* Translated by Chi-Chen Wang. Garden City, N.Y.: Doubleday Anchor, 1958.

Levy, Dore Jesse. *Ideal and Actual in The Story of the Stone.* New York: Columbia University Press, 1999.

Du Fu (Tu Fu) (712–770) *Chinese poet and philosopher*

A patriot and eyewitness to the imperial turmoil of the Tang dynasty, Du Fu (also known as Tu Fu) wrote from the heart lyrics of warfare and PROTEST. The grandson of a politician and poet, Du was native to Henan Province in east-central China. He grew up outside Luoyang but considered the capital city of Chang'an his home. Motherless, raised by an aunt and his scholarly father, he trained for the civil service, and traveled to Chinese cities. Although educated in standard Confucianism, he repeatedly failed imperial exams. After his marriage, his health worsened from respiratory disease and the effects of flood and famine. He wrote on a broad span of topics, including CREATION LORE in "Gazing at the Sacred Peak" (ca. A.D. 747) and the hardship of impressed soldiers in "The Song of the Wagons" (ca. A.D. 750).

Du Fu experienced a sustained series of disappointments. In vain, he courted imperial preferment by sending ceremonial verses to the Emperor Xuanzong. His life changed at age 43 following the An Lushan Rebellion in December 755, when the poet was employed in the residence of Crown Prince Li Cong. Du's flight from some eight years of civil war left him destitute. With his infant daughter in his arms, he, his wife, and three other children wandered mountain roads. In T'ung-chia Marsh, he dedicated a poem to a friend who sheltered Du's family. Famine, fear, and warfare produced in him sympathies with refugees and prisoners of war. The grim simplicity of his canon of some 1,500 poems influenced subsequent Chinese and Japanese lyricists.

Through lingual dissonance, strict metrics, and metaphoric ambiguity, Du Fu cultivated realism in impressions of his era. After his demotion to a desk job in the department of education in A.D. 757, he expressed the frustrations of bureaucracy, a disdain for court corruption, and his yearning for peace. The poem "Moonlit Night" (ca. 757) laments separation from his children in Chang'an; "Chen-Tao Lament" (ca. 759) recoils from young casualties, "forty thousand dead in a day" while Mongol veterans carouse in the marketplace and belt out lusty songs (Du Fu 1989, 25). The emotionally bruising "Peng-Ya Song" (ca. 757) describes survivors of imperial downfall as humbled beyond shame: "No one returned the way we came" (28). "Feng-Hsien Return Chant" (ca. 755) pities the elderly, wrapped in "harlequin rags," their minds twisted beyond repair (18). In "Facing Snow" (ca. 757), he sees himself as a "lone old grief-sung man" amid the ghosts of war (26). He complains of beggary in "Asking of Wu Lang Again" (ca. 768), in which his childless neighbor starves and ducks heartless tax collectors, who "[keep] her bone poor" (97).

Shifts about the country and reduction to a thatched hut in 762 elicited domestic verse on family and contentment, which Du pictures as lamplight over books and *koto* (zither) in "Facing Night" (ca. 768): With the empire returned to peace, hens roost for the night in his thatched ceiling. Two years later, the poet served as a combat adviser on the Tibetan frontier. On his return home by riverboat in spring 765, he grew feeble from asthma, deafness, and failing vision. At a stopover at Guizhou in south-central China, he rallied enough to work as a government secretary and to compose 400 lyrics. He regretted his low status: "Appointments / Advising lords are no certainty for my sons" (96). Amid a flood, when "lament seizes every district," he portrayed himself tottering in wooden clogs, "Adrift, slight as a flood-charm, I sail for peach / Branches of immortality" (9). Near the end of his lifetime of struggles, he asserted, "In idleness, I become real" (62). Before he could complete his return to Luoyang, he died at age 58 in Hunan Province.

Sources

Chou, Eva Shan. *Reconsidering Tu Fu: Literary Greatness and Cultural Context.* Cambridge: Cambridge University Press, 2006.

Du Fu. *The Selected Poems of Tu Fu.* Translated by David Hinton. New York: New Directions, 1989.

Hung, William. *Tu Fu, China's Greatest Poet.* New York: Textbook Publishers, 2003.

Dumas, Alexandre (père)   See NAPOLEONIC LITERATURE.

Edgeworth, Maria (1767–1849) *English novelist and essayist*

An Anglo-Irish feminist and political reformer, Maria Edgeworth voiced the unpleasant truths of English domination of Ireland. Born at her grandparents' home in Black Bourton, Oxfordshire, she was six when her father remarried and took her to Ireland, where she lived with a self-righteous stepmother, Honora Sneyd Edgeworth. At age seven, Edgeworth began mastering composition, French, and Italian while boarding at a Derby academy back in England. In her mid-teens, she replaced her father, writer and inventor Richard Lovell Edgeworth, as overseer of his property at Edgeworthstown (present-day Mostrim, Ireland). Free from gendered restrictions, she developed a writing career with children's cautionary tales, plays, a translation of a French novel, and letters to literary friends. She was most particular about her domestic novels and social spoofs, which required lengthy rewriting.

As Great Britain negotiated the Act of Union to join the English and Irish parliaments at Westminster, only months after the Irish Rebellion of 1798, Edgeworth risked political fallout by ridiculing British imperialism. Her satiric regional novel, *Castle Rackrent, an Hibernian Tale* (1800), England's first historical fiction, won her recognition among critics and readers. The vernacular narrative of "Honest Thady" Quirk, an octogenarian steward of the title estate, reveals the luxuries and vices that bring down a British landlord in 1782. The subtext discloses class conflict that presages the fall of the English landowners, dropping values of Irish estates, and the rise of the Irish Catholic middle class. The author acknowledges the cruelties of unfair taxation and disenfranchisement of tenant farmers who labor under Sir Condy Rackrent, M.P. Foreshadowing Sir Condy's future bankruptcy, the narrative pictures him borne through Dublin's streets in a sedan chair deluged by rain. As debts accrue, Quirk reports "hearing the doors clap for want of right locks, and the wind through the broken windows, that the glazier never would come to mend, and the rain coming through the roof and best ceilings all over the house for want of the slater" (Edgeworth 2007, 41). The extended image of British neglect of its possessions outside England bears obvious implications of ruin and squalor, both faults typically charged against the Irish rather than against their despoilers.

Edgeworth proposed cures for imperial malfeasance. Her *Essay on Irish Bulls* (1802), coauthored by her father, excuses the Irish for verbal blunders, newspaper gaffes, and conversational malapropisms by posting dialogues and models from masters of English including James Adams, John Lydgate, Samuel Johnson, Alexander Pope, and the translators of European fiction. In the short story "The Grateful Negro" (1804), she pictures a turnabout on a Jamaican plantation in which a fair-minded investor, Mr. Edwards, encourages slaves to better themselves.

In 1809, Edgeworth pursued the causes of economic decline among the wealthy in *Tales of Fashionable Life*, which predicts the collapse of the

Empire from sensual indulgences—gambling, gluttony, and arranged marriages based on monetary gain rather than the establishment of a family. She delights in overturning expectations by revealing that the aristocratic earl of Glenthorn was switched at birth for Christy O'Donoghoe, a robust blacksmith. With the voice of the prophet, she warns, "Epicurism was scarcely more prevalent during the decline of the Roman empire than it is at this day amongst some of the wealthy and noble youths of Britain" (Edgeworth 1832, 6). Her keen-edged satire of imperial greed glitters in a conversation in her last novel *Helen* (1834), in which she quotes Lord Chesterfield's quip that the lord of Ireland would want the Isle of Man for a cabbage bed.

Sources

Edgeworth, Maria. *Castle Rackrent*. Indianapolis: Hackett Publishing, 2007.

———. *Tales of Fashionable Life*. London: Baldwin & Cradock, 1832.

Edgeworth, Richard Lovell, and Maria Edgeworth. *Essay on Irish Bulls*. New York: J. Swaine, 1803.

Kenny, Kevin. *Ireland and the British Empire*. Oxford: Oxford University Press, 2004.

Nash, Julie. *New Essays on Maria Edgeworth*. Aldershot, U.K.: Ashgate, 2006.

Egyptian Book of the Dead   See BOOK OF THE DEAD.

Emecheta, Buchi (Florence Onye Buchi Emecheta) (1944–) *Nigerian fiction writer and journalist*

An Igbo feminist, Buchi Emecheta writes adult and children's works exploring the liberation of women from colonialism and tribal androcentrism. A native of Yaba outside Lagos, Nigeria, she grew up in the village of Ibuza, where Yoruba storytellers pounded drums while leading a stream of children about the streets. Although second in worth to her younger brother and therefore traditionally considered unworthy of schooling, she developed her own narratives while completing her education on a scholarship at the Methodist Girls' High School in Yaba. In 1960, the year her country attained freedom from the British, Emecheta discovered that nationhood for a country did not guarantee civil rights for women. She married unwisely, emigrated to London, and coped with a violent husband, Sylvester Onwordi, who burned her first manuscript in a show of male control. After leaving him in 1966, she raised three daughters and two sons while freelancing for journals and newspapers and majoring in sociology at the University of London. The title of her first novel *In the Ditch* (1972), serialized in the *New Statesman*, characterizes her life in an urban slum as marginalized flotsam from the backwash of a vanishing empire.

Emecheta developed a widespread and critical audience for her scenarios of female outrage at a tribally imposed identity. In her autobiographical novel *Second-Class Citizen* (1974), she characterizes the birth of Adah, her alter ego, as a blow to her father, who anticipated siring a boy. The erasure of Adah's personhood symbolizes the colonial devaluation of all black Nigerians: "Since she was such a disappointment to her parents, to her immediate family, to her tribe, nobody thought of recording her birth. She was so insignificant" (Emecheta 1983, 7). Ambition buoys her wounded spirit. She leaves her arrogant husband and publishes fiction that the white world ignores, a theme that recurs in Emecheta's autobiography, *Head Above Water* (1986).

After seven years of fieldwork in the London education system, Emecheta settled in Camden, New Jersey, and contributed articles to *Black Scholar, Essence, New York Times Book Review,* and *World Literature Today*. She dramatized the male-dominated marriage market in *The Bride Price* (1976), which echoes the themes of AMA ATA AIDOO's *No Sweetness Here* (1970). With *The Joys of Motherhood* (1979), Emecheta tackled issues of polygamy and male privilege. The protagonist, first wife Nnu Ego, fantasizes drowning herself in the river to carry her protests to the afterlife, the ultimate court of appeals for the silenced Nigerian female. Unaware of her infant son's death, onlookers recoil from the milk dripping from her breasts and upbraid her for abandoning "your husband, your father, your people and your son who is only a few weeks old" (Emecheta 1980, 61). Emecheta creates dramatic irony from the scolding of another female, who charges Nnu Ego with "disgracing the man who paid for you" and with violating "the tradition of our fathers" (62).

In 1985, Emecheta turned to the past with a fable of eden versus empire. *The Rape of Shavi* is the story of a fictitious nation of the African Sahel (the Saharan border region). The coming of white intruders into the passive kingdom of Shavi disrupts the lethargy of King Patayon and his tribe's contentment. There is irony in the need of Europeans to flee a nuclear catastrophe by flying to West Africa in a plane dubbed "Newark," a reference to Noah and the flood. The castaway motif creates opportunities for authorial commentary on racial superiority, sexually transmitted disease, and cultural stereotypes of African cannibals and leprosy, the Shavian diagnosis of the intruders' white skin. Emecheta expands on the metaphor by outlining the Western corruption that leads to violence and profiteering. Through Aesopic convention, the FABLE merges blacks and whites into a universal culpability. Late into the 20th century, she continued championing women battered by racism, sexism, and imperialism.

Sources

Emecheta, Buchi. *The Joys of Motherhood.* New York: George Braziller, 1980.

———. *The Rape of Shavi.* New York: George Braziller, 1985.

———. *Second-Class Citizen.* New York: George Braziller, 1983.

Sougou, Omar. *Writing Across Cultures: Gender Politics and Difference in the Fiction of Buchi Emecheta.* Amsterdam: Rodopi, 2002.

epic, African

The preservation of African oral history and poesy is a bardic tradition dating back to prehistory. Like the Hebrew CREATION text in GENESIS (ca. 500 B.C.), the Roman propagandist VIRGIL's AENEID (17 B.C.), and the Persian historiographer FIRDAWSI's *The Book of Kings* (ca. 1010), African compilations comprise empire building as well as HERO and quest tales, dynasty and genealogy, border strife, and economic and religious history. Among the Soninké of the southern Sahara in the Ghanian, or Wagadou

Empire, which according to some sources began around A.D. 600, the *Epic of Wagadu* (A.D. 750) takes the form of a medieval female rescue tale. A hero in the goldfields of West Africa's first empire, Mamadi Sefa Dekhote (Mamadi the Silent) wanders through India, Yemen, Israel, and other Islamic lands east to the utopian city of Wagadu. Like the Greek hero Perseus, who snatched Andromeda from a sea monster, Mamadi saves Sia Yatabere from sacrifice to Bida, a seven-headed serpent—black with red crests—living in a well at the Ghanian capital of Kumbi. The background episodes reprise stories from Genesis and the KORAN of Jacob's trickery of Isaac as well as the needs of the empire for magical sources of water during seven drought years, a parallel to the biblical account in EXODUS of Joseph's husbandry of Egyptian grain during a famine. The lack of a pure hero implies compromise in the Ghanian Empire (present-day Mali, Mauritania, and Senegal), where fragmented clans negotiate strategies for coexisting on a harsh land. In cinema form, Mauritanian scenarist Moussa Diagana's *la Legende du Wagadu vue par Sia Yatabéré* (The legend of Wagadu seen by Sia Yatabéré, 2001) describes a palace coup. The rescue motif and a gang rape supplant the book's ritual sacrifice of a virgin to a python. The film's orchestration of menace, violence, and heroism captures the tenor of the times.

In the late Middle Ages, Sundiata of the Keita clan (ca. 1217–ca. 1255) established the Mali empire, which supplied gold for European and Islamic coinage. According to African griots, the native archivists or storykeepers, it was prophesied that Sundiata would lead a great nation, the Mandinka of West Africa on the border between Mali and Guinea. According to oral tradition, he is unpromising at birth and lolls about for seven years, until his father sends Balla Fasséké, the royal griot, to train the boy. As with Aristotle's training of Alexander the Great and the readying of sons for manhood described in NIKOLAY GOGOL's Ukrainian folk epic *Taras Bulba* (1842), the inculcation of WISDOM trained Sundiata for leadership. At a climactic point in the legendary biography, he lifts an iron bar and bends it into a bow, the test of strength that symbolizes readiness for power, in the style of the Hebrew king David's trial battle with Goliath.

After the fall of Ghana, Sundiata was the focus of the 3,084-line *Sundiata: An Epic of Old Mali* (ca. 1255) as the hero who must grapple with his father's first wife and first son for power. The epic effectively tells a classic story of pastoral states fighting off rustlers. Like the untried Arthur Pendragon rousing Celts against invading Anglo-Saxons in late fifth-century Britannia, Sundiata lives in exile until he can muster enough cavalry and archers to march on the city of Tabon, a standard cooperative motif in medieval literature. By unifying the military force of 12 states, Sundiata becomes an emperor known as the Lion King of Mali, who controls tribes from the Niger River west to the Atlantic Ocean. Walt Disney Studios reprised the story of Sundiata in 1994 as an animated film, *The Lion King,* with animals substituting for the humans of Mali legend.

The Merger of Opposites

The intrusion of Islam on tribalism added global dynamics to the African epic. At the height of Mali's influence in West Africa, Mansa Musa (Emperor Moses, r. 1312–1337), Sundiata's grandson or grand-nephew, impressed the Muslim world in 1324 by making a hadj, or pilgrimage, to Mecca. Described in the seven-volume *Kitab al-ibar* (History of the Arabs, 1375) of Ibn Khaldun (1332–1406), Musa traveled via the Upper Niger River to Walata, Mauritania, and to the Mediterranean coast at Tuat, Algeria. In the 14th year of his reign, the emperor and 60,000 followers made a grand impression on North Africans, transporting gold carried by 12,000 slaves and 100 camels over the Sahara, a procession motif common to stories of such royal figures as the Queen of Sheba and Cleopatra. In the encyclopedia *Masalik al-Absar* (Voyage of the eyes, 1348), a summary produced by the Damascan chronicler al-'Umari (1300–49), Musa's arrival with so much wealth won the respect of emirs and sultans. As a result of his three-month stay in Cairo, the dispersal of some 15 tons of gold depressed the precious metals market throughout Egypt for the next decade. After Musa's return to Timbuktu, a stream of Muslim intellectuals followed him and turned his capital into a center of learning. In 1326, the Moroccan travel writer IBN BATTUTA (1304–ca. 1377) of Tangiers passed through Cairo, where people still marveled at Mali's gold supply. Battuta wrote in his *Tuhfat al-nuzzar fi*

ghara'ib al-amsar wa'aja'ib al-asfar (On the curiosities of cities and the wonders of travel, 1354) about Musa's reputation for opulence and generosity, the hallmarks of storied rulers such as Croesus of Lydia and Solomon of Jerusalem.

During the Renaissance, money and goods dominated global relations. At the time of the Bambara (Bamana or Segu) empire (1600–1861), a warrior state that based its income on slaves or captives, trade along the West African coast enabled the Bambara to outstrip the Mali in wealth and prestige. In *Epic of Bamana Segu,* (an oral folk history compiled about 1850), Bambarans expressed the collapse of earlier ideals of truth, honor, and nobility and the importance of wealth and commerce as the sources of political prestige. In place of a prophesied savior, citizens depended on a more realistic series of empire leaders. Along the Niger River, the maintenance of power, described in 7,585 lines of verse, passes back and forth between warriors equally matched with muskets, axes, and battle hammers.

During this same period, a second Bambaran empire of Kaarta took shape in the west in 1753 in part of the former Ghanian empire. The charismatic hero Sonsan dominates the *Epic of Sonsan of Kaarta* (an oral history compiled about 1850). In a parallel to the biblical story of Joseph's betrayal by his brothers, envious stepbrothers push Sonsan into a well. Jealousy and suspicion endanger Sonsan at an early age, but he survives by cunning and honorable dealings. As a goodwill ambassador, he founds a city, Sontiana, and a dynasty through his son Massa. A century later, in 1854, Islamic jihadists slaughtered the Kaartans and their imperial dynasty.

Epic Realism

Western warfare gradually subsumed the manly face-to-face encounters of African epic. During the competitive jockeying of European nations for control over African colonies, a war chief named Almami Samori Toure (ca. 1830–1900) established the Wassoulou empire (present-day Guinea), which warded off the French for 16 years until 1898. The warfare depicted in *Epic of Almami Samori Ture* (ca. 1900) resembles the wars for empire between walled cities during Europe's Middle Ages. Like Sonsan, Samori bears a significant birthmark and grows up daring and popular. After passing a test of worthiness on a par with the English legend Arthur's pulling the sword from the stone and the biblical David's defeat of Goliath with a stone from his sling, Samori urges his people to abandon paganism for Islam and to defend themselves against French usurpers.

As science and invention increased firepower, African military history lost its noble foundations and the grandeur of epic. The preservation of Guinean land in the Volta basin required negotiations with the British for firearms and a constant scorched-earth policy conducted by Samori's 12,000 soldiers. Triumphing on the border between Guinea and Mali and moving east to the Ivory Coast, Samori claimed gold mines before naming himself emperor. An unusual episode in the epic describes the rise of Demba, the one-breasted female warrior who, on April 2, 1883, led the battle of Woyowayanko, during which Samori's troops overcame French heavy artillery. The victory was short-lived as mechanized warfare led to trade-offs and concessions from African warlords. Since the early 1970s literary historians have contributed to western awareness of the African epic as a living tradition.

Sources

Belcher, Stephen Paterson. *Epic Traditions of Africa.* Bloomington: Indiana University Press, 1999.

Conrad, David. *A State of Intrigue: The Epic of Bamana Segu according to Tayiru Bambera.* Oxford: Oxford University Press, 1990.

Eisenstadt, Shmuel Noah, Michel Abitbol, and Naomi Chazan. *The Early State in African Perspective: Culture, Power, and Division of Labor.* Amsterdam: Brill, 1988.

Ibn Battuta. *Travels in Asia and Africa, 1325–1354.* Translated by H. A. R. Gibb. New Delhi: Manohar, 2001.

Niane, D. T. *Sundiata: An Epic of Old Mali.* Translated by G. D. Pickett. Harlow, U.K.: Longman, 1965.

epithalamium

For its celebration of human desire, the wedding poem or song known as the epithalamium is a constant feature in world literature, particularly for its preservation of details of imperial weddings and matrimonial alliances of nations. "The Courtship of Inanna and Dumuzi" (ca. 2800 B.C.), written during the time of the Sumerian empire, is GODDESS LORE honoring Inanna, the Queen of Heaven, which reaches heights of passion and physical specifics of sexual intercourse in her courtship of the shepherd Dumuzi. When she welcomes the groom to her inner sanctum, the epithalamium depicts the effulgence of female passion: "Inside the house she shone before him / Like the light of the moon" (quoted in Wolkstein and Kromer 1983, 36) a symbolic reference to both a moon cult and to womanly cycles and fecundity. The Sumerian agrarian culture dominates coital imagery, which describes the phallus as a plow and the vulva as a furrow. Appropriately for a patriarchal society, Inanna's brother Gilgamesh promotes her betrothal with a herder, whose breeding of animals for meat complements her supervision of grain fields, the source of Sumerian wealth. The celebration of fellatio compares seminal fluid to milk: "Make your milk sweet and thick, my bridegroom. / My shepherd, I will drink your fresh milk, wild bull, Dumuzi" (39). The postcoital scene pictures a sated groom and the seductive Inanna lolling in an atmosphere of sweet allure.

From the Hebrew empire (1050–920 B.C.), the scriptural anthology called the Song of Solomon (ca. 950 B.C.), Song of Songs, or Canticle of Solomon, is a nuptial anthem cycle comprised of mystic yet physically explicit odes to sexual attraction and conjugal love. Like the *Lakshmi Tantra* (ca. A.D. 950) (see TANTRAS), an Asian contribution to goddess lore, the anthology's love songs honor physical grace and desire. Traditionally, historians link the pastoral allegory to King Solomon's alliance with Egypt through a political marriage to a pharaoh's daughter, whose dowry was the city of Gezer, an ancient trading metropolis of the coastal plains west of Jerusalem. If so, about the time that Solomon was ending his great building project of a palace, temple, and a wall around Jerusalem, his African bride joined a harem of 700 wives and 300 concubines—Ammonites, Edomites, Hittites, Moabites, and Sidonians—none of whom is identified by name. The marriage to a member of a closed pharaonic dynasty, possibly the 21st, indicates Solomon's influence some 120 years after the decline of the Egyptian Empire (1550–1070 B.C.).

The benefit to the pharaoh is a direct link to the Davidic dynasty, a rising Middle Eastern power. The biracial, bicultural betrothal also exalts a scion of the Children of Israel, who served the pharaoh before the exodus to the Promised Land.

In the verses, the allure of a dark-skinned shepherdess from the north for an Israelite ruler results in a lavish royal courtship. In private, the beloved longs for a Shulamite man, whom she addresses in absentia in her night wanderings. To the king's favorites, voluptuaries jealous of her simple loveliness, she boasts, "I am black, but comely. . . . I am the rose of Sharon, and the lily of the valley," horticultural images applied to the anticipated messiah (Song of Solomon 1:5, 2:1). Her rivals accuse her of treachery for rejecting a king in favor of a shepherd. Fantasizing dialogues with her humble beau, she engages in visions enriched by anatomical euphemisms drawn from nature—for example, "Thy breasts shall be as clusters of the vine and the smell of thy nose like apples" (Songs of Solomon 7:8). The king, defeated by true love in chapter 7:10, relents and returns the peasant girl—still a virgin—to herding with the man of her dreams. In a village celebration, she reunites with a promise of faithfulness: "Set me as a seal upon thine heart" (Song of Solomon 8:6). One ironic interpretation of the song identifies Solomon, husband to 1,000 women, as the defender of monogamy.

To justify inclusion of the Song of Solomon in worship, priests and rabbis desexed the canticle by spiritualizing its lush images as symbols of God's commitment to his worshippers. The Spanish-Jewish poet YEHUDA HALEVI of Toledo returned to the original style and imagery for his "Marriage Song" (ca. 1125), a tender devotional to Tirzah for her charm and sweetness and for the speaker's anticipation of happy companionship after the wedding.

Variations on a Theme

The epithalamium also set a pattern for joyous union, as in the triple marriage of young chief Laa in David Kalakaua's compilation *The Legends and Myths of Hawaii* (1888); and for lamentations on nuptials that have failed or separated loved ones—for example, of Baldetta and Lindóia, a tragic bride in the New World epic *O Uraguai* (1769) by the Brazilian-Portuguese writer and former Jesuit novice José Basílio da Gama (ca. 1741–95), a rebel and statesman from San José, Brazil. The Greek playwright Euripides manipulated the tone of *The Trojan Women* (415 B.C.) by picturing the Trojan widows preparing to become Greek prisoners and leave Troy. Cassandra, the priestess of Apollo, falls into a trance and brandishes a torch while singing a marriage song to the god rather than to Agamemnon, the Greek king who has won her with a toss of the dice. In the AENEID (17 B.C.), VIRGIL, the imperial propagandist for Augustus, the first Roman emperor, incorporated the doomed alliance of the Trojan prince Aeneas with Dido, the widowed queen of Carthage, Rome's future enemy. The meddling of the goddess Juno produces a consuming passion in the queen after Eros wounds her with a love dart. In a nuptial scene similar in tone to the wedding scene in Valmiki's Hindu epic RAMAYANA (ca. 400 B.C.), Virgil depicts the queen and Aeneas retreating to a forest cave during a hail storm. In place of wedding anthems, "Lightning streaks; they couple; the skies shudder. . . . The nymphs from their hilltops shriek the cry of Hymen," the winged child-god who lights the way to the nuptial bedchamber (Virgil 1961, 93). The show of heavenly disapproval results in a dirge to presage Dido's suicide and self-immolation as Aeneas sails on to his destiny as the founder of Latium.

A Japanese nuptial verse offers a motherly variation on wedding hymns. Around A.D. 759, scholar and statesman Otomo no Yakamochi (ca. 717–785) compiled the Nara empire's 20-book MANYOSHU (*The Ten Thousand Leaves*, ca. 759), an imperial anthology of poetic models from Japan's golden age. Among its ritual prayers, patriotic odes, and erotic verses, he incorporated an emotive bridal song. At a dramatic moment following the newlyweds' departure, the mother of the bride recalls passing her jewel-like daughter into the groom's hands. The tender epithalamium melds the usual celebratory mood with the older generation's nostalgia. In place of post-wedding delight, the mother sinks onto the empty pillow in the bride's childhood bed.

Sources

Hawkins, Peter, and Lesleigh Cushing Stahlberg. *Scrolls of Love: Reading Ruth and the Song of Songs.* Bronx, N.Y.: Fordham University Press, 1999.

Song of Songs. In the Holy Bible. Iowa Falls, Iowa: World Bible Publishers, 1986.

The Ten Thousand Leaves, trans. Ian Hideo Levy. Princeton, N.J.: Princeton University Press, 1981.

Virgil. *The Aeneid,* trans. Patric Dickinson. New York: Mentor, 1961.

Wolkstein, Diane, and Samuel Noah Kramer, trans. *Inanna, Queen of Heaven and Earth: Her Stories and Hymns from Sumer.* New York: Harper & Row, 1983.

Equiano, Olaudah (Gustavus Vassa)
(ca. 1745–1797) *Beninian autobiographer*

A proponent of freedom, Olaudah Equiano expressed his detestation of slavery through his life story. He claimed to be an Igbo native from the village of Essaka, and to have grown up in a prestigious household on the Niger River under subjection to the Oyo empire of Benin. Documentation uncovered by later researchers indicated that he was actually born in South Carolina. During the 18th century, the Bight of Benin supplied British enslavers with one-quarter of their quarry. In 1756, according to Equiano's account, his own people kidnapped and enslaved him and a young sister, whom he later sought during his voyages as an able seaman. Initially traded to a sugar planter in Barbados, Equiano was sold several times, his small size being an impediment to the hard labor of plantations. Finally, he was dispatched as a domestic to the Virginia colony under a new name, Gustavus Vassa. One of the torments of his service was an iron bit that separated his jaws and impeded speaking, eating, and drinking. While traveling with his owner, Captain Michael Henry Pascal, during the Seven Years' War, Equiano worked as a powder monkey, dragging ammunition hogsheads to cannon. He also learned to read and write, and this, along with his skill at navigation, made him a valuable purchase for the Quaker shipper Robert King of Philadelphia. Under King's direction, Equiano worked as a clerk and managed to buy his freedom.

In 1766, Equiano left the Caribbean. After several years of travel and trading, he moved to London and began promoting abolitionism and outlawing of the slave trade. He made a strong impression with lectures, orations, and a slave narrative, *The Interesting Narrative of the Life of Olaudah Equiano, or Gustavus Vassa, the African, Written by Himself* (1789). The opening description of the slave trade pictures it extending from West Africa 1,500 miles east to Abyssinia. Descriptions of domestic life portray peaceful residences where polygamous families observe gendered customs but share a love of pomade. They abstain from alcohol and wash and pour a libation before meals. In the book, Equiano willingly serves the navy in engagements with the French and offers details of landfalls at Gibraltar, Barcelona, and the Levant and of piracy and press gangs in international waters. In his conclusion of racial dominion, he anticipates a time "when the sable people shall gratefully commemorate the auspicious era of extensive freedom" (Equiano 1837, 289).

Equiano eventually settled in Cambridgeshire, and in 1792 he married Susannah Cullen, with whom he had two daughters. Susannah died in 1796, and Equiano passed away the following year, at the approximate age of 52; his place of burial is unknown. Though modern scholarship has called many details of his autobiography into question, there is no doubt of his impact on the abolitionist movement in England. The film *Amazing Grace* (2007) starred the Senegalese actor-musician Youssou N'Dour as Equiano, reprising his belief in industry, commerce, and Christianity as civilizers of undeveloped nations.

Sources

Equiano, Olaudah. *The Life of Olaudah Equiano, or Gustavus Vassa, the African, Written by Himself.* Boston: Isaac Knapp, 1837.

Howard, Jennifer. "Unraveling the Narrative." *Chronicle of Higher Education* 52, no. 1 (September 9, 2005): A11.

Morgan, Philip D., and Sean Hawkins. *Black Experience and the Empire.* Oxford: Oxford University Press, 2004.

erotic literature

In much of the world's literature of empire, the artistic representation of carnal relationships explores universal human traits and intrigues. Models range from the sensual "The Courtship of Inanna and

Damuzi" (ca. 2800 B.C.) in Akkadian-Sumerian lore and the more sedate biblical book of GENESIS (ca. 500 B.C.) to the *Kama Sutra* (ca. A.D. 500), Vatsyayana's holy guidebook of lovers in the Gupta Empire. The Israelites celebrated parallel male and female desires in the EPITHALAMIUM Song of Solomon (ca. 950 B.C.), and WILLIAM SHAKESPEARE recreated the bicultural love affair of Antony and Cleopatra, victims of Augustus, the first Roman emperor. CRUSADER LORE such as the *Minnesang*, the GODDESS LORE of *Cantigas de Santa María* (Songs to the Virgin Mary, ca. 1283), and the *lais* of MARIE DE FRANCE all exalted male-female attraction in various ways.

A Sanskrit text from the Srivijayan empire, *Shuka Saptati* (*Seventy Tales of the Parrot*, ca. 1100) mimics the Persian frame story *The THOUSAND AND ONE NIGHTS* (ca. 942) with a cycle of plots drawn from disparate traditions of the Malayan realm. Narrated by Lord Shuka, who takes the form of a talking bird, the suite of 70 anecdotes dates as early as A.D. 500. The series ostensibly reminds a married woman named Prabhavati to honor monogamy by distracting her from trysts with her lover. Titillating episodes of bad company, prostitution, seduction, adultery, rape, violence to genitals, bestiality, and incest extract lore from Vishnu Sarma's *PANCHATANTRA* (ca. 200 B.C.) from the Mauryan empire of India to describe a variety of scenarios for infidelity on a par with the ribald stories of Giovanni Boccaccio, MIGUEL DE CERVANTES, and Geoffrey Chaucer.

Interspersed in the action are nuggets of wisdom about character, such as the roots of jealousy, envy, and possessiveness. Explicit details include a description of the best mattress for sexual intercourse to "bear the strong poundings of a couple's passion" (*Shuka Saptati* 2000, 183). By the time Prabhavati's husband, Madana Vinoda, returns from a 70-day voyage, she has remained chaste while learning moral lessons from the wise parrot. Through numerous versions and vernacular translations into Persian and Urdu, the *Shuka Saptati* remained a favorite folklore collection for its even-handed depiction of male and female foibles and forgiveness of straying mates.

Japanese Love Plaints

In a heavily structured court atmosphere, mournful Japanese mates waited out lengthy sea voyages that separated lovers depicted in the Nara Empire's 20-book *MANYOSHU* (*Ten Thousand Leaves*, ca. 759), an imperial anthology from Japan's golden age compiled primarily by the scholar and statesman Otomo no Yakamochi (ca. 717–785). His collection, pulling together poetry from the seventh and eighth centuries, ranged from ritual prayers, epithalamia, and odes to depictions of girls' flirtations with male idlers and oglers at the temple well. Memorable verses capture achingly carnal thoughts about secret trysts, breasts, genitals, and coitus. An anonymous text pictures the wet hemlines of young girls using their skirts to net sweetfish at the rapids of the Matsura River. Another narrative welcomes the stealthy lover who slips through the blinds to join his inamorata in her room without waking her mother.

Sexual frustration, a universal theme, also appears in Japanese court verses by a wide range of poets. Empress Iwa Hime compares a parting with Emperor Nintoku to torment on the rack; on the other end of the social spectrum, Sano Chigami, a clerk at the Grand Shrine of Ise, grieves over the exile of her lover, Nakatomi Yakamori, to Echizen Province. Princess Hirokawa, granddaughter of Emperor Temmu, describes herself as so laden with love's sorrow that she pulls a load of grief like seven carts uphill. Unrequited love disturbs Lady Otomo Sakanoue, who pictures a virgin as "the star lily that has bloomed/in the thick foliage/of the summer field" (*Love Songs* 2000, 42). Forbidden love troubles the poet Otomo Yasumaro, who muses on sexual temptation: "If men can touch / even the untouchable sacred tree, / why can I not touch you / simply because you are another's wife?" (65). A sophisticated erotic poem by Lady Ki views the restless female sleeper as a silk-tree blossom. With libertarian impertinence, she asks, "Should only its lord look upon it? / You too, my vassal, enjoy the sight" (41). The social position of both voyeur and unattainable lady layers amorous Japanese verse with the potential for personal and political disaster.

Eroticism and Colonialism

During the Italian Empire, the heroic poet and author GABRIELE D'ANNUNZIO popularized rhapsodic celebrations of sensual gratification. He publicized his love affair with the actress Eleanora Duse in a tell-all novel, *Il Fuoco* (*The Flame of Life*, 1900). In a garden tryst scented with jasmine, the lover

Stelio, the author's fictional persona, whispers, "I received you all into myself like a wave. And now it seems that I can no longer divide you from my own blood," a merger that stuns and overpowers (D'Annunzio 1900, 136). A year later, the author chafed censors with the tittle-tattle and scandal of the historical tragedy *Francesca da Rimini* (1901), set in 13th-century Italy amid the danger and spite of a love triangle involving the title figure, her husband, and his brother.

As Italy began to claim more territory from the Turks, D'Annunzio raised his iconic superman to new heights. The three-act play *Più che l'Amore* (More than love, 1906) portrays a cult figure through the manly explorer Corrado Brando, who abandons a paramour and unborn love child for a tragic fate. D'Annunzio extols his hero for exploits in unknown terrain in Italian East Africa and for standing firm on the wrong side of the law. The author's probings of modern tragedy bases heroism on Brando's rejection of social and political conventions for the greater good of his Italian homeland. At the play's debut on October 29, 1906, outraged theater-goers yelled, "Carabinieri, arrestate l'autore!" (Police, arrest the playwright) (Frese 2001, 78).

Sources

Benton, Catherine. *God of Desire: Tales of Kamadeva in Sanskrit Story Literature*. New York: State University of New York Press, 2005.

D'Annunzio, Gabriele. *The Flame of Life*. Translated by Kassandra Vivaria. Boston: L. C. Page, 1900.

Frese, Mary Ann. *The Search for Modern Tragedy: Aesthetic Fascism in Italy and France*. Ithaca, N.Y.: Cornell University Press, 2001.

Love Songs from the Man'yoshu. Translated by Ian Hideo Levy. Tokyo: Kodansha International, 2000.

Shuka Saptati: Seventy Tales of the Parrot. Translated by Aditya Narayan Dhairyasheel Haksar. India: HarperCollins India, 2000.

Ethiopian Book of the Dead   See BOOK OF THE DEAD.

Exodus (ca. 450 B.C.)

The scriptural epic of Exodus (Departure), the second book of the Torah and the Old Testament, describes the Hebrews' escape from servitude in the Egyptian Empire about 1250 B.C. during the late Bronze Age. At journey's end, they founded a priest nation in Canaan (present-day Palestine). Reprising the enslavement of Jews during Egypt's 19th dynasty, possibly during the rule of Ramses II (ca. 1303–1213 B.C.) the narrative is featured on 18 of the DEAD SEA SCROLLS. The original text focuses on the extraordinary life of Moses, a near victim of the pharaoh's order to drown Hebrew boys in the Nile. Like other mythic heroes, Moses has an unconventional childhood. The abandoned infant, set adrift in a cradle woven of reeds and reared as royalty by a princess, rescues his captive people and leads them to the fabled Promised Land. A saga of displacement and deliverance, the narrative dramatizes the slavery of the Jews and the parallel growth of Moses as a young lord of the household of the pharaoh, who "made [Hebrew] lives bitter with hard bondage" (Exodus 1:14). Compassion for suffering diverts Moses' attention from his own luxury and privilege to the bondage of Hebrew drones. In a flash of vengeance, he strikes and kills an Egyptian overseer, thus becoming an outlaw like Robin Hood and Rob Roy and bonding himself to the fate of a subject people.

The narrative recognizes Moses's godliness through a magical epiphany, the voice of Yahweh (God) emitted from a burning bush. Connecting divinity to Hebraic monotheism, the voice identifies himself twice as a single power honored by human patrilineage—"the god of thy father, the God of Abraham, the God of Isaac, and the God of Jacob" (Exodus 3:6). The drama pushes the text to a new level of personal identity with the Almighty, who proclaims, "I am that I am" (Exodus 3:14), an enigma of self-identity that has spawned unending theological contemplation. Like Arjuna, the self-effacing leader in the BHAGAVAD GITA, Moses declines the job of warrior or emancipator, but the voice refuses to rewrite Moses's fate. The coming battle against Pharaonic Egypt requires faith rather than weaponry or a display of military acumen. Moses convinces his followers of divine leadership by working wonders, turning a staff into a serpent and river water into blood. After nine pestilences subject the citizens to bloody Nile waters, frogs, lice, gnats, beetles, an epidemic among flocks and herds, boils, hail and thunder, locusts, and darkness, the Hebrews eat an unusual symbolic meal, the Passover, or "feast of unleavened bread" (Exodus 12:17), in preparation for the worst plague, the death of unprotected firstborn babes and beasts. In defeat, Pharaoh capitulates to Moses without having faced him on the battlefield.

A Nation on the Move

Following the Jews' escape, the combative narrative shifts to a peasant pilgrimage across the Red Sea, around the Philistine realm, and northeast to Mount Sinai. In Exodus 15:1–19, the Israelites raise a spontaneous anthem of praise as they leave the Red Sea. Feeding them in the desert are God's gifts, quail and manna, an unidentified subsistence food that falls from heaven in a symbolic gesture of support to the Israelites. At the appointed slope, Yahweh equips Moses with laws—a decalogue that opens with a monotheistic duty to reestablish order: "Thou shalt have no other gods before me" (Exodus 20:3). Amid acts of petulance, wrongdoing, and flouting of authority, the column marches on toward the Promised Land through a series of alien tribes, each posing a test of dedication to the emerging empire. As a focus of faith, they construct an incense altar and an ark of the tabernacle attended by vested priests. The portable ark bears sacred stone tablets inscribed with the Ten Commandments, "two tables of testimony, tables of stone, written with the finger of God" (Exodus 31:18), potent symbols of divine approval. The ark accompanies the Children of Israel across the Jordan River to Mount Shiloh in Canaan until its permanent location in the ninth century B.C. at the temple of Jerusalem built by King Solomon.

The composition of the KORAN (A.D. 633) echoes the drama of Moses' confrontation with Pharaoh, who accuses the Hebrew leader of sorcery. The Islamic version pictures Moses as a confrontational HERO: "Woe betide you! Invent no falsehoods against God, or He will destroy you with a scourge. Impostors will surely come to grief" (Koran 20:61). The Carthaginian polemist TERTULLIAN cites the Ten Commandments as proof that Christians respected life. In discussions of native-born heroes, NICCOLÒ MACHIAVELLI's Renaissance statecraft handbook *The Prince* (1514) lauds Moses as a political prodigy emerging from an enslaved people to lead them to freedom. The patriarchal bearded Moses has recurred throughout history in art, statuary, and bas-relief as well as in the Cecil B. DeMille screen saga *The Ten Commandments* (1956), featuring Charlton Heston as Moses and Yul Brynner as his adversary, Rameses II. Four decades later, Ben Kingsley and Christopher Lee reprised the roles of the Hebrew and Egyptian leaders in *Moses* (1996), an Emmy-nominated Turner Network TV film. In 1998, an animated version, *The Prince of Egypt,* cast Val Kilmer as the voice of Moses and Ralph Fiennes as the Egyptian pharaoh.

Sources

Compier, Don H., Pui-lan Kwok, and Joerg Rieger. *Empire and the Christian Tradition: New Readings of Classical Theologians.* Minneapolis: Fortress Press, 2007.

Exodus. In the Holy Bible. Iowa Falls, Iowa: World Bible Publishers, 1986, 90–158.

The Koran. Translated by N. J. Dawood. London: Penguin Classics, 2004.

F

fable

A source of timeless wisdom and sometimes indirect ridicule, fable, like anecdote and parable, preserves knowledge of human experience and history. Fabulists recorded the first written versions of ancient STORYTELLING during the Akkadian-Sumerian Empire, which began in 2350 B.C. Terse and insightful, like the agon or contest motif of the Babylonian CREATION story "Nisaba and Wheat" (ca. 1900 B.C.), the typical fable narrative takes place in an indistinct time and terrain. A prophetic biblical fable from Israel in the book of Judges 9:7–15 (ca. 1040 B.C.), composed in the early years of King Saul's reign, uses nature lore to demean Abimelech, a king from around 1700 B.C. who, like the briar, was a menace to productive kingdoms surrounding Shechem (present-day Nablus, Israel). When the prediction of internal unrest came true three years later, the civil war that overwhelmed the powermonger also destroyed surrounding settlements. Increasing the irony of his violent death was his felling by a millstone, dropped on his head from a siege tower by an elderly woman.

Throughout the ancient history of the Middle East, fable served more as an oral source of education than as mere amusement. The image of the briar and the tree recurs in 2 Kings 14:9 (ca. 535 B.C.) and again in 2 Chronicles 26:18 (400 B.C.) when Amaziah, king of Judah, threatens his father, Israel's king Jehoash. At a meeting of enemies around 800 B.C. to discuss a dynastic marriage, Amaziah, fresh from attacking south of the Dead Sea at Edom, plotted a raid on Israel. Jehoash quashed negotiations by promising to set a wild beast against the lone thistle. As the PROPHECY foretold, he overcame Amaziah, demolished the wall of Jerusalem, and plundered the palace and temple of their treasures.

The Greeks dominated the fable genre with the slave storyteller AESOP's models from the sixth century B.C. Following on Aesop, the Greek tragedian Aeschylus's "The Eagle and the Arrow," an ironic Libyan tale about empowering enemies incorporated into the play *Myrmidons* (ca. 470 B.C.), preceded his cautionary tale "The Man Who Reared a Lion's Cub" in the drama cycle *Oresteia* (458 B.C.). The latter fable alerted hearers to the nurturing of potential traitors, like the Trojan welcome to the Spartan queen Helen, the source of Troy's destruction. During the 29-year empire of Alexander III the Great of Macedon, Demosthenes of Athens told listeners the allegory of "The Wolf and the Shepherd" (ca. 336 B.C.), a tale warning Athenians to avoid risking Greek lives in the hands of an empire builder.

Middle Eastern Fable

In the next millennium, the fable archetype held its original form in the tales of Babrius, author of "The Rise of the Proletariat," written in Christianized Syria around A.D. 235. The characters of Eastern Mediterranean fables were often royalty and nondescript peasants of no discernible nationality or whimsical collections of animals and plants that English essayist Joseph Addison, producer of the newspaper the *Spectator*, termed "Brutes and Vegetables" (Addison and Steele 1907, 45).

Animal characters depersonalize the fable by setting the action outside the human realm. As the Parisian satirist JEAN DE LA FONTAINE explained in *Selected Fables* (1668), "When Prometheus wanted to create mankind, he took the dominant quality of each beast; of these pieces so diverse he composed our species; he made this work that we call the small world (microcosm). Thus these fables are a picture in which each of us finds himself portrayed" (quoted in Jewell 2001, 282). Fabulists chose beasts known for stereotypical behaviors—the pugnacious lion, the humble donkey, the predatory crow, the sly fox, the numbskull sheep, the nervous frog, the pesky fly, the shy dove. Thus, purveyors of animal logic, such as Babylonian and Hebrew court sages and the Greco-Libyan ambassador Apion of Alexandria, Egypt, the author of ANDROCLES AND THE LION—delighted hearers with the truism that character determines destiny. At the same time, the storyteller instructed or cautioned with provocative axioms revealed below surface caricature, such as the Chinese moral "He who rides the tiger cannot get off," a warning to despots who unleash mercenary armies as a means of conquest.

Before becoming anecdotes and miniature homilies, fables took the form of dialogues, such as in the Akkadian-Sumerian boast fables; the nature argument "The Tamarisk and the Palm" (2300 B.C.); and Babrius's "Show Me How" (ca. A.D. 235), a verbal disagreement between a baby crab and its mother. Around 1100 B.C., during the Sabaean empire, the forerunner of Ethiopia and Saudi Arabia, the sage Lokman the Wise, told pithy animal proverbs reduced to a few sentences of dialogue. Having survived a fall in status from prince to a maimed slave carpenter, Lokman infused his fables with a quiet humility gained from losing his fortune and family. Valued by Islamic aphorists, Lokman earned veneration for his faith in God and his willingness to accept destiny without complaint.

African Fable

The rise of West African empires of the Sahel on the south rim of the Sahara Desert encouraged the circulation of indigenous folk tales in the form of work chants, travel songs, dance rhythms, and group rounds. The Kanem-Bornu empire, comprising Cameroon, Chad, and Nigeria, attracted Arabic and Islamic scholars and moralists to the region around Lake Chad, a center known for its teaching tales. Timeless and anonymous logic puzzles, ethical debates, and trickster stories marked the folklore of the Songay, Hausa, Edo, and the Ashanti of Ghana. The Yoruba storyteller AMOS TUTUOLA reshaped stories of trial by ordeal for two Nigerian epics, *The Palm-Wine Drinkard* (1952) and *My Life in the Bush of Ghosts* (1952), both replete with Jungian threats and instinctive methods of self-preservation. Farther inland, *pourquoi* (why) or explanation stories such as "Pig's Long Nose and Greedy Mouth" flourished among the Congo and Loango along the Zaire River and northeast among the Aksumites of Ethiopia (fourth to 12th centuries) and the Semitic Kush of Nubia (present-day Sudan); 2000–1000 B.C.).

Humor lightens the WISDOM LITERATURE of sub-Saharan Africa. The Mbindu of Angola mocked polygamy with "The Frog and His Two Wives," a dilemma tale about a foolish husband trapped between two demanding cooks. A wittier form of fable colored the literature of the Malian empire (1247–ca. 1600). A mocking chorus, "The Song of Gimmile," describes the stingy king Konondjong of Gindo, who declines to pay his royal composer, a wandering musician from Korro. The king orders the man beaten and ejected from court. A harper named Gimmile the song-teller makes up a rude heptet that accuses the king of being ungainly, sagging in the belly, toothless, and bald. After the jingle gains popularity, the king attempts to suppress it. The bard he abused observes, "Who can stop a song that travels from country to country?" (quoted in Courlander 1996, 81), a reminder that memorable ditties move beyond political borders at the whim of the singer. Proving the wisdom of that rhetorical question were the dances, dramas, mumming, and Anansi the spider stories that slaves brought with them via the African diaspora to the Caribbean and the coastal Americas. By its very tenacity, diasporic literature proved that language preserves culture more surely than the sword.

In the last decade of the Roman Empire, the work of the elegist Flavius Avianus illustrated the decline of Roman style and purpose. His 42 Aesopic stories and fool tales, blending the materials of his predecessor Babrius with the ornate phraseology of OVID and VIRGIL, augment the metrical standards of all four influences. Around A.D. 400, Avianus composed a dedication explaining his preference for imaginary literature that anthropomorphized a pot, water jar, and battle trumpet as well as birds, domestic and wild animals, insects, and the gods Apollo and Jupiter. Among his morals for readers are warnings not to covet and not to make threats that cannot be backed up and a reminder that it is best to remain alone than to choose untrustworthy friends. One of the poet's most negative pieces, "The Soldier Who Burned the Weapons," pictures a warrior blaming the trumpet for turning Roman legions into killers without itself taking part in conquest.

Fable as Satire

Whether in home territory or throughout diasporas, fables soften the impact of SATIRE on its target—for instance, in the work of José Rosas Moreno (1838–83), a Mexican poet who composed "The Spider's Web" and "The Eagle and the Serpent" during the Second Mexican Empire (1864–67). To distance recitation of stories from the sphere of social PROTEST, the storyteller may set up an impersonal conflict, a word picture that leads directly to an *epimythium*, an abstract, often intuitive moral. The Arabian caliph Abu Bakr, a companion of the prophet Muhammad and conqueror of Syria and Iraq, retold "Strike on This Spot" (A.D. 630), an Egyptian exemplum or classroom model expressing the value of logic over hasty action. Into this same category falls the shepherd's comment on a sly wolf in sheep's clothing sneaking into the fold in Nikephoros Basilakis's *Progymnasmata* (Exercises, ca. 1175), written during the clash between the expansionist Mongols and Russian principalities preceding a national onslaught. Basilakis concludes, "Look for trouble and find it," a warning to would-be conquerors. Similar advice to monarchs about power and responsibility fills the WISDOM LITERATURE of Saadi (Sheikh Saadi, ca. 1210–ca. 1290), a Persian poet who produced under parables in *Rose Garden* (1258). In a tale of a Persian King, Saadi warns

that a tyrant resembles a wolf that superintends a sheep herd by sapping his empire's foundation.

The substitution of animals for people softens the didacticism and stresses right thinking without specifying incriminating political situations or scandals close to home, as is exemplified by the fox's conniving in *Sefer Meshalim* (*Book of Fables*, 1697) of the 17th-century rabbi Moses ben Eliezer Wallich (d. 1739) of Worms, Germany. Another writer from the latter days of the Holy Roman Empire, Gotthold Ephraim Lessing (1729–81) of Kamenz, Saxony, an imitator of the fables of Aesop and Phaedrus and of the PANCHATANTRA (ca. 200 B.C.) of Vishnu Sarma, pictured animal tyranny as a reflection of human conquest. His concise, utilitarian collection called *Fables* (1759) derides boasters in "Friendship without Envy" and "The Ox and the Calf" and mocks the strutting military poseur in "Dressed in Strange Feathers." Heavy with implications, Lessing's "The Briar" describes a plant that lives to destroy. Similarly, "The History of the Wolf" warns the unwary that the predator will not change its ways after rehabilitation. In a statement on the natural order of primacy, Lessing's "The Beasts Striving for Precedence" acknowledges ancient authority that some enemies always threaten.

Another cautionary tale about the claws under the velvet paw lies in the French fabulist Jean-Pierre Claris de Florian's "The Apes and the Leopard" (1792). In Florian's experience with leopards, an allusion to the French Revolution of 1789, "The people of such lofty tone / 'Twere well for us to let alone" (Florian 1888, 64). A more pointed accusation of aristocrats skewers Alfonso X the Wise, who ruled Castile in the last half of the 13th century. The king, an amateur astronomer, overlooks beggars while he moon-gazes. A poor man tugs on the royal robes and remarks, "You'll find men here, men who need bread: / You need not look for them up there; / They're here, around you, ev'rywhere" (Florian 1888, 119). The lessons came too late to save Louis XVI and Marie Antoinette of France, both of whom went to the guillotine in 1793.

The satirist Anatole France carried Florian's animal fables to a more chilling extreme with the novel *L'Île des pingouins* (*Penguin Island*, 1908), a fanciful diatribe against human barbarity. In one scene depicting mindless chauvinism, a shepherd explains to an outsider that a common tune, an antiporpoise war hymn, infects the minds of local children before they can talk. He justifies early corruption through hate music: "We are all good Penguins" (France 1921, xi). As society destabilizes and the empire falls, France remarks, "Anarchist attempts followed one another every week without interruption" (224). He adds that the typical victim is poor.

Fables and Universality

The similarity of fable themes and motifs derives from universal human psychology and from trade, religious conversion, and conquests that spread stories between peoples, such as the Hispanic storytellers throughout the Western Hemisphere and the Wolof stories of Senegal that the ethnographer BIRAGO DIOP transcribed into French. When the English satirist Samuel Johnson wrote "The Vulture" for the *Idler* on September 16, 1758, he referred indirectly to Great Britain's suppression of the North American colonies and of West Indians in the Caribbean. His allegory characterized war from the perspective of a bird profiting from carnage. The grotesque image casts the British Empire as food for corpse pickers. A contrasting bird *pourquoi* (why) story, ISAAC BASHEVIS SINGER's "Why Noah Chose the Dove" (1974), expresses the author's need for people to be more quiet and modest like the dove, a peace-loving messenger who carries God's promise of protection to Noah and his family. The dove, in a self-description, declares the importance of accepting individual differences: "Each one of us has something the other doesn't have, given us by God who created us all" (Singer 1974, n.p.). An allegory, the narrative explains why supporters of harmony are more valuable to society than its leopards, tigers, wolves, and vultures, symbols of Hirohito, Hitler, Mussolini, and Stalin, the causes of suffering during and after World War II.

As entertainment for children, fables conceal socioeconomic foibles under whimsy. A resilient tale, Hans Christian Andersen's "The Emperor's New Clothes" (1837) mocks the easily flattered ruler who believes he wears an outfit made from cloth that only the wise can see. The fabulist, a lover of youth for their truthfulness, has a child point out the obvious truth: "The emperor is naked." The fable marks an expansionist era in the Danish Empire and recurs in cinema version in *Hans Christian Andersen* (1952), a musical biopic starring Dannye Kaye.

On January 25, 1919, the journalist Louise Bryant (depicted years later in the film *Reds* [1981]) introduced the fall of the Russian and Austrio-Hungarian empires in the journal *Revolutionary Age* under the children's story "How the Revolution Began in America," part of a collection she entitled *Fables for Proletarian Children*. The Marxist parable characterizes President Woodrow Wilson's concept of a League of Nations as "a clever scheme for international policing to stop the further progress of revolution" (Bryant 1919, 6). The dreamscape of American socialism halts with the leap of an alley cat through the window, a droll conclusion to Bryant's tale.

See also GOETHE, JOHANN WOLFGANG VON; IRIARTE, TOMÁS DE; KAYLOV, IVAN ANDREYEVICH.

Sources

Addison, Joseph, and Richard Steele. *The Spectator.* Vol. 2. London: J. M. Dent & Sons, 1907.

Babrius. *Babrius and Phaedrus.* Translated by Ben Edwin Perry. Cambridge, Mass.: Loeb Classical Library, 1990.

Bryant, Louise. "How the Revolution Began in America." *Revolutionary Age* (January 25, 1919): 6.

Courlander, Harold. *A Treasury of African Folklore: The Oral Literature, Traditions, Myths, Legends, Epics, Tales, Recollections, Wisdom, Sayings, and Humor of Africa.* New York: Marlowe & Co., 1996.

Dijk, Gert-Jan van. *Ainoi, Logoi, Mythoi: Fables in Archaic, Classical, and Hellenistic Greek.* Amsterdam: Brill, 1997.

Fischer, Barbara, and Thomas C. Fox, eds. *A Companion to the Works of Gotthold Ephraim Lessing.* Rochester, N.Y.: Boydell & Brewer, 2005.

Florian, Jean-Pierre Claris de. *Fables of Florian.* Translated by J. W. Phelps. New York: John B. Alden, 1888.

France, Anatole. *Penguin Island.* Translated by A. W. Evans. London: John Lane, 1931.

Hobbs, Anne Stevenson, ed. *Fables.* London: Victoria and Albert Museum, 1986.

Jewell, Keala Jane. *Monsters in the Italian Literary Imagination.* Detroit: Wayne State University Press, 2001.

Kassis, Riad Aziz. *The Book of Proverbs and Arabic Proverbial Works*. Amsterdam: Brill, 1999.

Singer, Isaac Bashevis. *Why Noah Chose the Dove*. New York: Trumpet Club, 1974.

Fables of Bidpai See PANCHATANTRA.

feminism

Within the scope of the literature of empire, women authors such as the dramatist and poet APHRA BEHN, diarists MURASAKI SHIKIBU and IZUMI SHIKIBU, novelist MARYSE CONDÉ, journalists Nelly Bly and SANTHA RAMA RAU, autobiographer BUCHI EMECHETA, immigrant novelist ANZIA YEZIERSKA, and the frontier diarists of Canada fought battles of gender equity and autonomy. The topics are as old as Greek mythology, as indigenous to human debate as Greek playwright Aristophanes's sex comedy *Lysistrata* (411 B.C.), and as alluring as the GODDESS LORE of the Sanskrit *Lakshmi Tantra* (ca. A.D. 780).

In Sweden, the educator and romanticist Carl Jonas Love Almqvist (1793–1866) dismayed traditionalists with his masterwork, *Det går an* (*Sara Videbeck*, 1839), which lauds an ideal form of wedlock practiced in Britain, France, Germany, and Scandinavia. By her actions, the protagonist demonstrates the spunk of a female who makes her own arrangements, prefers friendship to a confining marriage, and accords Albert, her mate, the freedom to come and go without jealous questions. In a riposte to Almqvist's self-satisfied Sara, the Swedish dramatist August Strindberg (1849–1912) created *Miss Julie* (1888), depicting a battle between Kristin, a complacent peasant, and the title figure, an independent or New Woman who is willing to fight for the man of her choice. A bicultural American, PEARL S. BUCK (1892–1973), protested the disempowerment of women under the Chinese emperor in *The Good Earth* (1931) and in *The Mother* (1934), an experimental narrative focusing on female peasants. In the New World, the works of the Chilean Nobel Gabriela Mistral (1889–1957) and the Antiguan writer JAMAICA KINCAID (b. 1949) reflect on the residual effects of colonialism on family life in South America and the Caribbean. Among Americans of foreign heritage, the novelist AMY TAN stands out for compiling eyewitness recollections of the collapse of imperial China and the liberation of women from centuries of male domination.

An Early Pioneer

During the Italian Renaissance, Christine de Pisan (or Pizan) (1364–ca. 1434), a Venetian-born essayist and romantic balladeer, became the first European female writer to confront literary misogyny and the trivialization of women. Raised in Paris at the court of Charles V by her father, an astrology lecturer and court physician and counselor, Tomasso di Benvenuto da Pizzano of Bologna, she educated herself by reading chronicles, literature, and scientific treatises and by mastering French, Italian, and Latin. The death in 1390 of her husband, the court secretary and notary Étienne du Castel of Picardy, of bubonic plague left her the single parent of three children and also caregiver for her widowed mother. She supported them by publishing occasional verse—allegory, anecdotes, songs, and rondeaux. With the financial backing of the duc de Berry, the duchesse de Bourbon, the earl of Salisbury, Louis I of Orléans, Isabella of Bavaria, and Philip II of Burgundy, Christine issued essays on soldiery, court behavior, and hagiography and compiled a biography of Charles V of France. With *Epistre au dieu d'amours* (Letter to the god of love, 1399) and an AUTOBIOGRAPHY, *L'avision de Christine* (*Christine's Vision*, 1405), she tackled sexism promulgated by the conventions of courtly love. Her balanced arguments championed gender equality and a realistic understanding of human sexuality. She counted among her fans women of great influence—Anne of Brittany, Louise of Savoy, Leorna of Portugal, Marguerite of Austria, and Mary of Hungary.

Christine de Pisan rebuked historians in *Livre de la cité des dames* (*Book of the City of Ladies*, ca. 1405), an allegory that censures chroniclers for omitting women from world events. She defied the Catholic hegemony by refuting the interpretation of Eve in GENESIS as the cause of human miseries and by accusing Christian husbands of wife beating, drunkenness, and fortune hunting. With a sequel, *Le livre des trois vertus* (*The Book of the Three Virtues;*

1406), Christine addressed the concerns of "princesses and ladies honoured on earth" (Christine de Pisan 1985, 35) and warned of the evils of luxury and pride. The text criticizes poor female education and demands opportunities for women to fulfill their innate promise as a means of fighting frivolous stereotypes. Her apologia for female strengths lauds women for dignity and for devotion to peacemaking and justice.

The Hundred Years' War (1337–1453), a conflict of territorial claims and counterclaims between England and France, ignited a fierce loyalty in the author for her adopted homeland. In 1410, she took on the persona of Minerva, the Roman goddess of wisdom and war, to compose *Le livre des fais d'armes et de chevalerie* (*The Book of Deeds of Arms and of Chivalry*), a rare field-strategy manual compiled by a woman. In the second chapter, she defends the humanitarian position opposing unrestrained combat: "For in the exercise of arms many great wrongs, extortions, and grievous deeds are committed, as well as rapine, killings, forced executions, and arson" (Christine de Pisan 1999, 14).

After retiring to the Dominican abbey of Poissy at age 54, on July 31, 1429, Christine de Pisan composed *Le ditié de Jeanne d'Arc* (Hymn to Joan of Arc) in opposition to the seizure of French territory by Henry V of England. The heroic ode, the only tribute to Joan of Arc by a contemporary, honors the female folk leader for her intelligence and daring in reclaiming the Loire Valley. The poem salutes Joan's courage at the siege of Orléans on April 29, 1429, and the prophetic rise of a rural shepherdess to international fame.

The Feminist Pilgrim Abroad

An illiterate contemporary of Christine, the ecstatic visionary Margery Kempe (ca. 1364–ca. 1440) of Bishop's Lynn (now King's Lynn), Norfolk, freed herself from married servitude and composed the first autobiography of a woman in English. Born to John Brunham, mayor of Lynn, she wed John Kempe, a burgher and guildsman of her own class, in 1393. She suffered depression from intimate contact but bore her husband 14 children while she ran a brewery and grist mill. Her religious fervor advanced from ecstatic fasting, prayer, and confession to hallucinations, hysteria, and masochism. Suicidal thoughts that drove her to cling to a windowsill forced John Kempe to chain her to a bedstead for eight months. In solitude, she felt forsaken by God. In 1414, she fled her home to begin a pilgrimage to Canterbury, Leicester, Walsingham, and York. Her obsession with holy shrines took her to Assisi and Rome in Italy and to Santiago de Compostela, Spain's most popular religious site. After travels to view relics of Jesus, John the Baptist, and the Virgin Mary at Aachen in the Holy Roman Empire and to Jerusalem, a shrine of the Islamic hegemony, she returned to King's Lynn to nurse her dying husband. In 1431, their marriage ended at his death with duty and benevolence. Two years later, Kempe resumed her holy wanderings with religious ecstasies at Danzig, Poland, and Bergen, Norway.

Four years before her death, Kempe dictated a memoir to her son and a priest. *The Book of Margery Kempe* (1436) is an account of her emotional crises and the mysticism and theatrics that relieved her fervent religiosity. Key to her recovery were places that she venerated for their sanctity rather than their temporal significance. In fall 1413, robed in white and directed by visions of Christ, she joined a party of spiritual communers with the Virgin Mary in Jerusalem under the Mamluks, who encouraged restoration and tourism of religious sites as a boost to the imperial economy. Before reaching the Church of the Holy Sepulchre, a state attraction guarded by Muslims, she remarked, "I wepe sore in this holy place wher owyr Lord Jhesu Crist was qwyk and ded" (Kempe 2006, 161). She joined a candlelight procession led by friars bearing a cross. In the hands of Islamic exploiters, she paid a "Sarazyn" (173) to guide her to the site of the 40-day fast and crucifixion. Kempe's identification with the virgin's motherhood caused bouts of wailing, lamenting, and swooning on the Mount of Calvary, the site of Jesus' crucifixion. She subsequently looked back on Jerusalem as a source of succor and forgiveness. At Leicester in fall 1417, the mayor and others denounced Kempe's outbursts and jailed her. Because of her mental affliction, she viewed less fervent pilgrims with suspicion for chiding and threatening her.

As recounted in Book 2, on her third and last pilgrimage in spring 1433, Margery Kempe traveled with her Polish daughter-in-law by ship from southeastern England along the Baltic Sea. Fearing for Kempe's son's dissolute ways, Kempe and her daughter-in-law toured shrines in Danzig, Stralsund, and Wilsnack (present-day Brandenburg, Germany) and traveled by wagon to Aachen. The strength of the Catholic faith in northern Europe's Holy Roman Empire offered a strong contrast to her journeys in Islamic Palestine. However, in neither realm did she find sympathy for women or personal and sexual emancipation.

Feminism in the Spanish Empire

In 1669, a Hieronymite nun of New Spain, Sor (Sister) Juana Inés de la Cruz (ca. 1648–1695), flouted the Vatican by demanding human rights and education for females. In an era when men labeled women's minds and souls as second-class, Juana Inés Ramírez de Asbaje of San Miguel Nepantla, southeast of Mexico City, enjoyed the same run-of-the-library training that educated Christine de Pisan. Before she became Sor Juana, she taught herself Latin and Nahuatl and tried unsuccessfully to enter the Royal and Pontifical University of Mexico disguised as a boy. She spent her early teens as handmaiden to Leonor Carreto, the marquise de Mancera, whom Juana honored with a troubadour's passion. By age 21, having rejected suitors, Juana had only one option for independence: to take holy vows. To a disappointed wooer, she stated, "My body disinclined to this man or that, serves only to house the soul—you might call it neuter or abstract" (Cruz 1988, 9). In the woman-managed cloister, she learned logic, debated, taught music and theater, and kept the sisterhood's archives and ledgers. Simultaneously, she composed occasional verses, two farces, five sacramental plays, 16 carols, 62 ballads, 70 baroque sonnets, and religious allegories on the veneration of the Virgin Mary.

During the Golden Age of the Spanish Empire, Sor Juana fought the objectification of women with feminist verse and prose. She warned that physical beauty "is a corpse, is dust, is shadow, and is gone" (Cruz 1994, 147). Autocrats fumed at her theological knowledge when she cited the writings of St. Jerome and St. Paula, which prelates had falsely interpreted in order to demonize, shackle, and

dehumanize females. At age 43, Sor Juana rebutted the sexism of Manuel Fernández de Santa Cruz, the archbishop of Puebla, Mexico, by composing *La respuesta a Sor Filotea de la Cruz* (The reply to Sister Filotea of the Cross, 1691), the first feminist declaration of educational and intellectual freedom as the right of all Christians. She reasoned, "Being a Catholic, I thought it an abject failing not to know everything that can in this life be achieved, through earthly methods, concerning the divine mysteries" (53).

In the months preceding her death during a typhoid epidemic at the Convent of Santa Paula in Mexico City, Sor Juana dipped her pen in blood to disavow her writings and, under religious coercion, liquidated for alms her laboratory equipment, musical instruments, and some 4,000 books. Extant are four volumes of Sor Juana's correspondence, 100 books, and 185 manuscripts. In 1990, Assumpta Serna played the nun's role in the movie *Yo, la peor de todas* (I, the worst of all).

A Scots Rebel

A forerunner of the 19th-century independent or New Woman, the dramatist and poet Joanna Baillie (1762–1851) examined the gendered elements of heroism and imperialism. She was born in Bothwell, Scotland, to the Reverend James Baillie, a Presbyterian minister, and Dorothea Hunter Baillie. She counted among her ancestors the great Scottish hero William Wallace. After studying stagecraft at a boarding school in Glasgow and privately under Sir Walter Scott, Baillie composed 14 plays and one musical drama featuring psychological motifs and moral issues that featured male and female perspectives. Her narrative poem "The Legend of Lady Griseld [sic] Baillie," collected in *Metrical Legends of Exalted Characters* (1821), contributed to male-dominant Scots historical fiction a female of uncommon shrewdness and valor. Another ballad on Christopher Columbus surveys the logic of the visionary and concludes that "Earth's greatest son / That e'er earn'd fame, or empire won, / Hath but fulfill'd, with a narrow scope, / A stinted portion of his ample hope" (Baillie 1851, 732). Her sympathetic view emphasizes the fickleness of glory and the long-range shifts in historical appreciation of world exploration.

Baillie welcomed the ascension of Queen Victoria to the British throne and, in a letter written in spring 1837, wished for the empire an epoch of "peace and plenty" (Baillie 1999, 67). At literary maturity, she composed the metrical romance *Ahalya Baee* (1849), the tale of the legendary title figure, a Hindu queen who caught the interest of historian Sir John Malcolm, a diplomat and officer of the East India Company to whom the poet alludes. Beginning in 1735, according to the ballad, Ahalya reigned amid tribal turmoil on her borders, and yet, from age 30 to 60, she ruled at Maheshwar in the province of Mulwa in west-central India, without combat. A parallel to the imperial presence and control of Queen Victoria in British colonies, Ahalya puts down warlords and devotes herself to promoting prosperity, honoring Brahma, relieving poverty, and elevating the family. Baillie depicts a golden era in which urchins surround the rani's palanquin and chant, "She is our Mother, and she loves us all" (Baillie 1851, 842). At her death, a sage regrets that India's "restless chiefs" lack Ahalya's judgment and benevolence (847).

Joanna Baillie died in Hampstead, England, on February 23, 1851, leaving behind a wealth of poetry and plays she collected into one large volume published shortly before her death.

Indian Womanhood

A voice for the Indian woman, the civil libertarian and journalist Nayantara Sahgal (b. 1927) writes of imperialism as it spans southern Asian history from ancient times. A contemporary of the feminist author ANITA MAZUMDAR DESAI, Sahgal viewed the coming of independence for her country through the actions of prominent parents; her uncle, Prime Minister Jawaharlal Nehru; and her cousin, Indira Gandhi, a subsequent prime minister. Trained at a missionary academy at Woodstock, Mussoorie, and at Wellesley College, she edited Nehru's letters and worked as a freelance journalist, writing for the *Guardian*, *Frontline*, *Indian Express*, *Journal of Commonwealth Literature*, and the *Times*. She published two memoirs, *Prison and Chocolate Cake* (1954) and *From Fear Set Free* (1962); the polemical *The Freedom Movement in India* (1970), *A Voice for Freedom* (1977), and *Point of View:*

A Personal Response to Life, Literature and Politics (1997); and the biography *Indira Gandhi: Her Road to Power* (1982).

On the issues of violence against women, Sahgal denounced not only the wrongs of empire but also Hindu misogyny, the murder and cremation of female rebels by their kin, and suttee, or ritual burning of widow. Her novels *This Time of Morning* (1965), *A Situation in New Delhi* (1977), and *Rich Like Us* (1983) survey the price of feminist protest. The glib, witty *Mistaken Identity* (1988), set in 1929 during a period of arbitrary imprisonment, examines motivation and retaliation in northern India during protests against the British Raj. Of the empires that ruled his country, her protagonist, Bhushan Singh, a maharajah's son, titters about "the brilliant centuries between the barbarous hordes of Ghazni and Ghori, and the barbarous British" (Sahgal 1988, 26). The juxtaposition captures Sahgal's skill at denouncing imperialism.

See also GOTHIC LITERATURE; WOMEN'S JOURNALS, DIARIES, AND LETTERS.

Sources

Almqvist, Carl. *Sara Videbeck*. Translated by Adolph Burnett Benson. New York: American-Scandinavian Foundation, 1839.

Baillie, Joanna. *The Collected Letters of Joanna Baillie*. Edited by Judith Bailey Slagle. Cranbury, N.J.: Fairleigh Dickinson University Press, 1999.

———. *The Dramatic and Poetical Works of Joanna Baillie*. London: Longman, Brown, Green, and Longmans, 1851.

Christine de Pisan. *The Book of Deeds of Arms and of Chivalry*. Translated by Sumner Willard. University Park: Pennsylvania State University Press, 1999.

———. *The Treasure of the City of Ladies: or, The Book of Three Virtues*. Translated by Sarah Lawson. London: Penguin, 1985.

Cruz, Sor Juana Inés de la. *The Answer/La Respuesta: Including a Selection of Poems*. Translated by Electa Arenal and Amanda Powell. New York: Feminist Press, 1994.

———. *A Sor Juana Anthology*. Translated by Alan S. Trueblood. Cambridge, Mass.: Harvard University Press, 1988.

Forhan, Kate Langdon. *The Political Theory of Christine de Pizan*. Aldershot, U.K.: Ashgate, 2002.

Holloway, Julia Bolton, Constance S. Wright, and Joan Bechtold. *Equally in God's Image: Women in the Middle Ages*. Florence, Italy: Aureo Anello, 1990.

Kempe, Margery. *The Book of Margery Kempe*. Translated by Barry Windeatt. Rochester, N.Y.: D. S. Brewer, 2006.

Mehrota, Arvind Krishna. *A History of Indian Literature in English*. New York: Columbia University Press, 2003.

Sahgal, Nayantara. *Mistaken Identity*. London: Heinemann, 1988.

Firdawsi (Abolqasem Ferdowsi, Firdusi, Abu Ol-Qasem Mansur) (ca. 935–ca. 1020)
Persian poet and historian

The legendary historiographer Firdawsi won lasting acclaim for writing *Shahnameh* (*The Book of Kings*, ca. 1010), Persia's dynastic epic. Born Abu Ol-Qasem Mansur, in Tus (present-day Mashhad, Iran) he grew up privileged and was schooled in Shia Islam. At a transitional moment after throwing off three centuries of Arab rule, Persians of the Ghaznavid empire (975–1187) sought a revival of the culture and language that dominated the courts of the Achaemenid monarchs—Cyrus the Great, Darius, and Xerxes, the heroes of the Greek historian HERODOTUS's *Histories* (444 B.C.). Firdawsi began his masterpiece with the world's creation, taking his epic to the seventh-century Islamic conquest of Persia. The work took 35 years to complete. He declared, "I shall not die, these seeds I've sown will save / My name and reputation from the grave" (Firdawsi 2006, xi). Like the Roman poet VIRGIL, author of the AENEID (17 B.C.), Firdawsi assumed that the *Shahnameh* would assure his global fame and restore the sovereignty of the pre-Islamic Samanid dynasty of Khorasan in northeastern Iran. He presented the kingly saga at the court of his patron, Sultan Mahmud of Ghazni, who paid him only one percent of the original commission. Embittered and homeless, Firdawsi refused the pittance. He wandered the southern and northern extremes of the country before returning home to die in Tus and be buried in his yard.

Written in Pahlavi Persian, Firdawsi's sober, morally complex narrative of 120,000 lines upholds Islamic monotheism and honors Koranic CREATION LORE and mythos as the forefunners of FABLE and legends of tribal warfare and kingmaking. Like the suite of themes in Elias Lönnrot's KALEVALA (1836), the Finnish national story, the Persian epic covers Aryan civilization; Indo-Iranian history; the origin of Zoroastrian fire worship; the conquests of Alexander the Great, the Macedonian conqueror of Persia; and the feats of Rustam, the Persian Hercules. The narrative concludes with the fall of Zoroastrianism after Arab seizure of the Sassanid empire in A.D. 652, when the Umayyad caliph 'Uthman ibn 'Affan of Arabia supplanted the Iranian emperor, Shah Yazdegerd III. Over the reign-by-reign account, the poet scrutinizes a universal concern: What behavior behooves the good? Like the last words of the Hebrew king David in 2 Samuel 23:3, the poet exalts justice as the basis of rule, but he balances jurisprudence with celebration, dining, wine sharing, and Zoroastrian feast days that marked the Persian court as a place of enjoyment.

Firdawsi entwined familiar HERO tales with his perception of inborn ambition and hubris, a feature his writings share with those of GREEK DRAMATISTS, Confucius (see ANALECTS), and WILLIAM SHAKESPEARE. At the fall of the Persian Empire, the vizier Rostam interprets the stars and declares, "I am the time's most sad and sinful man; / This house will lose all trace of sovereignty / Of royal glory, and of victory" (833). The prediction foresees four centuries of fragmentation heralded in "the turning heavens—it's from there / That we are granted comfort and despair. . . . The stars are with the Arabs" (834, 835). The PROPHECY maligns Arab conquerors as liars, criminals, and brutalizers who lop off their enemy Mahuy's hands, feet, ears, and nose and seat him on a horse "left wandering the hot sands till he died of shame" (853). In a single sentence, Firdawsi foresees the fall of Persia and the rise of Arabs as a triumph of religion: "The pulpit replaced the throne" (853). His vivid epic influenced *Gulistan* (The Rose Garden, 1258), the sage parables of the Persian poet Saadi (Sheikh Saadi, ca. 1210–ca. 1290).

Sources
Curtis, John, and Nigel Tallis, eds. *Forgotten Empire: The World of Ancient Persia*. Berkeley: University of California Press, 2005.

Firdawsi, Abolqasem. *Shahnameh: The Persian Book of Kings.* Translated by Dick Davis. New York: Viking, 2006.

Forster, E. M. (Edward Morgan Forster)
(1879–1970) *English novelist and nonfiction writer*

Edward Morgan Forster, a London-born essayist and fiction writer, dramatized the social currents of British enclaves in India during the Edwardian age (1901–10). After completing his education at King's College, Cambridge University, Forster contributed short fiction to the *Albany Review, English Review, Independent Review, Pall Mall Magazine,* and *Putnam's.* He produced four novels between 1905 and 1910, and in 1921 he published *The Hill of Devi,* both a TRAVELOGUE and a treatise on Hindu life. While serving the maharajah of Dewas Senior as secretary in west central India, Forster gathered material for his fifth and most insightful novel, *A Passage to India* (1924), winner of the James Tait Black Memorial Prize for Literature and the Prix Femina Vie Heureuse. In *Aspects of a Novel* (1927), he stated the value of such scholarly research to civilization: "We (writers) are a very large and quite a powerful class, eminent in Church and State, we control the education of the Empire" (Forster 1956, 10). The assertion characterizes the scope and intensity of his Anglo-Indian fiction, with which he intended to stretch the imagination through unanswerable quandaries that demand analysis and debate.

Set in the decline of the British Raj during the independence movement of the 1920s, *A Passage to India* questions the complacency and arrogance that alienates races, religions, professions, social classes, and genders in the Indian subcontinent. A web of estrangement begins with a boring English stage play at the whites-only club and a tenuous encounter of English officials and Indian guests at an afternoon social that Mr. and Mrs. Turton of Chandrapore host at the club garden. Among whites, the jovial Muslim physician Dr. Aziz Ahmed "overrated hospitality, mistaking it for intimacy, and not seeing that it is tainted with the sense of possession" (Forster, 2002, 157), a gibe at English courtesies that maligns stilted manners as lace coverings for disdain. Group discomfort worsens with the judgments of the Hindu-Brahmin professor Narayan Godbole concerning Christians and Muslims, of Cyril Fielding the educator in the hectoring presence of Turton the tax collector, and of Adela Quested, a new arrival to the colony who has doubts about her upcoming wedding to Ronnie Heaslop and her own sexuality. Her future mother-in-law, Mrs. Moore, a dispenser of wisdom and proponent of inclusion, exclaims, "This to do and that to do and this to do in your way and that to do in her way, and everything sympathy and confusion and bearing one another's burdens" (207), a clue to Forster's disinclination toward Christian philosophy.

The author's disturbing allegorical novel jolted readers with the ironies and ambiguities of character interaction in fictional Chandrapore, which represents a crucible of Anglo-Indian relations in the decades following the death of Queen Victoria. In the courtroom, at a collision of personal prejudices and truth, Adela exhibits a brave honesty by recanting charges of rape against Dr. Aziz. Public atonement rids her of a subconscious echo, a Freudian upheaval of gender and social roles that ricochets from the unconscious to the conscious mind. The wounded sensibilities of British bigots and the jubilance of Indian nationalists erupt in a native celebration of the court judgment that winds through the streets like a pagan procession. Cyril Fielding realizes how quickly feigned decorum goes awry: "Everything echoes now; there's no stopping the echo. The original sound may be harmless, but the echo is always evil" (184). Like the civil servants who create a social pariah in RUTH PRAWER JHABVALA's *Heat and Dust* (1975), English bigots force Adela, the "addled quester," out of India's complex social order and out of the closed world of a British expatriate compound to the safe conservatism in London. In the inconclusive coda, Forster preserves a glimmer of idealism in Fielding, who marries Stella, a character bearing the Latin name for *star.* The novel was Forster's last to earn critical acclaim. Before his death at age 91, he accepted a Companion of Honour and an Order of Merit.

The Indian journalist SANTHA RAMA RAU wrote the stage play of *A Passage to India* in 1962; the BBC produced it for television three years later.

In 1984, David Lean directed a stimulating film version, which cast Judy Davis with Victor Banerjee, James Fox, Peggy Ashcroft, and Alec Guinness.

Sources

Forster, E. M. *Aspects of the Novel.* New York: Harvest Books, 1956.
———. *A Passage to India.* London: Macmillan, 2002.
Jay, Betty. *E. M. Forster.* London: Macmillan, 2003.

Frank, Anne   See CHILDREN'S LITERATURE.

frontier literature

The challenges of empire filled the personal writings of adventurers, dreamers, and newcomers to the outback. The allure of newness appealed to the British romancers Sir ARTHUR CONAN DOYLE, RUDYARD KIPLING, and H. RIDER HAGGARD, and to the Tasmanian historians James Fenton and John West, while it also introduced a subgenre known as the emigration text, a study of the hazards of settling in a foreign clime. Less optimistic on the topic, of JOSEPH CONRAD turned the plunder of the Congo jungle into a brain sickness in his classic novel *HEART OF DARKNESS* (1899), in which the outsider plunges into a toxic environment made savage by the exploiter rather than by the African native. Danish fabulist ISAK DINESEN's *Out of Africa* (1937), like OLIVE SCHREINER's *The Story of an African Farm* (1883) and G. B. Lancaster's *A Spur to Smite* (1906), aired concerns for the displaced pastoral tribes of Kenya and the paternalism that replaced their ancestral freedoms.

In Canada, the English-born sister authors Susanna Strickland Moodie (1803–85) and CATHARINE PARR TRAILL (1802–99) revealed a duality that informed the English-speaking readership of the glories and terrors of living in the wild. At the end of the Napoleonic wars, Traill, Moodie's older sibling and fellow provincial settler, settled outside Peterborough, Upper Canada (now Ontario), north of the Lake Ontario, in 1832 and collected her impressions in *The Backwoods of Canada* (1836). At peace in her home on the Otonabee River, she describes the frontier as a land of hope, newness, and anticipation. In a polite quibble with an Ohioan, she admits to prejudice against the rough plains behaviors to the south. His retort reminds her that "It would be hard if the English were to be judged as a nation by the convicts of Botany Bay" (Traill 1836, 293). To would-be pioneers, she warns that frontier life is not easy for genteel idlers and fortune hunters. She allies with pioneering "bush-ladies" (271) and alerts less hardy souls, "If people will not conform to the doctrine of necessity and expediency, they have no business in it" (140).

Susanna Moodie, a less contented emigrant arriving from Leith, Scotland, in 1832 at Douro, Upper Canada (present-day Ontario), covered rural life in *Roughing It in the Bush; or Life in Canada* (1852) and of community experiences in Belleville, Ontario, in *Life in the Clearings Versus the Bush* (1853). Unlike the Nova Scotian poet and journalist Joseph Howe (1804–73), who valorized native conditions with "The Song of the Micmac" (1874), a salute to the fortitude of aboriginal settlers, Moodie took the side of the imperial reformer. In the first volume, the cautionary text pairs "a peculiar charm in the excitement of improving a wilderness for the benefit of children and posterity" with homesickness for England's sophistication (Moodie 1852, 287). While living in a vermin-infested log cabin, Moodie pictures herself as a dutiful wife, homesteader, and parent. In the same imagery, she describes Canada as a foster mother to civilization's orphans, a reference to her Canadian-born daughter Agnes Dunbar and sons John Alexander Dunbar, Donald, and John Strickland. In a sobering balance, she treasures Ontario as the site of family graves, including John Strickland Moodie, who drowned in the Moira River in 1844 at age five.

The Poet's Canada

Other genres particularize the purpose and expectation of western settlers. The Irish poet Thomas D'Arcy McGee (1825–68), spoke in "The Arctic Indian's Faith" (1869) of the spirituality he gained from observing the animism of the Wapiti of Montreal, a view he shared with the British-Mohawk author PAULINE JOHNSON. Charles Mair (ca. 1838–1927), a native-born Ontarian from Lanark, honored a Shawnee warrior in the verse drama *Tecumseh* (1902), which revealed to white audiences the native belief in communal living on undeeded land. Mair's protagonist declares, "Our fathers commiserated [the whites'] distress, and shared freely with them whatever the Great Spirit had given to his red children" (Mair 1886, 7). Of Shawnee greatheartness, the text promotes sharing "all earthly goods / by the Great Spirit mean for common use" (13) and reminds the native to honor traditions of living off the land, loving wives and children, and respecting peace among nations.

To Samuel Mathewson Baylis (1854–1941), the romanticized era of the French woods runner in the poem "The Coureur-de-Bois" (1919), like the cowboy of the plains, favored the loner rather than the family man. In a time of all-male bonding and hardihood, the survivalist "roved a king / His untamed will his law" (Lochhead and Souster 1974, 93), a perspective supported by dime novels and early Hollywood screenplays.

William Henry Drummond (1854–1907), an Irish physician with a love of language, found much to admire in the Creole, particularly the off-and-on cadencing of Franglais, a pastiche of French and English. In "The Habitant" (1898), he agrees with a resident of Cheval Blanc (Whitehorse) about avoiding the city in favor of the wild. With the swagger of the backwoodsman, the speaker declares, "If you geev de fine house an' beaucoup d'argent (plenty of money)— / I rader be stay me, an' spen' de las' day me / On farm by de rapide" (101).

Poets who published in provincial newspapers and journals popularized nature verse as a vehicle for sermonizing. William Kirby (1817–1906), a journalist in Niagara-on-the-Lake, Ontario, and editor of the *Niagara Mail*, considered frontiering a form of character refinement. In the ode "Lord Lorne in the Northwest" (1881) and the didactic idyll "Thunder-Storm in August" (ca. 1876), he welcomes rough weather on the prairies and in the mountains as reminders of the creator's dominance over empires. In the latter poem, the speaker declares "reverses, poverty, disease, and death" a form of "purifying fire . . . To stay corruption's foul contagious breath, / To keep alive the spark of truth within" (17).

A Scots poet, Alexander MacLachlan (1818–96) of eastern Ontario, charged newcomers to Canadian with generating urban rot in a pristine environment that his poem "Indian Summer" labels holy. Like the conservationist Grey Owl (Archibald Belaney, 1808–1938) and the nationalist Mair, MacLachlan doubted that Canada would survive the waves of European immigrants that carried them from the Atlantic to the Pacific. In "We Live in a Rickety House" (1900), he thunders, "Our ignorance and crime / Are the Church's shame and disgrace" (21). The statement repudiates prevalent notions of empire building as a Christian duty to pagan lands.

Colonizing Australasia

Essential to accounts of frontier life in the provincial Southern Hemisphere, anonymous convict laments, settlers' diaries and journals, and verse scenarios often tinged colonial homesteading with nationalism. The canon espouses a love-hate relationship that portrays England as both nurturing founder and oppressor, as voiced in the seditious effrontery of the anonymous "The Wild Colonial Boy" (1830). Inhumanity dominates the action of Marcus Clarke's novel *His Natural Life* (1874), a tragedy of duty and personal ethics featuring British transportees imprisoned in alien spots such as Macquarie Harbour in Van Diemen's Land, an early name for Tasmania. The cruelty of living incommunicado emerges in the reminder that "No letters are allowed to be sent to the friends of prisoners without first passing through the hands of the authorities" (Clarke 2006, 242), a regulation more in keeping with the early history of Australasia's colonization. The core of later Australian literary themes rests on concepts of liberty and civil rights, themes in the work of the journalist Daisy Bates (1859–1951), who described infant cannibalism and trade in females in *The Passing of the Aborigines* (1938), an unsympathetic view of native nonwhites.

Establishing a continental identity, the folk ballads of Andrew Barton "Banjo" Paterson (1864–1941) and Henry Lawson (1867–1922), Australia's national poet, focused on bushrangers, cowboys, and raffish loners in rugged territory outside the bounds of European gentility and the control of Queen Victoria. In 1887, Lawson acknowledged fealty to both land and queen in "The Song of the Republic," an anthem to patriotism published in the *Bulletin*, Australia's oldest newsmagazine.

Both Lawson and Paterson depicted the first-generation Aussie as a model of bush pragmatism and self-reliance, subjects reflecting similar topics in the empire literature of H. Rider Haggard, Rudyard Kipling, and ROBERT LOUIS STEVENSON. The legendary outback hero, particularly the title figure in Paterson's "The Man from Snowy River" (ca. 1888), thrived in the high country and developed a mystic oneness with drought, heat, and aboriginal and animal elements of the grasslands and desert. In "Song of the Pen" (ca. 1885), Paterson declares that such outlanders thrive on cattle herding, sheep shearing, and horse breaking and avows, "Work is its own reward!" (Paterson 2004, 3), a statement ironically reflective of the values of late Victorian England.

The mythos of endurance in the wild colonial communities distanced from the mother country asserted grit and daring as tests of individualism, the theme of Lawson's short story "The Drover's Wife" (ca. 1892); "While the Billy Boils" (1896), an ode in prose to the overland stockman; and Paterson's "Waltzing Matilda" (1895), a poem used as an advertising ditty for "Billy" brand tea in western Queensland in 1902 that became Australia's unofficial national anthem. It symbolizes the outback swagman as the empire's reject. In "Old Australian Ways" (1902), Paterson emphasizes what separates the Aussie from Great Britain: "Our fathers came of roving stock / That could not fixed abide" (Paterson 1987, 27). Adrift from English jurisprudence, the frontiersman "must saddle up and go / Beyond the Queensland side, / Beyond the reach of rule or law" (27).

A Colonial Survey

Early in the 20th century, Edith Joan Lyttleton (1873–1945), a Tasmanian author who wrote under the pseudonym G. B. Lancaster, gained popular success in Europe and the United States for colonial fiction laced with scenic grandeur, slang, and outback jargon. From submitting short works to the *New Zealand Illustrated Magazine*, the *Australian*,

Everybody's Magazine, Harper's, and the *Bulletin*, she advanced to specific provincial challenges in the three novels, Aussie bushmen in *A Spur to Smite* (1905), pioneers and miners in *The Tracks We Tread* (1907), and Melanesian missions and the press gangs of European copra and lumber traders in New Caledonia and Vuataoni in the northern Solomon Islands in *The Altar Stairs* (1908). In Lancaster's ethical evaluation of the Royal North-West Mounted Police in *The Law-Bringers* (1913), the protagonist, Officer Jim Tempest, like GEORGE ORWELL in Burma in his autobiographical "Shooting an Elephant" (1950), bears the solitary burden of "regular patrols, the settlement of little sordid matters, the suggestion of law and order which he carried on his own body where he went" (Lancaster 1913, 76). His duties as a law enforcer take him from Grey Wolf, an outpost on the Athabaska River in north Alberta, to Hudson Bay and up Oregon's McKenzie River to the Arctic, a long trek made wretched by solitude and predators, human and animal.

Lancaster's one-woman empire survey continued with research into yellow fever and American imperialism in Cuba and Panama in *Fool Divine* (1917) and into Tasmanian convict labor in a Lyttleton family saga, *Pageant* (1933), a Literary Guild selection and winner of a Gold Medal for Australian literature. In the chapter entitled "Civilising" in the latter novel, she re-creates the preparations of locals for a visit from a British royal. In a deft aside, she adds, "At last the hated stigma of *convict* was erased, although it seemed likely that England would not discover this for another half-century" (Lancaster 1933, 328). Lancaster shifted her interests northeast to the Yukon for *The World Is Yours* (1934) and to the settlement of New Zealand for *Promenade* (1938), in which she criticizes the muddles of imperialism: "That infernal East India Company . . . trying to entangle us; and Stamford Raffles [the founder of Singapore] imploring us to hold on to Singapore— a worthless mud-flat; and Australia clamouring for protection and her own way" (Lancaster 1938, 34). The text honors the first generation of islanders, "those who were no exiles, to whom New Zealand was the only land they knew" (161). In her last months, Lancaster showcased provincial courage in Nova Scotia in *Grand Parade* (1944), a salute to female colonialists.

See also HURON CHIEF, THE; NATURE LORE; RICHARDSON, JOHN.

Sources

Clarke, Marcus. *His Natural Life*. London: Adamant Media, 2006.

Dixon, Miriam. *The Real Matilda: Woman and Identity in Australia 1788 to 1975*. Middlesex, U.K.: Penguin, 1976.

Lancaster, G. B. *The Law-Bringers*. New York: Hodder & Stoughton, 1913.

———. *Pageant*. Victoria, Aust.: Penguin, 1933.

———. *Promenade*. Sydney: Angus & Robertson, 1938.

Lawson, Henry. *Henry Lawson: Twenty Stories and Seven Poems*. Perth, Aust.: Angus and Robertson, 1947.

Lochhead, Douglas, and Raymond Souster, comps. *100 Poems of Nineteenth Century Canada*. Toronto: Macmillan, 1974.

Mair, Charles. *Tecumseh: A Drama*. Toronto: Hunter, Rose, 1886.

Moodie, Susanna. *Roughing It in the Bush; or, Life in Canada*. London: Richard Bentley, 1852.

Paterson, Andrew Barton. *Banjo Paterson's Poems of the Bush*. London: J. M. Dent, 1987.

———. *Saltbush Bill, J. P., and Other Verses*. Whitefish, Mont.: Kessinger, 2004.

Proudfoot, Lindsay J., and M. M. Roche. *(Dis)placing Empire: Renegotiating British Colonial Geographics*. Aldershot, U.K.: Ashgate, 2005.

Steenman-Marcusse, Cornelia Janneke. *Re-writing Pioneer Women in Anglo-Canadian Literature*. Amsterdam: Rodopi, 2001.

Sturm, Terry. *An Unsettled Spirit: The Life and Frontier Fiction of Edith Lyttleton*. Calgary, Alberta: University of Calgary Press, 2003.

Traill, Catharine Parr. *The Backwoods of Canada: Being Letters from the Wife of an Emigrant Officer, Illustrative of the Domestic Economy of British America*. London: Charles Knight, 1836.

G

Gandhi, Mohandas Karamchand   See
WISDOM LITERATURE.

Garcilaso de la Vega (El Inca) (1539–1616)
Peruvian historian
A learned Incan mestizo, Garcilaso de la Vega (El
Inca) preserved the history of two cultures in South
America. Born in Cuzco, Peru, to an Incan princess
and a Spanish conquistador, he accepted and promoted the Roman Catholic exoneration of imperialism. For events in his chronicle *Comentarios reales
de los Incas* (*Royal Commentaries of the Incas and
General History of Peru*, first part published in 1609,
second part in 1617), he drew on the STORYTELLING
of his mother and Peruvian relatives about dynasties, Amerindian pageantry, and local feudalism.
Using his classical education, he began constructing
a history of the Inca Empire in the style of European
CREATION LORE by picturing Manco Capac, the first
Inca, in the role of creator and governor of the first
Andean residents at Tahuantinsuyu (Peru). With
details from an uncle, Garcilaso summarized the
civilizing effects of Incan sun worship, agriculture,
herding, and spinning, weaving, and styling of cot-
ton, maguey, and wool into clothes and shoes. Of
the establishment of social order, he characterized
the first Inca king and queen as leaders of a savage
race and builders of Cuzco, the empire's capital.
The text describes native industry as strictly gendered, with the king leading men and the queen
superintending women. The myth of El Dorado
grew from descriptions of the reign of Huayna
Capac and stories of an Eden on Lake Titicaca, a
prize that enticed the Hapsburgs (rulers of Austria
1278–1918 and of Spain 1516–1700) to establish a
colony in South America.

Bilingual in Quechua and Spanish, Garcilaso
spent his adult life, from age 21, in exile in Madrid
and Cordoba, as a disinherited bastard of mestizo parentage. Critics accuse him of allowing
homesickness to inject sentiment into his writings, especially his belief that divine providence
selected the Inca as the New World receivers of
Spaniards and Christianity. On the contentious
differences between pagan Incas and orthodox
Catholic Spaniards, he defended Andean customs
and ancestral history, which Peruvians preserved
in oral history and recorded on quipus (knotted
strings). Of the Indian dream visions that appointed Mesoamerican women as midwives and hand-
maidens to the Earth Mother, his text vindicates
the profession from accusations of sorcery on the
grounds that each practitioner had to have given
birth twice to living children and completed ritual
training under priestly supervision.

The Price of Conquest

Garcilaso's narrative supplied the American historian William Hickling Prescott (1796–1859),
author of *History of the Conquest of Peru* (1847),
with details of the battle of November 16, 1532,
that enabled Francisco Pizarro and 150 soldiers to overwhelm the Incan king Atahualpa at
Cajamarca. At the initial confrontation with the
Inca, Fray Vicente de Valverde, a Spanish bishop

from Segovia, gave him no choice but capitulate to Holy Roman Emperor Charles V or else "be constrained with war, fire, and the sword, and all your idols shall be overthrown and we shall oblige you by the sword to abandon your false religion" (Garcilaso 1966, 102). The ensuing melee substantiated a dire PROPHECY of Viracocha, the god emperor of the 15th century, who foresaw national doom. Some 1,500 Inca died by trampling and the collapse of a wall that buried them alive. Drawing on the notes of Padre Blas Valera, a priestly scribe, Garcilaso recalls of the deaths, "I weep over them afresh" (108).

In the 1560s, after the Spanish abandoned the pretense of fair government for the Andes, Garcilaso ventured to approach King Philip II with objections to violence against Indians and to subjugation by Spaniards posing as Christian evangelists. Risking his reputation as a court translator, soldier, and historian, he denounced a labyrinth of laws controlling Inca choices of marriage, commerce, profession, and land ownership. He also supported the silver miners of Potosí and the laborers of Huanca who supplied the mercury for purifying gold ore: "If they ceased to do so, neither the silver nor the gold of the empire would be brought every year to Spain" (167). Unconscionable to Garcilaso were Viceroy Francisco de Toledo's abandonment of 300 Inca on the coast to starve to death, his claims of liberating Peru from paganism; and, in 1572, his sham trial and beheading of Tupac Amaru, the last Inca monarch, for rebelling against Spain and Christianity. Of Garcilaso's own identification as a half-breed Inca, he asserted, "I call myself [mestizo] in public and am proud of it" (88).

Reflecting on Florida

In 1599, well before the *Royal Commentaries*, Garcilaso completed *La Florida del Inca* (*The Florida of the Inca*), a six-book chronicle begun in 1567 and published in Lisbon in 1605 concerning Hernando de Soto's explorations of southeastern North America and a subsequent naval battle off Santiago de Cuba. The first book, based on incomplete cartographic knowledge, assumed that land north of Florida may have been part of New France, an established territory that spurred the

Spaniards to carve out their own colony. Garcilaso valorizes aboriginal habits and quashes rumors that Florida's Indians are cannibals. He describes Chief Hirrihigua's variation of the running of the gauntlet, during which white captives from the company of explorer Pámphilo de Narváez run across a courtyard to avoid arrows aimed at them. The chief spares a young Spanish expeditioner, Juan Ortiz, but saves him for a more bizarre torture, grilling over live coals. The chief's wife and daughters plead successfully for Juan's life and treat his burns with herbs.

The historian presents enough details to substantiate the exploration of the Americas as hardship duty. Low on salt and supplies, de Soto's forces tramp over rugged Appalachian terrain and through the marshes of the Mississippi Delta to reach the sea. The hardened Spaniards grieve the passing of Governor de Soto from fever on May 21, 1542, on the eastern side of the Mississippi River at Guyachoya (present-day McArthur, Arkansas). In the masculine style of Homer's *Iliad* (ca. 850 B.C.) and VIRGIL's AENEID (17 B.C.), they honor the warrior with stories of his "heroic feats and invincible spirit, his promptitude in battles and attacks, his patience in hardship, his strength and courage in fighting, and his caution, counsel and prudence in both peace and war" (Garcilaso 1951, 628). The lengthy history concludes with de Soto's burial in a weighted blanket in the Mississippi River and the abandonment of Florida as a likely colony. In 1780, Charles III of Spain suppressed Garcilaso's commentaries to prevent their use by Tupac Amaru II, leader of an Inca revolt against imperialism.

Sources

Arias, Santa, and Mariselle Meléndez. *Mapping Colonial Spanish America: Places and Commonplaces of Identity, Culture, and Experience.* Lewisburg, Pa.: Bucknell University Press, 2002.

Garcilaso de la Vega, Inca. *The Florida of the Inca.* Translated by John Grier Varner and Jeannette Johnson Varner. Austin: University of Texas Press, 1951.

———. *Royal Commentaries of the Incas and General History of Peru.* Translated by Harold Livermore. Norman: University of Oklahoma Press, 1966.

Genesis (ca. 500 B.C.)

The basis of the Torah and the first book of the Bible, Genesis (Beginning) is a Judaic CREATION text preceding the laws of Moses. Written at the beginning of the Persian rule of Palestine and replicated on 24 of the DEAD SEA SCROLLS, the action covers the arrival of Abram and Sarai in 1950 B.C. from Ur, a Mesopotamian city north of the Persian Gulf between the Euphrates and Tigris rivers (present-day south-central Iraq). A distillation of Ephraimite and Judean STORYTELLING, Genesis echoes the Sumerian account of the GODDESS LORE of Inanna, keeper of a sacred garden. The completed Hebrew book begins with the creation of Adam and Eve and advances to the lethal jealousies of their sons Abel and Cain, the latter a murderer marked as the eternal pariah. The high point of Genesis is the patriarchy of Abram, a nomadic tribal leader who sires the Jews and Arabs. From cosmology to a civilized monotheism, the story ranges from the mythic man (adam) formed from dust ('adamah) to a realistic drama of a family who travels more than 2,500 miles to Hebron, a homeland west of the Dead Sea.

Like the Hawaiian *Kumulipo* (The Beginning, 1897), translated into English by Queen Liliuokalani, the dynamics of Genesis incorporates politics and religion. In chapters 6–8, the classic flood motif set in Mesopotamia and Sumer during the Bronze Age depicts Noah as the model of righteousness. By chapter 11, impiety again distorts civilizing principles during construction of the Tower of Babel, a possible reference to the raising of a brick ziggurat temple to Ningal, the moon goddess, in Ur, located in present-day Iraq at the delta of the Tigris and Euphrates rivers. As a fable of international disunion, Genesis introduces nationhood, different language families, and the history of Abram and Sarai, who rename themselves Abraham and Sarah (Genesis 17:5, 17:15) for "father of nations" and "princess," an indication of elevation from nomads to royalty. ·

In Haran in southeastern Turkey, a PROPHECY of a stable nation precedes a divine covenant that establishes a race known to history as the "chosen people." Perhaps as propaganda for the nation of Israel, the Abrahamic covenant pledges, "I will make of thee a great nation, and I will bless thee, and make thy name great; and thou shalt be a blessing: And I will bless them that bless thee, and curse him that curseth thee: and in thee shall all families of the earth be blessed" (Genesis 12:2–3).

The First Conflict

Abraham's siring of Ishmael by the Egyptian handmaiden Hagar precipitates a family crisis emblematic of tribal blood feuds. The family survives the destruction of the cities of Sodom and Gomorrah, corrupt fleshpots that contrast the faith and clan commitment of Abraham's household. After Sarah conceives her first child at age 90, the couple welcome Isaac, whom they name the Hebrew word for "laughter" for their joy in parenthood in old age (Genesis 21:6). After fabulist Baroness Karen Blixen's sojourn in British East Africa (present-day Kenya), she wrote about empire building in Africa under the pseudonym ISAK DINESEN, an allusion to the centrality of the chosen people to the world family.

Genesis miniaturizes national antipathies in family disunion, an emblem of God's earthly lineage. Abraham's delight gives place to jealousy in chapter 21, when Sarah secures Isaac's primacy by ordering Hagar and Ishmael into desert exile in Beersheba, a hill town of southern Israel near Hebron, Sarah's eventual burial place between the Dead Sea and the Mediterranean. Destiny concludes the breakup of the household with God's promise to elevate Ishmael from wanderer to nation builder, a harbinger of the Arab hegemony. Implicit in the separation of sons lies a curse on Jews, Arabs, and the world at large, a universal burden deriving from a father's disinheritance of his firstborn. Crises in the next three generations of patriarchs—Isaac, Jacob, Joseph, and the 12 tribes of Israel—cover a multiplicity of envy, deceptions, and threats to justice and sanctity. The multigenerational history sets the stage for EXODUS, the Hebrews' retreat around 1446 B.C. from servitude to the Egyptian empire to new nationhood in Palestine.

Sources

Cross, Frank Moore. *From Epic to Canon: History and Literature in Ancient Israel.* Baltimore: Johns Hopkins University Press, 1998.

Genesis. In the Holy Bible. Iowa Falls, Iowa: World Bible Publishers, 1986.

genocide

Whether implied or overt, the threat to the survival of entire nations is the basis of terror scenarios in world epic poetry, fiction, and chronicles. The theme flourishes in a broad span of genres, including the Greek historian THUCYDIDES's *The History of the Peloponnesian War* (ca. 400 B.C.), Diego Durán's chronicle *Aubin Codex* (1576), the memoir *A Narrative of the Life and Travels of Mrs. Nancy Prince* (1850), the Nigerian dramatist Aimé Césaire's PROTEST play *A Tempest* (1969), and MARYSE CONDÉ's historical novel *I, Tituba, Black Witch of Salem* (1986). Imperiled peoples are standard figures in the literary APOCALYPSE and VISIONARY LITERATURE, including YEVGENY YEVTUSHENKO's threnody "Babi Yar" (1961), Jerzy Kosinski's surreal novel *The Painted Bird* (1965), and JOHN HERSEY's World War II reportage in *Hiroshima* (1946). Among the chilling examples stand two classics of the surreal, *The Trial* (1925) and *The Castle* (1926), meditations on injustice by Franz Kafka, a writer during the confused aftermath of the Austro-Hungarian Empire. Because of a distrust of governmental court trials and punishments, he envisioned the advent of perverted science in central Europe and the strategies of the Holocaust. A generation later, in "O die Schornsteine" ("O the Chimneys," 1947), German-Jewish playwright and poet NELLY SACHS commemorated the Jewish sufferings engineered by Hitler's perverted science. For her lyric threnodies, she earned the 1966 Nobel Prize in literature.

In early Hebrew literature, the biblical HERO epic Joshua (ca. 1050 B.C.) skirts ethical issues by incorporating mass murder and arson as punishments for the fallen city of Jericho. The core theme of the epic EXODUS (ca. 450 B.C.) is the plight of enslaved Hebrews under an unrelenting Egyptian pharaoh, possibly Ramses II. A more chilling atmosphere invades the book of Esther (ca. 175 B.C.), a later chronicle of a single hero standing between her people and annihilation. At the fall of Troy in VIRGIL's AENEID (17 B.C.), an epic composed as propaganda for the Roman emperor Augustus, the securing of a Greek victory around 1200 B.C. requires the slaughter of troops along with the murder of the royal children, the progenitors of future warriors against the Greeks. Because of the pervasiveness of vengeance as a family and clan duty in ancient literature, Agamemnon's warriors hack apart Priam's male relatives and toss infants from the battlements. The slaughter of the Trojan innocents recurs in three plays by Euripides (see GREEK DRAMA)—*Andromache* (ca. 425 B.C.), *Hecuba* (ca. 424 B.C.), and *The Trojan Women* (415 B.C.), pacifist dramas that commiserate with female and child noncombatants involved in wars between rival empires. *The History of the Peloponnesian War* (ca. 400 B.C.) by Thucydides reminded Greek readers that the slaughter of islanders on Melos in 416 B.C. continued a Mediterranean bloodlust that had changed little over the centuries.

In the five centuries after the Italian navigator Christopher Columbus led the way west from Iberia to new wealth and dominion in the late 15th century, New World epic showed little variation in its depiction of indigenous races in Antigua, Brazil, Hawaii, Hispaniola, Martinique, Mexico, and Peru. A series of lost-world stories fills the pages of BARTOLOMÉ DE LAS CASAS's *A Brief Report of the Devastation of the Indies* (1542), a summation of predations against the AZTEC of Mexico City in *The True History of the Conquest of New Spain* (1568) by Bernal Díaz del Castillo (1492–1584) and in *Royal Commentaries of the Incas and General History of Peru* (1617), written by the New World's first mestizo historian, GARCILASO DE LA VEGA (El Inca). In *O Uraguai* (*Uruguay*, 1769) Brazilian-Portuguese writer, former Jesuit novice, and rebel José Basílio da Gama (1740–95), narrated the one-sided victory of Portuguese-Hispanic firepower against the prehistoric weaponry of some 30,000 Guarani of Uruguay in 1756. In five cantos, the action begins with carnage and enslavement, raises hopes for negotiation, and then returns to the inevitable massacre. Some 130 years later, Polynesian royalty wrote of issues of ethnic survival in *Hawaii's Story by Hawaii's Queen, Liliuokalani* (1898), the last native monarch of the islands. In the postmodern era, the enormity of racial obliteration fueled "Ovando" (1989), a monster FABLE of imperial audacity by the African-Carib-Scots author JAMAICA KINCAID.

Cleansing Australasia

In ways both subtle and overt, exposés of ethnic cleansing in the South Pacific damned Anglo-Saxons for subjugating aborigines in Australia and

Tasmania and severely reducing their populations. In *The History of Tasmania* (1852), the Reverend John West (1809–73), the chronicler of the island originally called Van Diemen's Land, promulgated the view of black natives as an eyesore and scourge. To the dismay of settlers in rude huts, he lumped into one complaint the "idle and uncleanly men, of different civil condition but of one class; tribes of dogs and natives" (West 1852, 67). In subsequent discussion, he justified Caucasian prejudice on the grounds that native Tasmanians are heathens and attackers of farmers and herders. Some insurgents became "reckless oppressors of the natives; often the accomplices of the bushrangers (outlaws)" (132). Such comments justified European indifference to the decimation of the Tasmanian Palawa, whose population was reportedly reduced from 5,000 to 300 between 1803 and 1833.

A more sympathetic view in *A History of Tasmania* (1884) by James Fenton (1864–1950) shifts from West's contempt for native communities to compassion for a doomed race. Fenton admits the genocidal effects on aborigines of starvation, disease, war, and "European vices" (Fenton 1884, 23). After a mass land grab, aborigines were "scattered abroad in broken families to mix with hostile tribes in the most inhospitable and unproductive regions of the interior" (23). Fenton quotes Governor William Sorell, who branded the extermination of natives as "repugnant to humanity, and disgraceful to the British character" (98). Despite governmental condemnation, stockmen, herders, and freebooters roam the land and "indulge a demoniacal propensity to torture the defenceless" (98). Fenton acknowledged that, under threat from immigrants, "aborigines were rapidly becoming extinct" (381).

On July 22, 1933, an editorial in the *West Australian* dropped subtlety for overt promotion of genocide. Of the half-caste, the author declared, "On the ground alone that he is a nuisance to us, we should hurry on his disappearance" (quoted in Scott 1999, 7). On October 3, 1933, a corroborative editorial in the *Daily News* turned wishful thinking into a quasi-scientific image of "a small stream of dirty water entering a larger clear stream. Eventually the colour of the smaller is lost" (7).

Australia also suffered the severe depletion of native communities after British colonization began in the late 18th century. In 1938, Xavier Herbert (1901–84), a novelist from Geraldton, Western Australia, earned the Miles Franklin Award for *Capricornia*, a fictional microcosm of ethnic erosion in Darwin in the Northern Territory. He introduces his subject by pointing out the skill of the aborigine at blocking past invasions in 1642 from Batavia (present-day Jakarta) in the East Indies by the Dutch East India Company. Once European settlers established themselves, they displaced the black race from their heritage, but left the inexperienced colonists with a harsh desert on which aborigines had flourished from prehistory. The white males who ravished Binghi "black velvet" (female aborigines) sired half-breeds—"yeller-fellers" or "comboes"—who were of no more value than dingoes (Herbert 1943, 11). According to Herbert, further sexual intercourse weakened the black strain along with native language and oral literature.

In 1999, the Australian author Kim Scott (b. 1957), a half-caste descendant of whites and Nyoongar (west coast) aborigines, stirred new theories of genocide with a counter-history, *Benang: From the Heart*, winner of the Western Australian Premier's book citation and a RAKA (Ruth Adeney Koori Award). The linguistic tour de force also earned him the Miles Franklin Award, the first received by an indigenous author. Scott researched the social and economic oppression of aborigines from 1915 to 1940 under Auber Octavius Neville, the architect of a state system of taking aboriginal children from their grandparents in an effort to strip black Australian youth of ties with native dialects and ethnicity, the subject of the film *Rabbit-Proof Fence* (2002). His findings produced stories of land swindles, "up-breeding" (eugenics), and the erasure of indigenous peoples, whom he first examined in *True Country* (1993). Scott relates the story of *Benang* through the mind of Harley, a half-caste who yearns for a true accounting of his past: "I found myself wishing to reverse that upbringing, not only for the sake of my own children, but also for my ancestors, and for their children in turn. And therefore, inevitably, most especially, for myself" (Scott 1999, 21). Estranged from their homeland, old timers reminisce about the ancestors whom whites massacred and the ghosts that haunt Ravensthorpe, a region as bleak for Australia's aborigines as Warsaw for Polish Jews or as Wounded Knee or the Little Big Horn for Native Americans. Of native resilience, Scott exults, "I am part of a much older story . . . with its rhythm of return, return, and remain" (495).

World War II

The 1930s and 1940s revived humanitarian concerns from which world leaders had retreated after the "civilizing" measures of their predecessors. The predations of Nazi Germany stocked literature with gruesome images of the Holocaust, an attempt by the Third Reich to exterminate Jews, Gypsies, dissidents, homosexuals, the senile, the insane, and the handicapped. In *Ecrits de guerre 1939–1944* (*Wartime Writings, 1939–1944*), the French pilot and fabulist Antoine de Saint-Exupéry (1900–44) excoriated Adolf Hitler's egotistic vision of Pan-Germanism and criminalized Nazism for its exclusion of outsiders from a future master race of blue-eyed blondes. Simultaneously, from the upstairs window of a spice shop in Amsterdam, Holland, Anne Frank (1929–45), the teenage author of *The Diary of a Young Girl* (1947), a monument to realistic CHILDREN'S LITERATURE, viewed individual acts of kindness and cruelty during the pervasive terrorism of central and northwestern Europe. In PROTEST at the treatment of ethnic Jews, at age 12, she began recording the slow subjugation of citizens, whom SS officers and the German army deprived of rations while rounding up Jews for extermination in gas ovens.

The barbarity of Hitler's "final solution" permeated decades of verse, fiction, screenplay, and memoir. In 1971, the Dutch freedom fighter Corrie ten Boom (1892–1983) published *The Hiding Place*, a memoir of her concealment of Jews in Haarlem, the Netherlands. Postwar honors from the State of Israel listed her with the Righteous among the Nations alongside Oskar Schindler, a Sudeten German manufacturer who saved some 1,200 Jews from extinction. His life story was the subject of *Schindler's Ark* (1982) by Australian author Thomas Keneally (b. 1935) and Stephen Spielberg's film *Schindler's List* (1993). Substantiating Frank's and ten Boom's observations, the Dutch-American novelist Johanna Reiss (b. 1932) described the valor of the Oostervelds, a family of Gentile rescuers in *The Upstairs Room* (1990). In this story, through the couple's evasions and trickery, eight-year-old Annie de Leeuw survives to publish a children's memoir replete with privation and terror.

The lingering horrors of organized extermination flourished in the writings of ELIE WIESEL and ISAAC BASHEVIS SINGER. Similarly haunted by wartime inhumanity, the Russian poet Yevgeny Yevtushenko returned to an anti-Semitic killing ground in his threnody "Babi Yar" (1961), a monument to the more than 30,000 Ukrainian Jews mass-murdered on September 29 and 30, 1941, at a ravine in Kiev. Killings continued at Babi Yar into 1943, with an estimated 100,000 or more Jews murdered. Anatoly Kuznetsov (1929–79) expanded on the grotesque with *Babi Yar* (1967), a documentary novel personalized in the style of John Hersey's *Hiroshima* (1946). The action of August 13, 1943, when the Nazis forced prisoners to exhume and burn corpses, moves methodically through mass shackling and the digging up of remains—"the final phase of Babi Yar—the attempt to efface it from history" (Kuznetsov 1966, 302). One corps of laborers disinters and rips apart corpses, then hauls them to furnaces. A separate corps, the goldseekers, pried jewelry from fingers and, with tongs, gold teeth from skulls. From the mass cremation of remains, the workers moved on to crushing bone fragments and spreading ashes over vegetable beds. Kuznetsov adds, "Prisoners on their last legs, those who couldn't work anymore, were also dumped in—alive," a reference to the filling of a mass grave (306).

In 1965, the Polish-American novelist Jerzy Kosinski (1933–91) wrote of a young boy's travels through wartime Poland in *The Painted Bird*, a novel with disputed autobiographical roots. Through an imagistic narrative, the author avoided historical method to produce an episodic allegory. The text places the lone boy in a pseudo-medieval time and place parallel in tone and atmosphere to eastern Europe under Nazi occupation. When fact collides with the surreal, the narrative jolts the reader as the boy encounters unutterable evil. Traumatic scenes—mass sodomy, eye excision, garrotting, snarling dog packs, amputation, skinning alive—take on a picaresque sadism. Identified as a "gypsy bastard," the boy survives, but he "felt as empty as a fish bladder punctured again and again and sinking into deep, muddy waters" (Kosinski 1976, 157), the soullessness that Elie Wiesel described as "night." Ironically, the boy moves hopefully toward Joseph Stalin's Russian ranks and seeks safety among faceless survivors he embraces as "my friends, the night people" (232). For its powerful fictional depiction of Polish depravity, the Polish government suppressed the book for a quarter of a century. Both dramatist Arthur Miller and humanist scholar Elie Wiesel rank the novel among significant Holocaust literature.

Sources

Collingwood-Whittick, Sheila, and Germaine Greer. *The Pain of Unbelonging: Alienation and Identity in Australasian Literature*. Amsterdam: Rodopi, 2007.

Fenton, James. *A History of Tasmania*. Hobart, Tas.: J. Welch and Sons, 1884.

Gama, Basilio da. *The Uruguay: A Historical Romance of South America*. Translated by Sir Richard F. Burton. Berkeley: University of California Press, 1982.

Herbert, Xavier. *Capricornia*. New York: D. Appleton-Century, 1943.

Kosinski, Jerzy. *The Painted Bird*. New York: Grove, 1976.

Kuznetsov, Anatoly. *Babi Yar.* New York: Dell, 1966.

Scott, Kim. *Benang*. Fremantle, Aust.: Fremantle Arts Centre Press, 1999.

———. *True Country*. Fremantle, Aust.: Fremantle Arts Centre Press, 1993.

Vice, Sue. *Holocaust Fiction*. Westport, Conn.: Routledge, 2000.

Virgil. *The Aeneid*. Translated by Patric Dickinson. New York: Mentor, 1961.

West, John. *The History of Tasmania*. Launceston, Tas.: Henry Dowling, 1852.

Ghazali, al- (Abu Hamid Mohammad ibn al-Ghazali) (1058–1111) *Persian philosopher and theologian*

The Persian sage Abu Hamid Mohammad ibn al-Ghazali demanded more from Islam than a meaningless obedience to temporal powers and religious hierarchy. A native of Tus (near present-day Mashhad, Iran), a Persian city that flourished under the Seljuk dynasty, al-Ghazali enjoyed puppetry, which he later related to the relationship between humanity and God. He and his younger brother Ahmad acquired reverence for orthodox Islam from their father, a self-educated wool spinner, the source of the name *al-Ghazali*. Orphaned in boyhood, al-Ghazali and Ahmad received a more formal education from their foster father, a Sufi religious teacher who taught them piety, scripture, and hagiography.

Learning stabilized al-Ghazali's life. At Gurgan in what is now north central Iran, at age 12, he began seven years of scholarly study that included astronomy, law, logic, and scripture. After five years of postgraduate work in jurisprudence at Nishapur, he served Nizamul al-Mulk Tusi, a vizier, or administrator, of the Seljuk Empire. A respected philosopher and affable person who made friends easily, al-Ghazali debated with the intellectuals of his day. After 1091, he lectured in Baghdad at the Nizamiyyah College, which the vizier al-Mulk founded in 1065 to teach Islamic law. The excellence of al-Ghazali's teaching earned him the sobriquet of the people's imam (professor), but the demands of the classroom thrust him into depression, apprehension, and emotional collapse at a time when shifting alliances in the Seljuk family and civil wars arising over succession beset Persia.

Over months of a physical and spiritual crisis, al-Ghazali, then 37, received treatment from the caliph's personal physician. In 1095, leaving the college principalship to his brother Ahmad, he abandoned his possessions, made a pilgrimage to Mecca, worked as a sweeper in Damascus, and, in the guise of a peasant ascetic, meditated in the minaret of the city's great mosque. Two years later, he returned to his hometown to live as a recluse. Later wanderings took him to Jerusalem and Hebron in Palestine and, around 1099, among Coptic Christians in Cairo and Alexandria. In 1106, he returned to the theology department at Nizamiyyah College, then retired a second time to mentor Sufi teachers at his monastery until he died of a chronic illness on December 18, 1111. In his final hours, he dressed himself in his shroud and welcomed death as a future union with an eternal light, which he called the Beloved.

al-Ghazali's Texts

In an era of dispute between Shiites and Sunnis, al-Ghazali, like his Sufi successor RUMI, concentrated on the sanctity of the inner human. He set himself the task of reconciling Sufist individualism with an overbearing Islamic orthodoxy. For his classes, he wrote *al-Risalah al-Qudsiyyah* (The Jerusalem tract, 1097), a handbook to Islam. He also composed a valuable manifesto, *al-Munqidh min al-Dalal* (*Deliverance from Error,* ca. 1108), a medieval AUTOBIOGRAPHY rich in the philosophical insight of a brilliant religious skeptic. By defending Sufism, he rescued Islam from the esoteric and legalistic debate of extremists. He made religion more accessible to the average seeker by promoting a return to personal piety for comfort, direction, and salvation. At the core of his faith lay his trust in the individual soul.

Written mostly in Arabic and sometimes in Persian, al-Ghazali's 70 titles, from monographs and textbooks to multivolume treatises on philosophy and mysticism, dealt with the challenges of his day. Through lucid prose, subtle parables, and hypothetical conversations, he freed Islamic thought of Hellenistic atheism and rationalism and denounced those clerics who based their thinking on Aristotle, Plato, and Socrates. In *Kimiya-yi Sa'adat* (*The Alchemy of Happiness,* 1097), al-Ghazali proposed that in place of Greek philosophy, individuals should recognize themselves as weak humans reaching beyond base desires and delusions for oneness with the Almighty. He defined misfortune as the hand of God directing human affairs.

Critics charge al-Ghazali with an all-knowing arrogance but admire his transcendental spiritualism, which rose above disdain of Greek philosophy and of Sunni-Shiite squabbles and blood feuds. In *Mishkat al-Anwar* (*The Niche of Lights,* ca. 1105), the philosopher exalts human intuition as a means to enlightenment and ethical justice. Without hesitation, he declares, "God is the highest and furthest light. . . . He is the real, true light—He alone, without any partner in that" (Ghazali 1998, 3). He pictures humans as individual microcosms created through God's mercy. In place of undisciplined mysticism and wonder, the philosopher encourages a mindset in worshippers that their only earthly tasks are to love God and prepare for eternity. Translated into Arabic, English, Turkish, and Urdu, his profound views on law, theology, and worship influenced the Jewish Kabbalists, Saint

Thomas Aquinas, and the French philosopher René Descartes.

Sources

Abrahamov, Binyamin. *Divine Love in Islamic Mysticism: The Teachings of al-Ghazali and al-Dabbagh.* London: Routledge, 2003.

Ghazali, al-. *The Niche of Lights.* Translated and annotated by David Buchman. Salt Lake City, Utah: Brigham Young University, 1998.

Mitha, Farouk. *Al-Ghazali and the Ismailis: A Debate on Reason and Authority in Medieval Islam.* London: I. B. Tauris, 2001.

Gilbert, Sir William Schwenck
(W. S. Gilbert) (1836–1911) *English satirist and librettist*

A powerful satirist of the imperialist establishment, Sir William Schwenck Gilbert, the self-proclaimed "doggerel bard," teamed with the composer Sir Arthur Sullivan (1842–1900) to create comic operas that dominated the British musical stage at home and abroad. A Londoner trained at Great Ealing School and King's College, Gilbert began formulating witty patter and burlesque in late childhood. He contemplated behind-the-lines military chaos during his army service. He was clerking for the Privy Council when a legacy of £300 set him free from a mediocre civil service post in 1863. In *Fun, Piccadilly Annual,* and *Punch,* he published extravagant satires on railway moguls, magistrates, the clergy, and frivolous, overly decorated officers, as well as spoofs of legal pettifoggers and tedious, ineffective bureaucracy, all of which he knew firsthand.

In collaboration with Frederic Clay and, later, Arthur Sullivan, Gilbert leveled jest and puns against the British establishment with light fare that found favor with Queen Victoria and King Edward VII. Supplying books and lyrics set to his collaborator's music, he produced four works with Clay over seven years before his partnership with Sullivan at the Savoy Operas established their fame. In *Princess Toto* (1876), his last work with Clay, he chuckles at King Portico, an absurd stickler for protocol who fears making a fool of himself in front of his subjects. His comic opera *H.M.S.*

Pinafore, or The Lass That Loved a Sailor (1878) ridicules the Royal Navy and the promotion of political boobs and bumblers intent on easy money to positions of authority.

Gilbert grew bolder with *The Mikado, or The Town of Titipu* (1885), in which he ridiculed the British penal system by writing of torture and capital punishment, using Japan as his setting. For self-important ministers, he created the Noble Lord Pish-Tush and Pooh-Bah, Lord High Everything Else, a title that journalists found irresistible. The opening chorus chides the British for stereotyping Asians as "queer and quaint" and turns the jest on England's stiff courtesies with the reminder, "If you think we are worked by strings . . . It is simply Court etiquette" (Gilbert and Sullivan 1996, 559). Another sharp poke at imperial superiority occurs in the song of Nanki-Poo, the prince in disguise who charges, "Wher'er our country's banner may be planted, / All other local banners are defied!" (561). Despite Gilbert's intent to ridicule the British, Japanese court officials took umbrage at implied slurs against Meiji the Great, the emperor of Japan.

Gilbert lobbed more incisive witticisms in *Utopia, Limited, or The Flowers of Progress* (1893), a native opera that turns into farce the acquisition of colonies through capitalism and through the privilege of limited liability. By having Princess Zara spearhead the anglicization of her South Sea island home, the text mocks the aspects of England that colonists chose to emulate, particularly complacency and cultural smugness at appointments of "an Earl of Thackeray and p'r'aps a Duke of Dickens" to the peerage (1051). Gilbert concludes that his island utopia has reached its goal: "She is England—with improvements, / Which we dutifully offer to our mother-land!" (1051).

Gilbert's 14th and final opera with Sullivan was *The Grand Duke*, a failure produced in 1896. He went on to write three more plays, the last being *The Hooligan* (1911), a grim, one-act account of a prisoner awaiting execution that strayed from his satirical, lighthearted works with Sullivan. Gilbert died four months after its production, on May 29, 1911. His exuberant jabs at snobbery and racism combined with serious biography in the film *Topsy Turvy* (1999), an Oscar winner for costume and makeup, starring Jim Broadbent as England's best comic librettist.

Sources

Crowther, Andrew. *Contradiction Contradicted: The Plays of W. S. Gilbert.* Cranbury, N.J.: Fairleigh Dickinson University Press, 2000.

Gilbert, William, and Arthur Sullivan. *The Complete Annotated Gilbert and Sullivan.* New York: W. W. Norton, 1996.

Gilgamesh *(Epic of Gilgamesh)* (ca. 1800 B.C.)

The oldest known HERO tale, the *Epic of Gilgamesh* is the written version of a frame narrative that survives in the Akkadian language. Episodes detail the quest of Gilgamesh (ca. 2600 B.C.), a Mesopotamian god-king who raised the walled city of Uruk in Sumer (present-day Erech, Iraq) during the region's first dynasty. Traders and colonists spread his influence north of the Persian Gulf and built satellite cities with slave labor along the alluvial fan of the Fertile Crescent between the Tigris and Euphrates rivers (present-day southern Iraq). Written in cuneiform on 12 clay tablets, *Gilgamesh* survived in the archives of Assurbanipal, king of Nineveh around 650 B.C. The narrative reflects elements of the Perseus myth in which a young challenger escapes the plots of the Babylonian king to overcome a PROPHECY promising a hero of great strength and daring. An arrogant ruler who kills men and despoils women, Gilgamesh forms a brotherly friendship with Enkido, a literary foil. Unlike the sophisticated king, the semicivilized Enkidu, a fount of innocence and compassion, lives in the wild and roams the savannahs with gazelles and other beasts until a temple priestess introduces him to romance and carnality. He becomes friends with Gilgamesh after losing a wrestling match with the king. Together, in Syria on the Lebanese border, Gilgamesh and the outlander quell the sacred demon Humbaba in an archetypal battle of good against evil. The warriors' triumph over the Bull of Heaven, an embodiment of drought, raises threats from the gods for impiety, a charge shared by the Greek heroes Hercules and Odysseus and by the Hebrews Moses and Samson.

As a monument to empire building, the epic salutes ancient Mesopotamia as an urban civilization, which flourished with irrigated farming and river cultures in the Indus and Nile valleys. The narrative describes the quest of Gilgamesh for solace and immortality after his friend Enkidu dies and goes to the underworld as a sacrifice to compensate for the sins of Gilgamesh. Like Achilles mourning Patroclus in Homer's *Iliad*, Gilgamesh succumbs to sorrow. In outcries similar to the mourning of David for Jonathan in 2 Samuel 1:26, Gilgamesh honors his soulmate Enkidu as "the ax upon my belt and the bow in my weak hand, the sword within my sheath, the shield that covered me in battle, my happiest robe" (*Epic of Gilgamesh* 1992, 48–49). Twice thwarted in his effort to obtain eternal life, Gilgamesh despairs after a lengthy foray into the surreal land of the gods. The winemaker Siduri, like the Greek wine god Dionysus, offers pragmatic wisdom: She advises Gilgamesh to delight in the everyday joys of feasting, good company, cleanliness, and family life. She explains, "We frail humans die as you yourself must someday do. What is best for us to do is now to sing and dance" (64).

Literary historians revere the Mesopotamian epic for its humanistic theme of equality in death for all living beings, even god-kings. Chastened by loss, Gilgamesh returns to Uruk and contents himself with earthly conquest. Translator Danny Jackson renders the sensate pleasures of experiencing the architecture of Gilgamesh: "No one else ever built such walls. Climb Uruk's Tower and walk about on a windy night. Look. Touch. Taste. Sense. What force creates such mass?" (1). At the gates of Uruk, a lump of lapis lazuli establishes the role of art in empires by preserving the god-king's accomplishments carved for the edification of future leaders. In the final stave, Gilgamesh remarks, "Study the base, the brick, the old design. Is it permanent as can be? Does it look like wisdom designed it?" (84). The questions attest to a maturity in the king, who has experienced firsthand the transience of human powers.

Sources

The Epic of Gilgamesh. Translated by Danny P. Jackson. Wauconda, Ill.: Bolchazy-Carducci, 1992.

Mobley, Gregory. *Samson and the Liminal Hero in the Ancient Near East*. London: Continuum, 2006.

goddess lore

The literature of goddess cults expresses a view of worship that appeals to the human aspect of theology. The concept of the maternal nurturer invigorates much of the literature of empire, including prayers to the earth mother in the Atharva-veda, the fourth of the Hindu sacred texts; embrace of a world mother in the DAODEJING (*Tao-Te Ching*, ca. 300 B.C.); the Scots poet Joanna Baillie's honor to a Hindu queen in *Ahalya Baee* (1849); the Kikuyu reverence for the Danish planter and storyteller ISAK DINESEN in her memoir *Out of Africa* (1937); and the verses of BIRAGO DIOP, a Senegalese poet-storyteller. Veneration of the divine female permeated the Sumerian Empire with reverence for coitus, animal and plant fecundity, marriage, and death preceding rebirth. The supreme goddess Inanna, or Ishtar, a mythic superpower figure, appeared in Uruk (present-day Erech, Iraq) around 4,000 B.C. and starred in the world's first love story. She flourishes in poetic CREATION LORE as the orchardist of a holy garden and, in some versions, the sister of the warrior king Gilgamesh (see GILGAMESH), who arranges her betrothal. Similar in jubilant tone and rhapsodic style to the EPITHALAMIUM the Song of Solomon, "The Courtship of Inanna and Dumuzi" (ca. 2800 B.C.) rejoices in a physical union between a well-mated king and queen, he a shepherd and she the epitome of agrarianism in the Fertile Crescent between the Tigris and Euphrates rivers. Hymns to Inanna's power unite her with natural phenomena:

> Your quivering hand causes the midday heat to hover over the sea.
> Your nighttime stalking of the heavens chills the land with its dark breeze.
> Holy Inanna, the riverbanks overflow with the flood-waves of your heart.
> (Wolkstein and Kramer 1983, 95).

The urban Sumerian Empire archived clay cuneiform tablets extolling the valiant Inanna, passionate in bed and victorious, prestigious, and glorious in combat.

Native American lore perpetuated a similar glimpse of duality in goddesses. In the Mayan Empire, the "Hymn to the All-Mother" (ca. 1500

B.C.) honored Teteoinan, a maternal ancestor of Mexican aborigines who sprang from paradise to sprinkle the earth with yellow blossoms. A matriarch like the Greek Persephone and the Roman Ceres allied with abundance and delicate beauty, she exudes the radiance of the Sumerian Inanna: "Hail to the goddess who shines in the thorn bush like a bright butterfly" (quoted in Brinton 1890, 28). In a desert culture, where cactus sprouts tender blooms in delicate hues, Teteoinan symbolizes the resilience of the vulnerable. She protects wild animals and serves humanity as "an ever-fresh model of liberality toward all flesh" (29). The specifics of her benevolence center on fertility and midwifery. Christian proselytizers syncretized her cult with the Virgin Mary to produce Our Lady of Guadalupe, a less pantheistic goddess figure whose aura parallels the female mysticism of CRUSADER LORE.

The Female Divine in India
The *Lakshmi Tantra* (ca. A.D. 950), a treasured Indian text inscribed on Himalayan birch bark, contributes a womanly perspective to the TANTRAS (ca. 1050), scriptural Sanskrit writings of the Pala Empire (750–1174). The author seeks religious illumination through the sacred female, who achieved prominence during the rise of medieval feudalism and energized Buddhism and Hinduism during a period of challenge to orthodox Christianity, Islam, and Judaism. In the description of analyst Mandakranta Bose, "The goddess combines the dynamic polarity of contrasting traits: benign and terrific, erotic and demure, motherly and virginal, saintly and heroic, ferociously powerful yet calm and silent" (Bose 2000, 113). The supreme Vishnu's queen and bestower of grace, the goddess, like the maternal Haumea of Hawaiian lore, offers believers abundance, contentment, wellness, and the fullness of creation.

Unlike patriarchal scripture, the *Lakshmi Tantra* promotes self-discovery, gender equality, and an embrace of passion and humanism. Through poetic dialogue between seeker and sage, the narrative refutes the blood taboos of the menses and challenges orthodox notions of female guilt and sin, the wrongs committed by the Greek Pandora and the Hebrew Eve. The Indian narrative sanctions worship of the "goddess whose countenance radiates grace, fulfills every desire, satisfies the yearnings of the passionate, and leads to the state of self-realization" (*Laksmi Tantra* 1972, 5). The opening passage begs wisdom—"a boon, O great goddess, then reveal to me the nature of truth. . . . By what means canst thou be fathomed?" (6–7). Another version of the goddess cult appears in ode form in the *Saktisamagama Tantra* (ca. 1000), which takes its name from the creative energy of the goddess Sakti. The ode declares woman the universal creator:

> There is no jewel rarer than woman,
> There is not, nor has been, nor will be;
> There is no kingdom, no wealth, to be compared
>   with a woman;
> There is not, nor has been, nor will be, any holy
>   place like unto a woman
> (Saktisamagama Tantra 1978, 115).

As a result of the goddess cult, Indian women attained priesthoods, channeled sacred revelation, and taught female and male disciples Hindu principles.

The Goddess Cult in Europe
European depictions of goddess powers, including the graceful verse of MARIE DE FRANCE and LUÍS VAZ DE CAMÕES's Portuguese epic *The Lusiads* (1572), maintain contact with orthodox religion. Preceding Camoes's veneration of the goddess Venus in his epic, a tradition of cult worship of the Virgin Mary flourished among troubadours during the reign of 13th-century Spanish king of Castile-León, Alfonso X El Sabio (The Wise), the putative compiler of Iberian trouvère (troubadour) songs. The illuminated solo collection *Cantigas de Santa María* (Songs to the Virgin Mary, ca. 1283), 420 court tributes written in the Galician dialect of Castile, reflects Mary's patronage of Alfonso as well as peasant beliefs in *miragres* (miracles), honor to pilgrims, immersion in Spanish Catholic liturgy, and Andalusian festivals celebrating the mother of Jesus. Like the dual view of the wise and powerful goddess Athena in the Greek poet Hesiod's *Homeric Hymns* (ca. 520 B.C.), the song cycle pictures Mary as the maternal healer of the sick and the warrior rescuer of Constantinople from the Ottomans in the years following the Fifth Crusade and preceding Spain's full involvement in empire building.

A subset of violent verses focuses on persecution. The fifth poem characterizes Holy Mary as the rescuer of Beatrice, a Roman empress ousted by the emperor on the basis of lies told by his brother. The cycle of wrongs contains anti-Semitic expressions of Jewish persecution of Christians, as in "Christ Image Pierced by Jews" and "The Chorister Killed by Jews," as well as the Jews' torment of their own children. Inventive versification, such as the somber chant "Rosa das rosas" (Rose of roses), inflates sacred devotion to courtly love and subdued eroticism. The crossover from piety to lust marks "Rosa de beldad'e de parecer" (Rose of beauty and appearance), which ends with the singer longing to possess his idol, even if he has to swear off affairs with other women. The romantic subtext presages the emergence of the female icon from godhood to full womanhood, the object of Arthurian commentary on the flawed Queen Guenevere.

Sources

Alfonso X. *Songs of Holy Mary of Alfonso X, the Wise: A Translation of the Cantigas de Santa María.* Translated by Kathleen Kulp-Hill. Tempe: Arizona Center for Medieval and Renaissance Studies, 2000.

Bose, Mandakranta. *Faces of the Feminine in Ancient, Medieval, and Modern India.* Oxford: Oxford University Press, 2000.

Brinton, Daniel Garrison, ed. *Rig Veda Americanus: Sacred Songs of the Ancient Mexicans,* with a Gloss in Nahuatl. Philadelphia: D. G. Brinton, 1890.

Laksmi Tantra: A Pancaratra Text. Translated by Sanjukta Gupta. Amsterdam: Brill, 1972.

O'Callaghan, Joseph F. *Alfonso X and the Cantigas de Santa Maria: A Poetic Biography.* Amsterdam: Brill, 2000.

Saktisamagama Tantra. Translated by Binaytosh Bhattacharya. Baroda, India: Gaekwad Oriental series, 1978.

Wolkstein, Diane, and Samuel Noah Kramer. *Inanna, Queen of Heaven and Earth: Her Stories and Hymns from Sumer.* New York: Harper & Row, 1983.

Goethe, Johann Wolfgang von (1749–1832)
German poet, dramatist, and fabulist

A man of many interests and talents, Johann Wolfgang von Goethe epitomizes the writer's quandary at the fall of an empire. He was born to the lawyer Johann Caspar Goethe and raised among prominent intellectual burghers in Frankfurt, an imperial free city of the Holy Roman Empire. As a child, he studied with his father and a number of tutors, and received a far-ranging education. He read law at Leipzig University from 1765 to 1768 and wrote his first play, *The Lover's Caprice,* in 1767. After an illness, he finished his studies in Strasbourg and then began practicing law in 1771 while also pursuing his writing interests.

With his early verse, Goethe mocked the corruption and instability of the Holy Roman Empire, founded by CHARLEMAGNE on Christmas Day, A.D. 800, and then in its final years. As a citizen, Goethe recognized that politics could never fulfill its grandiose promises. In the tragic drama *Götz von Berlichingen* (1773), a chivalric tale that assured his fame, Goethe manages a tightrope act: Though he respects the then Hapsburg emperor Joseph II, he introduces *Zigeunerromantik* (Gypsy romanticism), a popular concept of the Rom as *Naturvölker* (nature people)—free-spirited wanderers and outcasts who prefer the freedom of nature to the confines of civilization. The poet indirectly charges the absolutist political federation with decadence, hedonism, and senility. The text portrays self-adulatory imperial portraits as a mockery, both of dignity and of artistic principle, and accuses judges of delaying justice through ineffective deliberation, settling only 60 out of 20,000 cases per year. The narrative attacks Holy Roman Emperor Maximilian I (1459–1519) as the last of the knights, a veiled criticism of outmoded ideals and governance since his accession as emperor in 1508. In the introduction to *Puppenspiel* (Puppet plays, 1774), a series of political farces, Goethe dismisses all emperors and their realms as, at best, illusory and temporary.

During the Age of Enlightenment, Goethe came under the influence of Gotthold Ephraim Lessing (1729–81), one of western Europe's revivers of the didactic FABLE. Goethe's bestiary *Reineke Fuchs* (*Reynard the Fox,* 1794), a complex frame narrative composed in the style of the Indian PANCHATANTRA (The Fables of Bidpai, ca. 200 B.C.), preceded by five years Napoleon Bonaparte's assumption of the post of first consul of France. In an animal court scene reminiscent of the Hohenstauffen dynasty

(1138–1254), the beasts tell Noble the lion their complaints against the fox's crimes:

> Nought sacred is there in his impious eyes:
> His soul is fixed upon ungodly pelf.
> Although the Nobles, nay, the King himself
> Should suffer loss of health and wealth and all
> And the whole State to hopeless ruin fall
> (Goethe 1954, 4).

Through the conventions of fable, Goethe illustrates the intrigue that underlies an empire. At the foot of the gallows, the fox cunningly escapes hanging by casually referring to buried treasure and to an assassination plot against Noble, a symbolic pairing of greed and fear, the emotions that impel rulers to the throne. Reynard compounds the image of venality by donning a pilgrim's robe and staff. He flees the court to kill again and to boast of his villainy by stuffing a rabbit head in his hunting pouch. The ongoing threat to Noble forces him to elevate Reynard to lord high chancellor, a promotion that satisfies his ambitions while keeping him under the eyes of the lion.

Harbinger of Chaos

In 1797, Goethe revamped a Syrian fable into "Der Zauberlehrling" ("The Sorcerer's Apprentice"), a folk tale, told in verse, about a foolish helper's lesson in abuse of power. The original, a product of the Roman Empire's second century, was the work of the Assyrian rhetorician and satirist Lucian of Samosata (ca. A.D. 125–ca. 180), who developed the story as an episode of *Philopseudes* (Lover of lies, ca. A.D. 175), an interlinking narrative of dialogues and supernatural tales. In an effort to halt a magic broomstick from drowning the necromancer's laboratory with water, Goethe's inept helper whimpers, "Stop, now stop! / You have granted / All I wanted" (Goethe 1871, 98). The master, a symbol of godly power, intercedes to supply the magic word to forestall catastrophe from a would-be magician's foolishness. Walt Disney used the fool tale as a segment of the animated feature film *Fantasia* (1940), featuring the music of Paul Dukas and Mickey Mouse as the water carrier.

Goethe's whimsical prediction of calamity came true in the first week of 1806 with the collapse of the Holy Roman Empire after Napoleon's recent victory at the battle of Austerlitz. In his AUTOBIOGRAPHY *Dichtung und Wahrheit* (*Poetry and Truth*, 1811–33), Goethe chooses the language of physical decline and infection to characterize a morbidity that had sapped the empire under its last leader, Francis II. However, during the Napoleonic era, the poet rejected liberalism and Prussian nationalism as threats to a vulnerable public order represented by Duke Karl August of Saxe-Weimar-Eisenach.

In parts 1 and 2 of his drama *Faust* (1826, 1831), Goethe lauded the rise of Frederick the Great during the Seven Years' War and mocked the tedium of the Augsburg court and of pro-imperial sloganeering. Probably his best-known work, the play is a classic study of ambition and dynastic pretensions as predecessors of downfall. Part 1 highlights the inhumanity of social standards in the stigmatizing of Margaret, an unmarried mother who drowns her infant to ward off the shame of bastardy. A broader commentary on rule occurs in scene five, when Brander, a minor character, scorns an imperial anthem: "A nasty song! Fie! a political song— / A most offensive song! / Thank God, each morning, therefore, / That you have not the Roman realm to care for!" (Goethe 1898, 85). Brander exults that he is neither the chancellor nor the kaiser of the Austro-German Empire.

During the writing of part 2, the playwright started to become nostalgic about the golden age of empire. In a prophetic scenario in act 3, he reenacts revolution as a Walpurgis Night, a hellish Viking holiday during which pygmies slaughter the aristocratic herons of Pharsalia. In the dark preceding the fight, the witch Erichtho comments on the establishment of political primacy: "No one grants the realm unto another: not him whose might achieved / And rules it, none; for each, incompetent to rule / His own internal self, is all too fain to sway / His neighbor's will, even as his haughty mind inclines" (Goethe 1899, 103).

The layering of past glories amid the follies of imperialism suggests that Goethe romanticized German history only so far as his imagination could substantiate its dreams. His romanticism impacted German-Jewish poet NELLY SACHS, and his GOTHIC outlook influenced the English terror writer MATTHEW GREGORY LEWIS.

Sources

Goethe, Johann Wolfgang von. *Faust: A Tragedy.* Translated by Bayard Taylor. Boston: Houghton, Mifflin, 1898.

———. *Faust: A Tragedy, the Second Part.* Translated by Bayard Taylor. Boston: Houghton, Mifflin, 1899.

———. *Poems and Ballads of Goethe.* New York: Holt and Williams, 1871.

———. *The Story of Reynard the Fox.* New York: Heritage Press, 1954.

Williams, John R. *The Life of Goethe: A Critical Biography.* London: Blackwell, 2001.

Gogol, Nikolay Vasilyevich (Nikolai Vasilievich Gogol) (1809–1852) *Ukrainian dramatist, essayist, and fiction writer*

A sharp and perceptive satirist, Nikolay Gogol used his writing to effectively level charges of imperial pomposity at the Russian Empire. Born in Ukraine, he aimed his sights beyond the confines of his native Cossack village of Sorochyntsi, north of the Crimea, and began his writing career in a boarding school at Nezhin on the Oster River. He read Homer in Greek and submitted his own poems to the school magazine, *Parnassian Dung.* At age 19, he left school and journeyed to St. Petersburg, where he began to attempt a literary career. Six years later, he revealed his poor education when he failed as a lecturer on medieval history at St. Petersburg University.

Gogol presented concepts of empire more forcibly and eloquently on paper than from the lectern. In his essay "On the Teaching of World History," published in the two-volume *Arabesques* (1835), he admired imperial power: "The first ruler of the world, Cyrus, with his fresh and powerful nation, the Persians, subdued and forcibly united nations of differing characteristics" (Gogol 1982, 46–47). He was less impressed with the methods of the Romans and Huns. His treatise accuses Julius Caesar of "[trampling] Britain underfoot" and charges Attila with unleashing "ominous retribution," like a predator lying in wait for prey. Into the breach left by the Huns' foray into the Roman Empire, the rise of Christianity provided a hold on citizens' minds that was beyond the ken of emperors.

Gogol developed his ideas on the Mongol hordes in "A History of Little Russia" and "On the Movement of Nations at the End of the Fifth Century" (both published in *Arabesques*) as the unforeseen salvation of his homeland from Lithuanian conquerors. The rescue began with the Tatars' scorched-earth policy: "Ancient Kiev razed to the ground; desolation and wasteland—that's how this wretched country looked! Frightened peoples fled either to Poland or Lithuania" (100). In his opinion, so great a challenge to survival resurrected a life force from squabbling Russians and "[shaped] an audacious, passionate nation of character" (101). To the south, the rise of the Slavonic Cossacks performed a similar service to Russia by using the cavalry to halt the spread of Islam into Europe.

Russian Nationalism

Like VIRGIL with the Roman Empire, Japanese poet KAKINOMOTO NO HITOMARO with the Nara empire, and RUDYARD KIPLING with the British Raj, Gogol exhibited a chauvinistic nationalism regarding Russia and anticipated the Russification of rural tribes through cyclical reform and solidarity. In two volumes of macabre short fiction and two of prose in arabesques, he developed his interest in empires as subjects for art, including admiration for Attila the Hun's magnetic leadership of a cavalry force in "A View of the Formation of Little Russia" (1835) and examination of early ninth-century Greek warfare with Arabs in the essay "Al-Mamun" (1835). The latter, set in a turbulent period of Khurasan history (present-day Afghanistan, Iran, Tajikistan, Turkmenistan, and Uzbekistan) during the rule of al-Mamun, the caliph of Baghdad, ponders the clash of ideas from markedly unlike civilizations on issues of social order. Gogol lauded the strengths of Harun al-Rashid, al-Mamun's father, a unifier whom the essay declares "a philosopher-monarch, a philosopher-politician, a warrior-monarch and monarch litterateur" (Gogol 1982, 135). The characterization anticipates later accolades to the hypothetical "renaissance man," the master of skills.

Gogol focused closer to his birthplace in a scathing three-act comedy, *The Government Inspector* (1836), a stage play similar in theme to GEORGE

ORWELL's classic anti-imperial essay set in Burma, "Shooting an Elephant" (1936). Gogol's premise, the unsuitability of the foppish clerk Khlestakov for high office, outraged conservative Russians but won the approval of Czar Nicholas I, who ordered an end to the play's suppression. Playgoers laughed at a case of mistaken identity that has a frontier mayor and his underlings kowtowing to the wrong man and offering bribes, a testimony to frontier corruption among civil servants far from the emperor's control. In explanation of the incognito visit, Judge Lyapkin-Tyapkin declares, "That's it. Holy Russia is going to war, and the ministers have sent this Official to find out if there is any treason here" (Gogol 1931, 8). The intelligentsia overreacted so lethally to the SATIRE that Gogol went abroad, journeying to Germany, Switzerland, and Paris before finally settling in Rome in a self-imposed exile that lasted 12 years.

Humanism and Suppression

Censors limited Gogol's access to the Russian press to publish a picaresque novel, *Dead Souls* (1842). A masterwork of social criticism, the narrative describes a buying spree by the intriguer Pavel Ivanovich Chichikov, who purchases 400 deceased serfs, still registered on the roll books of local landowners, to enhance his social status. State editors ameliorated the title by publishing the novel as *The Adventures of Chichikov; or, Dead Souls*, but they failed to soften the impact of Gogol's merciless censure of slavery. He characterized owners and traders of human chattels as monsters hiding behind the sanctity of Russian Orthodoxy, an elitist hierarchy that avoided questions of human rights for serfs. Of the privilege of serf owners, Gogol makes a stunning jab at proportional "hauteur and noblesse": "We have men so wise and adroit that they will speak to a landowner possessing but two hundred serf-souls in a way altogether different from that in which they will to one who possesses three hundred of them" (Gogol 1996, 44, 43). To achieve absurdism, the author carries the variations in courtesy to citing possession of one million serfs, a token of his outrage at the flesh market.

In 1842, Gogol completed a pictorial folk story, *Taras Bulba*, a short historical novel based on the brotherhood of Cossack hordes who raided and fought Poles and Jews in the 15th and 16th centuries. The theme of chivalric pride and divine mission along the Don and Volga rivers exemplifies Russian resistance to Poles, Tartars, and Turks. The soldier's sacrifice dominates the thunderous narrative with evidence of voluntary Cossack suffering for the common good: "All had laid down their heads, all were lost. Some had given their lives in honourable battle, others, bereft of bread and water, had perished amidst the Crimean salt marshes, whilst a few had fallen into shameful bondage" (Gogol 1907, 237). A grotesque story of war and retribution that costs the title character his sons and his own death tied to a tree and set aflame, the plot served as a film vehicle for the actor Yul Brynner in 1962. Confused in his last days, in late February 1852, Gogol burned unpublished writings that might have contributed to his commentary on imperialism.

Sources

Figes, Orlando. *Natasha's Dance: A Cultural History of Russia*. London: Macmillan, 2003.

Gogol, Nikolay. *Arabesques*. Translated by Alexander Tulloch. Ann Arbor, Mich.: Ardis, 1982.

———. *Dead Souls*. Translated by Bernard Guilbert Guerney. New Haven, Conn.: Yale University Press, 1996.

———. *The Inspector General*. Translated by John Anderson. New York: Samuel French, 1931.

———. *Taras Bulba: A Story of the Dnieper Cossacks*. Translated by Beatrice C. Baskerville. London: Walter Scott, 1907.

Goldman, Emma   See PROTEST LITERATURE.

Good Earth, The   See BUCK, PEARL S.

Gordimer, Nadine (1923–) *South African fiction writer*

A freedom fighter for native civil rights, Nadine Gordimer won the 1991 Nobel Prize in literature for a collection of humanitarian writings that three times incurred authoritarian censorship. Born of Lithuanian-Jewish and English parentage in Springs, Transvaal, a mining hamlet on the outskirts of Johannesburg, South Africa, Gordimer gained a perspective on the "otherness" fostered by imperialism from her father, Isidore Gordimer, a jeweler and watchmaker who left Lithuania in a self-imposed exile from the Russian Empire. Self-educated, she read the fiction of Russian authors Anton Chekhov and FYODOR DOSTOYEVSKY. After two semesters at the University of the Witwatersrand in Johannesburg, she advanced from juvenilia to publishing stories in the *Guardian*, *New Statesman*, *New Yorker*, and *New York Times*. Between 1961 and 1991, Gordimer won international regard for her denunciation of British depersonalization of blacks and of post-colonial obstacles to free speech and civil rights in South Africa.

Gordimer began examining motivations for activism with an autobiographical novel, *The Lying Days* (1953), a forerunner of her antiapartheid novel *Burger's Daughter* (1979), which captures the explosive emotions of the Soweto uprising, a series of riots of blacks in 1976. A decade later, she challenged the legality of antimiscegenation laws with *Occasion for Loving* (1963). Her regard for Zulu culture undergirds *The Conservationist* (1974), a Booker Prize winner that critics compare to OLIVE SCHREINER's settler novel *The Story of an African Farm* (1883). Gordimer's work expanded from village pettiness to compassion for the alien, the subject of *The Pickup* (2002). By placing South African cosmopolite Julie Summers in a bicultural relationship with Abdu-Ibrahim ibn Musa, an Afro-Arab immigrant, and resettling the couple in his unspecified homeland, the narrative examines from opposing angles the dilemmas and choices of a woman who experiences displacement.

Gordimer gripped readers' attention with her reversal of ethnic and cultural roles. The conflict in *July's People* (1981), a novel on human interdependence, prophesies the ultimate end to racism reminiscent of colonial times and the debunking of a master-servant relationship, symbolized by the possession of car keys. By following a white family to the village of the title character and examining their verbal exchanges, Gordimer replaces white pride with reliance on a petty chief for shelter. Maureen Smales, the white female protagonist,

accepts the reversal of roles in appealing to a black authority figure: "It's a question of courtesy, apparently. I don't think there's anything sinister. Paying respects to the chief—" (Gordimer 1982, 102). Her hesitance stimulates a shift in white perspective from their position as a privileged ethnic group to respect for a different race. Like her contemporary novelist Doris Lessing, Gordimer dramatized anticolonial struggle as a crusade for national identity.

Sources

Barnard, Rita. *Apartheid and Beyond: South African Writers and the Politics of Place*. Oxford: Oxford University Press, 2006.

Gordimer, Nadine. *Burger's Daughter*. London: Penguin, 1980.

———. *July's People*. London: Penguin, 1982.

———. *The Pickup*. London: Penguin, 2002.

Yelin, Rouise. *From the Margins of Empire*. Ithaca, N.Y.: Cornell University Press, 1998.

gothic literature

The double dealing and tyranny of imperialism suit the secrecy and conspiracy that characterizes gothic literature. A pervasive genre in world literature, gothic stories convey some classic themes, such as that of the strong bullying the weak, as seen in ROBERT LOUIS STEVENSON's writings of the Pacific, Nigerian author AMOS TUTUOLA's *The Palm-Wine Drinkard* (1952) and *My Life in the Bush of Ghosts* (1954), AMY TAN's Chinese historical novel *The Bonesetter's Daughter* (2001), ISAAC BASHEVIS SINGER's PROPHECY of the Nazi empire in *Der Sotn in Gorey* (Satan in Goray, 1935), and the Japanese ghost stories translated by Lafcadio Hearn. Subtextual implications of barbarism, racism, miscegenation, insanity, and xenophobia dominate RUTH PRAWER JHABVALA's novella *Heat and Dust* (1975) and JAMAICA KINCAID's conquest allegory "Ovando" (1989). The same themes undergird Oscar Wilde's biblical play *Salomé* (1893), which portrays necrophilia celebrated at Herod Antipas's Galilean palace. At the center of the action is the title character's sensual solo performance for which she claims the severed head of Jokanaan (John the Baptist), the harbinger of the Jewish messiah. In a similar stress on tone and atmosphere, the Argentine fiction writer Jorge Luis Borges, a purveyor of tales of victimization, anthologized episodes of robbery, piracy, and enslavement in *Historia universal de la infamia* (*A Universal History of Infamy*, 1935), a collection depicting crime in eighth-century Persia, late 17th-century Japan, and early 19th-century China.

In the postcolonial psychological novel *Wide Sargasso Sea* (1966), set in Jamaica's interior, the Caribbean author JEAN RHYS captured dance and ritual from the African diaspora in a rural setting. By sympathizing with Antoinette Cosway, the bartered bride, Rhys dramatizes feminist issues alongside the wrongs that English overlords commit against black islanders. Other examples of gothic terror and pathos, such as the body of Central American cautionary tales about "La Llorona," the weeping wraith of an AZTEC-Mexica sex slave and interpreter named Malinche, increase emotional involvement in the plight of indigenous characters whom society has muzzled and marginalized by race, class, or gender. In ballads and ghost stories, Malinche wanders the night after she has murdered her children to save them from Hernán Cortés and his Spanish conquistadores. Her presence in the darkness is both a warning for and a blessing on Indian and Mestizo women under the control of European adventurers.

Gothic Conventions

Gothic literary conventions display many stylistic details of the literature of empire. An ominous tone can project an author's attitude toward a work's subject and moral stance, as in NIKOLAY GOGOL's depictions of an outcast in his Cossack novel *Taras Bulba* (1842) and in Nathaniel Hawthorne's *The Scarlet Letter* (1850), a novel of ostracism exposing Puritan self-righteousness in the Massachusetts Bay Colony. Doom haunts anti-Semitic episodes about the wandering Jew in George Croly's *Salathiel: A Story of the Past, the Present, and the Future* (1828), a prophecy novel set in Jerusalem during the first-century regimes of the Roman emperors Nero and Titus. In an expression of hope, the exile observes the decay of his tormentors—Pompey the Great, Julius Caesar, and Mark Antony: "Every military genius, the natural product of a system that lived but on military fame, disappeared: the brilliant diversity of warlike talent, that shone on the very verge of the succession of the Caesars, sank, like falling stars" (Croly 1828, 224–225).

The establishment of Christianity increased the scope of surreal terrors. The somber, lethal atmosphere of Dan Brown's *The Da Vinci Code* (2003) suits a 21st-century reprise of medieval CRUSADER LORE. Gothic symbolism—codes, mazes, ambush, a mystic brotherhood—heightens ambiguous scenarios of alienation and stalking as well as calculated bloodbaths, all carried out to ensure the secrecy of Jesus's marriage to Mary Magdalene and their founding of a Christian dynasty. Similarly, Edgar Allan Poe's horror story "The Pit and the Pendulum" (1843) fantasizes about the Napoleonic general Antoine de Lasalle and the French army rescuing an unnamed prisoner from near death in a pit in Toledo during the Spanish Inquisition (then in its final years).

Popular Fiction

From the beginning of the romantic era, European and American readers clamored for exotic lore brought to their shores by seamen, mercenaries, traders, and civil servants of empires. Narratives laced with unusual settings and wish fulfillment paralleled a minor European revolution in architecture, landscaping, furniture, and table settings that saw the introduction of Chinese designs, pagodas, and dragon motifs on fabrics and murals. Home libraries displayed ornate editions of the *Rubáiyát of Omar Khayyám* (ca. 1130); *The* THOUSAND AND ONE NIGHTS (ca. A.D. 942); VOLTAIRE's *Candide* (1759); and Samuel Johnson's quest FABLE *The History of Rasselas, Prince of Abissinia* (1759), the story of royal Ethiopian siblings, Nekayah and Rasselas, who comb Egypt for utopian happiness. The English writer John Hawkesworth (ca. 1715–73) published a redemption plot, *Almoran and Hamet* (1761), set among Persian royalty; the English poet John Langhorne (1735–79) popularized Mesopotamian lore in *Solyman and Almena* (1762), a quest tale based on the exoticism and moralizing of *The Thousand and One Nights*. In the story, a gender turnabout in Delhi, India, capital of the Mogul Empire, has placed wives and concubines in charge of civil and military appointments. To find bliss with Almena, the protagonist Solyman sails with her on a seagoing trader to the Persian Gulf. The Irish romanticist Frances Chamberlaine Sheridan (1724–66) covered similar ground in her posthumously published *The History of Nourjahad* (1767), a tale of a Persian sybarite seeking happiness and fulfillment. Like Solyman, Nourjahad recoils from the thoughts of owning a harem and has no illusions about grandeur and sovereignty: "I shall there never aspire at high employments, nor would I be the sultan of Persia, if I might; for what addition would that make to my happiness?" (Sheridan 1822, 13).

As exemplified by the works of Poe, Kincaid, and Borges, colonial empires serve gothic literature as evocative settings for exotic ritual, barbarism, and segregation—for example, the epic violence between a father and son, citizens of the Ghaznavid empire, in Matthew Arnold's *Sohrab and Rustum* (1853); JOSEPH CONRAD's probe of the African ivory trade in HEART OF DARKNESS (1902); and the surreal time displacement of *The Kadaitcha Sung* (1990), a tale of South Pacific colonial horrors by Sam Watson, an Australian aborigine. William Beckford's oriental romance *Vathek, an Arabian Tale* (published in French in 1782 and in English in 1786) allegorizes the Persian sybarism of Caliph Vathek, who summons a giaour, or non-Muslim, to Samarah, Egypt, to provide forbidden pleasures. The caliph's depravity confirms British suspicions of Islamic countries and customs and substantiates rumors of Persian sexual indulgence, vice, and sacrilege. The torments of hell await Vathek, who is "sullied . . . with a thousand crimes" (Beckford 1970, 120). In 1816, the English romantic poet Samuel Taylor Coleridge pleased readers with "Kubla Khan; or, a Vision in a Dream, a Fragment," an ethereal terror tale contrasting an insular edenic garden with a future war in the Yuan dynasty during the rule of a 13th-century Mongol emperor. The suggestion of finite joys emphasizes that imperial glory and luxury are illusions soon destroyed by subsequent conquerors.

Gothic Cliché

Although reflecting popular tastes in escapist romance, 19th-century gothic adventure literature also maintained a grasp on themes of rapacity and collusion. An English crime story about the snatch-

ing of a yellow diamond from an Indian temple dramatized international thievery during British colonialism in Wilkie Collins's *The Moonstone* (1868), a best seller written at the height of Queen Victoria's reign. The heist of the diamond, a fictional version of the 105-carat Koh-I-Noor diamond from Golconda, India, as an addition to the British crown jewels attests to the usurper's desecration of an 800-year-old talisman. At the return of the moonstone to its source, the subtext implies that imperialists typically bungle their chance to acknowledge and learn from a another culture: "You have lost sight of it in England, and (if I know anything of this people) you have lost sight of it for ever" (Collins 1998, 472).

In the Americas, *colonial gothic* became an umbrella term for the multicultural lore of Canada, the Caribbean, Latin America, the American South and West, Alaska, Hawaii, and New England. An example of Amerindian historical fiction, JOHN RICHARDSON's Canadian romances *Wacousta; or, The Prophecy: A Tale of the Canadas* (1832) and its sequel, *The Canadian Brothers; or, The Prophecy Fulfilled* (1840), pit the 18th-century Ottawa chief Pontiac against British imperialists in a Cain-and-Abel story fraught with sibling animosity. In a more chilling tale, American writer Herman Melville (1819–91) depicted an African's revenge for wholesale kidnap and enslavement in "Benito Cereno" (1855), a ghoulish tale set on a Spanish slave vessel off the shores of St. Maria, Chile. In a subtle warning for Captain Delano, the title figure declares, "Ah, this slavery breeds ugly passions in man" (Melville 1856, 211), a statement that strikes the African villain Babo and influences Delano, the transporter of captive Africans to New World slave markets. The horror tale concludes with a visual token of revenge—the skull of the schemer Babo skewered on a pike.

Beyond Gothic Stereotypes

Farther north in the Western Hemisphere, Jules-Paul Tardivel, an emigré from Kentucky to Quebec, employed plots against French frontiersmen in the separatist novel *Pour la patrie* (*For My Country,* 1895) to create a vision of APOCALYPSE. The narrative refutes the idea of colonialism as a means of converting pagans to Christ. The action occurs at a nadir in Catholic conversions, when "Faith was declining. Everyone could see it" (Tardivel 1975, 11). Tardivel blames satanic plots of Freemasons for undermining French colonialism. During a meeting of dissidents, the Masonic master opposes preservation of nationalism and language "if by sacrificing them, we can destroy the Infamous One and uproot from the Canadian soil the cross of the priests, symbol of superstition and standard of tyranny" (12). The author proposes an alternative to the futuristic liberation of colonial Quebec through technological advances.

Into the full flowering of romanticism and beyond into impressionism, imaginative tales of gypsy curses, piracy, seraglios, African sloth, and Islamic decadence played out in the fantasies of authors such as Lord Byron (1788–1824), Sir ARTHUR CONAN DOYLE (1859–1930), Lady Caroline Lamb (1785–1828), and Louisa May Alcott (1832–88). In the critical treatise *Orientalism* (1978), Columbia University professor Edward Wadie Said, a Jerusalem-born culture critic, charged such purveyors of colonial orientalism with ethnocentrism. He denounced classic world authors as being on a par with the British explorer Sir Richard Burton, the English novelist George Eliot, the French novelist Victor Hugo, the English author RUDYARD KIPLING, the Scottish poet Sir Walter Scott, and the American humorist Mark Twain for repeating centuries-old stereotypes of the inscrutable Asian, the camel-riding nomad trader, fortune tellers, and harem residents menaced by armed eunuchs and lustful sheiks. Said charged Westerners with a subjectivity based on racism, religious bigotry, and a voyeurism that fed curiosity about global societies and sexual customs. He warned, "These are the lenses through which the Orient is experienced, and they shape the language, perception, and form of the encounter between East and West" (Said 2003, 58). Out of such wrongheadedness comes "a restricted number of typical encapsulations: the journey, the history, the fable, the stereotype, the polemical confrontation" (58), all of which strip the literature of empires of humanity.

Postmodern Gothic

In the second half of the 20th century, the merger of gothic conventions with social commentary renewed literary concern for the lingering effects of colonialism, racism, sexism, and human bondage. In the anticolonial historical novel *La Casa de los Espíritus* (*The House of the Spirits*, 1981), the Chilean writer Isabel Allende recaptured Hispanic exploitation of mestizo field laborers and house servants. For Chilean planter Esteban Trueba, after his rape of the virgin peasant Pancha García, retribution connects the blood-spattered dress with a shameful history: "Before her, her mother—and before her, her grandmother—had suffered the same animal fate" (Allende 1982, 57). The monstrosity of colonial concubinage gives birth to social unrest and revolution, realism's wages of sin. The narrative adapted well to screen in 1993 with an all-star cast—Jeremy Irons, Meryl Streep, Winona Ryder, Glenn Close, and Antonio Banderas as the peasant leader of a revolt against European oppressors.

Late in the 20th century, Africa and Australasia received their share of postcolonial survey. The Australian novelist Peter Carey resurrected issues of the GENOCIDE of aborigines in the symbolist novel *Oscar and Lucinda* (1988), the source of a 1997 screen version starring Ralph Fiennes and Cate Blanchett. The transportation of a whimsical glass chapel upriver in Australia to a parish of aborigines represents the transparency and fragility of British plans to suppress native culture by enforcing Church of England mores in the outback.

In Jane Campion's feminist novel *The Piano* (1993), the concubinage of Maori women is part of a program of domination. According to the villainous conqueror, Alasdair Stewart, "The bush, like the Maori people who inhabited it, needed to be brought to order" (Campion, 1995, 18), a free-floating statement of "need" implying coercion. The Oscar-winning film version captures the sullied morality of the colonizer ruling the colonized by engulfing the land that Stewart clears and torches with a blue haze, a symbol of hellish pollution.

In a more prophetic glimpse of world power struggles, the Sri Lankan-Canadian writer Michael Ondaatje reprised gothic conventions in a World War II romance, *The English Patient* (1996), a Booker Prize winner set in an Italian villa and a cave in southern Egypt during the fall of the Italian colonial empire. The bizarre retrieval of a corpse, subsequent plane crash, and catastrophic burns to the title character epitomize a familiar gothic motif, the triumph of love over violence, betrayal, suffering, and death.

Victimization and Feminism

The stereotype of the cowering female proved useful to feminist literature. Through images of timid, light-skinned women fleeing swarthy kidnappers, pirates, and warlords, gothic literature cultivated new territory as an opportunity for the New Woman, a late 19th-century feminist ideal. The adventurer freed of dependence on fathers, husbands, and male authority figures, fights misogynistic superstition and social obstacles to selfhood, the focus of the Danish memoirist and fabulist ISAK DINESEN's *Out of Africa* (1937) and *Babette's Feast* (1959).

For models, many authors followed two pinnacles of Victorian gothicism: Charlotte Brontë's *Jane Eyre* (1847) and Nathaniel Hawthorne's *The Scarlet Letter* (1850). Over a three-year period, readers altered their view of female self-sufficiency through the actions of two heroines. Jane Eyre, an orphaned English governess, empowers herself upon receipt of a colonial inheritance from her uncle. Motivated to succeed, she runs from the man she loves, a bigamist, and shapes her future through independent action. Hawthorne's Hester Prynne, an English settler of Puritan New England, escapes the stigmatizing of the mateless mother by establishing a home for her daughter Pearl in Massachusetts Bay Colony and by working as a seamstress and nurse. Amid misogyny, social ostracism, and prolonged loneliness, she liberates herself during a daily test of forbearance by refusing to be judged and intimidated, much like the heroines of medieval hagiography.

Female gothic themes suited the writers of new HERO stories. The Chinese-American author Maxine Hong Kingston battled Chinese patriarchy in a gothic saga, *The Woman Warrior* (1975), which immortalizes the female fighter against repression, female servility, foot binding, and the stoning of a madwoman during the Japanese invasion of Nanjing, China, during the winter of 1937–38. A healer like Hester Prynne, the midwife Brave Orchid challenges ghosts at a bridge, a symbol of the Chinese woman's difficult crossing from victim of male hypocrisy to self-actualization. The interpolated tale of Fa Mu Lan, an epic woman hero, supplies survival tactics that empower women, who arm themselves for opposition by sharing talk-stories.

In 1986, the French Caribbean writer MARYSE CONDÉ published a Caribbean version of the female hero story: *Moi, Tituba, sorcière noire Salem* (I, Tituba, Black Witch of Salem), a biography of victimization during the Salem Witch Trials of 1692. A black slave living far from her former home in Barbados, Tituba honors a matrilineage of female persecutions that include the burning of an African village and the stabbing of a grandmother who refused to enter the hold of a slaver's vessel.

In 1998, Barbara Kingsolver created the durable Orleanna Price, a missionary's wife, in *The Poisonwood Bible,* an American's glimpse of the emergence of the Belgian Congo out of imperial control. The text conjures horror stories of the fate of former European colonies as they pass into the hands of indigenous exploiters and despots, bringing female gothic literature into the late 20th century.

Sources

Allende, Isabel. *The House of the Spirits.* New York: Bantam Books, 1982.

Beckford, William. *Vathek.* London: Oxford University Press, 1970.

Campion, Jane. *The Piano.* New York: Miramax Books, 1995.

Carey, Peter. *Oscar and Lucinda.* New York: Vintage, 1997.

Collins, Wilkie. *The Moonstone.* London: Penguin, 1998.

Croly, George. *Salathiel: A Story of the Past, the Present, and the Future.* London: Henry Colburn, 1828.

Ketterer, David. *Canadian Science Fiction and Fantasy.* Bloomington: Indiana University Press, 1992.

Melville, Herman. *Piazza Tales.* New York: Dix & Edwards, 1856.

Said, Edward W. *Orientalism.* New York: Penguin, 2003.

Sheridan, Frances Chamberlaine. *The History of Nourjahad.* Philadelphia: Hickman & Hazzard, 1822.

Tardivel, Jules-Paul. *For My Country.* Translated by Sheila Fischman. Toronto: University of Toronto Press, 1975.

Granth (Adi Granth, Guru Granth) Arjan Dev (1604)

The Sikh scripture, the Granth (Book)—also called the Adi Granth (First Book) and Guru Granth (Holy Book)—provides literary evidence of an attempt to syncretize Hinduism with Islam in the Punjab. The anthology, a collection of 6,000 texts, took shape as the Mughal Empire spread from Pakistan to India and established territories as far north as Turkey and Mongolia. The finished book combines CRE-ATION LORE; evensongs; FABLES, verses; sermons; and WISDOM LITERATURE derived from missionary writings, Sufi mysticism, and hagiography in a variety of languages and dialects, including Arabic, Braj, Hindi, Marathi, Persian, Punjabi, Sanskrit, and Sindhi. The collection and its contributors cover centuries of Asian history. The legendary Namdev (1272–1350), a Hindu bard and wonder worker of Maharastra, India, amassed thousands of messianic songs that scandalized Brahmans. The wandering Tamil evangelist Ramanand (ca. 1400–1470) preached a one-world concept that welcomed females and slaves to his fold and revered God by the names Allah, Brahma, Hari, Lakshmi, Mohan, Ram, Sahib, Siv, and Vishnu. The saintly Ravi Das (Ravidas, 1376–1410) of Uttar Pradesh, India, joined Ramanand's circle and wrote devotional *ragas* (hymns) encouraging human fellowship in the style of the Zoroastrian AVESTA (ca. A.D. 530).

At a crucial shift in Sikh philosophy, the holy poet and seer Kabir (1398–1518) pressed for the merger of Hinduism and Islam. With 243 religious stanzas, he approached the mysticism of the Buddhist KOANs by exhorting the seeker of truth to consider states of being that merge with godhood and formlessness. The first Sikh guru, Nanak (1469–1539), a Pakistani miller and Vedic prodigy, anchored his text to the Sikh purpose by hybridizing Hindu-Muslim anthems and psalms that encourage penitence, pacifism, charity, and humility. In one brief aphorism, he inquires with a rhetorical question why people cultivate the illusion of permanence: "Like a dream and play consider the world! In these there is no reality without the Lord. . . . Why dost thou entertain false conceit; know, the world is like a dream. Among these things nothing is thine" (Adi Granth 1877, 707). His influence spread from Baghdad and Mecca to Assam, Basra, China, Sri Lanka, and Tamil Nadu. A contemporary, the blind epic poet Surdas (1479–1586), honored Krishna by contributing stories of the god's boyhood and by urging conversion to the true Sikh god.

A Complete Holy Book

After the Sikh faith took hold in Kartarpur, Pakistan, Guru Angad (1504–52) systemized Nanak's writings in the Punjabi alphabet. To the early ethical axioms on sanctity and human liberation, Angad added 869 liturgical works celebrating births, child namings, cremations, and funerals. Under Angad's direction, the faith took on an individual style, based on monotheism. He begged his teacher, "O Guru! let me know the One!" (3). His follower, the missionary Amar Das (1479–1574), of Amritsar, Punjab, exercised his faith in a communal feeding center that welcomed people from all social and economic levels, including the emperor Akbar (Akbar the Great, 1542–1605), a devotee of tolerance and syncretic faith who dined with street sweepers and beggars. As the scriptural collection reached its completion, Guru Ram Das (1534–81), a utopist from Lahore, Pakistan, added 679 worship songs. He and his son Arjan Dev (1563–1606) centered Sikhist instruction in Amritsar, a holy city. Ram Das's influence on Sikh liturgy includes chants for ritual bathing and for the Lavan nuptial rite, which directs a procession around the Granth to the singing of a verse extolling a peaceful family life.

In 1604, during the last months of Mughal tolerance, Arjan Dev recorded the original Sikh canon in two volumes. Like the paeans of whirling dervishes, his CREATION lyrics and psalms impart rhapsodic immersion in the Almighty: "O fascinating one! high are thy mansions, infinite thy palaces. O fascinating one! thy gates are beautiful. O Lord! the almshouse of the saints" (356). The rhetorical grace parallels David's Psalm 84:1–2: "How amiable are thy tabernacles, O Lord of hosts! My soul longeth, yea, even fainteth for the courts of the Lord: my heart and my flesh crieth out for the living God." In the months following the death of Akbar the Great on October 27, 1605, Arjan suffered imprisonment and torture in flames under orders of Akbar's son

Jahangir for refusing to rewrite the Granth to ortho-dox Muslim or Hindu specifications.

In 1704, Gobind Singh (1666–1708) of Patna, India, an anti-Mughal soldier and lawgiver, pro-vided an addendum of 59 hymns by his father Tegh Bahadur (1621–75), whom the Mughal emperor Aurangzeb had chained in an iron cage in Delhi and martyred with decapitation. Under threat of impe-rial brutality, Tegh speaks in otherworldly call-and-response his reliance on God: "By whom all worldly concerns are given up and who has taken the garb of retirement from the world" (706). He acquiesces to a greater power: "My strength is exhausted, fet-ters have fallen on me, there is no expedience whatever" (708). Gobind Singh, determined to overthrow Muslim power and avenge his father, wrote like a military man: "Strength is afforded, the fetters are loosened, everything becomes an expe-dient. Everything is in thy hand, even thou art thy own helper" (708). After Singh completed the holy book under the title of Guru Granth Sahib (Lord Book, 1708), he fought Mughal oppression, losing four sons while fighting 20 battles in 1705 against Muslim proselytizers. Singh himself, banished from the Punjab, died in combat in what is now Pakistan, before the full assimilation of Sikhism in India.

Following the British colonization of the Indian subcontinent, the new imperialists returned Singh's copy of the Granth to Arjan Dev's descendants at Lahore, Pakistan in 1849. The effort of immigration throughout the empire stimulated the Sikh dias-pora and weakened hopes for a Sikh state.

Sources

The Adi Granth, or, The Holy Scriptures of the Sikhs.
    Translated by Ernst Trumpp. London: Great Britain
    India Office, 1877.
Dass, Nirmal. *Songs of the Saints from the Adi Granth.*
    Albany: State University of New York Press, 2000.
Mann, Gurinder Singh. *The Making of Sikh Scripture.*
    Oxford: Oxford University Press, 2001.

Greek drama

In the fifth century B.C., at the end of Persian expansionism, Greek drama enjoyed a golden age. The stage offered a forum for public debate and a clearinghouse for doubts and unease among Athenian intellectuals concerning the future of their city-state. From its inception, Greek theater had its roots in the essentials of national pride. The festivals of Dionysus throughout the year were occasions for dramatic performances:

- The Lenaea, the winepress and wine-mixing festival, in late January, which in-cluded a religious procession and sacrifice along with plays, mainly comedy
- The Anthesteria, or "flower of the grape," a three-day tasting festival of casks, beakers, and pots in late February and the first days of March, which comprised drinking libations to the gods, rejoicing, dressing in costumes, and honoring the dead
- The six-day City Dionysia, the winemak-er's celebration, in April, which called for a display of weapons and phalluses, sacri-fice of bulls, street revelry, and dramatic performances
- The Rural Dionysia, a festival of vine cultivation, in the last days of December, consisting of thanksgiving for bread and wine, dancing, and singing of dithyrambs (exultant poems or hymns)

For the audience's edification, mythic and historical plots and characters reaffirmed beliefs in the gods, the nuclear family, and the city-state.

Greek playwrights made the most of their dramatic tools. The immediacy of dialogue and the subtleties of irony, allusion, and SATIRE enabled writers to examine threats to the status quo and to criticize the efforts of dignitaries and the mili-tary to maintain order and security against rogue empire assaults. Authorities excused from military obligations all members of the actors' guild, who served Dionysus, the god of wine and fertility, rather than Ares and Athena, the gods of war. As a gesture to soldiery, the Theater of Dionysus that Pericles rebuilt at Athens in 435 B.C. seated ephebi (18-year-old recruits) in a designated tier of rows behind the city officials and the Dionysiac priests.

The First Dramatist

Aeschylus (525–456 B.C.), a veteran of the battles of Marathon, Artemisium, Salamis, and Plataea, became the first superstar playwright in Athens. The Egyptian poet Constantine Cavafy (1863–1933) described Aeschylus as "a vivacious young man, mad about literature" (Cavafy 1992, 105). American mythographer Edith Hamilton called him the Western world's first dramatist and a writer with "soldier spirit" (Hamilton 1962, 173). Because of his basic decency and morality and his disdain for religious fanaticism, Aeschylus focused on humanistic questions. His only history play, *Persae* (*Persians*, 472 B.C.), the second of a tetralogy, draws on his eyewitness account of the Persian Wars (490 B.C. and 480–479 B.C.).

Aeschylus deliberately avoided turning stagecraft into a tool of the state. The lone extant Greek tragedy on a contemporary topic, *Persae* pictured international clashes from the perspective of the Persian leader Xerxes I (519–465 B.C.), Darius's son and the grandson of Cyrus the Great, all of whom HERODOTUS featured in his *Histories* (440 B.C.). Instead of gloating, Aeschylus extended pity to the vanquished by placing in the stage's center the tomb mound of Darius I (550–486 B.C.), who had led the Persians to defeat at the battle of Marathon five years before the play's action begins. An encomium to Cyrus interjects a common subject to imperial literature—the egotist's perception of assumed divine nepotism. According to the playwright, Cyrus overreached his potential by thinking himself "Heaven's favorite" for successfully merging the Medes and Persians into a single world power (Aeschylus 1991, 78). For balance, at the time the play was first staged, the performance featured the statesman Pericles, the playwright's benefactor, as *choregos*, or spokesman. Pericles led the chorus, the body of commentators who danced, gestured, chanted, and sang their interpretations and questions about each plot development.

Eschewing suspense in an age when everyone knew the results of the Persian Wars, the action of *Persae* depicts a character study of Xerxes' folly and embitterment. He returns home from the Greek victory at Salamis on September 29, 480 B.C., after a fleet of 1,200 Persian vessels attacked the Greeks' meager in-harbor armada of 310 ships. The king's hubris, a ruinous pride ungoverned by humility, had induced him to ignore omens and to commit to a war that generated "foundering awash dead men shrouded in sea-drowned cloaks" (53). The prominent speech of a combat messenger imparts to viewers its effects on distant Persian noncombatants, who rightfully fear for their nation, navy, and infantry.

Intertwined with military worries for the survival of young soldiers are the views of the overwrought dowager queen Atossa, Xerxes' 70-year-old mother. Because she is the daughter of Cyrus, and the widow of Darius for five years, she knows enough of war firsthand to fear for her son. The *choregos* honors her as "most blest among son-bearing women" (45), a salute to the homebound mothers who produced males for the Persian army. The chorus enhances the significance of female reactions to a faraway debacle that "so exceeds all bounds that one can neither tell, nor ask, about the suffering" (53). Rather than obsess over spears, shields, and cries of the fallen, the singers dread the sound of womanly mourning, which the playwright compares to "ripping falls on the fine-linen robes" (163), the first action of the female sorrower.

Aeschylus took an unusual tack in highlighting the remarks of a matriarch and a ghost. The queen of Persia knows too well Xerxes' penchant for risking disaster. Her queries about the nature of imperialism far from the motherland emphasize issues of drawn-out struggle and quests for power against nameless, helmeted alien warriors. Female commentary specifies the role of women as guardians of the hearth and upholders of religious piety and domestic sacrifice. Dutiful to her country, the queen reverences valiant male ancestry, even when it bereaves families.

The return of Darius's ghost from Hades recalls through early GOTHIC stagecraft his loss at Marathon, when the Greeks "crushed [his] huge and shining army" (51). The still-tender hurt from Marathon's combat toll prefigures the son's repeat of a fatal error and another round of postwar laments. The ghost charges his heir with "something so monstrous it twisted his good sense" (75). Like David's lamentation in the biblical books of Samuel over King Saul's death alongside his son Jonathan while fighting the Philistines at the battle of Gilboa in 1007 B.C., Aeschylus concludes the Persian loss with Xerxes' dirge. A flawed man, the king exalts Greek military might and blames himself for lack of foresight.

A Pacifist View

Aeschylus's successor, the introspective pacifist Euripides (ca. 484–406 B.C.) of Salamis supplied the classical stage at Athens with a series of imperial vengeance plays centering on the Trojan War: *Andromache* (ca. 425 B.C.); *Hecuba* (ca. 424 B.C.); and *The Trojan Women* (415 B.C.), winner of a second prize at the City Dionysia festival. His plays are the most poignant and enduring of the era. While *The Trojan Women* specifically arouses a sympathy for the female and child sufferings that occurred on the island of Melos in 415 B.C., when Athenian soldiers slew males and sold women and children at auction, all three plays are landmarks of the golden age of Greek theater that dramatize the unavoidable GENOCIDE that accompanies one empire's slaughter of another.

To prevent the emergence of a new generation of Trojan royalty, the triad begins, in *Andromache,* with a baby killing—Hector's widow's loss of the infant boy Astyanax and the enslavement of his mother, who becomes a Greek concubine. Myth increases the irony of female punishments for war by awarding Andromache as concubine to Neoptolemus, the savage son of Achilles who violates reverence for the gods by slaying the elderly King Priam on the altar and by murdering Queen Hecuba's daughter, Polyxene. Contributing to the protagonist's woes, Neoptolemus's wife Hermione charges Andromache with witchery as a means of explaining Hermione's barren womb and lack of sexual appeal. Perhaps because of his own two failed marriages, Euripides turns the dialogue into a verbal duel between Andromache and Hermione. He provides a subtext of insult to Sparta, the archenemy of Athens and homeland of Hermione.

Euripides' second Trojan tragedy, *Hecuba*, reignites the attack on the concept of war by featuring the widowed Trojan queen and her sorrow at the death of Princess Polyxene and Prince Polydorus, who epitomize the suffering inflicted by imperial conquest. The subtext honors elderly women who outlive their children and must bathe and shroud their remains for burial. With the trilogy's third part, *The Trojan Women*, the 65-year-old dramatist took a melodramatic look at the helplessness of noncombatants. They stand immobile as the citadel burns, Ajax drags the priestess Cassandra from the temple of Apollo, and Greek soldiers begin the lottery that will assign the women to sexual enslavement. After the departure of Andromache, Hecuba is left with the task of burying her grandson Astyanax, whose tiny corpse returns to the stage on his father's shield, a symbol of thwarted manhood and service denied the little prince. A 1971 film version starred Geneviève Bujold as Cassandra, Vanessa Redgrave as Andromache, and Katharine Hepburn as Queen Hecuba.

A Great Comedy Writer

To warn the nation of hubristic imperialism, Aristophanes (ca. 450–385 B.C.), Attica's audacious funny man, chose another route. Born during the Periclean age, he witnessed the moral decline of Athens's youth under increasingly rapacious demagoguery by the war party. To register his discontent at imperialism and the arms race against Sparta, he employed the aphorism "Laughter tells the truth." Although laws passed in 440 B.C. forbade the lampooning of public officials, he wrote gleeful satires for the Greek stage during a period rife with the buffoonery and greed of society's upper echelons. The playwright, whose plays are the only surviving examples of Greek Old Comedy, took on the worst of public parasites one by one. At the City Dionysia festival in April 426 B.C., he presented *Babylonioi* (The Babylonians, now lost), which leaders of the Athenian empire attended. The first scene opened on slaves at a mill, symbolic of cities yoked under Athenian oppression. The play portrayed Cleon (d. 422 B.C.), an Athenian statesman and *strategos* (general) as a demagogue. Cleon took offense and attacked Aristophanes in the senate, then charged him with treason for demeaning Athens before strangers attending the performance, a capital offense.

Aristophanes mined events of the late fifth century for anecdotes and lewd gags that he used in his plays to alert Attica to contemporary corruption. He specialized in mocking egregious political climbers, whose reckless attitudes took the Greeks to the brink of catastrophe. He satirized elements of the Peloponnesian War against Sparta

(431–404 B.C.) in *The Acharneis* (*The Acharnians*, 425 B.C.), which earned him a first place at the Lenaea festival. The action portrays a cynical Megarian (citizen of Megara, a small city near Athens) so down on his luck that he must sell his daughters to survive wartime famine. The allegory features Dicaeopolis (Just Citizen), a veteran wearied by combat and impoverished by the ravaging of his crops. He despises men like the hawkish Cleon, who sees the war as a chance to exterminate Sparta as a business competitor. The text threatens to hack Cleon into army boot soles and extols Dicaeopolis as a free agent brokering a citizen's truce and as a true Athenian for fermenting a wine called Peace. The playwright himself staged the performance, which concluded with 30 prostitutes dancing in honor of a 30-year cease-fire.

War and Wisecracks

In the comedy *Hippeis* (*The Knights*, 424 B.C.), a transparent allegory performed at the Lenaea festival in the seventh year of Athens's lengthy war with Sparta, Aristophanes revenged himself by mocking Cleon onstage. *The Knights* repackaged Cleon as the slave Paphlagonian (the tanner), a hanger-on eager to engage with ambassadors carrying fat purses. The dramatist ventures to say of his target, "a greater swine of a stool-pigeon never walked this earth" with "a voice like an overloaded sewer" (Aristophanes 1978, 30, 33). The comic masterwork failed to derail Cleon's political strivings and jury rigging, but it did preserve a sharp-edged sally picturing Nicias, Athens's senior general, as a sausage seller in verbal duel with Cleon. The play maligns Cleon for embezzlement by picturing a huge cake in his locker with only a sliver removed for the people.

Depicting greed at the public trough, *The Knights* anticipates that the higher-ups "intend to slurp down all the national gravy" (42). Aristophanes foresees that the tanner, the worst of bloodsuckers, will die in his own polluted brine, a slough of corruption symbolizing Athens's political miasma. To lessen the chance of being punished, the comedy writer himself played Cleon in a bloated portrait mask stained with wine. In a more serious vein, the historiographer THUCYDIDES took Cleon to task for

venality in *The History of the Peloponnesian War* (ca. 400 B.C.), a scholarly study of imperialism during Athens's cultural acme.

Aristophanes took offense at civil conflict requiring Attic Greeks to kill Corinthian, Megarian, and Spartan Greeks. For the City Dionysia festival in April 421 B.C., he based his topical play *Eiréné* (*Peace*) on the Athenian hope of a half-century accord with Sparta. The text demonizes arms dealers, fraudulent prophets, and the deceased officials Cleon and his enemy, Spartan general Brasidas, for seeking personal advancement at any cost. At a tenuous moment in the peace plan, Aristophanes grouses, "Desire to attain the rank of regimental commander shall begrudge, O holy Lady of Peace, thy return to the light" (105). To enable vintner Trygaeus to fly to heaven on a dung-beetle to rescue the title character, Aristophanes assembled a stage crane to lift the actor to the *skene* (backdrop) roof. In the play, country folk, the people most demoralized by warring, welcome peace with traditional fun. In the grand celebration, the plot toys with the connection between war's end and sex by describing a woman's fragrance as "the true scent of demobilization" (112), the introit to partying, drinking, and romancing, the normal forms of gaiety.

Women and War

In the 20th year of the Peloponnesian War, when Athens suffered a massive defeat against Sparta in Sicily, Aristophanes presented *Lysistrata* (411 B.C.), a play epitomizing his zest and the exuberance of Old Comedy. To relieve the despair caused by the empire's carnage, he created a ribald send-up on sex-deprived Athenian and Spartan husbands during intense truce negotiations. Filled with sight gags based on flirtations, coital boycotts, and the resultant priapism (persistent and painful erection), the play depicts a women's sex strike as an antidote to "soldiers in every grocery and potter shop, clanking around armed to the teeth" (Aristophanes 2007, 36). Through truth-telling obscenities and dialogue, the text weaves together the varied meanings of phallic imagery—as a symbol of fecundity and prosperity, as a salute to the human libido, and as a comic reminder of the weaponry, ambassadorial rod of office, and belligerence that forced Attica (the region of southern Greece and Athens) to the edge of extinction.

Lysistrata survives as the most controversial and most revived drama from the fifth century B.C. At a time when young men depart for battlefields in Pylos on the Peloponnese and the mountains of Thrace in northeastern Greece, leaving women untended and sexually unsatisfied, Athenian, Boeotian, Corinthian, Spartan, and Theban matrons dress in men's tunics and band into a pacifist political action group. The harried title figure, whose name translates as "disbander of armies," represents the feminist yearning for stability and amity. By collaborating with women from Boeotia and the Peloponnesus, she voices women's universal loathing of combat as a threat to the social order and the welfare of its children, whom governments encourage females to produce as fodder for war. Lampito, a Spartan woman, echoes the complaint with her own concern over multiple military rotations: "There's no discharge in this war" (15).

The humor of *Lysistrata* lies in the subversion of macho posturing by aggressive females who refuse to be silenced. Lysistrata musters her forces, taking them away from daily tasks of laundry, food work, and babysitting; in the voice of wise womanhood, she proclaims, "There are other things far far more important" (11). Lampito, her Spartan parallel, backs up a plan of total celibacy, but not without making a few gibes about Attic democracy being mob rule. The tit-for-tat implies that both sexes perpetuate the competition that sets one city-state against another. In the course of opposition from their husbands, Lysistrata's "market militia" (30) becomes a phalanx of swashbucklers. To promote solidarity, one amazon exhorts, "Sting them, Sisters, goad them into submission. You're in full sail" (35). Lysistrata seizes female momentum to create a paradigm of peacemaking based on the spindling of wool: "The colonies are loose threads; pick up the ends and gather them in. Wind them all into one" (37). Rather than debate her plan, the men reject orders from women as petticoat tyranny.

For battle preparations, the playwright arms the female half of the choruses with full mop buck-

ets and dresses his heroines in filmy nightdresses. Scented with come-hither perfumes, the women swear an oath by Aphrodite and sacrifice a wineskin rather than an animal. They take drinks from the punch bowl before the two female battalions face the enemy. Their tactics include the seizure of the citadel at the Acropolis and stopping the siphoning of funds from Athens's treasury to arms traders. During a confrontation with the city magistrate and a Scythian military squad, Lysistrata outrages vain males by proposing that women manage the public purse. The men's leader makes the clichéd plaint that men cannot live with women or without them, a bromide that strikes home with both Athenian and Spartan warriors. Only after both women and men begin to long for sexual reunion—painfully so in the men's cases—do the warring parties reach a peace accord, allowing the opposing armies and their wives to go home.

A realist and believer in forgiveness and compromise, Aristophanes depicted the restoration of social order through sociopolitical and conjugal reconciliation. The universality of *Lysistrata*'s themes resulted in its adaptation as rock opera and stage sex comedy, in addition to inspiring illustrations by the English artist Aubrey Beardsley. In the 1960s, first-wave American feminists embraced the bawdy dialogue for championing pacifism and full citizenship for women.

Sources

Aeschylus. *Persians*. Translated by Janet Lembke and C. John Herington. Oxford: Oxford University Press, 1991.

Aristophanes. *The Knights/Peace/The Birds/The Assemblywomen/Wealth*. Translated by Alan H. Sommerstein and David Barrett. New York: Penguin, 1978.

———. *Lysistrata*. Translated by Nicholas Rudall. Chicago: Ivan R. Dee, 2007.

Cavafy, Constantine. *Collected Poems*. Translated by Edmund Keeley and Philip Sherrard. Princeton, N.J.: Princeton University Press, 1992.

Forrest, W. G. "Aristophanes *Lysistrata* 231." *Classical Quarterly* 45, no. 1 (January–June 1995): 240–241.

Hamilton, Edith. *The Greek Way*. New York: Mentor Books, 1962.

Greene, Graham (Henry Graham Greene)

(1904–1991) *English novelist and journalist*

A writer of plays, short stories, criticism, and nonfiction work as well as the novels for which he is best known, Graham Greene delved into the moral ambiguities of 20th-century American and European imperialism. Born in Berkhamsted, Hertfordshire, England, his internal struggles with bipolar disorder began at age six, when he attempted to kill himself while enrolled at Berkhamsted School. In his mid-teens, he required psychological counseling before entering Balliol College, Oxford University, to study history. Upon graduating, he began a career in journalism, which ended in 1929 when he abandoned editing for the *Times* to write fiction. His often took as themes the collapse of Britain as a global economic and political force, and his fictional dialogues, rich with epigrams, analyzed the ebb of institutional loyalty, duty, and service.

Taking a personal approach to his stories, Greene engaged himself in colonial scenarios by creating a fictional alter ego. With his early socialist novels, he probed the waning of nationalism and turned fictional recruits to the foreign service into cynical, venal, and self-absorbed straw men, the victims of social isolation and government dilemmas. For the travelogue *Journey without Maps* (1936), he walked 350 miles of Liberia, one of Africa's few uncolonized lands. Because of Liberia's freedom from racist domination, he charged British imperialism in Kenya, Rhodesia, and South Africa with failure: "They were simply out to make money; and there was no hypocrisy in their attitudes towards 'the bloody blacks'" (Greene 1992, 43). The contrast between black-ruled and conquered nations seized his imagination. He mused, "To a stranger, I think, coming from a European colony, Monrovia and coastal Liberia would be genuinely impressive. He would find a simplicity, a pathos about the place which would redeem it from the complete seediness of a colony like Sierra Leone" (243).

His political acumen and hatred of indifference led Greene to serve during World War II in M16, the British intelligence agency. He was posted to Freetown, Sierra Leone, the source of one of his best novels, *The Heart of the Matter* (1948), set during the war. It won the James Tait Black Memorial Prize for depicting the internal struggle and eventual suicide of a police inspector, Major Henry Scobie, against West African smuggling, adultery, and blackmail, crimes the author connects with declining morality. A screen version in 1953 starred Trevor Howard, Maria Schell, and Peter Finch.

As it did GEORGE ORWELL, the postwar malaise confirmed for Greene the disrepute into which imperialism lapsed. In the early 1950s, he reported from Saigon to *Le Figaro* and the *Sunday Times* on the French colonial war, the source of his novel *The Quiet American* (1955), a PROPHECY of the American quagmire that began in Southeast Asia four years later. A love triangle hampers the efforts of a naive civil servant, Alden Pyle, to represent U.S. interests in Vietnam. An immature idealogue, he dismisses Indochinese politics as "only a damned colonial war anyway" (Greene 2002, 38). The author voices his own disgruntlement at colonialism in the jaded observation, "It's always the same wherever one goes—it's not the most powerful rulers who have the happiest populations" (49). Film versions in 1958, starring Audie Murphy and Michael Redgrave, and in 2002, featuring Michael Caine and Brendan Fraser, dismayed U.S. audiences for their anti-Americanism.

As a correspondent for the *Sunday Times*, Greene reported on the Mau Mau uprising against British colonial rule in Kenya (1952–60). Later, he gathered material for *The Human Factor* (1978), an exposé of imperialist paranoia regarding espionage and communism at the height of South African apartheid. The 1979 film version, shot in Kenya, combined the acting talents of top stars including Richard Attenborough, John Gielgud, and Derek Jacobi. In his autobiography *Ways of Escape* (1980), Greene characterized the British pull-out from Malaya in 1963 as a wise decision, unlike the American rush to occupy Vietnam.

Empire's End

Greene became a perceptive witness to faltering empires and the antiheroic behavior of some colonial civil servants. He anticipated the Cuban missile crisis of 1962 with *Our Man in Havana* (1958), an espionage thriller pitting treachery against survivalism. The statelessness of the civil servant emerges in a letter home, in which the protagonist declares, "Sometimes I fear going home to Boots and Woolworths and cafeterias, and I'd be a stranger now even in the White Horse" (Greene 2007, 62).

In January 1959, the author traveled to Leopoldville to explore the Belgian Congo. His visit to the Yonda, Imbonga, and Lombo Lumba leper colonies undergirded *A Burnt-Out Case* (1960), set in the fictional Congolese capital of Luc. Familiar with the Freudian concept of the repressed self, he symbolized the stifled subconscious with heat, sun, humidity, and claustrophobic boat cabin. As though referring to the unending duties of Europeans in service to the Belgian empire, Greene refers to the river as khaki-colored, a suggestion of drab uniforms set against a perpetually green forest.

The text pictures the cubicle occupied by the protagonist, Query, during a Conradesque journey upriver in search of the leprosy bacillus as "a nut at the centre of the hard shell of discomfort" (Greene 1961, 9). Heavy with suspense, the action suggests a symbolic subtext: the European's search for infection in a land that imperialism has corrupted. As a result of overlong contact with the outback, Querry sinks into a soulless despair worsened by atheism. Stymying Belgium's efforts to control the region, the jungle thwarts all movement except for that of snakes, insects, birds, primates, and pygmies, the only humans who thrive in the tropical environment. Greene symbolizes the failure of white incomers to function in the unyielding climate when he quotes the leper Deo Gratias. Knowing his case is incurable, the leper says, "I am too far gone, I can't feel at all" (31).

Sources

Greene, Graham. *A Burnt-Out Case.* New York: Viking, 1961.
———. *The Heart of the Matter.* London: Penguin, 2004.
———. *Journey without Maps.* London: Penguin, 1992.
———. *Our Man in Havana.* London: Penguin, 2007.
———. *The Quiet American.* London: Penguin, 2002.
Sherry, Norman. *The Life of Graham Greene.* Vol. 2: 1939–1955. London: Penguin, 2004.

Grey Owl   See NATURE LORE.

Grimm, Jacob (Jacob Ludwig Carl Grimm) (1785–1863) and Grimm, Wilhelm (Wilhelm Carl Grimm) (1786–1859) *German philologists and folklorists*

Born in Hanau, Hesse-Kassel, Germany, the scholars and story collectors Jacob and Wilhelm Grimm lived in an unstable milieu during an upheaval in northwestern European empires. Like the German poet and playwright JOHANN WOLFGANG VON GOETHE, the Grimm brothers lived during the dissolution of the Holy Roman Empire under Francis II and, until 1813, endured the occupation of Germany by the forces of Napoleon Bonaparte. In 1819, during a period of spying and censorship Jacob railed at the climate of mistrust, petty jealousies, and scandals among police, all features of the feudalism and rigid class system prevalent in Germany at that time. While Austria, France, and Prussia vied for territory, the brothers promoted the *Volk* (peasantry) and the solidarity and history of their German fatherland.

The Grimms earned respect from contemporaries for defending the arts. With Protestant fervor, Jacob declared the value of indigenous literature: "Nations hold fast by prescription: We shall never comprehend their tradition, their superstition, unless we spread under it a bed on still heathen soil" (Grimm 1883, vi). Like the Hawaiian story collector King David Kalakaua, the Australian FRONTIER LITERATURE writers A. B. Paterson and Henry Lawson, and the Polish-Jewish writer ISAAC BASHEVIS SINGER, the Grimm brothers envisioned that a single, all-encompassing language and a vigorous literary canon would supply a disparate German confederation with a common shared heritage. The writers' PROPHECY of a unified Germany came true in 1871 with the proclamation of the German Empire.

Germanic Treasures

The Grimm brothers rooted their careers in archival material and relived "olden times when wishing still helped one" (Grimm 2002, 17). In the estimation of the 20th-century author and literary analyst Padraic Colum, their stories concentrate on fear and a transcendent WISDOM that can free and validate humankind. Their ethnography and mythography drew on German antiquity for GOTHIC romance, beast FABLE, the 13th-century *Prose Edda* legends of the Icelandic bard SNORRI STURLUSON, and cautionary tales that warned the innocent of kidnap, abandonment, starvation, seduction, dungeons, torture, and death. The detail and naturalism of *Kinder und Hausmärchen* (Children's and household tales, 1812, 1815, 1822), *Deutsche Sagen* (*German Legends*, 1816, 1818), and the beast fable *Reinhart Fuchs* (Reynard the Fox, 1834) suited the education of children and established a sense of German nationhood in the minds of readers. In the preface to the first collection, Wilhelm extolled the purity of folktales, which reveal the marvel and blessing of childhood innocence. Story by story, the reading of ethnic treasures provided young minds with the "wonderful last echoes of ancient myths" that, according to the Grimm biographer Murray B. Peppard, preserved for future generations the "childhood of the race" (Peppard 1971, 48, 49). As a consequence of the Grimms' liberal politics, in 1837, after seven years on staff at the University of Göttingen, Jacob and Wilhelm resisted a constitutional violation committed by King Ernst August I and withdrew from Hanover as political victims.

The Grimm brothers expressed the extremes of international aggression through stories that paired obvious mismatches—a cat with a mouse, a wolf with a man, a bear with a wren, and a fox with bees. Their folktales put Rapunzel in a tower cell, Little Red Riding Hood in the clutches of a wolf, Snow White and Rose Red in peril of a black bear, a princess under the designs of the Frog Prince, Briar Rose under an evil spell, Thousandfurs in the hands of her lustful father, and Hansel and Gretel in the cage of a cannibalistic witch. The skewed balance of power leads to VIOLENCE, a given in world politics involving one nation's dominance over another. To public demands for bowdlerization of sexual implications and murder in their stories, the ethnographers softened the wording slightly but insisted that children face the truth about domestic violence, empire building, GENOCIDE, and war. Writing to Goethe in 1816, Wilhelm informed his contemporary that the stories "represent, without any additions by other hands, the characteristic poetic views and attitudes of the common people, since only a strongly felt need was ever the occasion for composing them" (70).

Through the importation of German storybooks to North America by German immigrants, Grimms' fairy tales passed to Hollywood. Individual stories and biography became sources of the films *Snow White and the Seven Dwarfs* (1937), *Cinderella* (1950), *Sleeping Beauty* (1959), *The Wonderful World of the Brothers Grimm* (1962), and *The Brothers Grimm* (2005), which features Heath Ledger and Matt Damon as Jacob and Wilhelm Grimm on a mission for the Napoleonic regime.

Sources

Grimm, Jacob. *Teutonic Mythology*. 3 vols. Translated by James Steven Stallybrass. London: George Bell & Sons, 1882–83.

Grimm, Jacob, and Wilhelm Grimm. *The Complete Grimm's Fairy Tales*. Introduction by Padraic Colum. New York: Routledge, 2002.

Peppard, Murray B. *Paths through the Forest: A Biography of the Brothers Grimm*. New York: Holt, Rinehart & Winston, 1971.

Toews, John Edward. *Becoming Historical: Cultural Reformation and Public Memory in Early Nineteenth-Century Berlin*. Cambridge: Cambridge University Press, 2004.

Zornado, Joseph L. *Inventing the Child: Culture, Ideology, and the Story of Childhood*. New York: Routledge, 2001.

Gulliver's Travels See SWIFT, JONATHAN.

H

Haggard, H. Rider (**Sir Henry Rider Haggard**)
(1856–1925) *British adventure novelist*

A reformer, chronicler, and storyteller, Henry Rider Haggard drew on the literature of colonial adventurers and his own experiences to initiate a new literary fashion known as the "Lost World" genre. His writing would influence contemporary and later writers such as Sir ARTHUR CONAN DOYLE (1859–1930), RUDYARD KIPLING (1865–1936), Edgar Rice Burroughs (1875–1950), H. P. Lovecraft (1890–1937), and Michael Crichton (1942–2008).

Born in Bradenham, Norfolk, England, Haggard was educated at a private day school in London and then at Ipswich Academy. In 1875, after having previously failing an army entrance exam, he went to Natal to become the secretary to Sir Henry Bulwer, the lieutenant governor of Natal, South Africa. This experience provided the source of local-color articles Haggard wrote for *Gentleman's Magazine* and *Macmillan's Magazine* and for his Allan Quatermain series. He traveled widely in Africa during the 1879 Anglo-Zulu War and the First Boer War (1880–81). During a return visit to England in 1880, he married Louisa Margitson; the couple went back to Africa for another two years before finally settling in Norfolk and then in London. Called to the bar in 1884, Haggard practiced law only occasionally, preferring instead to write novels.

Haggard created his signature characters from the adventures of a London-born contemporary, expeditioner and guide Frederick Courteney Selous (1851–1917), a forerunner of fictional heroes like Indiana Jones. While halfheartedly practicing law, the author romanticized the colonial rape of Natal, Zululand, the Transvaal, and Zimbabwe in *King Solomon's Mines* (1885), England's initial African adventure fiction and the first to feature Allan Quatermain. In a salute to the Victorian frontiersman, Haggard declares, "There is no journey upon this earth that a man may not make if he sets his heart to it" (Haggard 2004, 49), an expression of the can-do spirit of the explorers David Livingstone (1813–73), Henry Morton Stanley (1841–1904), and Mungo Park (1771–1806). Haggard tinged his settings with an ominous silence, such as that framed in *Black Heart and White Heart: A Zulu Idyll* (1900): "There seemed to be no life here and no sound—only now and again a loathsome spotted snake would uncurl itself and glide away, and now and again a rotten bough fell with a crash" (Haggard 1900, 27). The overblown heroics reflect the popular British conception of challenges to masculinity in a series of perilous treks through the bush.

Like Kipling and the Ukrainian dramatist and satirist NIKOLAY GOGOL, Haggard maintained firm beliefs in the civilizing capabilities of imperial conquest. His fiction made a substantial impact on gullible readers, and his popular swashbuckling novels shaped the attitudes of a generation of stay-at-homes concerning the South African frontier and the subjugation of nonwhite peoples in a foreign land. Vicariously, armchair travelers set off to live in the moment during safe fantasy forays in the exotic unknown typified by the titles

The World's Desire (1890), *Heart of the World* (1895), and *The People of the Mist* (1894). Freed of social constraint and decorum, the escapist reader experienced an atavistic past governed only by the demands of survival.

The Finite Empire

Presaging the Lost World motifs of the American writer Edgar Rice Burroughs's Tarzan saga, Haggard vindicated the prototypical big-game hunter, often accused of imperial villainy and waste. The Quatermain series placed such men on equal footing with the black bush dweller, a liberalization of attitude later represented by the safari organizers Bror Blixen, Berkeley Cole, and Denys Finch-Hatton in ISAK DINESEN's *Out of Africa* (1937). In *Allan Quatermain* (1887), the elephant stalker's dissatisfaction with African loot and with the decimation of animals reflects the growing British ambivalence toward the colonial pillage of Africa's natural resources and continental integrity. To the protagonist, avarice reveals the absence of true Christianity in people who are "fixed night and day upon Mammon's glittering image" (Haggard 2007, 469). In the introduction to *Allan's Wife* (1889), Haggard lamented the alteration of the Transvaal plains after the Boers seized the goldfields: "The game has gone; the misty charm of the morning has become the glare of day" (Haggard 1889, v). The complex character of Quatermain came to life on the screen in the acting of Stewart Granger in *King Solomon's Mines* (1950), George Montgomery in *Watusi: Guardians of King Solomon's Mines* (1959), Richard Chamberlain in *King Solomon's Mines* (1985) and *Allan Quatermain and the Lost City of Gold* (1987), Sean Connery in *The League of Extraordinary Gentlemen* (2003), and Patrick Swayze in a later reprise of *King Solomon's Mines* (2004).

By age 50, Haggard renounced his notoriety for penning best sellers and turned his attention to the decline of the African native under colonial rule. Like the English-Canadian FRONTIER writer Grey Owl (Archibald Belaney, 1888–1938), author of *The Men of the Last Frontier* (1931), Haggard recognized that despoliation of the wild was irreversible. As a supervisor for the Dominions Royal Commission in Australia, Canada, New Zealand, and South Africa, he began studying racism, land swindles, agrarian and herding conditions, and the plight of migrant Zulu laborers and miners. In his journal, *Diary of an African Journey* (1914), he speaks of battling the "darksome, unknown powers in Government offices" (Haggard 2001, 34), a bureaucratic combat far removed from the swagger of Allan Quatermain. Of the struggle to anglicize Rhodesia, he observed that, unlike the more hospitable regions of Australia and Canada, Rhodesia was not "a land suitable to the permanent establishment and reproduction of Europeans" (284). His tone discloses a race prejudice rooting blacks in lands that are uninhabitable by less robust white overseers. Nevertheless, he deplored the aim of the white race to govern Africa.

Sources

Haggard, H. Rider. *Allan Quatermain: The Zulu Trilogy, Marie, Child of Storm, and Finished.* New York: Wilder, 2007.

———. *Allan's Wife.* London: Spencer Blackett, 1889.

———. *Black Heart and White Heart.* London: Longmans, Green, 1900.

———. *Diary of an African Journey: The Return of Rider Haggard.* New York: New York University Press, 2001.

———. *King Solomon's Mines.* Whitefish, Mont.: Kessinger, 2004.

Hopkins, Lisa. *Giants of the Past.* Lewisburg, Pa.: Bucknell University Press, 2004.

Halevi, Yehuda (Judah Halevi, Judah ha-Levi, Yehuda ben Samuel Halevi) (ca. 1075–1141)
Spanish Jewish poet and theologian

A physician and writer during the Hebrew golden age (900–1200), Yehuda Halevi composed an overview of opposing agnostic, Christian, Hebraic, and Islamic theologies. He was born in Toledo in southern Castile, Spain, a territory that passed from Muslim control under the Abbasid Empire to the rule of Alfonso VI when Halevi was 11 years old. After his training at a seminary in Lucena, he entered the caliph's court at Castile. In his mid-teens, he began writing love ditties, riddles, drinking songs and nature verse in Arabic, Hebrew, and Spanish. His entry into medical practice in Cordoba brought him face-to-face with the Jews' position between Muslim expansionism and the Christian reconquest of Spain. He became a vigorous Zionist. Through 800 original elegies, laments, liturgical hymns, and prayers, he championed Judaism as a superior faith. He died during a voyage to Palestine, though details of his death are unclear.

Because of his balance of lyricism and gravitas, Halevi earned fame as the leading medieval Jewish poet. His secular verse includes a May-December EPITHALAMIUM that reminds the gray-haired philosopher of the span of time separating him from comely maidens. Of the materialism and pomp of empires, he warns, "He who lengthens the train of his coat, / easily stumbles over his own robe" (Halevi 2000, 126). Of his own fallibility, "The Sick Physician" suggests that piety relieves professional ennui and despair.

In the poem "Conquered Darkness," Halevi rhapsodizes on the vulnerability of the dove and, by extension, of himself. He intones, "May his light enter into my darkness!" and envisions the coming of the Messiah, the summation of light to a dark world (160). In liturgical stanzas similar in fealty and joy to Sufist verse, he replicates the tone and imagery of the Davidic PSALMS. Through worship, atonement, and praise, he seeks the sincerity and peace of the sabbath as an escape from the troubled politics of central and southern Spain as Christianity fought to regain it from Islam. The poet's spiritual escapism into a holy land takes literary form in his Lionide, odes to Lion that shape Jewish identity. The nationalistic poems appeared in translation throughout the late Middle Ages.

Through four-way debate, Halevi's great philosophical work, the *Kuzari* (written over 20 years and completed in 1140), vindicates the Jewish perspective on piety, biblical miracles, and the foundation of human history. The first of five chapters introduces CREATION LORE by naming Adam and Eve as the initial earth dwellers and honors Torah patriarchs, prophets, and chroniclers for their adherence to Mosaic law.

Sources

Halevi, Yehuda. *The Kuzari: In Defense of the Despised Faith.* Translated by Hartwig Hirschfeld. New York: E. P. Dutton, 1905.

———. *Ninety-Two Poems and Hymns of Yehuda Halevi.* Translated by Thomas Kovach, Eva Jospe, and Gilya Gerda Schmidt. Edited by Richard A. Cohen. New York: State University of New York Press, 2000.

Hamasa (Abu Tammam) (ca. 845)

An anthology of Arabic verse, the *Hamasa* (Courage) of the Abbasid poet Abu Tammam Habib ibn Aus, ca. 804–ca. 845, displays a breadth of interests and insights from the medieval Islamic world. Born in Jasim, Iraq, to Theodosius, a Christian wine merchant, Abu Tammam grew up in Hims in central Syria and apprenticed with a weaver. In Cairo, Egypt, he sold water at the Great Mosque and studied among the learned before beginning a career of court writing and reciting battle elegies for audiences in Damascus, Armenia, Baghdad, and Khorasan (present-day Afghanistan, Iran, Tajikistan, Turkmenistan, and Uzbekistan). While snowed in at the home of the Salamas at Hamadan, Iran, near a well-stocked library, he began assembling and categorizing the best of pre-Islamic Bedouin *qasida* (rhapsodic odes), tribal lays, and fragmentary gems in a 10-book collection organized by topic. At his death in Mosul, where he served as postmaster, the 3,760 verses contained in the *Hamasa*'s 882 entries remained unpublished in the private library of the Salama family. From there it passed to scholars in Baghdad.

Writing a century before the compilation of wonder tales and seduction scenarios in *The THOUSAND AND ONE NIGHTS* (ca. A.D. 942), Abu Tammam established a reputation for purity of style and for stark antithesis unclouded by philosophical gray areas. During the Crusades, Arab readers, including the Kurdish general Saladin, valued passages memorized from the *Hamasa* that counseled right thinking and behavior based on the values of desert nomads. During the Ayyubid dynasty in the 12th and 13th centuries, Abu Tammam's romanticized themes of valor, resilience, nobility, and masculinity endeared his writings to Muslim soldiers throughout Egypt and Syria. They quoted and sang tributes to fallen comrades and to the conquest of the fortified city of Amorium, which Caliph al-Mutasim captured in A.D. 838. In the ode "To Washal," the poet discloses Arab territoriality and militance by extolling the cool mountain spring and vowing to ward off the "base lip" from tasting it (Abu Tammam 1972, 147). Other subjects—fine wines, garden dalliances, and sexual fantasies—suited the needs and yearnings of the imperial warrior far from home.

Sources

Abu Tammam. *The Hamasa of Abu Tammam.* Translated by Felix Klein-Franke. Leiden: E. J. Brill, 1972.

Stetkevych, Jaroslav. *The Zephyrs of Najd: The Poets of Nostalgia in the Classical Arabic Nasib.* Chicago: University of Chicago Press, 1993.

Han Yong-un (Han Yu-cheon, Manhae)
(1879–1944) *Korean theologian and modernist poet*

A freedom fighter and religious progressive, Han Yong-un, who wrote under the pseudonym Manhae (Ten thousand seas), followed the shift of his ideals from revolution to the priesthood. A native of South Korea, he was born at Hongsong in Gyeongsang Province, southwest of Seoul. A member of the minor gentry, he read Cao Xueqin's court novel *The DREAM OF THE RED CHAMBER* (1791) and other classics of Chinese imperialism and learned a Confucian code of conduct from his father. Although he joined the Tonghak Revolt of 1894 at age 15, he fled the political backlash against Japanese aggression to study Buddhist scripture. He became a Buddhist monk in 1905, the same year Korea became a Japanese protectorate. Five years later, Japan's 35-year occupation began.

Han's travels to Kyoto and Tokyo in 1908 influenced his decision to adapt Chinese Buddhism to Western philosophy and Korean tastes with a visionary treatise, *Choson pulgyo yusin-non* (The restoration of Korean Buddhism, 1910), which predicts the death of Buddhism and Korea itself without immediate action to preserve liberty. Unlike the monks preferring hermitism and withdrawal from society, he insisted that all people alert themselves to threat and strengthen their faculties with an understanding of history. In fealty to the divine, he encouraged training in Buddhist principles without losing sight of the needs of ordinary citizens. Among his radical demands was the aboli-

tion of outworn ritual, of celibacy for monks, and of superstition. On the positive side, he foresaw "Minjung Buddhism" (the people's Buddhism)—a true enlightenment through guerrilla resistance of Japanese colonizers, restoration of normal peasant morals and institutions, and the creation of a free Korean state. In a line from his collected works, he identifies with the exuberant individual: "Coming in and out anywhere I please, crying and laughing cannot make any trace on my cheeks. In the ocean of suffering I want to make the lotus flower bloom in the fire" (Han 1999, 236).

On March 1, 1919, as his nation began its revolt against Japanese rule, Han codrafted and edited the Korean Declaration of Independence, an activist document that cost him three years in prison. Upon his release in 1922, he channeled his fervor into public oratory and essays. Influenced by Bengali author RABINDRANATH TAGORE, Han produced 163 poems in *sijo* (three-line stanzas of 14–16 syllables) and free verse in vernacular Korean. His 88 poems in *Nim ui ch'immuk* (*Love's Silence*, 1926) allegorize Korea as the beloved and press Koreans to embrace passive resistance and to rally for national independence. Refuting the orthodox Buddhist concept of disengagement, in "The Master's Sermon," he declares that tight bonds of love of nation are truly liberating. In "Your Touch," he pictures dynamic patriotism as a flame burning the heart, consuming cares, and satisfying longings.

The Manhae Prize, initiated in 1973 by the literary quarterly *Changjak gwa bipyeong* (Creation and criticism), preserves Han's ideals.

Sources

Han Yong-un. *Love's Silence & Other Poems.* Translated by Jaihiun Kim and Ronald B. Hatch. Vancouver: Ronsdale Press, 1999.

Yu, Beongcheon. *Han Yong-un & Yi Kwang-su: Two Pioneers of Modern Korean Literature.* Chicago: Wen State University Press, 1992.

Head, Bessie (Bessie Amelia Emery Head)
(1937–1986) *South African novelist and journalist*

A feminist libertarian, Bessie Head challenged apartheid as an inescapable hell for the biracial citizen. Born Bessie Amelia Emery of Scots-African ancestry in Pietermaritzburg, Head was the illegitimate daughter of a white mother committed by her family to the Fort Napier Mental Institution in punishment for sexual intimacies with a black stableboy. In "Notes from a Quiet Backwater I," the opening chapter of A *Woman Alone: Autobiographical Writings* (1990), Head pondered the destiny of children born of miscegenation "whose birth or beginnings are filled with calamity and disaster, the sort of person who is a skeleton in the cupboard or the dark and fearful secret swept under the carpet" (Head 1990, 3). After her mother killed herself, white foster parents gave Bessie a home until black characteristics marked her as a bicultural misfit. Under South African law, she became the ward of black parents. A few months before she turned 13, she entered St. Monica's Home, an Anglican boarding school near Durban.

After earning a teacher's certificate, Bessie began teaching at a primary school in Durban. In 1958, she moved to Cape Town, where she was hired as a reporter. She married Harold Head in 1961. Always a voracious reader, she investigated Hinduism, the religion of local Afro-Indians. She embraced motherhood but found marriage, teaching, and journalism in South Africa unsatisfying. Of the constant reminder of her mixed race, she lamented that the political situation was so untenable that she could not fashion it into fiction.

In 1964, Head took her son Howard and fled north to Botswana, which gained its independence from Great Britain in 1966. While raising Howard among the Bangwato in Serowe and writing for *Drum* magazine and the *Golden City Post*, she became an activist for other refugees from South African apartheid, and she began producing fiction about biracial misfits pressed to desperation and suicide. She spent 15 years at the Bamangwato Development Farm before becoming a citizen of Botswana.

Anguished Narratives

While living in poverty and mental torment, Head became the spokesperson for the racial pariah in self-exile from colonial and gender discrimination and injustice. At age 32, she published her first novel, *When Rain Clouds Gather* (1969), about

the residue of colonial racism that alters the fate of the Zulu ex-con Makhaya, an idealist who settles at Golema Mmidi, an agrarian commune. Paradoxically, in his flight from tribalism, he takes pride in his skill at language, a gift of the Zulu empire: "Since the days of Shaka we've assumed that the whole world belongs to us; that's why we trouble to learn any man's language" (Head 1995, 3). Far from the golden age of the Zulu hegemony, the narrative serves up the worst of starvation, picturing dying children, "their knees cramped up to their chins, their bony fingers curled into their palms like steel claws" (162).

Locked in mental turmoil and subject to episodes of schizophrenia, Head continued to battle her memories of childhood scandal and rejection. In 1971, she published *Maru* (1971), the story of a woman sired by a bushman with an Englishwoman. Mirroring Head's early womanhood, the orphaned protagonist, Margaret Cadmore, a teacher in Dilepe, suffers from alienation and a stifling malaise. Head's autobiographical novel A *Question of Power* (1973) enlarges on the solitude and ostracism of the expatriate through the fantasies of Elizabeth, a victim of mental disintegration. The phantoms that stalk her schizoid visions derive from the author's own battles with mental illness and from her fusion of tortuous hallucination with racist oppression and dispossession of self and country. After years of distress and heavy drinking, Bessie Head died in Serowe, Botswana, on April 17, 1986.

Sources

Head, Bessie. *Maru*. London: Heinemann, 1997.
———. A *Question of Power*. London: Heinemann, 1974.
———. *When Rain Clouds Gather*. London: Heinemann, 1995.
———. A *Woman Alone: Autobiographical Writings*. London: Heinemann, 1990.
Lewis, Desiree. *Living on the Horizon: Bessie Head and the Politics of Imagining*. Lansing: University of Michigan Press, 2007.

Heaney, Seamus (1939–) *Irish poet, translator, and essayist*

A child of the struggle to free Ireland from British dominion, Seamus Heaney has written works that testify to the paradox of violence and dissension in a bucolic green land. Orphaned in boyhood, he grew up in rural County Derry 40 miles northwest of Belfast in Northern Ireland. On scholarship, he studied English, Irish, and Latin at St. Columb's College in Londonderry. With a degree in English language and literature from Queen's University, Belfast, he joined the faculty at St. Joseph's Teacher Training College, submitted essays to magazines, and married the poet and mythographer Marie Devlin. In 1972, he moved to Wicklow in southern Ireland. A recipient of the 1995 Nobel Prize in literature, he has lectured at Harvard, the University of California at Berkeley, and Oxford.

With a simplicity and craftsmanship sometimes compared to the American poet Robert Frost, Heaney has woven into outstanding works—such as "Triptych," "The Strand at Lough Beg," and "Casualty"—a paradox of ancestral pride and willingness to compromise. In "After a Killing," modeled on Thomas Hardy's "The Man He Killed," Heaney eulogizes young men slain in the ongoing clash of Catholic against Protestant and loyalist against republican. In writing his musings on bog corpses, "The Tollund Man" and "The Grauballe Man," he reviewed the evidence of past efforts at empire—Viking, Anglo-Saxon, and British—that crop up in anthropological digs on rural turf. These poems of ancient bodies found in bogs suit the political quagmire that gobbled young energies and lives during the "troubles," the protracted conflict between British and Irish from the late 1960s until the Belfast Accord of 1998.

For a sonnet on farmer-soldiers, Heaney chose the scythe as a symbol of the agrarian resister facing cavalry and cannon in barley fields. In "Digging," a popular poem from *Death of a Naturalist* (1966), his imagery compares verse writing to peat cutting, a domestic task that occupied his grandfather and father. Like the Roman poets HORACE and VIRGIL, Heaney takes comfort in the cyclical rounds of planting, tending, and harvesting and in the one-on-one pleasures of friendship and sharing plates of fresh fare.

Poetry as Translation

In 1999, Heaney resurrected Viking ruthlessness, vanity, and melancholy in his translation of *Beowulf* (A.D. 800), an Iron Age heroic epic, from Anglo-Saxon. The text dramatizes the quasihistorical feats of a Geat warrior of Götaland (present-day southern Sweden) who aids the Dane King Hrothgar in quelling Grendel, a night-stalking beast. In the introduction, the poet notes that Beowulf voices the Scandic principles of honor as his personal code. First, he states the value of might over grief: "It is always better / to avenge dear ones than to indulge in mourning" (Heaney 2007, xiii). Bringing the concept of battlefield carnage down to the individual, he exhorts, "Let whoever can, / win glory before death," a pagan grasp on earthly life as the only reality (xiii). For the glory hunter Beowulf, the dismemberment and decapitation of Grendel underwater are the source of lasting fame, a he-man remembrance "as wide as the wind's home / as the sea around cliffs" (xiv). Nature-based imagery elevates Grendel to a natural phenomenon and his quelling on a par with subduing a force as unpredictable as a tornado. The poet amplifies the bloodbath with "loathsome upthrows / and overturnings / Of waves and gore and wound-slurry" (57).

Heaney's wording of the epic achieves a balance in the falling action. The approach of death shifts the mood from heroic to elegiac and prophetic. As the elderly warrior sits on a cliff like a wraith to await the fire dragon: "He was sad at heart, / unsettled yet ready, sensing his death. / His fate hovered near, unknowable but certain" (xvi). In death, Beowulf rejoins nature. From his pyre, the smoke carries his remains heavenward just as the sea brought him to land. The funereal coda takes a realistic measure of the era in terms of wartime devastation: A female mourner unleashes "a wild litany / of nightmare and lament: her nation invaded, / enemies on the rampage, bodies in piles, slavery and abasement" (xvii). Critics read into Heaney's virulent images the scarring of Ireland by centuries of British imperialism.

Sources

Beowulf: An Illustrated Edition. Translated by Seamus Heaney. New York: W. W. Norton, 2007.

Heaney, Seamus. *Death of a Naturalist.* London: Faber & Faber, 1966.

———. *Opened Ground: Selected Poems 1966–1996.* New York: Farrar, Straus, and Giroux, 1998.

Kabir, Ananya Jahansra, and Deanne Williams.
    *Postcolonial Approaches to the European Middle
    Ages: Translating Cultures.* Cambridge: Cambridge
    University Press, 2005.
Kennedy-Andrews, Elmer. *The Poetry of Seamus Heaney.*
    New York: Columbia University Press, 2000.

Hearn, Lafcadio   See TRANSLATION.

Heart of Darkness Joseph Conrad (1899)

JOSEPH CONRAD exposed imperial hypocrisy and
ethnic strife in his Congo novel *Heart of Darkness*,
a triumph of first-person STORYTELLING. After
witnessing European paternalism's downslide into
despotism, he hurled a rebuke at "deeds of empire"
and offered a grudging salute to the frontiersmen
who surrender body and soul for the sake of profit.
In the first year of his writing career, he introduced
the setting and themes of his future great novel in
the story "An Outpost of Progress," an ambivalent
tale printed in *Cosmopolis* magazine in July 1896
and anthologized in *Tales of Unrest* (1898). This
story of the demoralizing task of ivory trading
depicts two men as victims: the trading station's
assistant, Carlier, and the chief, Kayerts. The latter
accidentally shoots Carlier and then hangs himself
out of despair from isolation and a sordid involvement in the slave trade. The story introduces the
damaged conscience and sickness of guilt that
deranges and destroys.

Three years later, the author's exploration of
the sullied soul took shape in meatier form in *Heart
of Darkness* with the story of Kurtz, a crazed martyr
to the empire's depersonalization of natives and
apathy toward their fate. Choosing the Englishman
Charlie Marlow as narrator, Conrad begins the tale
of the extended voyage of a Belgian steamer on a
river in west Africa, the historic headquarters of
the slaving trade. Marlow's mission is to retrieve
Kurtz, a company agent who has been alone in
the interior for some time. As the newcomer loses
his urbane detachment during the journey, he
concludes that the business of imperialism in the
Congo is indefensible.

In the beginning of the story, before he sets
off on his mission, Marlow compares the Roman
concept of empire to savagery and marvels at
"the abomination—you know, imagine the growing regrets, the longing to escape, the powerless
disgust, the surrender, the hate" (Conrad 1983,
69). To heighten alienation on the frontier, the
author identifies few characters clearly but pictures the self-aggrandizement of imperialism as
an advancing monster, shapeless and menacing.
Marlow introduces himself as a nomad impelled by
boredom and intellectual curiosity to penetrate a
jungle so compact that it appears more black than
green, a suggestion of evil that defiles nature itself.
Moving toward the 20th century, he describes
colonialism as a "squeeze" and conquerors as
brutes who "grabbed what they could get for the
sake of what was to be got" (69). As the British
Empire displays its threadbare seams, Marlow
accepts the mission to bring Kurtz downriver from
his distant station. But ship repairs delay the journey. This image of breakdown haunts the entire
mission, threatening with destruction Marlow's
steamer and crew as well as Kurtz.

Confrontation with Evil

The text symbolizes racial and cultural misgivings
by picturing an impenetrable environment, the
source of the ivory trade, which develops from
commodity into a mystic icon. To extend the
atmosphere of barbarism to two fronts, the action
includes spears hurled from the bush and hints at
cannibalism among the ship's crew. Some 200 miles
upstream into the Congo River, Marlow observes
the chaining of moribund quarry laborers, "black
shadows of disease and starvation" (82). Pushing
15 days against the current, he reaches the Central
Station and is mesmerized by rumors and half-
tales about Kurtz, the company's top trader. The
trek becomes a retrogressive quest, "like travelling
back to the earliest beginnings of the world" (102).
Written 38 years after CHARLES DICKENS's *Great
Expectations* (1861), Conrad's view of colonial
opportunity scrutinizes the fiasco of those expectations at close range.

On the approach to Kurtz's compound, the
narrative describes an end to civilization and the
outskirts of the "heart of darkness"—the compound, which Kurtz has lined with human skulls.
Explaining the monstrosity of the stationmaster,

Conrad asserts, "All Europe contributed to the making of Kurtz" (122–123), who has become an icon of outlandish greed. Of Kurtz's damnation, Marlow notes, "The wilderness had found him out early and . . . had whispered to him things about himself which he did not know" (133), a paganism of soul more forbidding than the jungle itself. The retreat downriver requires constant repairs to Marlow's vessel—"an infernal mess of rust, filings, nuts, bolts, spanners, hammers, ratchet-drills" (147). Like the limping steamer, Kurtz, a "pitiful Jupiter," can only rave. At the end, his voice lapses into a whisper: "The horror! The horror!" as he sinks toward becoming a corpse for natives to inter in a "muddy hole" (148). The desolation and loneliness of Kurtz's life is the introit to madness, a severance from rationality that reduces him from man to beast—a punishment Conrad felt to be just retribution for his greed and cruelty.

Sources

Conrad, Joseph. *Heart of Darkness and The Secret Sharer*. New York: Signet, 1983.

Greaney, Michael. *Conrad, Language, and Narrative*. Cambridge: Cambridge University Press, 2002.

hero

Throughout the literature of empires, tales of bravery, physical strength, and ambitious quests set individuals apart in distinct historic epochs and locales, from the hardihood of the biblical Hebrew warrior Gideon, the Scandic hero *Beowulf* (ca. A.D. 800), and the Shawnee warrior in the Canadian poet Charles Mair's *Tecumseh* (1886) to the paddling and surfing gallants who woo a princess in the anonymous Hawaiian romance *Laieikawai* (1863). Over time, the literary survey of heroism emphasized character traits and difficult choices alongside physical prowess, a theme of JOSEPH CONRAD's antiheroic novels HEART OF DARKNESS (1899) and *Lord Jim* (1900) and of GABRIELE D'ANNUNZIO's criminal Corrado Brando; MARYSE CONDÉ's motherless Tituba; and PETER CAREY's Ned Kelly, the legendary Robin Hood of Australia. Over time, heroic values shifted away from the mythic and legendary to the victim of circumstances, a permanent fixture in the history of empires. One example is the work of combat reporter JOHN HERSEY, who shifted headline news into works such as *Men on Bataan* (1942) and *Hiroshima* (1946), which fed the American hunger for valor and grace under pressure.

Around 1200 B.C. at the beginning of the Israelite occupancy of Canaan (present-day Palestine), the late Bronze Age warrior Joshua stood out as a leader of the militaristic clan of Ephraimites. Mentored by Moses, the commander is the central character in the biblical book of Joshua, written about 1050 B.C. Linked to the patriarchs Abraham, Isaac, Jacob, and Moses of GENESIS (ca. 500 B.C.) and EXODUS (ca. 450 B.C.), Joshua faces the devotees of Asherah and Baal, divinities reverenced with sexual orgies, human disfigurement, and infant sacrifice, elements conducive to GOTHIC drama. In chapter 2, Joshua, a commander of pilgrims longing to cross the Jordan River and himself trained as a secret agent, assigns two spies to surveillance in Jericho, five miles west of the river. Before committing the Israelite army to siege, he observes religious custom by reinstating circumcision, a ritual passage of manhood required before his followers can enter "a land that floweth with milk and honey" (Joshua 5:6). Yahweh (God) readies the commander for battle through an epiphany. The seven-day encirclement of Jericho requires that the 12 clans select leaders. Launching forth with the cry "Shout; for the Lord hath given you the city" (Joshua 6:16), the decisive siege results in GENOCIDE and arson, a show of annihilation of the enemy that confers on Joshua the sovereignty of Moses (Joshua 6:27).

The Female Hero

In contrast to Joshua's male heroics, a subsequent hero saga, the book of Ruth (ca. 500 B.C.), a feminist narrative, prefaces the rise of the Davidic dynasty of Judah with female assertiveness. A simpler idyll than the Song of Solomon (ca. 590 B.C.), a love cycle and EPITHALAMIUM credited to King David's son Solomon, the book of Ruth departs from the nationalistic conquest motifs of Judges and 1 and 2 Samuel with a graceful and redemptive romance between a Jew and a foreigner—the Judaean landowner Boaz and the title figure, a Moabite widow from Syria. Coached by her mother-in-law Naomi,

Ruth openly courts the wealthy bachelor as a solution to homelessness and poverty. Set around 1100 B.C., the biographical narrative recounts the preservation of a genealogy through intermarriage with worthy immigrants.

The action begins with a triple tragedy, the widowhood of sister-in-laws Orpah and Ruth and their return with their widowed mother-in-law Naomi to her home in Bethlehem. Extending her marriage vows to include her husband's family, Ruth pledges to Naomi with tender parallelism, "Intreat me not to leave thee.... Thy people shall be my people, and thy god my god" (Ruth 1:16). Naomi reciprocates by matchmaking Ruth, a founding mother of Israel, to Boaz, a goodhearted barley farmer. By appealing to Boaz on his threshing floor, Ruth wins his love and becomes the great-grandmother of David. Bible historians conjecture that Ruth dates to period around 500 B.C. after Babylon's capture of Israel when xenophobic Jews attempted to preserve their racial purity under Persian rule, the love story encourages an open-mindedness toward bicultural relationships based on worthiness of heart and the willingness of a Gentile to convert to Judaism. This narrative of female risk-taking was the theme of the film *The Story of Ruth* (1960), starring Elana Eden and Peggy Wood as Ruth and Naomi and Stuart Whitman as Boaz.

Combat versus Domestic Valor

The history of strife among imperial factions in the Middle East extended to all faiths and cultures. With a minimum of self-adulation, in 721 B.C., Assyrian King Sargon II related in *The Fall of Samaria* his capture of the capital of northern Israel. Written in Khorsabad (east of present-day Mosul, Iraq), the war report covers a siege that resulted in 27,290 prisoners of war from the Ten Tribes of Israel. Included among the prisoners was King Iamani of the port city of Ashdod, Israel, where the troops led him away in chains. Sargon II headed a royal corps of 50 chariots and enriched his realm with an ongoing taxation of Samarians. With fishing imagery, the heroic king depicts the ease with which he netted the Ionian colonists of the western isles. Upon the betrayal of the Hittite pretender Ia'ubidi, Sargon moved against Qarqar, Syria, which he laid flat with fire. The impressment of local people added 200 chariots and 600 infantrymen to the Assyrian force. Sargon wisely installed Arab bedouin in Samaria and received tribute gifts from the Sabaeans of Yemen. Sargon's field text contains the gratitude of a king to the national god Ashur and characterizes the efficiency of empire building when backed by a dependable military.

In contrast to battlefield literature, a Cinderella tale, the book of Esther (ca. 175 B.C.), the source of the Jewish festival of Purim, relates from an insider's view the struggles of a captured people. The narrative contrasts Ruth's story with a more daring deviation from womanly submission during the Jewish diaspora. In 480 B.C. at Susa, an ethnically diverse city in present-day southeastern Iran, Ahasuerus, called by many Xerxes I (ca. 519–465 B.C.), inspects replacements for Queen Vashti, whom he divorces for disobedience, a paternal act of female disenfranchisement common to imperialism. The rest of the story depicts female subversion of supreme male authority. As a king's privilege, he selects an orphaned peasant girl for her beauty and modesty and celebrates their union with lavish entertainments and remission of taxes. Thus, in 480 B.C., Esther, the heir of King Saul and the beloved of Ahasuerus, becomes queen of Persia.

The plot of Esther's hero story turns on the power of a single malcontent to overcome racial issues. The brooding Haman, Persia's chief councillor, plots to exterminate Esther's guardian, her uncle Mordecai, by arranging the genocide of Jews, whom he dehumanizes as encumbrances to the empire. To rescue her people, Queen Esther breaches court protocol to approach the king and invite him and Haman to a private dinner. After the king discovers in an official chronicle that Mordecai saved him from assassination, Ahasuerus attends another private feast and learns from Esther that Haman plots to kill all her people. In a show of imperial ethics, the king rules against pogroms. In a twist of poetic justice, the king observes Haman entreating Esther for mercy, charges him with attempted rape, and has him executed on the gallows built to kill Mordecai. Film versions of Esther's life featured Joan Collins in *Esther and the King* (1960), Victoria Principal in *The Greatest Heroes of the Bible* (1978), Louise

Lombard in *Esther* (1999), and Tiffany Dupont in *One Night with the King* (2006).

Historical Heroes

In the KORAN (A.D. 633), separate passages reveal aspects of the heroism of Abraham, Ishmael, Ezekiel, Jonah, Joseph, and Job. Noah's story creates conflict out of the scorn of neighbors toward the builder of the ark. As a token of obedience, the scripture pictures the survivor of the flood as contrite before God: "Forgive me and have mercy on me, or I shall surely be among the lost" (Koran 11:47). Of the courage of Moses and his brother Aaron, the text refers to the 10 plagues of Egypt as "Our signs to Pharaoh and his nobles. But they responded with scorn, for they were wicked men" (Koran 10:75). In the introduction to the rise of the Davidic dynasty, the text asserts of the warrior king, "We taught him the armourer's craft, so that you might have protection in your wars" (Koran 21:80). David's successor, King Solomon, develops judgment over physical strength—from combat hero to intellectual and soothsayer.

Medieval heroic lore continued the bardic tradition of retelling feats of daring and acts of humility from past generations as the supreme compliment to the protagonist. In 1113, the earliest use of the Myanmar language preserved the Myazedi Inscription on a stone stele at a temple in Bagan, Burma. First published in 1919, the text, written like a royal proclamation or encomium, acknowledges the fealty of Prince Rajakumar, the royal love child of King Kyanzittha, who, around 1100, dedicated three slave villages to Buddha as a means of attaining wisdom and of propitiating the gods to improve his father's health. In 1298, the Venetian traveler MARCO POLO produced similar praise in *The Travels of Marco Polo* after his encounter with Kublai Khan, the emperor of the Tartars of Mongolia. As the focus of a lengthy odyssey narrative, the khan fulfills Plato's concept of a philosopher king for his self-control and noble aim. Excelling previous monarchs, he stands out as a wise organizer and innovator as well as the leader of a massive cavalry. To humanize his image of the Asian empire builder, Polo admits the khan's failures and balances them with incidents of mercy, generosity, and courtesy, such as his acceptance of the Christian cross as a symbol of goodness and justice.

Heroes of Southwestern Europe

The militant nature of feudalism produced a hero cult of the protector of agrarian society and the defender of the realm. Around 1175, the Anglo-Norman poet MARIE DE FRANCE lauded the virtues of the chivalric hero in chansons de geste, or French heroic epics, some reflective of Arthurian lore. To the northwest, the Icelandic mythographer SNORRI STURLUSON, a preserver of Viking lore, mentioned in the *Prose Edda* (1225) the importance of the champion to Norwegian monarchy. In a lengthy discourse differentiating between royalty and warriors, the text honors "Men of War, Brave Men, Valiant Men, Hardy Men, Overpowerers, Heroes" as opposed to "Coward, Skulker, Weakling, Qualmish, Caitiff, Scamp" (Sturluson 1916, 234). The poet applies grim diction to honor the "fair-piercing weapon, the render of blue birnies (chain mail),—with bitter thrusts and edges" (161). Mention of blood is frequent because of the many battles: "I see the heroes' slaughter on the fair shield-rim's surface" (161). In the later section, gift giving supersedes carnage and distinguishes the victor: "The king sows the bright seed-corn of knuckle-splendid gold rings," an overt public symbol of reward for loyalty (173).

In Iberia, the Castilian-Spanish knight-errant adventure tale *Amadis de Gaula* (*Amadis of Gaul*, 1508) narrates a Portuguese hero legend that was refined and extended by the Spanish author Garci Rodríguez de Montalvo (d. 1504), an alderman of Medina del Campo. A model of chivalric romance, the text bases conquest on an Arthurian motif of the abandoned bastard boy—the "Child of the Sea" (Montalvo 2003, 41)—reared by the Scots warrior Don Gandales and shielded by supernatural powers and PROPHECY, a standard token of promise from prehistory. Amadis develops into an invincible knight who fits the biographical outlines of an identifiable warrior, Simon IV de Montfort (1160–1218), a savage French fighter of the Fourth Crusade and the protagonist of William of Tudela's *Chanson de la croisade Albigeosie* (Song of the Albigensian Crusade, 1213). For four years, Amadis suffers the crusader's isolation and alienation while traveling through the Roman Empire and maintaining chivalry "at a higher level than in the house of any other king or emperor in the world" (110). He challenges Endriago, a satanic dragon that symbolizes the paganism and degeneracy of Islam. Throughout the 16th century, German, Italian, Portuguese, and Spanish writers added sequels to the popular cycle about a warrior "nothing short of wondrous" (176). The Spanish satirist MIGUEL DE CERVANTES mocked the super heroic Amadis in *Don Quixote* (1605), an antichivalric SATIRE.

New World Heroism

The prototypes of European epic writers set unlikely precedents for the characterization, action, and style of hero tales from the Western Hemisphere. The New World epic *O Uraguai* (*Uruguay,* 1769), composed in five cantos of blank verse by the Brazilian-Portuguese writer, former Jesuit novice, and rebel José Basílio da Gama (1740–1795), merged conventions of European romance with the near genocide of the Amerindian. The poem begins during the Guaraní Wars, or Jesuit Wars, of 1754–56, when some 30,000 Guaraní who had lived peacefully in Jesuit-run communities fought against Spanish-Portuguese armies who wanted their land. Da Gama opens on the carnage wreaked by General Gomes Freire de Andrada's Iberian army. Progressing to parlays at the Uruguay River in southern Brazil between the Spanish/Portuguese commanders and chiefs Cacambo and Sepé Tiaraju, the narrative tells of the one-sided warfare between bow-and-arrow soldiery and the advanced European firepower that kills the noble Sepé. Gama gains poetic momentum from wound descriptions: "The stript Sepé / Whose face was ghastly with the glaze of Death / Bathed in the flood of darkling gore that gusht / From the torn bosom while his livid arms, / Hoof-bruised, betrayed his miserable fall" (Gama 1982, 73).

Da Gama aimed his polemical epic of the colonial period at an exposé of the Jesuits of the Seven Missions for attempting to found an independent papal state in Uruguay. To raise the stakes for the outnumbered Guaraní, he introduces in canto 3 a vision of Sepé's spirit that convinces Cacambo to torch the Portuguese camp. Treachery in the form of assassination by the shaman Balda on behalf of his ambitious son Baldetta removes Cacambo

from the action. Preceding the destruction of the Guaraní settlement by Spanish-Portuguese forces, the poet inserts an ironic EPITHALAMIUM for the union of Baldetta and Lindóia, a tragic bride who grieves for Cacambo and who views Lisbon's destiny in a bowl of water. A conclusion to the 1,400-line epic contrasts the massacre of natives with the final humanitarianism of General Gomes Freire de Andrada to those Guaraní resisters who survive. Ironically, Da Gama's poem proved valuable to leaders of the Indianist movement of the mid-19th century. In 1986, the Oscar-winning film *The Mission* featured Robert de Niro and Jeremy Irons as clerics in a reenactment of the displacement of Brazilian mission Indians already weakened by smallpox epidemics.

The Byronic Hero

The romantic era in England popularized the Byronic hero, a literary cult prototype named for the controversial poet Lord Byron (George Gordon Byron, 1788–1824). In 1813, he depicted the outsider's abhorrence of the ritual execution of adulteresses in *The Giaour* (Infidel), which sets the Christian title figure against a vengeful Muslim husband. The protagonist suited a period of history in which European powers sought religious justification for attacking small nations of the crumbling Ottoman Empire. With flowery panache, the hero sweeps through a benighted culture: "He came, he went, like the Simoom (desert wind), / That harbinger of fate and gloom" (Byron 1826, 59), who bears the sorrow of a failed rescue attempt.

Delving into history, Byron's "The Destruction of Sennacherib" (1815), a rhythmic conquest narrative, surveys a doomed military quest—the Assyrian king's downfall while overreaching for conquest of Judah in 681 B.C. In the poem, Death engulfs Sennacherib: "For the Angel of Death spread his wings on the blast, / And breathed in the face of the foe as he pass'd" (590). By annihilating the Assyrian in the heat of action, Byron elevates the king's death as a measure of soldierly risk.

Byron described the self-absorbed heroic figure in the poem that made him famous, the autobiographical *Childe Harold's Pilgrimage* (1812–18). The lengthy TRAVELOGUE characterizes Europe's restlessness in the Napoleonic era's aftermath, when the title figure roams the eastern Mediterranean and views the Russian attacks on Turkish territory along the Danube River. With the adventurer's passion for live-or-die glory, Harold exults, "View us as victors, or view us no more!" (21). Of the endurance of empires, he admits to the unpredictability of history: "A thousand years scarce serve to form a state; / An hour may lay it in the dust" (22).

The brooding Byronic hero became fully developed in the poet's master narrative, *Don Juan* (1824), a 17-stage epic journey that begins, "I want a hero" (152). The poet salutes Greek islanders for trying to throw off the dominion of the Ottoman Empire for libertarian rather than religious reasons. Two cantos mourn shackled figures "chain'd and lotted out per couple / For the slave market of Constantinople" (212). A subsequent motif of female liberation from social and religious constraints depicts the picaresque hero as a champion of women, the pawns of empire: "Poor Thing of Usages! coerc'd, compell'd, / Victim when wrong, and martyr oft when right" (309).

The Byronic model influenced ALEKSANDR PUSHKIN's *Eugene Onegin* (1832); Charlotte Brontë's *Jane Eyre* (1847), in the form of Edward Rochester; and MARYSE CONDÉ's *La Migration des Coeurs* (*Windward Heights*, 1995), a restructuring of Emily Brontë's gothic feminism in *Wuthering Heights* (1847).

Sources

Beal, Timothy Kandler. *The Book of Hiding: Gender, Ethnicity, Annihilation, and Esther.* New York: Routledge, 1997.

Byron, George Gordon Byron, Lord. *The Works of Lord Byron Complete in One Volume.* Frankfurt: H. L. Branner, 1826.

Driem, George von. *Languages of the Himalayas.* Amsterdam: Brill, 2001.

Esther. In the Holy Bible. Iowa Falls, Iowa: World Bible Publishers, 1986.

Gama, Basilio da. *The Uruguay: A Historical Romance of South America.* Translated by Sir Richard F. Burton. Berkeley: University of California Press, 1982.

Harvey, G. E. *History of Burma.* New Delhi: Asian Educational Services, 2000.

Joshua. In the Holy Bible. Iowa Falls, Iowa: World Bible Publishers, 1986.

The Koran. Translated by N. J. Dawood. London: Penguin Classics, 2004.

Montalvo, Garci Rodriguez de. *Amadis of Gaul, Books I & II.* Translated by Edwin Place and Herbert Behm. Lexington: University Press of Kentucky, 2003.

Polo, Marco. *The Travels of Marco Polo.* Translated by Aldo Ricci. London: George Routledge, 1931.

Ruth. In the Holy Bible. Iowa Falls, Iowa: World Bible Publishers, 1986.

Stabler, Jane. *Byron, Poetics and History.* Cambridge: Cambridge University Press, 2002.

Sturluson, Snorri. *The Prose Edda.* Translated by Arthur Gilchrist Brodeur. New York: American-Scandinavian Foundation, 1916.

Sugirtharajah, Rasiah S. *The Postcolonial Biblical Reader.* London: Blackwell, 2006.

Treece, Dave. *Exiles, Allies, Rebels: Brazil's Indianist Movement, Indigenist Politics.* Westport, Conn.: Greenwood, 2000.

Herodotus (ca. 484–ca. 425 B.C.) *Greek historian*

During the Golden Age of Greece (ca. 500–300 B.C.), Herodotus, often referred to as the Father of History, was an appealing storyteller, ethnographer, and historian. The American mythographer Edith Hamilton dubbed him the "first sightseer" (Hamilton 1962, 98). He based his great work *The Histories* (440 B.C.) on the international conflicts of his time and recorded eyewitness commentary on the Persian Empire and the Greco-Persian Wars of 490–479 B.C.

Born to Lyxes and Rhaeo of Caria in the cosmopolitan coastal town of Halicarnassus, Ionia (present-day Bodrum, Turkey), Herodotus and his brother Theodore belonged to a well-educated, privileged class that could afford leisure and extensive travel. Because of Herodotus's soldierly perspective in his writing, he may have served as a hoplite, a volunteer militiaman who paid for his own spear, shield, helmet, and gear. He spent much of his adult life traveling the Mediterranean world. This was perhaps after the execution of his cousin, the epic poet Panyassis, in 454 B.C. for alleged treason under the tyrant Lygdamis. In his travels, Herodotus ventured as far west as Sicily, north to the Ukraine, south to the Nile River, and east to the Black Sea rim as far as the Dnieper River in southwestern Russia. He apparently spoke only Greek and relied on interpreters. Though he viewed the world from a Greek perspective, he took an interest in foreign customs and terms—for example, that cinnamon was a valuable trade item imported from China as a spice, pharmaceutical, and fragrance.

During his lengthy wanderings from 464 to 447 B.C., Herodotus established a reputation for impartial interviews, data collection, candid narratives, and pictorial episodes. Throughout his residency on the island of Samos off the coast of southern Turkey, he made lengthy voyages about the Mediterranean. En route, he perfected the rudiments of Western historical research, which covered social geography, trade, topography, and comparative politics. Unlike Homer's epic romanticism, Herodotus's innovative style derived from Ionian skepticism and a demand for hard data. The logic of his vigorous, scenic writings introduced the Western world to scholarly history.

In 444 B.C., while earning money for public readings of his entertaining episodes at the Olympic Games in Athens, Herodotus impressed the tyrant Pericles and the philosopher Sophocles; he also influenced the budding second-generation historian THUCYDIDES, who wept at the performance. Herodotus and the popular orator Lysias volunteered for a signal honor: to pioneer the Greek colony of Thurii in a part of southern Italy that the Romans called Magna Graecia. It was here, on the Tarentine Gulf, that Herodotus began compiling a chronicle on Assyria. He assembled his observations along with hearsay, anecdotes, myths, dreams and omens, and wonder tales into the irregular, absorbing narrative called *The Histories*. Before his death in his late 50s or early 60s, he divided his work into nine books, each named for one of the nine muses, beginning with Clio, the muse of history, and continuing through Euterpe (lyricism and music), Thalia (comedy and pastoral verse), Melpomene (tragedy), Terpsichore (dance), Erato (love poetry), Polyhymnia (hymns and oratory), Urania (astronomy), and Calliope (epic poetry).

The Histories

Paying little attention to the empire building of Carthage, Etruria, and Phoenicia, Herodotus's writings focus on a history of fifth-century B.C. Athens and the imperial ambitions of Persia, resulting in the Greco-Persian Wars. For style, he relied on *Ges periodos* (World travels, ca. 500 B.C.), a geography text by Hecataeus of Miletus, another famous traveler during the first half-century of the Persian rise to glory.

The Histories survey the crucial international disputes that had dominated the previous decades. As explained in his opening line, Herodotus hoped to preserve knowledge of the past and to show cause for the clash of dissimilar cultures. He describes the legendary origin of Troy and the subsequent antagonism between the Greeks and the Persians, whose great empire flourished from 550 to 330 B.C. In entertaining asides, he surmised a cause for the annual flooding of the Nile River, described the extent of Phoenician exploration of Africa, and discussed the behavior of Gelo, ruler of Syracusa, Sicily, who refused to take sides in the Greco-Persian conflict. For accuracy, the text introduces Persian expansionism with the rise of Cyrus II, or Cyrus the Great (ca. 585–529 B.C.), who brought the Medes and Persians together and converted to Zoroastrianism. The text covers the rise of Babylon (1:141–216) and the career of Croesus of Lydia (595–ca. 546 B.C.), the kingdom that stood between Greece and the advancing Persians.

Herodotus's anecdotes incorporate the social and economic value of women during the era. He maligned misogyny in the Babylonian custom of auctioning marriageable girls and of using the sums raised to subsidize poor men's weddings to ugly girls and cripples (1:196). He satirized the Lydian king Croesus's gifts in 547 B.C. to the Pythia, the cryptic priestess of Apollo at Delphi, to whom he gave cups made of precious metals, dyed garments, ingots, utensils, casks, ritual sprinklers, weapons, a statue of a female baker, and his own wife's necklaces and belts. The bribery failed to secure for Croesus a propitious forecast. The oracular consultation survives in history as a model of Pythian ambiguity: If Croesus should proceed against Cyrus, a great empire would fall. Misled by the oracle, Croesus interpreted his destiny as victor rather than victim (1:55–58). He failed to foresee that Cyrus would capture Sardis and add Lydia to the Persian Empire (546 B.C.). Later, while tied to a stake in anticipation of execution, the resigned Croesus expressed his agreement with the lawgiver Solon's belief that no man could be called lucky so long as he still lived (1:86). The text honors Croesus as "a good man whom the gods loved" (Herodotus 1961, 89), one of Herodotus's frequent lapses into subjectivity and moralizing.

Herodotus used this dramatic episode to compose an exemplum on the vagaries of fate and power. Cyrus, too, discovered too late the bitterness of defeat when the Massagetae of Iran destroy the Persian army. Herodotus blames the debacle on the weakening effect of empire on the loyalty of fighters. After the Massagetae queen Tomyris dishonored Cyrus's remains, she dropped his head in a sackful of gore with the cry, "You have your fill of blood" (100). As Herodotus predicted, following the death of Alexander the Great in 323 B.C., Lydia continued its downward spiral as a subject nation, passing through Seleucid and Attalid control before becoming a part of the Roman Empire in 133 B.C.

Like many Greeks, Herodotus was curious about Eastern customs and proclivities. His rambling discourse incorporated details of Massagetae cannibalism, the holy prostitution of Babylonian temple women, swineherds as social pariahs, the correspondence between the Greek deities Zeus and Dionysus and the Egyptian gods Amon and Osiris, and the bizarre burial of the Babylonian Queen Nitocris over a city entrance. In the historian's second book, digressions describe the topography of Egypt (2:1–34) and its customs, with emphasis on the hippopotamus and crocodile, the elevation of the hero Hercules, the royal genealogy from King Sesostris to King Amasis, and state funerals and monuments. The historian satisfied a controversy of his day by outlining the methods of Egyptian mummification for different classes of corpses (2:35–99). From his scientific details, readers learned the importance of cassia, gum, myrrh, natrum (a carbonate salt) and syrmaea (a mixture of cinnamon and senna) to corpse preservation, including the remains of crocodiles.

The Aim of Empire

Returning to his main theme in books 3–6, Herodotus continued exploring the resistance of Greeks, Ionians, and Scythians to Persian imperialism as a prelude to the warfare between the Easterners and mainland Greeks. In book 3, he accounted for the loss of Egypt to Cambyses II (d. 522 B.C.), Cyrus's son and successor, whom the Egyptian royal family cheated of marrying King Amasis's daughter Nitetis by sending another girl in her place. After summarizing Cambyses's excesses, the history returns to curiosities with tales of lions and flying snakes in Arabia and the ends of the earth beyond Ethiopia, a land of gold, ebony, and elephants. Book 4 reports on the unwise infiltration of the Persian king Darius I (550–486 B.C.) into Scythia (present-day southern Russia) and possibly as far as outer Mongolia. Following a side commentary on the Phoenician circumnavigation of Africa, the historian focuses on power mongering in the rise of Darius, who subjugated parts of Russia and Libya. In describing the Scythian strategy of living on horseback, Herodotus proposed a historian's summation of nomadism: "No one who invades their country can escape destruction, and . . . cannot by any possibility come to grips with them" (257).

Abandoning his campaign against the Scythians and taking a new interest in Greece, Darius began pushing into Ionia on his way toward Athens, the prize. Book 5 follows the Persians to victory in Thrace (present-day Bulgaria and the European side of Turkey), where Darius enriches his nation with the sale of prisoners of war. Herodotus warns that the sailing of the Greek fleet "was the beginning of trouble not only for Greece, but for the rest of the world as well" (350). He recounts the Persian route up the coast of Asia Minor to the Hellespont and Thrace, west to Samos and Icaria, and through the Aegean Islands to Naxos and Delos, a sacred isle in the Cyclades and clearinghouse for the Greek slave market. Ahead lies a major victory for Miltiades, commander of the Athenians at the battle of Marathon in 490 B.C., the beginning of the Persian reverses in Greece. One of Herodotus's most appealing secondary characters is the Athenian Pheidippides, the famed runner of Marathon. He raced to Sparta to request aid for the faltering Athenians, who risked the worst of destinies—being "crushed and enslaved by a foreign invader" (398). At the battle's finale, Herodotus records losses at 192 for Athens and 6,400 for the invaders.

Biographies of Empire Builders

Herodotus's final three books survey the end to Persian imperialism and closes with events preceding 479 B.C. He summarizes the megalomania of Xerxes I (519–465 B.C.), Darius's son and the grandson of Cyrus the Great, whom the Greek playwright Aeschylus had pitied in the drama *Persae* (*Persians*, 472 B.C.). During a two-decade reign from 485 B.C. to his death, Xerxes used a take-no-prisoners approach to quell revolt and tighten Persian control of Babylon and Egypt. Because of the threat to Greece, the mainland Greek city-states allied to protect their race, language, shrines, and the customs that set them apart from the barbaric Easterners. The chronicle exalts the Greek military and solidarity and impugns the Persian love of luxury and Xerxes's overreaching and barbarity.

To explain the supernatural power that overturned the Persian raid on the temple at Delphi, Herodotus reverts to Greek superstition. He explains that Apollo guarded the sacred precinct while the Delphians hid women and children on Mount Parnassus. At the burst of thunderbolts from the sky and the collapse of two rocky outcrops, the Persian army panicked and fled, with Delphians and two mysterious giant warriors slaughtering the stragglers. The historian damns the insurgents for subsequent sacrilege against Athena, goddess of wisdom and war. Let loose on Athens, the invaders climbed an escarpment and overran the Acropolis: "The Persians made straight for the temple gates, flung them open and butchered every man who had hoped to find a refuge there" (515). Nemesis is swift. The stirring text summarizes how a Greek coalition, led by the archon (chief magistrate) Themistocles, overwhelmed the Persian navy of 1,200 ships at the battle of Salamis on September 29, 480 B.C., and trounced the enemy infantry and cavalry months later in southern Greece at Plataea and Mycale.

The history concludes with the rise of the Athenian empire after years of threat from the East. In his summation of the grab for more territory, Herodotus quotes Artembares, grandfather of the crucified Persian commander Artayctes: "It is the natural thing for a sovereign people to do, and when will there be a better opportunity than now, when we are masters of many nations and all Asia?" (599).

Critical Views

Literary opinion diverges on the validity of Herodotus's concept of history. From Cicero, Dionysius, Longinus, and Quintilian, Herodotus earns kudos for his harmonious language, urbane wit and polish, copious details, and Homeric grandeur honoring Greek decorum. Of particular pleasure to young Romans was the story of Arion and the dolphin in book 2, one of Herodotus's most charming nature fables. Less positive critiques charged the historian with naïveté, moralizing, and interpolating fictitious oratory, such as the speech of Periander before the ghost of Melissa in book 5 and, in book 6, the betrothal of Cleisthenes of Sicyon's daughter Agarista, whose great-grandson was Pericles.

More than five centuries after writing his *Histories*, Herodotus received his most serious censure. Around A.D. 110, PLUTARCH, a biographer from Chaeronea, Boeotia, charged the historian with bias, error, and misleading commentary. The Assyrian rhetorician Lucian of Samosata (ca. A.D. 125–ca. 180) tweaked Herodotus for gullibility and for including wonder tales of India's giant gold-digging ants among serious chronicles of Greek warfare. However, he received a signal honor in Einhard's *Vita Caroli* (*The Life of Charlemagne*, A.D. 830), a biography of CHARLEMAGNE that emulates superstitious elements from Herodotus's *Histories* foretelling the triumphs, defeats, and deaths of kings.

An example of the historian's impact on the late 20th century is the Canadian writer Michael Ondaatje's World War II novel *The English Patient* (1992), a winner of the Canadian Governor General's Award and a Booker Prize. The text recounts Hungarian cartographer Laszlo de Almasy's obsession with *The Histories*. At the initiation of Almasy's affair with a married woman, Katherine Clifton, she recounts Herodotus's anecdote in book 1 of the disrobing of Candaules's wife before the security guard Gyges. The event reveals a point in history marking the elevation of women from possessions to persons with their own individuality and self-respect. The film version in 1996 featured the tattered copy of Herodotus's *Histories* as an ongoing study of hubris, imperialism, and violence as Almasy adds drawings, photos, and marginalia in his attempts to conceal his identity from the German Afrika Korps—a striking tribute to a historian of 2,000 years earlier.

Sources

Hamilton, Edith. *The Greek Way*. New York: Mentor Books, 1962.

Herodotus. *The Histories*. Translated by Aubrey de Sélincourt. Baltimore, Md.: Penguin, 1961.

Ondaatje, Michael. *The English Patient*. New York: Vintage, 1993.

Thompson, Norma. *Herodotus and the Origins of the Political Community: Arion's Leap*. New Haven, Conn.: Yale University Press, 1996.

Hersey, John Richard (1914–1993) *American journalist, novelist, and nonfiction writer*

John Hersey possessed the appropriate cultural and linguistic background to investigate a global war and the world's first military use of atomic power. Born in China to American missionaries, Grace Baird and Roscoe Monroe Hersey, he grew up in a bicultural household in Tientsin, where he attended elementary school and published his own neighborhood newsletter. He later reprised the life of a missionary's son in *The Call* (1985), a historical novel and fictional composite of a number of Protestant evangelists that included his parents. He was 10 when his family returned to the United States, where he later earned a journalism degree from Yale University. He also studied English literature at Clare College, Cambridge, as a Mellon Fellow. He began working for *Time* magazine in 1937.

Starting in October 1939, Hersey's unique background won him frontline postings to China, Guadalcanal, Sicily, and the Solomon Islands as a World War II combat reporter. The assignment coincided with the first on-site hourly news coverage of global events in history. As a specialist in Asian affairs, he headquartered at the Chungking bureau for *Life*, for which he interviewed the Chinese Nationalist leader Chiang Kai-shek; Generals Claire Chennault and Douglas MacArthur; and Lieutenant Jack Kennedy, hero of PT 109. Hersey accompanied the U.S. Marines to Guadalcanal in October 1942. He wrote articles for the *New Yorker* and *Time* during the Allied invasion

of Sicily, beginning July 10, 1943, and observed the brusque style of General George S. Patton, commander of the Seventh Army. Over the course of the war, Hersey traveled by destroyer and went down with four crashed planes, once in the sea.

With a survey of the walking wounded in *Men on Bataan* (1942), Hersey began turning headlines into war reportage focused on the individual. With *Into the Valley: A Skirmish of the Marines* (1943), he examined men and deeds on both sides at the Battle of Guadalcanal (August 7, 1942–February 9, 1943), a bloody chapter of the Pacific war that halted Japanese expansionism. His personal involvement including traveling aboard the aircraft carrier *Hornet*, loading stretchers, and sheltering with a company surrounded by the enemy. Writing of a sniper, he comments on the innocence of immature Japanese warriors: "Conscription had snatched him from his hopes, and young friends had sat at a banquet table and brushed arrogant characters on the little flag he was to carry to the front" (Hersey 1943, 36). His compassionate overview of male behavior under fire blended elements of Geronimo, Buck Rogers, Sergeant York, and frightened boys.

Hersey's Pulitzer Prize–winning novel *A Bell for Adano* (1944) featured the cruelty of Benito Mussolini's fascism against Sicilian townspeople by melting their tower bell to mold into rifle barrels. At a nadir of confidence, local scrappers fight back with a drunken orgy of glass smashing: "One of them would get up and shout; 'To hell with the son of a frog, Mussolini!' and he would throw a bottle as if he were throwing it at Mussolini" (Hersey 1988, 225). The pathos of civilian impotence elicits mugging and belly laughs to conceal the islanders' terror of being captured and shot. In 1945, a film version of the classic war novel starred John Hodiak, Gene Tierney, William Bendix, and Harry Morgan.

Researching *Hiroshima*

In 1945, Hersey covered news from China and Japan, giving him a prime vantage point for objective postwar reporting. The next year, he published *Hiroshima* (1946), an earnest literary monument to the immediate and long-range effects on citizens of Hiroshima, Japan, of the atomic bomb named "Little Boy," which destroyed the city on August 6, 1945. First printed as a story in the *New Yorker* on August 31, 1946, then read over the radio, and finally expanded into book form, the work has been called the world's most famous magazine article. The narrative opens on the "noiseless flash" of August 6, 1945, a firestorm that burns, blinds, and cremates citizens going about morning activities. The text examines the effect of the bombing on six Japanese citizens. The author cites without comment a Japanese opinion that "People of Hiroshima died manly in the atomic bombing, believing that it was for Emperor's sake" (Hersey 1946, 89). The book flourished worldwide except among Japanese readers.

In 1985, Hershey returned to the original interviewees in *Hiroshima* to assess the lasting damage to their health and careers. In the 1950s, survivors incurred diagnoses of carcinoma and leukemia. Unusual turns of events celebrated Sister Dominique Sasaki for operating the White Chrysanthemum Orphanage and lauded the Methodist pastor Kiyoshi Tanimoto on the television program *This Is Your Life*, where he met Paul W. Tibbets, Jr., the captain of the *Enola Gay*, the B-29 Superfortress that flew the atomic bomb to its first destination.

Hersey found more models of bravery for subsequent books. Another survey of wartime courage and waste, *The Wall* (1950), winner of a Daroff Award from the Jewish Book Council of America, commemorate 650 Polish Jews of the Warsaw ghetto for an uprising on April 19, 1943, against 3,000 members of the Nazi SS. Hersey's sources—tapes of diaries and documents translated from Polish and Yiddish—illuminated a desperate fight for dignity and solidarity that outweighed the obvious Nazi defeat of the resistance and their sending trainloads of survivors to the death camp at Treblinka, Poland. His narrative injects sympathy and humor for a community that for 26 days fought heroically without military aid and with no hope of victory. The wit of Rabbi Goldflamm makes light of incomprehensible horror: "All right, so we heard about the factory for making soap out of Jews in Lublin, we laugh and say, 'I'll be washing you!'" (Hersey 1950, 254–255). Hersey describes the selection process at the *umschlagplatz* (deportation center) as "Gehenna (hell). It is beyond life" (350). In 1982, the book inspired a Peabody Award–winning TV movie filmed on location at Sosnowiec, Poland, and starring Eli Wallach, Tom Conti, and Dianne Wiest.

Until his death, Hersey maintained his reputation for bringing global calamity down to a human level, for championing survivalism, and for his protests at the nuclear arms race.

Sources

Hersey, John. *A Bell for Adano*. New York: Vintage, 1988.
———. *Hiroshima*. New York: Random House, 1946.
———. *Into the Valley: A Skirmish of the Marines*. New York: Alfred A. Knopf, 1943.
———. *The Wall*. New York: Alfred A. Knopf, 1950.

Histories, The   See HERODOTUS.

Hitler, Adolf   See MEIN KAMPF.

Holocaust   See GENOCIDE; SINGER, ISAAC BASHEVIS; WIESEL, ELIE.

Horace (Quintus Horatius Flaccus) (65–8 B.C.)
Roman lyric poet and satirist
Born to a foundering world, Quintus Horatius Flaccus toward the end of the Roman Republic (ca. 510–27 B.C.), the Roman poet Horace wrote of stability and human contentment in an age of folly. A native of Venusia (present-day Venosa) in south-central Italy, he was the son of a freedman farmer and grain factor who had survived his own share of war. Although educated in Athens in literature and philosophy among elite young Romans, the poet remained touchy about his past to avoid being labeled a parvenu.

Horace was 21 when the assassination of Julius Caesar precipitated 17 years of civil war. In the period preceding the battle of Philippi in 42 B.C., he soldiered in Macedonia as a staff officer under Marcus Brutus, the enemy of Mark Antony and Caesar's nephew Octavian (later Augustus Caesar). Backing the losing side cost Horace his civilian job and his family's land. In reduced circumstance, he earned a living with a desk job in the imperial treasury; he depicted his displacement in "The City

Mouse and the Country Mouse" (30 B.C.), a gentle beast FABLE included in his *Sermonum* (*Satires*, 35–30 B.C.). Targets of his derision ranged from luxuries and sexual license (in the first satire) to the diminution of the peasant class. These humorous poems established Horace's fame.

Following the fall of the Roman Republic, Horace lived in two worlds: as a civil clerk and as an intellectual on a first-name basis with the arts patron Maecenas and the poets Lucius Varius Rufus, TIBULLUS, and VIRGIL, Rome's most revered epic poet and propagandist for Augustus, the city's first emperor (ruled 27 B.C.–A.D. 14). Augustus courted Horace's friendship. According to the Roman historian SUETONIUS's *De vita Caesarum* (*Lives of the Caesars*, ca. A.D. 121), the emperor said, "Enjoy any privilege at my house, as if you were making your home there" (Suetonius 1920, 487). Perhaps out of self-preservation, Horace exalted Augustus in verse as an *epiphanos* (god on earth) or sacred guardian of the people, a concept that risked the traditional Roman disdain for hereditary monarchy. Of two minds on the subject of the shift in sovereignty, the poet overtly thanked the *princeps* (chief) for grounding the new empire on law and morality; in the subtext, he laced his odes with attacks on the empire's prideful architecture, sexual promiscuity, secularism, and Persian frippery and incense, which debased a generation.

Propaganda and Practicality

Admired for his decorum, Horace was a mellow pragmatist who adopted wisdom from a long list of literary influences. At first, he saw no reason to regret the passing of republican Rome, but, by 23 B.C., over two decades after the murder of Julius Caesar, the poet edged a new optimism with caution. He endorsed the emperor's long-term vision for national rebirth and accepted Augustus's claim as Rome's savior and only choice for stability, peace, and prosperity. Horace's most diplomatic ode of the period, "Aurea Mediocritas" ("The Golden Mean," 23 B.C.), reminds the reader of Aristotle's precept—that balance guides the individual through good times and bad and steadies the mind for difficult decisions. He urged Roman leaders to halt unholy civil slaughter, Roman against Roman, and to direct military energies to the creation of an empire by subduing Arabs, Britons, Gauls, Parthians, and Scythians.

Horace's *Carmina* (*Odes*, 23–13 B.C.) voiced his wish to educate readers on morality. The text reprises the tone and atmosphere of classic Greek poets in their praise of state sovereignty. In book 3, the poet honors the military victories of General Drusus and his brother Tiberius against Alpine barbarians. The collection of 103 poems is best remembered for recommending carpe diem (seize the day, Ode 1.11), an epicurean aphorism encouraging enjoyment of the moment rather than postponing pleasure to an uncertain future. Horace scorned debauchery and requested a return to the moderate rites of Bacchus, the Roman wine god. In a rhetorical question, book 1 of the *Odes* reminds Romans that neglect of religion leaves them defenseless in time of catastrophe. The poet asks what god citizens will invoke when the empire tumbles, what plea will the Vestal Virgins raise to their divine patron, who no longer listens to their cries. In *Carmen saeculare* (*Secular Hymn*, 17 B.C.), a text intended for choral reading, he promoted patriotism, family values, and traditional worship of the gods, especially Apollo, Mars, Mercury, and Venus, the mythic mother of the Trojan hero Aeneas in Virgil's AENEID (17 B.C.).

At Horace's death at age 57, he willed to the emperor his estate outside Tibur (today's Tivoli) in the Sabine uplands. For Horace's compact verse and sunny epicureanism, Roman literati held him second only to Virgil. In the 17th century, Horace's verse influenced the elegant style and tone of the Parisian fabulist JEAN DE LA FONTAINE.

Sources

Boatwright, Mary T., Daniel J. Gargola, and Richard J. A. Talbert. *The Romans: From Village to Empire.* New York: Oxford University Press, 2004.

Horace. *Horace, the Odes: New Translations by Contemporary Poets.* Edited by J. D. McClatchy. Princeton, N.J.: Princeton University Press, 2002.

———. *Satires and Epistles of Horace.* Translated by Smith Palmer Bovie. Chicago: University of Chicago Press, 1959.

McNeill, Randall L. B. *Horace: Image, Identity, and Audience.* Baltimore: Johns Hopkins University Press, 2001.

Suetonius. *Suetonius*, J. C. Rolfe. London: William
   Heinemann, 1920.

Huron Chief, The (Adam Kidd) (1830)

An Irish-Canadian version of British romanticism,
the poet Adam Kidd's elegy *The Huron Chief* applies
Lord Byron's paradigm of the clash of empires to
Canadian FRONTIER LITERATURE. The long fictional
poem epitomizes the increasing subjugation of the
Canadian Indians. The Irish-born Kidd, a failed
candidate for the Church of England priesthood and
a contributor to the *Irish Vindicator, Quebec Gazette,*
and *Quebec Mercury,* apparently moved to Canada
as a teenager, around 1818. He wrote the poem after
challenging the secular and church authority in
Lower Canada. His aim, according to the introduction, was to expose the duplicity and transgressions
of Christian "Creeds-men" against North American
natives, some of whom fled American bigotry and
potential GENOCIDE in the lower Great Lakes region
to shelter in Ontario (Kidd 1830, 95). Kidd died in
Kingston in 1831 at age 29.

   In a pine grove in sight of Lake Erie, the murder of Chief Skenandow, committed by three whites
in 1816, takes on a demonic tinge. Revered for
wisdom and battle prowess, he falls to the treachery
of the outsider to whom the chief extends welcome
and kindness. The antiestablishment narrative,
related in the first person, has a Miltonic gravity
suited to its focus on imperialist sins committed in
an earthly paradise and, by extension, to the English
oppression of the Irish. Writing over 35 years before
the Canadian Confederation of 1867, Kidd defends
native love of nature and spiritualism from the
scorn of Europeans and vindicates himself being
sexually attracted to a Huron widow. He considers
the Huron well situated in an Edenic wilderness
"far, / from Europe's crimes, and Europe's errors"
(84). The Huron condemn as culprits the self-
righteous Christian invaders who think themselves
entitled to "a nigher way to march to heaven" (96).
Like the Canadian conservationist author Grey
Owl (Archibald Belaney, 1888–1938) and the Irish
travelogue writer Anna Brownell Murphy Jameson
(1794–1860), author of *Winter Studies and Summer
Rambles in Canada* (1838), Kidd regrets that "Our
hunting grounds—our streams—our lakes, / The
white usurper freely takes" (115). The closing lines
indicate that Skenandow has witnessed enough of
European barbarity to guess that his people will
survive only in stories of their noble past.

Sources

Bentley, D. M. R. *Mimic Fires.* Montreal: McGill-
   Queen's University Press, 1994.
Kidd, Adam. *The Huron Chief and Other Poems.*
   Montreal: Herald and New Gazette, 1830.

I

Ibn Battuta (Abu Abdullah Muhammad Ibn Battuta) (1304–ca. 1377) *Moroccan scholar and travel writer*

A native of the trading port of Tangier, Ibn Battuta, studied Islamic jurisprudence and flourished as a *qadi* (judge) of an Arabian law court, an ambassador to China, and one of the world's most-read travel authors. He set a record in his day for traveling through 15 empires. On June 14, 1325, he set out on a 30-year trek that began with an obligatory religious hajj (pilgrimage) by camel from Morocco to Mecca, the holiest city in Arabia. His odyssey of 73,000 miles took him across northern and western Africa and Zanzibar as well as through Iberia and Gibraltar, where he observed the Marinid Empire's struggle to control the straits between Mediterranean trade routes and the Atlantic Ocean. He traveled east from Morocco to Sardinia and into Palestine, Lebanon, Syria, Oman, Persia, Thrace, Turkey, the Genoese colony of Crimea and Ukraine, Armenia, Afghanistan, the Punjab, Ceylon, China, and Mongolia. His journey took him to Malaya and Sumatra in the Majapahit Empire, to Burma in the aftermath of the breakup of the Bagan Empire, and to Vietnam in the Khmer Empire.

Ibn Battuta's observations, pinpointing aspects of empires and historical events of the mid-14th century, are compiled in his *Tuhfat al-nuzzar fi ghara'ib al-amsar wa'aja'ib al-asfar* (On the curiosities of cities and the wonders of travel, 1354; translated into English as *Travels in Asia and Africa, 1325–1354.*). At the request of the Marinid sultan Abu Inan Faris of Fez, Morocco, the author dictated a TRAVELOGUE to Ibn Juzayy, a court scribe. Like the Greek traveling historian HERODOTUS and the Venetian adventurer MARCO POLO, Ibn Battuta mixed fanciful narrative with fact, including the peculiarities of the hippopotamus on the River Niger between Gao and Timbuktu in the Mali Empire, catapults firing coins to onlookers from the backs of elephants that he saw in Delhi, India, during the Tughlaq dynasty, and the meals of turmeric-stuffed lizard he refused in Siwasitan (present-day Sehwan, Pakistan). In Mamluk territory, he inspected the ruins of the famous *pharos* (lighthouse) of Alexandria, Egypt, one of the eight wonders of the ancient world.

Carrying only a KORAN, Ibn Battuta spoke with authority on the subject of shipping routes and piracy, epidemics, highwaymen, jurisprudence, civil wars, conquest, and international conspiracies and spying. His acquaintance with the Malian king Mansa Suleyman, the Seljuks of Turkey, and the unpredictable Sultan Tughluq of Delhi equipped Ibn Battuta with enviable political experience, including his knowledge of an attempted coup by the Malian queen. In return for his piety, courtesy, and wisdom, he heard STORYTELLING sessions by Malian griots and received gifts of slaves and concubines, horses, ceremonial robes, furs, jewelry, and gold. In the Maldives, Queen Khadijah's court conferred on him a deity's reverence and a magistracy. At Constantinople, under tight security, he met the Byzantine emperor Takfur, who questioned the visitor about his tour of Abraham's relics in Hebron and about Jesus's cradle and burial place in Jerusalem. Under the Mamluk regime, notable for economic and political stability in Asia Minor, Egypt, Palestine, and Syria, Ibn Battuta investigated hospitals, canals, colleges, and mosques, the fruits of wise government.

Dissension disturbed Ibn Battuta more than threats, robbery, foul salt mines, and house arrest. When a Singhalese sultan in Ceylon requested the traveler's advice on plotting a coup, Ibn Battuta hurriedly booked passage from the island. In Persian and Egyptian territory, he criticized the split of old empires among squabbling clans, particularly in Anbar, Iraq, on the Euphrates River. Of Egypt, then in political disarray, he reported archly, "The wretched subjects naturally suffered more severely than from the calculated extortions of a settled regime" (Ibn Battuta 2001, 24). In some Islamic states, he found outright banditry; in Damascus, he encountered a deadlier threat, the arrival of the Black Death. Most impressive of empires was the rule of Huizong, the Yuan emperor of China, a vast territory radiating out from an elegant wooden palace. Ibn Battuta's descriptions of processions and courts of the emperor's head wife substantiated the accounts in *Travels of Marco Polo* (1298), which some readers had doubted. Overall, Ibn Battuta enjoyed good company by being affable, trustworthy, and unobtrusive, and he left a unique legacy of travel writing.

Sources

Dunn, Ross E. *The Adventures of Ibn Battuta: A Muslim Traveler of the 14th Century.* Berkeley: University of California Press, 2004.

Ibn Battuta. *Travels in Asia and Africa, 1325–1354.* Translated by H. A. R. Gibb. New Delhi: Manohar, 2001.

I Ching (Book of Changes) (1144–206 B.C.)

A cosmological text developed over 21 centuries, the *I Ching* (*Book of Changes*) is one of the world's oldest written documents. Derived from oral tradition, it comprises both ethical advice and oracular symbology revealing the nature of the seasons, star systems, animal and plant kingdoms, and human cycles. Like the Hebrew Kabbalah teachings, the purpose of the Chinese work is to apply numerol-

ogy and diagrams as a guide to harmonize random, confusing elements of life. *I Ching* practitioners hoped that PROPHECY would encourage serene and blameless human behavior during periods of change and dynastic upheaval.

The text's mythic beginning bears elements of narrative similar to those of Ur in Iraq. Following a devastating flood, a Noah figure, Emperor Fu Xi (Fu Hsi, 2852–2737 B.C.), a semimythic civilizer of China from the lower Yalu River, looked for direction of human endeavors in celestial and earthly patterns. He identified the almighty as Tai Chi (the great absolute) and named opposing forces the yin and yang—abstract terms for the variables of light/dark, permanence/change, and male/female. He based their geometric shapes on a divine message, the markings on a tortoise shell (or horse) that he observed near the Hwang Ho River. From this, he derived a set of eight classifications of natural phenomena: heaven, lake, fire, thunder, wind, water, mountain, and earth. The next six rulers—the herbalist Shen Nong (fl. late 2700s), the warrior emperor Huang Di (2697–2598 B.C.), the religious reformer Zhuanxu (2514–2436 B.C.), the autocrat Ku (2436–2366 B.C.), the sage Yao (2358–2258 B.C.), and the peacemaker and musician Shun (2311–2211 B.C.)—applied *I Ching* patterns to healing, agriculture, marketing, inventions, animal husbandry, urbanization, security, and writing.

Formalizing Oral Tradition

Wen Wang (1199–ca. 1140 B.C.), the founder of the Western Zhou dynasty, standardized the concepts of north, south, east, and west with a fifth direction to the center, the source of balance. Augmenting the *I Ching*, he compiled the first written mystic guidebook, the *Zhou Yi* (Changes of Zhou, 1144 B.C.), which bases augury and necromancy on mathematical reconfiguration of the original symbols into 64 hexagrams, influencing prophets in China, Indochina, Japan, Korea, and the West. For the next millennium, the *I Ching* assisted formulators of court policy. Around 480 B.C., Confucius (551–479 B.C.), like the Greek priestess Pythia voicing Apollo's revelations through the Delphic Oracle, revised the interpretation of symbols from the supernatural basis to the ethical Tao (the way), which he revealed in the *Tuan Zhuan* (Commentary on the decision, 488 B.C.). The aphoristic wording, like the stoicism of classical Athens and Rome, urges patience: "Bear with things as the earth bears with us: by yielding, by accepting, by nourishing" (Walker 1993, 7). In the style of the Indian VEDAS, the Hebrew Proverbs, ANALECTS of Confucius (ca. 210 B.C.), BHAGAVAD GITA (ca. 200 B.C.), the *DHAMMAPADA* (ca. 50 B.C.) of Siddhartha Gautama, the writings of MARCUS AURELIUS, and the Sikh GRANTH (1604), subsequent WISDOM LITERATURE advises readers to avoid inner conflict, haste, egotism, and negativity.

In 213 B.C., during the Han dynasty, the *I Ching* was interpreted to confirm the concept of empire and advise on how to govern diverse cultures. That year, the text survived a campaign by Qin Shihhuang, the unifier of China, in which Confucius's followers were executed and his books burned.

The *I Ching* remained vital to future Asian empires. During the expansionist rule of the autocratic emperor Wu Di (156–87 B.C.), China doubled in size and made incursions into India, Korea, Mongolia, Parthia, Uzbekistan, and Vietnam. At the height of intellectual dispute on Confucianism's relation to other belief systems, the scholar Zong Zhongshu (Tung Chung-Shu, 179–104 B.C.) produced the *Chunqiu fanlu* (Luxuriant gems of the spring and autumn annals, ca. 100 B.C.), a treatise on the *I Ching* that made Confucianism dominant in China. The addendum systemized human behavior and the five elements—earth, fire, metal, water, and wood—with celestial numbers. The numerical matrix laid down standards of behavior for rulers and served the imperial university as a standard text on character building.

In the mid-1600s, Yamaga Soko, a Japanese military tactician and Confucian apologist, applied *I Ching* maxims to battlefield strategy. From its orderly arrangements of moral challenges and responses, he extracted soldierly codes of authority, power, courage, caution, endurance, order, duty, and survivalism for the training of the samurai class. The *I Ching* returned to influence state policy in 1715 during the Qing dynasty under emperor Kangxi (1654–1722), an encyclopedist who published an updated version.

Sources

Ritsema, Rudolf, and Shantena Augusto Sabbadini. *The Original I Ching Oracle: The Pure and Complete Texts with Concordance.* New York: Sterling, 2005.

Walker, Brian Browne, trans. *The I Ching or Book of Changes: A Guide to Life's Turning Points.* New York: Piatkus Books, 1993.

Iriarte, Tomás de (Tomás de Iriarte y Oropesa) (1750–1791) *Spanish fabulist and poet*

A clever Aesopic moralist of imperial Spain, Tomás de Iriarte composed didactic stories, WISDOM lore, and comedies of manners. A native of Orotava (present-day Tenerife), Canary Islands, he became a scholar in Madrid, where he worked as a state archivist under his uncle, the director of the royal library, and translated the Roman Horace's poetry and French drama. In *Fábulas literarias* (*Literary Fables*, 1782), Iriarte composed 76 original beast SATIREs such as "The Wallflower and the Thyme" and "The Frog and the Hen" to ridicule the pompous; all the FABLEs are rendered in verse. The impetus to his waspish wit derived from his scorn for court climbers who sought prestige and power by fawning upon rulers in Iberia, the Suez, the Philippines, Malta, and Tetuan, Morocco. One lengthy diatribe, "The Portrait," identifies by name Charles I, Ferdinand V, and Philip II and III, all pictured on coins. The subtextual gibe implies that portraits on money are far more valuable than pictures on canvas.

Iriarte's talents and irascible temperament suited the invective fable at its first appearance in Spanish literature. A seven-stanza insect story, "The Drones and the Bee," illustrates his impatience with deferential civil servants and court writers. The drones who fail at honey making turn their attention to honoring a dead bee with "funeral obsequies, brilliant and grand" and "panegyrics immortal" (Iriarte 1855, 9). Because the ritual is shallow and showy, an observer bee denounces the effort as the "fuss of your beggarly crew" (9). The ostentation, symbolic of courtly pretensions, epitomizes the vapid actions of courtiers who employ verbal flattery at the expense of sincerity. A similar theme invigorates "The Tea-Plant and Sage" by teasing the in-crowd for importing goods from the Spanish Empire while ignoring the quality of commodities grown on home soil. A similar conclusion rounds out "The Owl and the Toad" with the claim, "Conspicuous toads we rather would be, than modest owls in our own hollow tree" (132).

Iriarte saluted the fables of AESOP as "one which delights and instructs" (43), yet he chose to nettle and vex with his own models. His brusque allegory condemns the insidious wolf in "The Wolf and the Shepherd" and the ragman who blathers about dead villains but who flees "living dogs" (46). In "The Ostrich, the Dromedary, and the Fox," the poet tweaks aristocrats who rate others on the strength of family trees. He voices irritation with those who argue over trifles in "The Lion, Eagle and Bat," and he is equally annoyed with fools, whom he depersonalizes in the fable "The Muff, the Fan, and the Umbrella." With "The Rabbits and the Dogs," he ridicules those who fall victim to attackers because they waste time discussing trivialities. To boasters, he retorts, "Your brains are dark as the unlighted lanthorn" (14). To egregious fools, he chortles, "If one opens his mouth, then we know he's an ass" (16).

Perhaps because of Spanish phraseology, Iriarte's works translate poorly into English, thus limiting their inclusion in world literature anthologies. However, they continue the tradition of wise aphorisms that Aesop had begun 2,000 years earlier.

Sources

Iriarte, Tomás de. *Literary Fables of Yriarte.* Translated by George H. Devereux. Boston: Ticknor and Fields, 1855.

Kaufmann, Wanda Ostrowska. *The Anthropology of Wisdom Literature.* Westport, Conn.: Greenwood, 1996.

Izumi Shikibu (974–ca. 1033) *Japanese poet and diarist*

During the Heian period of Japanese history (794–1185), Izumi Shikibu recorded events and attitudes at the imperial court of Joto Monin. Born the eldest of several daughters of two families from the gubernatorial class, she married a middle-aged politician, Tachibana no Michisada, the governor of Izumi, the source of her surname, around 996. At age 23, she traveled to the provinces as a companion to her husband. Two years later, she chose to return to the urban capital and conduct affairs with powerful men. Scandal from her open romance with Prince Tametaka, son of Emperor Reizei, ended her marriage and estranged her from her father, Ôe no Masamune, the governor of Echizen. After her lover's death the next year at age 25, perhaps from plague, Izumi dallied with his married half brother, Prince Atsumichi, who died in 1007 at age 27, leaving her to raise their son Eikaku.

The following year, Izumi joined Queen Akiko's ladies-in-waiting at Kyoto and began composing confessional and emotional verse in *Izumi Shikibu Nikki* (*Izumi Shikibu Diary,* ca. 1008). Her style blends dialogue and mythic allusion with wit and short personal lyrics, of the sort that male and female courtiers exchanged in an ongoing game of flirtation. In competition with MURASAKI SHIKIBU, a more tasteful, discerning court poet, Izumi wrote poetry to please sophisticated readers and literary critics. She wed a general, Fujiwara no Yasumasa, and moved with him to Tango Province, where she mourned her daughter Koshikibu no Naishi, also a poet, who died in 1025 while giving birth to Izumi's grandchild. At her own death, Izumi asked that her dark path be lighted by the moon, a reference to Buddha.

Sources

Izumi Shikibu. *Diaries of Court Ladies of Old Japan.* Translated by Annie Shepley Omori and Kochi Doi. Boston: Houghton Mifflin, 1920.

Mulhern, Chieko Irie. *Japanese Women Writers: A Biocritical Sourcebook.* Westport, Conn.: Greenwood, 1994.

J

Jacobs, W. W. (William Wymark Jacobs)
(1863–1943) *English short story writer and playwright*

Edwardian horror and crime writer W. W. Jacobs earned a grudging regard from critics for mock-serious plots reflecting the influence of British imperialism on working-class characters. Jacobs's canon draws on his youth along the Thames estuary, where he absorbed the barroom stories and tall tales of sailors and merchant mariners returning from colonies in Asia and the Pacific. Employed in the Savings' Bank Department of the General Post Office, he simultaneously wrote for *English Illustrated, Pearson's, Strand,* and *To-day* some 150 humorous narratives and ghost stories that challenged the credulity of his readers. He depicted primitivism with animal imagery, similar to the squawking parrot in ROBERT LOUIS STEVENSON's *TREASURE ISLAND* (1883), Sir ARTHUR CONAN DOYLE's swamp adder in "The Adventure of the Speckled Band" (1892), and the lurking cobra in RUDYARD KIPLING's "Rikki-Tikki-Tavi" (1895). For GOTHIC exotica, he chose a Burmese murderer and his pet cobra in "The Brown Man's Servant" (1897) and the powers of a supernatural artifact imported to England from India in his frequently anthologized story "The Monkey's Paw" (1902), in which a military veteran advises against testing the power of a magical charm.

Jacobs made his mark on the literature of empire with "The Monkey's Paw," a suspense classic published in *Harper's* and anthologized in *The Lady of the Barge* (1902). A model of atmospheric STORYTELLING, the plot begins in a remote area of England on a rainy night. The conflict arises from a series of stories told by a veteran, Sergeant-Major Morris, who requires three whiskeys before he reveals his brush with an Indian curse. The mummified paw of the title animal, a symbol of the Indian monkey deity Hanuman, suggests an instrument of retribution from Asia against its invader. The tale tells the results of three wishes that ruin the lives of unsuspecting, gullible couple susceptible to natural greed. Set in 1870 at the height of Victorian imperialism, the narrative reveals a ghoulish revenge conjured up by sinister elements that colonials unwittingly import home like a native virus to safe, predictable England.

The mummified amulet in the title, the gift of a fakir, enters the story in the pocket of Morris, who notes that the first recipient to make a wish chose death as his final request. While making a wish, the host, Mr. White, reports, "It twisted in my hands like a snake" (Jacobs 2004, 16), an image suggesting the snake charmers of India. Jacobs connects the doom-laden talisman with man-eating technology in the death of the cottagers' son Herbert at his job at Maw and Meggins, a name suggesting the insatiable appetite of the factory system for laborers. The connection of pagan magic with England's progressive epoch indicates that the nation will pay for foisting its modernism onto innocent colonies.

Sources

Cloy, John D. *Pensive Jester: The Literary Career of W. W. Jacobs.* Lanham, Md.: University Press of America, 1996.

Jacobs, W. W. *The Lady of the Barge and Others.* Whitefish, Mont.: Kessinger, 2004.

Jahiz, al- (Abu Uthman Amr ibn Bahr al-Kinani al-Fuquaimi al-Basri) (ca. 776–ca. 869) *Arab encyclopedist and folklorist*

During cultural turmoil under the Abbasid caliphate, al-Jahiz, the first Islamic zoologist, surveyed life in some 360 works of folklore and nonfiction. A native of Basra, born Abu Uthman Amr ibn Bahr al-Kinani al-Fuqaimi al-Basri, he claimed Arabo-Ethiopian ancestry. He tended toward idleness, suffered being called "Goggle-eyes," and worked in boyhood to support his family, fishmongers living along an Iraqi canal. At the city mosque, he educated himself by attending lectures on history, lexicography, philology, poetry, and scripture and he became expert at diction, defining the meanings of words for clarity and understanding. At a time when Arab learning bore glimmers of the WISDOM LITERATURE of the Greeks and Persians, and when paper documents replaced parchment, he interspersed studies in orthodox Islam with Hellenic readings that favored the Greek philosopher Aristotle. When his mother urged him to choose a literary career, he began to write about a panoply of interests—agriculture, Arab cookery, board games, grammar, humor, language, oratory, physical handicaps, the seasons, versification, and zoology.

An upwardly mobile intellectual, al-Jahiz was readily accepted by the literary elite. He settled in Baghdad in 816 to study at the Bayt al-Hikma (House of wisdom), a library, institute of the humanities, and translation center established by Caliph al-Mamun in 813 to develop and study Persian astrology and mathematics and the Greek scientific treatises of Aristotle, Euclid, Hippocrates, Plato, and Pythagoras. Colleagues at the institute included al-Khwarizmi, the father of algebra and the algorithm, and three engineers and inventors known as the Banu Musa (Sons of Moses). In Baghdad and Samarra, the subsequent capital of the Abbasid caliphate, al-Jahiz produced monographs and texts. At age 40, he earned Abbasid patronage, in part by writing books on the caliphate and the military. Caliph al-Mamun considered hiring al-Jahiz as a household tutor, but declined because his bulging eyes amused the children. In advanced age, al-Jahiz, a partial paralytic, migrated back to his hometown. Legend describes his death in January 869 as, ironically, caused by a stack of tomes that fell on him. His work influenced RUMI, the touchstone of Persian Sufism.

Observation and Scholarship

Al-Jahiz devoted his life to observation, creating a medieval library of essay collections, epistles, and encyclopedias admired for their engaging style. He compiled a seven-volume bestiary, *Kitab al-Hayawan* (Book of animals, ca. 825), a masterwork covering snakes, foxes, hyenas, and the apes of Morocco. His zoology looks beyond the era's concepts of life to evolution, classification, embryology, diet, adaptation, camouflage, and environmentalism. He interspersed his scholarship with folk stories, anecdotes, and aphorisms based on animal behaviors as well as religious observations concerning god's reasons for making nature mutable yet orderly. Drawing on translations of works by Democritus, Euclid, Plato, and Ptolemy and anticipating Charles Darwin's theory of natural selection, al-Jahiz outlined the struggle of animals to survive and produce healthy offspring. The text influenced Islamic biologists as well as European scientists.

The encyclopedist's other works include a range of specialties that satisfied his intellectual curiosity. *Kitab al-Bukhala* (Book of misers, ca. 825) reveals a witty, teasing side of al-Jahiz in SATIREs of greed and eccentricity within numerous professions and lifestyles, including finance and begging. In *Kitab al-Bayan wa al-Tabyin* (Book of eloquence and exposition, ca. 825), he surveys oratory and the rhetoric of princes, politicians, and foreign ambassadors currying favor in the Islamic Empire. He ventured into erotica in *Kitab Moufakharat al Jawari wa al-Ghilman* (Book of dithyramb of maids and valets, ca. 825), a commentary on sexuality in the servant class. His classic propaganda text *Kitab al-Uthmaniyya* (Book of the Uthmaniyya, ca. 825) legitimizes the throne of the Abbasids against denunciation of the Shiites, Islam's vocal minority. Al-Jahiz's commentary accounts for the long-standing differences between Shia and Sunni, the opposing branches of Islam. His definition of the exemplary Arab leader values the veteran's experience over youth and cites hardihood and morality as essentials of nobility.

Political and Social Science

Al-Jahiz made astute remarks on conflicts and controversies. His *Manaqib at-turk* (Exploits of the Turks, ca. 825) pointed out that the rule of Turkish viziers depended on their army of mercenaries. He compiled treatises on contemporary difficulties with crime, priestly dissension, and slavery and on the merger of a Perso-Arab culture, which he attributed to the use of Persian scribes to disseminate Arab grammar, lexicography, and rhetoric. In his harsh commentary on client Christians and Jews, he described their antipathy to Islam and disrespect and hostility toward Muslims. Disdain for Jews is seen in his dismissal of a people noted for butchering, dyeing, metal work, and tanning, the lowliest of crafts. In *Al-Radd ala al-Nasara* (Refutation of the Christians, ca. 825), he claimed that Christian outsiders were hypocrites who considered themselves immune from the law. He accused them of worming their way into the professions and for stirring up squabbles by challenging the devout to interpret ambiguous scriptures and by baiting ordinary Muslims with provocative polemical questions. His accusations foretell a climate ripe for the Crusades, which began in 1096 and raged until 1272.

Al-Jahiz described the ethnic attitudes of Islamic and African empires of his time. Among his lost works are comparisons of horses and mules, of northern and southern Arabs, and of the animosities between pure and mixed-blood Arabs. He compiled *Risalat Mufakharat al-Sudan ala al-Bidan* (Superiority of blacks to whites, ca. 825), a history of Ethiopian rivalry with Arabs and a model of ninth-century stereotyping and Arab attitudes toward the Ethiopian Aksumite Empire. His conclusions include observations of Berbers, Chinese, Copts, Hindus, Moors, and Nubians. He characterized blacks as racially distinct because of their physical environment. Perhaps because his grandfather was Ethiopian, the author admired black people as great riders, dancers, and drummers and a more generous and contented race than whites.

Sources

Fisher, William Bayne. *The Cambridge History of Iran.* Cambridge: Cambridge University Press, 1993.

Jahiz, al-. *The Book of Misers: Al-Bukhala.* Translated by R. B. Serjeant. London: Garnet, 2000.

Jhabvala, Ruth Prawer (1927–) *German-Jewish screenwriter and fiction writer*

Far from her eastern European roots, Ruth Prawer Jhabvala lives in New York City and writes of colonial and postcolonial India, her adopted third home. Born Ruth Prawer to Polish-German forebears in Cologne, Germany, she grew up during the era of Nazi oppression. At age 12, she, her parents, and older brother Siegbert emigrated from Europe's anti-Semitic nightmare to England, but left behind 40 relatives who were victims of Hitler's "final solution." In a London bomb shelter during the blitz, she crouched over a copy of LEO TOLSTOY's *War and Peace* (1869). In 1948, the post-traumatic horror caused her father to kill himself. Among other fugitives from war, she developed the mindset of a displaced person at home anywhere but belonging nowhere.

In 1951, after earning her degree in English literature from London University, Ruth Prawer married Cyrus S. H. Jhabvala, a Zoroastrian and architecture professor from New Delhi, India. Settling into the social life of Delhi University, she became fluent in Hindi. She published her first novel in 1955 and short fiction printed in *Kenyon Review, Ladies Home Journal, London Magazine, New Statesman, New Yorker, Redbook,* and *Yale Review.* Other novels followed, and in 1963, she began writing for the screen in collaboration with the filmmakers James Ivory and Ismail Merchant. Her style, which would earn the regard of fellow author Salman Rushdie, displayed the influence of other writers of literature of empire, notably, JOSEPH CONRAD, CHARLES DICKENS, and E. M. FORSTER. In 1975, after raising three daughters with her husband, she settled in Manhattan, sought U.S. citizenship, and, like the Yiddish author ISAAC BASHEVIS SINGER, befriended other refugees of the Holocaust.

Critics began categorizing Jhabvala as a bicultural feminist after she wrote the Booker Prize–winning novella *Heat and Dust* (1975), a frank survey of female choices and dilemmas amid social misogyny in the Punjab of colonial and postindependence India. Told in framework style from letters and journals, the quest narrative is related by an unnamed female traveler searching for her matrilineage by tracing the history of her grandfather's first wife, Olivia Rivers, who rebelled against the constraints of a British community in Satipur, India, in 1923. A GOTHIC background sets Olivia in a colonial cemetery, outside a primitive abortion clinic, in a rural palace among women in purdah (female seclusion), alongside a female rescuer of untouchables, and amid barren women at the fertility festival at the Baba Firdau shrine. A moral pariah, Olivia decides to have an abortion of a fetus that could be the offspring of her English husband, Douglas, a minor civil official, or of Olivia's Muslim paramour, the nawab of Khatm. In choosing between a dreary mate and a manipulative lover, Olivia makes the feminist choice—herself and her own needs—and moves into the hills to live in solitude and self-fulfillment away from the petty patriarchy of the Indian raj.

With minimal extraneous detail, Jhabvala's two-layered story looks at a past and a passing empire. She mentions the outlawing of suttee (widow-burning), which the Welsh educator ANNA LEONOWENS described in *Life and Travel in India: Being Recollections of a Journey before the Days of Railroads* (1884), as well as poisoned wedding garments, the torment of a madwoman, and the Sepoy Rebellion of 1857, the uprising that forced the British government to remove the East India Company as ruler and install a regime that survived until 1947. At a climactic moment in Olivia's relationship with the nawab, who is in league with a band of dacoits (cutthroats) left over from the Mughal Empire, he charges the invasive British with heartlessness: "English people are so lucky—they have no feelings at all" (Jhabvala 1975, 144–145). Ironically, Douglas Rivers, the nawab's unwitting rival, makes a parallel assertion about the nawab's lawlessness: "He is a menace to himself, to us, and to the wretched inhabitants of his wretched little state" (148). Olivia, who blames both men for their misdirection of power against women, suffers the standard epiphany of the naive colonial by losing both her sexual and idealistic innocence and fending for herself.

In 1983, Jhabvala won a BAFTA award for adapting *Heat and Dust* for the cinema, featuring Greta Scacchi and Julie Christie. She also won Oscars for her screenplays of *A Room with a View* (1985) and *Howards End* (1992).

Sources

Jhabvala, Ruth Prawer. *Heat and Dust*. New York: Touchstone, 1975.

Smith, Andrew, and William Hughes. *Empire and the Gothic: The Politics of Genre*. London: Palgrave Macmillan, 2003.

Strongman, Luke. *The Booker Prize and the Legacy of Empire*. Amsterdam: Rodopi, 2002.

Johnson, Pauline (Emily Pauline Johnson, Tekahionwake) (1861–1913) *Mohawk poet and mythographer*

An Ontarian storyteller and freelance writer, Emily Johnson wrote of the mixed-race question in British North America. She was born on the Six Nations Indian Reserve near Brantford, Ontario, to a prominent family related to the Mohawk chief Joseph Brant and his sister Molly Brant as well as to Anglican missionaries. Her father was George Henry Johnson, a chief of the Six Nations (Cayuga, Mohawk, Oneida, Onondaga, Seneca, and Tuscarora); her mother was the English-born Emily Susanna Howells Johnson. Because of her ill health, Emily received tutoring in American and British classics from her mother and in Mohawk stories from her bilingual grandparents, Chief John Smoke Johnson and Helen Martin. In 1884, George Johnson died from pneumonia, a complication resulting from a clubbing by white bootleggers and clear-cutters of trees on Indian land. Beginning in the early 1880s, Pauline helped support her family by submitting populist verse to *Boy's World*, the *Brantford Expositor*, *Dominion Magazine*, *Gems of Poetry*, *Mother's Magazine and Family Journal*, *Saturday Night*, as well as to two verse anthologies, *The White Wampum* (1895) and *Canadian Born* (1903). The latter pairs regret at the loss of her people's heritage with verses admiring the British Empire. Her subtle indications of rebellion contrast the actions of Native heroes such as Joseph Brant and Red Jacket with the duplicity, plunder, and proselytizing of white settlers.

As a stage performer for 17 years (1892–1909), Johnson became Canada's first aboriginal writer and headliner. Taking the Mohawk name Tekahionwake (from her grandfather Jacob Tekahionwake Johnson), she earned stardom throughout Canada and the United States and in London for reciting dramatic monologues based on authentic knowledge of the Cree, Huron, Iroquois, Micmac, Mohawk, Ojibwa, and Squamish. Dressed in buckskin decorated with silver brooches, wampum, and ermine tails, she armed herself with an authentic skinning knife. She touched audiences with "As Red Men Die," "Cry from an Indian Wife," a tragic confrontation in "Wolverine," and "The Song My Paddle Sings," an apostrophe to nature and subtextual commentary on the terrors of white-dominated society. In the NATURE idyll "The Camper," in response to sin-obsessed evangelists, she described a sinless aborigine living in spiritual communion with the Almighty. In the vigorous verses of "The Riders of the Plains," she praised the Royal North-West Mounted Police for upholding British law on the North American frontier. Her tours raised money for the needy and, in 1900, supported Canadian soldiers fighting the Boer War.

Rheumatic fever, erysipelas, and respiratory fatigue cut short Johnson's public career. In retirement in 1909 among the Squamish in Vancouver, British Columbia, she wrote features and critical essays for the *Daily Province* and collected narrative poetry, short stories, and vignettes in *Legends of Vancouver* (1911). Her next work, *Flint and Feather* (1912), includes "The Pilot of the Plains," a melodramatic ghost story about the Indian maiden Yakonwita, who is coerced to marry among her own people and betray her "Pale-face lover" (Johnson 1913, 8), who tries to return to her but freezes to death with her in the snow. A more violent view of cultural clashes in "The Cattle Thief" aggrandizes Eagle Chief, a "monstrous, fearless" raider (13), and offers a chilling commentary on starving natives whom whites cheated of their land.

Johnson's last novel, *The Moccasin Maker* (1913), published after her death from breast cancer at age 51, describes the sorrows of native women insulted and belittled by their white partners. Devoid of spite, her writings reveal an authentic voice pleading for peaceful racial and cultural coexistence in central and western Canada.

Sources

Johnson, Pauline. *Flint and Feathers.* Toronto: Musson Books, 1913.

———. *The Moccasin Maker.* Whitefish, Mont.: Kessinger, 2004.

Peterson, Nancy M. *Walking in Two Worlds: Mixed-Blood Indian Women Seeking Their Path.* Caldwell, Idaho: Caxton Press, 2006.

Josephus, Flavius (Titus Flavius Josephus, Joseph ben Mattathias, Yoseph ben Matatyahu)
(ca. A.D. 37–ca. 100) *Jewish historian*

An uprooted Jew and contemporary of the Christian epistle writer PAUL, the scholar priest Flavius Josephus provided first-century Rome with an outsider's view of imperialism. Born Joseph ben Mattathias in Roman-occupied Jerusalem, he was the son of a Hasmonian aristocrat and Mattathias ben Gurion, a priest of Jerusalem who educated Flavius Josephus in Greek and Hebrew. Around A.D. 56, Flavius Josephus joined the Pharisees, a brotherhood of ascetic separatists. Because of his priestly lineage, in A.D. 64, he served his country as a legate (emissary) in negotiations with Emperor Nero to release Jewish clerics from Roman prisons. On the way to Italy, a shipwreck in the Adriatic Sea forced him and 600 other survivors to swim to shore.

Despite Flavius Josephus's doubts that Jews could win their liberty from Rome, during the First Jewish-Roman War of A.D. 66–73, he commanded a revolutionary militia at Galilee. His mother languished in prison; both his parents and wife perished in the onslaught that annihilated tens of thousands. When General Flavius Vespasian (Titus Flavius Vespasian, 9–79) marched on Jotapata, west of the Sea of Galilee, Flavius Josephus and his men retreated to a cave for 47 days under a blood pact to kill themselves rather than yield to Rome. In July A.D. 67, Vespasian captured Flavius Josephus, who surrendered under the ruse of bearing a prophecy that Vespasian would become emperor. By thus currying favor with the man who was indeed a future Roman ruler, Josephus saved himself from execution for fomenting revolt. He also managed to rescue his brother Matthias and some friends and relatives from bondage. Because Flavius Josephus, like the Chechen rebel in LEO TOLSTOY's novella *Hadji Murád* (1904), chose life with conquerors over death in his homeland, Hebrews obliterated the historian's name from written and oral discourse.

Josephus's PROPHECY came true in A.D. 69 when Vespasian became emperor, earning the historian a unique place in Rome's annals. With Vespasian as his patron, Josephus became a Roman citizen. He took the name Titus Flavius Josephus, received a pension and property in Judaea, and married a captured Hebrew woman from Caesarea, who abandoned him. He interpreted Aramaic and Hebrew documents for officials and provided Vespasian with counsel on Judaism and with privileged information on Palestinian uprisings. Scorned as a turncoat and toady by his rival historian Justus of Tiberias, author of *A Chronicle of the Kings of the Jews* (ca. A.D. 80), Flavius Josephus was powerless to negotiate with Jewish leaders at the Roman siege of Jerusalem in summer A.D. 70 or to prevent widespread mayhem and the destruction of the temple there. He married an Alexandrian Jew and sired three sons; only Flavius Hyrcanus survived childhood. After his wife's Hellenism caused a divorce and the defection of their son, in A.D. 75, Flavius Josephus married a Cretan Jew of royal blood and raised his sons Flavius Justus and Simonides Agrippa.

Jews and Romans

After he arrived in Rome in A.D. 70, Flavius Josephus turned to history and chronicled an international conflict in the seven-volume *Bellum Iudaicum* (*History of the Jewish War*, A.D. 75). Rather than write in his native Aramaic or the Latin of his new homeland, he chose refined, literary Greek. The chronicle, released to the public in A.D. 78, portrayed the clash of ideologies, the Roman based on military might and the Hebraic on devotion to Yahweh and the Torah. In book 3, chapter 5, he describes the Romans' bivouac style and their use of portable towers for launching arrows, stones, and darts. He admires how they "live together by companies with quietness and decency, as are all their other affairs managed with good order and security" (Flavius Josephus 1960, 505). Vivid scenes of famine, epidemics, and crucifixions served as propaganda for the Romans and as a warning to subject nations that revolt against the Roman Empire was foolhardy. He portrayed himself and his followers as peacemakers and blamed Jewish military aspirations on a fanatic splinter group led by corrupt manipulators. In book 6, the author credits Vespasian with the wisdom to wait out Jewish infighting, which saved the Romans the effort of quashing the revolution by fighting "hand to hand with men that love murdering, and are mad one against another" (536). The chronicle accuses rich Jews of buying their way to safety, leaving the poor to destruction, an accusation corroborated by the DEAD SEA SCROLLS. The historian also excuses Vespasian for burning the temple in Jerusalem,

an exoneration that the writer Sulpicius Severus rebutted more than three centuries later in his *Historia Sacra* (Sacred history, A.D. 400).

In the *History of the Jewish War*, book 7, chapters 8–9, Flavius Josephus describes a shocking episode in the Roman subjugation of Judaea: the defense of Masada, a tall butte in southern Israel overlooking the Dead Sea. Fleeing the procurator, Lucius Flavius Silva, in A.D. 72, Eleazar ben Yair, led Jewish refugees up two goat paths to a rock fort that Herod the Great completed as a royal retreat in 31 B.C. As Roman engineers inched their way up a rampart adjacent to a vertical slope and applied a battering ram to the walls, on April 16, A.D. 73, Eleazar delivered a heroic speech in the style of the Greek historian THUCYDIDES. As quoted by Flavius Josephus Eleazar claimed that suicide would save "our wives . . . before they are abused, and our children before they have tasted of slavery" (601). At his direction, the 936 Jews at Masada burned the buildings and killed themselves to cheat imperial Rome of victory. A television miniseries, *Masada* (1981), filmed on location, starred Peter Strauss as Eleazar, Peter O'Toole as the Roman commander Silva, and Anthony Quayle as the engineer Rubrius Gallus.

Preserving Jewish Culture

From issues of imperialism and subject nations, Flavius Josephus moved on to a broad view of Jewish history with his 21-volume *Antiquitates Iudaicae* (*Jewish Antiquities*, ca. A.D. 93). A derivative work, the text restructures Old Testament history and previous Judaic commentary into an explanation of Hebrew culture and ritual for the enlightenment of Gentile readers. Of the centrality of the temple at Jerusalem, founded by David and erected by his son Solomon, Flavius Josephus explains: "There ought also to be but one temple for one God; for likeness is the constant foundation of agreement" (631). He endorses the need for priestly supervision and for abstemious living among the devout: "And let our prayers and supplications be made humbly to God" (631). When the author died around A.D. 100, he left a brief AUTOBIOGRAPHY, *The Life of Flavius Josephus* (ca. A.D. 99), the first to survive from antiquity.

During an era of anti-Semitism promoted by the poet Juvenal, his fellow poet Martial, the rhetorician Quintilian, and the historian Tacitus, Flavius Josephus's *History of the Jewish War* is significant for its introduction of Judaism and Hebrew philosophy into the Greco-Roman world and for recording the background of Jesus' ministry and crucifixion. In a critique of Roman imperialism, the historian went to great lengths to demonstrate that the Judaean war erupted from Roman misrule. Key to Flavius Josephus's credibility are his knowledge of the Maccabaean dynasty, of the writings of the Essenes and Pharisees, and of priestly wisdom and political power. His canon expands on previous texts on the construction of temples, the geography of the Holy Lands, the reign of Herod the Great, and biographical details of Nero, Pontius Pilate, Kings Agrippa I and Agrippa II, John the Baptist, and Jesus' contemporaries. The historian's scholarship earned him a place in the Christian apologetics of the theologian Origen (ca. A.D. 185–ca. 254) and Eusebius of Caesarea (ca. A.D. 263–339).

Sources

Feldman, Louis H., and Göhei Hata. *Joseph, the Bible and History.* Tokyo: Yamamoto Shoten Publishing House, 1987.

Josephus, Flavius. *Josephus: Complete Works.* Translated by William Whiston. Grand Rapids, Mich.: Kregel, 1960.

Joyce, James (James Augustine Aloysius Joyce) (1882–1941) *Irish novelist and short story writer*

An exceptional author in the literature of empire, James Joyce chose exile from his rigidly Catholic country as a means of liberating his mind and spirit. Born in Rathgar, south of Dublin, to a failed distiller, John Stanislaus Joyce, and pianist Mary Jane Murray Joyce, the author was the eldest of a family of 15 children, five of whom did not survive to adulthood. Attending University College in Dublin, he studied English, French, and Italian and immersed himself in the dramas of the Norwegian Henrik Ibsen. In 1904, Joyce and his future wife, Nora Joseph Barnacle of Galway, moved to Trieste in the Austro-Hungarian Empire, where he taught English at the Berlitz School. In a newspaper essay in *Il Piccolo della Sera,* he railed against the hanging of an innocent Gaelic speaker who was unable to understand the charge of murder leveled by an Anglo-Irish magistrate. To support the couple and their son and daughter, Joyce delivered lectures on WILLIAM SHAKESPEARE and began composing an autobiographical work of fiction published in 1916 as *A Portrait of the Artist as a Young Man.* A film, *Nora* (2000), features Ewan McGregor as the author during a difficult time in his career and self-imposed exile to Europe to escape a colonized society encumbered with poverty and slavish devotion to Catholicism.

Joyce used his talents as a voice for nontraditionalists and rebels. His essay "Ireland at the Bar" (1907) bristles with outrage at injustice to the poor rural Irish who speak no English. He pictures an elderly defendant as "a remnant of a civilization not ours, deaf and dumb before his judge . . . a symbol of the Irish nation" (Joyce 2000, 146). Joyce spurned political parties and religious prelates and drew literary parallels between savagery toward the Jews during the Roman Empire and the subjugation of the Irish by the British Crown. During the Irish literary revival of the early 20th century, he mocked the Irish playwright John Millington Synge's three-act comedy *The Playboy of the Western World* (1907) as a propaganda play legitimizing Eurocentric sovereignty and cultural stereotyping of the Irish as drunken hicks and barflies. With literary finesse, Joyce's short stories "Araby" and "The Dead" from the collection *Dubliners* (1914) examines the outsider from the perspective of Joyce himself, a fellow pariah and expatriate in Zurich whom the British marginalized for his blatant Irishness and agitation for home rule. With marked despair for the author's homeland, the story "Ivy Day in the Committee Room" charges Irish politicos with failure to live up to the idealism and commitment of the Irish reformer Charles Parnell (1846–91). In *A Portrait of the Artist as a Young Man,* Joyce returns to extreme hero worship of Parnell, claiming "The priests and the priests' pawns broke Parnell's heart and hounded him into his grave" (Joyce, 2003 25).

Through jest, caricature, burlesque, and SATIRE, Joyce's complex stream-of-consciousness narratives treat issues of autonomy and the outsider's rule over the Irish Catholic peasant. With an historical quest novel, *Ulysses* (1922), the author pays tribute to the humble Irish yeoman as the backbone of the empire and honors Dublin, a largely ignored Catholic capital that merged ancient Celtic heritage with British additions. The text ridicules the character of the English imperialist Haines and castigates the London *Times* for being a colonial apologist in matters of Irish nationalism and civil liberties. Joyce's lingual wizardry wrings puns and gibes out of "imperial, imperious, imperative" (Joyce 1990, 131). To the character Stephen Dedalus, the enemy is the "brutish" empire (594). Heavy sarcasm between two characters describes the inglorious bureaucracy as "a dozen gamehogs and cottonball barons," "yahoos" who suppress "drudges and whipped serfs" (329). In agreement, the character Joe snorts that the Irish suffer in an empire "on which the sun never rises" (329), a subtextual comment on Ireland's despair. The exchange ends with a parody of the Apostles' Creed as it applies to Jack Tar, iconic British sailor.

Joyce suffered recurring eye problems and surgeries due to glaucoma, often hampering his work. Nonetheless, he threw himself into the composition of *Ulysses* as well as his other great novel, *Finnegans Wake*, the full version of which he published in 1939 to disappointing reviews. Having finally married Nora in 1931, he died in Zurich on January 13, 1941, still exiled from the country that had provided him with a rich source of material. Joyce's fiction was a vehicle for the actress Anjelica Huston, who starred in the film version of *The Dead* (1987).

Sources

Booth, Howard J., and Nigel Rigby. *Modernism and Empire: Writing and British Coloniality 1890–1940.* Manchester, Eng.: Manchester University Press, 2000.

Joyce, James. *Dubliners.* New York: Signet, 2007.

———. *Occasional, Critical, and Political Writing.* Oxford: Oxford University Press, 2000.

———. *A Portrait of the Artist as a Young Man.* London: Penguin, 2003.

———. *Ulysses.* New York: Vintage, 1990.

Judith (Yehudit) (ca. 590 B.C.) *Jewish hero*

A feminist HERO during the clash between Jews and the Assyrian Empire engineered about 593 B.C. by Nebuchadnezzar II of Nineveh, Judith is the title figure in anonymous historical fiction written around 150 B.C. and found in the biblical Apocrypha. In a model of Hebrew STORYTELLING, Judith averts destruction of the Jews by beheading Holofernes, an Assyrian siege commander whom the Babylonian king Nebuchadnezzar dispatched from Nineveh (in present-day southern Iraq) in the early sixth century B.C. Holofernes's raiding and pillaging reached west as far as Damascus. The book of Judith, usually included only in Catholic and Eastern Orthodox bibles, is set in the fortified Judean hill country outside Jerusalem. It describes Judith, the wealthy widow of Manasses, as a righteous zealot bearing a generic name meaning "Jewess." The narrative lauds her as a clever, sexually appealing nationalist who puts an end to Holofernes's marauding. When the Hebrew commander Uzziah ponders capitulating to the Assyrians, she impresses the ranks of male military leaders by proposing a cunning strategy to infiltrate Holofernes's tent.

Uncharacteristic of the usual literary wise woman, Judith exudes femininity. Cloaked in sackcloth and ash, the symbols of bereavement, she prays for divine guidance before perfuming her body, decking herself fetchingly "to allure the eyes of all men that should see her" (Judith 10:4) and posting herself at the gates of the hilltop city of Bethulia, possibly present-day Jenin on Palestine's West Bank. An unnamed but equally bold serving woman bears fruit, grain, bread, oil, and wine and accompanies her mistress past an Assyrian picket. The characterization of Judith depicts her as quick-witted and crafty. She promises to disclose a secret approach to the Jewish stronghold in exchange for safe passage away from the conflict. The patrol leader, fearing a ruse, sends 100 cavalrymen to accompany her to Shechem (present-day Salim, Israel). The book's author names the size of the force to emphasize the courage of Judith and her handmaiden in all-male terrain.

The tension mounts when the protagonist enters enemy territory. At the general's quarters, she beguiles Holofernes for four days by remaining modest while appealing to his vanity, a common trait in literature of empire in which women use trickery as a form of self-empowerment. After an evening of dining and imbibing, Holofernes passes out without seducing Judith, who eats only simple fare from her own foodstuffs, a symbol of self-control before opulence. Her approach to his couch precedes a cry to God for strength, the lopping of his head from the neckbone, and the destruction of bed hangings, proofs of his stature and vainglory as well as evidence of Assyrian decadence. Storing the severed head and bed canopy in her market bag, she returns to Bethulia to announce a triumph.

The psychological value of Judith's bold move serves a military purpose. To the surprise of neighboring nations, the Israelites rout the panicky Assyrians and plunder their camp. Extolled for her valor in slaughtering Nebuchadnezzar's general, Judith and her hymn of triumph (Judith 16:11–17) became a source of female iconography for paintings and statuary, tapestries, fresco, mosaic, stained glass, drama, and opera.

Sources

The Apocrypha of the Old Testament. King James Version. New York: American Bible Society, 1972.

Juvenal (Decimus Junius Juvenalis)

(ca. A.D. 55–ca. 140) *Roman poet and satirist*
A social critic who took a wittier approach to imperial license than found in the biographies of his contemporary PLUTARCH, Juvenal mocked the vices of the Roman emperor Domitian's rule with venomous verses. Details of the author's life are conjectural. The son or ward of an Iberian freedman or country squire, he was a native of Aquinum (present-day Aquino near Monte Cassino, Italy), southeast of Rome. He appears to have been an attorney after service as a military tribune on the Adriatic Sea in Dalmatia (present-day Croatia). Although he apparently circulated on the fringes of respectability due to his combative personality and invectives against the powerful, the emperor Vespasian allegedly elevated him to *flamen* (high priest). Under Domitian (ruled A.D. 81–96), Juvenal incurred banishment to Syene (present-day Aswan, Egypt) in A.D. 93 for maligning an actor. After his recall to Rome in A.D. 96 during Nerva's short reign, he launched a literary career by writing 16 SATIRES, perhaps to support himself after Domitian's confiscation of his inheritance. With extremes of vituperation and obscenity, his verses targeted cor-

rupt politicians, homosexuals, Greek immigrants, Jews, sadists, gladiators, gluttons, con artists, and male and female prostitutes. He is believed to have retired to an estate at Bilbilis (present-day Calatayud, Spain) and died in his 80s.

Juvenal's reactionary verse yields flashes of rhetorical greatness. Like SENECA, he excelled at succinct jewels of wisdom, some as short as two-word phrases, for example:

- a sound mind in a healthy body
- a rare bird
- Nobody becomes wicked overnight.
- Who's watching the watchmen?
- Revenge pleasures the narrow mind.
- Every neighborhood has its Clytemnestra.
- Morality is the only nobility.

For contrast, he held up the old aristocracy and their traditional values as models of behavior and mourned their eclipse in an iniquitous age. His often-vitriolic comments show that he harbored jealousy and resentment toward upstarts, cosmopolites, and poseurs who seized the spotlight and curried favor with the palace elite.

Juvenal bore a grudge against Domitian for curtailing civil liberties and for besmirching Rome's ruling dynasty through outrageous acts. In a graphic condemnation, the second book of Juvenal's *Satires* (ca. A.D. 127) calls the emperor "an adulterer stained by a union worthy of the tragic stage" (Juvenal 1992, 10), a charge citing Domitian's incest with his 27-year-old niece Julia Flavia, whom he murdered with an abortifacient. According to Juvenal in Satire 10, the decadence of the imperial family encouraged citizen apathy: "The people cast off its worries, when we stopped selling our votes" (88). The satirist concludes his 10th satire of Roman complacency with a cynical summation of Romans being bought with *panem et circenses* (bread and circuses, 89), a tragic replacement of principles by food for their bellies and tawdry amusements for their minds.

Sources

Hooley, Daniel M. *Roman Satire.* Oxford: Blackwell, 2007.
Juvenal. *The Satires.* Translated by Niall Rudd. Oxford: Oxford University Press, 1992.

K

Kafka, Franz   See PROPHECY.

Kakinomoto no Hitomaro (ca. A.D. 660–710)
Japanese poet

A revered bard of Japan's developing unification, Kakinomoto no Hitomaro wrote of a homogeneous folk culture unmarred by outside influences. A native of Nara in south-central Honshu, he married twice, the second time to the poet Yosami no Otome; traveled as an ambassador on state business; and died at his retirement home in Ihami south of Nara, a coastal city overlooking the sheltered bay he often described for its beauty. During his service as court poet and verse laureate to the emperors Temmu (673–80) and Mommu (697–707) and to Empress Jito (690–97), Hitomaro established himself as the nation's first major writer. As Confucianism and Buddhism altered the familiar foundations of Japanese society, later poets and scholars reflected on Hitomaro as a spokesman for a less confusing time.

Hitomaro crammed details into his odes and lyrics marking ceremonies, entombments, and royal hunts and processions. His verse found favor with Otomo Yakamochi, the poet and compiler of the MANYOSHU (*Ten Thousand Leaves*, ca. 759), an anthology of Japan's earliest lines, completed during the Nara Period (710–94). Among the 100 stanzas of Hitomaro's work collected in the text are tender love lyrics, memories of sibling love for his sister, and state poems, including the opening of a new palace at Yoshino southwest of Nara and a lament at the death of Prince Takechi, a fellow poet who died at age 42. In "On the Enshrinement of Takechi no Miko" (ca. 700), Hitomaro speaks in first person of his awe at the prince's wisdom, skill at bow and sword, and aptitude for reducing bellicose tribes into peaceful royalists, a talent Takechi shared with the Hebrew warrior-king David and Arjuna, hero of the BHAGAVAD GITA (ca. 200 B.C.). Another example of Hitomaro's writings for officialdom, "On the Sovereign's Visit to the Palace in Yoshinu" (ca. 700), contrasts a mansion in the royal compound with the wonders of flowing rivers and tall peaks surrounding Nara. The setting suggests the poet's preference for the eternal grandeur of nature over the temporal pomposity of state architecture.

In addition to inventive, soulful tankas (five-line verses with a set syllable count) on love, solitude, and death, Hitomaro wrote *chokas* (long narratives) encouraging patriotism. He honored his homeland by praising the natural beauties of a craggy country surrounded by shores and scattered islets. His reverence for Japan's past and for the integrity of peasant life permeates his most sophisticated works, which he composed to legitimate and dignify the position of Emperor Temmu, who seized power when Hitomaro was entering his teens. In "Prince Karu's Retreat to Remember His Father" (ca. 700), a wilderness idyll relieves the stress of court functions to allow the prince a private period. The poet respects the right of Karu (later to become Emperor Mommu) to normal expressions of sorrow by withdrawing to the Aki moors to grieve for his deceased parent, Crown Prince Kusakabe, who died in 689 when the boy was six years old. A tension between Hitomaro's public recitations and his personal existentialism invigorates "On Passing the Ruined Capital at Omi" (ca. 700), a pensive glimpse of the ruined halls of the legendary Emperor Jimmu, who ruled until 585 B.C. Like Homeric Troy at Hissarlik on the northwestern coast of Turkey and Tintagel, King Arthur's reputed birthplace in Cornwall, England, the Otsu Palace crumbled within sight of the pounding surf, an archeological monument to what the poet termed "this transitory world."

See also PRAYER.

Sources

Levy, Ian Hideo. *Hitomaro and the Birth of Japanese Lyricism.* Princeton, N.J.: Princeton University Press, 1984.

The Ten Thousand Leaves. Translated by Ian Hideo Levy. Princeton, N.J.: Princeton University Press, 1981.

Kalakaua, King David   See STORYTELLING.

Kalevala (Elias Lönnrot) (1836)

A literary monument to the soul's freedom, the *Kalevala* expresses the Finnish nationalism that inspired citizens in 1917 to free themselves from the foundering Russian Empire. The collation of *pourquoi* (why) stories and legends was the avocation of a public health officer and ethnographer named Elias Lönnrot (1802–84) of Sammatti, Finland. The 22,795 trochaic tetrameter lines exhibit the author's devotion to the rural folk tradition of the *suomilainen* (fen dwellers), to the Finnish and Russo-Karelian languages, and to competitive verse recitations accompanied by drafts of beer and strums of the five-string kantele, or zither. The absence of details about Danes, Germans, Russians, and Swedes suggests that the poet chose sources of enormous antiquity, taking them from a time when Finns lived free of imperial control. The value of the *Kalevala,* according to the linguist Eino Friberg, is immeasurable: "It is the shaper of our language; it is the inspirer of our independence; and it has been the source of the flowering of our art and literature" (Friberg 1988, 12).

The preface begins with an individual performer who declares to a circle of listeners, "I am ready now for singing . . . Songs of ancient wit and wisdom . . . legends of the times forgotten" (Lönnrot 1904, 1). Themes of the first 10 cantos first feature CREATION LORE of fecund whitecaps stilled by wind, the source of life for a seagoing people. The action covers the sorrow songs and stirrings of FEMINISM in the suicide of Aino, who drowns herself in the sea rather than marry an aged rhapsodist. Subsequent motifs of trickery and sedition create drama from hardihood and hospitality, which counterbalance violent episodes of trial by ordeal, bride capture, revenge, and blood oaths, all elements the text holds in common with Vyasa's *Mahabharata* (ca. A.D. 350) from the Guptan Empire and FIRDAWSI's *Shahnameh* (*The Book of Kings,* ca. 1010), Persia's dynastic epic. Throughout, Väinämöinen, a white-bearded wizard on a par with the Scandic Odin and the Arthurian mage Merlin, casts a spell over a credulous people. His enchantments use song and music to quell danger and to heal nature with a magic balsam, but the poet reminds his hearers that shamanism has its limits: "God alone can work completion / Give to cause its perfect ending" (124).

Like the *Chanson de Roland* (*Song of Roland,* ca. 1080), the oldest collection of French deed songs, and the Spanish epic EL CID (ca. 1150), the Finnish epic portrays the emergence of civilization in a savage race pitted against the domination of Tuoni, the kingdom of death. Issues of militarism and national order and defense give way to domestic catastrophe from epidemics and predations on moose and cattle, a disaster for a herding society. In the concluding allegory, the wonder-boy motif, a story of a virgin birth paralleling that of Jesus, pictures the threatened murder of a future king and the prodigy's wisdom in the face of a child killer. Following the boy's baptism, he advances to the Karelian throne. Because the people now turn to Christianity, Väinämöinen retreats across the sea, carrying in his craft the symbols of outworn paganism. He abandons to the Finns his kantele, a source of STORYTELLING and song for future needs.

The *Kalevala*'s heroic conventions parallel those of the poet Friedrich Reinhold Kreutzwald's *Kalevipoeg* (Kalev's son, 1853), the Estonian national epic. Väinämöinen was a source for Gandalf, the sage in J. R. R. Tolkien's *The Lord of the Rings* (1955). Russian filmmakers adapted the epic to the screenplay *The Day the Earth Froze* (1959); a Finnish-Chinese film, *Jade Warrior* (2006), introduced the *Kalevala* to Asian audiences.

Sources

Friberg, Eino, George C. Schoolfield, and Björn Landström, eds. *The Kalevala*. Chicago: University of Illinois Press, 1988.

Lönnrot, Elias. *The Kalevala: The Epic Poem of Finland*. Translated by John Martin Crawford. Cincinnati: Robert Clarke, 1904.

Kalilah and Dimnah   See PANCHATANTRA.

Kempe, Margery   See FEMINISM.

Kim (Rudyard Kipling) (1901)

Written for a British audience during the Second Boer War (1899–1902), RUDYARD KIPLING's young adult spy novel *Kim* humanizes the face of the cultural masquerader in the British Empire. The author introduced his boy HERO story in 11 installments in *McClure's Magazine* from December 1900 to October 1901 and simultaneously in *Cassell's Magazine* from January to November 1901, the year of Queen Victoria's death. The episodic narrative reveals Britain's rivalry with Russia over Central Asia as well as nostalgia for outmoded concepts of colonization and control. The setting is the Grand Trunk Road from Afghanistan to Bengal along the western Indian frontier, a crucible of global power struggle. Details emphasize an exoticism that panders to the European's oriental stereotypes, such as the romance of the Punjab, the seediness of a bazaar, and the affinity of Asians for lying, deception, and superstition. Kipling rhapsodizes on foreign strangeness: "All India is full of holy men stammering gospels in strange tongues; shaken and consumed in the fires of their own zeal; dreams, babblers and visionaries: as it has been from the beginning and will continue to the end" (Kipling 1901, 32). His idealization of the mystic prepares the reader for Kim's first encounter with the hypocrisy of white Christians.

The protagonist, Kimball "Kim" O'Hara, a plucky white waif and introspective errand boy, lives a rootless Peter Pan existence in Lahore, India (present-day Pakistan), where Kipling worked from 1882 to January 1888 as the assistant editor of the *Civil and Military Gazette*. His fictional boy is the result of the marriage of English nursemaid Annie Shott to Kimball O'Hara, an Irish color sergeant. At their deaths in 1878 from the standard colonial scourges—she from cholera and he from addiction to alcohol and opium—the 13-year-old "goes native" by slipping into Indian street society. He becomes what Kipling calls "the Two-Sided Man" (179), a person capable of understanding Eastern and Western perspectives. The text indicates that Kim's melding into an Indian milieu is made possible by the boy's wily nature and by his familiarity with local squalor and with British militarism, two extremes of Asian colonization. A scion of imperial servants, he bears multiple inner strengths: "Temperate, kindly, wise, of ungrudging disposition, a merry heart upon the road, never forgetting, learned, truthful, courteous" (255). More practical to his journey are his skill in spying and his fluency in Hindi and Urdu as well as English and dialects spoken by Afghans, Muslims, Sikhs, and Tibetans.

Imperial Threats

While composing the picaresque exploits of an Anglo-Indian teenager, Kipling feared the threat at that time from Russian expansion into India through the Bolan and Khyber passes. He prefigured Russian incursions into the British Raj in the short story "The Man Who Was" (1890), the poems "The Ballad of the King's Jest" (1890) and "The Truce of the Bear" (1898), and he continued that theme in the cloak-and-dagger scenes of *Kim*. When the character is introduced, he is sitting astride Zam-Zammah (lion's roar), a 14-foot cannon that is an icon of "might makes right" from the old Afghan Durrani Empire. He accompanies Teshoo Lama, a wandering Buddhist holy man from Tibet, on the first of the novel's three adventures. A standard literature ploy dating to classic Greek drama, the identification of an orphan by a totem, birthmark, or symbol, rescues Kim from living by his wits. Recognized by the chaplain of his father's British regiment, he turns to the lama's spiritual influence and mourns his alienation: "I am all alone in this land, I know not where I go nor what shall befall me" (122). Enrolled for three years at St. Xavier's, an English school in Lucknow, during his holidays Kim masters surveillance and the "Great Game" of espionage. He accepts recruitment by Babu, a Bengali British intelligence agent (205). Subtextually, Kipling criticizes the British for inveigling an underage orphan into dangerous underground assignments, a career that literature stereotypes as the lone work of the expatriate, and outcast.

The author echoes Arthurian lore—the neophyte warrior king's dilemma between love for the world (Guenevere and Camelot) and for the spirit of duty, embodied in the magician and sage Merlin. As a member of the British Secret Service, Kim, by now age 17, seeks a clear vision of empire, symbolized by a red bull on a green field, the insignia of his father's regiment. The boy spy finds himself split between quasi-Indian discipleship to the Holy One and his membership by right of blood in the imperialist sahibs. Literary historian Zohreh T. Sullivan explains: "The contradictory pattern of desire—to be loved and to control—underlying the familial trope of a world in which mother England would be caretaker to lesser children of imperial Gods was produced by the political machinery of empire" (Sullivan 1993, 2). At a high point in the action, Kim's journey to the Himalayas along the Indo-Tibetan border brings him into direct contract with two Russian agents posing as hunters. The successful outcome is achieved by skills that only a wanderer of the empire can claim—a familiarity with the crossroads of culture and language and a sophistication acquired from self-redeeming experience in a multinational contretemps that presages the cold war.

In 1950, Errol Flynn and Dean Stockwell starred in an MGM adaptation of *Kim*. A made-for-TV version in 1984 paired Peter O'Toole and Ravi Sheth.

Sources

Hopkirk, Peter. *Quest for Kim*. Ann Arbor: University of Michigan Press, 1999.

Kipling, Rudyard. *Kim*. London: Macmillan, 1901.

Simmons, Diane. *The Narcissism of Empire: Loss, Rage and Revenge in Thomas De Quincey, Robert Louis Stevenson, Arthur Conan Doyle, Rudyard Kipling, and Isak Dinesen*. Eastbourne, U.K.: Sussex Academic Press, 2007.

Sullivan, Zohreh T. *Narratives of Empire: The Fictions of Rudyard Kipling*. Cambridge: Cambridge University Press, 1993.

Kincaid, Jamaica (Elaine) (1949–)
Caribbean essayist and novelist

Essayist and fiction writer Jamaica Kincaid speaks the anger of the children of colonialism. Born Elaine Potter Richardson in St. John's, Antigua, an illegitimate child of African-Carib-Scots ancestry, she came of age in a British-dominated milieu that she describes in an autobiographical novel, *Annie John* (1985). Amid island storytellers, practitioners of the belief system called obeah, and worshippers of African animism, the author endured an insidious overlordship symbolized by tombstones "of long-dead people who had been the masters of our ancestors" before the emancipation of slaves in 1833 (Kincaid 1985, 50). Under compulsion from teachers, the emissaries of British culture during the last decades of British rule, she estranged herself from her black ancestry through gendered refinements and table manners and spoke proper English rather than her native West Indian patois. She later noted, "We got kind of the height of empire. They were trying to erase any knowledge of another history" (quoted in Ferguson 1994, 168). The inner battle of a devalued female against androcentric European rule resulted in a combative personality and caustic feminist canon.

A paradox of the author's upbringing derived from her condemnation of Christopher Columbus as well as her adoration of British poets, Anglo scripture, and the works of the Brontë sisters and George Eliot, the latter members of the privileged white caste. When the family's financial situation dictated that Kincaid quit school at age 16 and earn money, she emigrated from the Caribbean to New York in June 1965, completed high school, and entered night school at Westchester Community College in White Plains. Though she won a scholarship to Franconia College in New Hampshire, she left after a year, feeling herself too old to be a student any more, and returned to New York, where she embarked on a career in journalism. In 1973, she changed her name to Jamaica Kincaid as a way of freeing herself from her past.

In 1976, while writing for *Ingenue,* Kincaid obtained a staff position at the *New Yorker.* She dedicated herself to postcolonialism—an islander's anger at GENOCIDE and "the shameful qualities of imperialism and unjustified aggression" (Kincaid 1999, 148). She felt obligated to "remember not just the past—because there is no past—but the moment, and that moment is 500 years long" (quoted in Obejas 1996). In the *New Yorker* column "The Talk of the Town" and in fiction, she expressed black islanders' loathing for the British Empire, which stamped its domination on Antiguans through a constant English-based routine—Anglican church bells marking the hours, English teatime and eating habits, and even bulbs and plants from the British countryside. Her reason for concentrating on the corrupt history of the Western Hemisphere was survival—"getting something out of my head that if I don't will drive me absolutely insane" (quoted in Ferguson 1994, 174).

Ambivalence toward Home

Kincaid leveled abuse at the privileged white tourist in a short diatribe, *A Small Place* (1988), a counter-travelogue meant to insult rather than invite the outsider to Antigua. The text depicts recent arrivals at the airport as the "got-for-nothing" wealthy and includes the insulting comment, "We made you bastards rich" (Kincaid 1988, 10). Chapter two targets the British, who no longer exercise power over a quarter of the earth's people. Kincaid claims that the rulers of her own time seem unaware that "this empire business was all wrong" (23). The jeremiad won the approval of the critic and novelist Salman Rushdie, who applauded the author's acerbic lamentation and moralizing.

In autumn 1989, the author turned to allegory for another attack on colonialism. In "Ovando," an essay for the literary magazine *Conjunctions,* she envisions conquest as an arrogant ghoul rotting down to bare bone from the corruption that inhabits it. The GOTHIC wraith of Frey Nicolás de Ovando (1960–1518), whom the Spanish chronicler BARTOLOMÉ DE LAS CASAS reviled in *Brevísima relación de la destrucción de las Indias* (Brief report of the devastation of the Indies, 1552), enters

the home of a hospitable native of Hispaniola. Ovando, an early 16th-century military mentor to the Spanish conquistador Hernán Cortéz, the destroyer of the AZTEC empire, wears plate armor tinged with the blood of Arawak and Carib aborigines of the West Indies. Kincaid summarizes his governorship of the islands in a hellish litany comprised of "horror and misery and disease and famine and poverty and nothingness" (Kincaid 1989, 76). In the narrative, Ovando warns that he has allies—English, Dutch, French, Germans, and Iberians, all of whom threaten the Caribbean paradise with wholesale annihilation of indigenous cultures. The antithesis of the courtly knight, Ovando justifies his predations with the claim that discoveries are ordained by fate and sanctified by God, the conventional excuse for invasion. Kincaid's narrator defies the deluded warrior by smashing his mirror and destroying his map; her story preserves on natural tree fiber the seizure of the West Indies as a record for world history.

Personal Animosity

The cynicism that barbs Kincaid's work recurs in *The Autobiography of My Mother* (1996), in which the first-person protagonist describes her Carib ancestors as "defeated and then exterminated, thrown away like the weeds in a garden" (Kincaid 1996, 16). The protagonist, Xuela Claudette Richardson, voices the aphorism that good people are always poor because they have not committed enough sins to enrich themselves. At a pivotal moment in the four-year-old Xuela's life with Ma Eunice Paul, a surrogate mother and the family laundress, the child breaks the woman's only plate, which features an idyllic English countryside—a field of grass and pastel wildflowers beneath a mild sunlight. One word in gilt declares the scene to be "heaven," an identification linked to the island underclass concept of the British motherland, which enjoys "a life without worry or care or want" (9). For punishment, Ma Eunice forces Xuela's body into a servile pose holding rocks aloft in her hand beneath a pitiless Caribbean sun, an ironic posture that turns the impoverished laundress into an enforcer of bicultural standards that the young rebel Xuela defies. Subtextually, the laundress becomes a colonial apologist.

Kincaid's multilayered prose makes links between imperialism and the denigration of women and nonwhites. She muses on self-congratulatory males and their joy in not being born female and subservient like Ma Eunice Paul or the women whom raiders devalue through rape and bondage. Xuela extends the metaphor of androcentrism to racism by affirming male pride in being light-skinned. The accident of birth causes the male to feel "blessed and chosen to be [white] and it gives him a special privilege in the hierarchy of everything" (131). She summarizes the conqueror's sense of entitlement as an ipso facto awareness of "what makes the world turn" (132).

Travel introduced Kincaid to the extent of the British Empire and increased her compassion for the postcolonial poor demoralized by a legacy of cultural erasure and tourism, a modern version of SLAVERY. In August 1991, in the international review *Transition*, she published the personal essay "On Seeing England for the First Time," an explosion of rage at colonial racism and the pillage it created. Like the Trinidadian-British author V. S. NAIPAUL, she discovered that the reality bore little resemblance to the England about which she had fantasized. While working as garden editor for *Architectural Digest*, she analyzed botanic collections and horticultural traditions as evidence that imperialism sullies an innocent and joyful avocation. In her essay "Sowers and Reapers: The Unquiet World of a Flower Bed," published in the January 22, 2001, issue of *New Yorker*, she admitted to deliberate polarization in the gardening community by introducing postcolonial themes: "I had done something unforgivable—I had introduced race and politics into the garden" (Kincaid 2001, 41). The comment epitomizes her feeling of anger with every facet of colonialism, whether on the edenic island of Antigua or in the prim gardens of Europe and the United States.

Sources

Allen, Brooke. "Imperialism Is the Mama of All Sorrows," *Wall Street Journal*, 2 February 1996, A8.

Ferguson, Moira. "A Lot of Memory: An Interview with Jamaica Kincaid." *Kenyon Review* 16, no. 1 (Summer 1994): 163–188.

Kincaid, Jamaica. *Annie John*. New York: Farrar, Straus and Giroux, 1985.

———. *The Autobiography of My Mother*. New York: Plume, 1996.

———. *My Garden*. New York: Farrar, Straus, Giroux, 1999.

———. "Ovando." *Conjunctions* 14, no. 10 (Fall 1989): 75–83.

———. *A Small Place*. New York: Farrar, Straus and Giroux, 1988.

———. "Sowers and Reapers: The Unquiet World of a Flower Bed." *New Yorker* 76, no. 43 (January 22, 2001): 41–45.

Obejas, Achy. "Jamaica Bound: Imagining Lives of Those Never Let to Be," *Chicago Tribune*, 31 March 1996.

Kipling, Rudyard (Joseph Rudyard Kipling) (1865–1936) *British journalist, poet, novelist, and short story writer*

From Queen Victoria's reign through the uncertainties following World War I, Rudyard Kipling, a journalist, fabulist, balladeer, and fiction writer, exemplified the ambivalence of the British imperialist. Born in Bombay, India, he was the son of Alice MacDonald and John Lockwood Kipling, a sculptor and museum curator. Raised by a Portuguese nanny and a Hindu porter named Meeta, from his earliest years the bilingual author learned STORYTELLING along with a respect for the lower castes. In 1871, "Ruddy" and Alice Beatrice "Trix" Kipling, his three-year-old sister, traveled to the foster home of of Captain and Mrs. Holloway, a callous and uncaring couple living in Southsea, England. Until age 12, the author suffered a sadistic neglect that brought on psychological collapse. His only solaces were a month's vacation each December with his aunt Georgina and his uncle Edward Burne-Jones, a famous artist, as well as reading mysteries and adventure lore from the British Empire.

The author typified the life of the bicultural military child, as related in his autobiography, *Something of Myself, For My Friends Known and Unknown* (1937), left unfinished at his death. His mother finally rescued him from the Holloways, and in 1878, he entered a military prep school, the United Services College in North Devon. There he embraced a belief in British racial and cultural superiority. His schoolmates consisted mainly of fellow Anglo-Indians (British citizens born or residing in India), the sons of British officers: "Some seventy-five per cent of us had been born outside England and hoped to follow their fathers in the Army" (Kipling 1937, 23), a choice that severe myopia denied him. But life at Southsea in the Holloways' "House of Desolation" and at school far from the India of his birth made a survivor of him (8). He compensated for eyeglasses and bookishness by writing. In the young adult novel *Stalky & Co.* (1899), he captured the adventures and squabbles of his adolescent peers, whom he dubbed Beetle, Stalky, and McTurk.

The author's real education began at age 16 in Lahore, India (present-day Pakistan), on the editorial staff of the *Civil & Military Gazette*. His job was to turn reports from news agencies into vernacular and sensational news—abysmal sanitation standards, typhoid epidemics, murders, hoaxes, divorces from Egypt to Hong Kong, knighthoods in London, legislation from the British Parliament, and war diaries from Russia. In his AUTOBIOGRA-PHY, Kipling reported bouts of dysentery, ambient fevers of 104°, and bribes from underlings seeking advancement. Upon receiving cash, a shawl, and a fruit basket, he insulted the opportunistic sender by returning the gift via a low-caste sweeper. A canny servant, hired by Kipling's father as a bodyguard, declared, "'Till we get home you eat and drink from my hands" (28). A second fruit basket with money in it required more wit: Kipling pricked into the banknotes in Latin the words *Timeo Danaos et dona ferentes* (I fear Greeks bearing gifts), a line from VIRGIL's *AENEID* (17 B.C.). In Kipling's development into a writer, he became a bicultural specialist, and he predicted that he would never be fully English.

From Journalist to Published Author

From scouring for news and features, Kipling, then as earnestly patriotic as a raw recruit, proposed to enlighten the average English reader about the scope and purpose of the empire. He anthologized his first parodies of privileged white imperialists and their wives in a collection of juvenilia, *Departmental Ditties and Other Verses* (1886), issued by the *Gazette*. The anthology displays his gift for rollicking rhythms and rhymes conveying lower-class dialects and amusements common to soldiers. In

the estimation of the critic Diane Simmons, Kipling exposed the fallacies of imperialism—"a muddle of bored and sometimes desperate young men, a place where very little is accomplished" (Simmons 2007, ix). He followed with his first 40 stories in *Plain Tales from the Hills* (1888), the majority of them newspaper stories and all admired by some critics for their layering of heat waves, disease, bewildering circumstance, pointless servitude, and treachery. In "Thrown Away," the futility and venality of empire underlies a young English officer's shooting himself in the head in a place where "good work does not matter, because a man is judged by his worst output and another man takes all the credit. . . . Nothing matters except Home furlough" (Kipling *Plain Tales*, 1888, 15, 16). The major's cover-up of suicide exemplifies the author's obsessive motif—the heavy task of men charged with patrolling the empire, the topic of NIKOLAY GOGOL's *The Government Inspector* (1836) and GEORGE ORWELL's classic essay "Shooting an Elephant" (1936). A reverse image in Kipling's "The Story of Muhammad Din" enlarges on the trampling of a Muslim child's mud buildings, an emblem of India's vulnerability and innocence. The boys death follows his disillusion with the phony British pose of uplifting, Christianizing, and encouraging the Indian peasantry.

The anthology includes a variety of stories touching on aspects of Indian culture that were strange and fanciful to the average British reader. By setting fantasy fiction in India, Kipling coupled the refined European's fear of the irrational with the outré details of an incomprehensible Asian culture. The immediate result was an audience for Kipling's stories, which expressed his and the world's anxiety about imperialism and the posting of refined urbanites to global backwaters. For the reader, vicarious participation in British dominion fostered the illusion of power and triumph. For the author, anxiety developed into an emotional impasse.

In addition to the autobiographical "Baa Baa Black Sheep," at age 23, Kipling composed an adventure novella, "The Man Who Would Be King," anthologized in *The Phantom Rickshaw and Other Ghost Tales* (1888). The story discloses a mounting tension in the author's mind between a suspicion of individual motives and the supposed altruism of the British Raj. The narrative portrays the con artists Danny Dravot and Peachey Carnehan as presumptuous outsiders: "We have been boiler-fitters, engine-drivers, petty contracters . . . and we have decided that India isn't big enough for such as us" (Kipling *Phantom Rickshaw*, 1888, 252). The duo generates a deadly backlash by discounting the beliefs and taboos of a subject people on India's northwest frontier. Replete with episodic romance, marching songs, suspense, and situational irony, the quest tale follows the army pals to Kafiristan (in present-day Afghanistan) among "an all-fired lot of heathens" (128), a comment rich with working-class white disdain for Asians. The plot turns on local reverence for extremes of past and present—the conquests of Alexander the Great and the Masonic symbol, an emblem of male lodge membership that the author wore from his late 20s. Kipling concludes with a grisly paean to brotherhood in Peachey's return of Danny's dried skull to India, the result of a response by the uncivilized Asians to the bungled intrusion of British adventurers into an area even Alexander could not subdue.

From East to West

As a roving reporter for the Allahabad *Pioneer*, Kipling globetrotted from southern India to Rangoon, Singapore, Hong Kong, Auckland, Adelaide, San Francisco, Portland, Seattle, Yokohama, and Vancouver. After crossing the United States from west to east, he worked in London and wrote his first novel, *The Light That Failed* (1891), a study of the fictional artist Dick Heldar, whose eye injuries lead to blindness. The loss results after his service in the Sudanese War of 1881, when the Mahdi attempts unification of Sudanese tribes. Kipling subsequently chose the GOTHIC convention of transmutation as a punishment for sacrilege in "The Mark of the Beast," a cautionary tale in *Life's Handicap: Being Stories of Mine Own People* (1891), which features the desecrator of an Indian temple.

A romantic dirge, "Without Benefit of Clergy," published in the June 1890 issue of *Macmillan's Magazine* and anthologized in *Life's Handicap*, describes a biracial pairing that the author observed repeatedly and introduced in Danny Dravot's marriage to an Afghan and Trejago's romance with Bisesa in the story "Beyond the Pale" (1888). A racial cloud hovers over the pregnant woman Ameera, who fears that the love of John Holden, like other British commitments to non-white women, is "at the best an inconstant affair" (Kipling *Life's Handicap*, 1891, 132). Extolled by the writers GRAHAM GREENE, Henry James, Somerset Maugham, and Oscar Wilde; by the poets W. H. Auden, T. S. Eliot, and William Butler Yeats; and by the critics Kingsley Amis and Edmund Wilson, the elegy depicts Holden's double life as an ostensible bachelor and as the proud father of a mixed-race son. The auguries of a broken knife hilt and a blood sacrifice of two goats precede a cholera epidemic that robs him of his unofficial family. The combination of color prejudice and endemic tropical diseases highlights the threats to common-law Anglo-Indian marriage for colonial officials. The novelist Angus Wilson felt that the story's poignance hinted at its being autobiographical.

The Late Victorian Age

After his marriage to the American Caroline "Carrie" Starr Balestier in 1892, Kipling settled at her family's property outside Brattleboro, Vermont. For martial verse, march chants, and ballads in *Barrack-Room Ballads and Other Verses* (1892), he detailed the soldier's life of cheroots, gin halls, brothels, and murder, a capital crime charged against Danny Deever, a title figure in Kipling's most famous gallows tribute. In a salute to sacrifice, "That Day" honors the slaughter of British soldiers at Maiwand in south-central Afghanistan during the Anglo-Afghan War of 1880. "The Widow at Windsor," a view of royalty from the perspective of underpaid soldiers on the frontier, characterizes the social and economic gap between ordinary troops and the monarch they serve, Victoria, the queen-empress of India, then entering her fourth decade of grief for Prince Albert, her consort, who had died of typhoid fever in 1861. For "Mandalay," Kipling applies soldierly jocularity and infantry slang to the conquest of Burma; for the sentimental narrative poem "Gunga Din," dialect testimony enlivens the abuse of laborers employed by the colonial regiments. The author's sympathy for a fallen waterboy contrasts with the normal prejudice against Indians who served Britain well.

Kipling wrote CHILDREN'S LITERATURE as well, with the boy Mowgli featuring in two bestiaries, *The Jungle Book* (1894) and *The Second Jungle Book* (1895). The narratives compile allegories of animal daring based on the Roman myth of Romulus and Remus, the feral twins suckled by a she-wolf in 753 B.C. The motif of the "man's cub"—Mowgli is an abandoned male child raised by wolves, a panther, and a bear—echoes a common Kipling scenario, the protagonist's life as a fragile child of the empire. The two books anticipate the orphaned title figure of *KIM* (1901), a self-reliant young HERO on a par with Marie McSwigan's Norwegian sledders in *Snow Treasure* (1942) and the underground rescuers in Adeline Yen Mah's *Chinese Cinderella and the Secret Dragon Society* (2005). Another story from Kipling's collection, "Rikki-Tikki-Tavi," pictures the rescue of a small Anglo-Indian boy named Teddy from a krait (a venomous snake)and a pair of cobras by the title figure, a foundling mongoose named from the local slang for "hurry."

After leaving Vermont and returning to England in 1896, Kipling published *Captains Courageous: A Story of the Grand Banks* (1897), a standard coming-of-age tale dramatizing the maturation of Harvey Cheyne, a boy washed overboard and rescued by a fishing trawler off Newfoundland. As in much of Kipling's fiction about preteens, meeting the challenge on the edges of civilization is proof of manhood, a dare that the bespectacled author accepted in his own youth.

The Empire's Spokesman

In the last years of Queen Victoria's 64-year reign, Kipling wrote two famous works: the declamatory hymn "Recessional" (1897), which honors the queen's diamond jubilee, and the polemical verse "The White Man's Burden" (1899). Both poems debuted in the *Times* and, in 1903, appeared in *The Five Nations*. "Recessional" is a public apologia for British imperialism and hold on colonies around the globe. Kipling voices the common British view in his descriptions of the peoples of undeveloped countries as "heathen hearts" and lawless "lesser breeds" (Kipling 1999, 340), a phrase that the Indian novelist Nayantara Sahgal used for a title in 2007. "The White Man's Burden" champions the United States's appropriation of the Philippines

after the Spanish-American War. Phrases in the first stanza depicting nonwhite people as sulky, demonic children justify imperialism as a rescue of the uncivilized from their own benightedness. The terms precede a call to America to join Britain in tackling war, epidemic, hunger, and ignorance. The concept of a "white man's burden" has since become extremely unpopular as world opinion turned against Eurocentric leadership and American imperialism.

Also in 1899, the *Daily Mail* printed "The Absent-Minded Beggar," a salute to the soldier. Kipling intended his sentimental poem to elicit donations for the families of reservists fighting the Second Boer War (1899–1902). The popular line "Duke's son—cook's son—son of a hundred kings" (Kipling "Absent-Minded," 1899) precedes a reminder to civilians to support the wives and children left impoverished by Britain's struggle in South Africa.

At his peak during the bridge between the Victorian and Edwardian ages, Kipling, like Sigmund Freud and Mark Twain, battled skepticism and misanthropy. A dual bout of influenza and whooping cough weakened the author and killed his firstborn, seven-year-old Josephine. At the nadir of his pessimism, he noted, "When a man has come to the turnstiles of Night, all the creeds in the world seem to him wonderfully alike and colorless" (Kipling *Light That Failed*, 1891, vii). He extended his fame with more poetry, prose, and children's stories—*Kim* and *Just So Stories for Little Children* (1902), a collection of 12 *pourquoi* (why) tales that refute the British conceit that the empire represented the apogee of civilization. For a short time in 1900, Kipling was a roving reporter and associate editor of the *Friend*, a newspaper dedicated to military men published in Bloemfontein, Orange Free State. From close observation, he lambasted British leadership for the blunders of the Second Boer War and predicted apartheid, a subject that later absorbed the creative energies of NADINE GORDIMER.

Despite some concerns, Kipling remained an idealist about imperialism. The dystopian novelist George Orwell later claimed that Kipling had been naive about the money-making aims of world domination. In the poem "A Song of the White Men" (1900), the poet champions his race and gender:

"Well for the world when the White Men drink / To the dawn of the White Men's day" (Ralph, Doyle, and Kipling 1901, 301). Reluctant to accept official honors, he rejected a knighthood and, twice, the honor of being England's poet laureate, but he accepted honorary degrees from Cambridge, Durham, Edinburgh, McGill, Oxford, and Strasbourg universities and the Sorbonne. In 1907, he became the youngest writer and first Anglophone to receive the Nobel Prize in literature.

As well as speaking for Indian natives, civil servants, engineers, and soldiers, Kipling became the spokesman for Anglo-Saxon instincts. He sided with the average citizen against the world of the privileged and the cruel civil bureaucrats exposed in the short story "The Head of the District." He lost some respect due to his repudiation of machine gun and mustard gas use during World War I, which he named the Great War. In the story "The Vortex," published in *A Diversity of Creatures* (1917), one character admits that the military tax burden unfairly charges the average British subject with defending an ungainly empire, a size and distance problem that contributed to the fall of the Roman Empire. Another character proposes a federation by which each colony has a vote before committing its army to British wars.

After his 18-year-old son John "Jack" Kipling died on September 27, 1915, while serving with the Irish Guards on the Western Front at the battle of Loos, France, the author devoted himself to military monuments and graves and served as lord rector of St. Andrews University in Scotland. Orwell dubbed Kipling the unofficial historian of the British army and the "prophet of British Imperialism in its expansionist phase" (Orwell 1970, 118) but felt that Kipling never gave up allegiance to the ruling class: "This warped his political justment . . . and it led him into abysses of folly and snobbery" (132).

Loss changed Kipling. He struck back at the barbarism of Germany's clash with Britain in "Mary Postgate" (1915), a revelation of savagery in an otherwise sedate Englishwoman. In 1916, he published *Sea Warfare*, a collection of articles that commemorates efforts of the British navy in such clashes as the battle of Jutland on May 1, 1916. He takes the opportunity to censure British duplicity:

"The English are the worst . . . liars in the world, they have been rigorously trained since their early youth to live and act lies for the comfort of the society in which they move, and so for their own comfort" (Kipling 1916, 27). Without hedging, he charges the empire with "racial snobbery" (27). While composing "The Fabulists" (1917), a salute to AESOP and his imitators, Kipling stated that FABLE is less controversial than the realistic views of insanity, suicide, and death he recorded in "At the End of the Passage," "The Mark of the Beast," "To Be Filed for Reference," and "Thrown Away."

After Kipling's death from a perforated ulcer on January 18, 1936, his remains were cremated and his ashes interred in Poets' Corner of Westminster Abbey. The foundering of the British Empire reduced his reputation from skilled writer to propagandist, xenophobist, and Victorian chauvinist reviled by such critics as Lionel Trilling. Nevertheless, the vigor and simplicity of his verse has meant that he is still widely quoted at every level of British society.

Many of Kipling's writings survive on film: Shirley Temple as the female heroine in *Wee Willie Winkie* (1937); three versions of *Captains Courageous* (1937, 1977, 1996), the second starring Karl Malden and Ricardo Montalban; *Gunga Din* (1939), enacted by Sam Jaffe, Cary Grant, and Douglas Fairbanks, Jr.; *The Light That Failed* (1939), with Ronald Colman cast opposite Ida Lupino; several versions of *Kim*, including a 1950 film starring Dean Stockwell and Errol Flynn; a Disney adaptation of *The Jungle Book* (1967) and *Rudyard Kipling's The Second Jungle Book: Mowgli and Baloo* (1997); and the mythic tale of *The Man Who Would Be King* (1975), starring Michael Caine and Sean Connery as buffoonish standard bearers for the empire. In 2007 the television movie *My Boy Jack* depicted Kipling's distress over having helped his son enlist in the army.

Sources

Kipling, Rudyard. "The Absent-Minded Beggar," *Daily Mail* (London), 1899, n.p.

———. *Barrack-Room Ballads and Other Verses.* London: Methuen, 1892.

———. *Captains Courageous: A Story of the Grand Banks.* London: Macmillan, 1897.

———. *The Collected Poems of Rudyard Kipling*. London: Wordsworth Editions, 1999.

———. *Departmental Ditties and Other Verses*. Lahore: The Civil and Military Gazette Press, 1886.

———. *A Diversity of Creatures*. London: Macmillan, 1917.

———. *The Five Nations*. London: Methuen, 1903.

———. *The Jungle Book*. London: Macmillan, 1894.

———. *Just So Stories for Little Children*. London: Macmillan, 1902.

———. *Life's Handicap: Being Stories of Mine Own People*. London: Macmillan, 1891.

———. *The Light That Failed*. Philadelphia: J. B. Lippincott, 1891.

———. *The Phantom Rickshaw and Other Tales*. Allahabad, India: A. H. Wheeler, 1888.

———. *Plain Tales from the Hills*. London: W. Thacker, 1888.

———. *Sea Warfare*. London: Macmillan, 1916.

———. *The Second Jungle Book*. London: Macmillan, 1895.

———. *Something of Myself and Other Autobiographical Writings*. Cambridge: Cambridge University Press, 1937.

———. *Stalky & Co.* London: Macmillan, 1899.

Orwell, George. *A Collection of Essays*. Fort Washington, Pa.: Harvest Books, 1970.

Ralph, Julian, Arthur Conan Doyle, and Rudyard Kipling. *War's Brighter Side: The Story of "The Friend" Newspaper Edited by the Correspondents with Lord Roberts's Forces, March–April, 1900*. New York: D. Appleton & Co., 1901.

Simmons, Diane. *The Narcissism of Empire: Loss, Rage and Revenge in Thomas De Quincey, Robert Louis Stevenson, Arthur Conan Doyle, Rudyard Kipling, and Isak Dinesen*. Eastbourne, U.K.: Sussex Academic Press, 2007.

Sullivan, Zohreh T. *Narratives of Empire: The Fictions of Rudyard Kipling*. Cambridge: Cambridge University Press, 1993.

koan

An aphoristic brain teaser unique to Zen Buddhism, the koan is a form of religious teaching formalized in southern India during the Gupta Empire by the monk Bodhidharma in A.D. 520. The Chinese refined koans as *kung an* (public standards); the Japanese revered koans alongside Taoist mysticism. The liberalization of thought from rote study of scripture coincided with a period of expansion in eastern China, when challenges and perplexities assailed all levels of society. In 920, in the second decade of the Khitan Empire in northern China, the Zen master Nanyuan Huiyung recorded the first written koan, an enigma used to shake trainee monks from complacency. By exploratory rumination, like that triggered by AESOP's FABLES (ca. 550 B.C.), the ANALECTS of Confucius (ca. 210 B.C.), and MARCUS AURELIUS's *Meditations* (ca. A.D. 180), the novice philosopher could stretch his mind with glimpses of a higher perception. Nanyuan proposed to augment the routine of simple piety with insights that produced deeper awareness through abstruse questions. Bypassing scripture, ritual, and everyday logic, the koan produced what the Japanese called *satori*—an epiphany or awakening experience that startled the mind into new realms of understanding.

A unique addition to world WISDOM LITERATURE and wry wit, koans took a self-deprecating look at the thought processes of the serious holy man. A famous version describes a man clutching a rope dangling from a precipice while a tiger lurks above and mice chew at the cords. In a life-or-death predicament, the man notices the beauty of a wild strawberry. The koan emphasizes the importance of nature amid human struggle. The anthology of 1,700 koans amassed by the Chinese priest Yuanwu Keqin (Yuan-wu K'o-ch'in, 1063–1135) appeared as the *Pi-yen lu* (*Blue Cliff Record*, 1125), which the Japanese translator Setcho Zenji published as *Hekigan-roku*. By 1130, the Chinese teacher Dahui Zonggao (Ta-hui Tsung-kao, 1089–1163) of Anhwei Province was using collections of koans as a systematic verse curriculum that taught students to think independently and to rely on intuition. In a radical shift from simple engagement in silent Buddhist meditation, he added active intellectual discussion among some 2,000 disciples of realistic subjects extending from theology and philosophy to war and empire. He exhorted young philosophers to concentrate on word puzzles in anticipation of a flash of illumination. These transcendent moments transformed habitual thought patterns to insights into the self and to a spontaneous understanding of serenity in a troubled world.

In 1191, during the Kamakura empire, the Buddhist priest Myoan Eisai (1141–1215) imported Chinese Zen philosophy to Kyoto, Japan. At the Hoonji Temple in Kyushu, Japan's first Zen training center, he chose koans as a text for educating samurai warriors and intellectual Buddhists. Five levels of koans awakened the individual to sanctity, a true sense of being, and the steps to wisdom. In the late Song dynasty (960–1279), Wumen Huikai (Wu-men Hui-k'ai, 1183–1260), a Chinese priest from Hangchou, selected 48 of the original posers for the *Wumenguan,* or *Wumen Kuan* (*The Gateless Gate* or *The Gateless Barrier,* 1228), a classic collection that encourages the Buddhist neophyte to understand pure abstraction. In the preface, Wumen describes fools as people who depend on words for understanding. He exalts koans as "brickbats to batter at the gate, guiding monks in accord with their various capacities" (Wumen 1990, 3). The Chinese Zen master Hongzhi Zhengjue (Hungchih Cheng-chueh, 1091–1157) made his own selection, the *Tsung-jung lu* (*Book of Equanimity,* ca. 1240), which Japanese Buddhists published as the *Shoyoroku* (*Book of Serenity*). From 1336 to 1573, the Ashikaga clan of shoguns applied the koan to literature, art, and noh theatre.

In China's most famous novel, *DREAM OF THE RED CHAMBER* (1791), by the Beijing-born novelist Cao Xueqin, the text concludes with the elevation of Jia Baoyu, the spoiled protagonist, to Daoist monk. To questions about his mentor, he replies with a koan: "The place where he lives is far if you think it is far and near if you think it is near" (Cao 1958, 323). The statement reveals the young prince's intent to retreat from the Qing Empire to seek wisdom as a monk.

Sources

Cao Xueqin. *Dream of the Red Chamber.* Translated by Chi-Chen Wang. Garden City, N.Y.: Doubleday Anchor, 1958.

Heine, Steven, and Dale S. Wright. *The Koan: Texts and Contexts in Zen Buddhism.* Oxford: Oxford University Press, 2000.

Wumen Huikai. *The Gateless Barrier: The Wu-Men Kuan (Mumonkan).* Translated by Robert Aitken. New York: Macmillan, 1990.

Koran (Qur'an) (A.D. 633)

The holy book of Islam, the Koran (Recitation) attests in emotive Arabic to the goodness and majesty of Allah, the monotheistic creator and governor of the universe. The mythic revelation of scripture over a 22-year period by the angel Jibreel (Gabriel) to the prophet Muhammad (ca. 570–632) of Mecca (present-day Makkah, Saudi Arabia) introduced disciples to a moral and legal guide. The narrative bases its theology on the Abrahamic tradition founded in 1950 B.C. at Ur, a Mesopotamian city north of the Persian Gulf between the Euphrates and Tigris Rivers (present-day south-central Iraq). WISDOM LITERATURE intersperses hagiography, HERO stories, PROPHECY, BIOGRAPHY (including stories of the patriarchs Moses and Joseph), and CREATION LORE that pictures God shaping humankind "from clots of blood" (Koran, ix). Setting the tone and style of Islamic worship, Jibreel declared to the prophet: "Recite! Your Lord is the Most Bountiful One, who by the pen taught man what he did not know" (ix).

Like the Hebrew EXODUS (ca. 450 B.C.) and the Hindu BHAGAVAD GITA (ca. 200 B.C.), the Koran was born out of conflict. To escape assassins, at age 52, Muhammad crossed the desert northwest toward Medina, the cradle of Islam, and raised a Bedouin force of 30,000 that eventually overwhelmed the Arabian peninsula and crushed idolatry. Justifying Muslim militancy, a verse from the second sura (chapter), "The Cow," warns: "Guard yourselves against the fire whose fuel is men and stones, prepared for the unbelievers" (2:24). In 628, Muhammad sent evangelistic messages to the Christian emperor Heraclius at Constantinople (present-day Istanbul, Turkey), to the Aksumite king Amah of Ethiopia and Sudan, and to the Zoroastrian warrior king Khosrow II of Persia and Yemen. The letters encouraged each to convert to Islam (submission) to secure safety and peace. Heraclius declined the offer; Khosrow raged and destroyed the letter.

A Standard Text

A year after the prophet's death, Caliph Abu Bakr of Mecca, an early companion and disciple of Muhammad, arranged the divine communications in 114 chapters ordered by length, from longest to shortest. In the complete 6,236 *ayat* (verses), readers find explanations of natural phenomena and international events in terms of God's will. Like the Egyptian and Ethiopian versions of the BOOK OF THE DEAD, Koranic narrative lists honorifics for Allah, whom the faithful extol as the Peace, Forgiver, Creator, Compassionate, Provider, and Holy One as well as "Sovereign of the day of judgment" (1:2). The last term bears a subtextual alert to a required atonement of the sinful before they can attain forgiveness and after-life rewards.

The scripture states unequivocally that earthly power is a human illusion. According to the prophet, dominion resides only in heaven: "Did you not know that God has power over all things? . . . and that there is none besides God to protect and help you?" (2:7–8). In compliance with religious tradition, the penitent listens to oral recitation performed by trained readers, who elicit serenity, submission, and sanctity. Each service opens with the standard affirmation "Allahu Akbar! La ilaha illa Allah!" (God is great! There is no god but Allah). Used as the central textbook in the *maktab* (primary school), the collected verses use the royal "we" to exhort the young to respect law, justice, truth, and mercy.

Muhammad included a network of stories indigenous to the Middle East. In sura 18, "Al Kahf" (The Cave) unfolds into a complex, exemplary FABLE on surviving difficult times. The action depicts the endangerment of seven youths and their dog; the youths are known to Christian hagiographers as the Seven Sleepers of Ephesus (today a ruin on the west-central coast of Turkey). During the persecutions launched by the Roman emperor Decius in A.D. 245, the boys retreated to a cavern and allegedly slept for 300 years, a symbolic entombment of minorities in the Roman Empire suggestive of a living fetus awaiting birth. In a supernatural return from the dead, their resurrected spirits solace Muslims with a promise that Allah enfolds his believers in welcome and beneficence. Those who die in God's care awaken in Eden wearing gold bracelets and brocade and silk robes. The blessed lie on couches, a heavenly retreat out of range of profane tyrants and emperors.

Comfort to the Nations

As the Islamic kingdom expanded along trade routes over land and sea and challenged the hegemony of the Byzantine and Sassanid empires, the Koran became a source of inspiration and monotheism, especially for the laboring class and slaves. Worshippers sought safety in concealment and studied and prayed in private. Persecution of the devout by Christians, Jews, and pagans resulted in confinement of Muslims in dungeons. They incurred protracted torments, yet Muslims clung to their sacred book. In groups or alone, they read and recited slowly and respectfully in the original Arabic as a source of comfort and reassurance. A familiar verse asserts of Allah: "There is not a living creature on the earth whose destiny He does not govern. Straight is the path of my Lord" (11:53).

According to Antoine de Saint-Exupery's *Wind, Sand, and Stars* (1939), the Arabic scripture became the handbook that transformed desert dunes into an empire. Like the Hebrew warrior king David and the Chinese emperor Wu Di, Muhammad built an Arabic confederacy from disparate tribes and clans of nomads unused to the concept of citizenship in an empire. Of them, the prophet remarked, "Desert Arabs surpass others in unbelief and hypocrisy, and have more cause to be ignorant of the laws which God has revealed to His apostle" (9:97). The Koran unified them with the promise of an almighty deliverer from infighting: "He has power to let loose His scourge upon you from above your heads and from beneath your feet, and to divide you into discordant factions, causing the one to suffer at the hands of the other" (6:65). In an era of power struggles, the exhortations heartened followers of the new faith. They spread Muslim domination across Egypt, Iraq, Libya, Numidia, Persia, Phoenicia, and Syria and replaced paganism in Central Asia, North and Central Africa, and across Turkey into southern Europe as far north as the Danube River and as far west as the Iberian peninsula.

Sources

Cook, Michael. *The Koran: A Very Short Introduction.* Oxford: Oxford University Press, 2000.

The Koran. Translated by Nessim Joseph Dawood. London: Penguin Classics, 2004.

Krylov, Ivan Andreyevich (1769–1844)
Russian fabulist ands playwright

A satirist and fabulist, Ivan Adreyevich Krylov produced catchy aphorisms that spiced everyday Russian conversation. A product of the 18th-century Age of Enlightenment, he grew up in a humble military family in St. Petersburg, Russia. He educated himself by reading the French masters Nicolas Boileau, Molière, and Jean Racine and began writing in his mid-teens with *Cofeinitsa* (The fortune teller, 1785), a play about a gypsy who reads the future in coffee grounds. While coediting the literary magazine *Zritel* (Spectator) and the *Sankt-Peterburgskii Merkurii* (St. Petersburg Mercury), he produced a short SATIRE, "Eulogy to the Memory of My Grandfather" (1792), which ridicules pretentious aristocrats and corrupt bureaucrats. The squire in the caricature caters to hunting hounds and horses while ignoring the needs of serfs. The story prefigures the peasant unrest that resulted in 1917 in the overthrow of Czar Nicholas II, Russia's last monarch.

Krylov enjoyed tweaking his social superiors. During the golden age of Russian literature, he angered government censors with his caustic wit in an oriental quest story, "Kaib: An Eastern Tale" (1792), a denunciation of the czarist autocracy of Catherine the Great, who extended the Russian Empire into Ottoman and Polish-Lithuanian territories to control Belarus, Courland, Crimea, Lithuania, and Ukraine. Imperial police rifled Krylov's print shop and monitored his activities. Wisely, he stopped writing and left St. Petersburg. From 1797 to 1801, during the early reign of Czar Paul I, he remained in self-imposed exile and taught children in the household of Prince Sergei Galitzin of Riga on the Latvian coast south of Finland. In later travels, while observing the country folk of the Volga basin, he composed operas and stage dramas, beginning with a satire of Czar Paul (ruled 1796–1801) in *The Nibbler* (1804) and following with an attack on social fashion in *The Fashion Shop* (1807) and *Lesson for Daughters* (1807).

From Drama to Fable

As he approached age 40, Krylov began translating the FABLEs of the French satirist JEAN DE LA FONTAINE, but he soon began to write his own, initially in the style of both La Fontaine and AESOP. He ultimately composed 203 original beast tales in vigorous, mirthful vernacular. For the nine successful publications he began in 1809, Krylov earned the admiration of Czar Alexander I and received a government post as director of Russian literature at St. Petersburg's Imperial Public Library, where he lived and worked. In 1812, he published "The Wolf in the Kennel" and "The Crow and the Hen," two satires of the debacle of Napoleon Bonaparte in Russia that year that reduced the French army to consuming meals of crow soup. "The Division" and "The Pike and the Cat" mocked the disagreements of the Russian military hierarchy during the French invasion of Moscow. The author described the honor given to "snakes in hell" with "The Slanderer and the Snake" (1814). Tongue in cheek, he smirked that, in Satan's domain, names like Attila, Nero, and Napoleon "are inscribed on a tablet, and great solemnities are appointed in their honour" (Krylov 1883, 156).

Krylov's overt spite against the ruling class brought both notoriety and danger. "The Cask" scorns the residue of Russian admiration for French mannerisms and perspectives. He mocks affectations retained by Russians enraptured by Western European enlightenment and over-refined decorum. Stories such as "The Bear among the Bees," "The Rain Cloud," "The Council of the Mice," and "The Dog" skewered venal officials, who had the power to retaliate against a simple poet. Undeterred by their threats, in 1815, with "The Hare at the Chase" and "Canine Friendship," the fabulist scoffed at the ill-concealed hostilities during the Congress of Vienna, which remained in session from November 1, 1814, to June 8, 1815. After he incurred the displeasure of Czar Alexander I, and in 1824, Krylov stopped writing after the publication of the anticensorship tale "The Cat and the Nightingale," the antimonarchy fable "The Elderly Lion," and "The Grandee," a short gates-of-heaven dialogue in which St. Peter lauds a Persian satrap for indulging himself while leaving his subjects unburdened by royal interference. In spite of royal disapproval, by the 1830s, Krylov had become an honored figure in Russian literary circles. In 1838, a festival was held in his honor. He died in St. Petersburg on November 21, 1844.

From Censorship to Print

Over a decade after Krylov's death, his suppressed anticzarist, antielite plays and allegories such as "The Feast" went into print as textbooks for children and later as songs set to music composed by Sergei Rachmaninov and Anton Rubenstein. At the heart of Krylov's beloved cautionary parables, such as "Trishka's Caftan," "Fortune and the Beggar," "Demian's Fish Soup," "The Peasant in Trouble," were the famine, taxation, and injustices borne by the lowest level of Russian peasantry. In "The Leaves and the Roots," he reminded citizens that they should never stray too far from their ethnic beginnings. In "The Sheep's Petition," he dramatized the plight of the underclass under an impotent chain of command. When the sheep complains of the marauding wolves, Leo the lion king sends the sheep to state his case to the bear, who simply decrees that wolves should not eat sheep—but he does not enforce the decree. The droll conclusion declares that all must be well in the animal empire because there are few cases pending against wolves.

Krylov had much to teach royalty. His motif of the preparation of a prince in "The Education of the Lion," based on Catherine the Great's educa-tion of her grandson, Czar Alexander I, concludes with an expression of regret that most rulers lack an understanding of the wants and needs of their subjects, a theme found in the PANCHATANTRA (ca. 200 B.C.), the BHAGAVAD GITA (ca. 200 B.C.), and in Hans Christian Andersen's fable "The Emperor's New Clothes" (1837). One Krylov fable, "The Musicians," explains the inability of an ass, bear, goat, and monkey to form a musical quartet. They cannot agree on how to position themselves, but a nightingale tells them it does not matter, as they will never be musicians. Written in 1810, the text miniaturizes the disagreements of the four departments of the Russian Imperial Council. On the same theme, "The Swan, the Pike, and the Crab" describes the disunity of three unlike creatures as a team of dray animals. The description, like the PROPHECY of revolution in "The Horse and the River," hints at the uprising of the working class in 1917 to bring down the last Romanov czar. The fall of the Russian Empire restored one of Krylov's sayings to popularity: "To a head that is empty no art can add brains: / Though you place it in office—it empty remains" (182).

Sources

Krylov, Ivan. *Krilof and His Fables*. Translated by W. R. S. Ralston. 4th edition. London: Cassell & Co., 1883.

Tosi, Alessandra. *Waiting for Pushkin: Russian Fiction in the Reign of Alexander I (1801–1825)*. Amsterdam: Rodopi, 2006.

L

La Fontaine, Jean de (1621–1695) *French fabulist*

A worldly, lighthearted poet of the early years of the French Empire, Jean de La Fontaine revived the satiric intent, finesse, and clever badinage of the classic FABLE. A native of Chateau-Thierry in Champagne, a wine-growing region of west-central France, he completed his education in Paris, dabbled at law, and read Homer and the works of the Roman essayist Cicero, the playwright Terence, the poets Horace and OVID, and the epic poet VIRGIL. After an extended youth of gaming, womanizing, and indulgence in a fashionable wardrobe, in 1647, he inherited his father's position as royal inspector of waterways and forests and also made an unhappy arranged marriage. With plenty of time free from his official duties, he devoted himself to writing ballets, operas, dramas, salon trifles, and epigrammatic poetry. He was subsidized by Nicholas Fouquet, the superintendent of finances, but his insouciant lifestyle vanished with Fouquet's arrest and imprisonment for embezzlement.

In his late 30s, La Fontaine chose WISDOM LITERATURE as his métier. Unlike the later German writers Gotthard Ephraim Lessing and JOHANN WOLFGANG VON GOETHE, who valued the genre as a source of self-improvement and perfecting flaws, La Fontaine used the illustrative tale to improve public decorum and propriety. In company with Nicolas Boileau, Molière, Jean Racine, and Madame de Sévigné, La Fontaine refined his technique and devoted himself to the fable, which he collected in *Fables choisies* (*Selected Fables*, 1668,

1678). Around 1672, he sold his official position, and for the rest of his life, La Fontaine depended on the generosity of patrons. He was elected to the French Academy in 1684.

Advice to Power

Schooled in AESOP's style in the fables of Phaedrus published about A.D. 31 and drawing on the *PANCHATANTRA* (ca. 200 B.C.) and medieval tales, La Fontaine wrote dramatic nuggets based on models from Greece, Rome, Turkey, India, Britain, and the Islamic Empire as well as on bucolic French scenarios featuring dairymaids, cobblers, and shepherds. He dedicated his first book of fables to six-year-old Prince Louis, the Grand Dauphin, who was growing up in the royal court of Louis XIV, the self-indulgent Sun King. In "Education," La Fontaine warns, "Oft falls the son below his sire's estate; / Through want of care all things degenerate" (La Fontaine 1860, 117). The moral suggests that the fabulist considered his stories as words to the wise, especially to a future monarch.

In sophisticated French bearing an audacity similar to the Russian fabulist IVAN ANDREYEVICH KRYLOV, La Fontaine prodded the bastions of power in "The Man and the Flea," "The Dog That Carried His Master's Dinner," and "The Rat and the Oyster." With "The Bear and the Amateur Gardener," the moralist reminds the maker of alliances that false friends are more dangerous than enemies. A parallel, "The Funeral of the Lioness," states that the flatterer can easily amuse royalty: "No matter what you may have done, / Nor yet how high its wrath may run, / —The Bait is swallowed—object won" (91). In "The Lion's Court," the narrative advises the fawner on majesty of the value of plain speaking: "To gain the smile / Of kings, one must hold the middle place / 'Twixt blunt rebuke and fulsome praise / And sometimes use, with easy grace, / The language of the Norman race" (4). One of La Fontaine's most stirring "minidramas," "The League of Rats," derides the platitudes of would-be chivalric heroes facing a feline stalker named Raminagrab (Grimalkin in some versions). In "The Heron," La Fontaine abases the esthete for constantly expecting the best for himself. The stinger at the end proclaims, "Ye featherless people of the human race / —List to another tale as true, / And you'll hear the lesson brought home to you" (17).

Key to an appreciation of La Fontaine is his rejection of the didactic conclusion. He preferred compact scenarios and a subtle compassion. "The Rat Retired from the World" mocks state religions for cloistering the clergy from the horrors of international war. "The Dairywoman and the Pot of Milk" scolds monarchs for disbelieving that they can fall to the powers of "simple Jack" (32), a meditation on the Jacquerie that rebelled against King John II the Good of France at Poitiers in 1358. La Fontaine expresses pity for peasants in "The Hare and the Frogs," a meditation on lowly creatures who live in constant fear of larger, more aggressive beasts. In "The Animals Sick of the Plague," he denounces Renard the Fox's scapegoating of the ass, a bald, scabrous, scruffy beast hanged for eating grass. The moral frets, "Thus human courts acquit the strong, / And doom the weak, as therefore wrong" (10).

As a hint to crowned heads, La Fontaine composed "The Power of Fable," which warns the hypothetical emperor to listen to the wisdom of common folk. The fabulist's work influenced the writings of Krylov, a storyteller who teased a similarly decadent regime in Russia more than a century later. The Senegalese folklorist BIRAGO DIOP created his own version of La Fontaine's style by translating Wolof tales into French.

Sources
Hobbs, Anne Stevenson, ed. *Fables*. London: Victoria and Albert Museum, 1986.

La Fontaine, Jean de. *Fables of La Fontaine*. Translated by Elizur Wright. New York: Derby & Jackson, 1860.
Shields, David S. *Oracles of Empire: Poetry, Politics, and Commerce in British America, 1690–1750*. Chicago: University of Chicago Press, 1990.

Lancaster, G. B. (Edith Joan Lyttleton) See
FRONTIER LITERATURE.

Laozi (Lao Tzu) See DAODEJING.

Las Casas, Bartolomé de (1474–1566)
Spanish missionary and historian
Bartolomé de Las Casas was the first European author to condemn imperialism and enslavement in the New World. Born to the lower middle class in Seville, Spain, he was the son of a merchant who enriched himself by sailing with Christopher Columbus on his second voyage in 1493–94. Las Casas studied law and religion at the University of Salamanca, intending to become a priest. In 1502, he traveled to Hispaniola (present-day Haiti) with Governor Nicolás de Ovando, a commander of the Military Order of Alcantara, mentor to the explorer Hernán Cortés, annihilator of the indigenous Arawak and Carib of the West Indies, and despoiler of African slaves. He stayed in Santo Domingo for four years, during which time he witnessed the massacre of a large number of Indians. He returned to Spain in 1506 to resume his studies, and he was ordained the following year. He subsequently returned to Salamanca for a degree in Canon law, upon which he set sail for Hispaniola, arriving in September 1510. Though a property owner himself, he deplored the Spanish system of land development and forced labor (*encomienda*). The capture and burning at the stake of the Taíno chief Hatuey on February 2, 1512, so dismayed Las Casas that he dedicated his life thereafter to improving the lot of black and Indian slaves in the Greater Antilles, Guatemala, Mexico, Nicaragua, and Peru. He renounced his personal ownership of slaves in 1514; he later declared that the subjugation and exploitation of Indians was a mortal sin.

In the early 1520s, under the aegis of Holy Roman Emperor Charles V, Las Casas attempted to build a utopian community and mission in Cumaná on the north coast of Venezuela. He envisioned a trade relationship between peaceful farmers and European merchants as a New World crusade and a fertile ground for Christianization of pagans. Colonial Spanish investors undermined his work by fomenting an Indian uprising that climaxed in murder and arson. Discouraged, he returned to Hispaniola in 1522 and joined the Dominican order. He continued to campaign against slavery and the abuse of Indians, often angering his superiors. In his tract *Confessionario* (1545), Las Casas ordered new priests assigned to the Caribbean to deny forgiveness of sins to enslavers of Indians.

Eventually, while dividing his time between Spain and his work in the Americas, Las Casas accumulated the materials that would form the core of his great work, *Brevísima relación de la destrucción de las Indias* (Brief report of the devastation of the Indies, 1552). The chronicle, part of the humanitarian backlash against Spain's New World regime, offers the only eyewitness account of the indigenous tribes whom Columbus encountered and of the Spanish-made misery that developed in Central America and the West Indies, especially in mines and on plantations. Las Casas's virulent arguments against European exploiters of the Western Hemisphere were based on a humanist philosophy that deemed all people were created in God's likeness. In a blaze of indignation, he leveled charges of greed and GENOCIDE against ostensibly Christian investors and settlers under the *encomienda* system. He described the aboriginal labor pool controlled by European trustees as victims of a satanic form of usurpation and SLAVERY. He denounced "vexations, assaults, and iniquities" and "murder and torture inflicted on the natives in this relentless search for gold" (Las Casas 1999, 14, 35). Those who survived outright murder by impaling in pits or burning in locked buildings faced lives shortened by brutal labor, rape and concubinage, child enslavement, disease, accidents, and insufferable living conditions.

After the failure of a second utopia at Verapaz, Honduras, in 1545, Las Casas settled at Puerto de Plata, Santo Domingo. There he began composing a New World masterwork, his three-volume geological and social revelation, *Historia de las Indias* (History of the Indies), which he worked on for the rest of his life; it remained unpublished until 1875. In this work, Las Casas condemned maltreatment of the innocent and declared, "Indians descend from Adam our father, and this suffices for us to respect the divine principle of charity toward them" (Las Casas 1971, 66). One of his comments was a supreme insult to contemptuous Spanish—a belief that Indians were more spiritual and more respectful of divine powers than the Greeks and Romans, whom Europeans revered for philosophy and morality. He claimed that Indians displayed wisdom, political savvy, and jurisprudence based on their inclination toward peace and humility. As a model of evangelism gone wrong, he cited the defiance of Chief Hatuey, who chose public burning at the stake rather than baptism. His reasoning shocked the clergy: Hatuey spurned the sharing of heaven with blood-guilty Christians. Las Casas's summation proclaimed the right of Amerindians to eradicate Europeans from the earth.

A short time before his final illness and death, Las Casas outlined a legal brief condemning Spain for invasion and VIOLENCE in South America. In *De thesauris in Peru* (On treasure in Peru, 1562), he cited medieval precedent that upheld native sovereignty. Among European enslavers and criminals, his treatise castigated looters of native tombs and the conquistador Francisco Pizarro's strangulation of Atahualpa, the 31-year-old Incan Emperor, at Cajamarca, Peru. In 1566, writing directly to Pope Pius V, Las Casas predicted that God would damn Spain eternally for dispatching priests to the New World to enrich themselves at the expensive of suffering natives. In the priest's last days at Our Lady of Atocha monastery in Madrid, he entrusted to the Dominican staff his *History of the Indies*, the most severe criticism of Spanish imperialism of its time. For Las Casas's native rights activism, Cubans and Nicaraguans revere him as a national hero.

Sources

Adorno, Rolena. *The Polemics of Possession in Spanish American Narrative.* New Haven, Conn.: Yale University Press, 2008.

Castro, Daniel. *Another Face of Empire: Bartolomé de Las Casas, Indigenous Rights, and Ecclesiastical Imperialism.* Durham, N.C.: Duke University Press, 2007.

Las Casas, Bertolomé de. *History of the Indies.* Translated by Andrée Collard. New York: Harper & Row, 1971.

———. *A Short Account of the Destruction of the Indies.* Translated by Nigel Griffin. London: Penguin, 1999.

Orique, David. "Bartolomé de Las Casas: A Brief Outline of His Life and Labor." Available online. URL: http://www.lascasas.org/manissues.htm. Downloaded on January 9, 2009.

Lawrence, Thomas Edward (1888–1935)
Welsh archeologist, soldier, and memoirist

The legendary Lawrence of Arabia won mass appeal for his exotic blend of British stoicism and respect for Arabs. Born in Tremadog, Caemarfonshire, North Wales, he was the illegitimate son of Thomas Chapman, an Anglo-Irish baronet, and Sarah Junner, a governess. He was raised in Oxford with his four brothers and their parents, who called themselves Mr. and Mrs. Lawrence, and attended Oxford University. From an early age, Lawrence had an affinity for archeology and made trips to Europe and the Middle East even before he graduated. He abandoned postgraduate studies to take up an archeology post, working on excavations in Syria. Over time, he perfected his knowledge of Arabic and gained firsthand expertise in the Semitic world from explorations of Mesopotamia and Egypt.

Because of his familiarity with Iraq, Jordan, Palestine, and Syria in the Ottoman Empire and with British Sudan in northeast Africa, the British military enlisted Lawrence at the beginning of World War I to serve as an intelligence officer in Cairo for the Arab Bureau of the empire's foreign office. He advanced to the rank of major as a reward for leading Arab guerrillas against the port of Aqaba in southern Jordan on July 6, 1917, and advised Winston Churchill after the war on British colonial issues. Returned home a hero, he starred in a series of lectures delivered by journalist Lowell Thomas. For anonymity, Lawrence chose the name "T. E. Shaw" for enlistment in the Royal Tank Corps and, under the alias "John Hume Ross," he soldiered with the Royal Air Force in India on the Afghan border in the plane motor pool and reputedly as a spy. Of his military experience as an unknown recruit, he wrote in hard-bitten Joycean style *The Mint: A Day-Book of the R. A. F. Depot between August and December 1922* (1955), a diary of military life in the coarse camp idiom of his day. In 1923, after the press found Lawrence, he changed his name again, this time to T. E. Shaw, and joined the army. In 1925, he rejoined the RAF and served in Afghanistan. He died in a motor-cycle accident on May 19, 1935, soon after leaving the RAF.

Lawrence provided details of his wartime experiences in *Seven Pillars of Wisdom: A Triumph* (1922), named for a geological outcropping at Wadi Rum, a rugged valley northeast of Aqaba in southern Jordan. The narrative explains the author's part in the British plan to ally with the Arab Ali ibn Hussein, the sharif (governor) of Mecca, in an effort to beat the Germans and their Turkish allies, whom Lawrence describes as eager to "purge their Empire of such irritating subject races as resisted the ruling stamp" (Lawrence 1997, 28). The Ottoman Empire attacked Arab culture by scattering its leaders, forbidding secret societies and royal dynasties, and suppressing Arabic literature by a people who loved legend, song, and scripture. As a result, Middle Eastern Semites chafed at the denigration of clans and villagers, most of whom were fervent Muslims. In the author's opinion, the Arab revolt against Ottoman rule was a battle of ideologies: "They were fighting to get rid of Empire, not to win it" (86).

In his survey of cultural and territorial Arabic history, Lawrence made a case for an alliance of Britain with bedouin warriors. After 500 years of servitude "under the Turkish harrow" (57), desert dwellers recognized in world war an opportunity to shape an Arab world. His text introduces the commitment of British and Arab soldiers in the Middle East to one definition of victory: "We were a self-centred army without parade or gesture, devoted to freedom, the second of man's creeds, a purpose so ravenous that it devoured all our strength, a hope so transcendent that our earlier ambitions faded in its glare" (11). Peter O'Toole, Omar Sharif, Alec Guinness, Anthony Quinn, Jack Hawkins, Anthony Quayle, José Ferrer, and Claude Rains enacted autobiographical scenes from Lawrence's writings in the David Lean–directed film *Lawrence of Arabia* (1962), the first Oscar-winning movie to feature all-male dialogue. Ralph Fiennes starred in a subsequent TV screen version, *A Dangerous Man: Lawrence after Arabia* (1990).

Sources

Bivona, Daniel. *British Imperial Literature, 1870–1940: Writing and the Administration of Empire*. Cambridge: Cambridge University Press, 1998.

Lawrence, T. E. *The Mint*. New York: W. W. Norton, 1963.

———. *Seven Pillars of Wisdom*. London: Wordsworth Editions, 1997.

Léger, Alexis Saint-Léger   See PERSE, SAINT-JOHN.

Leonowens, Anna (Anna Harriette Edwards Leonowens) (1831–1915) *Welsh educator, journalist, and feminist*

In the course of her work as a schoolteacher and journalist, Anna Leonowens observed the maneuvering of southeastern Asians to avoid absorption into the British Empire. The daughter of Sergeant Thomas Edwards of the Royal Sappers and a Eurasian, Mary Anne Glasscott, the author claimed Caernarvon, Wales, as her birthplace, which later research found to be Ahmadnagar India. At age 18, she married Thomas Louis Leon Owens, a clerk in Poona, India. After his death from sunstroke in Penang, Malaysia, a decade later, she opened a school in Singapore under the surname Leonowens. In 1862, with her nine-year-old son, Louis Thomas, she moved on to Bangkok to teach the children and some of the 600 harem wives of Mongkut Rama IV of Siam (now Thailand). At the time, the 58-year-old king, the head of the Chakri dynasty, ruled an empire that included parts of Cambodia, Laos, and Malaysia.

In 1867, Leonowens became a devout abolitionist. She settled at Sunnyside in Halifax, Nova Scotia, and completed her memoirs with details of life in Asian colonies. In addition, she wrote travelogues for the *Halifax Critic* and the *Halifax Herald* and published for the *Atlantic Monthly* the

series *The English Governess at the Siamese Court* (January–June 1870) and articles on southeast Asian slavery and concubinage. Leonowens's contributions to 19th-century FEMINISM survive in Margaret Dorothea Landon's BIOGRAPHY *Anna and the King of Siam* (1944) and in composer Richard Rodgers and lyricist Oscar Hammerstein's romanticized Broadway musical *The King and I* (1951), originally starring Gertrude Lawrence and Yul Brynner. Contributing to Leonowens's lasting fame are the films *Anna and the King of Siam* (1946), starring Irene Dunne and Rex Harrison; *The King and I* (1956), featuring Deborah Kerr and Yul Brynner; and *Anna and the King* (1999), a reprise of the first films pairing Jodie Foster and Chow Yun Fat.

A Teacher's Insights

Like MARCO POLO in China, RUDYARD KIPLING in India, and ISAK DINESEN in Kenya, Leonowens came to terms with an exotic foreign setting. According to *The English Governess at the Siamese Court: Being Recollections of Six Years in the Royal Palace at Bangkok* (1870), during her years in the Siamese palace, she served as Mongkut's private secretary, translator, and negotiator with British and French consulates. In a rigidly male environment, Leonowens had to balance her influence as tutor to the nine-year-old crown prince Chowfa Chulalongkorn (later Rama V) with the impotence of a female in an androcentric nation. At her height, she encouraged educational reform and motivated Chulalongkorn to question dungeons, kowtowing, concubinage, and slavery. Of harem dwellers, she mourned, "How I have pitied those ill-fated sisters of mine, imprisoned without a crime!" (Leonowens 1870, 103). Her compassion underlies her most lyric passages on "the sickening hideousness of slavery . . . pain, deformity, darkness, death, and eternal emptiness, a darkness to which there is neither beginning nor end, a living which is neither of this world nor of the next" (104). Under her guidance, the prince came to realize, "It is we, the princes, who have yet to learn which is the more noble, the oppressor or the oppressed" (284). After his ascent to the throne in 1868, he modernized Siam by reforming slavery (it would not be completely abolished until 1915), disenfranchising the hereditary elite, equipping a modern army, founding the nation's first university, and maintaining his nation's sovereignty against European incursions.

Endangered health ended Leonowens's classroom career and began her dedication to writing, lecturing, the arts, and school administration. Near the end of her six-year employment in Bangkok, the encroachment of Burmese insurgents and of European imperialism increased pressure to compose neutral correspondence to protect Mongkut from British and French imperialists. Because of the contrast between her influence and her gender, Leonowens was an anomaly. She admitted to a serious depression from "the utter loneliness and forlornness of my life, under the load of cares and provocations and fears that gradually accumulated upon me" (282). Later, in *The Romance of the Harem* (1872), she continued attacking male primacy and the confinement and degradation of women, including Mongkut's numerous concubines. The narrative charges, "Polygamy—or, properly speaking, concubinage—and slavery are the curses of the country" (Leonowens 1872, 10).

Some 14 years after Leonowens began writing, she turned her thoughts back to India for *Life and Travel in India: Being Recollections of a Journey before the Days of Railroads* (1884). In a lengthy discourse on the Indian subcontinent, she censured the disinterest of "the great English grandees," who know and care little of the customs, religion, race, or languages of hundreds of provinces (Leonowens 1884, 321). To the credit of the British Raj, she claims, life improved for the poor in urban Bombay, Calcutta, and Madras, but not in the outback. The abolition of floating corpses on the Ganges River lessened outbreaks of disease. Outlawing of suttee, the practice of burning widows alive on the funeral pyres of their deceased mates, which RUTH PRAWER JHABVALA later deplored in the novella *Heat and Dust* (1975), limited the custom to remote communities. Her comments on restrictions on infanticide and suppression of *thuggees* (cult killers) augmented her view of the British Empire as a beneficial regime in India.

Sources

Dagg, Anne Innis. *The Feminine Gaze: A Canadian Compendium of Non-Fiction Women Authors and Their Books, 1836–1945*. Waterloo, Ont.: Wilfred Laurier University Press, 2001.

Leonowens, Anna. *The English Governess at the Siamese Court: Being Recollections of Six Years in the Royal Palace at Bangkok*. London: Trubner, 1870.

———. *Life and Travel in India: Being Recollections of a Journey before the Days of Railroads*. Philadelphia: Porter & Coates, 1884.

———. *The Romance of the Harem*. Philadelphia: Porter & Coates, 1872.

Lessing, Doris (Doris May Taylor Lessing)

(1919–   ) *British memoirist, polemist, and novelist*

A feminist, autobiographer, and writer of dystopian and speculative fiction, Doris Lessing examines the effects of snobbery and exclusion in multicultural societies. Born Doris May Taylor to British parents in Kermanshah, Persia (now Iran), she grew up on a remote grain farm in Mashonaland, Southern Rhodesia (present-day Zimbabwe). In her autobiography, *Under My Skin* (1994), she recalled, "I was part of an extraordinary time, the end of the British Empire in Africa, and the bit I was involved with was the occupation of a country that lasted exactly ninety years" (Lessing 1995, 160). At the Dominican Convent school in Salisbury, she retreated to the library and left at 14 without earning a diploma. In 1933, she took up jobs as a nanny, typist, and telephone operator. After two divorces, in 1949, she settled in London, became a Marxist, and, influenced by the New Woman fiction of the South African novelist OLIVE SCHREINER, began a freelance writing career.

Like other writers born or raised in foreign cultures, such as PEARL BUCK and JOHN HERSEY, Lessing loathed the idea of imperialism. She wrote, "How very careless, how lazy, how indifferent, the British Empire was, how lightly it took on vast countries and millions of people, not even bothering to inform itself about them" (Lessing 1998, 209). Her reunion with her Rhodesian and South African roots in 1956 proved so unpleasant because of police suspicions that she recorded her alienation in *Going Home* (1957). Her speculation on an easing of ethnic tensions proved wrong: "If you want to see the natives badly treated, then you should see the people just out from Britain: they are worse than anyone, much worse than the old Rhodesians" (Lessing 1996, 88). For her liberal views, Lessing remained persona non grata until the freeing of Southern Rhodesia from imperial control in 1980. As she explains in *Prisons We Choose to Live Inside* (1987), upon returning to Zimbabwe in 1982, she found the struggle for independence had been more lethal than news reports indicated. Starvation in the Sahel region south of the Sahara and murder in Afghanistan under the Soviet puppet government dismayed her, stirring her to write diatribes against such catastrophes resulting from "wild partisan passion," which she characterizes as "something very powerful and very primitive" (Lessing 1987, 42, 28). Nonetheless, in her second autobiography, *Walking in the Shade* (1997), she voiced a belief in the humanizing power of art—that "literature—a novel, a story, even a line of poetry—has the power to destroy empires" (Lessing 1998, 77).

In her best-selling debut novel, *The Grass Is Singing* (1950), a post–World War II addition to literature of the women's movement, Lessing examined the life of Mary Turner, a Southern Rhodesian farm wife and mistress of a domestic staff. In the story's action, Mary's life withers in tandem with the decline of humanity and trust among the peoples of British Africa. The author summarizes the social situation along class and color lines: "Afrikaners had their own lives, and the Britishers ignored them. 'Poor whites' were Afrikaners, never British" (Lessing 1973, 11). In the aftermath of the houseboy Moses's murder of Mary, locals take sides, exonerating her husband, Dick Turner, and lambasting her as "something unpleasant and unclean" (12), a hint of violated taboos of sanity, sex, race, and class. The corruption of the servant Moses from dependable domestic to vengeful spirit served as a vehicle for a Swedish film, *Killing Heat* (1981), starring Karen Black.

In commentary on perceived national superiority, Lessing scoffed at the notion that "God had elected us to rule the world" (Lessing 1995, 190). She blends didacticism with a sardonic tone in her autobiographical novel *The Golden Notebook* (1962), in which she creates a complex portrait of Anna Wulf, a writer, resident of Central Africa,

and member of the British Communist Party. The author makes light of colonial concerns in a racial observation about the security of white sovereignty in Central Africa: "Well of course, the blacks will drive us into the sea in fifty years' time" (Lessing 1999, 42). Her cynicism crops up later with the observation that boom times raise African incomes, "even in an economy designed to see that they had the minimum necessary to keep alive and working" (63). In her repudiation of history, she expounds on the hypocrisy of World War II, when Britain's assumptions about black Africans paralleled Adolf Hitler's outlook on ethnicity and human values.

Although heavy-handed in discussing ethics and morals, Lessing wins readers through her flexible scenarios and intriguing motifs. In a five-part science-fiction series, *Canopus in Argos* (1979–83), sermonizing threatens to overpower Lessing's plot. She creates an allegory of an advanced civilization to probe the ramifications of royalty, a gendered society, revolt against a ruling minority, and coercion. Canopus, her fictional milieu, mirrors Great Britain in its missionary zeal to colonize less sophisticated nations and to impose on them the institutions of the mother country—law, government, education, religion, and medicine. The Canopian method is familiar—the empire viewing its victims as naughty children in need of discipline and religious conversion. Lessing's concern for the underprivileged and global civil rights issues earned her a Somerset Maugham Award (1954), the W. H. Smith Literary Award (1986), a member of the Order of Companions of Honor (1999), and the 2007 Nobel Prize in literature. Her writing has inspired numerous feminists, notably the ecofeminist Barbara Kingsolver, author of *The Poisonwood Bible* (1998).

Sources

Klein, Carole. *Doris Lessing: a Biography*. New York: Carroll & Graf, 2000.

Lessing, Doris. *Canopus in Argos: Archives*. New York: Vintage, 1992.

———. *Going Home*. New York: Harper Perennial, 1996.

———. *The Golden Notebook*. New York: HarperCollins, 1999.

———. *The Grass Is Singing*. New York: Heinemann, 1973.

———. *Prisons We Choose to Live Inside.* New York: Harper Perennial, 1987.

———. *Under My Skin: Volume One of My Autobiography, to 1959.* New York: Harper Perennial, 1995.

———. *Walking in the Shade: Volume Two of My Autobiography—1949–1962.* New York: Harper Perennial, 1998.

Turner, Martha A. *Mechanism and the Novel: Science in the Narrative Process.* Cambridge: Cambridge University Press, 1993.

Levi, Primo Michele (1919–1987)
Jewish-Italian memoirist and essayist

A survivor of Auschwitz in Poland, Primo Levi augmented literature of the European Holocaust with eyewitness details. A native of Turin and the son of an engineer who encouraged his children to read, Levi grew up in a musical and intellectual environment. Homeschooled in his youth, he gained an understanding of language, history, and literature before majoring in chemistry at the University of Turin. The expansion of Nazi anti-Semitism into Italy in 1938 forced him to work under a false name. While fighting the Germans in the Alps with the Italian Resistance, he was arrested in December 1943 and interned in a Jewish concentration camp outside Modena; he was then 24. In 1944, Nazi troops transported him by cattle car to Auschwitz. From inmates, he learned enough German to work in the laboratory at Buna, where the need for press gangs "suspended killings at the whim of individuals" (Levi 1996, 9). Later, he wrote of the scramble for essentials—"a hiding place, a fire, a pair of shoes"—as his life devolved into "a collective, uncontrolled panic" (13, 16). Liberation in 1945 left him traumatized, malnourished, and weakened by scarlet fever.

Publication of Levi's *Se questo è un uomo* (*If This Is a Man*, 1947; published in the United States as *Survival in Auschwitz*) and *La truega* (*The Truce*, 1963; published in the United States as *The Reawakening*) as well as articles in *La Stampa* bear testimony to the vicious Nazi drive to exterminate European Jewry. The first narrative established the guile of prison comrades who smuggled in bread and soup for meals. The concept of community as a source of strength during the Holocaust infuses his only novel *Se non ora, quando?* (*If Not Now, When?*, 1984), a salute to Jewish partisans and their struggle for Zionism. The text muses on changes in the concept of empire in the modern era. After the Italian Fascist dictator Benito Mussolini is overthrown, Levi asks, "What is a king? a kind of czar, bigoted and corrupt, a thing of the past, a fairy-tale character with brain, plumes, and ornamental dagger, arrogant and base" (Levi 1986, 66). The complex relationship between English and Russian imperialism shifts dramatically as Hitler's hegemony approaches collapse. The character Jozek declares, "The Russians will help us, because in Palestine there are the English, and Stalin is trying to weaken them every possible way because he envies them their empire" (232).

In a book published posthumously, *The Black Hole of Auschwitz* (2005), Levi regretted that the collapse of Auschwitz, Buchenwald, Dauchau, and Mauthausen rid the world of one monster but did not halt subsequent hellholes in Brazil, the Soviet Union, and Vietnam. The survival of imperialism drove him to write more testimonials to rescue youth from a future of oppression and fanaticism. On April 11, 1987, Levi died by falling from the third story of his home. Whether the fall was an accident or deliberate is still debated.

Sources

Angier, Carole. *The Double Bond: Primo Levi, a Biography.* New York: Macmillan, 2002.

Levi, Primo. *The Black Hole of Auschwitz.* Translated by Marco Belpoliti and Sharon Wood. Cambridge, U.K.: Polity, 2005.

———. *If Not Now, When?* Translated by William Weaver. New York: Penguin, 1986.

———. *Survival in Auschwitz.* Translated by Giulio Einaudi. New York: Touchstone, 1996.

Lewis, Matthew Gregory ("Monk" Lewis) (1775–1818) *English playwright and gothic fiction writer*

A star of England's popular GOTHIC LITERATURE movement, Matthew Gregory Lewis become one of the first terror writers to demonize imperialism. Born to a wealthy father who became deputy secretary of war, Lewis had a lively imagination that was fueled by readings of demonology, witchcraft, melodrama, and orientalism. He favored Arabic romance in THE THOUSAND AND ONE NIGHTS (ca. A.D. 942), Teutonic gothic tales by JOHANN WOLFGANG VON GOETHE, and Friedrich von Schiller's romantic fiction, which he read at Oxford. He served briefly as a civil servant at the British embassy at the Hague in Holland in 1794 before abandoning his career to write professionally, a choice that enraged his father. His first novel, *Ambrosio, or the Monk* (1796), a lurid tale of lust and corruption in a Spanish monastery, shocked the country and became an immediate best seller, earning the approval of Lord Byron, Mary Shelley, and the marquis de Sade. The book's success earned him the nickname "Monk."

A member of Parliament from 1796 to 1802, Lewis inherited property and slaves in Jamaica after his father died. In 1815 and 1817, he traveled to Jamaica to inspect his estates and was moved by conditions there. In *Journal of a West India Proprietor* (published posthumously, 1834), he outlined his efforts to end the coercion and torment of Caribbean slaves. Yet of the double crimes of colonialism and bondage, he declared: "Every man of humanity must wish that slavery . . . had never found a legal sanction, and must regret that its system is now so incorporated with the welfare of Great Britain as well as of Jamaica, as to make its extirpation an absolute impossibility" (Lewis 1834, 402). Like other absentee landlords, he recoiled from the prospect of economic disaster following the abolition of slavery, which he did not live to witness. During a voyage home from a one-year sojourn in the West Indian colonies, he succumbed to yellow fever in May 1818, 15 years before the Slavery Abolition Act of 1833, which emancipated slaves throughout the British Empire.

Empire As Monster

In a varied collection entitled *Romantic Tales* (1808), Lewis pictured the demise of English colonialism in a masterly anticolonial cautionary tale, "The Anaconda: An East Indian Tale." Although he profited from real estate investments in a similar colony, he described the breath of the huge yellow and green she-monster as poisonous to the protagonist, Everard Brooke, an exploiter of the East Indies. Brooke encounters the massive reptile under shady palm trees in Columbo, Ceylon, where the reptilian symbol of colonialism stalks and strikes islanders. A proof of the anaconda's power is seen when it crushes a dog, which dies from the splintering of its entire skeleton. At the discharge of a musket, the anaconda, like the threatened colonist, grows more terrifying: "Her body swelled with spite and venom, and every stripe of her variegated skin shone with more brilliant and vivid colours" (Lewis 1808, 98). An encroaching demon infuriated by resistance, the snake comes to dominate Brooke, who gradually expires from fear and despair. Ironically, his elderly servant Zadi survives entanglement in the anaconda's coils, a proof of the resilience of an ancient Asian culture and a reward for loyalty.

The British gothic writer Roald Dahl reprised Lewis's snake symbolism in the collection *Someone Like You* (1953). The story "Poison" features the paralyzing fear experienced by Harry Pope, an Englishman living in India. He lies sweating and immobile, convinced that a venomous krait (snake) is crawling across his stomach. A sensational plot for both radio and television, the reptilian contact with skin panicked fans, who anticipated Harry's immediate death. Dahl carries the action through Dr. Ganderbai's efforts to inoculate Harry with antivenom and to anesthetize the snake with chloroform, at which point the protagonist realizes there is no snake in his bed or under his pajamas. Harry's humiliation in front of an Indian physician leads to a face-saving outburst that reveals the "poison" in the Englishman, a repository of racist snobbery. In outrage at the compassion of an underling, Harry spews out, "You dirty little Hindu sewer rat!" (Dahl 1992, 269). Dahl's story, with its strong reliance on terror of the unknown, returned Lewis's original image to television in 1980 as an episode of *Tales of the Unexpected*.

Sources

Dahl, Roald. *The Collected Short Stories of Roald Dahl.* India: Penguin, 1992.

Lewis, Matthew Gregory. *Journal of a West India Proprietor.* London: John Murray, 1834.

———. *Romantic Tales.* London: Longman, Hurst, Rees, and Orme, 1808.

Wright, Julia M. *Ireland, India, and Nationalism in Nineteenth-Century Literature.* Cambridge: Cambridge University Press, 2007.

Li Bo (Li Bai, Li Po) (701–762) *Chinese poet*
An ambitious Chinese courtier who wrote at the height of Tang dynasty culture, Li Bo left some 1,100 poems as evidence of his times. He came from Suyab (present-day Tokmok in northeastern Kyrgyzstan) in the Mongolian desert; from age five, he grew up influenced by Confucianism and Daoism outside Chengdu in Sichuan Province in southeastern China. He appears to have been bilingual in Chinese and Turkish or perhaps Persian and was an accomplished writer by age 10. Literary historians surmise that he was the grandson of an exile living on the country's western frontier. In his mid-20s, he journeyed across China and developed a liking for indolence, taverns, gaiety, and women. He admitted, "Three hundred sixty days a year / Drunk I lie, like mud every day" (Li Po 1922, 62). After marriage, he tried to establish a placement in civil service and wangled an appointment from the Emperor Xuanzong, a promoter of cultural opportunity for which the Tang dynasty was famous. Li Bo's wife's desertion from their home in Nanjing left him the job of rearing their daughter Bingyang and son Bojin.

In 742, Li Bo became a court darling in the capital city of Changan. Of his departure from Nanjing, in "On the Road of Ambition" (ca. 745), he chuckled, "I laugh aloud and go" (119). In one of his odes, "To His Friend Departing for Shuh" (ca. 745), he discredited the court prophet by declaring, "Go, my friend! Our destiny's decided" (36), an example of Li Bo's lax attitude toward morality and serious purpose. He cloaked skepticism about law and justice in a metaphoric couplet: "When the hunter sets traps only for rabbits, / Tigers and dragons are left uncaught," a model of his aphoristic style (37). While writing at the Hanlin Academy among the cream of Chinese scholars, the poet disgraced himself in drunken stunts and was dismissed. He spent the rest of his life traveling the country. At the suppression of the An Shi Rebellion against Xuanzong, Li Bo, then 54 years old, was believed to be implicated, and he was sent into exile in Yehlang (present-day Yunnan Province on China's south-central border). He died at Dangtu in Anhui Province near the coast, where the governor erected a monument on his grave.

With apparent ease, Li Bo produced short and long works, including *yue fu* (fantasy) about stars and butterflies, *jueju* (quatrains) on homesickness and leave-taking, and the *Changgan xing* (Song of Changgan), an ode to Chinese peasants who marry young. In his early years, he wrote "Gazing into Antiquity at Su Terrace" and "Gazing into Antiquity in Yüeh" (ca. 742) about the disappearance of the family of Empress Wu, who had held power in the poet's early boyhood before sinking into oblivion; both poems provide striking examples of NATURE LORE. In middle age, he pondered the death of a Japanese visitor in "Mourning Chao" (ca. 755). Daoism and Zen Buddhism infused his writings with stoicism and a willingness to accept change as the natural state of earthly life.

For Li Bo's skillful verse, admirers called him the "poem god." Once away from the intrigues and coteries of courts and palaces, he turned to nature, especially the moon and flowing water, as sources of solace for their predictable alterations of shape. For his own peace of mind, he claimed that he had withdrawn from troubled court life to "a jade green mountain . . . in another world / not among men" (quoted in Roberts 1991, 49).

Sources

Li Bo. *The Works of Li Po, the Chinese Poet.* Translated by Shigeyoshi Obata. New York: E. P. Dutton, 1922.
Roberts, Elizabeth, and Elias Amidon, eds. *Earth Prayers from around the World.* San Francisco: HarperSanFrancisco, 1991.

Liluokalani, Queen   See AUTOBIOGRAPHY.

Livy (Titus Livius) (59 B.C.–A.D. 17) *Roman historian*
A chronicler who wrote during Rome's golden age of literature, Livy (born Titus Livius) produced Rome's first complete history, *Ab urbe condita* (From the city's founding, A.D. 14), a best seller of its time, published in English as *The History of Rome.* A native Paduan from Cisalpine Gaul, Livy grew up among the elite of the provinces, received a classical education, and eschewed military training in favor of intellectual pursuits. He was in his

mid-teens when the assassination of Julius Caesar precipitated 17 years of civil war, effectively ending the Roman Republic. His more active years coincided with the consolidation of the Roman Empire under Caesar Augustus. While raising a daughter and son, he served the imperial household as history tutor to Claudius, Augustus's great-nephew and Rome's fourth emperor. As a writer, Livy chose to include anecdotal evidence of Roman personages within a chronology that drew on what he regarded as the most authoritative sources. His life's work required nearly four decades of constant research and composition.

In the second of 142 books, of which 35 survive, Livy's lengthy retrospect includes a famous cautionary FABLE, "The Mutiny of Body Parts," the source of which may date to 1250 B.C. As Rome grew accustomed to imperial rule, Livy's model of group cooperation advocated a higher state of governance. The story allegorizes the 494 B.C. people's revolt early in the establishment of the Roman Republic, when the consul Menenius Agrippa unified the Romans during the wars against the Volsci to the south. Livy ends the brief fable with a warning from Menenius Agrippa: "Whilst they wished under the influence of this feeling to subdue the belly by famine, the members themselves and the entire body were reduced to the last degree of emaciation" (Livy 1853, 117). The impact of these words on his listeners encouraged the commoners to elect two tribunes of the people as magistrates, a form of checks and balances against senatorial power and a paradigm that recurs in NICCOLÒ MACHIAVELLI's Renaissance statecraft handbook *The Prince* (1514). WILLIAM SHAKESPEARE reprised Livy's anatomy fable in the opening scene of his tragedy *Coriolanus* as a reminder to the English after the death of Elizabeth I that mob control was a threat the nation.

For information on the three Punic Wars (264–146 B.C.) and the clash between the Roman Republic and the Carthaginian Empire (present-day Libya), Livy drew on the Greek historian Polybius's *Histories* (ca. 145 B.C.). Livy's chronicle addresses the topic of empire and achieves heights of dramatic narrative in his account of the Punic Wars, the greatest threat to Rome up to Livy's time. It describes the success of the Carthaginian general Hamilcar from 249 to 228 B.C. and surmises that the Carthaginians would have taken Iberia and advanced into Italy if Hamilcar had carried out his master plan. Livy depicts the braggadocio of Carthaginian ambassadors in laughing at the Gauls for refusing to allow the North African army to pass through Gallic territory at Massilia (present-day Marseilles, France) on its way east over the Alps toward Rome.

The text promotes Roman patriotism by declaring the intent of Hannibal, son of Hamilcar, to destroy "the temple of Vesta, the eternal fire, and the fatal pledge for the continuance of the Roman empire" (1,055), a purpose that shook the very soul of the citizenry. Livy assigns to the Roman hero Publius Scipio Africanus an unwavering faith in the auspices that "portend entire success and joy" (1,075) in Hannibal's defeat at the battle of Zama in 202 B.C. Of Rome's strength, the historian postulates that "not only other kings and nations, but that even Alexander himself, would have found the Roman empire invincible" (583). The easy style of writing and the historian's enthusiasm for his subject meant that Livy's history remained a model of its genre for more than a thousand years.

Sources

Livy. *The History of Rome.* Translated by D. Spillan. London: Henry G. Bohn, 1853.

Miles, Gary B. *Livy: Reconstructing Early Rome.* Ithaca, N.Y.: Cornell University Press, 1995.

Lucan (Marcus Annaeus Lucanus) (A.D. 39–65) Roman poet

An indiscreet patriot during a perilous period in the Roman Empire, Lucan contributed insights into royal decadence. Born in Corduba (modern-day Córdoba) in a Roman province in Hispania (modern Iberia), he was the grandson of the rhetorician Seneca the Elder and nephew of the Stoic philosopher and statesman Seneca the Younger. At Rome, Lucan entered the school of the Stoic philosopher Cornutus before traveling to Athens to study rhetoric. At age 21, Lucan gained the approval of the 23-year-old emperor Nero, who appointed him magistrate and augur, the interpreter of natural omens. In the words of the Roman historian

SUETONIUS's *De vita Caesarum* (*Lives of the Caesars*, ca. A.D. 121), "He made his first appearance as a poet with a 'Eulogy of Nero' at the emperor's Quinquennial Contests [festivals of poetry and oratory] and then gave a public reading of his poem on the Civil War waged between Pompey and Caesar" (Suetonius 1920, 501). In the middle of the silver age of Roman literature, Lucan thrived as a court poet until the temperamental emperor became jealous of his facile verse. Forbidden to publish or recite his poetry, Lucan pursued the reckless course of insulting Nero in saucy lines. One notorious ode, *De incendio urbis* (*On the burning of the city*, A.D. 64), leveled a charge of arson at the emperor that generated the legend "Nero fiddled while Rome burned." Lucan defamed the imperial family more pointedly in book 9 of *Pharsalia* (A.D. 63), also called *Bellum civile* (*The Civil War*), his only surviving work.

Lucan chose history rather than mythology as the basis for epic and preferred grotesque and gory poetics over the classical style of VIRGIL, Rome's premier epic poet. He issued *Pharsalia*, a 10-book chronicle of the civil war a century earlier, in serial installments. The text covers the conflict between Julius Caesar and Pompey the Great, whom Lucan lionizes as the true defender of republican values. The epic poem reaches its height with the battle at Pharsalus, Greece, on August 9, 48 B.C., when Caesar overwhelmed Pompey, forcing him to take refuge at the court of the Egyptian pharaoh, Ptolemy XIII.

Nero took offense at Lucan's attack on his ancestor. After the poet moved from mere literary taunts into Senator Gaius Calpurnius Piso's coterie of anti-Nero conspirators, the emperor issued treason charges against Lucan on April 19, A.D. 65. Suetonius was aghast at Lucan's folly "making great talk about the glory of tyrannicides and full of threats, even going to the length of offering Caesar's head to all his friends" (Suetonius 1920, 503). At age 25, Lucan took the aristocratic Roman's way out of an execution order by slitting his arteries. He recited original verse while bleeding to death. His mother Acilia and wife, Polla Argentaria, escaped the proscription, which doomed the poet's father, two uncles, and 16 confederates. As the emperor intended, *Pharsalia* remained incomplete.

Lucan's Anti-Imperialism

Written in Homeric hexameters, Lucan's political epic proposed to reverse history. He seethes with hostility at the founders of the Julio-Claudian imperial line, who promoted civic chaos as a means of expunging the Roman Republic, and opens immediately on censure: "Wars worse than civil we sing . . . justice given over to crime" (Lucan 1993, 3). He decries nature "gone awry" and openly castigates the imperialists as "an everlasting dynasty [that] costs the gods dear" (24, 4). Lucan's explicit diction bristles with phrases stating disapproval—"crimes and evil," "glutted with blood, clash . . . at these massacres," "slave wars," "frenzied nation," "the whole discordant," "running head-on," "pact of tyranny," "Rome grown top-heavy." Foolhardy and yet admirable, the epic left little doubt of the poet's hatred of Nero and the whole concept of a Roman Empire.

Lapsing into the drama of Homer's *Odyssey* (ca. 850 B.C.), Lucan orchestrated an exposé of sources of public panic. His narrative summons metaphysical monsters: "Black Charybdis churned up blood-red brine from the sea-floor; Scylla's curs howled" (22). The text recalls the shield of Mars falling from the sky into the hands of King Numa and affirms a chosen spot in heaven for perfect men. For effect, Lucan juxtaposes necromancy and superstitions alongside realistic reportage about the embalming of Alexander the Great, the Egyptian lighthouse at Pharos in Alexandria, and Julius Caesar's redesign of the Roman calendar in 45 B.C. In company with soldiers and statesmen, Lucan placed the allegorical figures of Death, Fortune, Freedom, Liberty, and the towering phantasm of Roma. The latter, a colossal female, confronts Julius Caesar before he crosses the Rubicon River, an illegal entry of a standing army into city precincts. Roma reminds him of the city's sanctity and bids him rethink the transgression of sacred boundaries. At a peak of arrogance, Caesar exults to his foes, "You'll pay for your peaceseeking and learn there's nothing safer while I'm alive than war under my command!" (70).

In the opening lines, Lucan predicts that Caesar's effrontery to Roman law and custom will lead to the nation's suicide by a "sword-hand turned to strike its own vitals," a dramatic action known as "the Roman way of death" (1). In book 9, the poet returns to Caesar in Egypt when the commander in chief confronts Pompey's severed head and views him less as an enemy than as a son-in-law, the widower who was married to Caesar's daughter Julia. The image of Death delighting in carnage overdramatizes Lucan's bitterness toward the Republic's demise: "She gleans the things that fly up in the pitchy smoke—woodchips from the funeral bier, scraps of graveclothes crumbling to ash, cinders that stink of charred flesh" (158). A lengthy hyperbole depicts the female figure of Death waiting for corruption to eat into cadavers before she harvests icy eyeballs and gnaws yellow nails from hands.

The epic satirizes Cleopatra's exoticism and the luxuries and sexual extremes of the Egyptian court, striking close to public impressions of Nero's household. The 10th book pictures chiffon drapes, Tyrian purple, marble, onyx slabs, and veneer of agate and porphyry. Amid throngs of house slaves, Cleopatra poses in glory: "Red Sea spoils at her throat, a fortune adorning her—[trembling] beneath the weight of her ornaments" (274). Lucan predicts the collapse of the Roman Empire and the death of a "maniacal king" (271) who so ravages the citizenry that he leaves no survivors. A subsequent passage returns to Caesar's folly: "Such ambition! gift of the night that first bedded, first coupled the child of the Ptolemies' incest with a captain of ours" (272). For its vivid gothicism, *Pharsalia* appealed to Dante, who imitated in the *Inferno* (1321) snatches of Lucan's verbal mayhem in a literary descent into hell. Christopher Marlowe, Percy Bysshe Shelley, Robert Southey, and Thomas Babington Macaulay all praised Lucan's skill at apostrophe, epigram, and dramatic spectacle.

Sources

Lucan. *Pharsalia.* Translated by Jane Wilson Joyce. Ithaca, N.Y.: Cornell University Press, 1993.

Masters, Jamie. *Poetry and Civil War in Lucan's Bellum Civile.* Cambridge: Cambridge University Press, 2007.

Suetonius. *Suetonius.* 2 vols. Translated by J. C. Rolfe. London: Heinemann, 1920.

Lusiads, The   See CAMÕES, LUIZ VAZ DE.

M

Machiavelli, Niccolò (Niccolò di Bernardo dei Machiavelli) (1469–1527) *Florentine pamphleteer, historian, and political theorist*
Niccolò Machiavelli, the second son of a lawyer, was born in Florence at a time of political turmoil and warfare among the city-states of Italy. Homeschooled on the writings of the Greek historian XENOPHON, the Roman orator Cicero, and the historian LIVY, he devoted himself to statecraft. He worked as a state secretary for the city of Florence and served as ambassador to the courts of Caterina Sforza of Forli; Louis XII of France; Holy Roman Emperor Maximilian II; and Cesare Borgia of Rome, the prototype ruler for the author's *Il Principe* (*The Prince*, 1514; published posthumously in 1532). After a power shift restored the Medicis, Machiavelli's old enemies, in 1509, he was demoted and then falsely charged with conspiracy in 1512. For a year, he languished in prison, enduring torture on the rack before being released. In the small town of Sant' Andrea he worked as a chancery clerk and chronicled provincial life.

After writing his masterwork in exile at San Casciano outside Florence, Machiavelli was consulted in 1519 on a constitution for Florence. He subsequently compiled his seven-book *Dell'arte della guerra* (*The Art of War*, ca. 1520), the only manuscript published in his lifetime. The text recommends the mustering of a local militia rather than the hiring of mercenaries to defend the Italian city-states. In his final days, he worked on *Istorie florentine* (published in English as *The History of Florence and of the Affairs of Italy*, 1521–25), a vigorous treatise that reflects his knowledge of Genoan, Milanese, Neapolitan, and Pisan influence and of the Venetian empire. He cites examples of conniving, sacrilege, jealousy, and double-dealing among emperors and lesser monarchs, which marked the history of Italy from the Middle Ages throughout the Renaissance. In his tribute to Lorenzo the Magnificent (Lorenzo de' Medici, 1449–92), Machiavelli maintains that the death of a great statesman leaves a vacuum of leadership so vast that chaos is bound to erupt. Following the sack of Rome on May 6, 1527, by troops of the Holy Roman Emperor Charles V and the temporary expulsion of Pope Clement VII on June 6, the Medicis were banished. Machiavelli sought his old position in Florence but within weeks died of peritonitis.

A Guide for Emperors

Machiavelli's engaging manual *The Prince* differentiates among republics, monarchies, and empires conquered in war, such as Naples under Spanish rule, the Turkish control of Greece, Pisans under Florentine control, Milan under the control of Louis XII of France, and Venice menacing Alfonso d'Este, the duke of Ferrara. The author degrades the autocrat as the least admirable leader: "All the Turkish monarchy is governed by one ruler, the others are his servants, and dividing his kingdom into 'sangiacates' [small governments], he sends to them various administrations and changes or recalls them at his pleasure" (Machiavelli 1952, 43). With regard to established families such as the Sforzas and d'Estes, Machiavelli esteems the nobility and valor of the head of clan: "We have in Italy the example of the Duke of Ferrara, who was able to withstand the assaults of the Venetians in 1484 and of Pope Julius in 1510, for no other reason than because of the antiquity of his family in that dominion" (34). His claim equates clan stability with a successful long-term rule.

Focusing on 15th-century Italy, Machiavelli's rhetorical text covers difficulties in fortification and administration and incorporates elements of language, social class, religion, and customs. He reflects on the Spartan, Persian, Alexandrian, Roman, and Papal empires, particularly the Greek colony of Syracusa, Sicily. An admirer of the bold and the unscrupulous, the author cites as heroes the Greek Achilles, the Israelite Moses, Agathocles of Sicily, Hannibal and his conqueror Scipio Africanus, Julius Caesar, Lorenzo di Medici, and Cesare Borgia, the enemy of the warrior pope Julius II. Machiavelli's reverence for local forces over mercenary forces derives from the experience of Milan under threat of Louis XII of France: "The inhabitants who had willingly opened their gates to him, finding themselves deluded in the hopes they had cherished and not obtaining those benefits they had anticipated, could not bear the vexatious rule of their new prince" (35). Admirers of *The Prince* include the French regent Catherine de Médicis, the English essayist Francis Bacon, the English explorer Sir Walter Raleigh, the English playwrights Christopher Marlowe and WILLIAM SHAKESPEARE, and the Spanish epicist MIGUEL DE CERVANTES. The American libertarian Thomas Jefferson valued Machiavelli's work with the histories of the Athenian soldier XENOPHON. *The Prince* also inspired the French emperor Napoleon I, the Italian dictator Benito Mussolini, and Adolf Hitler, the author of MEIN KAMPF (1925–26).

Sources

Hörnqvist, Mikael. *Machiavelli and Empire.* Cambridge: Cambridge University Press, 2004.

Machiavelli, Niccolò. *The Art of War.* Translated by Christopher Lynch. Chicago: University of Chicago Press, 2003.

———. *The History of Florence.* Translated by Charles W. Colby. New York: Colonial Press, 1901.

———. *The Prince.* Translated by Luigi Ricci. New York: Mentor, 1952.

Mah, Adeline Yen (1937–) *Chinese-American memoirist and fiction writer*

Like the journalist and Holocaust survivor ELIE WIESEL, Adeline Yen Mah, an anesthesiologist turned memoirist and author of philosophical narratives and young adult literature, anchors her fiction and nonfiction to personal experiences during World War II. Born in Tianjin, China, she lost her mother to medical complications two weeks after her birth and grew up unwanted and abused after her father, a wealthy realtor and importer-exporter, married a Eurasian. After the family moved to Shanghai, Mah's emotional survival depended on the training in calligraphy and philosophy provided by Grandfather Ye Ye and the example of New Woman philosophy presented by her unmarried Aunt Baba, a clerk at the Women's Bank of Shanghai. As Japanese invaders penetrated Shanghai, the family had to sail to Hong Kong in a leaky boat. In 1947, Mah's father sent her to St. Joseph convent school in Tianjin, ironically in the path of communist soldiers pressing south from Manchuria; an aunt rescued her from the school in 1949. After training at London Hospital Medical School, Mah practiced anesthesiology in Hong Kong and in Anaheim, California, before becoming a writer of historical fiction and autobiography. Her narratives present an insider's perspective on the breakdown of empire and the threat of seizure by a rival empire.

Mah's canon examines the conflicts of the 1940s from a variety of viewpoints. Her first work, *Falling Leaves: The True Story of an Unwanted Chinese Daughter* (1997), a *New York Times* best seller, earned global renown for blending the menace of world war with child rejection. From a little girl's perspective, she recalls, "Japanese soldiers in armoured vehicles were ordered to roll over flimsy barbed wire barricades and take over the foreign concessions of Chinese treaty ports" (Mah 1997, 31). She recalls the shock that the Japanese could invade Malaya, bomb Singapore, defeat the American and British in Asia, and herd their citizens into concentration camps. An era of secret whisperings and plans to salvage the family fortune are common to children's lives during conflict: Like the Norwegian sledders in Marie McSwigan's *Snow Treasure* (1942) and Anne Frank, Dutch-Jewish author of *The Diary of a Young Girl* (1947) (see CHILDREN'S LITERATURE), Mah lost her innocence while she was still in grade school.

Mah rewrote her AUTOBIOGRAPHY for young readers under the title *Chinese Cinderella: The True Story of an Unwanted Daughter* (1999), an award-winning story of family dissension. She moved into historical fiction with an espionage novel, *Chinese Cinderella and the Secret Dragon Society* (2005), based on Japanese atrocities against collaborators with the Chinese resistance on Nan Tian Island in April 1942. Between these two works, she produced wartime philosophy in *Watching the Tree: A Chinese Daughter Reflects on Happiness, Traditions, and Spiritual Wisdom* (2000) and *A Thousand Pieces of Gold: A Memoir of China's Past through Its Proverbs* (2002). Mah's memories of Shanghai, an open city requiring no passport or visa, recall a safety zone for Jews fleeing Nazi Germany in the 1930s. She fills in background on Chiang Kai-shek's creation of a Chinese republic and on Colonel Jimmy Doolittle's raid on Tokyo on April 18, 1942, in retaliation for the December 7, 1941, bombing of an American military installation in Pearl Harbor, Hawaii.

Mah's writing reveals a childhood filled with uncertainty and low self-esteem. Her informed narrative blames the Versailles Peace Conference for allowing Japan to seize Germany's territories in Shandong Province and to advance occupation forces into Manchuria and Tianjin. From childhood observation of the Japanese secret police on the streets of Shanghai, she dredges up details of the Chinese underground that saved the Doolittle raid pilot Ted Lawson and his American B-25 crew from capture, torture, and possible execution at the Bridge House interrogation center. Mah's private gender war parallels her nation's struggles to throw off the invader at a time when "women in China were expected to sublimate their own desires to the common good of the family" (Mah 1997, 25). Details of female domestic life among the moneyed elite reflect the hardships of the servant class and of unwanted girls. Unlike those sold on the streets into concubinage at Shanghai brothels, Mah makes her own way in society through self-reliance. Critics value her contributions to young adult, feminist, and anti-imperial literature.

Sources

Davé, Shilpa, et al., eds. *East Main Street: Asian American Popular Culture.* New York City: New York University Press, 2005.

Grice, Helena. *Negotiating Identities: An Introduction to Asian American Women's Writing.* Manchester, U.K.: Manchester University Press, 2002.

Mah, Adeline Yen. *Falling Leaves: The True Story of an Unwanted Chinese Daughter.* New York: John Riley and Sons, 1997.

Manhae   See HAN YONG-UN.

Mansfield, Katherine (Kathleen Mansfield Beauchamp, Kathleen Mansfield Murry) (1888–1923) *New Zealand diarist, essayist, and short story writer*

A modernist fiction writer, Katherine Mansfield produced essays and stories that revealed the unassuming beauty of her homeland, New Zealand, as contrasted with the formality and soullessness of European settings. Born Kathleen Mansfield Beauchamp in Wellington, at the southern tip of North Island, she completed Wellington Girls' High School and Miss Swainson's School, a private academy for privileged teens, before entering Queens College in London. She read the outback verse of Henry Lawson, Australia's FRONTIER poet, and concurred with his view of Banjo Paterson's song "Waltzing Matilda" (1895) as a symbol of the trekker forever on the move in a menacing environment. During a three-week journey into the New Zealand bush with her father in 1907, Mansfield wrote of a contrast between the prissy regularity of English gardens and the splendor and savagery of the island outback, with its falls, rapids, ferny dells, and thermal valley, an opinion expressed in *The Urewera Notebook*, published posthumously in 1933. In her imagination lived "Visions of long dead Maoris, of forgotten battles and vanished feuds" (Mansfield 1997, 287). In the towns of Rotorua and Taupo, she recognized that immigrants threatened the integrity of Maori lands and the people themselves, whom she mourned for "passing, passing" (Mansfield, 2006 171) amid the moaning of swaying trees in the vignette "In the Botanical Gardens" (1907). In the poem "To the Memory of Stanislaw Wyspianski" (1910), she saluted the sketchy history of New Zealand and proclaimed herself a tainted pioneer, one of a horde of lawless intruders.

After settling in London in 1903, Mansfield felt herself cut off from the homeland she had once dismissed as petty and dull. Freelancing for *Athenaeum, Blue Review, Native Companion, New Age, Rhythm,* and *Signature,* she disclosed her sense of displacement and rootlessness by describing characters in transit, at doors or gates, on gangways or boats, or along sidewalks. Her letters and fiction reveal an unease among British citizens who appear judgmental of colonials. In the allegorical vignette "How Pearl Button Was Kidnapped" (1912), the welcoming of a white child to a Maori native hamlet transports the title figure to a less structured milieu than that of the British ruling class. Wading in the sea, Pearl's introduction to elemental nature, ends abruptly with an imperialist interpretation of danger. Uniformed police take her back to her parents, who prefer the safe sterility of a white social order (39).

While fighting tuberculosis Mansfield published only three more volumes of her work before her death in France from a pulmonary hemorrhage on January 9, 1923. She endured World War I, her mother's death, and the loss of a younger brother, an Anzac (Australian and New Zealand Army Corps) soldier, who was killed in a grenade accident. She symbolized the settler's alienation in a dreamscape dominating "Old Tar" (1913). The title character imagines that the building of a large home in territory bought from Maoris will satisfy his longing to possess a part of New Zealand. As his garish residence reaches completion, it takes on the gothic proportions emblematic of imperialism of an alien intrusion on the landscape.

Postwar shifts in attitudes toward the empire left Mansfield feeling estranged from the British ultra-colonials, as though she were a refugee. Knowing she was ill, and suffering a difficult relationship with her paramour and then husband, John Middleton Murry, she hurriedly issued fiction collections in the time she had left. In the story "Je ne Parle pas Français" (1918), she describes human spirits as "portmanteaux—packed with certain things, started going, thrown about, tossed away, dumped down,

lost and found, half emptied suddenly, or squeezed fatter than ever" (122). The demanding image suggests her personal changes of heart as she pursued her career in Europe while maintaining a secret self that longed for the South Pacific.

Sources

Mansfield, Katherine. *Katherine Mansfield's Selected Stories.* New York: W. W. Norton and Co., 2006.
———. *The Katherine Mansfield Notebooks.* Wellington, N.Z.: Lincoln University Press, 1997.
Smith, Angela. "Landscape and the Foreigner Within: Katherine Mansfield and Emily Carr." In *Landscape and Empire 1770–2000,* edited by Glenn Hopper, 141–158. Aldershot, U.K.: Ashgate, 2005.

Manyoshu (*Ten Thousand Leaves, Collection of Ten Thousand Leaves*) (ca. 759)

An artistic landmark of the Nara empire, the 20-book *Manyoshu* (*Ten Thousand Leaves*), a compilation of 4,500 poems, is Japan's most extensive and oldest extant imperial verse collection. Comparable to epigrams, PRAYERs, elegies, laments, and ballads, most of the entries are *banka* (threnodies), *choka* (rhymed lyrics), *sedoka* (conceits), *tanka* (odes), or *waka* (lyric poems) arranged chronologically by reign. The compilation begins with Emperor Tenji and lists Prince Otsu, Empress Jito, and the emperors Yuryaku, Mommu, and Jomei Temmu, thus forming a history of medieval Japan. Composed in ritual language in a hybrid form of Sino-Japanese character writing, the texts illustrate the influence of Chinese classicism on the Japanese literature written by Emperor Shomu's favorite poets, Yamabe no Akahito, Kakinomoto no Hitomaro, Sakanoe Iratsume, Princess Nukada, Yamanoue no Okura, and Otomo no Tabito. The star poet of the collection, Otomo Yakamochi (ca. 717–785), was a statesman, scholar, and the anthology's putative compiler in chief.

As a survey of Japan's first golden age, *Manyoshu* poetry reveals the essential order of court life through precise patterns of syllables that symbolize divine power over humankind and over the timeless natural landscape. Giving glimpses of life in the empire, the verses incorporate views of travelers, courtiers, monks, sentinels, commoners, housewives, courtesans, domestics, and lovers. A daring two-stage critique of imperial mismanagement, Yamanoue no Okura's elegy "A Question by a Poor Villager" (ca. 732) describes a sick peasant wrapped in a hemp quilt and lamenting his family's reduction to beggary. The answer, "A Reply by a Man in Destitute Poverty," voices the despair of a ragged farmer whose family gathers by a cold hearth with an empty rice pot, and eludes the village headman, the imperial tax collector.

Because the *Manyoshu* comprises a compilation of the best poets of the era, a wide range of verses encompasses personal views of courtship protocols, ritual coitus, naming taboos, journeys, and life passages and ghosts. They include the intimate thoughts of men and women in loving embrace and the disquiet of mates sleeping alone. The most poignant lines depict the sorrow and self-imposed seclusion of royal widows after the deaths of emperors. The funereal verses console individual sorrow and soothe sufferers with the promise of recurrent cycles of NATURE, symbolized by sunrise and ocean tides. In similar fashion, travel songs refresh the traveler's memories of home and ward off fears of dying far from loved ones.

See also EROTIC LITERATURE.

Sources

Bialock, David T. *Eccentric Spaces, Hidden Histories: Narrative, Ritual, and Royal Authority from The Chronicles of Japan to The Tale of the Heike.* Palo Alto, Calif.: Stanford University Press, 2007.

Ebersole, Gary L. *Ritual Poetry and the Politics of Death in Early Japan.* Princeton, N.J.: Princeton University Press, 1989.

The Ten Thousand Leaves. Translated by Ian Hideo Levy. Princeton, N.J.: Princeton University Press, 1981.

Marcus Aurelius (Marcus Aurelius Antoninus)
(A.D. 121–180) *Roman emperor and philosopher*

The salvation of Roman WISDOM LITERATURE, Marcus Aurelius Antoninus spoke on behalf of the era's "good emperors" the stoic philosophy of a prosperous, benevolent age. The grandson and heir of Rome's brick and tile manufacturer, he was born to consular status. His Iberian father, a judge who died in A.D. 124, claimed as relatives the emperors Hadrian, Trajan, and Antoninus Pius. At age 17, Marcus Aurelius received preferment for the throne and tutoring by scholars in drama, geometry, Greek and Latin grammar, literature, and oratory. During his three consulships, he prepared for rule, which he received in A.D. 161. In *Apologeticus* (ca. A.D. 198), the polemist TERTULLIAN praised Marcus Aurelius for protecting Christian soldiers who wrought a miracle—praying for rain to end a drought. After campaigns among the Germani and Sarmatii (Russians), he died in Vindobona (present-day Vienna, Austria) at age 59 from a plague that cost Rome millions of lives.

The emperor's *Meditations* (ca. A.D. 180), written in Greek and published posthumously, reveal a benefactor to the poor and sick and a contemplative parent bent on enlightening Commodus, his dissolute son and successor. The 12-book compilation opens on gratitude to a tutor, relatives, and icons who were models of exemplary character and who taught the philosopher the rudiments of composition. His ethereal visions of human goodness link humankind with god: "Observe how man touches the divine and with what part of his being this contact is made" (Marcus Aurelius, 2002, 30). While campaigning at Carnuntum (present-day Petronell, Austria) on the Roman front along the Rhine River from A.D. 172–175, the emperor pledged to purge his thoughts of aimlessness and gossip. He summarized the vices—greed, pandering, power mongering, licentiousness—that distract otherwise worthy people from reason and duty. As though addressing Commodus directly, Aurelius prioritizes human responses: "Body, soul, mind—the body for sensations, the soul for the impulse to act, the mind for guiding principles" (39).

Aurelius sought to teach his heir to honor public duty and to accept changes of fortune as one of life's givens. He urges Commodus to stand firm, like a rock against a pounding tide. For endurance, the father advises the repetition of a consoling mantra: "Bad luck borne nobly is good luck" (51). He forgives Commodus's minor failings and seeks to guide him to an inner peace with mortality and a harmony with nature, a common strand of the BHAGAVAD GITA and of Confucius's ANALECTS (ca. 210 B.C.).

After succeeding his father, however, Commodus regressed to the amorality of previous decadent emperors. Romans abhorred the son but kept statues of Marcus Aurelius on family altars and recited his aphorisms for their children's edification. In the film *The Fall of the Roman Empire* (1964), Alec Guinness voiced the wisdom of Marcus Aurelius as directed to his daughter Lucilla and son Commodus, played respectively by Sophia Loren and Christopher Plummer. A subsequent movie, *Gladiator* (2000), with Richard Harris and Joaquin Phoenix, contrasted the wisdom of Marcus Aurelius and the savagery of his son.

Sources

Birley, Anthony Richard. *Marcus Aurelius.* New York: Routledge, 2000.

Marcus Aurelius. *The Emperor's Handbook.* Translated by C. Scot Hicks and David V. Hicks. New York: Scribner, 2002.

Marie de France (fl. ca. 1175–ca. 1190)
Anglo-Norman poet and fabulist

In the chivalric era, the semilegendary poet Marie de France (Mary of France), a well-read Norman-French storyteller, satisfied medieval Europeans' obsessions with tales of power and violence. Little is known of Marie's life. She appears to have been an unwed bilingual intellectual probably residing in England at the court of Eleanor of Aquitaine and Henry II, ruler of the Angevin Empire from Ireland to the Pyrenees. Influenced by Indian exotica in the PANCHATANTRA (ca. 200 B.C.), she wrote 15 elegant *lais* (lays)—verse romances and feudal tales—and, around 1189, 103 FABLEs on timely topics related to the Crusades and *roman courtois* (courtly romance). In the Anglo-Norman dialect of northwestern France, Marie also translated Latin poems about St. Patrick and St. Audrey and wrote metrical love *contes* (stories). The *lai* narratives flow witty and light, reflective of AESOP's animal lore and intensely romantic in the style of OVID's love lyrics and of Arthurian lore detailing the doomed pairing of lovers resembling Tristan and Iseult.

Themes common to Marie's chansons de geste (French heroic epics) stereotype the male-female relationship through masculine deeds that Breton knights perform to impress women. Gendered motifs cover issues of sexual fidelity and the powerlessness of the *mal mariée* (mismated) woman to avoid a loveless union with an older man who wants a trophy wife or a fertile mate of noble lineage to build up a dynasty. Taking the woman's side in matters of passion, the poet tells of their resourceful responses to crises and suffering for love. Although some literary historians think Marie was a convent dweller, she offers keen insights into marital frustrations. In the fable "A Woman and Her Lover" and in the miniature romances in "Chevrefoil" ("Honeysuckle"), "Laüstic" ("The Nightingale"), and "Yonec," Marie exonerates lovers for illicit coupling. She rewards a HERO with union with his lady in *Lanval* while damning Queen Guinevere for being spiteful. The poet views the choices of the "other woman" in "Le Fresne" ("The Ash Tree") and in "Eliduc," which features the beautiful Guilliadun bidding for the affections of a knight married to Crown Princess Guildeluec. The dual tragedy that befalls a couple in "Les Deus Amanz" ("The Two Lovers") results from the ruthlessness of the king of the Pistrians in Normandy. To his grief, he demands a show of strength that kills a potential son-in-law and causes the king's daughter to die of sorrow, a genteel end for a thwarted female.

A highly skilled narrator, Marie de France contrasted courtesy and wooing with the negative side of medieval patriarchy and predicted in the epilogue of her fables that some male scribe would likely plagiarize her work. Her stories mocked the rigid social order. The fable "The Frogs in Search of a King" places a goddess in charge of animal destiny; "The Sun Who Wished to Wed" warns that the more powerful the lord, the more calamitous his downfall. A masculine perspective in the *lais* "Chaitivel" ("The Unfortunate"), "Eliduc," "Laüstic," and "Milun" emphasizes male exploits—a warrior's reputation, ambush, vengeance, tournament competition, hand-to-hand combat, sieges, the chastity belt, and abduction of damsels. In "Guigemar," the bonding of males in combat incurs dire consequences for disloyalty: "Each one pledged his support: they would accompany [Guigemar] wherever he went: the man who failed him now would be disgraced" (Marie 1999,

54). In a contrasting scene, Venus, the goddess of passion, tosses into the fire a copy of OVID's *Remedia Amoris* (Love remedies, ca. A.D. 2), which advocates that males control females. Marie repudiates macho stereotypes by stressing to readers that men like Guigemar are susceptible to love and willingly sacrifice themselves for the women of their choice.

Marie's canon reflects the callous traits of the Middle Ages. In her biography of Saint Audrey, the text opens on the conversion of Britannia to Christianity and the invasions of the aboriginal Celts by Germanic tribes of Angles, Jutes, and Saxons, the eventual conquerors of the British Isles. More chilling are the tragic, even savage conclusions in the *lais*—the ripping off of a nose in "Bisclavret" ("The Werewolf"), a beheading in "Yonec," and dual deaths in "Equitan," which retells the biblical account of David, the adulterous king of the Israelites, who disposed of Uriah the Hittite in battle to free Uriah's wife Bathsheba for marriage to himself. The latter *lai* ends a love triangle with the scalding to death of the title figure and the adulterous wife of his seneschal (steward). Supernatural details, such as magic flowers and potions in "Eliduc," shapes-shifting in "Bisclavret" and "Laüstic," and a lover's knot, tower immurement, and unhealed wound in "Guigemar" develop representations of romantic attachment that dominated the era's dance, drama, and STORYTELLING, as well as subsequent writings of Giovanni Boccaccio and Geoffrey Chaucer. The film romances *Lovespell* (1981) and *Tristan & Isolde* (2006) reflect Marie's classic tales and fables.

Sources

Larsen, Anne R., and Colette H. Winn. *Writings by Pre-Revolutionary French Women.* New York: Routledge, 2000.

Marie de France. *Fables.* Translated by Harriet Spiegel. Toronto: University of Toronto Press, 1995.

———. *The Lais of Marie de France.* Translated by Glyn S. Burgess and Keith Busby. London: Penguin, 1999.

Marinetti, Filippo Tommaso   See VISIONARY LITERATURE.

Markham, Beryl   See AUTOBIOGRAPHY.

Martí, José (José Julián Martí Pérez) (1853–1895) *Cuban poet, journalist, nonfiction writer, and translator*

Through his writings, the martyred freedom fighter José Martí led Cuba's fight to throw off Spanish imperialism. Born in Havana, he developed into a patriot at an early age. He hated slavery and Spanish tyranny as well as the threat of American imperialism. At age 16, while writing for the underground papers *El diablo cojuelo* (The crippled devil) and *La patria libre* (The free country), he went to jail in chains at hard labor for treason after police seized a letter he wrote, reproving a teenaged acquaintance of joining the Spanish army. Upon release a year later, he published *El presidio en Cuba* (*Political Imprisonment in Cuba*, 1871), in which he expressed his distaste for incarceration: "It drags with it this mysterious world that troubles the heart; it grows, nourished upon every somber sorrow" (Martí 1999, 5).

Martí began studying civil rights law at the universities of Madrid and Saragosa before returning to the Western Hemisphere in 1874. In Mexico, he reported for *Revista Universal* (Universal review), and at age 24, he taught history, literature, and philosophy at the University of Guatemala. The next year, authorities charged him with treason and deported him to Spain, where he lived apart from his wife, Carmen Zayas Bazán, and their infant José. After returning to Cuba and then being again deported to Spain, Martí escaped to Venezuela and then to New York in 1881. From that base, he worked with other exiled Cubans to win their country's independence, and over the ensuing years, he wrote and traveled extensively in pursuit of his causes.

During his long fight against Spanish imperialism, Martí supported himself by composing propaganda against political imprisonment and by translating literature from English, French, Greek, Italian, Latin, and Spanish. He wrote about Native American art and class war for Spanish and English newspapers and served as a consul to Argentina, Paraguay, and Uruguay. In his texts, he incorporated the SATIRE of Mark Twain and the transcendentalism of Ralph Waldo Emerson alongside paeans to the anti-imperialists through world history; yet, he also feared American territorial and economic designs on Cuba, Mexico, and Puerto Rico. Back in New York City, Martí mustered Cuban exiles from Key West and Ybor City, the Latino section of Tampa, Florida, to support Cuban liberation from both Spain and the United States. In 1895, with fellow patriot, he returned to Cuba to lead a rebellion against Spanish troops. On May 19, 1895, in Dos Ríos, he died in combat from three bullet wounds. His name and likeness can be seen today on a Miami radio station; the Cuban Club in Ybor City, Florida; Cuban coins; Havana's airport; and a monument in Havana's Plaza de la Revolución.

Called the "apostle of liberty," Martí earned a place in the world canon for his lyrics, particularly the words to the folk classic *Guantanamera* (1891), popularized in the 1960s by the folk singer Pete Seeger. Martí's popular *Versos Sencillos* (*Simple Verses,* 1891) apply color and imagery to describe the dangers to a sincere heart. His aphorisms, rich in NATURE references, champion liberty, civil rights, and compassion. In an essay on the American poet Walt Whitman, Martí pled the case for art: "Who is the ignoramus who claims that poetry is not indispensable to a people? . . . [It] is more necessary to a people than industry itself" (Martí 2002, 187). He declared his work necessary to the soul for initiating desire, faith, and strength. To promote his ideals, the United Nations Educational, Scientific, and Cultural Organization (UNESCO) awards the annual International José Martí Prize to champions of liberty.

Sources

Martí, José. *José Martí Reader: Writings on the Americas.* New York: Ocean Press, 1999.

———. *Selected Writings.* New York: Penguin, 2002.

———. *Versos Sencillos: Simple Verses.* Translated by Manuel A. Tellechea. Houston, Tex.: Arte Publico Press, 1997.

Rotker, Susana. *The American Chronicles of José Martí: Journalism and Modernity in Spanish America.* Lebanon, N.H.: University Press of New England, 2000.

Meditations   See MARCUS AURELIUS.

Mein Kampf (Adolf Hitler) (1925–1926)

A prelude to the formation of the Nazi empire, Adolf Hitler's two-volume *Mein Kampf* (*My Struggle*), a combination of autobiography and political manifesto, preceded his accession to power by seven years. Dedicating himself to the "resurrection" of the German motherland following the humiliation of World War I, at age 34, he began dictating an emotional, self-glorifying text. Influenced by the determinism of NICCOLÒ MACHIAVELLI's *The Prince* (1514), a Renaissance manual of statecraft, Hitler's work occupied his time after his arrest and imprisonment for treason committed during the Beer Hall Putsch of November 8–9, 1923. The failure of his brown shirt battalion to overthrow the Bavarian government earned him a cell at Landsberg am Lech, a fortress prison west of Munich, from April to December 1924. Despite the restrictions of incarceration, his dreams of power for Germany continued to draw disciples to his cause. He completed the first volume, *Die Abrechnung* (The settlement of accounts) in mid-July 1925 and the follow-up, *Die Nationalsozialistische Bewegung* (The National Socialist Movement), in December 1926. The Nazis gained political power in 1933. During Hitler's rule from then until 1945, he issued the combined autobiography in impressive editions. Readership increased dramatically in 1938, when the Nazi party adopted the work as a polemical guide to German national socialism.

Hitler's apologia begins with reflections on his peasant lineage and his education at the Realschule in Vienna, Austria, before setting out his views on propaganda, war, revolt, labor, foreign policy, and anti-Semitism. In the opening paragraphs, he introduces the pride of the self-made man, a prophetic concept that shapes his plans for the nation's future. His narcissism surfaces in repeated references to fate, immutable decisions, and firm resolve and in the qualifying of statements with the adverbs *entirely, certainly, firmly, never,* and *absolutely.* His loathing of the petty bourgeois and contempt for the manual worker reveal an even more disturbing arrogance. In a tirade of anti-Semitism in chapter 2, he loses rhetorical control in his image of lancing an abscess: "You found, like a maggot in a rotting body, often dazzled by the sudden light—a kike!" (Hitler 1939, 57). The chapter's text spews virulent diction—*pestilence, infected, garbage, filth, poison, germ-carriers, vice,* and *gutter.* Hitler's subjectivity rapidly degenerates into a display of mental and emotional derangement by one of the world's most despised despots. At a height of self-delusion, he vindicates his hate mongering as "the work of the Lord" (65).

In chapter 8 of volume 2, Hitler's dream of world conquest derives from his perspective on inferior or "parasite" people—Gypsies and Jews—and himself as the *Übermensch* (superman) or genius of the superior Aryan race, an idea borrowed from the German philosopher Friedrich Wilhelm Nietzsche's *Also Sprach Zarathustra* (*Thus Spake Zarathustra,* 1883–85), an anti-Judaeo-Christian treatise on willpower and self-mastery written during the Austro-Hungarian Empire. For Hitler, the notion of the dictator justifies his dismissal of democracy and elections and his respect for oratory as a means of swaying the gullible. He pictures himself in the grandiose role of rescuer: "Through a happy decree of Destiny, a man arises who is capable of liberating his people from some great oppression, or of wiping out some bitter distress, or of calming the national soul" (419). To claim control of the *völkish* (populist) right, he declares himself a genius by virtue of his ability to overcome humble beginnings and adversity. His conclusion sanctifies war as the purpose of human life. In closing comments, he defines diplomatic compromise as necessary to the advance of Germany to "lord of the earth" (281). Euphemistically, he dismisses his greed for land as a need for *lebensraum* (living space). A review by the British journalist and satirist GEORGE ORWELL in a March 1940 edition of the *New English Weekly* ridiculed Hitler's expansionism as "a horrible brainless empire in which, essentially, nothing ever happens except the training of young men for war and the endless breeding of fresh cannon-fodder," a PROPHECY of World War II (Orwell 2000, 13).

In an untitled, unpublished sequel, completed in early July 1928, Hitler repeated his initial rationalizations but exhibited increasing megalomania. Rediscovery of the manuscript in 1958 and publication of the *Zweites Buch* (Second book, 1961) gave a new generation of readers a glimpse of a monster bent on GENOCIDE and global conquest. According to a critique by Jeremy Noakes of the *Times Literary Supplement* on June 7, 1996, the one-man discourse discloses more psychoses. To stem "the de-Germanization, niggerization, and Judaization of our people" (Hitler 2006, 383), the author glorifies mass murder and aggression. He demands a suppression of "bastardization" of the Nordic races as the only way for a pan-Germanic Europe to thrive. To exonerate his heinous method, he ridicules statecraft and applauds the ancient Spartan devotion to militarism from infancy as the only strategy to develop national vigor. For an efficient imperialism, he envisions the colonization of Europe and a universal conscription of soldiers to the *Reichswehr* (state army). At the culmination of his epic delusion lay a short-term subjugation of "negroized" France, isolation of Poles, and an all-out confrontation against England and America for world power. Combating Hitler's paranoia and glory hunting, Danish-Norwegian author SIGRID UNDSET, a resistance volunteer and refugee, refuted the manifesto with *Return to the Future* (1942), which dismissed Nazi empire builders as lawless thugs.

Sources

Hitler, Adolf. *Hitler's Second Book.* Translated by Krista Smith. Minneapolis, Minn.: Consortium books, 2006.

———. *Mein Kampf.* Translated by Edgar Dugdale. London: Hurst and Blackett, 1939.

Kershaw, Ian. *Hitler: 1889–1936: Hubris.* New York: W. W. Norton, 2000.

Orwell, George. *My Country Right or Left 1940–1943: The Collected Essays, Journalism and Letters of George Orwell.* Edited by Sonia Orwell and Ian Angus. Boston: David R. Godine, 2000.

Mem-u Zin (Ahmed-i Hani [Ehmede Khani, Ehmedi Xani]) (1692)

The epic of Kurdistan, *Mem-u Zin* (Mem and Zin) stands out among Middle Eastern verse cycles as the first major declaration of Kurdish nationalism, a cause still pursued by a people whose ancestral lands passed to the control of Turkey, Iran, and Iraq. Derived from at least 18 strands of pre-Islamic ballads, the Romeo-and-Juliet love story confronts the Arabic and Persian hegemony by recounting Kurdish oral folklore in the Kurdish language. The 5,400-line narrative, rendered in *distiches* (couplets), expresses the ethnic traits that differentiate Kurds from surrounding Arabs, Persians, and Turks. Written by the poet and theologian Ahmed-i Hani (also Ehmede Khani or Ehmedi Xani, 1651–1707) of Bayazid, Kurdistan (present-day Hakkari, Turkey), the text captures the misery of the stateless, orphaned city dwellers of Jezira Bohtan on today's Iranian-Turkish border. The poet declares himself "a self-made man, not well bred ... a Kurd, a highlander from the foothills" (quoted in Chyet 1991, 147). He dedicated his efforts to Kurdish children, who needed to read native-tongue literature at mosque schools in tandem with learning Persian verse and reciting the KORAN in Arabic. To simplify the reading and comprehension, Hani compiled *Nubihara Bicukan* (The spring of children, 1695), an Arabic-Kurdish lexicon, to accompany the epic.

Hani impresses on Kurdish readers their cultural legacy of disunion—"always rebellion and split" (43). In the preface, "Derde Me" (Our ills), he regrets disunity of leadership and the Kurdish lack of education. The absence of a *padisah* (sultan) renders the Kurds targets of rapacious leaders of the Arab, Ottoman-Turk, Persian, Russian, and Safavid empires. If Kurdistan had a king, "he would extract us from the hands of the vile" (43). When greater nations fight, Hani laments, it is the disorganized Kurds who bleed and die. Massacres reduce their numbers, restricting their establishment of a stable nation. In metaphor, Hani pictures the slaughter of Mem and Zin's death from grief. The couple lie in adjacent graves separated by a deep-rooted thornbush, an allegory of perpetual separation.

Mem-u Zin was first printed in Istanbul in 1919. In 1996, the Turkish government arrested the publisher Mehmet Emin Bozarslan for issuing a children's version of the book. After its translation into English in Australia in 1983, the director Umit Elci made a film version of *Mem-u Zin* (1991) that presented the tragic romance in both Kurdish and Turkish.

Sources

Chyet, Michael Lewisohn. *"And a Thornbush Sprang Up Between Them": Studies on "Mem u Zin," a Kurdish Romance.* 2 vols. Berkeley: University of California at Berkeley, 1991.

Ozoglu, Hakan. *Kurdish Notables and the Ottoman State.* New York: State University of New York Press, 2004.

"Monkey's Paw, The"   See JACOBS, W. W.

Multatuli   See DEKKER, EDUARD DOUWES.

Murasaki Shikibu (Lady Murasaki)
(ca. 973–ca. 1025) *Japanese diarist and novelist*

Revered by feminists as one of the world's earliest feminist novelists, Murasaki Shikibu recorded observations of the Heian period (794–1185) of imperial Japan. Her real name is unknown; her pen name translates as "purple ceremonial." The motherless daughter of Fujiwara no Tametoki, who was appointed governor of Harima, Echizen, and then Echigo during the feudal period, she was a member of Fujiwara clan, a dominating faction of the period. She received an unusually fine homeschooling in Kyoto in an era that had no place for intellectual women and limited their access to learning. When she was around age 13, after the abdication of Emperor Kazan in 986, her father, a court appointee with an impressive scholarly background in Chinese literature, fell into disfavor, an event that changed her life. Scraps of information indicate that Murasaki gave birth to a daughter, Kenshi, in 999, two years before the death of her husband, Fujiwara no Nobutaka, during an epidemic. She became a lady-in-waiting to Empress Akiko around 1008, perhaps after her child began her schooling. Murasaki's brother Nobunori died in 1011. Their father worked at other civil appointments until 1016, when he became a Buddhist priest. It is not known how long Murasaki remained at court, nor exactly when she died. The last record of her is in 1013, though she may have lived as late as 1025.

The uncertainties of fortune and rapid changes in imperial patronage influenced Murasaki's writings. On scrolls in Chinese script, from 1008 to 1010, the author kept a diary, *Murasaki Shikibu nikki* (*The Diary of the Lady Murasaki*) featuring events and undercurrents in the cultured imperial court at the Tsuchimikado estate in Kyoto. From a Buddhist stance, she mocked the frivolity of the empire and the vanity and decadence of royals, whom the Japanese revered as "cloud dwellers" descended from the sun (Murasaki 1999, 59). A literary rival of the court diarist IZUMI SHIKIBU, Murasaki narrated acute vignettes of processions and entertainments, social mistakes, forbidden passions, and sexual dalliances. In her diary, she quotes the emperor's eldest son's world-weary sigh: "Ah women! Such difficult creatures at times!" (5). A woman at the whim of the self-indulgent imperial family, Murasaki scoffs, "You could imagine every Buddha in the universe flying down to respond" (8).

Murasaki turned what she saw around her into a fictional social saga, *Genji-monogatari* (*The Tale of Genji*, ca. 1008), an exposé of an egotistic man and his ruination of unwary women. The work illustrates the sophistication and prosperity at the height of the Heian period and the workings of fate on the title figure. In a leisurely society, the elite adorn themselves, luxuriate in elaborate gardens, and flirt on artificial lakes under colored lanterns to the sound of harp and flute music. The more fortunate inherit their status. Because of rigid court protocol, they are out of touch with life in Japan's provinces, which they visit only on administrative business or religious pilgrimages. Murasaki characterizes the helplessness of the individual as a leaf borne aloft by the wind. At the nadir of the fortunes of the protagonist Genji, the Shining One, he undergoes two years of exile on the rainy shores of Suma near Hiroshima, sailing there at age 26 to live incommunicado. Stripped of rank and privilege "from the world he rejected, a great deal of it seemed impossible to give up" (Murasaki 2002, 229). Murasaki strips the narrative of sophisticated behaviors to reveal the prince's true hurt and yearning. The story tells of his rehabilitation through Hamlet-like dreams that reunite him with the ghost of his father, the former emperor, and through the elevation of his son Yugiri to the throne.

Sources

De Bary, William Theodora, Donald Keene, George Tanabe, and Paul Varley. *Sources of Japanese Tradition from Earliest Times to 1600.* New York: Columbia University Press, 2001.

Murasaki Shikibu. *The Diary of Lady Murasaki.* Translated by Richard Bowring. New York: Penguin, 1999.

———. *The Tale of Genji.* Translated by Royall Tyler. New York: Penguin, 2002.

N

Naipaul, V(iadiadhar) S(urajprasad)

(1932–) *Trinidadian-British polemist, travel writer, and novelist*

A scion of British, Indian, and West Indian fore-bears, V. S. "Vidya" Naipaul won the 2001 Nobel Prize in literature for works in which he weighed the effects of imperialism on nations that decline to let go of old grudges. Born to an orthodox Hindu family of nine in Port of Spain in the British colony of Trinidad, Naipaul was the grandson of a sugar plantation laborer indentured by trickery into a new version of the slave system. He grew up among writers, attended Queen's Royal College, and departed at age 18 by plane to England, the land he had previously lived in only in his imagination. According to an autobiographical image in *Miguel Street* (1959), Naipaul left the southern Caribbean "not looking back, looking only at my shadow before me, a dancing dwarf on the tarmac," an image of diminution common to nonwhite colonials who venture into the mother country. (Naipaul 2000, 176). He studied English on a scholarship at Oxford University and worked for the BBC (British Broadcasting Corporation) on the program *Caribbean Voices*. In 1955, he wed a fellow student, Patricia Hale, who subsequently nursed him through nervous collapse. Upon recuperation, he dedicated his career to fictional and nonfictional treatises on the effect of forcing peoples and cultures into empires. He published his first novel, *The Mystic Masseur*, in 1957.

Naipaul developed his bent for irony, provocative farce, and SATIRE as they apply to the third world's neglected areas. Like the Polish-British author JOSEPH CONRAD and the Caribbean writer JEAN RHYS, he earned a reputation for ambivalence and skepticism toward the feasibility of human advancement through colonial evangelism and overt civilizing. From the outset, his blunt delivery offended idealists and social thinkers who campaigned for noble causes, particularly justice and equality. Of the survival of the fittest in a postimperial milieu, he stated, "The world is what it is; men who are nothing, who allow themselves to become nothing, have no place in it" (Naipaul 1989, 3). He made three tours of India and Pakistan to explore his ancestry first hand to determine why the two nations experienced waves of turmoil that reignited long-standing antagonisms between young and old, Hindu and Muslim, and Brahmin and illiterate. He concluded that "The world abrades one" (quoted in Dooley 2006, 12), a justification for his prickly fictional scenarios.

Naipaul had little sympathy for the situation in the Middle East. Of fanatical Muslims, he blamed fundamentalism for conversion methods that denied and erased previous cultural traditions. He believed that so limited a view "allows only to one people—the Arabs, the original people of the prophet—a past, and sacred places, pilgrimages and earth reverences. . . . It is the most uncompromising kind of imperialism" (118). Rather than launch a literary crusade, he declared himself devoid of cant: "I'm not interested in attributing fault. . . . I'm interested in civilizations" (118). In his late 40s, he toured the Muslim world to compile *Among the*

Believers: An Islamic Journey (1981), which contrasts fundamentalism in the former British and Dutch colonies in Iran, Malaysia, and Pakistan. Unlike the simplistic views of imperialism promulgated by the British apologist RUDYARD KIPLING, Naipaul saw too many variables in human and state relations to reduce imperialism to a simple paradigm. After a series of working tours and expatriate sojourns on five continents, at age 75, he resettled in Trinidad and began promoting a West Indian mindset to erase diasporic ties with ethnic homelands, particularly Africa, India, and Pakistan.

Cause and Effect
Inspired by a kaleidoscopic curiosity and an inborn identification with the underdog, Naipaul's works avoid the rigid ideology of the Marxist author Marjane Satrapi and the straightforward social scrutiny of anti-imperial authors such as JAMAICA KINCAID and DORIS LESSING. Rather than levy charges of exploitation in past epochs of colonialism, diaspora, and bondage, he ridicules the do-gooders who set out to save the third world and blames underdeveloped countries for apathy, superstition, and envy of industrialized nations. He began to address such multicultural concerns in a travelogue, *The Middle Passage* (1962), which covers his journey through British Guiana, Jamaica, Martinique, and Suriname. The core of this book is his survey of Indian and Pakistani immigrants in Caribbean and South American cultures, which required investigating their initial settlement in the New World and the intermingling of minority languages, skin colors, and customs. In *The Mimic Men* (1967), he followed the fate of minorities and disclosed the failure of native Caribbean communities to establish their own identities. In a fictional West Indian setting named Isabella, the name of the queen who sponsored Christopher Columbus on his first transatlantic voyage, a makeshift identity results in tragedy for the dispossessed, who have no choice but to imitate the ruling majority.

Naipaul, like Jamaica Kincaid, has identified New World colonies as paradise lost. With *The Loss of El Dorado* (1969), he looked specifically at the different values of British and Spanish colonizers along the Orinoco River in Venezuela. The text pictures the New World as a vulnerable Eden: a

"romance, a dream of Shangri-la, the complete, unviolated world. Such a world had existed and the Spaniards had violated it" (Naipaul 1970, 22). Instead of economic prosperity, Naipaul identifies agriculture under colonial governors as "a cynical extension of the developing old world, its commercial underside" (88), his term for the profit motive. His perusal of muddled lives in a collection of two short stories and three novellas, *In a Free State* (1971), winner of the Booker Prize, expands on this same theory. With succinct narration, he writes of individual immigrants in England, East Africa, and Washington, D.C., in untenable situations created by the wanton violence and bureaucracy that destroyed pre-Columbian contentment.

Naipaul specifies interracial sexual adventuring as a lighted fuse set to colonial tinder. A complex survey of interracial attraction in the Caribbean leads to social drama in *Guerrillas* (1975), the tragic story of Jane, a sybarite from London. Her death is the direct result of her flirtation with a Trinidadian hustler, Jimmy Ahmed, one of Naipaul's sleaziest characters, who sodomizes and murders her. Naipaul defines his enigmatic protagonists more clearly in *A Bend in the River* (1979), an outsider's view of the independence movement in central Africa, probably the Belgian Congo before it became Zaire. The speaker sets the action amid the cosmopolitanism of the coast, "an Arab-Indian-Persian-Portuguese place" (Naipaul 1989, 10) far removed from the dangerous primitivism of the interior in Conrad's HEART OF DARKNESS (1899). Of the many causes for violence, the narrative muses on subconscious vengeance against past empires: "Do you think we will ever get to know the truth about what has happened in Africa . . .? All the wars, all the rebellions, all the leaders, all the defeats?" (130). The author's tone anticipates a sure negative.

Throughout Naipaul's canon, he voices continual scorn for the world's whiners and ne'er-do-wells. His narratives depict means of survival as the underclass copes with poverty and as shopkeepers and small entrepreneurs contend with crime and bankruptcy. In contrast to the bottom rung of society scraping a living, he presents the sharpers, mercenaries, gold thieves, and ivory poachers as echoes of the Africans who sold their own flesh into slavery. He concluded a trilogy—*An Area* of *Darkness* (1964), *India: A Wounded Civilization* (1977), and *India: A Million Mutinies Now* (1990)—with the dim hope of purging English imperialism from the south Asian subcontinent. Growing progressively more despondent, he continued to analyze racial and cultural blending in *Half a Life* (2001), which pairs Willie Chandran, the son of an Indian Brahmin and an untouchable, with an Afro-Portuguese lover from an unidentified country, probably Mozambique. In his essay "Conrad's Darkness and Mine" in *The Return of Eva Perón and the Killings in Trinidad* (1980), Naipaul lauds Conrad's story of anticolonialism for its regard for realism and for describing events and situations beyond the power of the world to solve.

Sources

Dooley, Gillian. *V. S. Naipaul, Man and Writer.* Columbia: University of South Carolina Press, 2006.

French, Patrick. *The World Is What It Is.* New York: Knopf, 2008.

Hayward, Helen. *The Enigma of V. S. Naipaul.* Basingstoke, Hampshire, U.K.: Palgrave Macmillan, 2002.

Naipaul, V. S. *A Bend in the River.* New York: Random House, 1989.

———. *The Loss of El Dorado.* New York: Alfred A. Knopf, 1970.

———. *Miguel Street.* New York: Heinemann, 2000.

———. *The Return of Eva Perón and the Killings in Trinidad.* New York: Random House, 1980.

Napoleonic literature

For over half a century, European authors spun out tales, demilegends, and stage dramas based on the career of the Corsican militarist and French emperor Napoleon Bonaparte (Napoleon I). On a par with the exploits of Achilles, Alexander the Great, and Julius Caesar, the mythic details of Napoleon's fall from power stirred readers as well as the imagination of such writers as JOHANN WOLFGANG VON GOETHE, the folklorists JACOB and WILHELM GRIMM, the fabulist IVAN ANDREYEVICH KRYLOV, and the PROTEST writer Anne-Louise-Germaine de Staël (Anne-Louise-Germaine Necker, baronne de Staël-Holstein, 1766–1817), a French-Swiss intellectual and libertarian who angered Napoleon with her publication of *De l'Allemagne* (On Germany, 1810) (see PROTEST LITERATURE). While battlefield guides and trinket vendors raked in cash from tourists, artists painted murals, and the English poet Robert Southey (1774–1843) issued *The Life of Nelson* (1813) and the pro-Iberian epic *Roderick, Last of the Goths* (1814). Upon Napoleon's defeat and abdication, Lord Byron (1788–1824), immediately composed his "Ode to Napoleon Buonaparte" (1814) berating a brilliant upstart for his ignoble ambition.

Other writers expressed mixed sentiments about brilliance gone awry. The French George Sand (1804–76) wrote of contradictory views in her AUTOBIOGRAPHY, *Histoire de ma vie* (*Story of My Life*, 1855). The French fiction writer and dramatist Honoré de Balzac (1799–1850), a champion of individualism, recognized the rebel spark in Napoleon and admired his energy and brio as he advanced from soldier to emperor. Balzac's childhood and training at a school at Vendôme during the Corsican's rise to power provided details and observations of the shaping of imperialism. In the short stories "The Vendetta" and "A Shadowy Affair" (1850), Balzac depicts the emperor as a jovial fellow unspoiled by power and prestige and capable of dispensing justice and mercy to his subjects. The author contrasted opinions on patriotism in "The Napoleon of the People," anthologized in *Le medecin de campagne* (*The Country Doctor*, 1833), a polemic disguised as an exchange of ideas among local professionals—a physician, a justice of the peace, a notary, a wood merchant, a mayor, and a cavalry veteran. The doctor, in his dialogue on democracy and demagoguery, distinguishes the epochs of greatness—times when "There comes a Mirabeau, or a Danton, a Robespierre, or a Napoleon, or proconsuls, or an emperor, and there is an end of deliberations and debates" (Balzac 1895, 166).

Martial themes recur in a framework narrative, "Passion in the Desert," anthologized in Balzac's masterwork, *Le comédie humaine* (*The Human Comedy*, 1850). The text of the short story contrasts a panther and a lone French legionary who confront each other in the Egyptian desert. The soldier's solitude and the animal's friendliness lead to an unlikely attachment between the man and his beloved Mignonne (little one). In a fond retrospect, the protagonist looks back on his battle-field experience with Napoleon's Grande Armée: "I went through the wars in Germany, Spain, Russia, France; I have marched my carcass well-nigh over all the world; but I have seen nothing comparable to the desert" (Balzac 1905, 405–406). Weary of warfare, he concludes that the grand savagery of nature appeals to him because "God is there, and man is not" (406).

A Romanticist's View

Alexandre Dumas (Dumas père, 1802–70) used classic fiction as an outlet for anti-Napoleonic rage. The author's father, General Alexandre Dumas, suffered professional demotion during service in Napoleon's army. Alexandre was 13 when Bonaparte lost at Waterloo to the British under the duke of Wellington and the allied Austrians and Prussians. He later recalled the rejoicing at Louis XVIII's return from Ghent to the French throne.

As a law clerk to the duc d'Orléans at the Palais Royal in Paris, Dumas developed a parallel career as a crime analyst and dramatist. His classic vendetta tale, *Le comte de Monte-Cristo* (*The Count of Monte Cristo*, 1844) explores overlapping acts of greed and treachery that cover a 23-year span. In the novel, serialized in 18 parts in the *Journal des débats*, the author recalls the anti-Napoleon hysteria that leads to the imprisonment of 19-year-old Edmond Dantès, a merchant seaman based in Marseilles during the Bourbon restoration of 1814. The text, like Robert Southey's allegory "The Poet's Pilgrimage to Waterloo" (1816), begins with the political turmoil in France before and during Napoleon's escape from Elba. To Southey, Napoleon embodied evil, "Like Satan rising from the sulphurous flood, / His impious legions to the battle-plain" (Southey 1816, 19). In the opinion of Dantès's archenemy, the public prosecutor Gérard de Villefort: "Napoleon, in the island of Elba, is too near France, and his proximity keeps up the hopes of his partisans . . . [resulting in] duels in the higher classes, and assassinations in the lower" (Dumas 1889, 1: 70). Upon Napoleon's resurgence to power for 100 days, the chameleon-like survivalist Villefort admits glibly, "The miraculous return of Napoleon has proved that I was mistaken; the legitimate monarch is he who is loved by his peo-

ple" (145). Before Dantès can take revenge for the prosecutor's colossal crimes, he must escape from a dungeon in the Chateau d'If, a GOTHIC prison and emblem of medieval-style French oppression. To recoup his strength, Dantès involves himself with a panorama of Mediterranean characters: pirates and smugglers, the pope, swordsmen, and Haydée, the wronged daughter of the Ottoman ruler Ali Pasha. *The Count of Monte Cristo* has been filmed numerous times, including a 1975 version made for television, featuring Richard Chamberlain as the romantic swashbuckler avenging himself and his family against the villainies of Louis Jourdan, Tony Curtis, and Donald Pleasence.

Throughout his career, Dumas persisted in his anti-Napoleon writing. He followed *Monte Cristo* with the novella *Les frères corses* (*The Corsican Brothers*, 1844), which deals with the theme of vengeance. In 1855, the author wrote a subjective biography of the emperor entitled *Napoleon*. Another study of the usurper, *Le chevalier de Sainte-Hermine* (published in English as *The Last Cavalier: Being the Adventures of Count Sainte-Hermine in the Age of Napoleon*, 2005), remained forgotten for 125 years after the author's death. The novel exemplifies megalomania in Bonaparte's dialogue with Pope Pius VII: "You are pope, but I am emperor, an emperor like the Germanic emperors of old, like Charlemagne" (Dumas 2005, 633). Lost in reveries of triumph, Napoleon, like Adolf Hitler during World War II, affirms his dreams: "I would have marched to Constantinople and overthrown the Turkish Empire. I would have founded a great new empire in the Orient that would have guaranteed my placed in Italy" (56). The fantasy extends to grand promenades through European capitals and a proposed demolition of the house of Austria. While Napoleon spread his empire across Venice, Corinth, Athens, Smyrna, Cyrene, Carthage, Senegal, Ethiopia, Gibraltar, and Cadiz, his lust for plunder brought treasures from Alexandria, Egypt, and crusader caches from Malta.

The English View

The social novelist Jane Austen (1775–1817) was 28 years old when Napoleon breached the Peace of Amiens to reignite continental war. Over the next 12 years, the Corsican invader was checked at Trafalgar, exiled to Elba, and finally defeated at Waterloo. In the aftermath of European victory, Austen began composing a domestic romance, *Persuasion* (1817), after the dethroned emperor had gone into a second exile on August 8, 1815, this time at St. Helena, a British possession in the South Atlantic Ocean. A sense of inevitable change strikes the returning naval heroes, including the agreeable Admiral Croft, a veteran of Lord Nelson's forces whose valor contrasts with the snobbery and wartime profiteering of many of the ruling class. Parlor conversation—reminiscences of the sea and land battles of the immediate past—focuses on combat ironies. At a climactic moment in male-female discussion, Anne Elliot declares to Captain Harville the difference between extroverted warriors and the introversion of women's circumscribed energies: "We live at home, quiet, confined, and our feelings prey upon us" (Austen 1995, 179). As a modest celebration of Britain's victory, Austen rewards the dutiful Anne with an equally dutiful and rich husband, Captain Frederick Wentworth, who appreciates a steadfast mate.

Choosing the mockery of panache as his aim, the English parodist and satirist William Makepeace Thackeray (1811–63) described the Napoleonic era in the allegorical romance *Vanity Fair: A Novel without a Hero* (1848), serialized in 20 parts in *Punch* magazine. He set the narrative in a social context and highlighted the terror of civilian characters and the doubts of soldiers before the battles of Quatre Bras, on June 16, 1815, and Waterloo two days later. Unlike Leo Tolstoy's epic novel War and Peace (1869), Thackeray's fiction focuses on a social rather than historical outlook at a time when "The almost universal belief was, that the Emperor would divide the Prussian and English armies, annihilate one after the other, and march into Brussels before three days were over" (Thackeray 1848, 2:71). A model of the theory of the zeitgeist (spirit of the times), Thackeray's panorama of venality, panic, and opportunism demonstrates how wartime exigencies affect human attitudes and actions. Like Lord Byron's dramatic sound of fire that "strikes like a rising knell" (Byron 1854, 126) in "The Eve of Waterloo," Thackeray foresees catastrophe. Speaking through an English

cavalry officer, Major William Dobbin, the novelist gives a summary of the seriousness of the clash: "We're ordered to Belgium. All the army goes. . . . We shan't be home again before a tussle which may be fatal to many of us" (Thackeray, 1848, 1:320, 331). History substantiates Dobbin's estimate of the carnage: 4,000 French, and 4,800 English and Dutch were lost at Quatre Bras; at Waterloo, the cost was 25,000 French to 22,000 English and their allies.

Thackeray views the slaughter from a noncombatant perspective. After the enemy passes the Sambre River, "Boney" (Napoleon) becomes the monster whose approach stokes hysteria. A rout ensues among English civilians in Brussels, a vehicle for Thackeray's keen observations about human weaknesses. Amid disorder, two central characters, Amelia Sedley Osborne and Rebecca "Becky" Sharp Crawley, friends and military wives, react differently. Thackeray describes their thoughts after a cannonading announces the approach of the French army. Becky, an amoral social climber, capitalizes on her flirtations in Belgium and France to place herself among the elite and to plot an amour with one of Napoleon's marshals. Her old schoolmate Amelia, downcast by a battle that killed her husband, George Osborne, reevaluates her social and economic outlook. As a widow and single mother, she eventually chooses a realistic marriage with Dobbin, an old and faithful friend, when she discovers that George Osborne had betrayed her. In the 2004 film version, one of many made of *Vanity Fair*, Reese Witherspoon and James Purefoy starred as Becky Sharp and Rawdon Crawley, and Romola Garai and Jonathan Rhys Meyers played Amelia Osborne and William Dobbin, the idealized proponents of fidelity and stability.

Sources

Austen, Jane. *Persuasion*. Ware, U.K.: Wordsworth Editions, 1995.

Balzac, Honoré de. *The Comédie Humaine*. Translated by Katharine Prescott Wormeley. Boston: Little, Brown, 1905.

———. *The Country Doctor*. Translated by Ellen Marriage. Philadelphia: Gebbie Publishing, 1895.

Byron, George Gordon, Lord. *Childe Harold's Pilgrimage: A Romaunt*. Philadelphia: Henry Carey Baird, 1854.

Dumas, Alexandre. *The Count of Monte Cristo.* 2 vols. Translated by Pier Angelo Fiorentino. Boston: Little, Brown, 1889.

———. *The Last Cavalier: Being the Adventures of Count Sainte-Hermine in the Age of Napoleon.* Translated by Lauren Wayne Yoder. New York: Pegasus, 2005.

Hayward, Jack Ernest Shalom. *Fragmented France: Two Centuries of Disputed Identity.* Oxford: Oxford University Press, 2007.

Maurois, Andre. *Alexandre Dumas—A Great Life in Brief.* Maurois Press, 2007.

Southey, Robert. *The Poet's Pilgrimage to Waterloo.* London: Longman, Hurst, Rees, Orme, and Brown, 1816.

Thackeray, William Makepeace. *Vanity Fair.* 3 vols. Leipzig: Bernhard Tauchnitz, 1848.

nature lore

The literature of empire frequently features the escapism found in the outdoors and in natural phenomena, a convention demonstrated by the pastoral settings in the *Rubáiyát of Omar Khagyam* (ca. 1130) and idyllic scenes set among Bohemian peasants in Rainer Maria Rilke's *Offerings to the Lares* (1895), on the Russian steppes in poems by BORIS PASTERNAK, and in rural Norway in the domestic novels of SIGRID UNDSET. To his earth prayer "Those Who Are Dead Are Never Gone" (1985), the Senegalese poet BIRAGO DIOP asserts that death reunites all beings with nature—trees, water, rocks, even fire. His verse affirms the soul in a world that snatches life from the powerless. A yearning for oneness with nature underlies the Japanese poet Yamanoue no Okura's "Hinkyu mondo" ("Dialogue on Poverty," ca. 733). Envying the freedom of animals, a suffering peasant mourns that he lacks the mobility of a bird to fly away to a less dismal milieu than Nara-era Japan. In contrast to the stationary life of hunger and distress, a German Gypsy poem, "Jolly Is the Gypsy's Life" (ca. 1900) states that the itinerant Rom pay no tax to the Kaiser and live under clan rule amid the forest green. The two perspectives on submission to constraints illustrate the difference between a peasant mentality and the open-road point of view of the nomadic Gypsy.

Rural settings suit the feigned naïveté of FABLE in the Mesopotamian "The Tamarisk and the Palm"

(ca. 2300 B.C.) and in AESOP's beast story "The Frogs and Hares," a mirror image of human terror under threat. In David's Hebrew PSALMS (ca. 900 B.C.), the freshness and liberation of the pasture offers rest and spiritual repose, as in this affirmation of divine safekeeping: "If I take the wings of the morning, and dwell in the uttermost parts of the sea; / Even there shall thy hand lead me, and thy right hand shall hold me" (Psalms 139:9–10). In 2 Samuel 12:1–7, the bucolic background of the Judaean priest Nathan's fable "The Rich Man and the Poor Man's Lamb" (ca. 950 B.C.) is a prelude to an accusation against King David for murder and adultery; within the serenity of a pastoral culture lies a subtextual comment on a monarch endowed with a harem of wives and concubines. The moral is obvious: A ruler blessed with his pick of women should justify to his subjects his desire for Bathsheba, the widow of Uriah the Hittite, whose death David engineered. The seduction illustrates empire at its worst in the story of a king's greed.

For chroniclers of warfare, nature often symbolizes refuge. In "The Destruction of Sennacherib" (1815), the British poet Lord Byron creates irony out of nature images that forestall a siege in 701 B.C. He pictures Sennacherib's Assyrian force descending on a Hebrew encampment at Galilee in late evening like a wolf targeting passive sheep. By morning, destruction ends with a return of God's beneficence, which quells the Gentile army before it can attack the Jews. The iconic "Angel of Death" intercedes against the Baal worshipers' might, which "melted like snow in the glance of the Lord" (Byron 1826, 589), a light image that accords God omnipotence over Babylonian empire builders. In 450 B.C., the Greek historian HERODOTUS reprised Sennacherib's losses in prose with an improbable explanation, the onslaught of field mice that chew the Assyrian bowstrings and eat the leather thongs of their shields before the army can carry its pillaging farther south into Egypt. The chronicler's fable implies an all-encompassing power of nature that the overconfident tend to minimize as inconsequential.

In Retreat from Dominion

The literature of empire also describes nature as an antidote to human disappointment and sorrow. The

Chinese poet LI BO summons faith in the resilience of nature in "Gazing into Antiquity at Su Terrace" and "Gazing into Antiquity in Yüeh" (ca. 742). Both poems tell of looking at ruined imperial palaces and contemplating their gradual absorption into the landscape. Li Bo's contrast of the fallen timbers with the patient earth emphasizes the planet's permanence as an abode that mocks the temporary structures erected by sovereigns.

In VIRGIL's AENEID (17 B.C.), the epic HERO Aeneas takes to the sea with faith in the PROPHECY that a new land lies waiting for the defeated Trojans. Escaping from Troy, the refugees sail west to reestablish domestic peace and piety in new homes and temples. In book 8, Aeneas locates a white sow suckling 30 piglets, a "marvelous portent" of fecundity and a prophecy of the tributary states that would feed off the empire (Virgil 1961, 172). A miracle reveals divine blessing—the Tiber River "did . . . reign / His thrusting stream and the water was silent-still" (212), giving Aeneas's rowers an easy approach to the site of the future city of Rome.

Writing a decade after Augustus transformed a troubled republic into the Roman Empire, Virgil acknowledges the prerequisite of conquest of the indigenous Latins before Rome could take shape. By accepting the need to subdue a settled people and take their land, Virgil uses verse to defend the virulence of Roman colonizing. Under Aeneas's leadership, the Trojans begin seizing and carving out an empire that will eventually surround the Mediterranean Sea and move into three continents.

Subsequent authors took their cue from Virgil and other early defenders of imperialism. The shift toward rationalizing militarism in later literature of empire reduced nature to a mere backdrop, the proportion allotted in the Scandic epic *Beowulf* (A.D. 800), FIRDAWSI's Iranian epic *The Book of Kings* (ca. 1010), and CRUSADER LORE. As conquest grew more destructive, writers took issue with the Virgilian glorification of conquest and alerted readers to the fragility of the planet and to a growing perception of nature as finite. Ecosensitive works such as JOHN HERSEY's *Hiroshima* (1946), Nevil Shute's *A Town Like Alice* (1950), YEVGENY YEVTUSHENKO's "Babi Yar" (1961), and AMY TAN's *The Kitchen God's Wife* (1991) pictured soil, water, and air as victims on a par with human casualties of war.

Canadian Conservationism

Since its discovery by Europeans, the Western Hemisphere has produced literature that acknowledges both its pristine beauty and the role of native animism in preserving the land. One of the oddities of Canadian FRONTIER LITERATURE, the works of Grey Owl or Wa-sha-quon-asin (He who walks by night), reflects on the ravages of colonizers bent on personal enrichment in a new frontier. He introduced the reading public to a sanctuary that his publisher, Lovat Dickson, described as "a cool, quiet place, where men and animals lived in love and trust together" (Dickson 1973, 14). A mystic wanderer wearing moccasins and snowshoes who traveled by canoe over Alberta, Ontario, Quebec, and Saskatchewan, Grey Owl gained a reputation as a Byronic HERO, a storyteller who claimed Apache-Scots ancestry and revered Henry Wadsworth Longfellow's American epic *Song of Hiawatha* (1855), a preface to the Christianizing of the Great Lakes Objibwa by French Jesuits. During World War I, Grey Owl enlisted and served in France with the Black Watch in the Canadian Expeditionary Force. In 1935, he overtaxed war-damaged lungs and a shrapnel wound to the foot by lecturing across England. At Buckingham Palace in 1937, he informed King George VI of the danger that overtrapping, blood sports, and industrialization posed to the Canadian wilderness. At the author's death in 1938 at age 49, his publisher revealed that Grey Owl was a false Indian persona adopted by Archibald Stansfeld "Archie" Belaney of Hastings, England, who in 1906 had emigrated to Canada, where he had assumed his Native identity.

Grey Owl treasured natural grandeur. He established his authority as a naturalist for the Canadian Parks Branch and his literary reputation with STORYTELLING of Cree, Mohawk, Ojibwa, and Saulteau animal tales. Conservationists extolled his children's book *Sajo and the Beaver People* (1935) and his AUTOBIOGRAPHY *Pilgrims of the Wild* (1934). For the sake of the environment, after the annihilation of the beaver and buffalo to the south, his vituperative first book, *The Men of the Last Frontier* (1931), attacked hunters from the United States who ventured north to find pristine landscapes and ample fish and game. He denounced interlopers as "get-rich-quick vandals" and demonized humankind as "the only profane thing, an ogre lurking to destroy" (Grey Owl 1931, 150, 142).

The author's 27 essays on naturalism in *Tales of an Empty Cabin* (1936) promoted laws and national preserves protecting Canada's resources and wildlife. He thundered at amateurs, "Man should enter the woods, not with any *conquistador* obsession or mighty hunter complex, neither in a spirit of braggadocio, but rather with the awe and not a little of the veneration of one who steps within the portals of some vast and ancient artifice of wondrous architecture" (Grey Owl 1936, vii). In a retort to bumbling campers, his essay "Rivermen" ridicules "kitchen-garden woodsmen" and "carpet knights" (152); "The Mission of Hiawatha" canonizes the "Man the Beasts Loved," a woodsman who becomes "a very Messiah of the Wilderness" (71), a St. Francis surrounded by birds and small animals. In 1999, Pierce Brosnan played the would-be Ojibwa in a biopic, *Grey Owl,* which dramatizes the author's one-man effort to prevent further destruction of the Canadian landscape.

Sources

Byron, George Gordon Byron, Lord. *The Works of Lord Byron, Complete in One Volume.* Frankfurt: H. L. Broenner, 1826.

Dickson, Lovat. *Wilderness Man: The Strange Story of Grey Owl.* New York: Atheneum, 1973.

Grey Owl. *The Men of the Last Frontier.* Toronto: Macmillan, 1931.

———. *Tales of an Empty Cabin.* Toronto: Macmillan, 1936.

Margalit, Gilad. *Germany and Its Gypsies.* Madison: University of Wisconsin Press, 2002.

Scott, Jamie S., and Paul Simpson-Housley. *Mapping the Sacred: Religion, Geography and Postcolonial Literatures.* Amsterdam: Rodopi, 2001.

Virgil. *The Aeneid.* Translated by Patric Dickinson. New York: Mentor, 1961.

oral tradition   See STORYTELLING (ORAL TRADITION).

Orwell, George (Eric Arthur Blair)
(1903–1950) *English novelist, essayist, and polemist*

A scion of the British Empire, George Orwell, like his predecessor RUDYARD KIPLING, knew the burden of the imperialist servant. Born Eric Arthur Blair in Motihari, Bengal, India, Orwell was the only son of a British narcotics officer in the Indian Civil Service. He and his sisters Avril and Margaret came of age in Eastbourne, England, in boarding schools where they incurred bias and sneers for their poverty. A reduced-fees pupil at St. Cyprian's School, Orwell suffered canings for minor infractions by a headmaster prejudiced against the children of civil servants in the empire. In 1949, shortly before Orwell's death, he wrote an antischool essay, "Such, Such Were the Joys," in which he satirized the academy under the name Crossgates and reprised his "sense of desolate loneliness" (Orwell 1970, 5). The text makes grim humor of his admiration for Cain and Jezebel in the Old Testament and of "Ananias, Caiaphas, Judas and Pontius Pilate" (37) in the New Testament, all participants in the crucifixion of Christ in the early years of the Roman Empire. To escape unhappiness, Orwell read Indian FABLEs, the poems and stories of Kipling, and the SATIREs of Jonathan Swift.

In his teens, Orwell developed an anti-intellectual, apolitical mindset. He hated adulation of money and position, contempt for the laboring poor, and xenophobia toward outsiders born in the colonies. In the same essay, he tried to make sense of the imperialist's primacy: "How could the rich, the strong, the elegant, the fashionable, the powerful, be in the wrong? It was their world and the rules they made for it must be the right ones" (36). He concluded that he was inherently conflicted: "Always at the centre of my heart the inner self seemed to be awake, pointing out the difference between the moral obligation and the psychological fact" (36).

At age 24, Orwell entered the Indian Imperial Police at Moulmain in Lower Burma, but he quit his post out of disgust at the imperialist model. In an essay on British colonies in Asia, he commented that "the job of administering the Empire had ceased to appeal. Few able men went east of Suez if there was any way of avoiding it" (274). With a "dirty hands" paradigm, he explained how colonialists undermined the humanity of subject peoples as surely as the subjects' attitude toward racism, opportunism, and despotism sapped the morale of civil servants.

The Tottering Empire
During the decline of the British Empire between the world wars, Orwell, in the mode of the Polish-British novelist JOSEPH CONRAD, satirized the position of the colonial outsider in Southeast Asia in the novel *Burmese Days* (1934). In a contrived dialectic, the timber merchant Flory insults proper Englishmen as abusers and despots steeped in Indian blood: "British prestige, the white man's

burden, the pukka sahib sans peur et sans reproche [the true gentleman without fear and without blame]—you know. Such a relief to be out of the stink of it" (Orwell 2004, 37). In the "Kipling-haunted Club" (65), Flory calls alcohol "the cement of empire" (35) and describes secret rebellion as a hidden poison menacing the health of the British sahib. Flory compounds the outrage with a pun: "Pox Britannica, doctor, Pox Britannica is its proper name" (41), a suggestion that the British invade other countries like an epidemic.

During World War II, Orwell turned from pacifist fiction to essays for BBC overseas radio and for the *London Tribune, Manchester Evening News, New Leader, Observer,* and *Partisan Review.* One treatise, "The Lion and the Unicorn: Socialism and the English Genius" (1941), charges the British with "world-famed hypocrisy—their double-faced attitude toward the Empire" (Orwell 1961, 251), with a veneer of patriotism covering any doubts about the morality of colonizing third-world nations. In summer 1946, his personal essay "Why I Write," explained his scorn for imperialism. In reference to patriotic sloganeering during two global wars, in "The Lion and the Unicorn" (1941) he bristled, "The English have absorbed a quarter of the earth and held on to it by means of a huge navy. How dare they turn round and say that war is wicked?" (Orwell 2005, 19).

From Journalism to Dystopianism

Immediately after World War II, Orwell, like GRAHAM GREENE, focused on the collapse of imperialism and the invasion of literature by politics. He satirized Nazi fascism and Russian totalitarianism in *Animal Farm: A Fairy Story* (1946), a dystopian beast FABLE that established Orwell's place as a moral force promoting the dismantling of empire. The allegory casts pigs, sheep, horses, dogs, ducks, and a goat, donkey, and raven to act out a chronology of European history: the overthrow of the Russian Czar Nicholas II, the last Romanov emperor, in 1917; the rise of the Communist Party; and the alliance on August 23, 1939, of the Russian dictator Joseph Stalin with the master race theorist Adolf Hitler. In chapter 7, the narrative outlines the plotting of demagoguery, terrorism, and public

slaughter to quell opposition: "When [the sheep] had finished their confession, the dogs promptly tore their throats out, and in a terrible voice Napoleon demanded whether any other animal had anything to confess" (Orwell 1946, 83). As the barnyard haven gravitates toward a police state, the conniving pigs subdue the rest of the livestock with insidious lacklogic: "All animals are equal but some animals are more equal than others" (123). In a final twist, Orwell describes how the dominant, goose-stepping pigs and cunning humans are so similar that they have become identical. An animated film of *Animal Farm* features the voices of Kelsey Grammer and Ian Holm, among others.

As Orwell sank toward death from tuberculosis and the after-effects of a sniper's bullet to the throat while fighting for the Republicans in the Spanish Civil War, he completed *Nineteen Eighty-four* (1949), a darker PROPHECY of world absolutism originally titled *The Last Man in Europe.* The action, a reminder of the Stalinist purges that featured in the anti-Soviet verse of ANNA AKHMATOVA and YEVGENY YEVTUSHENKO, features unending war waged by the people of Oceania against Eastasia, a symbolic name for the British colonies on the Pacific Rim. At Airstrip One, a repressive state monitored by telescreens, Londoners have no choice but to admire war planes and a group of Asian prisoners of war or to suffer vaporization into "unpersons" (Orwell 1983, 38). Beyond London, ongoing international clashes unify and robotize the citizenry into jingo-spewing sycophants. Supporting the expanding empire, science and technology generate more vicious weaponry as well as methods of thought coercion to rid potential rebels of objectivity. At his job, protagonist Winston Smith sits, alone and dehumanized, in a cubicle at the Ministry of Truth, where clerks rewrite truth as "doublespeak" to substantiate the predictions of state propagandists (42). Under torture, Smith proclaims Orwell's view on the longevity of tyranny: "It is impossible to found a civilization on fear and hatred and cruelty. It would never endure. . . . It would have no vitality. It would disintegrate. It would commit suicide" (221). A film version, shot in London in 1984, features John Hurt as the protagonist and Richard Burton as O'Brien, his nemesis.

The Dying Empire

Shooting an Elephant (1950), Orwell's posthumous collection of essays, bears the name of his most pungent anti-imperialist entry, written in 1936. It has since become a standard literary riposte to imperialism. A skillful polemist who learned in his 20s the cost of colonialism, he destroyed the myth of British protection of the weak. From his police work, he knew of the empire's civil rights infractions in caging prisoners and lashing their bare backsides with bamboo. In "Shooting an Elephant," he writes of the seething anti-British hatred that boils over with betel juice spit on white women's dresses and with the Burmese mockery of European police officers. Recalling his street patrol at age 23, he asserts in the second paragraph, "Imperialism was an evil thing" and remarks that colonial civil servants "[see] the dirty work of Empire at close quarters" (Orwell 1950, 236). While experiencing the decline of British hegemony and forecasting even worse empires to replace it, he longs to strike back with a bayonet against his tormentors. The paradox of sympathy mixed with spite captures his untenable position as a colonial lawman.

Orwell's portrait of a male elephant gone "must" introduces mixed gender imagery by comparing it to a cow. Because a mob of 2,000 expects him to shoot the rampager, Orwell realizes that the nonwhite majority controls him with their collective will, even though he is the only white male and the only armed person on the scene. He shoots three times with a rifle, causing the animal to fall to earth like a tree or boulder. With sober regret for its protracted death, he acknowledges that the white executioner "wears a mask and his face grows to fit it" (239). The female qualities of the elephant become a subtextual image of the widowed Queen Victoria in her last days: "He looked suddenly stricken, shrunken, immensely old . . . he sagged flabbily to his knees. His mouth slobbered. An enormous senility seemed to have settled upon him" (240). Like the empire on its last legs, the elephant manages to reach up for a final trumpet. The last sentence, explaining Orwell's face-saving method of animal extermination, manages to end on the word *fool.*

Sources

Ingle, Stephen. "The Anti-Imperialism of George Orwell." In *Literature and the Political Imagination,* edited by John Horton and Andrea Baumeister, New York: Routledge, 1996.

Orwell, George. *Animal Farm.* New York: Signet, 1946.

———. *Burmese Days.* Fairfield, Iowa: 1st World Publishing, 2004.

———. *A Collection of Essays.* Fort Washington, Pa.: Harvest Books, 1970.

———. *My Country Right or Left 1940–1943: The Collected Essays, Journalism and Letters of George Orwell,* ed. Sonia Orwell and Ian Angus. Boston: David R. Godine, 2000.

———. *1984.* New York: Signet, 1983.

———. *The Orwell Reader: Fiction, Essays, and Reportage.* Fort Washington, Pa.: Harvest Books, 1961.

———. *Shooting an Elephant and Other Essays.* New York: Harcourt, Brace, 1950.

———. *Why I Write.* New York: Penguin, 2005.

Woodcock, George. *The Crystal Spirit: A Study of George Orwell.* Toronto: Black Rose Books, 2005.

Ovid (Publius Ovidius Naso) (43 B.C.–A.D. 17)
Roman poet and mythographer

An eyewitness to the social and political chaos that led to the formation of the Roman Empire, the elegaic poet Ovid captured in verse his heartache over personal disgrace and exile. The son of aristocrats, he was born on March 20, 43 B.C., at Sulmo, 90 miles east of Rome along the Pescara River in the Abruzzi high country. In boyhood, he shunned military training and weaponry. His ambitious father arranged two unsuitable marriages for him—both were short-lived—and rebuked him for choosing an unremunerative career in literature. In preparation for a legal career, Ovid's father had him and his older brother educated in rhetoric under two Roman teachers, the eminent orators Arellius Fuscus and Porcius Latro. In Ovid's teens, Augustus awarded him a key of distinction and a fine steed as tokens of his promise. After his brother's death, Ovid abandoned his job as a court magistrate, studied ethics and Epicurean philosophy for a year in Athens, and, with the poet Aemilius Macer, toured Sicily and Troy (present-day Hissarlik, Turkey).

At the founding of the Roman Empire in 27 B.C., Ovid became a court wit and man about town, financed by the family estate. He built homes and gardens on the Capitoline Hill and between the Claudian and Flaminian Ways and, under the patronage of the orator Messalla Corvinus, initiated a career in poetry, giving public recitations of his sparkling verse. At age 33, he issued the *Amores* (Loves, 10 B.C.), the forerunner of erotic verse in *Ars amatoria* (*The Art of Love*, ca. 3 B.C.), a guide to men and women in pleasing and keeping the affection of their beloved. The venture into blatant carnality affronted Emperor Augustus, who sought to reinforce his position with laws against adultery, in a return to old republican values.

At his height, Ovid published the *Metamorphoses* (Transformations, A.D. 8), an imaginative overview of 250 Greek and Roman myths similar in pre-civilized customs and behaviors to the Japanese mythographer Ohono Yasumaro's *Kojiki* (A.D. 712) and to the Mayan *POPUL VUH* (ca. 1558). Prophetically, Ovid's poems mused on the undeserved incarceration of Proserpina and Eurydice in the underworld and on the excessively ambitious Tiresias, the prophet who offended Juno, and Phaeton, the doomed youth who drove Hyperion's sun chariot. For Phaeton, Ovid composed a pensive epitaph: "Though he greatly failed, more greatly dared" (Ovid 1984, 1:83).

The Blunder

Ovid's downfall illustrates the need for discretion within the imperial state. Allegedly blaming the poet for corrupting the emperor's granddaughter, Julia the Younger, in A.D. 7, Augustus banned the poet's books for indecency and, for some still-unknown offense, exiled him to Tomis (present-day Constanta, Romania), a fogged-in sea town near the Danube River on the Black Sea. Julia, too, was exiled for her affair with Decimus Junius Silanus. Subsequent theorists surmise that Ovid learned some damning secret, perhaps a conspiracy, in the imperial household. On a bleak shore apart from his adored wife Fabia and daughter Perilla, he expressed thanks for avoiding execution or obligatory suicide, confiscation of his estate, and loss of civil rights. In a shaky sociopolitical era, Ovid's advice in A.D. 8 struck Romans as sound: "In medio tutissimus ibis"

(You will go safest in the middle), a restatement of Aristotle's Golden Mean, "Nothing in excess."

The poet ceased work on *Fasti* (Calendar of holidays, A.D. 17), a month-by-month compilation of the foundations for Roman religious customs and rituals. The work had given the poet an opportunity to ingratiate himself with the imperial descendants of the Julio-Claudian line, whom a new, amended calendar exalted. Ovid's text propagandizes Augustus as *pater patriae* (father of his country), a replacement for the mythic Romulus. The 12-book project, which Ovid dedicated to Germanicus, Augustus's grandson, required research in Rome's three public libraries, which came to an end upon the poet's exile.

Lacking source material for research, Ovid consoled himself with personal writing and spent the rest of his life composing autobiographical *carmina* (poems). Spiritually isolated among the boorish Getae of Thrace (present-day eastern Romania, European Turkey, northeastern Greece, and southern Bulgaria), he had no audience who understood his Latin recitations. To reconcile himself to living among aliens, he learned Dacian-Getian, the local language. He felt that residence in Tomis required service in the home guard, an onerous duty for a melancholic exile in his late 50s. Eventually, the Getae valued him as poet-in-residence, absolved him of taxes, and freed him from civic duties. At his death and burial on an island in Lake Siutghiol, citizens raised a monument to him at the city gates.

Work in Exile

On the way east by sea, Ovid immediately began writing *Tristia* (Sorrows of an Exile, A.D. 10) and followed with *Epistulae ex Ponto* (Letters from Pontus, A.D. 10), a survey of the sorrows incurred by an unwitting enemy of the state. In *Tristia*, the poet denied the emperor's charge of wickedness but confessed to folly. Ovid imbued his verses with a lugubrious tone. In self-pity, he mourned, "I must lose my native land for ever" (Ovid 1995, 15). He hinted that Augustus himself deserved blame for encouraging public immorality by sponsoring gladiatorial spectacles, where open seating was unsegregated by gender and where men arranged trysts with their lovers. To the emperor, Ovid proclaimed the injustice of banishment: "My tongue has told no secrets. I've said nothing, nor in my cups were words profane unfurled" (53). He confessed thoughts of suicide, which a friend prevented.

Ovid's disgrace ate at his composure and eroded his health, hope, and vigor. He allowed himself to vent his spite in *Ibis* (A.D. 11), a literary curse that lacerates an unnamed villain for defaming the poet, who had no opportunity for rebuttal. Other poems express his yearning for his wife Fabia, his grandchildren, and old friends; and for forgiveness from Augustus and Tiberius, the first emperor's successor. Despite pleas for amnesty or a change of location to "somewhere safer" (31), however, Ovid died at Tomis. An elegant lyricist of universal themes, he influenced generations of readers and writers with his views on imperial grudges and capricious exercises of power. His eloquent style influenced MARIE DE FRANCE and Chrétien de Troyes, the popularizers of CRUSADER LORE, as well as the Parisian fabulist JEAN DE LA FONTAINE.

Sources

Habinek, Thomas N. *The Politics of Latin Literature: Writing, Identity, and Empire in Ancient Rome.* Princeton, N.J.: Princeton University Press, 1998.

Herbert-Brown, Geraldine. *Ovid and the Fasti: An Historical Study.* Oxford: Oxford University Press, 1994.

Ovid. *Metamorphoses.* 2 vols. Translated by Frank Justus Miller. Cambridge, Mass.: Harvard University Press, 1984.

———. *Sorrows of an Exile.* Translated by A. D. Melville. Oxford: Oxford University Press, 1995.

P

Panchatantra *(The Fables of Bidpai)* **(Vishnu Sarma)** (ca. 200 B.C.)

A collection of the earliest Hindu STORYTELLING compiled during the beginnings of the Mauryan Empire, the five-book *Panchatantra* (also called *The Fables of Bidpai*) earned the title of mother of Asian folklore. The anthology was the work of the Brahmin intellectual Vishnu Sarma of Varanasi (present-day Benares in southern India). A minister named Sumati proposed to educate the sons of Amarashakti, king of Mahilaropaya—Anantashakti, Bahushakti, and Ugrashakti—in the arts of logic, diplomacy, and statecraft. Sumati hired Sarma, an aged *acharya* (professor) of Sanskrit WISDOM to spend six months teaching the princes ethics and practical politics. This undertaking resulted in his compilation of the *Panchatantra*, a manual of ethics and realpolitik. Translated into Persian, Arabic, Syriac, Greek, Slavic, Turkish, Chinese, Latin, Hebrew, and Spanish, the compendium of five tantras (books)—"The Loss of Friends," "Gaining Friends," "Union," "Separation," and "Causing Dissension among Friends"—consists of a complex interlinkage of fool tales, beast FABLES, exempla, dialogues, aphorisms, allegories, admonitions, and stories of the Buddha's youth.

The compendium, the first Indian folklore to reach Western readers, comprised the princes' lessons over six months of classroom reading and discussion. The anthropomorphic actions of animal characters—foxes, cats, mice, herons, ducks, doves, owls—resemble the stories of the Greek fabulist AESOP, who depicted animals in their normal settings and behaviors rather than as courtiers in a palace. In one episode, a king troubled by dreams ponders reversals of fortune. He feels compelled to question the cavalier cruelties of empires toward peasants, a motif that appears in the Greek chronicler HERODOTUS's *Histories* (440 B.C.) and the Japanese poet Yamanoue no Okura's "Dialogue on Poverty" (ca. 733). At a high point in one story, a victor "lifted his neck on high, exalted his mind heavenwards, trampled on the ground, trod upon things with his foot, set his heel on a lofty rock, and sought to crush both the king and his subjects" (*Kalilah* 1885, 73), an Indian model of extreme hubris. A piece of advice to rulers states, "A king who is pure in mind and far from iniquity, devoid of impurity and cleansed from lasciviousness, and finally has a soul unsmitten with greed, and far from envy, . . . this king attains to all things, spends the days of his life with all satisfaction, overcomes all oppositions and subdues all fortified places" (220). The admonition echoes advice to sovereigns contained in "The Last Words of David" (2 Samuel 23:1–3, ca. 900 B.C.), Laozi's DAODEJING (300 B.C.), and Confucius's ANALECTS (ca. 210 B.C.).

A Literary Touchstone

Throughout history, the wise have treasured the *Panchatantra* for its simple truths. It inspired a Buddhist masterwork, Aryasura's *Jatakamala* (*Garland of Birth Stories*, ca. A.D. 350), 34 traditional Sanskrit stories about Gautama Buddha's incarnations and the impact of his ethics on India's peasantry, Brahmins, and royalty. An evangelist living in Bengal in eastern India and present-day

Bangladesh, Aryasura created a popular aphorism: "The fortunes of the world depend on the behavior of its rulers" (Aryasura 1989, 94). A later story advised, "Inspire a love of virtue in all creatures by your own practice of self-discipline" (152).

In A.D. 570, during the Sassanian dynasty, King Khosrow I the Just of Ctesiphon (near present-day Baghdad, Iraq), a patron of culture and star science, commanded his physician Burzoe to travel to India to translate the Indian story cycle into Persian as an example of prudence. The result was *Kalilah and Dimnah*, an influential version of the *Panchatantra*. An edition from the Umayyid dynasty around A.D. 750, also named *Kalilah and Dimnah*, was the work of the Syrian Abdullah Ibn al-Muqaffa of Basra, who translated it from Middle Persian into Arabic. EROTIC LITERATURE in the anonymous Sanskrit suite *Seventy Tales of a Parrot* (ca. 1100) draws episodes directly from the parent text.

The lessons of the *Panchatantra* are still with us. Pilgrims have carried the stories of the monkey gardeners, wily jackals, and the lion king Fierce-Heart to Tibet and China; European crusaders brought home episodes of the *Panchatantra*, the first Indian text of Indian lore to affect to Europe. During a period of plotting and violence in Kashmir, the Brahmin storyteller Somadeva created the 18-book *Kathasaritsagara* (*The Ocean of the Streams of Stories*, 1070) as a chapbook for Queen Suryamati. The advice to rulers applied to all castes: "A wise man should not serve fools: he should serve wise men. Discontent also does harm. . . . Discontent produces in both worlds intolerable and unceasing grief" (Somadeva 1884, 75, 76). In France, the brevity and wit of the *Panchatantra* influenced the style of the fabulists MARIE DE FRANCE and JEAN DE LA FONTAINE. A German version of the *Panchatantra*, *Reineke Fuchs* (*Reynard the Fox*, 1794), a bestiary by JOHANN WOLFGANG VON GOETHE, predicts the rise of Napoleon Bonaparte to first consul of France. One of the stories of Hans Christian Andersen, "The Princess and the Pea" (1835), features an original Indian theme about an Asian princess whose royalty is obvious in her delicacy and vulnerability to physical pain. One of the original tales served as the basis of an animated children's film, *Manpasand: The Perfect Match* (2008), produced by the Children's Film Society of India.

Sources

Aryasura. *Once the Buddha Was a Monkey.* Translated by Peter Khoroche. Chicago: University of Chicago Press, 1989.

Kalilah and Dimnah: or, the Fables of Bidpai. Translated by Ion Grant Neville Keith-Falconer. Cambridge: Cambridge University Press, 1885.

Pancatantra. Translated by Visnu Sarma. London: Penguin Classics, 2007.

Somadeva. *The Katha Sarit Sagara; or, Ocean of the Streams of Story.* Translated by C. H. Tawney. Calcutta: J. W. Thomas, 1884.

Pardo Bazán, Emilia (Emilia, Cantessa de Pardo Bazán) (1851–1921) *Spanish novelist and nonfiction writer*

A dynamic feminist and antimilitarist, Emilia Pardo Bazán voiced the disillusion of a generation of late-colonial Spanish Europeans. Born to aristocratic parents at La Coruña in Galicia in northwestern Spain, she treasured early memories of the Spanish annexation of northern Morocco. In *Autobiographical Sketches* (1886), she recalls a Spanish seizure of territory bordering the Strait of Gibraltar after the battle of Tétouan on February 6, 1861, a high point of the Spanish-Moroccan War of 1859–61. At a triumphal march, which she viewed at age 10 from a balcony on Real Street, "A Splendid sun shone on the bayonets and naked swords; it rendered the colors of the national flag—pierced by bullets—gayer, shinier, and bolder" (Pardo Bazán 1992, 264). She read world literature from a well-stocked library containing the works of Dante Alighieri, Alexandre Dumas, JOHANN WOLFGANG VON GOETHE, George Sand, LEO TOLSTOY, and Émile Zola. During the political exile of her father, the conde de Pardo-Bazán, she traveled with him, acquiring fluency in English, French, German, and Italian. She wrote 580 short stories for journals and newspapers—*Los contemporáneos, El cuento semanal, El libro popular, La novela corta,* and *Nuevo teatro critico.* At age 28, she advanced to novel writing with *Pascual López: The Autobiography of a Medical Student* (1879), followed by *La tribuna* (The tribune, 1882), which portrays the factory workers as New World replacements for the peons of old.

At a time when Spain's intellectual life suffered, Pardo Bazán, like the Polish-born JOSEPH CONRAD, depicted the effects of imperialism on the imperialists themselves rather than on the colonized. She achieved fame with a novel, *Los pazos de Ulloa* (*The House of Ulloa*, 1886), which surveys the decadence of Galician aristocrat Dom Pedro and the demise of the Spanish nobility. From a woman's viewpoint, Bazán realistically depicts the corruption of the church and the vitiation of the upper classes from centuries of dependence on unearned wealth— "plenty of talk about revolution, freedom, human rights . . . And in the end, only tyranny, privileges, and feudalism, for what is this but a return to the days of bondage and the injustice of slavery?" (Pardo Bazán 1992, 138). The false morality and class rigidity of the time plunges the Spanish, especially women and the peasant class, into despair.

By championing the underdog in fiction, Pardo Bazán alienated friends and broke her ties with the ruling class. Conversely, in a literary history, *La revolución y la novela en Rusia* (*Russia: Its People and Its Literature*, 1887), the author found much to praise in the depotism of Ivan the Terrible and Peter the Great, who introduced a standing navy and infantry, public education, commerce, and European enlightenment to a backward empire. Nonetheless, three decades before the Russian Revolution of 1917 and the assassination of Czar Nicholas II, Czarina Alexandra, and their five children, Pardo Bazán foresaw the danger of a restless peasantry: "Countryfolk, patient as cattle, but fanatical and overwhelming in their fury, once let loose, will sweep everything before it" (Pardo Bazán 1890, 152). In 1908, King Alfonso XIII conferred on the author the title of countess in acknowledgement of her endeavors for literacy and culture. A statue in the main park of La Coruña honors her service to Spain.

Sources

Balfour, Sebastian. *The End of the Spanish Empire, 1898–1923.* Oxford: Oxford University Press, 1997.
Pardo Bazán, Emilia. *The House of Ulloa.* Translated by Roser Caminalas-Heath. Athens: University of Georgia Press, 1992.
———. *Russia: Its People and Its Literature.* Translated by Fanny Hale Gardiner. Chicago: A. C. McClurg and Co., 1890.

Park, Mungo   See TRAVELOGUE.

Passage to India, A   See FORSTER, E. M.

Pasternak, Boris Leonidovich (1890–1960)
Russian poet, novelist, and translator

In a modern epic, Boris Pasternak dramatized the fall of Czar Nicholas II and the rise of corruption of the Soviet empire. A Jewish Muscovite, he was the son of a professional pianist, Rosa Kaufman, and a postimpressionist art scholar, Leonid Pasternak. As members of the intelligentsia, his parents encouraged innovation and debate among visitors, including the German poet Rainer Maria Rilke and the Russian composers Sergey Rachmaninoff and Aleksandr Scriabin. Of the influence of the novelist LEO TOLSTOY, a family friend, at the residence in Odessa, Pasternak stated, "His spirit pervaded our whole house" (quoted in Shapiro et al. 1994, 326). The author attended a German-run high school in Moscow. At age 15, he sustained an attack by a mounted Cossack during a period of revolution brought on by a workers' strike. He studied musical composition at the Moscow Conservatory, but in 1910 he enrolled in philosophy studies at the University of Marburg, Germany.

At age 24, Pasternak began a career as a poet. His poetry reflected the political ferment of anarchy, Bolshevism, and Menshevism. During World War I, a draft board rejected him for conscription because of a broken leg. In the Ural Mountains at Vsevolodovo-Vilve (outside present-day Perm in southwestern Russia), he clerked in a factory making acetic acid, acetone, and chloroform. Soon after the collapse of the Russian Empire, his sisters Josephine and Klara and parents fled to Berlin. Pasternak settled farther south at Saratov, an arts center and port on the Volga River, and ran a library while developing his talent for alliteration, dialect, and startling, surreal conceits. During the soul-numbing years of Stalinist fervor, Pasternak compared the reign of terror to the pre-Christian Roman Empire and the 16th-century reign of Ivan the Terrible. The author's creative endeavors forced him to maintain secrecy about his works and his association with other artists and freethinkers, with whom he exchanged drafts and critiques. He predicted that his persistence would survive shifting political conditions. In his words, "Time will preserve my handwriting from the historians' curry-combs" (quoted Barnes in 2004, ix).

Pasternak revitalized native verse with his first anthologies, *Sestra moya zhizn* (My Sister—Life, 1921) and *Temy i variatsii* (Themes and variations, 1923). His devotion to art and individualism swells in "The Image" (1921), which exults, "Although life wears out all ties / and pride warps the mind, / we will die with the pressure / of what we strive for in our blood" (Pasternak 2002, 29). Against the tide of communism, he demands in "Diseases of Earth" (1921), "Are these poems fermented/enough to stun the thunder?" (43). His collection *Vysokaya bolezn* (*A Sublime Malady,* 1925), a polemical series on the rebellion of Sevastopol in 1905, preceded two long poems on the event, *Leytenant Shmidt* (Lieutenant Schmidt, 1927) and *Devyatsot pyaty god* (The Year 1905, 1927). To make his poetry more acceptable to his Russian readers, Pasternak experimented with populist themes and styles in *Vtoroye rozhdenie* (The second birth, 1932). After a trip to Paris in 1935 to attend the Anti-Fascist Congress, he completed a nationalistic collection of poetry, *Na rannikh poyezdakh* (On early trains, 1943). He also made a living translating foreign drama and verse—William Shakespeare's tragedies *Cleopatra, Hamlet, King Lear, Macbeth, Othello,* and *Romeo and Juliet* and JOHANN WOLFGANG VON GOETHE's *Faust*—but he bore guilt that his peers faced the confiscation of their works, gulags, and execution.

At the end of World War II, Pasternak began his autobiographical saga, *Doctor Zhivago* (1956), a tragic love triangle derived from experiences during his residency in Peredelkino, a writers' colony outside Moscow. Because Soviet censors branded as traitorous a story of the author's wife Evgenia and mistress, Olga Ivanskaya, and vilified Pasternak as an anti-Marxist, editors of *Novy Mir* (New world) refused to serialize the novel. The Italian journalist Sergio D'Angelo smuggled the manuscript out of Russia in 1957 for publication in Italy, and subsequent translation into 18 languages. Authorities expelled the author from the Writer's Union, which monitored manuscripts that might slander the Soviet Union or violate communist precepts. Subservient colleagues followed the government's

lead by denouncing Pasternak's libertarian ideals. However, worldwide acclaim for the novel resulted in Pasternak being awarded the 1958 Nobel Prize in literature. Pressures from the Communist hierarchy and the exigencies of cardiac disease forced him to decline the honor, which his son Yevgeny accepted 29 years after his father's death from lung cancer.

In his last months, Pasternak wrote "Nobel Prize" (1958), a confessional verse comparing his life under communism to that of a criminal with a noose around his neck. He died on May 30, 1960, at his home in Peredelkino. Some 2,000 mourners attended his funeral and heard readings of his verse. His home later became a museum.

Conscience of a Nation

During an epoch of police terrorism and on-the-spot executions, Pasternak's *Doctor Zhivago* became an allegorical conscience for the Russian people living in what the author called "the time of Pharisees" (Pasternak 1962, 3). The protagonist, Yuri Andreievich Zhivago, a Muscovite physician and poet, lives for love, work, and country. During a world war, the Bolshevik Revolution, and civil war, his passions sustain him and invigorate his organic verse. In the lyric "Winter Night," he symbolizes the humanistic quest as a single candle flame melting a spot in an ice-covered window pane, an image of Russia's frozen soul that the director David Lean developed in his 1965 film starring Omar Sharif as Zhivago. The author summarizes the agony of survival: "His own ideas and notes also brought him joy, a tragic joy, a joy full of tears that exhausted him and made his head ache" (28).

Pasternak depicts his tragic hero with Christ-like pathos. At an emotional nadir recorded in Zhivago's poem "Hamlet," he prays, "Abba Father, / I beg you, take this cup from me," a restatement of Mark 14:36 (3). In an atmosphere of tyranny, fanaticism, and carnage, the physician clings to his humanity by traveling to northern Siberia, away from the urban fray and paranoia of Moscow. Such personal neutrality comes at a cost—isolation from his wife and family and the temptation of adultery with Lara Guishar Antipova, a married combat nurse who assists him during World War I. He compensates for a disjointed existence with the belief that a divine power, "the movement of universal thought and poetry in its present historical stage and the one to come" used him as a fulcrum (364). Zhivago's ideals are a testament to the author's determination to remain true to his native land and to withstand threats of exile and annihilation. Of the soul of Mother Russia, Pasternak predicted a resurgence: "By midnight denizens and dreamers / Moscow most of all is cherished. / Here is their home, the fount of all / With which this century will flourish" (quoted in Figes 2003, 216).

Sources

Barnes, Christopher. *Boris Pasternak: A Literary Biography.* Cambridge: Cambridge University Press, 2004.

Figes, Orlando. *Natasha's Dance: A Cultural History of Russia.* London: Macmillan, 2003.

Pasternak, Boris. *Dr. Zhivago.* New York: Pantheon, 1958.

———. *In the Interlude: Poems, 1945–1960.* London: Oxford University Press, 1962.

———. *My Sister—Life.* Translated by Mark Rudman and Bohdan Boychuk. Chicago: Northwestern University Press, 2002.

Shapiro, Michael, Daniel Shapiro, and Nancy Hartman. *The Jewish 100.* New York: Citadel, 1994.

Paul (Saint Paul, Paul of Tarsus, Saul of Tarsus)
(ca. A.D. 4–ca. 67)

A Jewish tentmaker of the early Roman Empire, Paul of Tarsus, Cilicia (present-day southern Turkey), produced at least seven and maybe as many as 14 epistles of encouragement to followers of a revolutionary new faith. Originally called Saul, he was a contemporary of Jesus and of the Jewish historian FLAVIUS JOSEPHUS; he converted to Christianity and adopted the name Paul following a vision that blinded him on the way to Damascus, Syria. Like the Roman poets OVID and VIRGIL, the Numidian philosopher AUGUSTINE of Hippo, and the modern Russian writers ANNA AKHMATOVA and BORIS PASTERNAK, Paul wrote of his beliefs at a time of social and economic unrest under the emperors Caligula and Nero. As a missionary, he traveled to Antioch, Corinth, Crete, Cyprus, Greece, Malta, Sicily, Turkey, and Thessalonica in southwestern Macedonia to recruit converts and encourage the Christian faith. He gained renown for spirited sermonizing, very different from tradi-

tional Judaism, on topics of predestination, good deeds, faith, atonement, salvation, impurity, diet, and divine grace.

Paul had an advantage over his brother evangelists. When in conflict with religious and civil authorities in Jerusalem, Caesarea, and Rome, he claimed Roman citizenship, a privilege that established his rights, guaranteed him a proper trial, and saved him from arbitrary execution. The letters he sent to new Christians defined elements of faith that remain pivotal to followers. His simplicity touched troubled hearts with practical guidance: "Hold fast to that which is good" (1 Thessalonians 5:21). Concerning the redemptive power of the Messiah, he challenged his audience with a rhetorical question in the context of Roman imperialism: "Who shall separate us from the love of Christ? shall tribulation, or distress, or persecution, or famine, or nakedness, or peril, or sword?" (Romans 8:35). The affirmation of hope in his words comforted women, slaves, prisoners of war, lepers, and members of minor sects—those most vulnerable to Roman prejudice.

Composing in koine, or dialect Greek, around A.D. 53, Paul took into account the multicultural turmoil created by Rome's subjugation of Jews, coupled with attacks by Jews on Jesus Christ's followers, a new sect that threatened conservative Judaism and the dominance of their priests. Of his own past role as a Pharisee persecuting Christians, Paul emphasized the importance of benevolence over law in one of his most quoted verses: "Though I speak with the tongues of men and of angels and have not charity, I am become as sounding brass, or a tinkling cymbal" (1 Corinthians 13:1). He outlined the style and tone of communion, a peaceful sharing of bread and wine with fellow Christians. He established the act as a sacrament and an anticipation of the messiah's second coming: "For as often as ye eat this bread, and drink this cup, ye do show the Lord's death till he come" (1 Corinthians 11:26). One of his lyrical visions of life after death carries the poet's ecstatic vision: "Behold, I shew you a mystery. We shall not all sleep, but we shall all be changed, in a moment, in the twinkling of an eye, at the last trumpet: for the trumpet shall sound, and the dead shall be raised incorruptible, and we shall be changed" (1 Corinthians

15:51–52). To a people conquered and controlled by Roman legions, the promise of transformation in the afterlife held great appeal.

Paul demanded the constancy and inclusion of all converts to Jesus's teachings. To squabblers over the admission of both genders and disparate sectarians to Christian fellowship, he exulted, "There is neither Jew nor Greek, there is neither bond nor free, there is neither male nor female: for ye are all one in Christ Jesus" (Galatians 3:28), a rejuvenating proclamation to victims of Roman harassment. He popularized the use of the Greek descriptor *Christos* (the anointed) as Jesus's official title and challenged marginalized minorities to think of themselves as religious warriors: "Put on the whole armor of God, that ye may be able to stand against the wiles of the devil" (Ephesians 6:11). The bold equating of Roman despotism with satan put backbone into disciples by allegorizing their daily miseries as the eternal war of good against evil.

Paul's WISDOM reflects the thoughts of a realist running out of time. In his 60s, he observed, "We brought nothing into this world, and it is certain we can carry nothing out," an existential commentary on mortality (1 Timothy 6:7). To heighten an argument against materialism, he declared, "For the love of money is the root of all evil" (1 Timothy 6:10). At the time of his beheading in Rome in or before A.D. 67, Christian fervor had aroused sufficient disquiet in Emperor Nero to warrant persecutions, including the torture of Christians who allegedly confessed to starting the Great Fire of Rome on July 18, A.D. 64. According to book 15 of the *Annals* (A.D. 116) of the Roman historian TACITUS, a roundup of adherents resulted in "mutilation by dogs or, fixed to crosses and made flammable, on the dwindling of daylight they were burned for use as nocturnal illumination" for the imperial gardens, around which Nero drove his chariot (Tacitus 2004, 326).

In his last years, with serenity and grace, Paul conferred a benediction on his beleaguered followers: "Now the god of peace, that brought again from the dead our Lord Jesus, that great shepherd of the sheep, through the blood of the everlasting covenant, make you perfect in every good work to do his will, working in you that which is well-pleasing in his sight" (Hebrews 13:20–21). The blessing is still used to strengthen congregations' patience and faith.

Sources

Bruce, F. F. *Paul, Apostle of the Heart Set Free.* Grand Rapids, Mich.: Eerdmans, 2000.

Holy Bible. Iowa Falls, Iowa: World Bible Publishers, 1986.

Tacitus. *The Annals.* Translated by Anthony John Woodman. Indianapolis: Hackett, 2004.

Peake, Mervyn (Mervyn Laurence Peake)
(1911–1968) *English fantasy writer, artist, and poet*

A GOTHIC symbolist, set designer, and illustrator, Mervyn Peake recast the grimness of World War II into literary phantasms of evil. He was born to British parents, a medical evangelist and a missionary nurse, in Kuling, Jiangxi Province, China. A case of encephalitis in his early months precipitated the tremors, insomnia, irritability, hallucinations, and melancholia that eventually took his life. The family returned to England during the first two years of World War I but then returned to China in 1916. Peake was a childhood reader of CHARLES DICKENS and ROBERT LOUIS STEVENSON. His early introduction to grotesquerie occurred during his admission to a ward at McKenzie Memorial, a Congregationalist clinic in Tientsin southeast of Beijing, where he sketched physical malformations. During the early years of the Chinese Republic, he observed more wretchedness among malnourished and abused peasants. Upon his return to England in 1923, he attended the Croydon School of Art and the Royal Academy. At age 21, he joined an artist commune on the Channel Isle of Sark off the northern coast of Normandy, where he escaped from feelings of alienation and otherness resulting from his Chinese upbringing. He married Maeve Gilmore in 1937; the couple had three children.

During World War II, Peake served as a sapper and war artist in the Royal Artillery and Royal Engineers of the British army. In the poem "May 1940," he summarized the mayhem of the second world war in a rhetorical question, "Where has lost sanity a resting place / These days" (Peake 1981, 144). In 1945, after seeing Bergen-Belsen, a Nazi death camp in northern Germany, he wrote poems such as "Digging a Trench," "The Consumptive, Belsen 1945," and "Victims." He lapsed into morbid imaginings about the ruthless realities of Hitler's Holocaust, which had filled the camp with 13,000 corpses and 60,000 moribund inmates whose "eyes like great hearts of black water / Shone in their wells of bone" (168).

Aided by memories of medical research on patients, Peake brought black humor into a medieval sequence of gothic novels, beginning with *Titus Groan* (1946) and followed by the Heinemann Prize–winning *Gormenghast* (1950), which reprises settings from Beijing's walled compounds. In the landscape of Gormenghast, Peake envisions suffocation from septic traditions: "It lay inert, like a sick thing. Its limbs spread. It took the shape of what it smothered" (Peake 2007, 358). After freelancing as an illustrator on *Grimms' Fairy Tales, Alice in Wonderland, TREASURE ISLAND,* and *Dr. Jekyll and Mr. Hyde,* Peake continued fiction writing with *Boy in Darkness* (1956), *Titus Alone* (1959), and the fragment *Titus Awakes,* which the author abandoned in 1960 after his health failed from neurodegenerative dementia.

Peake excelled at visual innovation. Using gothic convention, he fleshed out plots with dreamscapes, claustrophobic towers and dungeons, the treachery of a shadowy SS elite, perverted scientists like Dr. Josef Mengele, neurotic fetishes and phobias, and ritual execution throughout the Nazi empire. His musings on human-animal hybrids, as in H. G. Wells's science fiction novel *The Island of Dr. Moreau,* show the bestiality in the worst of humanity and anticipate medical experiments placing animal parts in human bodies. For characters, he created allegorical figures—Dr. Alfred Prunesquallor, Flay, Fuchsia Groan, Lord Sepulchrave, Pentecost, Rottcodd, Nannie Slagg, Sourdust, Steerpike, and Chef Abiatha Swelter. Set over lesser figures, the ogreish Steerpike, a Hitleresque villain from *Titus Groan* and *Gormenghast,* looks through eyes the rust-red color of dried blood. The surreal series earned a cult readership that included the novelist GRAHAM GREENE and the poet Dylan Thomas. The BBC presented radio versions of *Titus Groan and Gormenghast,* in 1984, 1992, and 2003. BBC-TV presented *Gormenghast,* starring Ian Richardson

and Christopher Lee, in 1999 and *Boy in Darkness,* featuring Terry Jones as the Storyteller, in 2000.

Sources

Peake, Mervyn. *Gormenghast.* Woodstock, N.Y.: Overlook, 2007.

———. *Peake's Progress.* Edited by Maeve Peake. Woodstock, N.Y.: Overlook, 1981.

Peake, Sebastian. *Mervyn Peake: The Man and His Art.* London: Peter Owen, 2006.

Perse, Saint-John (Alexis Saint-Léger Léger)
(1887–1975) *French poet and translator*

Under his pen name of Saint-John Perse, Alexis Saint-Léger Léger won the 1960 Nobel Prize in literature for somber nationalistic poetry as well as celebrations of silence and solitude in NATURE. Born to wealthy French cane and coffee planters on the island of St. Léger des Feueilles off Pointe-à-Pitre, Guadaloupe, he was 10 years old when the French Antilles separated from the French Empire. In 1899, as the political situation grew threatening for colonialists, his family returned to France and settled in the Pyrenees in Pau. After an education at the law school of the University of Bordeaux, Léger initiated translations of Pindaric odes and of Daniel Defoe's adventure classic *Robinson Crusoe* (1719) in *Images for Crusoe* (1909), a story of the castaway that foreshadows the poet's last years as a refugee from Hitler's Europe. He followed with *Élogues* (Elegies, 1910). At age 24, he joined the foreign office and worked for the media during World War I. Afterward, he served in the French embassies in Beijing and Washington, D.C.

By 1938, Léger (or Perse, his pen name) was a senior official at the Munich conference, where, over his protest, Germany formally annexed part of Czechoslovakia. He lost his French citizenship after expulsion in 1940 by the Vichy government, which also revoked his French Legion of Honor. While Nazi investigators pillaged his Paris residence and destroyed his unpublished writings, he escaped near-certain execution by fleeing to England. He lamented the impermanence of a government career: "I have built upon the abyss and the spindrift and the sand-smoke" (Perse 1982, xiv). He refused a position in the government-in-exile of

General Charles de Gaulle and rejected a teaching position at Harvard University. From 1941 to 1945, he worked at the Library of Congress as the consultant on French literature, a post obtained for him by the poet Archibald MacLeish. He lived out his retirement in Provence and the United States. He died on September 20, 1975, at his villa in Provence and was buried in Giens.

Writing from Experience

Influenced by the novelist Victor Hugo (1802–85) and by literary colleagues Paul Claudel (1868–1955), André Gide (1869–1951), and Paul Valéry (1871–1945), Léger established a literary persona, Saint-John Perse, to separate his writing from his diplomatic career. His adopted surname translated as the exotic "Persia," and his canon began with the publication of a Homeric epic, *Anabase* (*Anabasis*, 1924). The poem is a grand conquest narrative reflective of the influence of the Greek historian XENOPHON, author of the combat memoir *Anabasis* (*The Expedition of Cyrus*, 354 B.C.). Perse's story of the protagonist, a tribal despot who journeys to an allegorical interior, draws on the poet's experiences in the Gobi Desert. The text features egotistic idealizations of the unidentified conqueror's campaign: "Glory at the threshold of the tents, and my strength among you, and the idea pure as salt holds its assize in the daylight" (Perse 1982, 31).

Perse wrote timeless verse on the subject of homelessness, alienation, transience, and spiritual drift. The dynamic sweep of his style, which he called *parole de vivant* (the living word), suggests an active involvement of the writer in the action, an identity with words and movement that sustains the long narrative. In each poem, an underlying continuity aims an unnerving focus, a view ahead that refuses to flinch. Perse established a following with *Exil* (*Exile*, 1942), an impersonal meditation on world war. In the "great feat of arms on the march across the world" he envisioned a gothic terror, "This huge muffled thing loose in the world, and suddenly growing huger like drunkenness" (47). His protests against the "monsterhead" seek an end to pursuit of "my Numidian soul" (49), a color image of his dark spirit in flight from Nazi-occupied France. In *Vents* (*Winds*, 1946), his commentary on Columbus's discovery

and exploration of the Western Hemisphere and on World War II prefigured his voyage imagery in *Amers* (*Seamarks*, 1957), a rumination on the human desire for challenge and exploration of the unknown. Upon receipt of the Nobel Prize at age 73, Perse summarized his view of art as an expression of human ambivalence toward injustice: "It is enough for the poet to be the guilty conscience of his time" (xi).

Sources

Baker, Peter. *Obdurate Brilliance: Exteriority and the Modern Long Poem*. Gainesville: University Press of Florida, 1991.

Perse, Saint-John. *Selected Poems*. Edited by Mary Ann Caws. New York: New Directions, 1982.

Phaedrus (ca. 15 B.C.–A.D. 50) *Thracian-Greek fabulist*

In the formative decades of the Roman Empire, the freedman poet Phaedrus, a former Thracian slave, made a name for himself in one genre, his retellings of AESOP's beast FABLES. A mountain boy, he was born at Pydna in Macedonia (northeastern Greece), but grew up in Rome as a domestic servant in the imperial palace of Augustus, who freed him. During his years under three successive emperors, he had access to education and literature. In five volumes, Phaedrus published 150 allegorical best sellers refined from the *Aesopia* (ca. 225 B.C.), tales collected by the Athenian orator Demetrius Phalereus of Alexandria. Although a pet of the literati, Phaedrus retained an underclass perspective in his droll STORYTELLING, which subtly undercuts a vice-ridden society. The needling of Lucius Aelius Sejanus, Tiberius's palace prefect, with stories in *Fabulae Aesopiae* (Aesopic fables, ca. A.D. 31) put the writer in danger. Sejanus suppressed his last 55 stories, which included the moral "Vulgare amici nomen sed rara est fides" (The name of friend is common, but loyalty is rare) (Phaedrus 1876, 24). The final collection remained unpublished throughout the reigns of Claudius and Nero.

A tutor to Lucius, the grandson of Augustus, Phaedrus used court favor as a means of prodding lapsed morality. A simple model of his updated parables and anecdotes, "The Weasel and the

Mice," illustrates that all citizens, even common folk, have their place in society. One of Phaedrus's targets, the Athenian tyrant Demetrius Poliorcetes, earned scorn for encouraging favor seekers, the scourge of the Julio-Claudian dynasty. A retelling of Aesop's fable of frogs in search of a king reminds the reader that those who hated the Greek tyrant Peisistratus risked a revolution that might put someone worse in charge. For the author's audacity, the satirist Martial quipped in his *Epigrammata* (ca. A.D. 85) about "inprobi Phaedri" (wicked Phaedrus). The former slave's works influenced later moralists, medieval preachers, the fabulist JEAN DE LA FONTAINE, and the Dutch humanist Desiderius Erasmus, who was fond of the SATIRE of foolish intellectuals in the story "The Cock and the Pearl."

Phaedrus stands out as a Roman bondsman who made a cultural impact. He credited the fable as a form of satire through which the lowest slave could express outrage and mockery. Posing as a naif, during the reigns of Augustus, Tiberius, Caligula, and Claudius, Phaedrus turned the sober Greek moral tales into stylized satires, *promythia* (introductory morals), dialogues of law-court bribery, and commentary on palace scandal during the empire's early years. With a sick joke in "The Ass and the Priests of Cybele," Phaedrus rages against the cruelty of slavemasters and, subtextually, exonerates slaves for looking out for their own welfare. The story "Tib. Caesar ad Atriensem" (Tiberius Caesar to a flunky) warns curriers of favor that their ingratiating ways are annoying; "Milvus et Columbae" ("The Kite and the Doves") summarizes the menace that authoritarianism holds for the lowly. At the conclusion of "The Ass and the Old Man," an *epimythium* (moral) observes that, following a shift in government, poor people change nothing but the names of their masters.

Sources

Anderson, Graham. *Greek and Roman Folklore.* Westport, Conn.: Greenwood, 2006.

Fitzgerald, William. *Slavery and the Roman Literary Imagination.* Cambridge: Cambridge University Press, 2000.

Henderson, John. *Telling Tales on Caesar.* Oxford: Oxford University Press, 2001.

Phaedrus. *Fabulae Aesopiae.* Translated by J. T. White. London: Spottiswoode & Co., 1876.

Pharsalia See LUCAN.

Pliny the Younger (Gaius Plinius Caecilius Securdus) (ca. A.D. 61–ca. 113) *Roman writer*

An eyewitness to the flourishing empire of A.D. first-century Rome, the Roman writer of letters called Pliny the Younger held subjective views of customs and government. Born Gaius Caecilius, he was the nephew of Pliny the Elder, Rome's first encyclopedist; the son of a cavalry officer posted to the Rhine River; and a member of the knight class. After his father's death, Pliny was raised and homeschooled by his mother at Novum Comum (present-day Lake Como, Italy) during the mental decline of Emperor Nero and the enthronement of Vespasian, a successful soldier, in A.D. 69. On August 24, A.D. 79, Pliny was a student of rhetoric at Rome. His uncle, then commander of a fleet, saw the eruption of Vesuvius and died of suffocation. As heir to Pliny the Elder's fortune, the teenager received a priceless legacy—his uncle's estate, a massive library, and research notes, which he housed at his country villa at Laurentinum, south of Rome.

Of the settled life, Pliny declared, "For my part I like a well-ordered course of life . . . just as I admire the regular order of the stars" (Pliny 1872, 114). Of particular value to him, intellectual discussions, good manners, and friendship offered the most solace during the empire's difficulties. At a time when he felt "harassed by a thousand troubles," he confided to a friend the need to retreat from Rome "with its idle pursuits and laborious trifles" (125) to enjoy relaxation and private reading. After becoming a lawyer, Pliny worked as accountant to the III Gallica legion in Syria, the palace quaestor (magistrate), and treasury supervisor under Emperor Domitian. After joining his friend TACITUS in prosecuting Marius Priscus, governor of Africa, for malfeasance, Pliny became consul and chair of the senate. He accepted promotions to the provinces, where he judged cases of gubernatorial graft and embezzlement. Accompanying him to Bithynia (present-day Turkey) in A.D. 109 was his mentor, the historian SUETONIUS.

From boyhood, Pliny dedicated himself to serious writing, beginning with verse and, at age 15, a Greek tragedy. By A.D. 80, he had pled his first court case. In the *Panegyricus Traiani* (Encomium to Trajan, A.D. 100), an address to the senate praising Emperor Trajan, Pliny, then aged 39, emulated the speaking skills of Cicero. The text emphasizes contrasts between Trajan's skill at governance and fiscal control and the failures of his predecessor Domitian. In the *Epistulae* (*Letters*, A.D. 97–113) Pliny describes contemporary events—for instance, the details of his uncle's attempted rescues by sea of Pompeiian citizens and his death from the eruption of Vesuvius; the Roman quandary over the rising popularity of Christianity, which he considered a ridiculous superstition. In an investigation of Christians, Pliny admits, "I judged it necessary to try to get at the truth by putting to the torture two female slaves" (153). He gives up interrogating the cultists and turns the issue over to the emperor. His last letters to Trajan complained of the lackluster supervision of Roman provinces by venal officials. Pliny's reputation for veracity was so respected that the Christian apologist TERTULLIAN of Carthage quoted his letters in essays on religious faith and worship styles.

Sources

Hoffer, Stanley E. *The Anxieties of Pliny the Younger.* Philadelphia: American Philological Association, 1999.

Pliny. *Pliny's Letters.* Translated by Alfred Church and W. J. Brodribb. Edinburgh: William Blackwood and Sons, 1872.

Plutarch (Lucius Mestrius Plutarchus)

(ca. A.D. 46–ca. 120) *Greek biographer and essayist*

Plutarch, a model writer for world essayists, chose a comparative biography for illuminating human excellence and frailties. A Romanized Greek from Chaeronea, Boeotia, near Mount Parnassus in east central Greece, he was one of three brothers born to a wealthy family. At age 20, he studied mathematics, philosophy, rhetoric, and science at the Academy of Athens. As a senior priest at the Oracle of Delphi, he interpreted the prophecies of the Pythia. Surviving from his early life is a letter to his wife Timoxena, who mourned the death of their two-year-old daughter, also named Timoxena. A renowned friend-maker, Plutarch was elected magistrate and won multiple terms as mayor of his district. On diplomatic missions, he traveled the Mediterranean and studied Egyptian theology in Alexandria. His work earned him Roman citizenship and, under Emperor Hadrian, an honorary post as the provincial governor of northern Greece. In an essay on traditional worship, he regretted the ebb of the Roman mores into secularism and decadence.

In his 60s, Plutarch devoted his energies to writing character studies. Although formally untrained in history, he chose to write a BIOGRAPHY of Alexander the Great and to criticize *The Histories* (440 B.C.) of HERODOTUS. Plutarch's *Moralia* (Customs, ca. A.D. 110) investigates theological concerns, including the widespread worship of Isis and Osiris and the decline of reverence for the Delphic oracle. Extending religious concerns to matters of governance, he mused on the unifying effect of public worship and on the problem of emperors at choosing a deity for a nation to esteem. His essays on brotherhood and marital and parental love reflect an abiding humanism and a respect for women and children and for long-standing friendships.

Plutarch compiled 46 tandem biographies in *Bioi paralleloi* (*Parallel Lives,* ca. A.D. 110), a best seller in the Roman world. A reflection of contemporary prejudices and mores, the pairings, one Greek with one Roman, begin with King Theseus of Athens and the mythic king Romulus, the twin of Remus; and the Spartan lawgiver Lycurgus, whom he paired with the Roman lawgiver Numa Pompilius. Plutarch extends the comparisons through the leading figures of the late republic—Brutus, Cicero, Julius Caesar, Mark Antony, and Pompey. The text concludes with Galba and Otho, who attempted to restore Rome's finances after the extravagant reign of Nero, the former emperor. Of Galba's reign, Plutarch summarizes the venality and barbarity that preceded the death of Nero and the discontent that precipitated the beheading of Galba. Of the disastrous three-month rule of Otho, Plutarch pities the second ruler who tried to cleanse Rome of corruption: "Though [Otho] lived no more decently than Nero, he died more nobly" (Plutarch 1926, 486). The text implies that any ruler following a madman like Nero had little hope of flourishing in office.

The 1579 TRANSLATION of Plutarch's biographies by Sir Thomas North, *Plutarch's Lives of the Noble Grecians and Romans*, provided details for WILLIAM SHAKESPEARE's five-act tragedy *Julius Caesar* (1599). Based on Plutarch's details and analyses, the Elizabethan stage play surveys secret maneuvering precipitating the end of the Roman Republic and a period of political proscription resulting in death sentences for the most distinguished and powerful of Roman republicans. The playwright returned to Plutarch's summation of a pivotal era—the founding of the Roman Empire—with *Antony and Cleopatra* (ca. 1605). The popular tragedy is fraught with rhapsodic passion and treachery as two Roman generals fight to the death for power and vastly differing views on imperial rule.

Sources

Duff, Timothy E. *Plutarch's Lives: Exploring Virtue and Vice.* Oxford: Oxford University Press, 2002.

Plutarch. *Moralia.* Translated by Frank Cole Babbitt. Whitefish, Mont.: Kessinger, 2005.

———. *Parallel Lives.* 11 vols. Translated by Bernadotte Perrin. Cambridge, Mass.: Harvard University Press, 1926.

Polo, Marco (1254–1324) *Venetian explorer and travelogue writer*

A merchant and traveler, Marco Polo provided the Western world with a late-medieval best seller, a documented description of the fabled Silk Road of Cathay (China) and a memoir of Kublai Khan, the emperor of China. In company with his well-traveled father, Niccolò Polo, and uncle Maffeo, traders with the Byzantine Empire, 17-year-old Marco set out in 1271 to east central Asia with letters and oil from the lamp at the Holy Sepulchre, a gift from Pope Gregory X at the khan's request. The Polos made their odyssey overland via some 5,600 miles through Jerusalem, Armenia, Turkey, and Georgia,

where they traversed battlegrounds once commandeered by Alexander the Great. They continued east to Persia, from where the New Testament writer Matthew indicated that the three magi set out to visit the Christ child, an apocryphal trio unnamed in the Christian gospels but in later western works called Balthasar, Caspar, and Melchior.

Because of an innate intellectual curiosity, Polo adapted naturally to travel. After admiring the silk needlecraft of Persian women, he traveled over Afghanistan's rugged terrain, the fine pasturage of Tibet, and Muslim enclaves skirting the Gobi Desert. He arrived in Inner Mongolia at Sachiu (present-day Dunhuang, China) in the fourth year of his trek. Along the route, he survived hostility on the strengths of his grace, lingual skill, and STORYTELLING ability, all of which later impressed the great khan, who entrusted him with diplomatic missions. For three years, Polo held the governorship of Yangzhou. He conducted a diplomatic mission to the Bagan empire in Burma, a rich coastal property that the Tartars considered adding to their empire. After 17 years, in 1291, the khan dispatched Marco Polo with Princess Koekecin and a fleet of 14 ships from Quanzhou to sail the South China Sea and around Vietnam to Java, Sumatra, Sri Lanka, and India before delivering the princess to Persia to be married. The final sea leg introduced Polo to Madagascar, Mozambique, Zanzibar, and Abyssinia.

A Traveler's Stories

After his tour of many of the world's empires—Abyssinian, Bagan, Islamic, Majapahitan, Mamluk, Mongolian, Papal, and Persian—Polo arrived in Venice in 1295 and described his journeys to incredulous listeners. He admired his mentor, Kublai Khan, the sixth lord of the Tartars and ruler of the world's largest land-based empire. Most impressive to the traveler were the khan's valor, wisdom, and suitability to the offices of emperor and commander of 360,000 cavalry and 100,000 infantry. Polo spoke of the khan's failed expedition against Japan's Kamakura shogunate in 1274 and again in 1281, when typhoons destroyed the Mongolian armadas. Among the marvels of China, a few stand out for their ingenuity—the khan's portable silk and cane palace, paper currency and bank credit, bathrooms, and asbestos table napkins. The napkin that the Polos returned to the pope displayed the Petrine Supremacy worked in gold: "Tu es Petrus et super hanc petram aedificabo ecclesiam meam" (You are Peter and upon this rock I will build my church; Polo 1931, 74), a reference to the commissioning of the beloved disciple that is sheathed in gold on the dome of St. Peter's Basilica in Rome. The gesture illustrates the khan's willingness to study the beliefs of other cultures and to respect their symbols and scriptures.

To curious Venetians, Polo reported details of life in China, including priority mail service, canal transportation, and coal fires. He recited a memoir of Kublai Khan, whose power lay in charisma and sincerity toward his subjects: "When these peoples saw how worthily this lord exercised his dominion, and how good he was, they went most willingly with him" (79). He surprised his listeners by claiming that the size and complexity of the Chinese Empire dwarfed the realms of Europe.

Polo later commanded a war galley for Venice, which lost to the Genoese fleet at the Island of Curzola. In 1298, during incarceration as a prisoner of war of the Genoese, the romance writer Rustichello of Pisa wrote in Old French the travelogue dictated by his cell mate, later entitled *The Travels of Marco Polo*. At age 66, Polo wrote a new version of his travels in Italian. Among his fans was the explorer Christopher Columbus, who jotted notes in the margins of his copy. An Emmy-winning television series, *Marco Polo* (1982), starred Ken Marshall as the title figure alongside a star-laden cast that included Burt Lancaster as Pope Gregory X and John Gielgud as the doge of Venice. A TV remake in 2007 cast Brian Dennehy as the great khan.

Sources

Haw, Stephen. *Marco Polo in China: A Venetian in the Realm of Khubilai Khan.* New York: Routledge, 2006.
Polo, Marco. *The Travels of Marco Polo.* Translated by Aldo Ricci. London: George Routledge, 1931.

Popol Vuh (ca. 1558)

A scriptural monument to native Mesoamerican culture, the *Popol Vuh* (Council book) preserves the myths, hymns, prayers, chronology, royal genealogy, astronomy, and prophecies of the Quiché-speaking Maya. A compilation of CREATION LORE, saga, ancestral WISDOM, and inventive STORYTELLING, the original text is older than the law codes of Moses and Hammurabi, the Harappan lore compiled in the Rig Veda of India (1700–1400 B.C.), and the AVESTA of Persia (ca. A.D. 530). The Mayan codex surveys tales of the supernatural from tribes of the Sierra Los Cuchematanesa Mountains in north-central Guatemala, which stretch from southern Mexico south to Guatemala and east into northern Belize. In 1558, only three decades after Spanish conquistadores seized Central America, Diego Reynoso, an Indian Christian convent and a historian, translated the complicated narrative from the Quiché alphabet into Spanish. In both languages, the two-stage text recalls the Meso-American agrarian culture and religion from 1500 B.C. to the classical period from A.D. 250 to 900, which saw the construction of Chichén Itzá, Mayapán, and Uxmal.

The *Popol Vuh* follows native fortunes up to 1523, when a 28-year-old conqueror and looter, Captain Pedro de Alvarado of Badajoz, Spain, began pacifying the Guatemalan highlands under the command of explorer Hernan Cortés, conqueror of the Aztec of Mexico in 1521. After the Spanish burned two native kings, buildings, and all hieroglyphic manuscripts, Quiché speakers preserved their heritage by memorizing segments of the *Popol Vuh* to pass on to their children along with native dance and ritual. In 1722, a Dominican scholar, Francisco Ximénez (or Jiménez), discovered Reynoso's bark-paper manuscript in El Calvario Church, at Chichicastenango, Guatemala, but dismissed the pagan allegory as stories for Mayan children. Ethnographers have since refuted church literary analysis and treasured the manuscript as the equivalent of the Hebrew creation lore of Genesis (ca. 500 B.C.) and the Hindu epic *Ramayana* (ca. 400 B.C.). Archeologists validated the Guatemalan text by comparing literary episodes to iconography on a 1,500-year-old Mayan temple complex.

The Beginnings of Life

Like the Japanese *Kojiki* (A.D. 712) of Ono Yasumaro and Navajo creation lore, the cosmogeny of the *Popol Vuh* depicts the earth's beginnings from a single beneficent deity. The plumed serpent Gugumatz, or Q'uk'umatz, earned reverence as the "maker and modeler, bearer and begetter of all living things, heart of lake and sea, plate and bowl shaper, midwife and matchmaker, defender and protector. He is mother-father of life and humankind, breathgiver, heart-giver, upbringer of a lasting light, and knower of all, whatever there is" (*Popul Vuh* 1996, 64). The fluid verse depicts a primeval nothingness, like soup in a pot, humming and bubbling with potential. Gugumatz takes pride in the unfolding of primordial earth from a mist and the separation of water from land. The cosmos reaches fruition with the planting of seeds and the shaping of living creatures, who master the first human task—to speak the god's name. The assignment resounds with the majesty and severity of the first commandment in EXODUS 20:2–3: "I *am* the LORD thy God, which have brought thee out of the land of Egypt, out of the house of bondage. Thou shalt have no other gods before me." The *Popol Vuh* describes a trinity of gods who choose a gardener to tend the hills and plains. For material, the trio builds their model out of maize growing on Guatemala's northern border with Mexico, where the first hunter-gatherers lived. The single crop becomes a symbol for all food plants that sustain humankind.

The Mayan codex follows a universal theme. The second stave of the *Popol Vuh* honors the first farmers, whom the gods mold out of clay. The purpose of the agrarian prototype is both procreative and devotional: The first tiller of the soil serves God as "a giver of praise, giver of respect, provider, nurturer" (68). Unlike the sonorous Hebrew account of Adam and Eve in GENESIS 2:7, 21, a humorous Mayan passage derides the faults of a clay being who stands lopsided, crumbles, and dissolves in rain. The gods replace their practice model with a figure carved from coral wood (the tropical *guibourtia*), but it, too, disappoints because of its stiffness and lack of feeling. The gods dispatch jaguars to demolish the wood man and scourge the earth with a hurricane and flood. The third try results in men shaped from maize and women from *espadana*, or tassel grass, a resilient swamp ground cover. Because the paired models prove flimsy, the gods send a bird and jaguar to devour them. Until better earthlings appear, the planet returns to a state of darkness and lifelessness, the author's allegorical image of the precreation status of Earth.

The Heroic Era

The *Popol Vuh* balances issues of sustenance and worship with fun and competition. Part two sanctifies *tlachtli*, or pok-a-tok, the onomatopoetic name for handball played on an earthen court and batted by shoulder, elbow, or hip through stone goals at each end. Twin players, Hun Hunahpú and Vucub Hunahpú, protect their heads with feathered helmets and pad their hips, elbows, and forearms for striking a sphere molded from rubber, a substance tapped from the trees indigenous to South America. Like the early anthropomorphism in OVID's *Metamorphoses* (Transformations, A.D. 8), the players' match against envious gods results in divine cheating and the slaughter of the human team. The disposal of the martyrs' heads leads to the positioning of Venus, the evening star, and the emergence of the skull-shaped calabash, a traditional Mayan bowl for serving cacao drinks. Thus, the mythic sacrifice serves a triple purpose, as revenge for the gods, a heavenly guide, and a useful vessel for humanity.

As in the account of the Virgin Mary's divine impregnation in Luke 1:26–35, the Mayan codex elevates womankind in biblical style by empowering females through parthenogenesis, or reproduction without fertilization. The severed heads of the twins puzzle Ixquic, the curious female equivalent of the Hebrew Eve and the Greek Pandora. She ponders the waste of two human lives: "What? Well! What's the fruit of this tree? Shouldn't this tree bear something sweet? They shouldn't die, they shouldn't be wasted. Should I pick one?" (98). The myth describes how saliva from the decapitated head of Hun Hunahpú becomes seminal fluid that impregnates Ixquic. From the virgin's dilemma in a merciless male-dominated society comes a scriptural substitute for ritual heart excision as punishment for her supposed adultery: Instead of lopping open her chest, the executioners accept a red model heart formed from the crimson resin of a cochineal croton tree. To win the love of the future grandmother of her children, Ixquic becomes the prototype of the female harvester. In response to her reverence for fruits of the soil, the gods give her twin sons, Hunahpú and Xpalanqúe, incarnations of their deceased father and uncle, who suffered beheading to rid the world of divine animosity. In a similar act of acceptance, the grandmother institutes Quechéan rituals to ensure the annual corn cycle, a symbol of regeneration similar to the Isis and Osiris stories of ancient Egypt and the Greek Dionysian cycle.

The complicated story line of the *Popol Vuh* intersperses sacramental vignettes with trickster tales, accounts of salvation and shape-shifting, and the gymnasts and holy jesters of the Totonac, the Indian people inhabiting eastern Mexico. Centuries before Charles Darwin predicated human evolution from apes in *Descent of Man* (1871), Mayan mythographers posited the reverse, the evolution of simians from early Guatemalans. Domestic scenarios justify a conundrum in world theology, the replacement of matriarchal-horticultural dominion with an all-encompassing patriarchal-agrarian regime. Ixquic's twins retrieve their fathers' remains from ignominy and promise perpetual reverence to fatherhood: "Your name will not be lost. So be it" (141). The two boys, ballplayers like their father, ascend into the heavens to become the sun and moon, the illuminators of the human world below. In part 4, a thanksgiving PRAYER venerates the divine sustainer for providing a "greening path," the source of a "good life and beginning" (150). The poet's use of *greening* implies a cycle of renewal, a theme that permeates creation stories with the promise of perpetual beginnings.

Mayan Civilization

Like the book of Exodus (ca. 450 B.C.), the *Popol Vuh* accounts for the migration of the Quiché from mountains and caves of central Guatemala south to a warmer climate. Along the way, they feed a constant fire, the basis of sun worship similar to the Greek and Roman adoration of Apollo as light bringer, prophet, healer, and patron of the arts. From penitence and propitiation of the gods evolves Mayan civilization and a cessation of blood savagery. Tribe communicates with tribe. The sinful learn to weep and repent, a catharsis of sin that introduces the blessing of self-reclamation and spiritual healing, a gift that Aristotle extolled in GREEK DRAMA. As Guatemalan history succeeds legend, the account advances from myth to a chronicle of wars, fortified cities, spying, assassinations, and celebrations of triumph over enemies. At the height of tribal rivalry, the *Popol Vuh* speaks of the importance of self-defense against a race of canyon people: "Their lineages came to be bled, shot full of arrows at the stake. Their day came to nothing, their heritage came to nothing" (188). The expunging of the enemy's culture, like the flood that overwhelms earth, signifies the worst of God's punishment and a rationalization of imperialism.

In the last centuries of the Mayan Empire, violence becomes the dominant factor in the *Popol Vuh*. After overpopulation, environmental damage, and chronic combat sapped the Mayan empire after A.D. 900, survival involved aggression against rivals and cultic bloodletting, persecution, and sacrifice. The narrative concludes with Spanish invasions and the torture and burning of natives who refuse to convert to Catholicism. Mourning the rise of a Spanish empire in Meso-America, the poet laments cultural annihilation: "This is enough about the being of Quiché, given that there is no longer a place to see it" (198).

By analyzing the details of chronology and genealogy in the text, proponents of Quichéan mythology disproved the contention that Native Americans, unlike European cultures, developed no concept of history or nationalism. In 1999, the Mayan teacher Victor Montejo tackled the problem of ethnic oblivion by composing a children's version of the text, *Popol Vuh: A Sacred Book of the Maya* (1999), an effort to preserve the aboriginal legacy for future generations.

Sources

Joseph, Gilbert Michael, and Timothy J. Henderson. *The Mexico Reader: History, Culture, Politics*. Durham, N.H.: Duke University Press, 2003.

Popol Vuh: The Mayan Book of the Dawn of Life. Translated by Dennis Tedlock. New York: Touchstone Books, 1996.

prayer

Supplications from earth dwellers to divine powers mark the world's earliest literature of empires. Both meaningful and mystical, whether recorded in GREEK DRAMA, the Hindu *Atharva Veda* (Lore of the fire priests, 800 B.C.), the Sufist verse of RUMI, or the scriptures of Abyssinians,

Aztecs, Buddhists, Egyptians, Christians, Jews, Quechuans, and Zoroastrians, expressions of spirituality and confession pervade the human relationship with the unknown. In the Hittite empire of ancient Anatolia (present-day Turkey), from 1460 to 1180 B.C., propitiation of gods at feasts, magic exorcisms, and state cult ceremonies includes blessings on royal brides and grooms, oaths of devotion, chants accompanying libations and sacrifices of oxen on holy altars, intercessory petitions, and thanksgiving for military victory. Recovered clay tablets record straightforward appeals and offerings to the sun deities of the underworld to deflect evil gossip, slander, and curses from enemies. A ruler indicated his humility by kneeling and exclaiming, "Incline your good eyes, lift your thousand eyelashes, and look kindly upon the king" (quoted in Singer 2002, 22). The prayers acknowledged the divine right of kings, which derived solely from the Hittite pantheon, headed by the storm deity Teshuba and his consort Hebut, goddess of the sun.

Babylonian prayers in the Sumero-Akkadian tradition reprised texts calling on the aid of Shamash, the Assyrian god of light and justice. An entreaty for mercy from Prince Kantuzzili from around 1425 B.C. speaks to the sun god, the great judge, of the anguish of a lethal medical problem. The suppliant claims to be "the servant of your body and your soul" and begs absolution of sins (32). Early in his reign, dictating to the court scribe, the boy king Mursili II (ca. 1321–1295 B.C.) composed multiple invocations to the sun god Arinna that called down protection from the epidemic that killed his brother Arnuwanda and asked for victory over Assyrian forces from the Upper Tigris River that were besetting the Hittite realm. To appease the benevolent spirit, Mursili's priest asks that "the sweet odor, the cedar and the oil, summon you" (50). Mursili prayed to Lelwani, queen of the underworld, to cure his wife, Princess Gassuliyawiya, of sickness in exchange for constant devotion and praise to the holy goddess. The emperor boasts, "To you, my goddess, there are temples only in Hatti, but in no other land is there anything for you" (73). The I-thou relationship of a petitioner with the divine emphasizes the sense of fervent communication with invisible celestial powers.

An existential plea recognizes the sins of the fathers as an ongoing curse on humankind. Like the cries of the Hebrew Job, the Hittite suppliant asks if the divine "takes vengeance on his wife, his children, his descendants, his family, his male and female slaves, his cattle and sheep together with his crop? Will he not destroy him utterly?" (quoted in Bryce 2002, 140). Mursili II begs forgiveness for court impiety in past administrations and asks for an assurance of future prosperity and grace. On Mursili's behalf, paid temple reciters entreat the gods to offer the emperor an idyllic afterlife in a meadow, a parallel to the Hebrew Eden in GENESIS (ca. 500 B.C.), the Roman Elysian Fields described in VIRGIL's AENEID (17 B.C.), and the Gardens of Paradise in the KORAN (A.D. 633). The Hittite text seeks an end to struggle in a sunny place where "cows, sheep, horses, and mules graze for him" (183). The subtext indicates the stabilizing influence of herding on nomadic hunter-gatherer clans.

Self-Empowering Invocation

Jewish mysticism, an obscure and controversial branch of ritual that emerged from unwritten Babylonian and Egyptian folklore, relies on the Kabbala (Tradition), a system of thought that employs arcane methods of knowing the infinite. To satisfy curiosity and longing to learn the secrets of nature and creation, early Kabbalists speculated on ecstatic worship and methods of escaping the physical boundaries of the visible world. Despite the danger of damnation, they longed to look God in the face. Because of the dangerous conditions of Jewish residency in hostile or apathetic empires in Babylonia, Syria, Persia, Spain, Rome, and Egypt, Kabbalists paid little heed to the society around them and honored only the power of Yahweh (God). Through specific rabbinic versions of invocations, hymns, cosmology, and written enigmas, the devout opened channels to the god whose image provided the model for humankind. By strengthening their faith, Kabbalists sought to rid themselves of pride and hatred of the rulers who tormented followers of minority religions.

Kabbala was based in oral tradition that was written down in several texts over the centuries. These texts outline hidden links to creation and to marvels and enchantments that unlock the heart and plan of the universe. In Jerusalem, Rabbi Akiba (or Akiva) ben Joseph, a martyr to Roman oppression, produced a work on mysticism, *Hékhalot zutarté* (The smaller book of celestial palaces, ca. A.D. 100), a handbook for the seeker of godly wisdom through human self-empowerment. A subsequent prayer manual, *Sefer yetzirah* (*Book of Creation*, A.D. 200–500), expanded on sacred numerology, formulae, and spells as psychic means of secret communication with God. In A.D. 905, an Egyptian Kabbalist named Saadiah ben-Joseph (882–942) journeyed from Jerusalem to Persia in the Ghaznavid Empire to establish a yeshiva (academy) of disciples. As *goan* (principal) and director of curriculum, he translated the Torah into Arabic, compiled a dictionary, and wrote Kabbalistic texts that legitimized peasant myths about God through scientific law and analysis. Among his most-used works was the *Siddur* (Prayer book, ca. 940), a compendium of invocations, confessions, and thanksgivings that he compiled while living in Baghdad, Syria. His followers researched scholasticism, dream interpretation, confession and atonement, the ascetic lifestyle, charms and magic phrases, and extreme forms of prayer and supplication.

Imperial Prayers

A monument to Japan's Nara culture, the 20-book MANYOSHU (*Ten Thousand Leaves,* ca. 759) includes the works of an ostensible poet laureate, KAKINOMOTO NO HITOMARO. Among the 4,500 verses illustrating courtship protocols, naming taboos, journeys, and life passages, Hitomaro's farewell prayers cover a variety of losses, from a mother's nostalgia for her recently married daughter to a threnody in which parents sorrow over the death of a child lost to plague. In the latter, the speakers describe a ritual plea for a cure before a mirror and futile prostrations on the hearth. Like the disconsolate personal verses on Roman tombstones, the Japanese odes admit that humankind has little choice but to accept suffering and grief. The choice of the mirror and hearth imply that the speaker must look inward for truth and anchor family life to a homesite, an emblem of permanence and protection constructed with human hands rather than a shelter in nature provided by the creator.

Hitomaro's many prayers for travelers stand out as emotive entreaties during separation, especially sea voyages. The Japanese text acknowledges the control of the gods over human events, but the poet feels compelled to plead for the wanderer's safety and fortune. The compulsion to beg for divine intervention pours from the poet's spirit like waves caressing a rocky shore, a cyclical pounding of crags by water. The verse itself becomes a mantra, a verbal amulet rich with empathy for the one who departs from a familiar setting. The traveler conveys his own urge to renew his spirit at mountain passes, geological representations of the cleavage between life and death. As he journeys on, he looks back on a dismaying sight: "My home farther and farther recedes" (*Ten Thousand Leaves* 1981, 81). Such visual images break the continuity of home and realm and emphasize the frail tether that links humans to their clan and motherland.

Another travel poem regresses to old-world superstition for solace on the departure of an imperial ambassador on a mission to the Chinese court. The speaker summons myriad protective spirits and asks "The great deities who dwell / Between heaven and earth / And especially [the god] Okunitama / Of Yamato" to perch on the ship's prow or fly overhead to guide the traveler safely (101). The ritual of summoning protective gods requires that the traveler clap his hands before embarking from Cape Chika for home at Mitsu Harbor in Otomo (present-day Okoyama on the island of Honshu, Japan). With a touch of wishful thinking, the poet envisions the sea journey as being straight as a taut black rope, a hint at the voyager's intent to make no detours with a subtextual linking of the traveler and his home. In the closing lines, the suppliant begs for both luck and a speedy return. The traveler finds comfort in the first sight of the capital city of Nara, a subtle connection between the beneficence of the gods and the sovereignty of the emperor.

Travel prayers favor women's perspectives, especially those from Japan's east coast. Poems by female writers list the wife's obligations to custom—leaving their hair uncombed and floors unswept until the voyager returns. The avoidance of such tasks implies disorder in a household when the husband's absence upsets the domestic balance. A more intimate gesture is the placement of "a sacred *sake* bottle" (189) by the bedside as a plea for the husband's physical and spiritual wholeness. In one of Hitomaro's travel poems, the voyager thanks his wife and parents for observing the appropriate separation ritual. As a romantic gesture, he promises to keep tied the traveling sash that his mate wove him for the trip, a subtle suggestion of sexual fidelity.

Prayer and Nationalism
Supplication on behalf of the state and its rulers is a standard in the literature of empires. The verbal connection between divinity and sovereignty implies heavenly blessing and approval of the state and an appropriate humility in the ruler, who expresses an overt gratitude for the divine right to govern. Models permeate BIOGRAPHY and chronicle—for example, Einhard's memories in *Vita Caroli* (*The Life of Charlemagne*, A.D. 830) of Pope Leo III's crowning of the Carolingian king Charlemagne as the first emperor of the Romans (Holy Roman Emperor) and the blessing of Rodrigo Díaz de Vivar, called El Campeador (the champion) in the Spanish epic *El Cid* (ca. 1150), for defending Iberians against Muslim invaders. During the final decades of a Japanese occupation of Korea that began in the 1870s, the intellectual and modernist author YI KWANGSU (1812–1950) published allegorical fiction and historical works that appeased the ruling government while stirring patriotism in Koreans.

Yi incorporated old-fashioned duty and patriarchy in the nation's first modern novel, *Mujông* (The Heartless, 1917), a bestselling allegory of turning points in Korean history. When the protagonist, Hyông-sik, an instructor in English at a Seoul middle school, proposes liberal Western notions of betrothal to Yong Chae, an obedient traditionalist, she is dumbfounded at the concept of romantic love. Representing an old-fashioned nation faced with an inevitable advance into modernism, she turns to prayer to ease their estrangement. She pleads for forgiveness, guidance, and defense from temptation and concludes, "Make me love my husband with all my heart" (Yi 1990, 7). Through the couple's contretemps, Yi demonstrates an element of Confucian self-discipline in the bride-to-be, who has no expectation of immediate affection for the groom, a symbolic situation that Koreans face as

captives of imperial Japan. Hyông-sik, a modernist, astounds his male friend by declaring that he "cannot deny his wife's freedom to do as she wishes (8)," a libertarian view imbued with the author's fervor for civil rights.

Sources
Bryce, Trevor. *Life and Society in the Hittite World.* Oxford: Oxford University Press, 2002.

Plutschow, Herbert E. *Chaos and Cosmos: Ritual in Early and Medieval Japanese Literature.* Amsterdam: Brill, 1990.

Roberts, Elizabeth, and Elias Amidon, eds. *Earth Prayers from Around the World.* San Francisco: HarperSanFrancisco, 1991.

Singer, Itamar. *Hittite Prayers.* Amsterdam: Brill, 2002.

The Ten Thousand Leaves. Translated by Ian Hideo Levy. Princeton, N.J.: Princeton University Press, 1981.

Yi Kwang-su. *Modern Korean Literature: An Anthology.* Translated by Peter H. Lee. Honolulu: University of Hawaii Press, 1990.

Prince, Mary (1788–ca. 1833) *Bermudian autobiographer*

Mary Prince, a slave from Brackish Pond in the British crown colony of Bermuda, composed England's first AUTOBIOGRAPHY of a black female. Until her liberation in England, she was the property of five different owners. The daughter of a domestic and a sawyer, she passed in infancy into servitude to Betsey Williams and, 12 years later, to Captain John Ingham and Mary Spencer Ingham at Spanish Point. To ridicule her lowly station, they called her "Mary, Princess of Wales." Of the sadism of her master and jealous mistress, Prince declared, "The stones and timbers were the best things in [the house]; they were not so hard as the hearts of their owners" (Prince 1831, 54). In despair, Prince wished to die rather than suffer "the whip, the rope, and the cow-skin" (59). The testimonial impressed on readers the daily threat and execution of punishments on top of wounds still fresh from previous lashings.

At age 18, Prince suffered more terrifying displacement. Under new ownership, she joined the rakers at the saltworks on Grand Turk in the Caicos Islands, from which the English extracted up to 75 shiploads of salt annually. General maltreatment and the labor of breaking up coral and tufa and diving for stones elicited her sympathy for other drudges: "In telling my own sorrows, I cannot pass by those of my fellow slaves" (62). Of her misery, she explained that boils on her feet impeded her wheeling of a barrow through sand, which so incensed the overseer that he tormented her with whippings. Out of duty to the slave, she insisted on compiling the narrative, which exonerates the British for their ignorance of slave torments. Her autobiography also describes old Daniel, an elderly cripple whom the master strips, beats with a briar, then soaks in saltwater until the victim writhes like a worm. With naive faith in human benevolence, she desires "all the good people in England to know that they may break our chains, and set us free" (11).

By 1818, under the slave name Molly Wood, Prince moved south to Antigua in the Leeward Islands to work as a nanny and laundress for the planter John Wood, who rescued her from Robert Darrell, a sexual predator. At Spring Gardens, she learned to read at the Moravian Church, and in 1826, she married Daniel Jones, a widowed freedman, woodworker, and cooper. In 1828, bent with arthritis at age 40, she served a master in Leigh Street in London, until she escaped to a Moravian church a few weeks later. In 1831, with the aid of Thomas Pringle, secretary of the Anti-Slavery Society, she compiled *The History of Mary Prince, a West Indian Slave,* transcribed by stenographer Susanna Strickland. Rather than exploit the pose of the female victim, the narrative displays dignity and pride in accomplishment and asserts, "Oh the Buckra people who keep slaves think that black people are like cattle" (71). Leading to three unsuccessful lawsuits against the publisher and author, Prince's autobiography created a sensation and proved critical in the dispute between proslavery factions and the emancipation movement. The Slavery Abolition Act was passed in 1833, the year in which Mary Prince disappears from history.

Sources

Ferguson, Moira. *Subject to Others: British Women Writers and Colonial Slavery, 1670–1834.* New York: Routledge, 1992.

Prince, Mary. *The History of Mary Prince, a West Indian Slave.* London: F. Westley and A. H. Davis, 1831.

Prince, Nancy Gardner (1799–ca. 1856)
American ethnographer and evangelist

Nancy Gardner Prince, an ethnographer and American Baptist preacher, wrote an AUTOBIOGRAPHY and a TRAVELOGUE of her adventures in Russia and the West Indies. A freeborn native of Newburyport, Massachusetts, she was the granddaughter of a female Indian captive and of Tobias "Backus" Wornton of Gloucester, a slave kidnapped from Africa who served in the Continental Army in 1775 at the battle of Bunker Hill. After her marriage in 1824 to Nero Prince, a black cook, the pair sailed to Copenhagen, Denmark, and traveled overland to St. Petersburg, Russia, where her husband became a footman or guard at the royal palace. According to Nancy's travelogue, *A Narrative of the Life and Travels of Mrs. Nancy Prince* (1850), Russians adored the imperial family, Czar Alexander I and Czarina Elizabeth Alexeyevna. When a member of royalty died, "the criminals that have rebelled against the imperial family are placed in cells, thus combining the prison and the tomb; and in sailing by, these miserable creatures are exposed to the careless gaze of unfeeling observers" (Prince 1850, 26). Among the prisoners suffering flogging and exile to Siberia were the fomenters of the Decembrist Revolt on December 14, 1825. Nancy Prince's attempts to establish an orphanage and school in St. Petersburg proved unworkable. A similar project in Boston for black foundlings also failed.

In 1833, Prince returned to the United States, but her husband died before he could join her. Widowed at age 41, Prince, like the nurse-herbalist MARY JANE SEACOLE in the Crimea, became an anomaly—a free black female agent. Backed by white philanthropists, she targeted the West Indies as fertile ground for missionary work. A self-reliant traveler and social dissident, she was outraged by imperial neglect of islanders. She visited Jamaica to encourage ethnic pride among former slaves. In a candid view of the Kingston market, she found black women dependent on weaving straw bags and hats and entering disastrous competitions to keep from starving. Of the bargaining with the destitute of her own race, she complained about the adversarial relationship forced by black women's penury in the Western Hemisphere: "We are not particularly women anymore; we are parties to a transaction designed to set us against each other" (40–41).

Prince reported an American prejudice that "emancipation has been of no benefit to you; I wish to inform myself of the truth respecting you, and give a true account on my return" (50). She found American immigrants discontented in the Caribbean and ex-slaves illiterate and underpaid. Concerning disgruntled maroons, slaves from Sierra Leone, Prince cited the plan of Queen Victoria to resettle them in Jamaica. While laboring as a volunteer settlement worker, Prince formed a negative opinion of maroons as "full of deceit and lies, this is the fruits of slavery, it makes master and slaves knaves" (62). On a disastrous return trip to New York, diverted by storm to Key West and New Orleans, she commiserated with gangs of southern slaves as "We poor blacks" (62). Prince's writing is a firsthand account of the problems that ensued from slavery even after its laudable abolition by the British.

Sources

McLeod, Jacqueline. *Crossing Boundaries: Comparative History of Black People in Diaspora.* Bloomington: Indiana University Press, 2001.

Prince, Nancy. *A Narrative of the Life and Travels of Mrs. Nancy Prince.* Boston: Wm. A. Hall, 1850.

Scott, Jamie S., and Paul Simpson-Housley, eds. *Mapping the Sacred: Religion, Geography and Postcolonial Literature.* Amsterdam: Rodopi, 2001.

Prince, The   See MACHIAVELLI, NICCOLÒ.

prison literature

The literature of empire is replete with coercion, house arrest, concentration camps, atrocities, and imprisonment. Examples span the centuries, from the New Testament APOCALYPSE literature of the New Testament's Revelation (A.D. 95), reputedly written by John the Divine in a cell on Patmos island, to the Carthaginian apologist TERTULLIAN's consolation *Ad martyras* (To the martyrs, A.D. 197) and LEO TOLSTOY's "A Prisoner in the Caucasus" (1872). Incarceration scenarios appear in many genres, including the Scottish explorer Mungo Park's TRAVELOGUE *Travels in the Interior Districts of Africa* (1799); the Russian author FYODOR DOSTOYEVSKY's social novels *The House of the Dead* (1862) and *Buried Alive; or, Ten Years of Penal Servitude in Siberia* (1881); and Sir ARTHUR CONAN DOYLE's Sherlock Holmes mystery *The Sign of Four* (1890), which features a lockup in Agra, India. For the surrealist Franz Kafka (1883–1924), a writer in Prague during the Austro-Hungarian Empire, cell confinement seemed less frightening than a grotesque machine that inscribed the court's judgment on the defendant's body, a GOTHIC image from *In the Penal Colony* (1919) that prophesies the perverted science of Adolf Hitler's war machine. The orator Emma Goldman, an exile from the United States, published *My Further Disillusionment in Russia* (1924) after viewing the squalor and hopelessness of Russian prisons, particularly the concentration camp at Ryazan southeast of Moscow. Such incarceration ended her illusions about Russia as a workers' haven replacing the Romanov dynasty.

The Trinidadian poet and satirist Alfred Hamilton Cruickshank (1862–1927) viewed colonialism in the islands as a form of incarceration. He shocked British sensibilities in 1933 with a rebuke to the abolitionists who congratulated themselves for ending slavery in the West Indies. The poet insisted that the aftermath of slavery was still an issue: "Upon our limbs / Still hang the shackles, clanking, hellish hymns / To greedy Mammon, whom our masters serve on bended knee" (quoted in Neptune 2007, 33). From black work songs, he simulated rhythms and phrasing for "The Convict Song" in *Poetry: Poems in All Moods* (1937), an androcentric plaint against "manhood draining" that turns a number of male inmates into hardened, hate-filled anti-imperialists (Burnett, 1986, 138).

World War II Prisoners of War

In 1950, the British writer Nevil Shute (1899–1960) reflected on Japanese militarism in a diary novel, *A Town Like Alice.* Set in the British colony of Malaya, the book's historical basis is the 1,200-mile forced march of 80 Dutch residents of the Dutch East

Indies from Padang around Sumatra. The story focuses on the survivalism of the heroine Jean Paget after the Japanese invasion of Malaya. Infiltration by the enemy at first seems unlikely: "Even when the Japanese landed in the north of Malaya there was little thought of danger in Kuala Lumpur" (Shute 2002, 35). The Japanese make it clear there is little hope of mercy for the 17 surviving women: "You do good things, obedience to orders, you will receive good from Japanese soldiers. You do bad things, you will be shot directly" (40). From the prison staff, inmates learn that "all prisoners are disgraceful and dishonourable creatures in the eyes of the Japanese" (86). Guards express their contempt with callous treatment, terrorism, and deprivation of food, beds, and drugs. The author notes a factor common in prison literature: "Men and women who are in great and prolonged distress and forced into an entirely novel way of life . . . frequently develop curious mental traits" (98), including religious thoughts and fantasies of home and family. To the surprise of a Japanese sergeant, the women prisoners assist him after he falls ill with fever by carrying his load, an act of compassion derived from common humanity.

Throughout the narrative, dual threads of brutality and romance link Paget with Sergeant Joe "Ringer" Harman, an Aussie soldier and would-be rescuer. He suffers crucifixion at Kuantan for aiding the female prisoners by providing stolen chickens, Lifebuoy soap, bandages, splints, and antidotes for dysentery. Before her journey to Kota Bharu on the northern Pacific coast of Malaya, Jean recalls Japanese retaliation: "They nailed his hands to a tree, and beat him to death. They kept us there and made us look on while they did it" (95). Two film versions of A Town Like Alice recreated the concentration camp atmosphere and the secularized image of the prisoner of war as a Christ figure: a 1956 edition, starring Virginia McKenna and Peter Finch, and an Australian made-for-TV reprise in 1981, pairing Helen Morse with Bryan Brown.

A gripping fictional account of Japanese wartime cruelty was Pierre Boulle's World War II novella Le Pont de la rivière Kwai (The Bridge over the River Kwai, 1952), winner of the Prix Sainte-Beuve. It was appreciated for its depiction of the contrast between the national pride and imperial styles of Great Britain and Japan, symbolized by the inter-

action between the impeccably dignified Colonel Nicholson and the sadistic Colonel Saito, a minor dictator who knows that "a high-level Japanese inspection was imminent" (Boulle 1954, 50). A member of the French Resistance in Burma, China, and French Indochina, Boulle wrote from memories of capture and forced labor superintended by the Vichy French. He had languished in a Saigon prison during the bridging of the Mekong River for the 258-mile Burma Railway between Bangkok, Thailand, and Rangoon, Burma. He knew from personal acquaintance with the enemy the pride of a man like Saito, who resents his job for keeping him out of front-line action and from the glories of imperial victory.

Like Nevil Shute, Boulle emphasized the communal mentality of the shared miseries of prisoners of war. The novel tells of the 500 inmates as being one part of the "sixty thousand English, Australians, Dutch, and Americans assembled in several groups in one of the most uncivilized corners of the earth, the jungle of Burma and Siam" (10), a milieu that mirrors the barbarity of the Japanese army. Balancing themes of discipline and destruction, Colonel Nicholson finds himself torn between setting an example of steadfastness under pressure and outfoxing the Japanese by sabotaging the bridge that has cost the prisoners their energy and health. In the rush to complete construction, he worries about the growing effects of beri-beri, dysentery, malaria, and slow starvation: "Bit by bit, day by day, hour by hour, some of the living substance of each prisoner came apart from its individual organism to be swallowed up in the anonymous material universe" (141). Wartime decision making requires an assessment of possible gain against probable loss—how much work completed on the bridge versus how many lives ruined. David Lean's 1957 film version, The Bridge on the River Kwai, won an Academy Award for screenplay and a second Oscar for Alec Guinness, who played Colonel Nicholson opposite Sessue Hayakawa as Colonel Saito.

Soviet Torments

The chronicler of prison torments in Soviet Russia, Aleksandr Isayevich Solzhenitsyn (1918–2008) earned the 1970 Nobel Prize in literature for his accounts of imperial brutality. While serving in the Russian army in East Prussia in February 1945, he posted a criticism of the Soviet dictator Joseph Stalin in a letter that censors intercepted. This resulted in Solzhenitsyn's arrest, interrogation, and beating at Lubyanka prison, headquarters of the KGB, the Soviet secret police. After his trial in absentia, his incarceration began at a labor camp where he worked as an installer of parquet floors and concluded with a three-year carpentry and masonry detail in 1953 at Ekibastuz in Kazakhstan.

The misery of subfreezing weather, whiteouts, and a starvation diet of bread and gruel pervades Solzhenitsyn's fictional prison memoir *One Day in the Life of Ivan Denisovich* (1962), which he first published in the Soviet journal *Novy Mir* (New world). The narrative voices the unrest resulting from suppression of civil rights under Stalin, a vain, emotional tyrant given to paranoid spying, forced confessions, petty vengeance, terrorism, meaningless hearings, and capricious executions. Victims vanish into gulags, an acronym for the government agency that ran remote lumber and mining camps reserved for *zeks* (political dissidents). Through the horrifying detail of the life of inmate Ivan Denisovich Shukhov, the author describes work-gang sufferings from scurvy, overwork, and callous treatment. Aiming machine guns at prisoners' heads, guards order the men to stand bootless on frozen ground. The text enumerates repetitive head counts and outdoor body searches for hidden food, civilian clothes, and contraband letters: "When it was freezing, the frisking routine was not so tough in the morning—though it still was in the evening" (Solzhenitsyn 1963, 35). Inmate complaints of violations of the criminal code prove unwise. Old timers learn to cope, hiding their trowels from confiscation, cadging treats and cigarettes, and retreating to the infirmary to recover from fever and aching muscles. The author salutes the typical survivor for endurance: "His mind was set on one thing—never to give in" (172).

Solzhenitsyn reiterated his charges against Stalin in *The First Circle* (1968), an exposé of gulag conditions at a technical work camp, the subject of a 1973 Polish film and television miniseries in 1991 and 2007, starring F. Murray Abraham as Stalin. In 1973, Solzhenitsyn returned to prison fiction with his satiric masterwork *The Gulag Archipelago*,

a three-volume work banned in the Soviet Union until 1989. The narrative charges dictator Vladimir Lenin with using punitive work camps as sources of slave labor, the backbone of the Russian public works system. Solzhenitsyn wrests humor from the terrain of the mother country, which was "not slow to discover exile. . . . Our great spaces gave their blessing—Siberia was ours already" (Solzhenitsyn 2007, 421). Within such prison microcosms, the ferment of barrack conspiracies, strikes, and internal banishment creates a pervasive hopelessness and despair for a normal life.

Prison in Postcolonial Africa

In Nigeria, the poet and playwright Wole Soyinka (b. 1934), a Yoruban from the southwestern coastal town of Abeokuta, wrote from a Kaduna prison cell of the plight of postcolonial Africans. He was 26 years old when his nation won independence from the British Empire. In the political turmoil after independence, he tried to negotiate peace within warring tribes and to protest fraud in a radio broadcast. During 22 months of solitary confinement on a charge of spying from 1967 to 1969, like Shukov in Solzhenitsyn's *One Day in the Life of Ivan Denisovich*, he developed cunning skills of self-preservation and a loathing for the "power prostitutes," the vicious leaders who sought to rule Nigeria by force (Soyinka 1988, 36). To issue *Poems from Prison* (1969), he scribbled intertextual lines on the pages of seven smuggled books. He continued baiting his warders with verse in *A Shuttle in the Crypt* (1972), picturing civil war as a crucible "to force impurities in nationweal / Belly-up, heat-drawn by fires / of truth" (Soyinka 1972, 6). He lionizes the courage of the rebel as a "passive valour," a simmering nemesis awaiting release from prison (21). Despite Odyssean hardships, the oppressed plot "burnt offerings" to reinvigorate Nigeria's "violated visions" (89). In *The Man Died: Prison Notes of Wole Soyinka* (1972), he outlines his way of coping with filth, odors, and treachery. He does so through mental disengagement: "Reality is killed and buried with memories of the past" (Soyinka 1988, 128). At a time when he wants to write about the collective plight of postcolonial peoples, he voices outrage at arbitrary isolation, degradation, and repression. He states his object to be a "denunciation of war . . . to repudiate and end both the secession of Biafra, and the genocide-consolidated dictatorship of the army," which he vilifies as an "anti-human barrier" (19). Nigerian authorities banned his memoir because of its demand for full disclosure of government documents.

In *Mandela's Earth and Other Poems* (1988), Soyinka sought a renewal of what he called "race retrieval" from the "life-usurpers" by mocking the elaborate protocols of military regimes. By relating the god Ogun and the Zulu hero Shaka to 20th-century conflicts, he reminds the world of "our pride once boasted empires / Kings and nation builders" and of the power of defiance embodied by imprisoned South African freedom fighter Nelson Mandela, "a black, unwilling Christ" (Soyinka 1989, 15, 1). Soyinka's poems nominate prisoners of conscience as martyrs for enduring sleep deprivation, starvation, shackling in an upright position, lunacy wards, slow-acting poison, and electric shocks to the genitals. Through verse, he recounts his own tenuous grip on sanity during a hunger strike and his resolve to remain whole, physically and mentally. For his humanism, in 1986, Wole Soyinka became the first African to receive the Nobel Prize in literature. During four years of self-imposed exile from his homeland, he returned to the issues of administrative corruption and illicit jailing and torture in *The Open Sore of a Continent; A Personal Narrative of the Nigerian Crisis* (1996) and its sequel, *The Burden of Memory, the Muse of Forgiveness* (1998).

Sources

Boulle, Pierre. *The Bridge over the River Kwai.* Translated by Xan Fielding. New York: Bantam, 1954.

Burnett, Paula, ed. *The Penguin Book of Caribbean Verse.* Middlesex, U.K..: Viking Penguin, 1986.

Jeyifo, Biodun, ed. *Perspectives on Wole Soyinka: Freedom and Complexity.* Jackson: University Press of Mississippi, 2001.

Kato, Megumi. "Typical Evil? The Japanese Represented in Australian War Writings." In *Beyond Good and Evil?: Essays on the Literature and Culture of the Asia-Pacific Region,* edited by Dennis Haskell, Megan McKinlay, and Pamina Rich, 65–78. Claremont: University of West Australia Press, 2006.

Neptune, Harvey R. *Caliban and the Yankees: Trinidad and the United States Occupation.* Chapel Hill: University of North Carolina Press, 2007.

Shute, Nevil. *A Town Like Alice.* Callington, U.K.: House of Stratus, 2002.

Solzhenitsyn, Aleksandr. *The Gulag Archipelago 1918–1956.* New York: Harper Perennial, 2007.

———. *One Day in the Life of Ivan Denisovich.* Translated by Max Hayward and Ronald Hingley. New York: Bantam, 1963.

Soyinka, Wole. *Mandela's Earth and Other Poems.* Ibadan, Nigeria: Fountain, 1989.

———. *The Man Died: The Prison Notes of Wole Soyinka.* New York: Noonday, 1988.

———. *A Shuttle in the Crypt.* London: Methuen, 1972.

Procopius (ca. A.D. 490–ca. 563) *Byzantine historian*

As an attorney and military aide to the Byzantine general Flavius Belisarius, Procopius of Caesarea (present-day Israel) reported accounts of wars against Goths, Ostrogoths, Persians, and Vandals. He gained a knowledge of the politics of Italy, North Africa, Persia, and Sicily from some 15 years of military campaigns. In retirement, in his early 50s, he served Constantinople as prefect or security officer. In the style of the Greek historians HERODOTUS and THUCYDIDES, he recorded in classic Attic Greek the details of the Nika riots and massacre at the Hippodrome in A.D. 532; the fall of Carthage (present-day Tunis, Tunisia) in 533; the capture of Rome from the Goths in 538; and the plague of 542, which infected the Eastern Roman Emperor Justinian I. In the next decade, Procopius completed the *Anecdota* or *Historia arcana* (*Secret History,* ca. A.D. 550), an exposé of the court intrigues of Belisarius and his wife Antonina and a model of invective directed at the emperor and his wife, the Empress Theodora. Beyond the maligning of Belisarius as henpecked and the pornographic details of Theodora's sexual excesses, the historian focuses on the emperor's ineptness and conceit. Procopius dares to charge, "Of the forcible seizure of property and the murder of his subjects [Justinian] could never have enough" (Procopius 1966, 94). To maintain the flow of tribute, the emperor fomented foreign wars, though their cost weakened his empire.

His next compendium earned Procopius the title of leading Byzantine historian. In the opening chapter of an eight-volume history, *De bellis* (On the wars, A.D. 552), the text characterizes Justin's seizure of the empire by "forcing aside all the kinsmen of [the former Emperor] Anastasius, although they were numerous and also very distinguished" (Procopius 1914, 24). When the business of governing fell to Justin's nephew, Justinian I, Procopius notes that pestilence bore political implications for the inexperienced ruler: "Work of every description ceased, and all the trades were abandoned by the artisans" (109). In more upbeat passages, the historian returns to his first love, the siege tactics, tunneling, and undermining that marked the Roman army corps of engineers as the world's most efficient. The narrative outlines the destruction of King Totila of Treviso, Italy, and his Ostrogoths by the 74-year-old Armenian-Roman general Narses and his force of Armenian, German, Hun, and Slavic mercenaries. For background, Procopius juxtaposes physical and geographic details with wise observations and instructive passages written in his own individual style.

A peacetime project, the six-volume *De aedificiis* (On buildings, A.D. 561), a panegyric on civic and church projects, covers architect Anthemius of Tralles's creation of the Hagia Sophia, the architectural jewel of the Eastern Roman Empire. A more amenable tone credits God with inspiring the floor plan and exalts Justinian for organizing construction crews and for employing Anthemius and a deputy designer, Isidorus of Milesia. Their work impresses Procopius as "a most glorious spectacle, extraordinary to those who beheld it, and altogether incredible" for its dome and the interior lighting of sacred mysteries (Procopius 2004, 6). The structure set the model for basilicas and sanctuaries that Justinian erected throughout the empire to honor the Virgin Mary. Byzantine liturgy and anthems by Romanos the Hymnographer assimilate Christian worship with exaltation of the emperor himself, whom Christ protects and blesses. Procopius's comment on church music implies that Romans furthered the concept of the divine right of kings.

Sources

Cameron, Averil. *Procopius and the Sixth Century.* New York: Routledge, 1996.

Procopius. *History of the Wars.* Translated by H. B. Dewing. London: Heinemann, 1914.

———. *Of the Buildings of Justinian.* Boston: Adament Media, 2004.

———. *The Secret History.* Translated by Geoffrey Arthur Williamson. London: Penguin, 1966.

Propertius, Sextus (ca. 50–15 B.C.) *Roman elegist*

An enthusiastic poet and critic during Rome's golden age of literature (83 B.C.–A.D. 17), Sextus Propertius wrote elegies regretting the fall of the Roman Republic and the rise of Caesar Augustus's empire. Propertius retained much of the rural perspective he gained in early childhood on his family estate at Mevania near Assisi in Umbria. Reared in Rome from age 10 by his widowed mother, he received a good education and made friends among the privileged class. He was an impressionable six-year-old when conspirators stabbed Julius Caesar in the Senate chamber. Propertius retained a zeal for republicanism and a horror of civil war, which threw Rome and its provinces into turmoil for 17 years. In his late teens, he began writing reflective verses on the rise of Augustus from Caesar's nephew and heir to *princeps* (first man), the sole ruler of Rome. At a height of military opportunity for the enlistee, in the 92 poems of his four-book *Carmina* (*Elegies*, 15 B.C.), Propertius declared himself "ill-equipped for glory or for arms" (Propertius 1996, 9), a distaste he shared with the contemporary poets HORACE and TIBULLUS.

After the deaths of Cleopatra and Mark Antony 11 days apart in August 30 B.C., Propertius abstained from public adulation of Augustus, the murderer of Cleopatra's son Caesarion. In a subdued elegy, the poet ventured a muted criticism of imperialism: "Caesar is great in war, but conquered nations mean nothing in love" (34). The 10th poem of the second book of *Carmina* launches into sarcasm at the larger-than-life statue of Augustus, which is too tall for the poet to reach with garlands. A more desultory praise colors the fourth elegy in the third book, in which the poet portrays himself in the crowd on the Sacred Way while viewing "Caesar's axles heavy-laden with spoil and his horses often halted at the mob's cheers" (76). Again, Propertius applies visual perspective to place him at ground level looking up at an oversized ruler.

In detailed surveys of the city skyline, the poet criticized imperial finery and flashy building projects, a palpable form of imperial self-adulation. He turned the myth of Tarpeia, betrayer of the Roman Citadel during the Sabine War (750 B.C.), into a cautionary tale to remind Rome that rot from within exacts a terrible punishment. In "Luxury Is Destroying Rome," his 13th elegy in the third book, he abandons tentative criticism to confront the greed and venality that Roman courtiers manifested under Augustus. Plutocrats wealthy from civil war and property confiscations relax with showy extravagance; their ostentation ranges from pomades to purple dyed robes and vices from impiety to public lewdness. Injustice reigns in courts where corruption buys judges. Echoing Tibullus's lore of pastoral retreats, the poet repines, "Lucky of old the country youth, living in peace" (89). With bold defiance, Propertius reproaches his proud homeland for rotting away under prosperity, but he predicts that, like the prophecies of Cassandra, his scolding will go unheeded.

Sources

Propertius. *The Poems.* Translated by Guy Lee. Oxford: Oxford University Press, 1996.

Welch, Tara S. *The Elegiac Cityscape: Propertius and the Meaning of Roman Monuments.* Columbus: Ohio State University Press, 2005.

prophecy

A significant element in epics, history, and polemics, predictions of future events expressed in such genres as APOCALYPSE and VISIONARY LITERATURE exemplify the value to rulers of those who can foretell the future. Literary accounts of prophecies go back to the Chinese I CHING (1144 B.C.), the Carthaginian apologist TERTULLIAN's *Apologeticus* (*The Apology,* ca. A.D. 198), and the Yiddish folklore of ISAAC BASHEVIS SINGER. The stereotype of the seer as a source of hope and promise emerges often in the literature of empire, including the Hebrew CREATION LORE in GENESIS (ca. 500 B.C.), Malian heroics in *Sundiata: An Epic of Old Mali* (ca. 1255), the Qing dynasty in Cao Xueqin's novel DREAM OF THE RED CHAMBER (1791), the anonymous Hawaiian romance *Laieikawai* (1863),

and King David Kalakaua's *The Legends and Myths of Hawaii* (1888), a collection of folklore from prehistoric Oceania. A poignant model, the *Aubin Codex,* written in 1576 and published in 1867, contains the forecasts of the Dominican monk and translator Diego Durán that Spanish conquistadores will overwhelm the Aztec empire in unparalleled carnage. A similar volume, *Royal Commentaries of the Incas and General History of Peru* (1617), by GARCILASO DE LA VEGA describes a harbinger of the downfall of Cuzco, Peru, at the hands of Spanish adventurers.

The scriptural book of 1 Samuel (ca. 920 B.C.) places the priest Eli in an intimate scene at the temple of Shiloh (north of present-day Beit-El, Israel). Oblivious to Eli's presence, Hannah, in "bitterness of soul" (1 Samuel 1:10), prays directly to the Almighty for an end to her barren state. The priest Eli implies a positive answer to her plea with a simple benediction, "Go in peace" (1 Samuel 1:17). After his foretelling comes true with the birth of a son, Hannah acknowledges the future Israelite leader by naming him Samuel, meaning "God has heard." Prefiguring the Magnificat (Luke 1:46–55), the Virgin Mary's New Testament canticle honoring her cousin Elizabeth's begetting of John the Baptist, Hannah's song blends the elements of the Te Deum with an affirmation that God is capable of remedying the misfortune of individuals. Of the fall of empires, she sings, "The bows of the mighty men are broken and they that stumbled are girded with strength" (1 Samuel 2:4). The episode elevates Samuel to a supreme rabbinical role in Israel involving the anointing of the empire's first kings, Saul and David, who established his capital at Jerusalem.

Prophecy and the Holocaust

Between the late 19th and early 20th centuries, literary prophecy, such as the Russian poet Anna Akhmatova's "Petrogard, 1919," corroborated citizens' apprehensions about global instability. A contemporary of the Czech PROTEST poet Rainer Maria Rilke, the author Franz Kafka (1883–1924), born in Czechoslovakia and writing in German, sensed the future reintegration that awaited Europe as it shook off outworn empires and entered the modern age. He turned to existentialism and surrealism to describe the individual's entanglement in central European politics. A citizen of Prague in the Austro-Hungarian Empire, Kafka worked at an Italian insurance agency while writing tortured fiction about bureaucracy and the decline of citizens' rights under the Emperor Franz Joseph. For material, in 1915, Kafka drew on the scarcity of commodities under the Hapsburgs and the dominance of the black market during a winter famine. Looming in the background, the Russian occupation force, like vultures, patrolled Bohemia's borders.

In 1917, Kafka viewed the collapse of the Russian and Austro-Hungarian Empires through a dual perspective, that of an alienated Jew and a tuberculosis patient awaiting death. His loathing of dehumanization overwhelms the narrative of *Der Verwandlung* (*The Metamorphosis*, 1915), in which the protagonist, Gregor Samsa, a low-level clerk, changes overnight into a giant insect, a symbol of helplessness and lost humanity. A more chilling view of incarceration and the grotesque, the short story *In der Strafkolonie* ("In the Penal Colony, 1919"), introduces a device that inscribes the court's judgment on the defendant's body. The mechanization of judgment foresees control of humanity by malignant technology, a theme dominating the works of science-fiction writers such as Arthur C. Clarke, Robert A. Heinlein, Isaac Asimov, and Ray Bradbury a half century later.

Two of Kafka's protagonists, K. in *The Trial* (1925) and Josef K. in *The Castle* (1926), portray the victimization of ordinary people by heartless, largely invisible governmental powers. An artist's summation in *The Trial*, which opens with impersonal passive verbs, implies the Byzantine maze of bureaucracy: "The rules for painting the various levels of officials are so numerous, so varied, and above all so secret, that they simply aren't known beyond certain families" (Kafka 1999, 151). In *The Castle*, the narrative describes an atmosphere of suspicion, paranoia, and retribution where simple questions risk "inadvertently breaking some unknown rules" (Kafka 1998, 182). Kafka's method of incorporating eerie, unforeseen twists of fate added the term *Kafkaesque* to the English language, meaning "nightmarishly illogical," a fair summation of the coming GENOCIDE of the Holocaust. His warning to his readers of totalitarianism proved prescient, prophesying the rise of Adolf Hitler's SS in the

1930s and the Nazi regime in the early 1940s, when the lethal gas Zyklon B provided the "final solution" to unwanted citizens and gas ovens disposed of remains. Kafka's own three sisters languished in the Łódź ghetto and died in death camps.

In their illogical dreamscapes and scenarios of impersonal torment to the individual, Kafka's writings mirrored the shift in literary forebodings toward the surreal evil of the future. An admirer of Kafka, Anna Akhmatova, echoed the persecution of citizens in her play *Prologue: A Dream within a Dream* (1923). In her struggle to survive the purges, insane asylums, and gulags of Soviet dictator Josef Stalin, she acknowledged Kafka's authenticity as a prophet of modern history, and art. His works also influenced the Holocaust writings of ELIE WIESEL and MERVYN PEAKE and the Australian FRONTIER LITERATURE of PETER CAREY.

Sources

Kafka, Franz. *The Castle*. Translated by Harmon. New York: Schocken, 1998.
———. *The Trial*. Translated by Breon Mitchell. New York: Schocken, 1999.
Holy Bible. Iowa Falls, Iowa: World Bible Publishers, 1986.
Stach, Reiner. *Kafka: The Decisive Years*. Translated by Shelley Frisch. New York: Harcourt, 2005.
Tsumara, David Toshio. *The First Book of Samuel*. Grand Rapids, Mich.: Eerdmans, 2007.

protest literature

The literature of empire owes much of its potency and initiative to protesters of tyranny, a fitting description of the Russian-American immigrant author Mary Antin, German theologian DIETRICH BONHOEFFER, anti-Nazi polemist SIGRID UNDSET, Martinican dramatist Aimé Césaire, Cuban libertarian JOSÉ MARTI, and antistate Russian poet YEVGENY YEVTUSHENKO. In the eras of Asian despotism, protest required subtle phrasing, for example, the esoteric musings of the fourth-century Chinese poet TAO QIAN, a court expatriate during the Eastern Jin dynasty. In the 20-book MANYOSHU (*Ten Thousand Leaves*, ca. 759), the oldest imperial verse collection from Japan's Nara Empire, YAMANOUE NO OKURA created a two-part peasant dialogue. Composed around 732, the elegies "A Question by a Poor Villager" and "A Reply by a Man in Destitute Poverty" lament hard times that reduce villagers to cold hearths and illness for young and old. Stalking the poor are hunger, epidemic plague, and the imperial tax collector. The indirect denunciation typifies Japanese protest writings, which made their case without vilifying Emperor Shomu, whom patriots revered like a deity.

A fervent anti-British propagandist, playwright, and chronicler of the Massachusetts Colony, Mercy Otis Warren (1728–1814) ridiculed King George III's representatives with allegorical SATIRE. Homeschooled with her brother James in Latin, French, and English classics, she later studied the collapse of the Roman Empire in the first volume of the English writer Edward Gibbon's *The History of the Decline and Fall of the Roman Empire* (1776) and observed the ongoing efforts of the British and French to exploit the New World. In 1754, she wed a merchant (who later become a politician) and settled on a farm along the Eel River at Plymouth to raise their five sons. After launching a popular salon, she joined the colonial independence movement; networked with other revolutionary wives, including Abigail Adams and Martha Washington; and debated politics with prominent patriots such as Samuel Adams, John Hancock, Patrick Henry, and Thomas Jefferson. Anonymously, she produced pamphlets that circulated beyond America to Great Britain and Europe.

In two plays, serialized in the *Boston Gazette* and the *Massachusetts Spy*, Warren used her pen as a liberating force. Her paired tragedies, *The Adulateur* (1772) and *The Defeat* (1773), mimicked Governor Thomas Hutchinson in the pomposity and short-sightedness of the fictional Rapatio, governor of Servia. A year later, *The Blockheads: or, The Affrighted Officers, a Farce* (1774), mocked royal appointees, naming them Dapper, Dupe, Meagre, Paunch, Puff, Shallow, Simple, and Surly. Shortly before the battle of Lexington, fought on April 19, 1775, Warren published *The Group*, a salute to the Boston Tea Party that ridiculed the Crown for its inept administration of the colonies through royal stamp agents. The prologue anticipates the triumph of rebels to "dash the proud Gamester from his gilded car," a gibe at King George and his entourage, whom she lumps into the company of "court syco-phants, hungry harpies, and unprincipled danglers" from "blunderland" poised over Massachusetts like biblical locusts (Warren 1775, 1).

In postcolonial Massachusetts, the playwright altered her anti-British agitation to demands for civil rights and women's equality, the subject of her farce *The Motley Assembly* (1779) and a treatise, *Observations on the New Constitution, and on the Federal and State Conventions* (1788). She honored her hero, President Washington, as the dedicatee of *Poems, Dramatic and Miscellaneous* (1790). Among the plays in the collection, she included *The Sack of Rome* (1790) and *The Ladies of Castile* (1790), the latter set during the rule of Holy Roman Emperor Charles V and issued at the urging of Abigail Adams. Warren's preface salutes "principles that instigated their patriots, and glories in the characters of their heroes, whose valour completed a revolution that will be the wonder of ages" (Warren 1790, 100). In composing the three-volume *History of the Rise, Progress, and Termination of the American Revolution* (1805), she gloated over the global effects of the revolt in neighboring states, "not as an object of curiosity, but with views and expectations that might give a new face to the political and commercial systems of a considerable part of the European world" (Warren 1805, 171). She saw King George's profligacy and the support of God as the opposing powers that led to the patriots' victory at the battle of Lexington. Alluding to the writings of Gibbon and the Italian political theorist NICCOLÒ MACHIAVELLI, she belittled the British political effort to forestall the mustering of the Continental Army and the "dismemberment of the empire" (282).

A Swiss Rebel

A contemporary of Warren, Mme de Staël (Anne-Louise-Germaine Necker, baronne de Staël, 1766–1817), a French-Swiss intellectual and libertarian debater, examined the effect of Napoleon Bonaparte's territorial exploitation on women and families. In her childhood, she encountered at her mother's Paris salon the elite thinkers of her day, and she would later meet the German poets JOHANN WOLFGANG VON GOETHE and Friedrich von Schiller, the romantic poet Lord Byron, and the ethnographers JACOB and WILHELM GRIMM.

At age 20, she married a Swedish ambassador and increased her political influence until the French Revolution forced her from Paris. In 1792, her egalitarianism sparked the first of three banishments for denouncing Napoleon's empire.

In October 1789, de Staël praised the French women and children who shouldered farm tools to launch the Women's March to Versailles in search of bread. The author's pamphleteering vindicated Marie Antoinette following the August 1793 trial that charged the French queen with capital crimes. Napoleon censored Staël's perceptive treatise *De l'Allemagne* (On Germany, 1810) for accusing his followers of fanaticism. He exiled her once more along with two of her friends, limiting ports of embarkation to four southern routes to forestall her possible complicity with the English. After the British triumph over Napoleon at Waterloo, Belgium, on June 18, 1815, and the restoration of Louis XVIII to the French throne, Staël returned from exile, during which she had resided in Germany, Scandinavia, Russia, and Poland.

Staël recuperated from a stroke while crusading for the abolition of slavery and for the French republic in a best-selling chronicle, *Considérations sur la révolution française* (*Considerations on the Principal Events of the French Revolution*, 1818). In an attack on militarism, she charged that "the victorious flags of the army covered the crimes of those who governed" (Staël 1818, 125). With a bold aphorism, she declared that slaughter was not the same as national destruction. In the posthumously published *Dix années d'exil* (*Ten Years' Exile*, 1820), she summarized the pettiness of the Bonapartists. Chapter 18 mocks Napoleon's self-crowning and charges that "Terror, which formed the background of the picture, prevented the grotesque of the front from being laughed at as it deserved to be" (Staël 2007, 83). In her estimation, citizens made the new emperor a butt of humor for his lack of culture and for his inability to conduct administrative business with the rest of Europe. In book 2, she enjoys the irony of encountering the French army on June 22, 1812, on its doomed invasion of Russia.

Conflict and Art

The decline of the Hapsburg Empire sent central European writers and artists fleeing over the eastern borders to the ethnic purity of Russia. In Prague, Czechoslovakia, the poet Rainer Maria Rilke (1875–1926), a contemporary of the Czech writer Franz Kafka and idol of the Russian novelist BORIS PASTERNAK, feared the nihilism generated by Friedrich Nietzsche's "God is dead" theory. During the decline of the Austro-Hungarian Empire, Rilke separated himself from the ruling German minority and wrote protests against the ominous expansionism of German politicians and the greed of Austrian capitalists. Through criticism and poetry, he rejected his Germanic ethnicity, developed bilingualism in German and Czech, and wrote in admiration of the folklore of Bohemia, the western half of today's Czech Republic. Preferring the simplicity of peasants over the arrogance and faux sophistication of German cosmopolites, he rejected imitation of the West to express his ethnic roots. He accused Czechs, Slavs, and Yiddish speakers of losing spontaneous styles of speech and native idioms by emulating the rigid verse forms and politically correct prose of England, France, and Germany.

In an era of material ambition, the poet searched fruitlessly for contentment and was a crusader against Eurocentrism, which he called a "kingdom of decay." In "Mir zur Feier" ("To Celebrate Myself," 1899), Rilke pictured himself as an unconventional youth strolling the paths of Bohemia's past (Rilke 1987, xii). He called for a cultural revival of Czech art based on Pan-Slavism, a movement seeking Eastern European unity. His stories, odes, and sonnets exalted the biblical prodigal son from Jesus's parable in Luke 15:11–32, the wanderer in search of a homecoming and forgiveness for profligacy. Rilke found grace, authenticity, and hope in the harmony of rural Bohemia, where nature blessed the farm laborers who laughed, sang, and danced to the fiddle music of their ancestors.

With the collection *Larenopfer* (*Offerings to the Lares*, 1895), Rilke looked back on the daily devotions of Romans to their ancestral gods rather than to the trumped-up emperors—Augustus, Tiberius, Caligula, Claudius, Hadrian, Commodus, Constantine, and Julius—who made themselves gods through public acts of self-deification. The verse portrait "Land and Folk" insists that forest, field, orchard, and pasture enrich Bohemians as God intended. Rilke called the country lifestyle

"Volksweise" (the folk way) and exalted folk celebrations as "Freiheisklänge" (sounds of freedom). He repudiated the glory of the standard HERO warrior in a popular work, *Die Weise von Liebe und Tod des Cornets Christoph Rilke* (The Day of the Love and Death of Cornet Christophe Rilke, 1899), a stylized dreamscape that contrasts carnal love with the bleakness of soldiery. In his mystic dreams in *Das Stundenbuch* (*The Book of Hours*, 1903), an idealization of Czech nationhood, Rilke yearned for a sublime empire devoid of pomposity and social differences.

A Radical in America and Russia

At the beginning of the 20th century, Emma Goldman (1869–1940) a labor agitator, lecturer, and memoirist, impressed audiences with her fiery egalitarianism and antiwar efforts. A Jew born in Kovno, Lithuania, she came of age in czarist Russia when persecution, military impressment, and pogroms endangered lives. After arriving in Rochester, New York, in 1885 with a sewing machine under her arm, she worked in the garment district and supported pacifists. Goldman developed an anarchistic philosophy and served 12 months at Blackwell's Island penitentiary for rioting. In Harlem in 1906, she founded *Mother Earth*, a periodical that featured the feminist and radical thoughts of the journalist Louise Bryant, orator Voltairine De Cleyre, utopist Charlotte Perkins Gilman, reproductive rights activist Margaret Sanger, and radical English novelist Mary Wollstonecraft, author of *A Vindication of the Rights of Woman* (1792).

Goldman anthologized a series of platform lectures in *Anarchism and Other Essays* (1910). In "Patriotism," she declares the true nationalists to be the working class, whether they be rebels against Porfirio Díaz in Mexico, Czar Nicholas II in Russia, or the American imperialists in Cuba during the Spanish-American War. In her essay "Francisco Ferrer," she salutes the Spanish republican rebel for struggling against the dual evils of imperialism and Catholicism. Of the Russo-Japanese War of 1904–05, she asserts financial motives as the true call to combat: "We see again that back of the fierce Moloch of war stands the still fiercer god of Commercialism" (Goldman 1910, 140). She supports her charge against the czar with accusations

of profiteering on investments in the Korean war industry. Further denunciation of Russian despotism in the speech "Woman Suffrage" pictures Finland as a subjugated state.

On December 21, 1919, at 6:00 A.M., U.S. authorities deported Goldman under military guard aboard the steamer *Buford* to Finland and by rail to Russia. The twofold charge against her consisted of promoting birth control and abetting World War I era draft resistance. At first, she rallied to the singing of the "Internationale," the international Communist Party anthem and exulted, "All my life Russia's heroic struggle for freedom was as a beacon to me" (Goldman 1923, 3). Her exuberant prose honored the *dubinushka* (peasant), "the modern Samson, who with a sweep of his mighty arm had pulled down the pillars of decaying society" (4). Aghast at the persecution of workers in Petrograd (present-day St. Petersburg), she departed within two years to Sweden and Germany. Goldman's polemic *My Disillusionment in Russia* (1923) vented anger at the Bolshevists' collusion with imperialist Germany, political harassment, socialized industry and state monopolies, surveillance, and forced labor. In a sequel, *My Further Disillusionment in Russia* (1924), she found Jews in Kiev and Odessa still suffering from starvation and pogroms. Among the beggars at rail stations, she deplored the sight of "emaciated and ragged children, pleading for a crust of bread at the car windows" (Goldman 1924, 2). Her writings told the free world of manhunts for anarchists under the dictator Vladimir Lenin and of the stifling of dissidents and their imprisonment in foul lockups such as the concentration camp at Ryazan southeast of Moscow, where inmates battled filth, bedbugs, and lice.

Goldman demanded courage from journalists. In her autobiography, *Living My Life* (1931), she charged the world media with concealing from readers "the inhumanities committed by the Czar (Nicholas II)" (Goldman 1931, 70). She admired the Scottish dissident Tom Bell, who rebuked Nicholas on his arrival at Leith, near Edinburgh. As the entourage passed, the protester yelled, "Down with the Russian tyrant! To hell with all the empires!" (264). Her memoir exalts the revolution of 1905, when "The subdued social forces and the pent-up suffering of the people had broken and had at last found expression in the revolutionary tide that swept our beloved *Matushka Rossiya* (Mother Russia)" (372), an event that unified New York's East Side with radical glee. She wrote that President William McKinley was "the willing tool of Wall Street and of the new American imperialism that flowered under his administration" (309–310), a reference to the annexation of the Philippines. The charge implicates McKinley in an American effort to found its own empire.

In 1981, Maureen Stapleton projected Goldman's passion in *Reds,* a film that earned her an Oscar. Central to the historical scenario was Goldman's influence on the journalist John "Jack" Reed (1887–1920), played by Warren Beatty. Reed authored *Ten Days That Shook the World* (1919), an eyewitness account of the October Revolution of 1917 that precipitated the fall of the Romanovs and the rise of Soviet Russia. He spoke with an insider's understanding when he charged that "The corrupt reactionaries in control of the Tsar's Court deliberately undertook to wreck Russia in order to make a separate peace with Germany" (Reed 1919, viii). Reed's journalistic style describes socialist splinter groups and refutes global misinterpretations of motivations and actions. His eyewitness reportage incorporates dramatic confrontations of opposing groups, such as the sailors and Red Guards who overrun the Petrograd telephone office. They face down idealistic young operators, girls who romanticize the notion of "passing up cartridges and dressing the wounds of their dashing young defenders, the *yunkers,* many of them members of noble families, fighting to restore their beloved Tsar!" (197). Late in the night of November 18, 1917, the fractious party leaders reach a workable solution. They confirm that "the union of all the workers and all the exploited will consolidate the power conquered by them" (312). Reed concludes with a backward glance at what he saw as a just peace and the triumph of socialism.

Sources

Davies, Kate. *Catharine Macauley and Mercy Otis Warren: The Revolutionary Atlantic and the Politics of Gender.* Oxford: Oxford University Press, 2005.

Fairweather, Maria. *Madame de Staël.* New York: Carroll and Graf, 2005.

Goldman, Emma. *Anarchism and Other Essays.* New York: Mother Earth Publishing, 1910.

———. *Living My Life.* New York: A. A. Knopf, 1931.

———. *My Disillusionment in Russia.* Garden City, N.Y.: Doubleday, 1923.

———. *My Further Disillusionment in Russia.* Garden City, N.Y.: Doubleday, 1924.

Reed, John. *Ten Days That Shook the World.* New York: Boni and Liveright, 1919.

Rilke, Rainer Maria. *Sonnets to Orpheus.* Translated by David Young. Middletown, Conn.: Wesleyan University Press, 1987.

Staël, Madame de. *Considerations of the Principal Events of the French Revolution.* Edited by Duke de Broglie and the Baron de Staël. London: Baldwin, Cradock & Joy, 1818.

———. *On Germany.* Translated by John Murray. London: John Murray, 1813.

———. *Ten Years' Exile.* Edited by Auguste Louis de Staël. London: BiblioBazaar, 2007.

The Ten Thousand Leaves. Translated by Ian Hideo Levy. Princeton, N.J.: Princeton University Press, 1981.

Travis, Anna A. *Rilke's Russia: A Cultural Encounter.* Chicago: Northwestern University Press, 1997.

Warren, Mercy Otis. *The Group.* Boston: Edes and Gill, 1775.

———. *History of the Rise, Progress, and Termination of the American Revolution.* Boston: E. Larkin, 1805.

———. *Poems, Dramatic and Miscellaneous.* Boston: I. Thomas and E. T. Andrews, 1790.

Psalms (ca. 900 B.C.)

At the literary height of the Israelite empire, the compiling of 150 psalms (hymns) preserved lyrical praises, war hymns, call and response, antiphonal doxologies, communal and personal laments, ritual marches and worship processionals of the royal house of Judah, messianic encomia, righteous testimonials, penitential songs and meditations, and thanksgiving anthems sung to the music of flute and string and percussion instruments. Collected by King David (ca. 1037–967 B.C.) and subsequent hymnographers in the style of Hindu collectors of the VEDAS (1700–1400 B.C.), the psalms address the nature of godhood and kingship. Specific lines confirm the monarch's role as guardian of justice and the royal duty to divinity with themes of terror, panic, vengeance, bondage, mercy, majesty, and victory. A theocratic psalm pairs wisdom with godliness as the pillars of rule: "Be wise now therefore, O ye kings: be instructed, ye judges of the earth. Serve the Lord with fear, and rejoice with trembling" (Psalm 2:10–11). A similar admonition emphasizes the difference between pagan warriors and the armies of Yahweh: "Some trust in chariots, and some in horses: but we will remember the name of the Lord our God" (Psalm 20:7).

The psalter, some of which appears in 39 sheets of the DEAD SEA SCROLLS, attests to the expansionism of Israel under god's regent, who reigns in Jerusalem. Psalms 72:8 and 89:25 foresee David's empire spreading to the ends of the earth. As explained by the German theologian Hans-Joachim Kraus, a ruler perches on the juncture of two domains: "The emperor stands at the center of a universal view of the world. He finds himself at the intersection of sacral enthronement and mythical cosmology" (Kraus 1992, 121). A specific assault on Israel in its postempire years occurs in Psalm 74 with the desecration of the cult shrine at Bethel 10 miles from Jerusalem in the Northern Kingdom. During a Persian raid, "They break down the carved wood thereof at once with axes and hammers. They have cast fire into thy sanctuary" (Psalm 74:6–7), an unconscionable defilement of the holy of holies.

The Psalms continue to console, uplift, and encourage readers and to inspire art, drama, cinema, and poetry. Antiphonal readings undergird liturgical music and dance. During the late A.D. second century, the Carthaginian polemist TERTULLIAN cited David's verse in *De spectaculis* (Of public shows, ca. A.D. 201). He used Psalm 1 as a rebuke against brutal gladiatorial events and as a testimony of Hebrew pacifism, piety, and humility. Lines from the Psalms appear in the films *David and Bathsheba* (1951), *Solomon and Sheba* (1959), two versions of *A Story of David* (1960, 1976), *King David* (1985), and *David* (1997).

Sources

Kraus, Hans-Joachim. *Theology of the Psalms*. Minneapolis: Fortress Press, 1992.
Psalms. In the Holy Bible. Iowa Falls, Iowa: World Bible Publishers, 1986, 819–920.

Saebo, Magne. *On the Way to Canon: Creative Tradition History in the Old Testament*. New York: Continuum International, 1998.

Pushkin, Aleksandr Sergeyevich (Alexander Pushkin) (1799–1837) *Russian poet and novelist*

A radical writer and social reformer, Aleksandr Pushkin wrote romantic tragedies and narrative verse caricaturing the social standards of czarist Russia. Born to Muscovite aristocrats, he began reciting original verse at age 14 while enrolled at the Imperial Lyceum outside St. Petersburg, an institution established in 1811 by Czar Alexander I. In the writer's early autobiographical poems, he delighted in his Boyar (Bulgarian) heritage and in the free-spirited Rom (Gypsies) and attempted to alter the way that Russians viewed themselves. In the short story "The Shot" (1830), he examined the code of dueling practiced during the first Napoleonic empire. In reaction to social climbers scrambling for noble rank, he justifies his rise to fame and influence in "My Pedigree" (1830): "How then aristocrat am I to be? / God be thanked, I am but a citizen" (Pushkin 1888, 62).

Pushkin's poem "Ode to Liberty" ruffled the imperial court with its disrespect for royalty and its affronts to the church. Exiled on May 1820 to the Ukraine, then the Crimea, Moldavia, and finally to Odessa, he negotiated a reprieve with Nicholas I in 1826 but continued to feel pressure from censors and government spies who read his mail. Drawn southwest by reports of the Greek Revolution in 1821 and hostilities against the Ottoman Empire, Pushkin wrote of unrequited love in *The Captive of the Caucasus* (1821) and of an Oriental legend in *The Fountain of Bakhchisaray* (1823), romantic ballads that earned him acclaim as the "Russian Byron." In 1825, the author began serializing *Eugene Onegin*, which he based on the folk tales told to him by his nurse and completed in 1832. The plot contrasts the aristocratic Onegin, a Byronic HERO, with Tatiana Larina, a naive country girl who develops finer instincts and morals than he. Under government surveillance, the poet completed the verse tragedy *Boris Godunov* (1825), the story of the boyar-emperor who ruled from 1598 to 1605 following a period of murderous court intrigues under Czar Ivan IV the Terrible. Because of the author's criticism of imperial autocracy, censors suppressed the play until 1866.

Pushkin advanced to subversive motifs and themes reflecting on the evils of despotism. He honored Peter the Great in the long narrative poem *Poltava* (1828), which commemorates the Russian triumph over Charles XII, emperor of Sweden, in 1709, in the central Ukraine. He made a more direct attack on imperial authority with *The Bronze Horseman* (1833), a ballad about the dreamer Yevgeny, a grief-stricken flood survivor who blames a monument to Peter the Great for the wretchedness of commoners. After cursing the equestrian statue, Yevgeny has to face the retaliation of the bronze figure, a symbol of autocracy and suppression of free speech that springs to life and pursues him to his death. According to the 20th-century Russian poet ANNA AKHMATOVA, the milieu of gloom and decay in St. Petersburg presented in *Eugene Onegin* explodes into stark GOTHIC fantasy in *The Bronze Horseman*. Pushkin describes the city as a sociopolitical hellhole that looms pitiless and overbearing on Yevgeny's horizon. Beginning at line 207, the narrative typifies the czar as immobile as he surveys the flood, a national calamity and a PROPHECY of the Romanovs' inaction in the final days of the Russian Empire.

In his last years, Pushkin angered Czar Nicholas I by researching the life of Peter the Great in the imperial archives as the model of a worthy ruler.

In "The Captain's Daughter" (1836), Pushkin openly castigated the "old days," when "torture was so ingrained a part of the judicial process that the beneficent order abolishing it remained a dead letter for a long time" (Pushkin 1999, 146). The unfinished narrative *Peter the Great's Feast* was a blatant criticism of royal pretension. The ironic narrative ridicules Russian commoners for their trust in the autocrat's nobility and benevolence.

A court intrigue forced the author into a duel that resulted in his death at age 37. To avoid a political demonstration, the government concealed the location of Pushkin's funeral and interment. His works have been adapted to opera by Modest Moussorgsky, to oratorio by Nikolay Rimsky-Korsakov, and to ballet by Pyotr Ilich Tchaikovsky, and they influenced the lyricism of Anna Akhmatova. In cinema, Ralph Fiennes and Liv Tyler starred in an English film, *Onegin* (1999).

Sources

Andrew, Joe, and Robert Reid. *Two Hundred Years of Pushkin.* Amsterdam: Rodopi, 2003.

Pushkin, Alexander. *Eugene Onegin.* Translated by Charles Johnston. London: Penguin, 2003.

———. *Poems.* Translated by Ivan Panin. Boston: Cupples and Hurd, 1888.

———. *The Queen of Spades and Other Stories: A New Translation.* Translated by Alan Myers. New York: Oxford University Press, 1999.

R

Ramayana (Valmiki) (ca. 400 B.C.)

The oldest poetic work of Sanskrit literature, the *Ramayana* (The deeds of Rama), India's beloved Hindu epic, dramatizes an imperial struggle between good and evil. In six cantos and an epilogue, a total of 24,001 *slokas* (lines), the work took shape orally between the eighth and fifth centuries B.C. The setting is Ayodhya, the capital of Kosala and a center of pilgrimage to the birthplace of Prince Rama in northeastern India. Along the Ganges River basin south of the Chinese border, priests used the sacred water from the river to consecrate hereditary kings and to administer oaths. Composed in four-foot lines of eight syllables each, the formulaic classic passed from the STORYTELLING of the mythical ascetic seer Narada to the written narrative by the poet Valmiki of Allahabad. The narrative's flow complemented the dignity and sincerity of Hindu prayers, hymns, chants, ritual sacrifice, and adages on the subjects of duty and righteousness.

Like Homer's *Iliad* (ca. 800 B.C.), the *Ramayana* is an action story that expresses the Hindu character of Valmiki's times. He framed the epic poem to portray the HERO Rama, a fighter of demons and ogres. Through chronological episodes, the narrative describes king making, beginning with Rama's youth, education, selection as heir apparent, and preparation for court duties under his father, King Dasaratha. The story impressed its audiences, who took inspiration and courage from the account of the protagonist's virtues. Subtextually, Rama's marriage to Sita, a pure nature spirit who springs from a fresh furrow, commemorates the establishment of an agrarian society. The breaking of clods with a plow represents coitus and establishes the strict gendering of the narrative, which depicts Sita as a willing handmaiden to her groom.

Nature also bears elements of danger and peril. Like the portentous EPITHALAMIUM of VIRGIL's *AENEID* (17 B.C.), ominous bird calls follow Rama's nuptials, and foretell trial by an archery competition and a 14-year exile in central India. Sita embodies the duties of the Hindu consort by pleading to share Rama's banishment as a marital obligation. In book 3, the main conflict, the hero must battle monsters from Ceylon to retrieve his bride from an abductor. At the core of evil, Ravana, Rama's nemesis, takes on satanic qualities: "He sometimes walks on foot and moves about like the wind—he shines like fire and spreads heat like the sun. . . . He does not know fear" (Valmiki 1894, 1632). Poetic hyperbole intensifies Ravana's threat, enhancing Rama's victory over consummate evil and thus begging the question of conducting a just and necessary campaign. After Rama passes the tests of manhood and defeats Ravana, he accepts his destiny by replacing his deceased father on the throne. False slanders force him to exile Sita, a wife allegedly soiled by her kidnapper, to the forest when she bears Rama twin sons. She returns to face her accusers and vindicates herself.

Rama as Divinity

Unlike the heroes of the Hebrew book of EXODUS (ca. 450 B.C.) and the Greek chronicler HERODOTUS's

Histories (440 B.C.), India's epic glorifies a two-dimensional protagonist free of the complexities and frailties of humankind. Because the hero manifests remarkable might, radiance, sinlessness, austerity, and self-mastery, later Brahmin intellectuals revered Rama as an earthly incarnation of Vishnu, the supreme deity. In a passage on the majesty of royalty, Valmiki's text provides a prayer for a just ruler: "O lord of creatures, do thou also confer upon us a king who shall be foremost among men; by worshipping him we shall be freed from all sins" (1,566). The blend of respect with deification identifies a civilization that holds an emperor in higher esteem than later concepts of respected, but fallible rulers. Like the Essenes who compiled the DEAD SEA SCROLLS (150 B.C.–A.D. 70) in the Middle East, Valmiki anticipates a messianic age marked by the omnipotence of a savior of humankind.

The story of Rama suited the performance of itinerant bards, who carried it west to Benares and on to other nations where citizens regarded hereditary monarchy as the bulwark of the state. The text passed on to the Chinese, Tibetan, Japanese Khmer, Lao, Malay, Maranao (Philippine Islands), Burmese, and Thai realms, each of which interpolated local legend, ballads, laws, allusions to royalty, and genealogy.

- From the middle of the Tang dynasty, the Chinese version (Dunhuang [ca. 787]) consists of six manuscripts found in Dunhuang (Tun-Huang), northwest China. These were the result of a command of Governor Wei Chu of Shoa-chou to monastery scribe Fa-hai, a collaborator on the translation.
- The Chinese narrative was the source of the Tibetan *Ramayana, Tongbao (T'oung Pao)* (ca. 800), the work of Buddhist translators toward the end of the Tibetan empire during the reign of Trisong Detsan at a time when Tibetan forces ventured into China and suffered a crippling defeat.
- Near the end of Japan's classical Heian Period, Taira no Yasuyori translated the *Ramayana* into the *Hobutsushu* (Collection of jewels, ca. 1100). Issued at the height of Japanese court life, this rendition emphasizes the era's refinement of art and verse.

- At the end of the Majapahit empire from 1293 to 1500, Tamil transcriptors altered the character of Rama for the Malay version, *Hikayat seri Rama* (Legend of the great Rama, ca. 1500). The Malayan version inserts Javanese court romance for the amusement of audiences in Bali and the Malay peninsula.
- In the period of civil unrest following the collapse of the Khmer Empire, the *Reamker* (ca. 1550), a Khmer version of the *Ramayana*, became the Cambodian epic. It reflects the adaptation of Hinduism to Buddhism, a religion that alters Rama's earthly strivings to embrace indifference to combat and loss. To Khmer readers, the hero is Buddha himself. The poem's action summarizes daily decision making by a king who rules rice farmers.
- Initially transcribed on palm fronds, the Lao version, *Phra Lak Phra Lam* (Beloved Lakshma and Beloved Rama, ca. 1600), confirmed legends of the royal lineage. The narrative, a model of the *jataka* (godhood story), served the national ballet as a source of sacred stories about Prince Rama. Images from the story decorate Angkor Wat, a temple complex built in about 1112 in northwestern Cambodia.
- The Burmese version of the Rama tales, the *Rama Thagyin* (1775), was a translation completed by U Aung Phyo in the Mon language preceding a period of invasions by Chinese armies of the Qing dynasty.
- A later adaptation, the Thai Ramakien (1797) was the translation of King Rama I the Great (1782–1809), founder of the Chakri dynasty, who added CREATION lore and the tenets of animism. His son and successor, Rama II, applied the narrative to mime or dance drama, a native art form featuring choral readers, themes of vengeance and carnal love, and a dance troupe wearing oversized masks and costumes.

The *Ramayana* has dominated culture and the arts in India and Southeast Asia up to the present. Segments of the epic undergird sculpture, painted scrolls, shadow plays, and puppetry as well as the film *Ramayan* (1986) and the animated cartoon *Ramayana: The Legend of Prince Rama* (1992).

Sources

Bose, Mandakranta. *The Ramayana Revisited.* Oxford: Oxford University Press, 2004.

Dumoulin, Heinrich, James W. Heisig, and Paul F. Knitter. *Zen Buddhism: A History.* Bloomington, Ind.: World Wisdom, 2005.

Valmiki. *The Ramayana.* Translated by and edited by Manmatha Nath Dutt. Calcutta: H. C. Das, 1894.

———. *Reamker: The Cambodian Version of the Ramayana.* Translated by Judith M. Jacob. New York: Routledge, 1986.

Rau, Santha Rama (Vasanthi Rama Rau Wattles) (1923–) *Indian biographer, essayist, travel writer, and journalist*

A feminist and Brahmin, Santha Rama Rau writes of imperialism from a cosmopolitan perspective. A native of Madras, she is the daughter of Sir Benegal Rama Rau, a civil servant and diplomat, and Dhanvanthi Handoo Rama Rau, a memoirist and the international president of Planned Parenthood. Rau's family occupied embassy quarters around the world. She entered primary school in England at St. Paul's Girls' School, London. When she was in her mid-teens, the Raus began an assignment to the South African embassy, then moved to Bombay during World War II. With an English degree from Wellesley College, she established a journalistic career as editor of *Trend* magazine. Her AUTOBIOGRAPHY, *Home to India* (1944), describes her mother and grandmother's lives and the reaction to the loosening of restrictions on Indian female behaviors and choices. Another autobiographical work, *Gifts of Passage* (1961), set during the decline of the British Raj, reveals a loss of respect for the English as the "we" versus "they" mentality marginalized even high-caste Indians. One of Rau's personal embarrassments occurred at the Bombay Yacht Club, where staff banned her because of her race.

Rau made her name by studying ethnic quandaries under colonialism. While her father served as India's first ambassador to Tokyo, she taught English at a Christian academy, Mrs. Moto Hani's Garden School of Freedom. As Japan recovered from the collapse of its empire, Rau became a devotee of Kabuki theater and acting troupes, recognizing them as the cultural voice of the Japanese people. In 1951, she married Faubian Bowers, an American theater expert, former interpreter, and aide to General Douglas MacArthur during the American occupation of Japan. From tours of Afghanistan, Bali, Burma, Cambodia, China, Indonesia, Laos, the Philippines, Sri Lanka, the Suli islands, Thailand, and Vietnam, she gathered themes and travel topics for *East of Home: The Discovery of Asia by an Asian Educated in the West* (1950). The debut on Broadway in January 1962 of her stage version of E. M. Forster's sociopolitical novel *A Passage to India* preceded a 1965 BBC television production and influenced director David Lean's 1984 screenplay. In 1966, Rau divorced her husband, with whom she had had one son, born in 1952. In 1977, she married Gordon Wattles, a legal counsel at the United Nations.

While covering news for *Holiday* magazine in Africa, Asia, and Russia, Rau composed vignettes and serialized novellas for *Eros, Flair, Horizon, New Yorker, New York Times Magazine, Reader's Digest, Reporter, Saturday Evening Post,* and *Vogue.* She ghostwrote Gayatri Devi's biography, *A Princess Remembers: The Memoirs of the Maharani of Jaipur* (1974), the story of one of the last of queens of Jaipur, who defied purdah, the forced seclusion of women. Rau summarized "The Trial of Jomo Kenyatta" (1976), a detailed essay on the Kenyan leader's banishment from British East Africa five years before it gained independence. Police arrested him in 1952 in Nairobi, Kenya, for conspiracy and abetting an uprising of the Mau Mau, a secret Kikuyu society feared for its terrorism, murder, and the plunder of land and herds belonging to colonists. The text charges whites with monopolizing the coffee- and sisal-growing central plateau and with forbidding land purchase by blacks and Asians. In tribute to Kenyatta's contribution to black nationalism, Rau characterized him as "the only African to emerge as anything approaching a national leader in that curious association of colonies, trust territories, and protectorates" (Rau 1969, 176). Her subsequent works repudiate the residue of British imperialism.

Sources

Klein, Christina. *Cold War Orientalism: Asia in the Middlebrow Imagination, 1945–1961.* Berkeley: University of California Press, 2003.

Mehrotra, Arvind Krishna. *A History of Indian Literature in English.* New York: Columbia University Press, 2003.

Rau, Santha Rama. *A Princess Remembers: The Memoirs of the Maharani of Jaipur.* Philadelphia: J. B. Lippincott, 1976.

———. "The Trial of Jomo Kenyatta." In *The Reporter Reader,* edited by Max Ascoli, 176–201. New York: Doubleday, 1969.

Rhys, Jean (Ella Gwendolen Rees Williams)
(1890–1979) *Dominican-Welsh novelist and short story writer*

A West Indian feminist and gothicist, Jean Rhys revisited classic 19th-century English fiction from a colonial perspective. Born Ellen Gwendolen Rees Williams of Creole, Scots, and Welsh ancestry in Roseau, Dominica, she lived isolated from the largely black population. In childhood, she absorbed elements of miscegenation, bigotry, and voodoo that animated her adult fiction. Her education began at an island convent school and progressed to the Perse School for Girls, a British boarding academy in Cambridge, England. In 1909, she entered the Academy of Dramatic Art. From work as an artist's model and a stage dancer in musical comedy at age 29, she escaped into a marriage with Jean Lenglet, a French-Dutch journalist, that would bring little happiness and end in 1932. She had an affair with the editor and novelist Ford Madox Ford in 1923–24, and in 1947, she married Max Hamer. Though she issued stories and novels in the 1930s and 1940s, she didn't achieve real fame until the publication of her novel *Wide Sargasso Sea* in 1966. She died in England on May 14, 1979, having visited her native Dominica only once in her adult life. Her uncompleted AUTOBIOGRAPHY was published after her death.

While living in Vienna, Rhys published her first short story, "Vienne" (1924), in the *Transatlantic Review,* and then a collection, *The Left Bank and Other Stories* (1927), in which she layers glimpses of West Indian negritude excluded from belonging in French cafes and parks.

Like the Indian journalist SANTHA RAMA RAU and the Trinidadian-British author V. S. NAIPAUL, Rhys had discovered a colonial vibrance within uprooted cultures that survived vicari-ously through transportable institutions and beliefs. Unlike Naipaul, however, she outlined the minority islander in bold relief against a white cosmopolitan background. In "Trio," she generates a flash of island nostalgia with her description of meeting a woman from the Antilles. The Afro-Caribbean style of a white chemise and Martinique turban complement thick lips and "fuzzy, negress' hair" (Rhys 1992, 34), a combination the author finds intriguingly lively and life-affirming. The speaker muses, "From the Antilles, too. You cannot think what home-sickness descended over me" (34). Like JAMAICA KINCAID's essays for the *New Yorker,* Rhys's stories "Again the Antilles" and "Mixing Cocktails" repeat themes of creole displacement against a white milieu. In a racial overlay, black character and behavior contrast the enervation and degeneracy of "old money" colonials, who enrich themselves off the toil of slaves.

When she was in her mid-50s, Rhys wrote a prequel to Charlotte Brontë's *Jane Eyre* (1847). *Wide Sargasso Sea* is a psychological novel that details the victimization of Antoinette Cosway, a sensual Jamaican Creole heiress. The arranged marriage and rejection of Antoinette precipitates her departure from her island home and her incarceration by her husband Edward in rural England under the name Bertha Mason Rochester. Her vulnerability to patriarchy derives from naïveté. On her wedding day, she protects herself with a feminine gesture: "I am wearing a long dress and thin slippers, so I walk with difficulty, following the man who is with me and holding up the skirt of my dress. It is white and beautiful and I don't wish to get it soiled" (Rhys 1967, 59–60), a foreshadowing of their doomed wedlock. Antoinette's diminution by a self-centered white Englishman seems inevitable, the result of colonialism and male-dominated society. Displaced on England's moors, she feels a pervasive chill, a symbol of the British disdain for nonwhite people and for her Afro-Caribbean culture. The social quandary limits her to escapism through mad scenes in which she dresses in red and relives a childhood exuberance. Like a moth in a bell jar, she turns manic, beating her wings against her impersonal confines. Film versions made in 1993 and 2006 contrast the lush freedoms of the West Indies with the frigid realities of English society.

Sources

Rhys, Jean. *The Collected Short Stories.* Edited by Diana Athill. New York: W. W. Norton, 1992.

———. *Wide Sargasso Sea.* New York: Norton, 1967.

Savory, Elaine. *Jean Rhys.* Cambridge: Cambridge University Press, 1998.

Thomas, Sue. *The Worlding of Jean Rhys.* Westport, Conn.: Greenwood, 1999.

Richardson, John (Major John Frederick Richardson) (1796–1852) *Canadian journalist and novelist*

English Canada's first novelist, John Richardson wrote dramatic historical romances based on his exploits on the battlefield and his observations of biculturalism. Born in Queenston, Upper Canada (now Ontario), he was the grandson of a Scots fur trader, John Askin, and Nanette, an Ottawa Indian. After his education in Detroit, Michigan, and Fort Malden, Amherstburg, Ontario, he joined the British 41st Welsh Regiment of Foot, heroes of the War of 1812. In 1813, following his capture at the Battle of Moraviantown, he spent nine months in a prisoner-of-war penitentiary at Frankfort, Kentucky. After his release, he went to Europe to fight but arrived too late for the Battle of Waterloo. During his time in military service, he developed expertise in guerrilla tactics. After switching regiments several times, serving in Barbados and Grenada, he received invalid pay for medical reasons. He stayed in London and Paris, supporting himself through journalism, writing dispatches for the London *Times.* His first novel, *Écarté, or the Salons of Paris* (1829), was a social study of gambling in the Paris demimonde. In the years to come, he would write articles, novels, short stories, and even songs, and he started but failed to complete a history of the War of 1812. He returned to Canada in 1838 but left for good in 1848 and died in New York City on May 12, 1852, broke, depressed, and mostly unappreciated in his native country.

Richardson contributed to battlefield literature and colonial FRONTIER LITERATURE with *Wacousta; or, The Prophecy: A Tale of the Canadas* (1832) and *The Canadian Brothers; or, The Prophecy Fulfilled* (1840), paired novels set during the French and Indian War and the war of 1812.

Traditionally compared to the American frontier novelist James Fenimore Cooper's Leatherstocking Tales, Richardson's twin narratives have earned respect as a colonial Canadian epic. They dramatize British military errors during battles with the Ottawa chief Pontiac from 1763 to 1766 in the wilderness of the Sinclair River environs of Fort Detroit and Fort Michilimackinac as well as events of the War of 1812.

In his books, Richardson appears ambivalent toward the displacement of first peoples. Graphic confrontations between Indian and European contrast methods of reconnoitering and fighting, especially the Indian kidnap and terrorizing of women. The English garrison believes that the "savages" have several methods of isolating and capturing outposts. A proof lies in Pontiac's "bloody atrocities in all the posts that have fallen" and in his war tent, which he rings with scalps of men, women, and children (Richardson 1832, 317). In chapter 3, white pickets fail to spy a single unarmed Ottawa floating by the fort to observe the size and location of their force. Because of the swimmer's stealth, the English must admit, "The bird is flown, and we have only to thank ourselves for having been so egregiously duped" (72). In a later admission of short-sightedness, Richardson declares that the insurgents originally seemed as nonthreatening "as a mite among the numerous nations that were leagued against the English" (162). Counterbalancing the desperate military situation is the friendship of Miss de Haldimar with her rescuer Oucanasta, a wordless woman-to-woman synergy that eases tensions on the frontier.

The sequel of *Wacousta,* Richardson's *The Canadian Brothers; or, The Prophecy Fulfilled,* foresees the rise of Canadian nationality. Set on Lake Erie in summer 1812, the narrative opens in celebration of the British possession of Amherstburg, "one of the loveliest spots that ever issued from the will of a beneficent and gorgeous nature" (Richardson 1840, 1). Needing assistance against the Americans, white Canadians ponder the arrival of the Shawnee chieftain Tecumseh and the possibility of a British alliance with Great Lakes tribes. In the ensuing debate, colonial officials, in the presence of black slaves, use wartime scalping and pillaging as justification for refusing the proposed treaty. The response from the general reminds the white naysayers that "Indian cruelty does not exceed that which is practiced even at this day in Europe, and by a nation bearing high rank among the Catholic powers of Europe" (78). The statement is a testimonial to Richardson's evenhandedness in representing the clash of empires and cultures.

Sources

Moss, John. *Future Indicative: Literary Theory and Canadian Literature*. Ottawa: University of Ottawa Press, 1987.

Richardson, John. *The Canadian Brothers; or, The Prophecy Fulfilled*. Montreal: A. H. Armour and H. Ramasay, 1840.

———. *Wacousta; or, The Prophecy: A Tale of the Canadas*. London: T. Cadell and W. Blackwood, 1832.

Rig Veda   See CREATION LORE; VEDAS.

Rubáiyát of Omar Khayyám, The   See TRANSLATION.

Rumi (Mawlana, Jalal ad-Din Muhammad Balkhi, Maulana Jalal al-Din Rumi, Mevlana Jalaluadin Rumi) (1207–1248) *Persian philosopher and poet*

The Persian philosopher and theologian Mawlana Jalal ad-Din Muhammad Balkhi, who wrote under the pen name Rumi, represented the golden era of Sufism. At a time when the Persian nation and culture were under attack, he provided Muslims of the Seljuk Empire with the *Mathnawi* (*Spiritual Couplets*, ca. 1270), a masterwork of Islamic teachings. Born on September 30, 1207, Rumi was the son of Mumine Khatun, who came from the caliphate line of Abu Bakr in Balkh, Ghurid, in eastern Persia (present-day Afghanistan); his father, Baha ud-Din Walad, a mystic essayist and teacher, earned the favor of the Seljuk sultan Al-oddin Kay Qobad. The family journeyed west in 1218 to Nishapur, Iran, to escape Genghis Khan and his Mongol invaders. Behind them, the raiders conquered Balkh and Samarkand and spread their empire west over Transoxiana (present-day Kazakhstan, Tajikistan, and Uzbekistan). Episodes of burning, starving, looting, torturing, and murdering earned this era the name of "Islamic holocaust" for reducing the indigenous Muslim population to 10 percent of its original number.

Safe in Konya, Anatolia (present-day Turkey), as Mongols pressed into Persia and destroyed the Abbasid Caliphate in Baghdad, Rumi was able to complete his education. At Aleppo and Damascus, he delved into Sanskrit folklore, the encyclopedias of AL-JAHIZ, and Persian collections of odes, meditations, and pious confessionals. Rumi mastered versification in Arabic, Greek, Persian, and Turkish and led a religious academy while training himself in Sufism, an asceticism rejecting human restraints and religious orthodoxy. At age 37, he met the wandering dervish Shams-e Tabrizi (Shams of Tobriz, Iran), a religious visionary with whom he lived and studied until Shams's disappearance on December 5, 1248. Historians surmise that Rumi's students may have martyred Shams.

Persuaded by the goldsmith Salah ud-Din-e Zarkub and the scribe Hussam-e Chelebi, Rumi, like his predecessor AL-GHAZALI, made a dramatic midlife break from formal teaching. He expressed his beliefs and faith in the *Diwan-e kabir* (The great divan, ca. 1240), a six-volume compendium of lyrics that transcend warfare and cultural destruction. He contradicted the widespread view of Mongols made "drunk on wine of violence": "Their war and peace are made upon illusion, their glory and their shame are from illusion" (Rumi 2007, 116, 13). One of his most famous short works, the perceptive FABLE "The Blind Man and the Elephant" (ca. 1270), describes the limited range of human understanding. He urges the sorrowing to accept death as a form of change rather than extinction. In a prediction of cellular biology, he explains that "God's joy moves from unmarked box to unmarked box, / from cell to cell. / As rainwater, / down into flowerbeds" (quoted in Roberts and Amidon 1991, 44). He muses, "Whatever came from Being is caught up in being, drunkenly forgetting the way back" (40). Of the wonder of both earth and the afterlife, he urges individuals to remain alert to natural phenomena and joy.

Over 12 years, the poet dictated the *Mathnawi* to his scribe. Revered as the Persian KORAN, the

six-volume classic is composed in *ghazals*—10-
or 12-line odes or love lyrics linked in a lulling
monorhyme, *aa, ba, ca, da*. The anthology drew
on scripture, superstition, and fable and stressed a
universal longing for wholeness and unity with passion and beauty.

To achieve the sublime states described in
Rumi's verse, the sufist *mevlevi* (whirling dervishes)
developed a mental and physical frenzy during
their sacred dance. The ecstatic gyration produced
fana (euphorias) that, according to the poet,
"liberate the spirits from the body's trap and wipe
the records clean" (Rumi 2007, 41). The whirling
generated a mystic release from time and space and
a call to "Behold the power of God in his composure!" (12). The rapid rotation of the trunk and
limbs freed the mind of idol worship, rid the soul of
guilt, and intoxicated the spirit with an epiphany
of self-surrender. Enraptured with thoughts of God
and universal love, the dancer became free of
formal religious forms and the greed and power-
mongering around them.

Venerated as the height of Persian poesy, the
Mathnawi revived Islam after an era of Mongol
suppression. The text praises fascination with
nature and stresses an intuitive sanctity. Verses
give only God control of earthly events. Rumi
warns the usurper, "Do not pretend to rulership

and power" and invites, "Come in and see the
power and grace of God" (65, 79). When set to
drum rhythms and flute strains, the poems mimic
the motions of stars and the regular cycle of
planetary orbits. The universality of moral uplift
served soldiers before and during combat, lovers
at weddings and in sexual union, and pilgrims at
shrines. Through recitation of the verses, worshippers stripped themselves of fault, repented of sin,
and lifted clean hearts to God.

At Rumi's death in Anatolia on December
17, 1273, his eldest son, Sulfan Valad, replaced
him as leader of Sufism. Rumi won recognition
for the Sufi ideal—zealotry and abandonment of
worldly distractions to become one with divinity
and eternal truths. Holy men still recite his utopian
verses in monasteries, sanctuaries, and synagogues
and in the mosques of Afghanistan, Iran, Pakistan,
Tajikistan, and Turkey.

Sources

Lane, George. *Genghis Khan and Mongol Rule*. Westport,
    Conn.: Greenwood, 2004.
Roberts, Elizabeth, and Elias Amidon, eds. *Earth
    Prayers from Around the World*. San Francisco:
    HarperSanFrancisco, 1991.
Rumi, Mevlana Jalaluddin. *Spiritual Verses*. Translated by
    Alan Williams. London: Penguin, 2007.

Sachs, Nelly (Leonie Sachs) (1891–1970)
German Jewish playwright, poet, and translator

Nelly Sachs spoke through verse and letters of the grief and powerlessness of fellow Jews murdered during the Holocaust. Born Leonie Sachs, the daughter of an inventor and businessman, she grew up in the affluent Tiergarten section of Berlin and was homeschooled until her entry into the Aubert Academy in 1903. In childhood, she wrote puppet plays and short stories with medieval themes. She began submitting poems to magazines and newspapers when she was in her mid-teens. Timid and reclusive, she developed friendships through correspondence with the Romanian Jewish poet Paul Celan, the German Jewish expatriate poet Hilde Domin, and the Swedish educator and CHILDREN'S LITERATURE author Selma Lagerlöf. After a call-up to a concentration camp and a five-day interrogation at Nazi headquarters, Sachs, then 49, escaped with her widowed mother, Margarete Sachs, to Stockholm through the intervention of Lagerlöf and Prince Eugen of Sweden.

The uprooting redirected Sachs's ethnic, religious, and literary outlook. The horrors of Jewish suffering and GENOCIDE and the failure of her inquiries about dead and missing persons plunged Sachs into paranoia and nervous collapse requiring hospitalization. She renounced her German citizenship to become a Swedish citizen, but she continued to write in German as a way of retaining ties to her homeland. In place of agnosticism, she sought a spiritual reprieve through Hasidism and a study of Kabbala, a form of scripture-based divination. Both sources of traditional wisdom influenced her emotionally stark verse. Four years before her death from cancer, she received the Peace Prize of the German Book Trade and shared the 1966 Nobel Prize in literature for her lyric identification with a victimized race. Her works circulated among Ashkenazi Jews in central and eastern Europe and among diasporic communities in the Middle East and Switzerland.

Reminders of the Holocaust

As a witness to conspiracy to mass murder, Sachs, like ELIE WIESEL, used universal metaphors to visualize her emotional wounds and those of departed spirits, the "dead brothers and sisters" to whom she dedicated her work (Sachs 1967, 1). She commiserated with Paul Celan on his "sulphurous epiphanies," her term for the corrosive memories of Nazi Germany (Celan and Sachs 1995, 17), and she inveighed against survivors' silence. From her brush with annihilation, she wrote the mystical collection *In den Wohnungen des Todes* (In the habitations of death, 1947), in which she addressed death camps and the calculated barbarity of Hitler's "final solution." The poem "But Perhaps God Needs the Longing" conjectures that death meshes with reincarnation to keep stars burning in the night sky. Her most famous poem, "O die Schornsteine" ("O the Chimneys," 1947), allegorizes the erasure of Israel as smoke drifting up "the ingeniously devised habitations of death" into a pitiless sky (Sachs 1967, 3). Her words for the voiceless fill a trio of antiphonal poems, "Chorus of Orphans," "Chorus of Stars," and "Chorus of Things Left Behind." In "Chorus of the Rescued," she pictures herself and other survivors forever haunted by dangling nooses and gnawed by worms of fear. On the solace of the written word, "Chorus of Comforters" questions the right of poets to record so appalling an atrocity against European Jewry.

In the tradition of psalmists and visionaries, Sachs's poetry covers the extremes of human suffering from torture and torment to an earthly reconciliation and redemption in the afterlife. Her titles create mind pictures of terror: "Even the Old Men's Last Breath," "Landscape of Screams," and "Death Still Celebrates." The GOTHIC poem "What Secret Cravings of the Blood" turns Hitler into a cartoon figure—"the terrible puppeteer . . . with foaming mouth" who reduces "Sinai's people" to ashes and dust (17). "O the Night of the Weeping Children!" describes Nazi minions as "terrible nursemaids" (7) suckling small children with panic. The cry in "A Shoe" echoes the rootlessness of postwar refugees in Israel.

Sachs's stage play *Eli, ein Mysterienspiel vom Leiden Israels* (*Eli: A Mystery of the Sorrows of Israel,* 1951) merges a pervasive sorrow over a child's murder with the joy of living in a Jewish homeland free of Hitler's imperialistic aims. The poem "And No One Knows Where to Go" (1957) captures the post–World War II displacement and spiritual vacuum of genocide survivors. Sachs envisions sprigs of hope in the budding branches a woman collects in the poem "White in the Hospital Park" (1962). Setting her apart from other post-Holocaust writers was her unwillingness to seek vengeance against German Nazis. In place of bitterness, she cultivated a spiritual transcendence that infused her poetry with images of fire, flame, dust, sand, and heavenly constellations.

Sources

Bower, Kathrin M. *Ethics and Remembrance in the Poetry of Nelly Sachs and Rose Auslander.* Rochester, N.Y.: Boydell and Brewer, 2000.

Celan, Paul, and Nelly Sachs. *Correspondence.* Translated by Christopher Clark. Berlin: Sheep Meadow, 1995.

Langer, Lawrence L. *Art from the Ashes: A Holocaust Anthology.* Oxford: Oxford University Press, 1995.

Lorenz, Dagmar C. G. *Keepers of the Motherland; German Texts by Jewish Women Writers.* Lincoln: University of Nebraska Press, 1997.

Sachs, Nelly. *O the Chimneys: Selected Poems, Including the Verse Play, Eli.* Translated by Michael Hamburger, Christopher Holme, Ruth Mead, Matthew Mead, and Michael Roloff. New York: Farrar, Straus and Giroux, 1967.

Sahgal, Nayantara   See FEMINISM.

Sand, George   See AUTOBIOGRAPHY.

satire

Satire serves the anti-imperialist as a comedic shield for the writer's assault on the oppressor. The genre proved useful to a variety of ages and writers who produced classic social and governmental criticism, including the Greek fabulist AESOP and his Roman counterpart PHAEDRUS, the French anticolonialist VOLTAIRE, the Trinidadian-British polemist V. S. NAIPAUL, the Javanese anticolonial iconoclast EDUARD DOUWES DEKKER, and the Ghanian playwright AMA ATA AIDOO. Verbal irony and exposés, and mockery of the mighty can take many forms: the Buddhist mockery in *Dohakosha* (Treasury of songs, ca. A.D. 790), the comedy of Aristophanes (see GREEK DRAMA), the CRUSADER LORE of the trouvères, the aphorisms of the Roman muckraker JUVENAL, the Carthaginian TERTULLIAN's invectives against Rome, the STORYTELLING of the Nigerian ethnographer CHINUA ACHEBE, the novels of French writer Anatole France, the stage librettos of the English lyricist WILLIAM SCHWENCK GILBERT, and the bitterness of Aleksandr Solzhenitsyn's gulag novels (see PRISON LITERATURE). Appealing to common sense and reason, satire uses obvious exaggeration to express public acrimony at dominion and to belittle the usurper and overlord. Near the end of Rome's first century of imperial rule, the epic poet LUCAN defamed the imperial family of Nero in *Pharsalia* (A.D. 63), a venture that cost the satirist his life. In the second century of the Islamic empire, *Kitab al-Bukhala* (The book of misers, ca. 825) revealed the scampish nature of the Arab encyclopedist and folklorist AL-JAHIZ, who attacked greedy plutocrats. On a more daring scale, the Russian author IVAN ANDREYEVICH KRYLOV mocked Catherine II the Great and the czarist aristocracy in snide FABLEs.

Throughout history, ridicule has played a part in culture, language, and national literature. Spaniards quote from TOMÁS DE IRIARTE's fables and the antichivalric jests of MIGUEL DE CERVANTES, author of *Don Quixote of La Mancha* (1605), source of the term *quixotic*, meaning "outrageously impractical." In 1729, the English writer JONATHAN SWIFT's *A Modest Proposal* defended the rural Irish against the heartless mercantilism of Great Britain. Before the American Revolution, while the colonies labored under the taxation of England's George III, the Massachusetts libertarian Mercy Otis Warren allegorized the conflict. Her droll stage plays, a seemingly harmless form of PROTEST LITERATURE, were full of malignant puns and aspersions against the British Crown and its colonial representatives. In Ireland, MARIA EDGEWORTH published the regional novel *Castle Rackrent, an Hibernian Tale* (1800), England's first historical fiction, as an attack on vice-ridden British landlords. With a direct sally against the British regime, Edgeworth asserted, "There is no danger in the present times, that any individual should exercise such tyranny as Colonel M'Guire's with impunity, the power being now all in the hands of government and there being no possibility of obtaining from parliament an act of indemnity for any cruelties" (Edgeworth 2007, 85).

On a broader front, writers satirized the clergy, bureaucracy, and international catastrophe. In *The Pickwick Papers* (1837), the English social novelist CHARLES DICKENS included episodes mocking missionaries for their fervid soul-saving among the bereft of the British Empire. The Ukrainian author NIKOLAY GOGOL aroused the censor's ire in the staging of *The Government Inspector* (1836), a three-act exposé of government corruption on the Russian frontier. Even though the play had the approval of Czar Nicholas I, Gogol exiled himself to Rome for 12 years to avoid retaliation. In this same era, parodist William Makepeace Thackeray lampooned

European social climbers during the Napoleonic era in the allegorical romance *Vanity Fair: A Novel without a Hero* (1848) (see NAPOLEONIC LITERATURE). At a moment when civilians are desperate to flee, the author tweaks the condescension of Lady Bareacres, who offers to purchase Mrs. Crawley's horses: "Mrs. Crawley returned a note with her compliments, and an intimation that it was not her custom to transact bargains with ladies' maids" (Thackeray 1848, 280–281).

Opportunities to caricaturize the interloper cropped up throughout the late 19th and early 20th centuries. RUDYARD KIPLING, the most prominent surveyor of British imperialism, turned satire into tragedy with the seizure of tribal power by two bumbling army buddies in "The Man Who Would Be King" (1888). The protagonists, tricksters Danny Dravot and Peachey Carnehan, follow the trail of Alexander the Great to Kafirstan (present-day Afghanistan). A blow against fascism by the radical Italian polemist and poet Filippo Tommaso Marinetti impugned the foppish dress and militarist posturing of "Il Duce," Benedetto Mussolini, the Italian dictator during World War II. The Irish-born playwright George Bernard Shaw reached back to imperial Rome to flay the over-zealous Christians and their imperial persecutors in the two-act stage adaptation of the fable ANDROCLES AND THE LION (1912). Like JAMES JOYCE's *Ulysses* (1922), Shaw's play carried a subtextual salute to the Irish, the underdog of the British Isles. In this same between-the-wars era, English humorist Evelyn Waugh ridiculed the efforts of British aid to Emperor Haile Selassie in modernizing Ethiopia in *Black Mischief* (1932), a jovial send-up set on the fictional isle of Azania. A keen manipulator of allegory and invective, the English novelist GEORGE ORWELL spoke from experience about the alienation of a colonial outsider in Southeast Asia in the novel *Burmese Days* (1934). More gripping, his classic dystopian animal fable *Animal Farm: A Fairy Story* (1946) paired irony with pathos in a tableau of Marxism and fascism in an English barnyard.

The rise of the Soviet Union proved fertile ground for humor and more pungent sarcasm. In 1953, the English fabulist, archaeologist, and historian Jacquetta Hopkins Hawkes mocked the Soviet ideal with "The Unites," a dystopian tale in the collection *A Woman as Great as the World and Other Fables.* The narrative, an example of modern WISDOM LITERATURE, employs irony using a fragmented inscription, "Unites the Human Race," a section of the opening stanza of "The Internationale" (1888), the Communist Party workers' anthem. A peaceful dawn illuminates an atomic disaster, the relics of technological advancement, enslavement, and civil war. Additional irony depicts the remnants of humankind eager to establish a pastoral haven. The fable turns to wisdom lore as a sage admonishes the survivors to distinguish themselves from insects and beasts by aiding the weak and devoting themselves to God. His message refers indirectly to the Soviet menace: "Those great men who have been put at the head of society are as grains of dust at the foot of the colossal mystery of this universe" (Hawkes 1953, 169).

Sources

Edgeworth, Maria. *Castle Rackrent.* Edited by Susan Kubica Howard. Indianapolis, Ind.: Hackett Publishing, 2007.

Hawkes, Jacquette Hopkins. *A Woman as Great as the World and Other Fables.* New York: Random House, 1953.

Snodgrass, Mary Ellen. *Encyclopedia of Satire.* Santa Barbara, Calif.: ABC-Clio, 1996.

Thackeray, William Makepeace. *Vanity Fair.* 3 vols. Leipzig: Bernhard Tauchnitz, 1848.

Schreiner, Olive (Olive Emilie Albertina Schreiner) (1855–1920) *South African novelist*

A radical feminist writer, polemist, and pacifist, Olive Schreiner denounced the arrogance of white South African usurpers. The daughter of Gottlob Schreiner, a Wesleyan missionary, she was born one of 12 children in rural Wittebergen, Basutoland, South Africa. She grew up in a background of restrictive Calvinism and received homeschooling from her mother. She fled her father's illusions of righteousness to board with a brother, Theophilus, and to work as a governess. At age 19, she completed *Undine,* a feminist novel about a rebellious bluestocking that was published posthumously in 1929.

In 1881, Schreiner enrolled in Edinburgh University to study medicine, but asthma forced her to leave. Departure from Africa had enabled the author to view her homeland objectively. After moving to South Kensington, London, in 1882, she sold her autobiographical masterwork, *The Story of an African Farm* (1883), under the pseudonym Ralph Iron. The book is a settler novel depicting South African colonial life that influenced the themes and motifs of NADINE GORDIMER's *The Conservationist* (1974) and the anti-imperial writings of DORIS LESSING. Schreiner's text mocks the attempt of Gregory Rose to attain gentility by naming his colonial farm Rose Manor "in remembrance of the ancestral domain, and the claim of the Roses to noble blood . . . in their own minds at least" (Schreiner 1888, 203). The illusions of nobility and a family crest characterize the statelessness of settlers who occupy Hottentot territory while theoretically advancing their social status in their mother country.

On her return to South Africa in 1889, Schreiner settled at Winberg outside Cape Town during political upheaval over ethnocentrism, white supremacy, and apartheid. She viewed the British Empire as an unwieldy monster suffocating and poisoning the peoples entangled in its limbs. Her egalitarianism toward Indian residents later won the regard of Mohandas Gandhi, the era's model of pacifist protest against the British raj. Schreiner and her husband, politician Samuel Cronwright, whom she had married in 1894, professed libertarian ideals in *The Political Situation in Cape Colony* (1895). She continued warring against imperialism with the allegorical fool tale *Trooper Peter Halket of Mashonaland* (1897), an exposé of child rape, sexual bondage, and flogging as the standard white mistreatment of black Rhodesians. At the root of the title character's dreams lies a sense of entitlement and a belief that all white colonists profit in South Africa. In his description of the despoiling of a black concubine, Halket expresses amazement that the woman would choose a black mate over him: "They've no hearts; they'd rather go back to a black man, however well you've treated them" (Schreiner 1897, 31).

At the onset of the Second Boer War (1899–1902), Schreiner, like ISAK DINESEN in Kenya during World War I, sharpened her denunciation of colonialism. She abandoned fiction to write *The South African Question* (1899), a pro-Boer diatribe in which she imagined the British scorched-earth policy as a form of imperial suicide. The treatise allows full range to sarcasm directed at "the greatest empire upon earth, on which the sun never sets" as it "[rises] up in its full majesty of power and glory and [crushes] thirty thousand farmers" (Schreiner 1899, 104). The text charges the empire with the waste of lives and cynicism in replacing their losses with a new influx of unsuspecting settlers and civil servants. At her death from heart disease, Schreiner left unpublished *Thoughts on South Africa* (1923), which champions multiculturalism and the complex harmony of racial diversity.

Sources

Burdett, Carolyn. *Olive Schreiner and the Progress of Feminism: Evolution, Gender, Empire.* London: Palgrave Macmillan, 2001.

Schreiner, Olive. *The South African Question.* Chicago: Charles H. Sergel, 1899.

———. *The Story of an African Farm.* Boston: Roberts Brothers, 1888.

———. *Trooper Peter Halket of Mashonaland.* Boston: Roberts Brothers, 1897.

Seacole, Mary Jane (Mary Jane Grant Seacole) (1805–1881) *Caribbean herbalist and memoirist*

Mary Jane Seacole, an herbalist and combat nurse from Jamaica and a compatriot of the English nurse Florence Nightingale, compiled eyewitness accounts of SLAVERY and racism in the West Indies and the ravages of the Crimean War. Born Mary Jane Grant in Kingston, she was the daughter of a Scots soldier and a Creole Jamaican mother who was descended from slaves. She grew up among British army officers who boarded at her mother's inn in Kingston and later said she valued "good Scotch blood coursing in my veins" (Seacole 1857, 1). From her mother's care of boarders, Seacole learned folk treatments for malaria and yellow fever, the sources of seasonal Caribbean epidemics. While tending invalids, she developed a vigorous work ethic and strong imperial loyalties. In 1836, she married Edwin Seacole, who died in 1844, leaving her to raise their two children.

Seacole turned her practical skills into a career. In 1850, as a young widow, she joined her brother in Cruces, New Granada (now Panama), to nurse victims of cholera. During a sojourn in Chagres, Panama, she faced coarse comments and contempt from American men who disdained the authority of a lone black woman. She grieved that Americans and Europeans were more likely to recover from cholera than Central American Indians, who had no natural immunity to the microbe. Amid the sufferings, she opened a store at Navy Bay and sold West Indian preserves and pickles to pay for bandages and medicine. Yet in a salute to the civil engineering of imperialists, she took pride in the completion of a rail line across swamplands on the Isthmus of Darien: "It was reserved for the men of our age to accomplish what so many had died in attempting, and iron and steam, twin giants, subdued to man's will, will put a girdle over rocks and rivers, so that travellers can glide as smoothly . . . as they can from London to Brighton" (10).

In 1853, back in Jamaica, Seacole ran a hospital during the virulent yellow fever epidemic that ravaged the island. The following year, she traveled to London to volunteer for the nurse corps in the Crimea, a prize on the Black Sea fought over by British, French, Ottoman, and Russian imperialists. Because the military medical corps rejected her for being a mulatto, she journeyed overland to the combat zone outside Balaclava on her own funds and opened the British Hotel, an inn and canteen that funded her medicines, buggy, and driver. Before an armistice ended the war in March 1856, Seacole ventured into bombardments within range of cannon fire to rescue the fallen, whom she transported to her wards. She treated battle wounds as well as cholera, pneumonia, scurvy, typhoid fever, and typhus. Of her treatment of English, French, Russian, Sardinian, and Turkish patients, she remarked, "All death is trying to witness—even that of the good man who lays down his life hopefully and peacefully; but on the battlefield, when the poor body is torn and rent in hideous ways, and the scared spirit struggles to loose itself from the still strong frame that holds it tightly to the last, death is fearful indeed" (138). Her commentary provided the most valued glimpses of war by a black female autobiographer of her century.

In nursing's infancy, Seacole valued freedom of movement and unrestricted professional practice, which combined traditional medicine from the Americas, Europe, and the West Indies. Soldiers preferred her care to army hospitals because of her standards of cleanliness and nutrition and her kindness to patients of all backgrounds and ranks. In her journal, *Wonderful Adventures of Mrs. Seacole in Many Lands* (1857), she boasted that the typical casualty called her "Mother Seacole" because he "knew very well that I should not ride up in answer to his message empty-handed" (167). A wounded Russian officer was so grateful for Seacole's gentle boost into a field ambulance that he gave her his ring and kissed her hand. By the time she returned to London, she, like Florence Nightingale, was herself a recovering veteran. Her four campaign medals, her work later as masseuse to the princess of Wales, and the success of her book recouped the financial losses of her Crimea dispensary and rescued her from bankruptcy. She died a respected figure in London on May 14, 1881.

Sources

McLeod, Jacqueline. *Crossing Boundaries: Comparative History of Black People in Diaspora.* Bloomington: Indiana University Press, 2001.

Robinson, Jane. *Mary Seacole: The Black Who Invented Modern Nursing.* New York: Carroll & Graf, 2004.

Seacole, Mary. *Wonderful Adventures of Mrs. Seacole in Many Lands.* London: James Blackwood, 1857.

Seneca (Lucius Annaeus Seneca, Seneca the Younger) (ca. 4 B.C.–A.D. 65) *Roman playwright, satirist, essayist, and philosopher*

The ascetic and conservative writer Seneca—sometimes called Seneca the Younger to distinguish him from his father, the rhetorician Seneca the Elder—was a major figure in Rome's silver age of literature (A.D. 14–117). His biography is sketchy. He was probably born in Corduba (present-day Córdoba, Spain); his parents were Etrusco-Italian intellectuals. Seneca grew up in Rome, where he displayed remarkable curiosity and perception while studying philosophy and rhetoric under Attalus the Stoic. As a young man, he appears to have recuperated from chronic illness among relatives in Egypt and returned to Rome to run for a local magistracy in A.D. 31. For a quarter of a century, he conducted his public career while also writing some 10 tragedies, 10 dialogues, letters, and expository essays. Maintaining a stoic philosophy and pragmatic outlook, he lived through the consolidation of the Julio-Claudian dynasty under its first five emperors—Augustus (ruled 27 B.C.–A.D. 14), Tiberius (14–37), Caligula (37–41), Claudius (41–54), and Nero (54–68). Seneca's admirer, the historian TACITUS, declared that the orator's skills suited the demands of the day. His skill at public speaking roused jealousy in Caligula, who lacked the author's grace, courtesy, and suasion, particularly as it related to the rules of war and the justification of peace. Years later, in "De beneficiis" ("On Benefits," A.D. 63), the author wrote, "How came Caligula to be emperor of the world? a man so cruel, that he spilt blood as greedily as if he were to drink it" (Seneca 1882, 68). In his last year, Seneca saluted survivors of perilous times with a brief essay, "De providentia" ("On Providence," A.D. 64).

After Caligula's death, because of a conflict with the emperor Claudius's wife Messalina, Seneca entered an eight-year exile on Corsica in A.D. 41 on a charge of adultery. He later consoled himself in "De vita beata" ("On the Happy Life," A.D. 58) with the fact that Aeneas, Rome's mythic progenitor, was a refugee from Troy. In exile, Seneca composed "Ad Helviam matrem" ("To My Mother Helvia," A.D. 42) as a filial solace during his absence. The moral treatise "Ad Polybium de consolatione" ("To Polybius on Consolation," A.D. 44) vindicates the imperial form of government but attacks Caligula, Claudius's predecessor, for self-absorption and gambling. The author returned to the imperial court as tutor and counselor to young Nero in A.D. 49, perhaps because of the author's reputation for phrasing sententiae (aphorisms) in his moral essays—for example:

- Great wealth is great slavery.
- A realm established on injustice never lasts.
- A gem cannot be polished without friction, nor a man refined without trial.
- All cruelty derives from weakness.

- After a failed harvest comes more sowing.
- Shame may restrain what the state does not outlaw.
- The most powerful man controls himself.
- Wisdom does not come by accident.

Seneca served Nero grudgingly as councillor and adviser, acting as go-between with a disapproving Senate. His version of the FABLE ANDROCLES AND THE LION in De beneficiis ("On Benefits," A.D. 64) reflects his doubts about Nero's ability to govern mercifully and equitably. The author retired at age 58 and lived out his last three years in intellectual pursuits.

Scolding Emperors

Seneca's essay topics range from providence and caution to leisure, tranquility, blessings, pardon, and the brevity of life. He condemned imperial faults with the lively "Apocolocyntosis divi Claudii" ("The Pumpkinification of the Divine Claudius," A.D. 54), a Merippean SATIRE that consists of ridicule in alternating prose and verse mocking the deification of Claudius. The text taunts the imperial cult by which emperors were believed to ascend to heaven and, on the strength of their achievements on earth, become gods. Claudius arrives at the gate of the underworld in range of Cerberus, the hellish guard dog. Seneca smirks at his diffidence: "He saw that black, shaggy dog, which was certainly not the sort of thing you'd like to meet in the dark, and in a loud voice he cried out: 'Claudius is on his way!'" (Arbiter and Seneca 1986, 231). At a dramatic moment in the emperor's presentation, the ghost of Augustus opposes the elevation of Claudius, whose beheadings of enemies demeaned the title of Caesar. Seneca proposes that the deification of a man as vice-ridden as Claudius endangers Roman faith in all the gods. The satire mocks the dead emperor by decreeing that he will spend eternity rattling dice in a bottomless box.

A later essay addressed to Nero, "De clementia" ("On Clemency," A.D. 56), encourages him to agree to amnesty for Seneca to clear his reputation of a sex crime. The author describes the ideal emperor as one who embraces mercy as a model of equity and beneficence for Roman citizens. Seneca asserts, "It is for low and vulgar spirits to brawl, storm, and transport themselves: but it is not for the majesty of a prince to lash out into intemperance of words" (382). His essay admonishes an empire that suppresses freedom of speech, another form of SLAVERY. Tragically, Seneca died after Nero ordered his former teacher to commit suicide for his alleged involvement in conspiracy. Seneca's development of the essay as a clarification of personal moral views and behavior influenced later writers including St. Jerome, Francis Bacon, and Michel de Montaigne.

Sources

Arbiter, Petronius, and Lucius Annaeus Seneca. *The Satyricon; The Apocolocyntosis.* Translated by John Patrick Sullivan. London: Penguin, 1986.

May, Larry. *War Crimes and Just War.* Cambridge: Cambridge University Press, 2007.

Seneca, Lucius Annaeus. *Seneca's Morals of a Happy Life, Benefits, Anger and Clemency.* Translated by Roger L'Estrange. Chicago: Belford, Clarke, 1882.

Shakespeare, William (1564–1616) *English playwright*

An actor and dramatist from Stratford-on-Avon, William Shakespeare came of age at the height of the Elizabethan era of voyaging and conquest and before the founding of the British Empire. He was around 23 when he left his wife, Anne Hathaway, and their three children and moved to London, where he acted and wrote for the Lord Chamberlain's company, later named the King's Men. While portraying statesmanship in drama, he employed engaging stagecraft, salting his stories with disgruntled ghosts, assassins, and royalty beset by court treachery, as exemplified in NICCOLÒ MACHIAVELLI's *The Prince* (1514), a political manual that the playwright admired. Shakespeare chose settings on the far edge of English awareness, including Bermuda in *The TEMPEST* (ca. 1610–11), reputedly his literary farewell to the London stage. His rise to prominence coincided with the defeat of the Spanish Armada on August 8, 1588, the beginning of a multinational state and the outset of its mastery of the sea, leading to English colonialism. Literary historians note that, despite the playwright's obvious Englishness, he never overtly sided with the dominant culture.

Shakespeare's admirers included sophisticated theatergoers and drama patron Queen Elizabeth I, whose father, Henry VIII, had rid England of Rome's papal authority. At the queen's death on March 24, 1603, Shakespeare won the regard of King James I, the Scottish king who ruled both England and Scotland. Before the playwright's retirement in 1611, he produced chronicle plays about Celtic, English, and Scots history as well as comedies, tragedies, and romances that incorporated elements of SLAVERY, court and military intrigues, favor currying, and empire building. The perceptiveness of his canon won kudos in 1840 at a critical time in the British Empire, when the Scottish essayist Thomas Carlyle exclaimed in "The Hero as Poet": "Indian Empire will go, at any rate, someday; but this Shakespeare does not go, he lasts forever with us" (Carlyle 1895, 134). The declaration attests to the continued popularity of Shakespeare throughout British colonies, language groups, and educational institutions.

Shakespeare and the Roman Empire

The conventions of imperialism imbue Shakespeare's early writings with the events and strife of the Roman Empire. His first revenge tragedy, *Titus Andronicus* (ca. 1588–1594), describes a royal struggle in Rome after the death of an emperor in the final years of Roman power. The title figure, a Roman captain-general, returns in triumph from a decade in the field battling the Goths of East Germany, the fourth-century invaders of Rome. After Andronicus's election to emperor, he rejects the notion of being *candidatus*, the Latin term for the politician clad in a symbolic white toga, and spurns a request that he "help to set a head on headless Rome," an allusion to the recycling of sculpted imperial torsos with new heads (1.1.185–186). The protagonist mourns the death of Bassianus, Emperor Saturninus's brother, whom a Moorish agent and the two sons of the Gothic Queen Tamora, Chiron and Demetrius, kill in the forest. A forged letter implicates Andronicus's sons Martius and Quintus, who suffer a wrongful execution. More shocking for playgoers is the despoilation of Andronicus's daughter Lavinia, whom Tamora's minions rape and disfigure by lopping off Lavinia's hands. The internecine plot, Shakespeare's most revolting, concludes after 14 brutal deaths, a sop to lovers of GOTHIC drama and a glimpse of the carnage of war and blood that shore up empires. The vicious tragedy took on new life as *Titus* (1999), a film starring Anthony Hopkins and Jessica Lange as the Roman general and Goth queen.

Early in 1599, Shakespeare apparently perused Sir Thomas North's translation of PLUTARCH's 46 tandem life studies in *Bioi paralleloi* (*Parallel Lives*, ca. A.D. 110) for details of the March 15, 44 B.C., assassination plot against Julius Caesar. Because of the source material available, the play *Julius Caesar* is a more correctly drawn historical drama than *Titus Andronicus*. In the second funeral speech, the play's rhetorical peak, Mark Antony summarizes Caesar's climb up the political ladder from field commander to dictator for life and his refusal to wear a crown. Antony resumes by citing Caesar's victory over the Nervii in Belgic Gaul in 57 B.C., reported in the second book of Caesar's *Commentarii de bello Gallico* (*Gallic Wars*, ca. 50 B.C.). Shakespeare's chronicle is a testimonial to the grueling campaigning, hostage taking, and SLAVERY in northwestern Europa and Britannia that laid the groundwork for imperial expansion. With considerable expertise and guile, Antony stirs plebeian unrest with an alleged recitation of the dictator's will and a rallying cry: "Here was a Caesar! when comes such another?" (3.2.251). Shakespeare dramatizes the rhetorical challenge as a farewell to republican government and as an introduction to a 17-year period of administrative quandary and civil war preceding the formation of the Roman Empire in 27 B.C. In the interim, Antony, in concert with Octavius and Lepidus, Rome's first triumvirate, cynically initiates a political purge by proscribing citizens with a stab into a scroll: "These many then shall die; their names are prick'd" (4.1.1). Another testimony to opportunism, Antony's examination of Caesar's will, provides means "to cut off some charge in legacies" (4.1.9), the promised inheritance with which Antony baited his rabble-rousing funeral speech. The bloodlust, chicanery, and venality anticipate the corruption of the Julio-Claudian dynasty.

The idealism of Marcus Brutus, the prize catch of Cassius's conspirators, lends pathos to the two suicides—Brutus and his seducer Cassius—that end the five-act tragedy. In the final scene,

Shakespeare changes the tone from self-serving negotiation to a vestige of traditional Roman values. Antony concludes with a more magnanimous speech—a salute to Marcus Brutus, a defender of traditional republican Rome: "This was the noblest Roman of them all: / All the conspirators save only he / Did that they did in envy of great Caesar; / He only, in a general honest thought / And common good to all, made one of them" (5.5.76–80). The death of other leaders leaves Octavius, Caesar's nephew, adopted son, and successor, in a position to shape the national destiny. The concluding line reveals that Octavius, not yet self-proclaimed as Augustus Caesar, considers international conflict and the loss of many Romans to civil war the necessary sacrifices to an imperial future. Shakespeare's play saw two film remakes, casting Marlon Brando, James Mason, and Louis Calhern as Mark Antony, Marcus Brutus, and Caesar in 1953 and Charlton Heston, Jason Robards, and John Gielgud as the same triad in 1970.

Roman Imperialism in Africa

Shakespeare returned to the foundation of the Roman Empire with *Antony and Cleopatra* (ca. 1605), a familiar tragedy in popular history, also based on Plutarch's writings, about events following Julius Caesar's assassination. Because of the demands of compressed stage action, the text shortens to a few weeks the period between the battle of Actium in the Ionian Sea on September 2, 31 B.C., and the suicides in Alexandria, Egypt, of contenders for control of the eastern Mediterranean—Mark Antony on August 1, 30 B.C., and Cleopatra VII 11 days later. Shakespeare stresses the uniqueness of Cleopatra as lover of both Julius Caesar, the former dictator of the Roman Republic, and of Antony, one of the interim triumvirs who grappled for power before the formal establishment of the empire under Octavius.

In the play, Agrippa, the seasoned warrior, refers derogatorily to the Egyptian queen's sexual allure: "Royal wench! / She made great Caesar lay his sword to bed, / He ploughed her, and she cropped" (2.2.234–236), a reference to the siring of the twice-royal child Caesarion. Shakespeare moves from the dynastic mutterings of Agrippa about a political marriage between Antony and Octavius's sister Octavia to focus on real passion. At a crisis in Antony's life, having been dismissed as an ambitious politician, he rejects power and patriotism for love: "Let Rome in Tiber melt, and the wide arch / Of the ranged empire fall! Here is my space" (1.1.34). The inevitable ruinations of the title characters became a vehicle for the film stars Charlton Heston and Hildegarde Neil in 1972 and for Timothy Dalton and Lynn Redgrave in 1983. The historical screen version, *Cleopatra* (1963), a $44 million Hollywood extravaganza based in part on Shakespeare's tragedy, starred Richard Burton and Elizabeth Taylor and featured Rex Harrison, Roddy McDowall, Martin Landau, and Hume Cronyn as characters destroyed in the death throes of the Roman Republic.

Shakespeare and the Venetian Empire

A popular drama set in Venice, Shakespeare's *The Merchant of Venice* (ca. 1596–98), praises justice, mercy, friendship, and romance as superior to worldly aims. The action pictures a battle of wits in the rich Queen of the Adriatic, a crossroads of trade, avarice, and intrigue early in the Italian Renaissance. A subplot concerns the loss of convoys at sea to "land-rats and water-rats, water-thieves and land-thieves" (1.3.23–24), a risk common to speculators equally culpable for milking distant lands of their commodities. Along with money, the theme of European dynasty dominates the play. Among suitors for the orphaned heiress Portia are the princes of Aragon and Morocco, western Mediterranean nationalities that lend cultural and racial exoticism to the cast and introduce the power of Suleiman I the Magnificent, the lawgiver and sultan of the Ottoman Empire. Because the Aragonese and Moroccan princes fail to solve a prenuptial puzzle, they lose the lovely Portia and their right to marry and procreate (2.1.38–42). The lapse curbs the expansionism of Aragon and Morocco but foretells longevity and wealth for Portia's aristocratic bloodline.

In a parallel subplot, the moneylender Shylock and his nubile daughter Jessica are Jews living in an alien Italian realm dominated by a questionable Christian morality and by unions based on economics and social position. As a satiric highlight, Shakespeare turns into comic relief Shylock's cry, "My daughter! O my ducats! O my daughter! /

Fled with a Christian! O my Christian ducats! / Justice! the law! my ducats, and my daughter!" (2.8.15–17). Before Portia appears disguised as the sage Balthasar, Gratiano delivers an understated authorial comment on Britain's dream of world power, demonizing commercial empires as "wolvish, bloody, starved and ravenous" (4.1.138). By declaring that mercy "becomes / The thronéd monarch better than his crown," Portia begins solving a verbal conundrum (4.1.188–189). With clever legal sparring, she thwarts Shylock's bloody tribute of a "pound of flesh" from the debtor Antonio (4.1.232). Her courtroom oratory resounds with denunciation of Venetian xenophobia and of ethnic and religious bias. She earns for herself the sobriquet "a second Daniel" (4.1.334), a comparison to a Hebrew hero whose name means "judge by God." Of the value of her own debating skills, Portia exults, "So shines a good deed in a naughty world" (5.1.91), an apt description of the dishonorable status of Venice among competing nations. For the screen, the play served the talents of Sir Laurence Olivier and Joan Plowright in a 1973 film and of Al Pacino, Jeremy Irons, and Joseph Fiennes in a 2004 remake.

A Venetian Clash with the Turks

A broader view of Venetian imperialism marks *Othello* (ca. 1603–04), one of Shakespeare's more astute studies of human psychology and of the struggle for control of international sea power. Othello, a Moorish general and member of a North African royal dynasty, holds the position of commander in chief because Venetian law bars its citizens from the post in order to prevent a military junta from seizing governmental control. According to the villain Iago, Venice "cannot with safety cast him" (1.1.148), a curious comment suggesting a tenuous relationship between the black mercenary and white Europeans. In the second act, a newsbearer exults on fate, which delivers to the Turks a deadly blow: "The desperate tempest hath so bang'd the Turks / That their designment halts; a noble ship of Venice / Hath seen a grievous wrack and sufferance / On most part of their fleet" (2.1.25–28). Shakespeare's subtext implies that the weather, an unpredictable factor controlled by divine will, deserves more credit than the fleet for securing the island of Cyprus for Venice against

Turkish naval forces dispatched by the Ottoman Empire. While Othello takes control in a twist of imperial power, his detractors ridicule his thick lips and ram-black coloring, as well as the pagan taint of an infidel race called blackamoors, whom racists equate with Satan. The dialogue indicates that race is a virulent issue at any time.

Like *The Merchant of Venice, Othello* contains overt cultural stereotyping and is one of the bard's most troubling probes of evil. Venetians reproach each other for "turning Turk" (2.3.189), a reference to the different ethnic and religious rules and customs within the Ottoman Empire, which threatens a Christian hegemony. Othello's moral subversion undermines his recent marriage to Desdemona, a Venetian noblewoman. His love match destroyed by lies, he admits that his bride has reason to hate him, for "I am black" (3.3.267), an admission of fault caused by skin color. The play's contrasting roles—a military leader at a pinnacle of fame for combat service, made wretched by the entrapment of the malcontent Iago—were played by Anthony Hopkins and Bob Hoskins in a 1981 television version and by Laurence Fishburne and Kenneth Branagh in a 1995 film.

Shakespeare and the Danish Empire

The tragedian produced a monument of English theater with a study of international conniving in *Hamlet* (ca. 1599–1600), set in the Danish Kingdom at the beginning of a 750-year span of imperial rule. It is thought that Shakespeare set the play in the mid-11th century during the reigns of Harald III Sigurdsson of Norway and Sweyn II of Denmark. At the helm in Denmark is Claudius, a fratricidal monarch and wife despoiler, whom Hamlet debases as "a cutpurse of the empire and the rule . . . a king of shreds and patches" (3.4.91, 102). Hamlet scolds his tremulous mother, Queen Gertrude, for accepting a "bloat king" into her bed (3.4.182). The prince expresses his outrage that a vice-ridden lecher and crown thief should flaunt illicit power in the place of the murdered King Hamlet, the prince's father and ideal of a noble and valiant sovereign. By supporting young Hamlet's intention to unseat Claudius, Shakespeare sets a bold authorial precedent—endorsement of revolt as the Danes' right and obligation.

The bard's view of retribution within family and state suits the genre of tragedy. As in the tests of Shylock's resolve and Othello's mettle, Prince Hamlet falls victim to his innate faults. Rather than bring a criminal charge against a miscreant, he employs symbolic oratory, both his own and that of the players producing the play-within-the-play, *The Murder of Gonzago*, into "something like the murther of my father" (2.2.595). The trick serves as the prince's trap to catch a rat. Because he lacks a sovereign's resolve, Hamlet can only picture himself as an avenger: "Now could I drink hot blood / And do such bitter business as the day / Would quake to look on" (3.2.390–392). The absence of belligerence in his makeup proves him unworthy of his role as Denmark's crown prince.

At a time when Catholic Spain menaced Protestant England, Shakespeare portrayed Hamlet's downfall within a doomed royal clan. The hiatus in Danish leadership tempts power-hungry contemporaries encircling the Scandinavian nation. The young prince Fortinbras of Norway, sensing the "state to be disjoint and out of frame" (1.2.20), moves decisively toward conquest and finds a horrifying prostration of the Danish power structure. As Fortinbras enters the great hall at Elsinore Castle, he sees corpses of King Claudius and Queen Gertrude, the courtier Laertes, and the title character. The astonished prince differentiates between war and palace intrigue: "Such a sight as this / Becomes the field, but here shows much amiss" (5.2.412–413).

The complex role of a princely regicide attracted cinema greats for over a half century—among them, Sir Laurence Olivier in 1948, Richard Burton and Christopher Plummer in 1964, Richard Chamberlain in 1970, Derek Jacobi in 1980, Kevin Kline and Mel Gibson in 1990, Kenneth Branagh in 1996, and Ethan Hawke in 2000.

Sources

Carlyle, Thomas. *Heroes, Hero-worship and the Heroic in History*. Philadelphia: Henry Altemus, 1895.

Lupton, Julia Reinhard. *Citizen-Saints: Shakespeare and Political Theology*. Chicago: University of Chicago Press, 2005.

Maley, Willy. *Nation, State and Empire in English Renaissance Literature: Shakespeare to Milton*. London: Macmillan, 2003.

Shakespeare, William. *Antony and Cleopatra*. New York: Washington Square Press, 2004.

———. *Hamlet*. New York: Washington Square Press, 2003.

———. *Julius Caesar*. New York: Washington Square Press, 2004.

———. *The Merchant of Venice*. New York: Washington Square Press, 1995.

———. *Othello*. New York: Washington Square Press, 2004.

———. *Titus Andronicus*. New York: Washington Square Press, 2005.

Tennenhouse, Leonard. *Power on Display: The Politics of Shakespeare's Genres*. New York: Routledge, 1986.

Woodbridge, Linda, ed. *Money and the Age of Shakespeare: Essays in New Economic Criticism*. London: Macmillan, 2003.

Shahnameh   See FIRDAWSI.

Singer, Isaac Bashevis (1904–1991) *Polish-American journalist, novelist, and storyteller*

Isaac Bashevis Singer, the most prominent Yiddish author of his time, turned the insanity of the Third Reich's bloodtide and Stalin's purges into the elements of GOTHIC fiction and FABLE. A Hasidic Jew native born in Leoncin (near Warsaw), Poland, he grew up in Radzymin under control of czarist Russia. He and his brother and sister, authors Israel Joshua Singer and Hinde Esther Singer Kreitman, were the children and grandchildren of rabbis. Singer learned STORYTELLING and eastern European mysticism in Warsaw and, during the German occupation of World War I, in Lublin province at Bilgoray, a target of the German high command in World War I. In addition to the Torah, he read golem monster tales, fantasies about evil spirits, the Russian fiction of FYODOR DOSTOYEVSKY and LEO TOLSTOY, Talmudic wisdom, and the form of scripture-based divination through numerology known as Kabbala. At age 16, he studied at the Tachkemoni Rabbinical Seminary in Warsaw, but he rebelled against his conservative upbringing and left to work as a translator and editor for *Globus*, a Yiddish journal. In the years preceding the formation of the Nazi Empire, he published the novel *Der Sotn in Gorey* (*Satan in Goray*, 1932), a tale of illusion he serialized in his Polish literary journal. In the narrative about vibrant 17th-century folk life, a menacing false prophet arises together with satanic rituals and mass terror from the Cossack pogroms of czarist Russia—Hitlerian motifs Singer repeated in the parable "The Destruction of Kreshev" (1942) and *The Slave* (1962).

At age 31, Singer abandoned his common-law wife Rachel and son Israel and immigrated to New York City. Like his fellow expatriate Jew, NELLY SACHS, who resettled in Sweden, he supported himself as a translator and foreign correspondent for the Yiddish newspaper *Der Forverts* (*The Jewish Daily Forward*). In the months preceding World War II, he grappled with the horrific situation in Europe, which he described in *Enemies, a Love Story* (1972) as demonry: "Wasn't it possible that a Hitler presided on high and inflicted suffering on imprisoned souls? He had equipped them with flesh, blood, teeth, claws, horns, anger" (Singer 1988, 53). The author began his fiction career by befriending a lost generation, the traumatized Hungarian, Polish, Romanian, and Russian survivors of the Holocaust who fled to Lower East Side tenements and clustered at coffee shops to whisper their stories of terror.

In his tragicomic novel *Meshugah* (1994), published posthumously, Singer confessed that, because of the murders of friends and relatives, he lived on the edge: "I had driven myself into isolation and despair. But new springs of energy seemed to have opened up in me" (Singer 1994, 10). He feared that the onslaught of the Nazis on Warsaw Jewry preceded a piecemeal assimilationism in New York, but he clung to the hope that "neither religious nor worldly Jewishness was ready to become extinct" (10). He foresaw the disintegration of orthodoxy in a pre-Holocaust saga, *Di familye Mushkat* (*The Family Moskat*, 1950), a vision of a culture being destroyed. He shared dramatic ironies with his readers, who knew what awaited his protagonist, Asa Heshel Bannet, one of the metropolitan Jews who constituted a third of the population of Warsaw. The author's memories of a thriving Hasidic citizenry enabled him to relive a civic solidarity obliterated by "the Nazi hordes" (Singer 2007, 595) poised for attack on the border and to write of conditions in Poland that foreshadowed the

Nazi occupation. At the height of savagery, Singer ponders on "Mussolini, Hitler, every Nazi lout who lustily sang the *Horst Wessel* song [the Nazi Party anthem] and howled for Jewish blood to spurt from the knife" (558). The author also describes his surprise at the numbers of naive Jews who expect a miraculous deliverance.

Years after World War II, Singer used survivors' stories to recreate the lost world that East European emigrés left behind. In *Short Friday* (1964), he fused past and present threats in the stories "Alone," "The Last Demon," and "A Wedding in Brownsville," a tale of a Nazi murder that destroys the expectation of a marriage and new life. In *Shosha* (1978), he turned an alter ego, protagonist Aaron Greidinger, into a refusenik who chooses to remain among urbanites doomed by Hitler, Mussolini, and Stalin rather than flee the coming catastrophe. Bashele, Shosha's mother, warns, "These days you can't be sure of your life" (Singer 1982, 105). As proof, she cites a radio speech: "That madman Hitler . . . screamed so, you could go deaf" (105), an ironic choice of terms for a community filled with Jews who live in denial of virulent anti-Semitism.

The Voice of Suffering
Singer tried to assuage the misgivings of Jewish survivors of the Holocaust by writing in Yiddish, a language blended from German and Hebrew that he feared would soon die out. His dedication to Polish/Jewish tradition helped him cope with his sorrow at the loss of Jews in gas ovens and Soviet gulags and to the assimilation of former Jews to secular society. He envisioned a hellish microcosm in the short story "The Little Shoemakers." The narrative depicts Abba witnessing the Nazi test-run bombing of the southeastern Polish village of Frampol on September 13, 1939: "A black cloud rose over the courtyard of the synagogue. . . . The apple trees were blossoming and burning" (Singer 1960, 50). Like the conflagration of Sodom and Gomorrah, flames consume the holy books in Abba's house. He departs Poland without his shoemaking equipment, losing both his trade and Jewish identity. In his travail, he pictures himself as Jonah, whom God tested in the belly of the whale.

Through jeremiads against world dictatorship, Singer longed to free his family and all humanity from exploiters and murderers like Nazis, Black Shirts, and the NKVD, Stalin's secret police, and to reward Jews with their own homeland in Israel. His objective succeeded when the next generation of Jews began reading Yiddish writings for answers to the sufferings of their parents and grandparents. His selection as a Nobel laureate in 1978 surprised even his publisher, Farrar, Straus and Giroux, who thought that a specialist in Yiddish fiction had too small a readership to be influential. His readership increased with a revival of his fiction, mainstream theatrical versions of his stories, and film adaptations of his work, notably *The Magician of Lublin* (1979); *The Cafeteria* (1984); *Enemies, a Love Story* (1989); and *Yentl* (1983), a vehicle for Barbra Streisand, Mandy Patinkin, and Amy Irving.

Sources

Hadda, Janet. *Isaac Bashevis Singer: A Life.* Madison: University of Wisconsin Press, 2003.

Singer, Isaac Bashevis. *Enemies, a Love Story.* New York: Farrar, Straus and Giroux, 1988.

———. *The Family Moskat.* New York: Farrar, Straus and Giroux, 2007.

———. *An Isaac Bashevis Singer Reader.* New York: Farrar, Straus, & Giroux, 1960.

———. *Meshugah.* New York: Farrar, Straus and Giroux, 1994.

———. *Shosha.* New York: Farrar, Straus and Giroux, 1982.

slavery

The fate of the slave and prisoner of war echoes through the literature of empire. Scripture and chronicle resound with empathy for bondsmen and serfs, the heroes of the Hebrew book of EXODUS (ca. 450 B.C.) and the underdogs in HERODOTUS's *Histories* (440 B.C.); THUCYDIDES' *The History of the Peloponnesian War* (ca. 400 B.C.); and Euripides' *Andromache* (ca. 425 B.C.), *Hecuba* (424 B.C.), and *The Trojan Women* (415 B.C.), the latter a resilient GREEK tragedy mourning the defilement of female prisoners of war. In *History of the Jewish War* (A.D. 75) and *Jewish Antiquities* (A.D. 93), the historian FLAVIUS JOSEPHUS, an adopted Roman citizen, sorrowed at the despair of Jews under the imperial sword of the emperors Vespasian and Titus. Like

the Nigerian ethnographer AMOS TUTUOLA, the Russian writer IVAN TURGENEV, and the Bermudan autobiographer MARY PRINCE, Josephus knew sadism and menace from experience with arrogant slave owners. Another source of bondage lore, *The Last Journals of David Livingstone in Central Africa* (1874), turned the TRAVELOGUE into fuel for world abolitionism. A postcolonial backlash, the PROTEST play *A Tempest* (1969) by Nigerian dramatist Aimé Césaire, refocused WILLIAM SHAKESPEARE's *The TEMPEST* (ca. 1610–11) by sharpening images of abasement and bondage in the Caribbean, where slaves enriched European cane planters.

During the rule of the Roman emperor Antoninus Pius, Rome's first novelist, Lucius Apuleius Platonicus (ca. A.D. 123–ca. 180), a philosopher, wit, and orator from the Roman colony of Numidia (present-day Algeria), wrote SATIREs of the moneyed classes. He produced an episodic fool tale, *Metamorphoses* (A.D. 158) commonly known as *The Golden Ass*, the first work of the Roman Empire to assess the lives of the underclass. The aristocratic protagonist, Lucius the magician, overshoots his powers by turning himself into an ass, thus introducing him to the sufferings of beasts of burdens, herders, and slaves. The narrative depicts the crude tests of a sound body and mind in captives offered for inspection at the slave market. To bolster his argument for civil rights, the author dramatizes the immurement of a maidservant in a cave and the scorn of a slave's testimony against nobles in criminal court. In the 13th episode, a bondsman becomes the dowry of an aristocratic bride. After she uses him as a cat's-paw to purchase poison for the murder of a son-in-law, she suffers exile while the slave, who has no choice but to obey her, dies on a cross.

Enslavement and pillaging were the expected rewards of the Viking conquests, which spread terror over coastal Europe from 775 to 1100. In the Icelandic bard SNORRI STURLUSON's *Heimskringla* (Orb of the world, 1220), a blind sage remarks on the worthlessness of a bondsman: "Red gold and clay are things very unlike; but the difference is still greater between king and slave" (Sturluson 1833, 123). In Sturluson's *Prose Edda* (1225), the Norse imperialist pictures routine torture and on-the-spot execution of those captives not worth selling into bondage: "He who put to shame the

Host-Duke thrust out the eyes of prisoners,—he who speeds the sacrifices; in song I chant his praises" (Sturluson 1916, 226). The welcoming of death attests to the gruesome torments awaiting the hapless prisoner of war.

New World Bondage

Literary achievements struck a blow for equality and against white European supremacy. BARTOLOMÉ DE LAS CASAS, the first European author to condemn imperialism and enslavement in the New World, studied law and religion before mounting a defense of the oppressed of the Spanish Empire. Having served as a priest in the New World, he expressed revulsion at the capture and burning at the stake of the Taíno chief Hatuey on February 2, 1512, and he dedicated his literary canon to the liberation of black and Indian slaves in the Greater Antilles, Guatemala, Mexico, Nicaragua, and Peru. To convince complacent courtiers on the inhumanity of their New World enterprise, Las Casas issued a confrontational history, *Brevísima relación de la destrucción de las Indias* (A brief report of the devastation of the Indies, 1542), in part expressing European outrage against Spain's atrocities against the indigenous tribes whom Columbus encountered and whom Spanish overlords in Central America and the West Indies worked to death in mines and on plantations.

In 1782, publication of *The Letters of the Late Ignatius Sancho, an African* introduced a black perspective to British abolitionism. Born on a slave vessel on the way from Guinea to the West Indies, the author, dramatist, and essayist Ignatius Sancho (ca. 1729–80), lived in New Granada, the broad expanse of territory in the far north of South America, until his preferment at age 20 by the Duke of Montagu to the post of valet. In 1772, Sancho urged a friend to show kindness to blacks. In his last two years, he declared in a letter, "The grand object of English navigators—indeed of all Christian navigators—is money—money—money" (Sancho 1782, 149). He surmised that the vices of nonwhite Caribbeans derived from lessons learned from deceitful white colonials who introduced Christianity, greed, firearms, and liquor.

The French human rights champion Victor Marie Hugo (1802–85) chose the Haitian Revolution of 1791 for his second novel, *Bug-Jargal* (1826), a jungle melodrama begun in 1818 and featuring a noble black martyr. Set at a sugar plantation on Cap Français, Saint Domingue (present-day Haiti), in the days leading up to a wedding on August 22, 1791, the action dramatizes the destruction of Fort Galifet. A slave insurrection rings the death knell of African forced labor and of easy money for European exploiters of New World resources. Symbolizing the romantic ideal of the aristocrat, Marie's bower, the shooting of a menacing alligator, and the blossoms crushed by a black serenader presage disillusion about the permanence of French imperialism. The text exploits both the motif of the noble displaced African prince and the myth of African males sullying white womanhood. At the climax, Hugo depicts Pierrot, a giant black rebel from Kakongo, kidnapping the bride-to-be, whom he clutches while his dog Rask carries off a white infant in a cradle. From the perspective of the French hero, Captain Léopold D'Auverney, the slave represents not only a threat to the colony but also "the loathsome ravisher of Marie" (Hugo 2004, 101). By reversing the normal racial stereotypes, Hugo accuses the French of contradicting their own slogan *liberté, fraternité, egalité*.

Slavery and Vulnerability

In literature worldwide, the impressment of children into bondage echoes a distaste for dehumanizing the innocent. In *Travels in the Interior Districts of Africa* (1799), Mungo Park (1771–1806), an explorer of the Niger River, describes the blistering of feet and rubbing of chained ankles during the 30-mile-a-day passage of a slave coffle. The slave Nealee is so wearied that she is unable to flee a hive of bees on the rampage. Park describes how she "crept to the stream, in hopes to defend herself from the bees by throwing water over her body, but ... was stung in the most dreadful manner" (Park 1816, 323). Because she fails to rally, guards whip her pitilessly until she can travel only by litter. Contributing to her collapse is the daily ration, which slave mongers limit to a handful of meal and sips of water. The slaves who bear her litter and her load raise a cry, "*kang-tegi, kang-tegi* (cut her throat, cut her throat)" (325). The slave driver chooses instead to leave her behind to starve or be eaten by beasts.

With his adventure novel *Kidnapped* (1886), the Scots author ROBERT LOUIS STEVENSON recalled the previous century, when "white men were still sold into slavery on the plantations" of the Carolinas (Stevenson 1921, 61), a fate awaiting hero David Balfour. Over a decade before American abolitionist Harriet Beecher Stowe denounced bondage in *Uncle Tom's Cabin* (1852), the Cuban fiction writer Gertrudis Gómez de Avellaneda y Arteaga (1814–73) attacked native-born slavery within a creolized people when she published the melodramatic novella *Sab* (1841), the ill-starred love story of a mulatto slave who adores his white master's daughter Carlota. The story centers on the exploitation of nonwhite laborers to ensure Cuba's vast sugar industry, a cornerstone of Spanish imperial wealth and aristocratic luxury. To Teresa, an Ursuline nun, Sab grieves that his children "will be condemned to see fortune and ambition facilitate a thousand ways to glory and power for men no better than themselves" (Gómez, 1993, 107). Although published in Madrid in 1841, the story was banned in Cuba until 1914.

The inhumanity of the imperial slave era lives on in the postcolonial age. The Guadaloupian historical novelist MARYSE CONDÉ earned a Grand Prix Littéraire de la Femme for *Moi, Tituba, sorcière noire Salem* (*I, Tituba, Black Witch of Salem*, 1986), originally a research project completed at Occidental College in Los Angeles on a Fulbright scholarship. The story examines multiple crimes against Tituba, an Anglo-Ashanti martyr conceived by white-on-black rape of her mother Abena on a slave galley on the Middle Passage. In 2001, JAMAICA KINCAID, an Antiguan columnist and novelist of Afro-Carib-Scots ancestry, mused on conquerors and the conquered in her essay "Sowers and Reapers: The Unquiet World of a Flower Bed," published in the *New Yorker*. She remarked on the daybook that the U.S. founding father Thomas Jefferson kept at his home at Monticello, Virginia. A meticulous survey of herbs and vegetables, Kincaid's writing has a minor footnote on the 12 slaves who did Jefferson's bidding during planting, hoeing, and harvesting. The future president referred to a mixed-race cultivator, Beverly Hemings, a son whom Jefferson allegedly sired on Sally Hemings, his concubine. To Sally, Beverly, and Sally's other three half-white children who worked the neat terraced gardens, Jefferson provided shoes and linen and wool yardage for clothing but withheld both acknowledgement of his paternity and manumission. At a Methodist church door in Kincaid's novel *The Autobiography of My Mother* (1996), the protagonist, Xuela Claudette Richardson, imagines entering the church to remind worshippers of the Caribbean status quo. She asserts that the sources of world power lie within the usurper's triad: "connive, deceive, murder" (Kincaid 1996, 134).

Sources

Apuleius. *The Golden Ass.* Translated by P. G. Walsh. Oxford: Oxford University Press, 1999.

Gómez de Avellaneda y Arteaga, Gertrudis. *Sab* and *Autobiography.* Translated and edited by Nina M. Scott. Austin: University of Texas, 1993.

Hugo, Victor. *Bug-Jargal.* Translated by Chris Bongie. Buffalo, N.Y.: Broadview, 2004.

Kincaid, Jamaica. *The Autobiography of My Mother.* New York: Plume, 1996.

———. "Sowers and Reapers: The Unquiet World of a Flower Bed." *New Yorker* 76, no. 43 (January 22, 2001): 41–45.

Park, Mungo. *Travels in the Interior Districts of Africa.* London: John Murray, 1816.

Raser, Timothy Bell. *The Simplest of Signs: Victor Hugo and the Language of Images in France, 1850–1950.* Cranbury, N.J.: University of Delaware Press, 2004.

Sancho, Ignatius. *Letters of the Late Ignatius Sancho, an African.* Translated by Joseph Jekyll. London: J. Nichols, 1782.

Stevenson, Robert Louis. *Kidnapped.* New York: Blue Ribbons Books, 1921.

Sturluson, Snorri. *The Heimskringla; or, Chronicle of the Kings of Norway.* Edited by Samuel Laing and Rasmus B. Anderson. London: Longman, Brown, Green, and Longmans, 1833.

———. *The Prose Edda.* Translated by Arthur Gilchrist Brodeur. New York: American-Scandinavian Foundation, 1916.

Solzhenitsyn, Aleksandr Isayevich   See
PRISON LITERATURE.

Soyinka, Wole See PRISON LITERATURE.

Staël, Anne-Louise-Germain de See PROTEST LITERATURE.

Stevenson, Robert Louis Balfour
(1850–1894) *Scots novelist and poet*
A beloved fabulist and adventure writer at the height of the British Empire, Robert Louis Stevenson harbored a Scots skepticism about the merits of colonialism. A scion of three generations of lighthouse engineers, he deviated from the family career to unleash an active imagination. While immersed in the Bible, WILLIAM SHAKESPEARE's plays, Sir Walter Scott's romances, and *The THOUSAND AND ONE NIGHTS*, he rejected his family's Church of Scotland teachings and failed—or refused—to seriously pursue civil engineering coursework at the University of Edinburgh. After travels around Scotland with his father, he agreed to a compromise: law school, travel, and a career in fiction. He journeyed to Europe and witnessed the downside of commercial exploitation and Calvinist proselytizing. At age 24 in a personal letter, he summarized the depravities of empire as "tax gatherers, slaves, cheatery, chicane, poverty; suddenly drums and sunlight and the pageantry of imperial violence" (Stevenson 1997, 84).

Like many of his Irish and Welsh contemporaries, Stevenson took an ambivalent view of the colonizer and the colonized. In *An Inland Voyage* (1878), he commiserated with German imperialists for their loss of Alsace-Lorraine to France by comparing German nationalism to that of the British: "We shall never know we are Englishmen until we have lost India" (Stevenson and Osbourne 1905, 98). He added his personal regret over losing the English colonies during the American Revolution, a defeat that made him "remember what our empire might have been" (68). While treating a persistent cough and respiratory infections in his weak lungs at spas in France, Scotland, and Switzerland, Stevenson entertained his stepson, Lloyd Osbourne, with escapist episodes of *TREASURE ISLAND* (1883), an adventure story that presaged H. RIDER HAGGARD's creation of the "Lost World" genre. When the author serialized the blood-and-thunder tale as *The Sea-Cook* in *Young Folks* magazine from October 1881 to January 1882, he developed a new subgenre appealing to young men still innocent of the empire's profiteering.

Imperialism, Slavery, and Loss
Stevenson employed political intrigue in his next novel, *Kidnapped* (1886), which casts as the HERO David Balfour, the author's alter ego. The action, also serialized in *Young Folks*, features a Jacobite Catholic, Alan Breck Stewart, fleeing from the turmoil in Scotland after 1745 (Bonnie Prince Charlie's Jacobite rising). Among episodes of lost inheritance, gambling, and regicidal plotting lie character issues—for example, the depiction of Captain Hoseason, "rough, fierce, unscrupulous, and brutal," and trade in child slaves to plantations in the Carolinas, "unhappy innocents who were kidnapped . . . for private interest or vengeance" (Stevenson 1921, 43, 44). A star-packed film version in 1971 featured Donald Pleasence, Michael Caine, Jack Hawkins, and Trevor Howard.

A similar plot energizes *The Master of Ballantrae: A Winter's Tale* (1889), which Stevenson completed while he lived in the Hawaiian Islands. The story depicts the involvement of the Stewart clan in the Jacobite rising on behalf of Bonnie Prince Charlie, the exiled Stuart pretender. A subplot sets the title character in India, the British adventurer's Mecca. In 1953, the swashbuckling intrigue suited the screen image of actor Errol Flynn; a 1984 remake for television starred Sir John Gielgud.

During the Stevenson family's voyage in 1888 aboard the schooner *Casco* in the Marquesas Islands, Fakarava Atoll, Tahiti, Hawaii, the Gilbert Islands, the Solomon Islands, and Samoa, the author sought relief from his illness. In serious physical decline, he compared his malaise to the colonial threat that England, France, Germany, and the United States posed to the Pacific islands. A dying man viewing a dying paradise, he shifted his focus from masculine romance to proselytism. While surveying the colonial pillage of the islands of Oceania, especially those under German imperialistic rule, he wrote of liberty, his own and that of islanders. In prose and verse, he depicted them by lamplight, in darkness, and under a shadowed moon, all representations of their failure to understand their peril from rapacious world powers. With *In the South Seas* (1891), Stevenson lauded Samoans for lightheartedness by calling them "the gayest and the best entertained inhabitants of our planet" (Stevenson 1891, 42).

The Writer as Social Critic

In the posthumously published story "The King of Apemama" (1896), Stevenson depicted Tembinok, an island king who resisted after England colonized the Gilbert Islands. He charged the English with narrow-mindedness and blatant discourtesy to a host culture, a slight that islanders shared with highland Gaels. Both Polynesian and Gael suffered the belittling leveled by the English colonizers. Stevenson stressed the accusing eyes and the silent glare that expressed the Polynesian's outrage. After spotting a sentinel in a palm tree, he remarked, "The thought that perhaps at all hours we were similarly supervised, struck us with a chill. Talk languished on the beach" (Stevenson 1891, 22).

With the diatribe *A Footnote to History: Eight Years of Trouble in Samoa* (1892), Stevenson grew bolder. The text refutes the British hypocritical belief of freeing the savage from ignorance by drawing European characters revitalized through contact with the Samoan islander. Ironically, the self-centered imperialist profits from the Polynesian's natural goodwill and industry.

In the 1890s, Stevenson began translating island folklore for European readers. Reverting to traditional STORYTELLING, he reset the genie-in-the-lamp motif from Scheherazade's *The Thousand and One Nights* stories as "The Bottle Imp," featured in *Island Nights' Entertainments* (1893). The magic bottle formerly owned by the emperor Napoleon I and by Captain James Cook, passes in and out of the life of the hero Keawe, a Hawaiian mariner who travels from the Kona shore to Tahiti, an island of French Polynesia. Part of the curse of wish fulfillment is leprosy, a disease that turns Keawe into a pariah. The author's visit to Father Damien's leper colony on Molokai so impacted his imagination that he referred to the disease throughout his South Seas writings. The infection represents a dual torment—a medical curse and imperial encroachment. Subtextually, it replicates the horror of whites at contamination through close or intimate contact with nonwhites.

While living at Vailima, a plantation manse in Samoa, the author lobbied for islanders against the imperialistic plans of Germany, England, and the United States and from the proselytizing of missionaries, the subject of the anticolonial tales "The Four Reformers" and "Something in It" in *Fables* (1888). With the story "The Beach of Falesá" (1892), he damns Wiltshire, the white male trader, for originally viewing Uma, an island female, as a sexual commodity and for considering their half-caste children unsuitable for "white man's country" or white husbands (Stevenson 1917, 148). In *The Ebb-Tide* (1894), written with his stepson Lloyd Osbourne, Stevenson pictured the inglorious British intruder as a bearer of pestilence, a microbe less virulent than the moral pollution sweeping the beach at Papeete, Tahiti. Washed up on shore lies the detritus of empire—timbers, rigging, harpoons, rusted tanks, ladders, "a whole curiosity shop of sea curios"—a parable in junk guarded by "the commonplace ghosts of sailormen" (Stevenson and Osbourne 1905, 166–167). His sociological TRAVELOGUE, *The Amateur Emigrant from Clyde to Sandy Hook* (1895), recounts "legends of the steerage" (Stevenson 1895, 60) about passengers and stowaways escaping the Old World to better lives in the New World. The very different conditions aboard an ocean liner are a miniature version of the wealth of England's elite contrasted with that of its underclass. With a Jekyll-and-Hyde paradigm, Stevenson proposes a Conradian "heart of darkness" within the English, an evil basis of the British Empire. His view of hypocritical agendas influenced the writings of CHINUA ACHEBE, Sir ARTHUR CONAN DOYLE, GRAHAM GREENE, H. Rider Haggard, and MERVYN PEAKE.

Sources

Ambrosini, Richard, and Richard Dury. *Robert Louis Stevenson: Writer of Boundaries*. Madison: University of Wisconsin Press, 2006.

Edmond, Rod. *Representing the South Pacific: Colonial Discourse from Cook to Gauguin*. Cambridge: Cambridge University Press, 2005.

Mack, Douglas S. *Scottish Fiction and the British Empire*. Edinburgh: Edinburgh University Press, 2006.

Simmons, Diane. *The Narcissism of Empire: Loss, Rage and Revenge in Thomas De Quincey, Robert Louis Stevenson, Arthur Conan Doyle, Rudyard Kipling, and Isak Dinesen.* Eastbourne, U.K.: Sussex Academic Press, 2007.

Stevenson, Robert Louis. *The Amateur Emigrant from the Clyde to Sandy Hook.* Chicago: Stone and Kimball, 1895.

———. *An Inland Voyage.* New York: Charles Scribner's Sons, 1905.

———. *In the South Seas.* London: S. S. McClure, 1891.

———. *Island Nights' Entertainments.* New York: Charles Scribner's Sons, 1917.

———. *Kidnapped.* New York: Blue Ribbons Books, 1921.

———. *Selected Letters of Robert Louis Stevenson.* Edited by Ernest Mehew. New Haven, Conn.: Yale University Press, 1997.

———, and Lloyd Osbourne. *The Ebb-Tide: A Trio and Quartette.* New York: Charles Scribner's Sons, 1905.

storytelling (oral tradition)

An art thousands of years older than writing, oral tradition began with the human sharing of anecdotes, testimonials, cautionary tales, and hero boasts. Its style and themes undergird world scripture—for example, the Ephraimite and Judean narrations that form the Hebrew CREATION story in the book of GENESIS (ca. 500 B.C.), the Mayan POPOL VUH (A.D. 1558), and Persia's epic *Shahnameh* (*The Book of Kings,* ca. 1010), FIRDAWSI's exaltation of dynasties. The entertainment of court officials flourished with Scheherazade's telling of the stories of *The THOUSAND AND ONE NIGHTS* (ca. A.D. 942). Her skill at narration and suspense saved her life and enriched the marriage of her mate, King Shahryar, a notorious woman-hater whose antipathies softened from hearing tales and parables. The practice of pleasuring the community's ear with stories thrived among the Assyrian war camps of Sargon II, the Polynesian islanders whom ROBERT LOUIS STEVENSON entertained in Samoa, and the aboriginal sand tracers of Australia. Stories from oral tradition were recorded by Afro-Caribbean mythographers in Barbados and Trinidad, absorbed by English audiences reading the Canadian NATURE LORE of PAULINE JOHNSON and Grey Owl, and reported by the fictional Marlow's in JOSEPH CONRAD's *HEART OF DARKNESS* (1899). In the rhapsodic essay "The Songs of the Ukraine" (1834), the Russian writer NIKOLAY GOGOL lauds peasant folklore, which mingles with the birdsong of the steppes. He asserts that folk songs are "the vibrant, clear, colorful, truthful history of a nation, revealing the whole life of the people" (Gogol, 1982, 1986), especially the stories of past power structures and the evolution of survival strategies.

Inventive, rhythmic, and immediate, live storytellings by a harper, griot, jester, kahuna, minstrel, or seanachie incorporate different elements to heighten the impact of words, chant, call and response, animal sounds, and tunes. Essential to repetitions of familiar *pourquoi* (why) FABLES, such as RUDYARD KIPLING's *Just So Stories for Little Children* (1902), is the teller's ability to shape the narrative to the age span, interest, and needs of the audience. For refugees and the victims of diaspora, stories create the illusion of home and the familiar. For the anguished colonial, the masking of outrage with parody, trickster deceit, and mimicry, such as the Anancy the Spider tales of Jamaica and the Nigerian Hausa story "Spider and the Lion," offer an outlet for pent-up frustration and fear of the oppressor. The teller's tone can vary from sober WISDOM LITERATURE, as in the biblical book of Esther (ca. 175 B.C.), to simplistic jests in the PANCHATANTRA (ca. 200 B.C.), wry incongruities in stories by WILHELM and JACOB GRIMM, gripping narratives of battles and narrow escapes in the Babylonian *GILGAMESH* (ca. 1800 B.C.), and the verse stories and fables of MARIE DE FRANCE and JEAN DE LA FONTAINE.

Reclamation

Some Polynesian oral tradition found a bilingual preserver in King David Kalakaua (1836–91), a would-be emperor of Oceania who recorded the myth, legends, fables, and folktales of the Hawaiian realm. Born a quarter century after Kamehameha the Great united the island string under one dynasty, Kalakaua was educated in English. In addition to starting a Hawaiian-language newspaper, he amassed *The Legends and Myths of Hawaii: The Fables and Folklore of a Strange People* (1888) for translation into English. Like the Russian ethnographer Nikolay Gogol and the Grimm brothers, the island king valued oral tradition as a nation-building tool for his Hawaii-for-Hawaiians campaign. In the style of the Greek rhapsode, he incorporated oral genealogies, GODDESS LORE, taboos, PROPHECY, and hula and worship chants along with outrigger voyages, tattooing, sacrifice of prisoners of war, and cannibalism as true elements of the Polynesian culture that spread from Hawaii to New Zealand and east to west from Rapa Nui (Easter Island) to Fiji. In an artistic renaissance, he masterminded a comprehensive collection of pre-Christian lore before islanders lost touch with their pagan past.

Kalakaua amplified tales that encompass nature lore and history, particularly the arrival of pioneers from Tahiti and the rapacity of Captain James Cook and the European explorers who followed him. A phenomenon myth recounts how an immigrant family took refuge on a volcano and shape-shifted into lava that overwhelmed their pursuers and drove them into the sea. Voyage lore in "Moikeha and the Argonauts" describes the reunion of Polynesian dynasties from Hawaii, Samoa, and Tahiti. It concludes with an EPITHALAMIUM involving the young chief Laa's triple marriage and feast and followed by "the sacred first-born children of Laa, / Who were born on the same one day" (Kalakaua 1972, 135). "The Iron Knife" describes the first war of conquest. At a height of zeal, "the Hawaiian army, cheered by chants of battle and beating of war-drums, is buffeting the waves on its way to Maui" (182).

In the late 20th century, the Australian author Kim Scott (b. 1957) rejoiced in oral tradition as the antidote to the savagery of imperialism. He created a fictional story keeper in Harley, protagonist of *Benang: From the Heart* (1999). In a deliberate act of reclamation of the past and reunion with lost peoples, the bard chants to a circle of listeners at a campfire. Benang claims that his words channel voices annihilated by invaders of the island: "I touch the earth only once in my performance—leaving a single footprint in white sand and ash—through me we hear the rhythm of many feet pounding the earth, and the strong pulse of countless hearts beating" (Scott 1999, 9). His oral seance mesmerizes hearers with the exuberance of ancient spirits. He assures them, "I am alive. Am bringing life" (10).

Sources

Beckwith, Martha Warren. *Hawaiian Mythology.* Honolulu: University of Hawaii Press, 1977.

Gogol, Nikolay. *Arabesques.* Translated by Alexander Tulloch. Ann Arbor, Mich.: Ardis, 1982.

Kalakaua, David. *The Legends and Myths of Hawaii: The Fables and Folklore of a Strange People.* Rutland, Vt.: Charles E. Tuttle, 1972.

Scott, Kim. *Benang.* Fremantle, Aust.: Fremantle Arts Centre Press, 1999.

Sturluson, Snorri (1178–1241) *Icelandic mythographer and genealogist*

Toward the end of Viking colonial expansion west from Scandinavia into Iceland, Greenland, and Newfoundland, Snorri Sturluson, a historian, orator, and bard, compiled alliterative myth into the *Prose Edda* (1225), a repository of pagan culture and wisdom. His work prefigured the role of such antiquarians and romanticists as Sir Walter Scott, the preserver of Scots folklore, and Henry Wadsworth Longfellow, who depicted Iroquois heroism in his epic poem *The Song of Hiawatha* (1855). Born into a powerful clan of the Icelandic Commonwealth, Sturluson was educated by Jon Lopson, a chief of Norway's royal family at Oddi on the southwestern coast of Iceland. Though he wrote poetry and became famed for it, he was also a lawyer of some importance. By age 38 he had risen to a position of authority during a period of national ambition, venality, and revenge killings, when Norway's King Haakon IV sought to add Iceland to his realm. Sturluson visited Norway from 1218 to 1220, and within two years of his return to Iceland, he had once again become lawspeaker of the Icelandic parliament, a position he held until 1232. Objections to his close relationship with the Norwegian king ignited a period of armed confrontations verging on civil war, with Sturluson pitted against both his own brother and nephew. He returned to Norway to join forces with Haakon, but the king mistrusted him, and after Sturluson returned again to Iceland, Haakon ordered his death for conspiracy. He was killed on September 23, 1241.

As a tribute to Norse power, Sturluson anthologized 16 king stories into the *Heimskringla* (Orb of the world, 1220), written in Old Icelandic, a branch of Old Norse. Reordering disjointed sagas, the text chronicles the Norse monarchy up to the year 1177, including Halfdan the Old, a raider-king from late fifth-century Denmark who recurs in the folk epic *Beowulf* (A.D. 800). In heroic style, Halfdan was legendary for seizing in combat a war bride who gave him 18 sons, nine from a single birth. More recognizable as historic figures are Harald I Fairhair (860–940), Haakon I the Good (920–961), and Olaf Tryggvason (964–1000), who introduced Christian beliefs to Viking society.

The *Prose Edda*, Sturluson's collection of myths, is a tribute to skaldic or traditional minstrelsy and to the preservation of genealogy, court verse, and a great romantic cycle. Reflecting the politics of his age, the anthology comprises 29 long poems—11 lays about gods and 18 sagas of Germanic heroes. It includes many of the myths and poems of the *Poetic Edda*, a much older collection of Norse Songs and legends. The ethnographer JACOB GRIMM, in his preface to *Deutsche Sagen* (*German Legends*, 1816), praises both *Eddas*, "whose plan, style and substance breathe the remotest antiquity, whose songs lay hold of the heart" (Grimm 1883, v–vi). Sturluson filled terse lines with muscular verbs and images of natural phenomena and human resolve, as with descriptions of sailing, "The Comber fell headlong o'er me; the main called me home unto it: I accepted not the Sea's bidding" (Sturluson 1916, 221). Sturluson portrayed the harsh truth of empire in the abasement of the loser: "O Norway's gracious Signor, grant the wretched, as the happy, may now enjoy thy wise laws; give greatly, hold thy word" (226). Like the Greek tragedians, Sturluson considered his work sacred to the Allfather, who sat on high and viewed mayhem below. Sturluson warned young bards, "Remember always that these old legends are to be used to point a moral or adorn a tale. . . . Tampering with tradition is a crime against scholarship" (Sturluson 1916, xvii).

In the style of the Hebrew book of GENESIS, Viking cosmology blames the CREATION of woman for earthly strife and human downfall. According to the *Poetic Edda*, the origin poem "Voluspa" ("The Sibyl's Prophecy") describes the curiosity of the omnipotent Odin to know the past and future of the universe. The touchstone of Viking mythology, the text is the word of a female prophetess. As in

the Indian Rig Veda (ca. 1200 B.C.), the original Hindu scripture, and the Japanese *Kojiki* (*Records of Ancient Matters*, A.D. 712), written by the scribe O no Yasumaro, she harkens to a mystic time of nothingness when "Earth was not found, nor Ether-Heaven—a yawning gap, but grass was none" (16). She revisits the hoisting of land from the sea, a manly task that exalts Norse brawn. The creation of the first human couple, Ask and Embla, involves shaping bodies from wood, a holy material honored by tree worshippers. At the center of the new cosmos grows the ash tree Yggdrasil, which shelters the well of fate. The seer looks beyond human empire builders to the Ragnarok (Doom of the gods), a cataclysm of flood and fire when a final earthly battle destroys a pantheon of gods and leaves earth bare for a rebirth. The heroic strivings of humanity in Sturluson's narrative influenced the collection of Germanic lore by Jacob and Wilhelm Grimm, and the medieval sagas of the Danish-Norwegian novelist SIGRID UNDSET, recipient of the 1928 Nobel Prize for Literature. *Edda* prototypes suited Hollywood for the films *The Vikings* (1958), starring Kirk Douglas; *The Long Ships* (1964), a vehicle for Richard Widmark and Sidney Poitier; and *13th Warrior* (1999), based on a a retelling by novelist Michael Crichton featuring Antonio Banderas.

Sources

Grimm, Jacob. *Teutonic Mythology*. Translated by James Steven Stallybrass. London: George Bell & Sons, 1883.

Nejmann, Daisy L. *A History of Icelandic Literature*. Lincoln: University of Nebraska Press, 2007.

Sturluson, Snorri. *The Heimskringla; or, Chronicle of the Kings of Norway*. London: Longman, Brown, Green, and Longmans, 1833.

———. *The Prose Edda*. Translated by Arthur Gilchrist Brodeur. New York: American-Scandinavian Foundation, 1916.

Suetonius (Gaius Suetonius Tranquillus)
(ca. A.D. 69–after 130) *Roman historian, biographer, and essayist*

Writing toward the end of Rome's silver age of literature, the chronicler known simply as Suetonius reviewed the lives of emperors up to the accomplishments of Hadrian, the 14th emperor. Born in North Africa, Suetonius was the son of a soldier and lived a boyhood of some privilege, including a superior education. His father, a war hero from Hippo Regius (present-day Annaba, Algeria), set him an example of civic duty. After purchasing a modest estate in Italy, Suetonius observed Roman customs and politics as a civil servant during the reigns of Trajan and Hadrian. In his early 40s, he took a moderate stance by siding with the Roman senate in matters of principle and choice. He joined the government entourage of PLINY THE YOUNGER to the Black Sea at Pontus (present-day eastern Turkey), where both observed the workings of imperial rule in a remote territory. At age 53, Suetonius lost his position as imperial clerk because of an alleged discourtesy to Hadrian's wife, Empress Vibia Sabina. In retirement, the author wrote on biography, history, customs, politics, Greek linguistics, grammar, Pliny's letters, and the verses of HORACE, LUCAN, and VIRGIL. The date of his death is not known.

Like the Greek biographer PLUTARCH, Suetonius obsessed over personal details of great leaders. His list ranged from Julius Caesar, Rome's first dictator for life, to the first 11 emperors—Augustus, Tiberius, Caligula, Claudius, Nero, Galba, Otho, Vitellius, Vespasian, Titus, and Domitian. In *Divus Augustus* (The divine Augustus), book 2 of his famous *De vita Caesarum* (*Lives of the Caesars*, ca. A.D. 121), the historian characterizes the first emperor as an idealist who established the empire in 27 B.C. as the best solution to the turmoil left by Julius Caesar's assassination in 44 B.C. and the ensuing 17 years of civil war. With obvious favoritism, the author lauds Augustus for reviving senatorial prestige and for initiating the Pax Romana, two centuries of territorial growth and prosperity. The narrative reprises Rome's humiliation under Germanic forces on September 11, A.D. 9, in the Teutoburg Forest (present-day Saxony), where local tribes slew 20,000 members of the 17th, 18th, and 19th legions. Suetonius reveals the emperor in a frenzy, banging his head against palace walls and wailing for his soldiers' return. As a result of the loss, the Roman military those three legion numbers retired.

Imperial Contrasts

More damning than his account of an emperor's despair at a signal defeat for the Roman army are Suetonius's explicit judgments of Augustus's successors. The narrative reveals disgrace and degradation succinctly and impartially. Book 4 examines the basis of Caligula's faults and charges him with innate hostility, viciousness, and resultant mental degeneracy. Book 6 condemns Nero as a grandiloquent exhibitionist, a sexual deviant, and a despoiler of the innocent. The narrative asserts that Nero molested freeborn boys, sullied married women, and raped Rubria, a vestal virgin. As his sanity deteriorated, his vices worsened: "He castrated the boy Sporus and actually tried to make a woman of him; and he married him with all the usual ceremonies, including a dowry and a bridal veil . . . and treated him as his wife" (Suetonius 1920, 131). The final book also impugns Domitian for cunning and spur-of-the-moment executions of people who displeased him. Suetonius asserts that "the penalty which Domitian paid for his avarice and cruelty was fully merited" (281).

In contrast to the worst of the Julio-Claudian line, Emperor Vespasian, a general who rose from the ranks, stands out among Suetonius's more positive histories. Because of the rubble left by a devastating fire and public rioting, Vespasian led a clean-up crew and began restoring records dating to the city's foundation. He broke ground for a temple of peace adjacent to the Forum and another to the memory of the Emperor Claudius. Of public altercations, Vespasian commanded, "Unseemly language should not be used towards senators, but to return their insults in kind is proper and lawful," a gesture toward freedom of speech (303).

In *Scorpiace* (Antidote for the scorpion's sting, ca. A.D. 211), the Carthaginian polemist TERTULLIAN used Suetonius as a source by quoting *Lives of the Caesars* as proof that Nero was the first Roman emperor to murder Christians. The dignified style of Suetonius's literary biography influenced Einhard's *Vita Caroli* (*The Life of Charlemagne*, ca. 840), a personal memoir of CHARLEMAGNE, and Robert Graves's palace tell-all *I, Claudius* (1934), the subject of an award-winning 1976 television series starring Derek Jacobi in the title role.

Sources

Griffin, Miriam T. *Nero: The End of a Dynasty*. New York: Routledge, 2000.

Kelly, Christopher. *The Roman Empire*. Oxford: Oxford University Press, 2006.

Suetonius. *Suetonius*. Translated by J. C. Rolfe. London: William Heinemann, 1920.

Swift, Jonathan (1667–1745) *Anglo-Irish essayist, poet, and satirist*

A deft hand at sarcastic SATIRE, Jonathan Swift championed the Irish against English conventionality. A Dubliner born fatherless, he began his education at Kilkenny Grammar School and continued his studies at Trinity College, Dublin. He weathered the anti-Irish backlash during the Glorious Revolution of 1688 (when King James II was overthrown) by leaving home to attend graduate school at Oxford University and to work as an estate secretary. In his mid-30s, he entered the Anglican clergy and sought a doctorate in theology. During his free time, he edited the *Examiner* and issued broadsides, parodies, and invective condemning the British government for heartless mercantilism and for lengthy imperial wars against Spain.

During the reign of Queen Anne (1702–14), Swift failed to secure a church appointment, upon which he returned to Ireland. There he vexed the queen and her ministers with humanitarian tracts. His most famous, the persuasive pamphlet "A Modest Proposal" (1729), vilified England's treatment of the Irish and proposed an investment in livestock that would turn Irish children to profit as table delicacies for discriminating English gentry. For the sake of irony, he subtitled the essay "For Preventing the Children of Poor People in Ireland from Being a Burden to Their Parents or Country, and for Making Them Beneficial to the Publick." With a tweak at the Western Hemisphere, the fictional speaker remarks, "I have been assured by a very knowing American of my Acquaintance in London; that a young healthy Child, well nursed, is, at a Year old, a most delicious, nourishing, and wholesome Food; whether Stewed, Roasted, Baked, or Boiled; and, I make no doubt, that it will equally serve in a Fricasie, or Ragoust" (Swift 1958, 490).

Asides charge landlords with victimizing the Irish through high rents and taxes and with limiting sources of income for able-bodied workers. A proposal to turn human skin into gloves and summer boots anticipates the Nazis' recycling for profit of gold teeth, hair, and skin of death camp victims during the Holocaust.

Swift's best-selling masterwork, the mock TRAVELOGUE *Gulliver's Travels* (1726), allegorizes imperial pettiness and court fiascos under George I through the wanderings of a naïf, Lemuel Gulliver, a ship's surgeon, among the pygmy Lilliputians, giant Brobdingnagians, and horse-people called Houyhnhnms. The shortsighted surgeon, an unreliable narrator, satirizes the idea of empire through disjointed episodes of chauvinism. Occasional epiphanies remind him that his homeland and church veil colossal flaws, which he symbolizes by the high-wire acts of courtiers seeking promotion and by the fanatic antipathies between diners who crack their eggs on the small end or the large end. In Lilliput, in a description of the rearing of infant males, Gulliver admires training "in the Principles of Honour, Justice, Courage, Modesty, Clemency, Religion, and Love of their Country" and notes as an aside, "They are never suffered to converse with servants" (39), a direct jab at the treatment of Irish domestics in English employ. Upon the surgeon's return to England, he bridles when "a little contemptible Varlet, without the least Title to Birth, Person, Wit, or common sense, shall presume to look with Importance and put himself upon a Foot with the greatest Persons of the Kingdom" (93). Implicit in Swift's criticism of imperial snobbery is his faith in Irish individualism and his distaste for the British lordliness toward its tributary nations. The imaginary voyages influenced the imaginative satires of the French writer VOLTAIRE, screenwriters of a cartoon series in 1992, and a television miniseries in 1996, featuring Ted Danson and Mary Steenburgen.

Sources

Brown, Laura. *Ends of Empire: Women and Ideology in Early Eighteenth-Century English Literature*. Ithaca, N.Y.: Cornell University Press, 1993.

Swift, Jonathan. *Gulliver's Travels and Other Writings*. New York: Modern Library, 1958.

T

Tacitus (Publius Cornelius Tacitus, Gaius Cornelius Tacitus) (ca. A.D. 56–ca. 117)
Roman historian, biographer, and essayist

A brilliant successor to the essayist SENECA the Younger, the statesman and chronicler Tacitus mirrored the compression and conciseness of the Greek historian THUCYDIDES. Believed to have been born in northern Italy or in southern Gaul, he was the son of the governor of Belgic Gaul. Tacitus enjoyed the privileged education of the knight class, but he was not too gentrified to be unsympathetic toward barbarian tribes who suffered under the control of imperial Rome. He served as a mentor and friend to the essayist PLINY THE YOUNGER and, at age 22, married Julia, daughter of General Gnaeus Julius Agricola. After studying rhetoric and law, Tacitus exhibited the influence of the orator Cicero on his dignified speaking style. By age 32, he achieved a judgeship and membership in a priestly college and advanced within the year to a provincial governorship.

The jurist's worst experience with imperialism occurred after A.D. 93, when Emperor Domitian executed at least 20 senators. In the BIOGRAPHY *De vita et moribus Julii Agricolae* (On the life and character of Julius Agricola, A.D. 98), Tacitus, then a consul, accused the emperor of squeezing the life's blood from the nation. That same year, he raised questions of Roman moral and cultural differences with tribal Germans in "De origine et situ Germanorum" ("On the Origin and Situation of the Germans," A.D. 98). He retired to write for pleasure but returned to his law practice at age 44 during Trajan's term to join Pliny in the joint prosecution of Marius Priscus, a corrupt proconsul in Lepcis, Africa (present-day Al Khums, Libya). At age 56, Tacitus accepted appointment to the governorship of western Anatolia (present-day Turkey).

History as Critique

Tacitus excoriated the decline of Roman nobility into imperial squalor. Set in the reign of Vespasian, the 14-book *Dialogus de oratoribus* (*Dialogue on Orators*, ca. A.D. 105), is a paean to the quality and high moral tone of public oratory during the last years of the Roman Republic. In an attack on imperial high-handedness, he decried the loss of civil rights and freedom of speech during Rome's previous generations. In the quick-paced *Histories* (A.D. 107), he critiqued imperial failings over a half century from the reign of Nero to Domitian by focusing on A.D. 69, the year of four rulers—Galba, Otho, Vitellius and Vespasian. The narrative reminds the reader that hereditary monarchy lacks assurance of quality. Of Nero, Tacitus charges, "It was his own profligacy, his own brutality, and that, though there had been before no precedent of an emperor condemned by his own people" (Tacitus 1876, 9). In the quick succession of three despots followed by the election of Vespasian, the founder of the Flavian dynasty, the historian acknowledged that the army had more power over selection of an emperor than did the senate or citizenry. Tacitus particularized the dangers of selling official posts for money and the calamity of mob uprisings and bloodbaths climaxing with heads hoisted on poles for public viewing. He raged at the destruction of the temple of Jupiter Optimus Maximus, a long-standing emblem of Roman piety.

A broader scan in Tacitus's 16-book *Ab excessu divi Augusti* (*Annals*, A.D. 116) covered the entire empire to A.D. 116. An ambivalent text, the narrative recognizes the precarious state of Rome's line of succession by cataloguing a series of scandals, conspiracies, and crimes. Tacitus commended Augustus for making the transition from civil war to empire but held out little hope that succeeding emperors would maintain the quality of life and justice of the previous century. The history depicts Tiberius, Augustus's successor, as a sexual libertine and the puppet of Lucius Aelius Sejanus, an officer of the Praetorian Guard whom the Roman mob dismembered in A.D. 31. Of the much flaunted successes of the popular general Germanicus, Mark Antony's grandson, in central Europe, Tacitus strips the myth of glitter by balancing victories with losses. Rather than praise Roman achievements against the Germani, the chronicler concludes that the Germani made the Rhine an unyielding northern boundary of Rome's aspirations.

Sources

Haynes, Holly. *The History of Make-believe: Tacitus on Imperial Rome.* Berkeley: University of California Press, 2003.

Tacitus. *Annals of Tacitus.* Translated by Alfred John Church and William Jackson Brodribb. London: Macmillan, 1906.

———. *The History of Tacitus.* Translated by Alfred John Church. London: Macmillan, 1876.

Tagore, Rabindranath (1861–1941)
Indian poet, novelist, and short story writer

The Bengali dramatist, lecturer, composer, and peace poet Rabindranath "Rabi" Tagore of Calcutta, India, hoped his writing would become the epitaph of world imperialism. He was born to an artistic and intellectual family shortly after the Indian Mutiny of 1857, a revolt of Indian soldiers that presaged the end of southeast Asian domination by the British. A child prodigy, he devoured WILLIAM SHAKESPEARE's plays and other British works of fiction, but he abandoned fighting the Anglo-Bengali

political problem in favor of human rights for all. He stigmatized the English for ruling over India but living separately from its people. He also observed the intransigence of narrow Indian sectarianism in a time that demanded national unity. In an era of Westernized progress that brought the railroad and telegraph to India, he became a social and cultural modernist by writing verses, essays, narratives, some 2,000 songs, and SATIREs in popular Bengali vernacular. He later mocked rote religious schools in "The Parrot's Training" (1918), a beast FABLE about a bird killed after being force-fed pages of scripture. The story expressed his impatience with narrow-minded fundamentalists.

After law studies in London, Tagore returned home at age 19 without a degree. On December 9, 1883, he married Mrinalini Devi, with whom he had five children. While superintending his family's estate in Shilaidaha, he resided in a houseboat on the Ganges River along the present boundary between India and Bangladesh and observed the hardships of his family's rural tenants. Influenced by the spiritualism of the Hindu Upanishads and by the religious verses of the Sikh poet Kabir of Benares (1440), Tagore pressed for the merger of Hinduism and Islam. In the poem "Now Turn Me Back" (1893), he sought a pragmatic end to the imperial quagmire in India and to the plight of dispossessed and starving Indians who gained nothing from orthodox extremism or from mechanization of transportation and industry. He determined that the rescuer of India had to be an artist rather than a politician or military leader. In the tone of the American poet Emma Lazarus's ode "The New Colossus" (1883) inscribed on the Statue of Liberty, he demanded of himself, "Rise O poet, and give voice to these dumb, haggard and stupefied faces, bring hope to these tired, emptied and broken hearts" (quoted in Majumdar 1993, 101).

Viewing Empires

Tagore traveled the world to observe cultures. His collection *Gitanjali* (*Song Offerings*, 1912) recommended freedom of thought in "Where the Mind Is without Fear" and "Walk Alone," two of his most popular didactic poems, on a par in idealistic tone and intensity with RUDYARD KIPLING's "If" (1895). A refrain from "Silent Steps"—"He comes, comes, ever comes" (Tagore 1996, 26)—bears the poet's hope for a messiah, a rescuer to set Indians free. During Tagore's stay in the United States in 1912, he delivered eight lectures in English at Harvard University containing lessons of the Upanishads on soul consciousness, the self, and love and beauty in action; the lectures were published as *Sadhana: The Realisation of Life* (1913). He intended the texts to shake complacent Americans free from their materialism and lack of interest in the world's poor. In 1914, the year after Tagore received the first Nobel Prize awarded to a writer from India, World War I brought him to despair. He mourned in verse that "All the sorrows of the earth, all its sins and crimes, its heartbreaks and its lust for violence have swelled like a tidal wave overlapping the banks, blaspheming the skies" (112).

From 1912 to 1932, Tagore traveled widely, lecturing throughout Europe and the Americas and visiting China, Malaysia, Iran, and Egypt. Like the Jewish humanist Albert Einstein, Tagore saw apathy as a threat to survival of the human family. He was particularly sensitive to the plight of women and girls in patriarchal societies, where females lived circumscribed lives controlled by self-indulgent males. A compassionate short story, "The Fruitseller from Kabul" (1892), pities the outsider Ramun, an Afghan grape seller in Calcutta who yearns for his family. Benevolence at last neutralizes a life of bitterness as Ramun, enriched by a gift of cash after years in jail, is able to return home to the daughter he left behind.

Tagore's feminist novel *The Home and the World* (1916), the subject of a 1984 screenplay, pits the easygoing Sandip against the radical thinker Nikhil in competition for Nikhil's wife Bimala, who becomes mature enough to make her own choice. A more intense study of Hindu misogyny, the story "Haimanti" (1916) contains the motifs of dowry and of the suttee, the title figure's obligatory self-immolation on her mate's funeral pyre.

Contributing to Tagore's sensitivity to human need was a lengthy term as a widower who had lost two children. In the lyric "Shah-Jahan" (1916), he pictures the demise of the great Indian ruler, the grieving widower who built the Taj Mahal to honor his wife Mumtaz: "You are gone, now, Emperor— / Your empire has dissolved like a dream / Your throne is shattered, / Your armies, whose marching / Shook the earth, / Today have no more weight than the windblown dust on the Delhi road" (Tagore *Selected Poems* 2005, 79).

The Citizen as Individual

In 1915, Tagore received a knighthood, but he renounced the honor four years later after the Amritsar massacre of April 13, 1919. Because of the British Indian Army's attack on 1,800 unarmed men, women, and children with 10 minutes of gunfire, killing 379 (and possibly more), Tagore devoted his life and art to the underclass, whose dignity and values he ranked above political concerns. In 1923, he wrote the story "The Editor," a touching salute to a widower who gives up journalistic sniping to rescue his daughter from a fever. In 1928, Tagore wrote a letter to a Methodist missionary on the waste of Indian lives and talents under imperial rule. He declared, "The best way of keeping a people permanently under foreign subjection is to kill their humanity" (Tagore 1997, 362). He dedicated his remaining 13 years to writing to alleviate the plight of the underclass.

Tagore cultivated serenity in his *Collected Poems* (1937). His verses acknowledge the control of the almighty over earthly strife: "Away from the sight of Thy face/My heart knows no rest or respite" (quoted in Roberts and Amidon 1991, 312). In physical decline in his late 70s, he feared the rise of Adolf Hitler's Nazi empire in 1939. In the poem "Those Who Struck Him Once," he compared Fascists to those who killed Christ: "In their roaring mingles the music of their hymns, while the Son of Man in his agony prays, 'O God, fling, fling far away this cup filled with the bitterest of poisons'" (quoted in Majumdar 1993, 123). In 1940, Tagore supported Mohandas Gandhi in seeking an end to the British Raj and demanding relief for India's poor. In a final speech delivered a few months before the formation of the Quit India Movement, he looked to World War II as the dawn of a global power shuffle: "The time has arrived to prove that the power, vanity, and conceit of the very powerful also are not secure" (98). Tagore's writings influenced the screenplays for *Kabuliwala* (1956, 1961), *The Lonely Wife* (1964), and *Sand in the Eye* (2003); his life was the source of the documentary

Rabindranath Tagore (1961). Tagore's belief in self-determination influenced HAN YONG-UN, a Korean independence fighter, and ANNA AKHMATOVA, a poet of the Russian Empire.

Sources

Majumdar, A. K. Basu. *Rabindranath Tagore, the Poet of India.* New Delhi: Indus, 1993.

Roberts, Elizabeth, and Elias Amidon, eds. *Earth Prayers from Around the World.* San Francisco: HarperSanFrancisco, 1991.

Tagore, Rabindranath. *Gitanjali.* Introduced by William Butler Yeats. London: Branden, 1996.

———. *Sadhana: The Realization of Life.* New York: Three Leaves Press, 2004.

———. *Selected Letters of Rabindranath Tagore.* Edited by Krishna Dutta and Andrew Robinson. Cambridge: Cambridge University Press, 1997.

———. *Selected Poems.* Translated by William Radice. London: Penguin Classics, 2005.

———. *Selected Short Stories.* Translated by William Radice. London: Penguin Classics, 2005.

Tan, Amy (An-mei Tan, Amy Ruth Tan)
(1952–) *Chinese-American writer*

By voicing her mother's eyewitness account of Japanese conquests in China, Amy Tan recorded the postimperial collapse of Nationalist China and the liberation of many women from male oppression in the diaspora preceding Mao Zedong's communist takeover. She was born in Oakland, California, to Chinese parents who were part of that diaspora. Of the flight to America of her parents, Daisy Du Ching and John Tan, Tan explained, "Immigrant parents come to America with the idea that they're going to lose ground, economically and socially, but that their children will eventually benefit from what they've done" (quoted in Chatfield-Taylor 1989, 178). To express hope for propitious times, her parents gave her a Chinese name, An-mai, meaning "blessing from America" and expounded Chinese WISDOM for her edification from traditional sources. Bringing up a bicultural family taxed the parents, especially as their daughter preferred independence over obedience. Amy struggled against the claustrophobic mother-daughter bond that generated constant and deep-seated antipathies. She absorbed

Western culture through reading AESOP's FABLES, Bible stories, *Grimm's Fairy Tales,* and the prairie memories of Laura Ingalls Wilder. With degrees from San Jose State University and the University of California at Santa Cruz, Tan epitomized the postimperial liberalization of Chinese women.

After working several years as a technical writer, Tan began to explore the feminist aspects of prewar China, a culture that had vicariously influenced her life and language. She examined ethnic clashes between Chinese mothers and first-generation American daughters in *The Joy Luck Club* (1989), her popular first novel. Tan's account of the erosion of traditional social mores begins with the fall of the Qing dynasty (1644–1912), China's last feudal royal house, when Marxist and Christian perspectives began to question feudal marriage and female depersonalization. The first women seeking independence suffered many hardships. During a flight west to Chungking from Japanese invaders of Kweilin, the most tragic character, the war widow Suyuan Woo, survives starvation and dysentery by abandoning twin infant girls, Chwun Hwa and Chwun Yu Wang. Suyuan's contemporary, Gu Ying-ying, endures statelessness in the hands of a California office of the Immigration and Naturalization Service: "She stayed there for three weeks, until they could process her papers and determine whether she was a War Bride, a Displaced Person, a Student, or the wife of a Chinese-American citizen" (Tan 1989, 107). The journey ends with an expatriate life in San Francisco's Chinese-American enclave, where cultural elements like American given names, social games of mah jong, the formation of an investment club, and the reunion of Suyuan's first and second families illustrate their adaptation to the West. In 1991, the novelist coauthored the screen version filmed in part in Guilin, China; a stage adaptation debuted at Theatre Works in San Francisco in 1998.

Generational Stories and Sisterhood

In the female-driven *The Kitchen God's Wife* (1991), an intimate talk-story and winner of a *Choice* best book citation, Amy Tan exonerates her mother's hasty choices. Like PEARL BUCK's *The Good Earth* (1932), the narrative depicts female lives from a noncombatant female's point of view against a backdrop of refugee displacement and economic uncertainty. For material, Tan drew on long conversations with her mother that revealed a series of long-kept secrets. In their talks, Daisy Tan spoke of the unhappiness of a seven-year marriage to the villainous Wang Zo and the relief of escaping from the constraints of unfeeling male domination. According to Winnie Louie, the fictional version of Daisy Tan, traditional Chinese courtship "was like buying real estate" (Tan 1991, 164), a father-to-groom negotiation conducted by a marriage broker to settle dowry and bride price. Seeking freedom from such patriarchal matrimony, in the 1930s, Winnie and others of Nationalist China's New Women abandoned the old-rituals of Chinese customs to embrace egalitarianism.

Amy Tan established a bicultural rapport with her mother that produced accounts of the anger and outrage of a wife-prisoner in a feudal marriage and domestic abuse resulting in the deaths of two infants. To characterize the dismal captivity of concubines in polygynous marriages, the author sympathizes with the paramours of a womanizer who chooses to abort fetuses rather than raise unwanted children. Through the book, she lionizes her widowed maternal grandmother, Gu Jingmei, forced to marry a wealthy industrialist, the sexual and financial dominator of five women, seven children, and their individual servants. Her character opts for a suicidal meal of rice cakes laced with bitter opium rather than struggle for domestic dignity as a replacement wife. Such use of food contradicts the typical womanly offering of sweets as a love token; instead food becomes a release from unbearable servitude.

Contemporary with husband's bullying and marital rape was the Nanjing Massacre, a series of appalling atrocities committed by Japanese forces from November 1937 to early February 1938. In their advance south from Manchuria to Shanghai and after occupying Beijing and Tianjin, the invaders raped and murdered some 260,000 Chinese peasants, who cowered in a state of *taonan*, a nearly untranslatable term roughly equivalent to "scared to death."

The next generation of Chinese, epitomized by the author's mother, Daisy Tan, moved further away from domination by establishing careers and stable marriages. Daisy's counterpart, Winnie Louie, works as a vocational nurse and hospital technician in Shanghai. To circumvent Wen Fu, an abusive philandering husband and a pilot for the Kuomintang air force during the Sino-Japanese War (1937–45), she aborts three pregnancies to spare future children the menace of a psychopathic father "hungry to feed his own power" (325). Essential to her blossoming, a period of fifteen months in a women's prison for adultery and a divorce and remarriage redirect her life from Tientsin to American justice in California. Heightening the suspense, a period of civil war ending in the Communist takeover compels the fictional Winnie Louie to rely on a female rescuer, Auntie Du, enabling her to escape during the last five days that the Chinese borders remain open.

Tan depicted sisterhood as a major factor in her subsequent works. In the two-part plot of *The Hundred Secret Senses* (1995), she describes the initial gap in understanding between half sisters as the older one, Kwan Li, tells ghost stories and FABLES in pidgin English to her sibling, the Amerasian protagonist (and the book's narrator) Olivia Yee Laguni. In a past life that Kwan recalls, Olivia was interpreter Nelly Banner and Kwan was Nunumu, the laundress for an English mission compound in Changmian, China. The climax occurs during the Taiping Rebellion of 1864, when Manchu soldiers patrol rural villages to exterminate God worshippers, roast a human leg over a fire, and torch the caves of Thistle Mountain to suffocate or burn alive villagers who take refuge in subterranean passages. Tan depicts the real American mercenary leader Frederick Townsend Ward of Massachusetts as General Warren, but she omits Charles George Gordon, a British Army major general who completed the mission to quell the rebellion after Ward's death in battle in 1862.

The lack of communication between a female ghostwriter and her mother, the attempted suicide of a nanny, and a woman's punishment of her illegitimate daughter are the main elements of *The Bonesetter's Daughter* (2001). Set in Hakka hamlet near Thistle Mountain outside Guilin. The narrative equates 21st-century bad blood with spiritual unrest from previous centuries, particularly the slaughter of 30 million Chinese in 17 provinces during the emperor's war against anti-Confucian

Christian revivalism, which lasted from 1850 to 1864. The concurrent accounts of past lives and recovered memories incorporate situational irony alongside GOTHIC elements—brigandage; bride capture; and a stalker, the drug-addicted Chang Fu Nan. Crucial to a tale of communication between generations is the brush-and-paper script writing method passed patrilineally through apprenticeships limited to the family's sons. Thanks to an illicit matrilineal heritage, the character LuLing at last communicates with her daughter using calligraphy, a symbolic representation of truth.

Sources

Chatfield-Taylor, Joan, "Cosmo Talks to Amy Tan: Dazzling New Literary Light." *Cosmopolitan* 207 (November 1989): 178–180.

Ma, Sheng-mei. *The Deathly Embrace: Orientalism and Asian American Identity.* Minneapolis: University of Minnesota Press, 2000.

Palumbo-Liu, David, ed. *The Ethnic Canon: Histories, Institutions, and Interventions.* Minneapolis: University of Minnesota Press, 1995.

Tan, Amy. *The Joy Luck Club.* New York: Penguin, 1989.

———. *The Kitchen God's Wife.* New York: Penguin, 1991.

tantras

During the European Middle Ages, The Tantras (Weaving), a syncretic Sanskrit encyclopedia of the Pala Empire (750–1174), proposed a philosophy of unifying creation. In the third century A.D., Buddhism altered its orthodoxy to accommodate a literary exploration of the body and the psyche. Influenced by vernacular romance and inspirational verse, writers of the resulting texts offered Brahmans of Assam, Bengal, and Kashmir a means of satisfying their desire to unite with the divine. In a period of widespread translation into other Asian languages, writers of nonsectarian tantras gave guidance to practitioners of Hinduism and Buddhism in Bhutan, Cambodia, China, Japan, Korea, Mongolia, Nepal, and Tibet. Among such writers was Padmasambhava, a Tibetan evangelizer and lama who also composed the Tibetan BOOK OF THE DEAD (ca. A.D. 775).

Tantras consist of chants, collections of psalms, legends, FABLEs, dialogues, parables, incantations, and charms based on the tensions between yin and yang, a universal polarity. The *Lakshmi Tantra* (ca. A.D. 950), an Asian contribution to GODDESS LORE, enshrines the divine female in glory and, in the EPITHALAMIUM, wreathes her with human gratitude for passion and sexual satisfaction. An attack against pious exhibitionism, the *Hevajra Tantra* (ca. A.D. 790) uses mysticism to express human freedom at all social levels through direct knowledge. The *Kularnava Tantra* (Ocean of Tantrism, ca. A.D. 1000) scorns bookishness for depriving the scholar of such concrete experiences as ritual coitus. The *Sarada Tilaka Tantra* (ca. 1000) summarizes CREATION LORE, godhood, and magic. Compiled after the fall of the Pala Empire and during the rise of Islam in India, the *Mahanirvana Tantra* (1295) speaks of the blessings of earth and fosters an enjoyment of food. A guide to pleasure in NATURE, superstition, passion, food, and alcohol, the text advocates a controlled indulgence in earthly joys devoid of shame or fear.

Sources of Tantric Wisdom

The forerunners of the tantric canon, written during the Guptan Empire (ca. A.D. 280–550), use poetry and aphorisms to identify the duties of Buddhism and Hinduism. A parable in the *Yogacara Bhumi Sutra* (A.D. 284) recommends reconciliation and forgiveness as prefaces to contentment. The *Guhyasamaja Tantra* (Total of mysteries), which the sage Asanga wrote around A.D. 350, outlines the value of meditation and standardizes the tantric tradition. Saraha, a Bengali arrow maker, monk, and poet, compiled 280 verses in the SATIRE *Dohakosha* (Treasury of songs, ca. A.D. 790), which mocks ascetics and the religious hierarchy for public posturing. Sahara extols the human form and encourages seekers to celebrate the physical senses with the wonder and delight of children. At the command of Emperor Junna, the Japanese cleric Kukai (774–835) composed 10 volumes on Buddhist spiritual illumination entitled the *Juju Shinron* (Ten stages of religious consciousness, A.D. 830), a parallel to Indian and Tibetan tantric writings.

Tantric WISDOM encompasses the extremes of the human condition. The *Kalachakra Tantra* (Wheel of time tantra, A.D. 966), a collection of initiation and purification rites from northwestern India, describes in Sanskrit the cycles and rhythms of phenomena, both in the body and the universe. From the Buddhist perspective on life, the aphorisms comment on the inevitability of pain:

> In the womb there is the suffering of dwelling in the womb;
> at birth and while a child there is also suffering.
> Youth and adulthood are filled with the great sufferings of
> losing one's mate, wealth, and fortune, as well as the great suffering of the afflictive emotions.
> The old have the suffering of death.
> (quoted in Dalai Lama 1999, 39–40).

While acknowledging suffering, the spiritual movement called Tantra instructed ordinary worshippers to refrain from needless hurt. Texts revolutionized social convention by honoring women and branding womanizers and wife beaters as sinners. Tantric writing elevated wives to equal partnership in marriage, accepted females in positions of authority, and denounced suttee, the obligation forced on widows to share their dead husbands' funeral pyres.

Sources

Dalai Lama XIV. *Kalachakra Tantra: Rite of Initiation.* Edited and translated by Jeffrey Hopkins. Somerville, Mass: Wisdom Publications, 1999.

Roberts, Elizabeth, and Elias Amidon, eds. *Earth Prayers from Around the World.* San Francisco: HarperSan Francisco, 1991.

Urban, Hugh B. *Tantra: Sex, Secrecy, Politics, and Power in the Study of Religion.* Berkeley: University of California Press, 2003.

Tao Qian (Tao Chien, Tao Yuanming)

(A.D. 365–427) *Chinese poet and essayist*

A classical scholar and liberal Daoist (Taoist) philosopher, Tao Qian (Tao Chien) explored in verse his views on life's unremitting struggle. Virtually unknown in his day, he was born Tao Yuanming of noble lineage during the Eastern Jin dynasty in Jiangxi, southeastern China. According to his AUTOBIOGRAPHY, *Biography of the Gentleman of Five Willows* (date unknown), after 13 years of city life, he wearied of court corruption and jockeying for power. Contributing to his discontent was sorrow at

the death of his brother Zhang's wife in Wuchang at a young age. In winter 400, Tao gave up a civil service post to live simply in a ramshackle thatched hut and support his wife and five sons by farming. He chortled, "I'll take this farmland life anytime, anytime" (Tao 2000, 10).

Like the Greek agrarian poet Hesiod, Tao found his work taxing and unremunerative. Lacking an ox, he pulled his own plow while his wife guided it down the furrows. After his home burned, poverty drove him back to bureaucracy in the capital. He briefly served in the army and took a magistracy in the town of Peng-tse 30 miles to the northeast before returning six years later to his rural roots in the village of Chai-sang, six miles southwest of Jiujiang. The ode "Returning to My Old Home" pictures his first glimpse of terraced fields and plots where houses vanished after neighbors died. Literary historians deduce that the poet's love of independence and seclusion led to alcoholism and a disavowal of his youthful Confucianism. Leaning his walking stick on the brushwood gate, he retreated into reading, reciting poems, and plucking the *koto* and took Dionysian delight in sipping wine and being himself.

Like the Roman poets HORACE, JUVENAL, and VIRGIL, in retirement from public life, Tao Qian rejoiced in solitary walks in the hills in sight of flocks of birds and South Mountain. He anticipated death as inevitable. At "home day-in day-out, taking things easy" (22), he grew chrysanthemums, vegetables, millet, herbs, bamboo, and shade trees and contemplated old age in an area where villagers "make mornings and evenings pure joy" (48). He put little faith in emperors and advancement and declared, "Getting rich isn't what I want" (18). He grieved that he was born too late to attain the high moral tone of "thousand-year-old books" written by "timeless exemplars" (28).

Tao's publications survive as evidence of a structured life relieved on occasion by wine drinking with friends and enjoyment of song and small talk. He composed a utopian essay in prose, "Tao Hua Yuan Ji" ("Peach Blossom Spring," ca. 420). Revealed to a fisherman through a cleft in the mountains, the Shangri-la of Peach Blossom Spring represents rural happiness based on work and modest rewards. To avoid war, the people settled the remote haven two centuries earlier after 221 B.C. during the Qin (Ch'in) dynasty. Fortunately for their peace of mind, no followers of the fisherman's trail located the valley.

Historians interpret Tao's hermitism as overt scorn of the ruling class. His ascetic philosophy found strength in the timelessness of earth and heaven and in cycles that never end. Of the dangers of empires, he groused, "Ch'in's First Emperor ravaged the sense/heaven gives things, and wise people fled" (Tao 2000, 71). The poet scorns that "Great men want the four seas" (74). In contrast to greed and power, he describes the detached Daoist lifestyle as worry-free, a reference to his ragged robe and bare rooms overlooking a shady country lane. Like the Greek warrior-poet Archilochus, Tao acknowledged the finality of mortal life with equanimity: "There's no doubt about it, death's death" (39). He discredited the permanence of Daoism and noted that the human legacy must be good works founded on love. To foolish time wasters, he urged an embrace of nature's abundance and of the precious moments that quickly fade into "the empty sorrows of distance" (80). Tao's lyrical writings later influenced poets of the Tang dynasty (608–907), who took comfort in his relaxed but earnest anti-imperial verse.

Sources

Tao Qian. *The Selected Poems of T'ao Ch'ien.* Translated by David Hinton. Port Townsend, Wash.: Copper Canyon Press, 2000.

Zongqi, Cai, ed. *Chinese Aesthetics: The Ordering of Literature, the Arts, and the Universe in the Six Dynasties.* Honolulu: University of Hawaii Press, 2004.

Tao-te Ching   See DAODEJING.

Tempest, The **William Shakespeare** (ca. 1610–1611)

WILLIAM SHAKESPEARE's stage romance *The Tempest* pictures a common figure in imperial literature, the outcast ruler in exile. Drawing from 17th-century seafaring lore, the play alludes to the wrecking of the 300-ton flagship *Sea-Venture* on Bermudan shores on July 24, 1609. A nor'easter off the Azores separated the ship from a convoy of seven armed merchant ships and two pinnaces or tenders bound from Plymouth, England, with supplies for Jamestown, Virginia. After three days of buffeting, the *Sea-Venture*, England's first purpose-built emigrant ship, and its 150 passengers survived a miraculous beaching on the reefs at Gates Bay, an unidentified inlet. On July 28, Admiral George Somers, Sir Thomas Gates, and the crew of the Virginia Company of London retrieved the cargo and sheltered on the "Devil's Islands," which they began colonizing. Some 142 survivors retrieved rigging and fittings from the *Sea-Venture* and sawed cedar trees into two boats—the *Deliverance* and the *Patience*—that carried them to Jamestown on May 23, 1610. The arrival saved the dwindling colony from starvation and disease.

In the early years of the rule of James I over England and Scotland, William Shakespeare's interest in historical literature led him to *A True Declaration of the Estate of the Colonie in Virginia* (1610), possibly written by an investor named Dudley Digges. English translations were also available of the French essayist Michel de Montaigne's "Of Cannibals" (1580), which offered a bloodthirsty view of the New World's primitive societies, based on his meeting with a Brazilian native. Additional data from Sylvester Jourdain's "A Discovery of the Barmudas, otherwise Called the Ile of Divels" (1610)—an eyewitness account in a letter by William Strachey, a survivor of the *Sea Venture*'s mishap, and a pamphlet by Sir Thomas Gates, governor of Jamestown—supplied enough background for Shakespeare's composition of *The Tempest*. For romanticism, the playwright drew on Italian street drama, the commedia dell'arte, for the stereotypes of the villainous Caliban, the ingenuous Miranda, and the buffonish Stephano and Trinculo, who augment a cast of nobles striving for control of wealthy Italian duchies. Literary critics identify Caliban as a symbol of the diasporic victim, the disgruntled slave of West Indian entrepreneurs. In a retort to Prospero, Caliban sneers, "You taught me language, and my profit on't / Is, I know how to curse" (1.2.363–364).

After the King's Men debuted the allegorical play at the Globe and at Blackfriars, a reprise at

Whitehall on November 1, 1611, delighted King James I and the Jacobean court with the fairy tale plot. The setting, a magical land to Europeans, bears "subtleties o' th' isle, that will not let you believe things certain" (5.1.124–125), a description of the allure of North America to explorers, readers, and playgoers. The title represents the human predilection for VIOLENCE; the action turns to comedy with a series of plots and counterplots interwoven with magic spells carried out by the wizard and master manipulator Prospero and his sprite Ariel. With its combined themes of atonement, forgiveness, and conciliation between conspirators and castaways, *The Tempest* was, perhaps fittingly, Shakespeare's last play, and therefore is called his "farewell to the theater." The popular work continued to please royal audiences for the nuptials of Elizabeth, the princess royal, to Frederick V, Count Palatine, on February 14, 1613. John Dryden's version of *The Tempest* in 1667 received mention in the diary of Samuel Pepys. Seven years later, the playwright Thomas Shadwell presented the drama in opera form, which the composer Henry Purcell rescored in 1695.

Staged Imperialism

Shakespeare's romance is a miniature version of the imperial clashes of his era and the abrupt unseating of rightful rulers. The dramatic conflict off the "still-vexed Bermoothes" (1.2.229) reflects an imperial conflict of the dramatist's day: the Hapsburg and Bourbon jostling for the duchy of Milan and the kingdom of Naples. The playwright describes a similar struggle for power in the coup d'état by which Antonio usurps his brother Prospero's rule of Milan, a plot abetted by King Alonso of Naples. The text is one of family treachery, guilt, and repentance. Resolution of a political wrong rests on a Romeo-and-Juliet romance between Prospero's daughter Miranda and Ferdinand, the crown prince of Naples. Shakespeare has Sebastian say of Prospero's domain: "I think he will carry this island home in his pocket and give it to his son for an apple" (2.1.89–90), a double image of inherited rule that implies its success needs tending and nurture. The cynical summation attributes to the wizard Prospero the power-mongering of both the speaker and Antonio, his fellow plotter.

To emphasize the absence of greed and conspiracy in Prospero's New World realm, Shakespeare frees Miranda of earthly ambition by isolating her on the shores of Bermuda, far from Europe's cabals and power struggles. The three evildoers—Caliban, Trinculo, and Stephano—undergo a trial by ordeal as punishment for their plotting murder. The romantic conclusion illustrates how purity of motive and innocent love renew humanity and reaffirm the best in the "brave new world" (5.1.205), which Shakespeare depicts as Europe's second chance for self-redemption. Antonio envisions the start of an English toehold in North America as "sowing the kernels of [empire] in the sea, bring forth more islands" (2.1.91–92). The Shakespearean romance and its allegory of repentance and forgiveness flourished in movie format in *Tempest* (1982), featuring John Cassavetes, Molly Ringwald, Susan Sarandon, and Raul Julia; and in *Prospero's Books* (1991), starring John Gielgud.

A Power Shift

In 1969, a proponent of black Antillean nationalism, Aimé Césaire (1913–2008) of Martinique, adapted Shakespeare's romance into the drama *Une Tempête* (*A Tempest*), a surreal cleansing of the West Indies of British colonialists. He invigorated his Creole French play with subversion of British egotism and condescension through the enchantment of Afro-Caribbean animism. Dialogue represents the opposing philosophies of Malcolm X and Martin Luther King, Jr., in the characters of Caliban and Ariel, one a bitter black African and the other a thoughtful maroon. When the storm rages, the captain feels the presence of Shango, a monstrous, whirling *orisha* (divinity) carried west with the diaspora from the Oyo Empire (present-day Nigeria). Shango's phenomena hover over the action like black rage at postcolonial racism and treachery. Unlike Shakespeare's benign view of Renaissance colonialism, Césaire's power structure lies in the hands of nature, which dwarfs the buffeted ship and entwines Prospero in a jungle grotto, a symbol of the white illusionist's self-exile in enemy territory.

Césaire delighted in humbling the European imperialist. While the wizard Caliban wields magic, the seagoing adventurers crouch in their cabins.

The storm humbles the crew and passengers for their effrontery in an expedition that threatens to contaminate the New World with greed, SLAVERY, and GENOCIDE. Expressing his outrage, Caliban accuses Prospero of the worst of betrayals, "Imposing on me an image of myself: underdeveloped, in your words, incompetent" (Césaire 1985, 16). Following the radical orator Malcolm X, Césaire accuses Prospero of robbing blacks of their self-esteem, true names, and history. Caliban commands, "Call me X" (18), a rejection of the identity forced on him by Europeans. In 1998, Césaire's adaptation opened on the London stage on the 150th anniversary of the abolition of slavery in the French Antilles.

Sources

Césaire, Aimé. *A Tempest.* Translated by Richard Miller. New York: Borchardt, 1985.

Maley, Willy. *Nation, State and Empire in English Renaissance Literature: Shakespeare to Milton.* London: Macmillan, 2003.

Nutall, A. D. *Two Concepts of Allegory: A Study of Shakespeare's The Tempest and the Logic of Allegorical Expression.* New Haven, Conn.: Yale of University Press, 2007.

Shakespeare, William. *The Tempest.* New York: Washington Square Press, 1961.

Ten Thousand Leaves   See MANYOSHU.

Tertullian (Quintus Septimius Florens Tertullianus) (ca. A.D. 155–after 220)
Carthaginian essayist and polemist

The first notable apologist for Christianity, Tertullian formalized many standard Christian religious terms and agitated for religious freedom. The son of a Roman centurion based in Carthage (present-day Tunisia), he apparently was a trial attorney and spirited forensic orator. His scholarship and command of rhetoric attests to a good education in grammar, literature, logic, oratory, and philosophy. In his late teens and early manhood, Tertullian studied law. After a conversion from paganism to Christianity in A.D. 196, he spurned Athenian philosophers for their worldliness and attacked the Roman culture of barbaric sport at gladiatorial events. He became a disciple of the prophet Montanus, a millennialist, and a teacher of orthodox theology. Some biographies surmise that Tertullian was ordained into the priesthood, a preface to his rise to prominence as one of the early Latin fathers. During the disastrous reign of Septimius Severus and the improved conditions under Caracalla, Tertullian's essays in both Greek and Latin, "Ad martyras" ("To the Martyrs," A.D. 197), "De idolatria" ("Of Idolatry," ca. A.D. 200), "De corona" ("Of the Crown," A.D. 201), "Scorpiace" ("Antidote for the Scorpion's Sting," ca. A.D. 211), and "Ad Scapulam" ("To Scapula," A.D. 214), reviled Roman attitudes on religion, the soul, and morality and shamed the persecution of Jews and Christians, even though their loyalty to Rome was unimpeachable.

The thrust of Tertullian's reasoned essays gave insight into concepts of nationhood and ethnicity during the Roman Empire. He defended a maligned faith by recalling the crucifixion of Peter, the stoning of Stephen, the beheading of James, and the imprisonment of Paul, a Roman citizen. His *Apologeticus* (*The Apology,* ca. A.D. 198), a forceful attack on imperial persecution of minority faiths, declares martyrdom the foundation on which the church would grow and survive. The text lauds Emperor Tiberius for recognizing Christians as a sect in the years following Christ's death. Tertullian accuses later Roman emperors of cowardice for fearing the worshippers they condemned and crucified: "Men cry out that the state is beset, that the Christians are in their fields, in their forts, in their islands" (Tertullian 1854, 2). As proof of disquiet over the sect's growth, Tertullian lists the pagan faiths of tribes throughout the empire who incur no reproof from Rome for clinging to traditional gods and altar sacrifices. To substantiate his allegations, he quotes the letter that Emperor Trajan received from PLINY THE YOUNGER, a respected attorney for the imperial court during hearings on Christian worship and hymn singing.

Tertullian made his points with irony, pun, and SATIRE as well as invective. His range of topics covers problematic sources of religious antipathy, particularly the sacraments of baptism and the eucharist. In defense of Christians, his "Ad nationes" ("To Nations," ca. A.D. 197) repudiates the charges against the sect of infanticide, bestiality, and incest and identifies the anti-Christ—the beast predicted in the biblical book of Revelation—as the Roman Empire, which he equated with the sinful empire of Babylon. "De spectaculis" ("Of Public Shows," ca. A.D. 201) denies that Christians court death sentences and use executions in the arena as masochistic displays of religiosity. For scriptural support, the author quotes the prohibition against killing from the Ten Commandments in the book of EXODUS and cites the PSALMS of David for blessing Hebraic piety, humility, and peacekeeping. In contrast, he maligns imperial dynasties for public vulgarity, "a pomp preceding, proving in itself whose it is, by the long line of images, by the host of statues, by the chariots, by the sacred carriages, by the cars, by the chairs, by the crowns, by the robes" (197). He concludes that the imperial grandeur and cruelty of the Roman circus "offends God" (197).

Sources

Dunn, Geoffrey D. *Tertullian.* New York: Routledge, 2004.
Tertullian. *Tertullian: Apologetic and Practical Treatises.*
    Translated by C. Dodgson. Oxford: F. & J.
    Rivington, 1854.

Thackeray, William Makepeace   See NAPO-
LEONIC LITERATURE.

Thousand and One Nights, The *(Alf Laylah Wa Laylah, The Arabian Nights, Tales from the Arabian Nights)* (ca. A.D. 942)

The Persian frame story *Alf Laylah Wa Laylah (The Thousand and One Nights)* is an eclectic folk collection of works by storytellers from the centuries-old lore of empires in Arabia, Egypt, Greece, India, Iran, Iraq, Mesopotamia, Persia, Syria, Turkey, and Yemen. The text overlays tribal customs and 10th-century situations with Koranic law to create moral lessons for a just and virtuous ruler. Its stories derive from numerous contributors, beginning with the Abbasid government secretary and storyteller Abdus al-Jashyari, who, at his death in A.D. 942, left his intended collection of 1,000 entries less than half complete at 480. Oral recitations of the popular tales enthralled desert dwellers, who lived harsh lives under rigid religious fundamentalism,

with images of beauty, abundance, sexual surrender, and passion.

Introducing the saga of *The Thousand and One Nights* is the peril of Scheherazade, the vizier Shirazad's daring daughter, who volunteers to marry the Persian sultan Shahryar, the ruler of lands from Persia to India. Suspecting disloyalty in all women, he renounces romance as an infirmity of the spirit and rejects the concept of a consort as a lifelong companion, even less as an adviser and equal. Over a period of three years, he treats his brides as expendable and executes each after only one night. Royal paranoia threatens the future of the kingdom, which can produce no crown prince under the steady annihilation of potential mothers.

The goal of *The Thousand and One Nights* is the transformation of Shahryar from his devaluation of women and the rescue of his domain from the lack of a worthy queen and a male successor. In the opinion of the scholar M. E. Combs-Schilling, among androcentric Arabs, "When it comes to the really important dimension of man's being, man is to keep his eyes on the prize—on the God who exists beyond this world—and not turn back to gaze at this world's women," (Combs-Schilling 1989, 268). Fortunately, Shahryar has loved stories from boyhood, and Scheherazade regales him nightly with tales that she never completes until the following night, when she begins a new one. By beguiling him for 1,001 nights with intricate cliffhangers, she turns literature into ransom. She manages to give birth to three princelings while entertaining her husband and indirectly instructing him on the family's need for stability and nurturing. Transformed by his trickster bride, Shahryar grants her a reprieve from execution and, to his subjects' relief, orders a 30-day celebration marking his repentance for killing some 1,100 innocent female citizens. He orders scribes to collect Scheherazade's stories in 30 volumes, a symbolic homage to female integrity and ingenuity. In a landmark of world literature, the preservation of oral treasures retained such aphorisms as "Who seeketh Fame without toil and strife / Th'impossible seeketh and wasteth life" (*Arabian Nights* 2001, 402).

The strands of *The Thousand and One Nights* stray from court life under Abbasid caliphs to fantasy figures—djinns, magi, giants, devils, cheats, angels, sorcerers, poisoners, and wonder workers. Other elements include a lynx hunt, the seven sages, talking birds, a valley of serpents, trapdoors, magic lamps, sapphires as big as fruit, and the eggs of the roc, a huge flying predator. Amid the exotica are facets of medieval life in the Middle East—racism, auguries and omens, live burials, foot washing and bath fetishes, elaborate makeup and perfume, immurement of virgins, weddings and widowhood, veiling, circumcision, inheritance laws, and daily Muslim prayer ritual. The core of the story network emphasizes the powerlessness of the peasantry, fisher folk, crafters, traders, poets, and bandits under an unforgiving caste system. But might has its limits. Beast FABLEs such as "The Sparrow and the Eagle," the story of a sparrow that tries to snatch a ram from a barnyard, illustrate the dangers of overreaching, a lethal flaw in the governance of empires. A grim reminder of nemesis engraved on a tablet warns "By Allah, the Destroyer of delights and the Severer of societies and the Devastator of dwelling places came down upon them and transport them from the spaciousness of their palaces to the straitness of their burial places" (517).

Gendered Motifs and Themes

A century after Abu Tammam's compilation of warrior stories in HAMASA (Courage, ca. A.D. 845), *The Thousand and One Nights* displays a misogynistic motif of female dependence on men for existence that underlies a feminist staple, the survival of women through self-subordination. Clever women pleasure men by denying their own needs and by adopting male standards of attraction and sexual dalliance. In "The Porter and the Three Ladies of Baghdad," in a poetic adulation of the male, the female versifier proclaims the intoxicating power of the male glance and gait and admits, "His coiling curl-lets my soul ennetted / And his cruel will all my wits outwitted" (70). The tales acknowledge an Islamic hypocrisy that stereotypes women as carnal voluptuaries, connivers, and traitors capable of sabotaging a kingdom's dynasty. In "The Hermits," a shepherd charges an angel, "How much of foulness hidest thou under thy beauty, and how many a pious man hast thou seduced from his duty and made his end penitence and perdition?" (256). Like the myths of Eve, Pandora, and Lilith (the bearer of disease and death), the question assumes the worst of women.

Confrontations between perfidious males and fearful females dominate the Arab narrative. One account of self-preservation, "The Wily Dalilah and Her Daughter Zaynab," dates to the time of Harun al-Rashid of Tehran, a patron of the arts and the contemporary and host of CHARLEMAGNE. The story pits two clever females against the double-dealers of Baghdad, who condemn the women to crucifixion. Scheherazade subverts the misperception of the Eve myth and the loss of paradise from GENESIS and the KORAN as the destiny of all gullible males. Her mastery of oriental WISDOM, jest, and anecdote illustrates the centrality of women to the empire as mothers and educators of royal children, humanizers of patriarchy, and advisers on mate selection to assure the longevity of the royal household.

The Book in Translation

In 1717, the translator and orientalist Antoine Galland of Rollet introduced to Europe a French version of the Arabic classic. It preceded a multivolume English version produced in 1885–88 by the explorer and linguist Sir Richard Francis Burton, the translator of the Indian *Kama Sutra* and of LUIS DE CAMÕES's *The Lusiads*. Burton justified the work as requital of England's "forgetting that she is at present the greatest Mohammedan empire in the world" and that "she has systematically neglected Arabism" (Burton 2001, 28). Among the adventure lore, revenge motifs, and crime stories, European writers added classic narratives about the beggar boy Aladdin and his genie from a magic lamp, Ali Baba and the 40 thieves, and the voyages of Sinbad the Sailor, a Persian adventurer from Basra during the Abbasid Empire and a forerunner of JONATHAN SWIFT's protagonist in *Gulliver's Travels* (1726).

In Europe and North America, the themes in *The Thousand One Nights* of brotherhood, good faith, ethical purity, and fidelity influenced hosts of composers, artists, and authors, including the playwright WILLIAM SHAKESPEARE; the poet Alfred, Lord Tennyson; the adventure writer ROBERT LOUIS STEVENSON; and the GOTHIC master MATTHEW GREGORY LEWIS. A feminist author, the Danish raconteur ISAK DINESEN, valued the empowerment of females via seductive words. The Arabo-Sicilian writer Muhammad ibn Zafar al-Siqilli (1104–69) followed *The Thousand and One Nights* with his *Sulwan al-Muta' Fi' Udwan al-Atba'* (*Consolation for the Ruler*, 1154), a forerunner of NICCOLÒ MACHIAVELLI's *The Prince* (1514). Film versions include *Arabian Nights* (1942), starring Maria Montez as Scheherazade; the voiceovers of Robin Williams in Walt Disney's *Aladdin* (1992); and the cartoon feature *Sinbad: Legend of the Seven Seas* (2003), narrated by Brad Pitt and Catherine Zeta-Jones.

Sources

The Arabian Nights: Tales from a Thousand and One Nights. Translated by Richard Francis Burton. New York: Modern Library, 2001.

Combs-Schilling, M. E. *Sacred Performances: Islam, Sexuality, and Sacrifice.* New York: Columbia University Press, 1989.

El Saadawi, Nawal. *The Hidden Face of Eve: Women in the Arab World.* London: Zed Books, 2007.

Hovannisian, Richard G., and Georges Sabagh. *The Thousand and One Nights in Arabic Literature and Society.* Cambridge: Cambridge University Press, 1997.

Thucydides (ca. 465–ca. 395 B.C.) *Greek historian*

The inheritor of HERODOTUS's pioneering cultural history, Thucydides elevated the genre to the more scholarly discipline of political historiography. A native of a fishing village in Helimous, a region southwest of Athens, Greece, he was the son of Hegesipyle and Olorus, a substantial landowner. He may also have been a nephew of Miltiades the Younger, the victor at the battle of Marathon, and a cousin to Miltiades' son Cimon, a hero at the battle of Salamis. In boyhood, Thucydides studied under the rhetorician Antiphon of Rhamnus and under Anaxagoras, the philosophy teacher of Euripides, Pericles, and Socrates. His wealth came from ownership of gold mines at Scapte Hyle in Thrace, the home of his wife, with whom he had a daughter and a son, Timotheus. Because of the estate's distance from Athens, the historian was later able to take a dispassionate view of imperialist struggles in Greece. His fastidious use of cause and effect derives from teachings of the peripatetic Sophists and perhaps

from his contemporary Hippocrates, the famed diagnostician of Cos. In 444 B.C., he reputedly wept at the Olympic Games during Herodotus's reading from his *Histories*.

Thucydides took part in the Peloponnesian War (431–404 B.C.), the bitter struggle between Sparta and Athens that involved every other city-state in Greece in a series of constantly changing alliances and conflicts. Being in the thick of things, he compiled details that gave his writings immediacy. In summer 430 B.C., he survived a plague—possibly epidemic typhus or typhoid fever—that had moved north from Ethiopia, Egypt, and Libya into Athens via the harbor at Piraeus. During a Spartan siege that confined citizens behind the walls of Athens, the pestilence swept the city. As conditions worsened from close contact and unsanitary conditions, infection and suicide killed a third of the populace, including many soldiers and also the statesman Pericles, Thucydides' political idol.

The historian criticized battlefield atrocities for undermining Athenian humanity and openly disparaged the Athenian demagogues Hyperbolus and Cleon. The latter was the butt of stage SATIRE by the comedy writer Aristophanes in *The Knights* (424 B.C.). That same year, Thucydides was elected *strategos* (general) on the island of Thasos in the north Aegean. After the Spartan general Brasidas forced a surrender from the people of Amphipolis (present-day Amfipoli in Macedonia) in 422 B.C. at a cost of 600 Athenian soldiers, Athenians blamed Thucydides for arriving too late with his fleet of seven ships. Cleon exiled him to Thrace, a 20-year banishment that Thucydides accepted, perhaps as an alternative to execution.

Biographers portray Thucydides as a principled, rational historiographer. Supported by income from his gold mines, he apparently traveled widely, reaching the Athenian colony of Syracusa, Sicily. After Athens lost its Aegean empire along with its sources of revenue, he seems to have returned to Athens in 404 B.C., but he left in a few months to work on his history at leisure, free from urban political turmoil. At the historian's death, reputedly murdered at about age 40, survivors honored him with burial southwest of the Acropolis at Koile in the Cimon clan's vault alongside his sister Elpinice. Thucydides left his history incomplete. His daughter Archedice finished Book VIII; XENOPHON, a cavalryman during the Peloponnesian War, added the *Hellenica,* an inferior account of subsequent events from 411 to 362 B.C.

The History

Thucydides is remembered today for his uncompromising life work, *The History of the Peloponnesian War* (ca. 400 B.C.), a disciplined study of the decline of Athens shortly after the building of the Parthenon and the sculpting of its gold-clad statue of Athena. The impartial, frankly realistic chronology ignores artistic developments and examines all but the last six years of the 27-year conflict from 431 to 404 B.C. between Sparta and Athens, a nation obsessed by over-ambitious imperial objectives. Freedom of speech under Pericles allowed for public dispute about the nature of Athenian imperialism, which threatened the trade routes of rival states Corinth and Sparta to Aegean ports. The historian correctly predicted that the clash would be catastrophic for Greece and destabilize and jeopardize its environs. For research, he undertook a lengthy overview of prewar debates and embassies, verbatim speeches, interviews with informants on both sides of the conflict, and his own eyewitness view of events. He deviated from Herodotus's style by omitting superstition and references to anthropomorphic gods and focused on causes of Athens's downfall, which he put down to human greed and stupidity.

In the opening book, Thucydides establishes his belief in the "great men" theory of history, a concept in vogue when the Jewish chronicler FLAVIUS JOSEPHUS wrote *Bellum Iudaicum* (*History of the Jewish War,* A.D. 75). Thucydides' text lauds Pericles as the brilliant and decisive leader whom Athenians needed to counter the Spartan threat. Rivalry sharpened the military might of both nations, but dogged diplomacy promoted coexistence, an achievement that marked civilized behavior between adversary states. During a period of imperial affluence that followed the Greek-Persian wars, Athenian aristocrats substituted money for commitment: "The majority of them shirked military service to escape absence from home.... The Athenian navy was increased as a result of their contributing to its cost while they themselves were always untrained and unprepared for war" (Thucydides 1963, 40). The visible threat to the rest of Greece forced Spartans to prepare for an inevitable conflict by land and sea. By emphasizing the moral lapse in Athenians, Thucydides demonstrates his grasp of objectivity.

Accounting for War

In Book II, Thucydides illustrates the unforeseeable factors that affect the destiny of empires. He cites the collapse of 14 years of peace with the outbreak of war on the north slope of Mount Cithaeron in southern Greece, where Athens supported Thebes against the Boeotian city of Plataea (a Spartan ally). In retaliation, Sparta attacked Athens; Athens, in turn, sent a fleet against Sparta. Thucydides stresses the cost of warfare with the crowding of peasants into the safe confines of Athens's walls and in the winter memorial to fallen warriors, whose bones filled the cypress coffins of individual tribes. Pericles eulogized Athenian heroes as models of a unique national character that "respects the majority and not the few" (66–67). He lauded Athens for strength at home and on foreign soil and belittled Sparta for its fanatic training of warriors from childhood through old age. In summary, Pericles declared Athenians contenders "for a higher prize" (69), an allusion to imperial ambition. As though speaking through the leader's oratory, Thucydides offers us his view of the importance of right thinking and honor.

From the height of oratory, the historian moves to the devastation of the epidemic in Athens and the death of Pericles from fever in 429 B.C., two causes of social and moral breakdown. The Spartans, under the command of Archidamus, directed some 65 percent of their forces into Attica (the area around Athens), but the pestilence halted their advance. Against an insidious infection that doctors could not treat, the Spartans withdrew. The Athenians faced the sapping of their strength from death and terror as well as the rise of hedonism. The chronicle reflects on the fact that "life and riches were alike ephemeral" (65) in a land where survivors feared neither God nor the law. While the Spartans seized the advantage to plunder the Laurion silver mines south of Athens, the Athenians remained behind city walls, as Pericles had advised. Thucydides allows himself a burst of hero worship: "[Pericles] kept Athens safe, and she reached the height of her greatness in his time" (83). The historian's concern for ordinary Athenians reflects his regret that imperial decision makers often sacrifice citizens for token victory.

The Spread of Violence

With Book III, Thucydides characterizes the imperial struggle as a political epidemic that afflicted neighboring peoples. The first to fall was Mytilene, the capital of the island of Lesbos, which capitulated to Athens in autumn 428 B.C. The victors under Cleon killed only the 1,000 rebels who caused Mytilene's revolt; Cleon then subdivided Lesbos into 3,000 plots designated for colonial occupation and subjugation. One by one, the Aegean states of Corcyra, Megara, and Aeolus yield to Athens, followed by Messina, Leucas, and Ionia. Sparta took Plataea through a scorched-earth method and converted it to public land as a sop to their allies, the Thebans. In a vivid account of the civil war on Corcyra, Thucydides comments on the extremes of wartime barbarity. Describing constant killing, he notes that "the whole Hellenic world, one may say, was in commotion" (115), spreading senseless violence and a first-strike mentality among men eager to establish their battlefield reputations. The author blames vengefulness and lack of scruples on "the love of power, originating in avarice and ambition" (116), one of the bolder indictments of imperialism in ancient history.

At the height of international conflict, Thucydides meditates on the shift in imperial hopes in Book IV, which opens in spring 424 B.C. At a pivotal point, Sicily revolted against Athens under the influence of the Spartan general Brasidas, who deliberately ran his own ship aground, giving his soldiers no choice but to fight. A subsequent Athenian defeat in Boeotia at Delium (outside present-day Tanagra, Greece) forced the truce of 423 B.C. Here Thucydides inserts his own small part in the lengthy war by explaining how loss of confidence in Athens caused the people of Amphipolis, which Thucydides had failed to protect, to surrender to Brasidas. In his own behalf, he describes his dilemma as being "on the spot" (159). Two more years of fighting concluded in 421 B.C. by the Peace of Nicias. The competition for an alliance with the Argives, Sparta's neighbors, caused a debilitating struggle on both sides. Minor conflicts between small cities allied to Athens or Sparta led to a renewal of war. Book V concludes with the Melian controversy, Thucydides's critique of Athenian savagery at Melos in 416 B.C. The onslaught resulted in GENOCIDE through killing all the men and in the sale of women and children into SLAVERY.

A Critique of Empires

Book VI demonstrates a pervasive theme of imperialism: overreaching ambition based on delusions of grandeur and shortsighted projections of risks and losses. The Athenian attack on Sicily began without the scouting necessary to assure success. The historian puts into the mouth of General Nicias a warning that Athens should complete old business before venturing so far from home. The blunder, which Thucydides compares to the folly of the entire Peloponnesian conflict, forced an Athenian leader, Alcibiades, into the Spartan camp. He galvanized them with a depiction of Athens as a military monster bent on devouring all of Hellas. In explanation of his betrayal of Athens, Alcibiades defined patriotism with a fervor anticipating the American pamphleteer Thomas Paine's PROTEST treatise "The Crisis" (1776): "The patriot is not one who would not attack his own country when unjustly deprived of her, but one who in warmth of his passion would try to win her back by every means in his power" (242). In 414 B.C., turmoil in Sicily during the Peloponnesian War forced the Athenians to send a fleet to fortify Syracuse while Sparta sent forces to support the Sicilians. Following a sea battle at Syracuse, Demosthenes and the Athenians were defeated and surrendered to the Sicilians. The victors executed Demosthenes and Nicias and sold survivors as slaves. Thucydides honors Nicias as "[undeserving] of so miserable an end, for he had invariably conformed to the rules of good conduct" (306).

The chronicle turns to another theme: the inability of imperialists to rein in rogue leaders. Racked by military losses and desertions, the Athenian citizenry abandoned democracy for oligarchy under a consortium of plutocrats known as the Four Hundred. At this low point in national unity, Sparta seized the advantage to mount a coastal invasion. Although Athens recovered hope with a victory at the Hellespont, by 411 B.C., the Athenian empire faced doom. Thucydides seizes the historian's right of retrospect to contrast Athens and Sparta as adversaries: "The two peoples were of very different tempers; the one quick, the other slow; the one enterprising, the other deficient in daring; and this was of the greatest service to the Athenians" (332).

Critical Opinion

Critics tend to lionize Thucydides as a brilliant but modest and impeccably objective war historian. With utter detachment, he described scenes of moral decline and of the erosion of traditional values. Unlike Herodotus, who looked to the past, Thucydides, from line one, looked at the effects of disastrous imperialism. Like the 20th-century battlefield journalist JOHN HERSEY, author of *Hiroshima* (1946), the Greek historiographer apparently took notes day by day, but in his history he remains aloof and nonjudgmental. He admits that eyewitness accounts differ on both sides, but he accepts contradictory memories as a natural outgrowth of battlefield confusion and misinformation. He recognizes the conflict between the individual and the state by depicting Pericles as an egalitarian who pursued Athenian national aims while hiding his personal disapproval of conflict against Greek neighbors.

Thucydides' unemotional, densely packed reportage is relentless in its search for truth. He constantly winnows out details, and avoids embellishments to maintain a microscopic focus. Because he absorbed himself in details of embassies, fleets, and the military, his work remains one of the most perceptive perspectives of war in the ancient world. His precision and control earned the respect of Xenophon, who narrated the events of the last seven years of the war. Later critiques by Dionysius of Halicarnassus and the Roman satirist Lucian belittle Thucydides' history as overly grim and the speeches pompous and melodramatic. Nonetheless, the historian's incisive method inspired a series of historical analysts, including Polybius, Josephus, Sallust, TACITUS, PROCOPIUS, and ANNA COMNENA, the Byzantine author of the *Alexiad* (1148).

Sources

Crane, Gregory. *The Blinded Eye: Thucydides and the New Written Word.* Lanham, Md.: Rowman & Littlefield, 1996.

Sahlins, Marshall. *Apologies to Thucydides: Understanding History as Culture and Vice Versa.* Chicago: University of Chicago Press, 2004.

Thucydides. *The Peloponnesian Wars.* Translated by Benjamin Jowett. New York: Washington Square Press, 1963.

Tibetan Book of the Dead   See BOOK OF THE DEAD.

Tibullus, Albius (ca. 55–ca. 19 B.C.) *Roman poet*

With serene elegies, Albius Tibullus, an ambassador and literary lion of Rome's golden age of literature (83 B.C.–A.D. 17), repudiated imperial power-mongering by the Julio-Claudian dynasty. Like HORACE, JUVENAL, PROPERTIUS, and VIRGIL, Tibullus witnessed the vulgarity of preferment-seeking among Rome's post-republican nouveau riche. Born southeast of Rome in the Sabine hills outside Praeneste (present-day Lazio, Italy) to old-fashioned parents of the knight class, he developed character and refinement, both treasured by his wealth of friends. He was 10 years old when Julius Caesar's assassination ended the Roman Republic and initiated 17 years of civil war. He was 13 when, like others favoring the losing side, he suffered the confiscation of the Tibullus family's estate outside Tivoli, which he mourned in verse.

A colleague of Horace and OVID and a protégé of the orator Messalla Corvinus, Tibullus survived ruin and swore off striving for court distinction and affluence. At age 20, he set out with Messalla on a military mission to the Middle East, but he halted at Corcyra (Corfu) to recover from illness. He used the respite as an opportunity to write his third elegy, which mocks augury for assuring him of a successful expedition. The fiasco caused him to avoid future involvement with the army; he asserted, "Hence flags and trumpets! me you'll never have; / Bear wounds and wealth to warriors bent on gain" (Tibullus 1872, 10). He spurned temple building and imperial sloganeering about the *aeternae urbis* (eternal city) and ignored Augustus's rationale for dismantling the republic in 27 B.C. in favor of an empire. Tibullus's death at age 36 stirred the public with sorrow and regret for lost talent. Ovid mourned him in his "Lament for Tibullus's Death" (15 B.C.)

Tibullus's *Carmina* (*Elegies*, 19 B.C.), a collection of pastoral dirges, declarations of love, and occasional verse, mourns the upheaval in Rome through Nemisis, a personification of fate. He reveals a languor and nostalgia nourished by withdrawal into quiet contemplation free of the contention of the empire's climbers. He declares himself free of grudges: "The wealth and harvest-stores my sires possessed / I covet not" (9). "The Simple Life," which opens the first book of his poems, disclaims the silk couches of the vainglorious Augustan Age and advocates a return to the *lares* (household gods), the domestic protectors clustered at the individual homeowner's hearth shrine. A companion piece, the tenth elegy, repudiates bloodshed for the sake of military titles and loot. Of the victims of Rome's disastrous civil war, Tibullus views them as pigs drawn from the sty to the sacrificial altar.

Sources

Lee-Stecum, Parshia. *Powerplay in Tibullus: Reading Elegies Book One.* Cambridge: Cambridge University Press, 1998.

Tibullus, Albius. *Elegies.* Translated by James Cranstoun. Edinburgh: William Blackwood, 1872.

Tolstoy, Leo (Count Lev Nikolayevich Tolstoy)
(1828–1910) *Russian novelist and essayist*

A moralist and pacifist reformer during the decline of the Romanov dynasty, Leo Tolstoy wrote passionately about VIOLENCE, Christianity, and anarchism. The son of Count Nikolai Tolstoy, the author claimed descent from one of Russia's oldest and most respected noble families. In 1844, he left the family estate at Yasnaya Polyana in the Caucasus to study Asian philology and law at Kazan University in Tatarstan north of the Kazakhstan border. His time in the imperial army as a gunnery officer earned the sympathy of the British writer GEORGE ORWELL, a child of empire who noted that the Russian author came of age in a militarist epoch during which most young males from good families spent time in uniform.

After service along the Danube and in a war of annexation fought in present-day Chechnya between the Black and Caspian Seas north of the Iranian borders, Tolstoy began the first of his semiautobiographical war fictions. He won the regard of the newly crowned Czar Alexander II for vignettes of the Crimean War in *Sevastopol Sketches* (1855), which describes the tenacity of the Russian Empire against an alliance of the British, French, and Turks. In realistic glimpses, Tolstoy turned personal experience into propaganda promoting moral individualism and civil disobedience. *Sevastopol Sketches* dramatizes the mental torment of Volodya, an ambivalent soldier who serves under the imperial eagle of Nicholas I. With unflinching introspection, the character berates himself: "Lord! Can it be that I am a coward . . . can it be that I so lately dreamed of dying with joy for my fatherland, my tsar?" (Tolstoy 1888, 181), a reference to the recently deceased Nicholas I. To the author, military life derived from hypocrisy—a form of disciplined bondage forcing men like Tolstoy and Volodya to loot and destroy. Rather than the epitome of patriotism, service to the czar sapped spirits of honor and courage and pushed sensitive men toward madness. To the author's chagrin, government censors revamped one vignette, "Sevastopol in May," into prowar propaganda for dissemination in the September issue the magazine *Sovremennik* (The contemporary), published by Tolstoy's fourth cousin, ALEKSANDR PUSHKIN.

Tolstoy displayed integrity and courage in revealing his innermost beliefs. In the novella *The Cossacks: A Caucasian Story of 1852* (1863), he reprises his own maturation from spoiled aristocrat to battlefield veteran through the eyes of the protagonist Olenin, a parallel to Volodya. The narrative explores the contrast between NATURE and the battlefield, which became a motif of the post–World War II era central to the libertarian novels of Anatoly Kuznetsov, BORIS PASTERNAK, and Aleksandr Solzhenitsyn (see PRISON LITERATURE) and to the verse of ANNA AKHMATOVA and YEVGENY YEVTUSHENKO. Because the memory of battlefield carnage haunted Tolstoy, *The Cossacks* required over a decade of composition and revision. It earned the regard of his contemporary, the novelist IVAN TURGENEV, who classed the autobiographical piece among Russian masterworks.

Benevolence and Historical Fiction

During a period of altruism beginning at age 31, Tolstoy sheltered the homeless and jobless, served as a magistrate on his estate, and opened 13 schools for peasants. He wrote an alphabet book, didactic children's literature, primers, and a pedagogical journal entitled *Yasnaya Polyana* (Clear glade). He explored the moral and cultural changes in his country in *Voyna i mir* (*War and Peace*, 1869), an epic example of NAPOLEONIC LITERATURE featuring Russian resilience under the threat of the French general's expansionism in 1812. Tolstoy's text deals with the influx of Western European ideas and behavior at the court of Czar Alexander I and the fastidious dress, mannerisms, and bilingualism of aristocrats who converse in French. For all their illusions of wealth and control, the Bezukhovs, Bolkonskys, Kuragins, and Rostovs, four of the five central households featured in the story, suffer the random cruelties of the French invasion, diminution of property and wealth, and disillusion.

In Tolstoy's last years before the collapse of the Russian Empire, he ceased writing sophisticated novels to compose folklore similar to stories treasured and recited by illiterate peasants. He wrote treatises and adapted Aesopic and Hindu FABLES and European fool tales—"The Big Oven," "The Fool and His Knife"—into illustrative commentary on a perilous period of history. At the core of his didacticism was his aristocratic distaste for middle-class materialism, insincerity, profligacy, and progressivism that threatened Russian tradition. His admiration for the free-spirited peasant energizes *The Living Corpse* (1900), a six-act drama lauding the decision of Fedya, a dissatisfied St. Petersburg aristocrat, to drop out of society. He offers to marry Masha, a Gypsy singer, whom the text describes as a pure dove offering "pure, self-sacrificing love" (Tolstoy 1919, 74).

Tolstoy's obsession with the senselessness of combat underlies "A Prisoner in the Caucasus" (1872), a war memoir that Turgenev prized for its artistic quality. The shackling and escape attempts of Zhilin, a prisoner of the Tartars, contrasts the exigencies of war with the humanity and piety of Muslim Tartar villagers. As in *The Cossacks*, the author refuses to debase the enemy, whom he portrays in appealing family, religious, and community scenarios. The crux of "A Prisoner in the Caucasus" prefigures Tolstoy's conversion to a radical form of Christian brotherhood, a result of incarceration that FYODOR DOSTOYEVSKY glorified six years earlier in *Crime and Punishment* (1866).

The Power of the Individual

In his last two decades, Tolstoy crusaded for nonviolence. Following two years of famine and Asiatic cholera outbreaks, he produced a bold criticism of Czar Alexander III, known as the Peacemaker. With the pacifist diatribe *The Kingdom of God Is within You* (1894), Tolstoy railed against universal military service and international bloodshed. He took the title from Christ's words: "Neither shall they say, Lo here! or, lo there! for, behold, the kingdom of God is within you" (Luke 17:21). Of Russian imperialism, the author notes that "from the Roman Caesars to the Russian and German Emperors," power has always required favoritism toward soldiers, the robotic agents of imperial will (Tolstoy 1894, 241). To the dismay of the czar, the text repudiates the power of the empire in favor of the rule of Christ's Sermon on the Mount, which blesses peacemakers. Tolstoy repudiates despots and demands equality for all classes with a rhetorical question: "Without justice, what is an empire but a great band of brigands?" (181). The Indian nonresistance leader Mohandas Gandhi admired Tolstoy's treatise for its validation of the human conscience as a source of benevolence more trustworthy than either church or state.

In the 10th year of the reign of Czar Nicholas II, Tolstoy denounced the Russo-Japanese War and wrote his final work, *Hadji Murád* an antimilitary HERO novel written during 1896–1904 and published in 1912. He based the title figure on a real Islamic warrior who led Chechen guerrillas during a Russian invasion of the Caucasus in 1851. After Murád's capture, Cossack forces slew him and sent his embalmed head to Czar Nicholas. Tolstoy symbolized Murád with a thistle and immortalized him in a fable about a falcon slain by fellow birds because contact with humans had changed the falcon's true identity. The author extolled his hero for courage under fire, reviled the officers under Nicholas I for corruption and bloated triumphalism, and pitied the peasants of southern

Russia for the demands of grain cultivation and for the loss of farm income during conscription by the army. The posthumously published narrative was banned in 1912, but it appeared unabridged in a German edition released in Berlin. The original text remained unpublished in Russian until the Bolshevik Revolution of 1917.

Tolstoy stated his notion of passive resistance in "A Letter to a Hindu" (1908), an editorial reply printed in the *Free Hindustan*, leading to an exchange of letters with Mohandas Gandhi. To convey his fellowship with humanity, the author quotes Krishna and cites lines from the Upanishads (Lessons, 1000–600 B.C.) and the VEDAS (Knowledge, ca. 150 B.C.). His moral integrity impressed his countrymen, fellow authors ANTON CHEKHOV and Fyodor Dostoyevsky; the Korean modernist YI KWANGSU; and two writers who escaped the Holocaust, RUTH PRAWER JHABVALA and the Yiddish Nobel laureate ISAAC BASHEVIS SINGER.

Sources

Said, Edward. *Culture and Imperialism.* New York: Knopf, 1993.

Simmons, Ernest Joseph. *Tolstoy.* New York: Routledge, 1973.

Tolstoy, Leo. *Hadji Murád.* Translated by Aylmer Maude. Alexandria, Va.: Orchises Press, 1996.

———. *The Kingdom of God Is within You.* Translated by Constance Garnett. London: Heinemann, 1894.

———. *The Living Corpse.* Translated by Anna Monossowich Evarts. New York: Nicholas L. Brown, 1919.

———. *Sevastopol,* Isabel Florence Hapgood. New York: Thomas Y. Crowell, 1888.

———. *War and Peace.* London: J. M. Dent & Sons, 1915.

Traill, Catharine Parr (Catharine Parr Strickland) (1802–1899) *British autobiographer and children's writer*

A pioneer of Canada before the formation of United Province of Canada in 1840, author-naturalist Catharine Parr Traill produced a classic settler's handbook and guides to North American plants. Born Catharine Parr Strickland in Surrey, England, and raised in Suffolk, she was the sister of Susannah Strickland Moodie, who also wrote accounts of life in early Canada (see FRONTIER LITERATURE). In her youth, Traill studied botany, debate, geography, history, and mathematics with her father, and she became a children's author at age 15. After marrying a Scots widower, Lieutenant Thomas Traill, at age 30, she emigrated to Upper Canada, where she compiled *The Backwoods of Canada: Being Letters from the Wife of an Emigrant Officer, Illustrative of the Domestic Economy of British America* (1836). In a gendered environment where males performed the outdoor work of clearing land, planing lumber, planting crops, and tending and trading livestock, the feminized text covers her adaptation to bush country while making a home and giving birth to the first of nine children. During 60 years away from England, she contributed feature stories on the frontier to *Anglo-American Magazine, Chambers' Edinburgh Journal, Home Circle, Literary Garland, Maple Leaf,* and *Sharpe's London Magazine,* and she issued children's pioneer stories—*Canadian Crusoes: A Tale of the Rice Lake Plains* (1852) and *Lady Mary and Her Nurse: or, A Peep into the Canadian Forest* (1856).

As Canada's first female journalist, Traill surveyed the purpose of emigration from the motherland. She explains in the introduction to *The Backwoods of Canada* that economics drives Europeans into the colonies: "The emigrants to British America are no longer of the rank of life that formerly left the shores of the British Isles. It is not only the poor husbandmen and artisans, that move in vast bodies to the west, but it is the enterprising English capitalist, and the once affluent landholder" (Traill 1836, ii). For the sake of investment opportunity, outdoor living, and personal liberty, newcomers, particularly the young, accept the solitude and hardships of leaving home to settle the Western wilderness in a "Robinson Crusoe sort of life" (123). The transition offers adventure, but requires compromise. On forested land on Lake Katchawanook outside Peterborough, Ontario, with her sister living a mile away, Traill misses English hedgerows, rosebeds, and riverside vistas. Accepting new and different challenges, she learns from the Great Lakes Chippewa how to dig Indian turnips, dye and decorate willow baskets with quillwork, boil maple sap into sugar, ice fish for pike, and sew sheets of birch bark into a canoe. Her descriptions introduce readers to a positive image of Native Americans as peaceful, productive people.

Based on middle-class Christian values, Traill's epistolary memoir defines the role of the settler wife. In an era that threatened the traditional British caste and class systems, the text looks to the confident, industrious gentlewoman to ameliorate the crudeness of cabin life. Traill, a forerunner of the independent "new woman" of the mid-19th century, declares that the true lady, even humbly dressed, can never be vulgar. She sets about refining the outback: She hangs maps and prints on rough walls, paints wildflowers and birds, embroiders petit point by the fire, bakes bread, stitches moccasins from animal pelts, and plants hops along the porch for decoration. Lacking a frontier tradition, she regrets so great a shift from Britain to a country where the imagination starves because of "no historical associations, no legendary tales" (153).

Traill's memoir emphasizes a love of the unspoiled outback, to which vigorous emigrants are drawn. From an ecological perspective, she, like such writers of NATURE LORE as Grey Owl (Archibald Belaney, 1888–1938), John Muir (1838–1914), and Henry David Thoreau (1817–62), longs for a pristine environment. She explains in *Pearls and Pebbles* (1894) that she wants to protect the Canadian wild from sodbusters clearing and plowing land and introducing alien plantings—corn and grain fields, potato and turnip patches, and clover pastures. Her pragmatism advises the wise use of wood lots by chopping out old trees for firewood and leaving saplings to flourish with sunlight and added root room. To distract squirrels from the corn crib, she offers them a basket of sunflower heads. Her writing and coping mechanisms rescued her from loneliness and displacement that must have been increased by her husband's death from depression in 1859.

For the remainder of her widowhood, Traill drew on colonial Canada for popular works— *Canadian Wildflowers* (1868) and *Studies of Plant Life in Canada: or, Gleanings from Forest, Lake and Plain* (1885). In the latter, she extols the courage of settlers, who "spread themselves along the then unbroken forests on the shores of the St. Lawrence, and bore hardships and privations of which there are few parallel cases" (Traill 1906, 121). Writing almost to the end of her life, she was 97 when she died on August 29, 1899. A campus of Trent University, Catharine Parr Traill College, bears her name.

Sources

Chilton, Lisa. *Agents of Empire: British Female Migration to Canada and Australia, 1860s–1930.* Toronto: University of Toronto Press, 2007.

Hessing, Melody, and Rebecca Sue Raglon. *This Elusive Land: Women and the Canadian Environment.* Vancouver: University of British Columbia Press, 2005.

Traill, Catharine Parr. *The Backwoods of Canada: Being Letters from the Wife of an Emigrant Officer, Illustrative of the Domestic Economy of British America.* London: Charles Knight, 1836.

———. *Studies of Plant Life in Canada: Wild Flowers, Flowering Shrubs, and Grasses.* Toronto: William Briggs, 1906.

Whitlock, Gillian. *The Intimate Empire: Reading Women's Autobiography.* New York: Continuum, 2000.

translation

The advancement of translation as a literary science assists nations in learning from each other, particularly through scripture, FABLE, STORYTELLING, and WISDOM LITERATURE. For example, the Persian and Syriac versions of the Sanskrit PANCHATANTRA (*The Fables of Bidpai*, ca. 200 B.C.) allowed the Sassanian and Umayyad dynasties to profit from a classic anthology of fool tales, beast fables, exempla, dialogues, aphorisms, allegories, admonitions, and jataka tales. As the Crusades ended in 1272, returning European warriors carried home Indian legends and cautionary tales like souvenirs of Asian treasure. Similarly, the KOANs that the Buddhist monk Bodhidharma collected in A.D. 520 passed through translation into the Chinese *Pi-yen lu* (*Blue Cliff Record*, 1125) and the Japanese *Mumonkan* (*The Gateless Gate* or *The Gateless Barrier*, 1228) as models of mind-stretching logic and solutions to dilemmas. In 1717, the French translator and orientalist Antoine Galland of Rollot introduced to Europe a French version of the Arabic folk collection *The* THOUSAND AND ONE NIGHTS (ca. A.D. 942), which amasses works by storykeepers from centuries of the lore of Arabia, Egypt, India, Mesopotamia, Persia, and Syria.

A touchstone of literary excellence, the King James Bible marks a significant accomplishment of British literature. In 1611, 750 reformers of the Church of England asked James I of England to issue an authorized scripture. He appointed 54 scholars to translate the Hebraic Old Testament and the Aramaic and Greek of the New Testament into a version carrying the king's imprimatur. At Cambridge, Oxford, and Westminster, the nine committees translated both sections of the canon bible plus the Apocrypha or noncanonical writings. As the height of Jacobean English, the finished King James Bible, or KJB, won regard for poesy and textual uniformity. The text glimmers with unique phrasing: "all things to all men," "at their wit's end," "the blind lead the blind," "fight the good fight," "filthy lucre," "in the twinkling of an eye," "a lamb to slaughter," "a man after his own heart," "my brother's keeper," "my name is legion," "the patience of Job," "pearls before swine," "the prodigal son," "suffer fools gladly," "thorn in the flesh," "tongues of men and angels." In the Apocrypha, the HERO tales in Maccabees (ca. 125 B.C.), written in Judea during a revolt against the Seleucid dynasty, resonate with the majesty of Israelite piety in Mattathias's evaluation of godliness and earthly sovereignty: "Though all the nations that are under the king's dominion obey him and fall away every one from the religion of their fathers, and give consent to his commandments: yet will I and my sons and my brethren walk in the covenant of our fathers" (Maccabees 1:19–22). Biblical phraseology and cadence influenced subsequent works in English for more than 300 years including those of John Milton, John Dryden, and RUDYARD KIPLING.

One work to undergo a series of poetic restatements, the *Rubáiyát* (Quatrains, ca. 1130) of the mystic, astronomer, mathematician, and philosopher Omar Khayyám (1048–1122) dates to the rise of the Seljuk dynasty in the Turco-Persian Empire in 1037. The intrusion of secular Turks into the strict Muslim theocracy of Persia introduced themes of agnosticism, hedonism, and sexual delight. Omar Khayyám, a native of Nishapur, Khorasan (present-day Iran), allowed his imagination full play, counter to Conventional Islamic interpretations of the KORAN. Like the Mesopotamian god king Gilgamesh (see *GILGAMESH*), he developed a fatalism based on his fears of mortality and earthly impermanence; like the DAODEJING (*Tao-Te Ching*; Classic of the way of power, 300 B.C.) of Laozi, Omar reduced life to a series of questions, a perpetual puzzle. Not an adherent to religious fundamentalism, he came into conflict with fanatics who scorned his enjoyment of life as defiance of Islamic hierarchy, prophecy, and taboos against alcohol. In 1957, a Hollywood biopic, *The Life, Loves and Adventures of Omar Khayyam*, featured Cornel Wilde as the poet, Debra Paget as his love interest, and Yma Sumac performing Persian songs. A new version of the poet's life, *The Keeper: The Legend of Omar Khayyam* (2005), displays the work of director Kayvan Mashayekh and Bruno Lastra as the poet.

In 1859, Edward FitzGerald (1809–83) of Suffolk, England, published the first of five editions of *The Rubáiyát of Omar Khayyám*, which spans three decades of work on the Persian original. In the second edition, he arranges stanzas in an implied chronological order that opens on early morning worship and presses the reader to "Oh make haste" (Omar 1888, 67), an injunction to wrest joy from mortal existence. By the seventh quatrain, the speaker renounces repentance and demands wine and an immersion in human delights. In rejecting blind allegiance to the sultan, he demands, "Ah, take the Cash, and let the Promise go / Nor heed the rumble of a distant drum!" (58). Of the powerful, the speaker reminds the reader of the temporal nature of empires—"How Sultan after Sultan with his Pomp / Abode his destin'd Hour, and went his way" (59). He comments on the fate of "some buried Caesar" and laments his own inability to unravel "the Master-knot of Human Fate," a death image (60, 63). Literary historians question FitzGerald's stress on the futility of life and his redirection from Omar's heterosexuality to the translator's admiration for young males. Infringing on the ancient manuscript are fusions of individual quatrains and some original verses by FitzGerald written in Persian style.

A notable later translator of Eastern works transferred to the West, Lafcadio Hearn (Patrick Lafcadio Hearn, 1850–1904) stressed the GOTHIC conventions of Japanese ghost tales. Born in Greece, he grew up in Dublin and attended Ushaw Roman Catholic College in Durham, England, where a sports accident blinded his left eye. He worked as a crime reporter for the *Cincinnati Daily Enquirer* and, in 1877, for *Harper's New Monthly* and the New Orleans *Times Democrat*. In 1889, at age 39, he grew restless and migrated to the West Indies. A year later, he traveled to Matsue, Japan, to teach at Shimane Prefectural Middle School while also publishing mystery stories in *Atlantic Monthly* and *Harper's*. Feeling himself at home in the country, he obtained Japanese citizenship, wed Setsu Koizumi, and adopted the name Koizumi Yakumo. He subsequently taught English literature at the Imperial University of Tokyo, studied haiku, and translated into English the stories of the French authors Theophile Gautier and Guy de Maupassant.

Hearn's skillful interpretation gave the European and American reading public access to Japanese literature. His nonfiction work *Glimpses of Unfamiliar Japan* (1894) introduces concepts of home shrines, emperor worship, gardening, educational systems, and funeral ritual. With Setsu's help, he translated the macabre tales "The Goblin Spider" and "The Old Woman Who Lost Her Dumpling" for *Japanese Fairy Tales* (1898) plus 14 stories and vignettes about superstitions and Buddhism for the anthology *In Ghostly Japan* (1899). He assembled 17 naturalistic Asian ghost cameos in *Kwaidan* (Ghost stories, 1904), the subject of a 1965 film. His collection opens on "Mimi-Nashi-Hoichi," the story of a blind court musician who plucks a lute while recounting the events of a Samurai battle. He recalls the destruction of the Heiké clan, who "perished utterly, with their women and children, and their infant emperor likewise—now remembered as Antoku Tenno" (Hearn 1904, 3). The drowning of the royal household results in seven centuries of haunting by imperial ghosts. The story "Butterflies" narrates how butterflies choose Emperor Genso's concubines.

Sources

The Apocrypha of the Old Testament. King James. New York: American Bible Society, 1972.

Hearn, Lafcadio. *Glimpses of Unfamiliar Japan* Boston: Houghton, Mifflin, 1894.

———. *In Ghostly Japan.* Boston: Little, Brown, and Co., 1899.

———. *Kwaidan.* Boston: Houghton, Mifflin, 1904.

Omar Khayyam. *Rubáiyát of Omar Khayyám.* Translated by Edward FitzGerald. 1888. Reprint, Oxford: Oxford University Press, 2009.

travelogue

World exploration generated curiosity in armchair travelers about exotic places. CRUSADER LORE such as Graindor de Douai's *Song of Antioch* (ca. 1180) and Geoffrey de Villehardouin's *The Conquest of Constantinople* (1207) brought information about food, dress, customs, and the arts from the Middle East to Europe. Later, *The Travels of Marco Polo* (1298) astounded Europe with its account of MARCO POLO's 17 years in China. Arab readers treasured *On the Curiosities of Cities and the Wonders of Travel* (1354), IBN BATTUTA's survey of Christian, Hindu, and Islamic port cities and the customs of 15 empires. The SATIRE of JONATHAN SWIFT made an account of mock voyages in *Gulliver's Travels* (1726), a sustained send-up of ethnocentrism, the blindness of people to the perspectives, mores, and aims of other nations and ethnicities.

White authors found readers eager for details of the black races. Mungo Park (1771–1806), a Scots surgeon, aroused interest in Africa, which he visited on three expeditions. As physician to the African Association, at age 23, he joined a trek to find the source of the Niger River. Imprisonment for four months at Ludamar on the southern edge of the Sahara and a seven-month recuperation from fever in Bambara country in the Malian empire delayed his return until December 22, 1797. He wrote up his observations in a popular memoir, *Travels in the Interior Districts of Africa* (1799). His sociological inquiries covered empire building in the Fulani territory in Guinea and as far north as Timbuktu in Mali. Of the encroachment of Europeans, he described people on the Senegal River as traders who "carried on a great commerce with the French in gold and slaves, and still maintain some traffic in slaves with the British factories on the Gambia" (Park 1816, 62).

Park exhibited his subjectivity by taking an instant dislike to the Moors. He accused them of thievery and savagery toward Mandingo bondsmen, whom Moors openly kidnapped. He disclosed that Arab conquest resulted in the conversion to Islam of black enclaves from Senegal to Abyssinia (present-day Ethiopia). Of Arabs, he declared, "They are a subtle and treacherous race of people; and take every opportunity of cheating and plundering the credulous and unsuspecting Negroes" (110). Enslavement affected three out of four blacks, most of them prisoners of petty wars: "They claim no reward for their services, except food and clothing; and are treated with kindness or severity, according to the good or bad disposition of their masters" (280). Just before sailing from the slave warehouse on the island of Goree, Senegal, to St. John's, Antigua, Park witnessed a swap of rum and tobacco for slaves. His eloquent narrative on the miseries and deaths of some 130 blacks in the hold of an American slave ship, the *Charlestown,* confirmed accounts of cruelties that killed off Africans and lessened Captain Charles Harris's profits.

Another Scots physician, David Livingstone (1813–73), became the first European to cross central Africa and was a fellow observer of the flesh trade. Recruited by the London Missionary Society, from 1848 to 1856, through negotiation and kindness, he made a peaceful trek from the Atlantic to the Zambezi River on the Indian Ocean. He returned to East Africa in 1866 to press into the interior from Zanzibar west to Lake Tanganyika. He failed to locate the source of the Nile and died in Zambia from dysentery and malaria 15 years before the British added the territory to its empire. His two-volume travelogue, *The Last Journals of David Livingstone in Central Africa* (1874), delved more poignantly than Park's writings into the African's plight, either as an Islamic pawn or a slave. Of the slave trade as a business, he damned it as "an accursed system" (Livingstone 1874, 114). He maligned Muslim husbands of the Comoro Islands as "more like jailers than friends of their wives. . . . They thus reduced themselves to the level of the inferior animals, and each was like the bull of a herd and not like a reasonable man" (214). Livingstone's writings led to renewed calls for the abolition of SLAVERY and a growing intolerance of Islamic misogyny.

Reporting on a Grand Scale

A bold seeker of headlines, investigative reporter Nellie Bly (1864–1922), the pen name of Elizabeth Jane "Pink" Cochran, earned renown for traveling around the globe in 72 days. The trip established her position as one of the "New Women" of the suffrage era. At age 21, she became one of the few female writers to cover a city beat for a major newspaper, the *Pittsburgh Dispatch,* for which she interviewed Marxists and factory workers. As one of the first international female reporters and war correspondents and a born muckraker, she reported graft and poverty under President Porfirio Díaz in *Six Months in Mexico* (1888), a view of the country two decades after the collapse of the second Mexican Empire. In an exposé for Joseph Pulitzer's *New York World,* she had herself admitted among the 1,600 inmates at the Women's Lunatic Asylum on Blackwell's Island in Manhattan. Her eyewitness report yielded *Ten Days in a Mad-House* (1887). She crusaded for women by posing undercover as a domestic for the story "Trying to Be a Servant" (1890) and as a sweatshop girl for "Nellie Bly as a White Slave" (1890).

On November 14, 1889, the reporter, billed as "Bly on the Fly," challenged the French science fiction writer Jules Verne's fictional 80-day world voyage by embarking from Hoboken, New Jersey, on the *Augusta Victoria.* The bet attested to the improvement in transportation: She sped around the world in 72 days and six hours. Her foreign stops began with London and included Amiens, France, where she met Verne, and Brindisi on the southeastern coast of Italy. Arriving in Africa at Port Said, Egypt, which was a recent acquisition of the British Empire, she ventured beyond Ismailia into Asia at Aden, Yemen, at a time when Britain and the Ottoman Turks vied for control of traffic through the Suez Canal. She voyaged across the Indian Ocean to Colombo, Ceylon, and, aboard the *Oriental,* want on to Penang, Malaya, and through the Straits of Malacca to Singapore. From there, she passed through a monsoon on her way to Hong Kong and Yokohama, Japan. On horseback and burro, in ricksha, and by rail, sampan, and steamer through 10 countries and from San Francisco by train to New Jersey, she covered 24,000 miles, issuing regular telegraph updates along the route. Afterward, she published *Nellie Bly's Book: Around the World in 72 Days* (1890) before giving up journalism for lecturing. Ever the feminist, she admired

Japanese geishas for their serenity and saluted Queen Victoria for guiding the British Empire.

See also WOMEN'S JOURNALS, DIARIES, AND LETTERS.

Sources

Bly, Nellie. *Around the World in 72 Days.* Brookfield, Conn.: Twenty-First Century Books, 1998.

Livingstone, David. *The Last Journals of David Livingstone in Central Africa.* London: John Murray, 1874.

Park, Mungo. *Travels in the Interior Districts of Africa.* London: John Murray, 1816.

Treasure Island Robert Louis Stevenson (1883)

For his classic adventure novel, *Treasure Island,* the Scots writer and poet ROBERT LOUIS STEVENSON chose a title that suited the 19th century. His story portrays a period when England, Spain, and France claimed entitlement to the world's treasures, regardless of the bloody work of securing them. As in writings by the Danish storyteller ISAK DINESEN, RUDYARD KIPLING, the TRAVELOGUE authors David Livingstone and Mungo Park, and the FRONTIER writer CATHARINE PARR TRAILL, the text describes European risk takers in far-flung nooks of the globe. Set in 1745, the sea adventure story makes no overt claims for the British Empire beyond a break from urban ennui and an open-ended indulgence in intellectual curiosity. With GOTHIC allure, the voyage begins with the discovery of a map belonging to Captain Billy Bones. A forerunner of H. RIDER HAGGARD's "Lost World" genre, the fantasy features lawless ruffians who enrich themselves from piracy and plunder of a sea trade spawned by colonialism in North, South, and Central America. The subtext links greed to the progressive mindset, "a shrill voice [that] broke forth out of the darkness . . . without pause or change, like the clacking of a tiny mill" (236).

Belittled by Haggard as mere propaganda for the true-blue British lad, Stevenson's allegory served classrooms as a model of good fun overlaid with patriotism, audacity, and wholesome character building. The criminal element—for example, J. Flint, captain of the *Walrus*—reflects real privateering in the Caribbean. Historically, the pirates Howell Davis, Edward England, William Kidd,

Bartholomew Roberts, and Edward "Blackbeard" Teach and the national hero Sir Francis Drake preyed on the Spanish gold and silver mines and mints in Central and South America. At a crucial epiphany in the coming to knowledge of the book's HERO, Jim Hawkins, he realizes that he straddles the divide between civilization and lawless avarice. He states, "If I'm to choose, I declare I have a right to know what's what, and why you're here, and where my friends are" (Stevenson 1918, 244). At the adventure's end, Jim distances himself from treasure hunting and vows, "Oxen and wain-ropes would not bring me back again to that accursed island" (306), a Jekyll-and-Hyde hellhole that haunts his dreams. The stirring pictorial novel was the basis of numerous films, including one starring Jackie Cooper and Wallace Beery as Jim Hawkins and Long John Silver in 1934 and another with Bobby Driscoll and Robert Newton in a 1950 Disney remake. Forty years later, the pairing of Christian Bale and Charlton Heston suited a television version filmed in part in Jamaica.

Sources

Ambrosini, Richard, and Richard Dury. *Robert Louis Stevenson: Writer of Boundaries.* Madison: University of Wisconsin Press, 2006.

Edmond, Rod. *Representing the South Pacific: Colonial Discourse from Cook to Gauguin.* Cambridge: Cambridge University Press, 2005.

Mack, Douglas S. *Scottish Fiction and the British Empire.* Edinburgh: Edinburgh University Press, 2006.

Stevenson, Robert Louis. *Treasure Island.* New York: Charles Scribner's Sons, 1918.

Tu Fu See DU FU.

Turgenev, Ivan Sergeyevich (1818–1883)

Russian novelist, short story writer, and playwright

A contemporary of FYODOR DOSTOYEVSKY, NIKOLAY GOGOL, and LEO TOLSTOY and a literary star across Europe during the golden age of the Russian novel, Ivan Turgenev wrote long and short fiction that promoted the Westernization of the czarist Russian Empire. Born in Oryol, Russia, he was the son of a colonel in the Russian imperial cavalry who died when Turgenev was 16 and a wealthy heiress who suffered from her husband's philandering. As a boy, Turgenev had a standard education, followed by studies at the universities of Moscow, Saint Petersburg, and Berlin. His time in Germany convinced him that Russia could benefit from Western ideas and attitudes, especially the evil of serfdom. He began writing plays and short stories and first attracted public attention with *A Sportsman's Sketches*, a collection of stories published in 1852. It was his novels, however, that brought him the greatest fame. Later in his life, Turgenev lived little in Russia, preferring to spend his time in Paris or Baden Baden; his preference for western Europe threatened his friendships with Tolstoy and Dostoyevsky. Though he had a long-term affair with a Spanish singer, and an illegitimate daughter with a serf, he never married. He received an honorary degree from Oxford University in 1879. Four years later, he died in Bougival, France, near Paris, and was buried in the Volkov Cemetery in Saint Petersburg.

A retiring, fair-minded man, Turgenev nurtured a rebel's heart and yet displayed goodwill as well as integrity. At the same time that abolitionists in the United States, Great Britain, and the Caribbean wrangled over abolition of SLAVERY, he supported serfs and denounced Czar Nicholas I and his arbitrary suppression of civil rights. In his novel *Fathers and Sons* (1862), the author advocated "active patience, not without some cunning and ingenuity" (Turgenev 1975, 43), a suggestion of the stealth and strategy that brought down Nicholas II and the Romanov dynasty in the Russian Revolution of 1917. Turgenev's championing of liberal authorship caused him to remind Tolstoy that literature should have a political aim, although he admitted: "You loath this political morass; true, it is a dirty, dusty, vulgar business" (16).

In the 25 realistic short stories and two fragments serialized in the magazine *Sovremennik* (The Contemporary) and anthologized in *A Sportsman's Sketches*, Turgenev criticized the imbalance between the elite's self-indulgence and the wretched conditions of an enslaved peasantry. In the opening story, he describes Orel and the typical life of a serf: "He lives in wretched little hovels of aspen-wood, labours as a serf in the fields, and engages in no kind of trading, is miserably fed, and wears slippers of bast (hemp)" (Turgenev 1895, 1). As a result of Turgenev's love of liberty and his praiseworthy obituary of Gogol, Turgenev spent four weeks in a St. Petersburg prison and then 18 months in exile at Spasskoye, the family estate in west-central Russia. During his incarceration, he composed "Mumu" (1852), the story of a wealthy widow's cruel treatment of Gerasim, a deaf-mute farm laborer.

Turgenev wrote more pointedly of his backward country after Russia's defeat in the Crimean War in 1856. He serialized *Rudin* (1855), his first novel, about an ineffectual scholar frustrated by the barriers posed by Czar Nicholas I to social and land reform. Of the dangers of foreign education to Rudin, defamers charge, "His eloquence is not Russian," evidence of the protagonist's estrangement from his native land (Turgenev 1908, 99). After Alexander II issued an edict on February 19, 1861, emancipating serfs, the novelist created a stir the next year with the publication of *Fathers and Sons*, a novel of ideas that he began writing as an expatriate on the Isle of Wight. The narrative debates the generational clash between a recent university graduate, Arkady Nikolaevich Kirsanov, and his elders—his father Nikolai and paternal uncle Pavel—concerning the rising democratic movement. The appeal of the nihilistic pre-med student Yevgeny Bazarov shocked and dismayed the older generation of readers, who promoted traditional values and gradual modernization of Russia rather than revolution and abandonment of serfdom.

Turgenev's last novel, *Virgin Soil* (1877), begun during a visit to England, anticipates by four decades the end of the Russian Empire. The action prophesies a vigorous Russian generation that will lead a rebellion against the aristocracy. One character worries about backlash: "It's such as you that the inspectors of the Czar are ever eager to clap in custody" (Turgenev 1920, 113). The idealist Nezhdanov replies with an apologue: "If you choose to be a mushroom, you must go in the basket with the rest" (114). In 1878, Turgenev turned to didacticism and wrote a series of first-person FABLES. The best examples—"The Sparrow," "Cabbage Soup" and "The Fool"—honor humble folk and deride the adulation of the mighty. In his 60s, Turgenev wished that his epitaph would note his activism on behalf of serfs. At his funeral, the imperial police suppressed dissent by concealing the time of his interment from Turgenev's admirers.

Sources

Baring, Maurice. *An Outline of Russian Literature.* New York: Nova, 2006.

Turgenev, Ivan. *Fathers and Sons.* Translated by Rosemary Edmonds and Isaiah Berlin. London: Penguin, 1975.

———. *Rudin: A Romance.* Translated by Isabel F. Hapgood. Boston: Jefferson Press, 1908.

———. *A Sportsman's Sketches.* Translated by Constance Garnett. London: Heinemann, 1895.

———. *Virgin Soil.* Translated by Constance Garnett. London: Heinemann, 1920.

Tutuola, Amos (1920–1997) *Nigerian ethnographer, novelist, and storyteller*

A facile teller of Yoruba FABLEs and folk stories, Amos Tutuola surveyed social history and wrote on African survivalism during Nigeria's emergence into the modern world as an independent nation. A native of Abeokuta near the southwestern coast of Nigeria, he was raised by Yoruba Christians on a cacao farm. With only six years of primary education, he based his untutored writings on a reading of The THOUSAND AND ONE NIGHTS (ca. A.D. 942) and on the bedtime STORYTELLING of fables and deity tales of his grandmother. During World War II, Tutuola served in the Royal Air Force as a coppersmith; he subsequently operated a labor department message relay and, at age 36, clerked and stocked shelves in a store owned by the Nigerian Broadcasting Network. While living in Lagos, he found spare time to jot stories on scraps of paper.

At age 32, eight years before Nigeria negotiated independence from Great Britain, Tutuola published *The Palm-Wine Drinkard* (1952), an episodic fantasy novel told through the perspective, dreamscapes, and bizarre dialect of a Nigerian naïf. In the book, riddling and shape-shifting in the style of Dante's hell and JONATHAN SWIFT's

Gulliver Travels (1735) parallel the contradictions of colonialism in an unsophisticated African nation where exorcism, polygamy, oral education, and tribal clashes are common. The protagonist asserts manhood through a trial by ordeal. On his flight through "Deads' Town," he explains: "If one is captured, he or she would be sold into slavery for foreigners who would carry him or her to unknown destinations to be killed for the buyer's god or to be working for him" (Tutuola 1994, 18). By equating ritual sacrifice with forced labor, Tutuola expresses the long-term African terror of enslavement.

A similar atmosphere of controlled panic overlays the author's second Jungian novel, *My Life in the Bush of Ghosts* (1954), a GOTHIC mythography that draws on Yoruban cultural symbols, *pourquoi* (why) stories, and cautionary tales. The structure replicates the quest motif of Tutuola's first novel in a vision of the flight of a child from slave catchers, the Satan-on-earth figures of Nigerian nightmare. A pell-mell plunge into the jungle forces the boy to rely on animal instincts. Trusting to self, he relies on intuition and sense of smell. In his precipitate venture into the unknown, he observes the threat to age-old Yoruban traditions, which he pictures as spirits: "These ghosts were so old and weary that it is hard to believe that they were living creatures" (24). The wanderings of his protagonist amid anthropomorphic animals, metaphysical perils, ogres, and demons illustrate the confusion of Yorubans in the grip of European values and other predations on the black race. The crises force Tutuola's characters to emulate attitudes that draw on the preliterate history of the Benin, Ife, and Oyo empires for relief from the diminution of West African culture.

Sources

Gérard, Albert S. *European-Language Writing in Sub-Saharan Africa.* Amsterdam: John Benjamins, 1986.

Quayson, Ato. *Strategic Transformations in Nigerian Writing.* Bloomington: Indiana University Press, 1997.

Tutuola, Amos. *The Palm-Wine Drinkard; and My Life in the Bush of Ghosts.* New York: Grove, 1994.

U

Undset, Sigrid (1882–1949) *Danish-Norwegian novelist and polemist*

A feminist writer, lecturer, and translator, Sigrid Undset reprised details from the medieval Danish Empire. According to her autobiography, *Elleve Aar* (*The Longest Years*, 1934), she learned folk narrative in her native Kalundborg, Denmark, and mastered two defunct Scandic languages, Old Danish and Old Icelandic. The invalidism of her archeologist father, Ingvald Undset, and his death from malaria in 1893 depleted family finances and ended her plans to attend a university. With certification from Christiana Commercial College, she worked in the office of a German electrical engineer while extending her knowledge of world fiction by reading such works as the Icelandic *Njals Saga* (ca. 1250), medieval German CRUSADER LORE, and SNORRI STURLUSON's Teutonic *Heimskringla* (Orb of the world, 1220) as well as the fiction of Jane Austen, the Brontë sisters, and the Scandinavian playwrights Heinrich Ibsen and August Strindberg.

On a government scholarship, Undset traveled through Germany and Italy and published *Gunnar's Daughter* (1909), a feminist historical novel set during the 10th-century expansionism of Olaf I of Norway and Iceland. The text depicts the androcentrism of Scandic rule in state, church, and clan, an exaltation of machismo that disempowers and discounts females. The heroine, Vigdis, describes the male egoism that dates to the Viking era: "My father believes in nothing but his own power and strength, nor had my grandfather any other faith" (Undset 1998, 7). Using parallel themes and motifs,

Undset created a three-volume masterwork, *Kristin Lavransdatter*, comprised of *Kransen* (*The Bridal Wreath*, 1920), *Husfrue* (*The Wife*, 1921), and *Korset* (*The Cross*, 1922), set during early 14th-century Norwegian feudalism. The trilogy, a diatribe against patriarchal marriage, pits the title character against her promiscuous mate, the knight Erlend Nikulaussøn. She describes the feudal customs of King Haakon the Old, who awarded Kristin's father the manor of Skog, the family estate. Competitive Norwegians serve royalty and vie for positions at court, the height of ignoble ambition according to STORYTELLING about Nordic history.

Undset structures action to reflect on the faults of imperialism. In the second volume, scandal ballads recall a military traitor who was hanged for selling out Haakon's forces for seven barrels of gold. A more pressing contretemps involves King Magnus's bankruptcy while trying to gain control of Skaane, Sweden. In Kristin's search for salvation in the last volume, she rejoices in the selection of a monarch who does more than "[squander] his time, energies, and the wealth of the kingdom on incursion in other lands" (Undset 2001, 306). She regrets the "wicked and turbulent times that had descended upon the realm after the death of blessed King Haakon" (385), when nobles abandoned religion. The motif of the "good old days" reflects not only a shift away from imperialism but also Kristin's advancing age and inability to cope with modernity.

Undset followed *Kristin Lavransdatter* with a tetralogy of medieval Norway, *Olav Audunssøn* (*The*

Master of Hestviken, 1925–27), which won her the 1928 Nobel Prize in literature. The narrative features the political maneuvering between Denmark and Norway over Iceland.

The War Years

The Nazi occupation of Undset's home in Oslo on April 9, 1940, and the combat death of her son Anders in World War II induced her to support the Resistance and to spy for the U.S. government. Her anger at the onset of World War II repudiates Adolf Hitler's self-glorification in MEIN KAMPF (1925–1926), an apologia for racism and for his fantasy of a master race. Before fleeing by trawler across Sweden to Siberia, Japan, and San Francisco, she composed *Tillbake til Fremtiden* (*Return to the Future,* 1942), a wartime memoir suppressed during Josef Stalin's tyranny in Russia. At the sight of Siberians forced into beggary, she shuddered at the effects of rickets on undernourished children, who peddled raspberries and blueberries at the depots: "From out their rags protruded ugly chicken-breasts and the rows of knobs in crooked, humped backbones. Legs and arms like matches, with large knobby joints" (Undset 1942, 135). Her eyewitness account reveals random arrests of foreigners, particularly those foolish enough to photograph military terrain.

Undset's anti-German polemic begins with a recall of Norway's stone borders, "silent witnesses of our right to this land which our forefathers for more than two thousand years have toiled to conquer so that homes for man could be built" (2). She honors Viking oarsmen as Norwegian farmboys are put to the test. The memoir catalogs disbelief and panic as Nazi invaders entered Oslo, German ships seized major ports, and Luftwaffe bombers loomed overhead in blatant intimidation of noncombatants. She outlines the shrewdness of the Wehrmacht general Richard Pellengahr, who ordered confiscation of every vehicle, sled, and pair of skis in Norway as a form of house arrest. Of his forces, she regards their robotic predations as a testimonial to the "legend of the Pied Piper of Hamelin" (224) and proof that the goodheartedness of the Hohenzollern era was absent from the Panzer divisions.

At the same time that Undset noted international concerns that Germans were, by nature, evil megalomaniacs, she strove to preserve global fairness and good memories of her motherland. She joined the American Commission for the Protection and Saving of Historical and Artistic Documents, an international effort to rescue irreplaceable writings from Hitler's bonfires. At the request of First Lady Eleanor Roosevelt, at the war's height, Undset wrote *Lykkelige Dager* (*Happy Times in Norway,* 1942), an introduction to life with her children at Bjerkebaek in Lillehammer, Norway, before the German occupation. King Haakon VII awarded the author the Grand Cross of the Order of Saint Olav in 1947, both for her patriotism and her literary work. She died in Lillehammer on June 10, 1949. In 1995, the Norwegian actress Liv Ullman directed the film version of *Kristin Lavransdatter.*

Sources

Stone, Harry. *Writing in the Shadow: Resistance Publications in Occupied Europe.* New York: Routledge, 1996.

Undset, Sigrid. *Gunnar's Daughter.* Translated by Arthur G. Chater. New York: Penguin, 1998.

———. *Kristin Lavransdatter: The Cross.* Translated by Tiina Nunnally. New York: Penguin, 2001.

———. *Kristin Lavransdatter: The Wife.* Translated by Tiina Nunnally. New York: Penguin, 1999.

———. *Kristin Lavransdatter: The Wreath.* Translated by Tiina Nunnally. New York: Penguin, 1997.

———. *Return to the Future.* Translated by Henriette C. K. Naeseth. New York: A. A. Knopf, 1942.

V

Vedas (ca. 150 B.C.)

The four Vedas (Knowledge), the world's oldest religious texts, narrate the traditional WISDOM LITERATURE of the ancients in 10,552 Sanskrit verses. Nomadic Aryan bard-priests from Persia carried the oral invocations, ritual, and praise songs east to the Harappan civilization of northern India. From as early as 2100 B.C., preliterate Hindus reverenced the word of God as recited by Brahmans, the most educated class of their society. Vedic followers migrated into the Indus valley and settled the Punjab by 1500 B.C. Listeners to the Vedas celebrated the holy word with dance, song, and the playing of cymbals, drums, flutes, harps, and zithers, the same instrumentation accompanying recitation of the Davidic PSALMS (ca. 900 B.C.) of the Israelite Empire. Although committed to parchment by scribes for the Maurya emperors of India, the written text circulated empire-wide two millennia later. Sages, priests, and prophets learned from the corpus Hindu edicts on beneficence, self-denial, divinity, and right thinking. Recitations explained transmigration of the soul to merge with the sacred atman (oversoul). From Vedic aphorisms, the righteous learned to accept destiny and a place in the feudal caste system, which ranked intellectuals and warriors above farmers, traders, crafters, and serfs. Among those who respected Vedic teaching was the Russian author LEO TOLSTOY, who cited ancient Indian scriptural authority in "A Letter to a Hindu" (1908).

The first collection, the Rig Veda (Praise stanzas), is the fount of Indian religious belief and literary achievement. Compiled among pastoral-agrarian clans in northern India from 1700 to 1400 B.C., it speaks in veneration of a fire god, of the first man, and of the healing power of soma, a hallucinogenic beverage. Of Yama, the first human and child of the sun god, the text conveys his primacy as "spying out the path for many . . . the first to find the way for us" (Rig Veda 1981, 43). Because of the sanctity of his mission, Yama is the first king and defender of humanity. As tribalism gave place to monarchy, Vedic anthems accompanied coronations, royal births, funerals, and cremations and honored charity, morality, and thanksgiving. War anthems exalted the confederacy of chiefs who warded off enemies from the southern Punjab. In the evocative "Burial Hymn," the survivors spurn death, comfort the widow, and "[go] forward to dance and laugh, stretching farther our own lengthening span of life" (52).

The Growth of the Vedas

The compilation of subsequent Hindu verse added three collections to the Rig Veda. Around 1000 B.C., priests anthologized a separate hymnbook, the Sama Veda (Chant lore), comprised of 1,549 liturgical verses, incantations, and feasting and drinking tunes similar in tone to the Bacchic verse and Homeric hymns of ancient Greece. In a more pragmatic mode, the Yajur Veda (Sacrificial prayers, 1000–600 B.C.) suited the needs of the altar guild. A prayer for victory implores the fire deity, "May we win by thy help, O Agni, our wish . . . May

300

we win booty, seeking for booty; May we win, O deathless, undying glory" (Yajur 2004, 51). A folkloric compendium of 6,000 verses, the Atharva Veda (Lore of the fire priests, 800 B.C.), was a fount of spirituality and otherworldliness. Based on the teachings of the mythic healer Dhanvantari, it offers mantras and prayers on the subjects of danger, fear, love, witchcraft, sin, forgiveness, crop culture, diet, disease, snakebite, and family blessings. One plea requests peace to the earth through appeasement of the dreadful, cruel, and evil, an all-encompassing reference that includes imperialist adversaries. Accompanying a love charm is the ritual incantation, "I dig this herb, of plants the strongest, with which one drives off her rival; with which one wins completely her husband" (Atharva 1905, 118). In a retreat from earthly miseries, a prayer asks, "O Earth, O Mother, dispose my loss in gracious fashion that I may be at ease, and in harmony with your powers" (quoted in Roberts and Amidon 1991, 52), a displacement of concerns of sovereignty to oneness with creation. To assure a unity of all endeavors, the collection asks the goddess: "Breathe fearlessness into us: / fearlessness on earth / and fearlessness in heaven" (114).

The Vedas address the nature of conflict. One prayer from the Rig Veda seeks life's sweetness in nature; another regards God as the "scatterer of ignorance and darkness" (267), a thanksgiving for the ultimate power over human frailties. In place of governmental maltreatment, a nationalistic plea requests, "Let us be united, / Let us speak in harmony ... Unified be our hearts; / Common be our intentions" (93). On the subject of domestic discord, like the gentle AZTEC priest-poet Nezahualcoyotl and Jesus in the Sermon on the Mount, the priest intones God's commandment with maternal fondness: "Like-heartedness, like-mindedness, non-hostility do I make for you; do ye show affection the one toward the other, as the inviolable cow toward her calf when born" (138). A hymn to the war chariot extols the stout tree trunk that builders turn into a vehicle. In a subdued paean to the chariot, the poet declares, "Let him who mounts thee conquer things unconquerable" (374). A parallel anthem honoring the war drum implores a victory: "Thunder against them ...

drive, O drum, misfortune away from here; / Indra's fist art thou; be stout" (375).

Interpreting Wisdom

Accompanying each of the four Vedas are interpretive ancillary texts that are similar in pairing to the Hebrew Talmud and the Torah and guidebooks to the *Analects* of Confucius (ca. 210 B.C.). The *Brahmanas* (Godly discussions, 1000–600 B.C.) order intricate ceremonies. The most poetic of the ancillaries, the Upanishads (Lessons, 1000–600 B.C.) comprise 108 sections in which a guru explains the wondrous nature of the inner self.

Forerunners of the *Mathnawi* (*Spiritual Couplets*, ca. 1270) of RUMI, the Vedic verses encourage ecstatic worship. Extolling the generations who followed Yama, the first man, the narrative of the Upanishads marvels at the mathematic possibilities of reproduction: "He is one, he becomes three, he becomes five, he becomes seven, he becomes nine; then again he is called the eleventh, and hundred and ten and one thousand twenty" (Upanishads 1897, 124–125). Originated during an era of change, the lessons exhibit the emergence of humanism among the Hindu hierarchy. The *Aranyakas* (Forest treatises, 600 B.C.) are treatises for the meditation of hermits on natural phenomena in the wilderness. The *Sutras* (Rules, 800–350 B.C.), legalism codified during the late Indo-Gangetic empire, apply Hindu teachings to daily domestic situations and to the responsibilities of emperors. The *Kama Sutra* (450 B.C.), written by the ascetic monk Vatsyayana, summarizes the elements of courtship and conjugal love, a token of the advancement of gender equality in India.

The beauty of Hindu mysticism influenced the Bengali poet RABINDRANATH TAGORE, a spokesman for world peace. Of immersion in godliness, Tagore exulted, "I touch by the edge of the far spreading wing of my song thy feet which I could never aspire to reach. Drunk with the joy of singing I forget myself and call thee friend who are my lord" (Tagore 1996, 13–44).

Sources

Atharva Veda Samhita. Translated by William Dwight Whitney and edited by Charles Rockwell Lanman. Cambridge, Mass.: Harvard University, 1905.

The Rig Veda. Translated and edited by Wendy Doniger. Harmondsworth, U.K.: Penguin Classics, 1981.

Roberts, Elizabeth, and Elias Amidon, eds. *Earth Prayers from Around the World.* San Francisco: HarperSanFrancisco, 1991.

Sama Veda. Translated by S. V. Ganapati. Delhi: Motilal Banarsidass, 1992.

Tagore, Rabindranath. *Gitanjali.* London: Branden, 1996.

The Upanishads. Translated by Friedrich Max Müller. Oxford: Oxford University Press, 1897.

The Yajur Veda Taittiriya Sanhita. Whitefish, Mont.: Kessinger, 2004.

violence

The destructive power of human villainy is a pervasive motif in the literature of empire. Writers who recreate history often concentrate on dramatic or evocative scenarios—for example, the spread of first-strike militarism in THUCYDIDES's *The History of the Peloponnesian War* (ca. 400 B.C.), the description of severed limbs in *Pharsalia* (A.D. 63) by the Roman epic poet LUCAN, and the deaths of lovers in the Kurdish poet Ahmed-i Hani's MEM-U ZIN (Mem and Zin, 1695). Alexandre Dumas, père (1802–70) earned the disapproval of the Russian czar Nicholas I for serializing in the *Revue de Paris* a heroic romance, *Le maître d'armes* (*The Fencing Master; or, Eighteen Months in Saint Petersburg,* 1840), a fictional glimpse of the imperial capital during a historic venting of liberal unrest by army officers. Rage produced the uprising of December 26, 1825, a day after the czar's accession.

Creative plottings and killings invigorate GOTHIC court intrigues in William Makepeace Thackeray's *Barry Lyndon* (1844), imaginative murder in Sir ARTHUR CONAN DOYLE's "The Adventure of the Speckled Band" (1892), poisonings in the Roman imperial household in Robert Graves's *I, Claudius* (1934), and the land grabs and pilfering of the landed gentry during a famine in imperial China in PEARL S. BUCK's masterwork *The Good Earth* (1931). In revelatory passages about an agrarian mother's upbringing of sons, Buck characterizes the lure of the military for boys dazzled by the glory of war and the desire for a uniform decorated with medals. The marauding of undisciplined troops overwhelms a villager: "There

were soldiers in the very room where his wife lay ill, and he protested and they ran a knife through him as though he were made of lard—as smoothly as that—and it came through him clean to the other side" (Buck 1931, 234).

All too often, mayhem and catastrophe set the tone, mood, and atmosphere in the earliest recorded texts. During the Babylonian Empire from 1900 to 1600 B.C., court sages shared FABLEs and agons, or contest stories, as models of WISDOM. Along with narratives on stalking animals—snakes, foxes, and wolves—are human death penalties, burning, disemboweling, rending of limbs, and blood sucking. According to Laozi (Lao-Tze), the Chinese antiquarian who wrote the DAODEJING (*Tao-Te Ching*) (Classic of the way of power, 300 B.C.), the cause is inherent: Violent people condemn themselves to unnatural deaths. The compilation of the Tibetan BOOK OF THE DEAD (ca. A.D. 775), describes savagery in the underworld in the first weeks after death before the soul can attain purification before reincarnation. Confrontation with demons threatens the naked spirit with a lord of death who can disintegrate the individual—"cut off thy head, tear out thy heart, pull out thy intestines, lick up thy brain, drink thy blood, eat thy flesh, and gnaw thy bones" (*Tibetan* 2000, xlvi)—all without killing the victim.

Women and Guile

Involvement of female heroes in violence enlivens the biblical book of Judges (ca. 1040 B.C.), which features the prophet and judge Deborah, the assassin Jael, and the seductress Delilah. In individual tales dating to 1100 B.C. and collected in an anthology during the Israelites' exile in Babylon, the story of Deborah honors her for wisdom and bravery. She serves Israel as the strategist who sends General Barak against Sisera, leader of the Canaanite infantry. Deborah foresees a horrific conclusion to 20 years of enemy action—the volunteering of Jael, a self-appointed assassin and one of the mothers of Israel, to drive a tent peg into Sisera's head. In the style of JUDITH, slayer of Holofernes, Jael accomplishes her task by posing as a submissive hostess and by beguiling Sisera with a bowl of milk and a dish of butter before hammering the spike into his temple. The two-stage episode concludes with a scriptural gem, the Song of Deborah, an ancient paean. The self-assured judge exults with General Barak, "I *even* I, will sing unto the Lord" (Judges 5:3). Of female daring in a border war, she boasts, "I Deborah arose, that I arose a mother in Israel" (Judges 5:7). The song contrasts her literary foil by celebrating Sisera's demise with a triumphal repetition: "At her feet he bowed, he fell, he lay down: at her feet he bowed, he fell: where he bowed, there he fell down dead" (Judges 5:27).

In chapters 13–16, the introduction of Delilah, a sexually autonomous Philistine, pictures female strength on the opposing side. At the end of a hero cycle, Delilah's betrayal of her lover Samson, a Nazirite strongman, to secret agents precedes his shearing and blinding. After the female double-dealer recedes from the story, Samson's recovery allows him to pull the temple of Dagon at Gaza onto his own head as well as those of his adversaries, but the narrative says nothing of Delilah's fate. Mirroring the downfall of womanizers described throughout Hebrew scripture, the sacrifice of Samson is necessary to the establishment in 1050 B.C. of an Israelite empire. Above the righteous Deborah and Jael, art chooses Delilah as the femme fatale for representation in painting, statuary, epic, opera, and the film *Samson and Delilah* (1949), which pairs Hedy Lamarr with Victor Mature.

Male carnage far surpassed women's roles in murder and the slaughter of combat. The he-man motif, a basis of patriarchal literature, dominates the Viking lore of SNORRI STURLUSON, author of the *Rose Edda* (1225), a compilation of Iceland's mythology. Of the earth's creation from a giant's remains in the section called the *Voluspa*, Sturluson describes the filling of earth's "yawning void" with body parts of Ymir the giant: "Of his blood the sea and the waters; the land was made of his flesh, and the crags of his bones; gravel and stones they fashioned from his teeth and his grinders and from those bones that were broken" (Sturluson 1916, 20). The skull becomes the dome of heaven and the sparks that burst from the bloody fight light the night sky. The inventive dismembering concludes, "And of his brain the bitter-mooded clouds were all created" (21). In Norse battle lore, mercy lacks merit, and the vulnerability of women is unavoidable: "The sturdy king's bright Flare soared above the cattle's bulwark; the vikings burst in grimly: grief on the maid descended" (224).

Violence in the Caribbean and Latin America

A Spanish priest, BARTOLOMÉ DE LAS CASAS (1474–1566), warned European imperialists that their greed and carnage in the New World doomed the conquerors in the sight of God. In *Historia de las Indias* (*History of the Indies*, published in 1875), he honored Indian martyrs who had fallen since Christopher Columbus's first voyage to the West Indies in 1492 under the ensign of Spain's King Ferdinand and Queen Isabella. The chronicle compares Spanish atrocities in Hispaniola to barnyard killings: "They pitilessly slaughtered everyone like sheep in a corral" (Las Casas, 1971, 94). Persecutors chop hands, leaving them dangling by shredded skin, and place bets on how many slices they require to lop off heads or sever torsos. Among the chiefs they burn and hang is an elderly female Indian named Higuanamá. The priest commiserates that the people "understood themselves to be so injured, so persecuted and so hopelessly desperate about finding a hiding place" that they surrender (95). In his summation of loss, Las Casas estimates that 2 million natives died during the invasion of Hispaniola. His poignant writings did little to stem New World violence.

The cruelty of conquest inspired defenders of humanity against racism and classism. In Latin American romantic novels, the Nahua poet and writer Ignacio Manuel Altamirano (1834–93) stressed that the essence of a country is the rooted peasantry rather than the race-pure usurper and ruling class who lacked ties to the soil. His articles for *El Renacimiento* (Renaissance) supply details of manners, native ritual, dress, and diversions during the Mexican empire, when a growing indigenous sense of belonging coincided with bursts of anarchy and nationalism. In *Clemencia* (Mercy, 1869) and the short story "La navidad en las Montañas" ("Christmas in the Mountains," 1871), Altamirano pictures the turmoil in Guadalajara during the invasion of January 7, 1864, when the French attempt to move inland from the sea. The invaders arrive under the flag of the Hapsburg-Lorraine emperor Maximilian I of Mexico, who died with dignity in 1867 before a Mexican firing squad. The coup illustrates the power of indigenous people to throw off a short-lived foreign dominion.

Altamirano employed native sources of rural banditry and civil abuse to depict lawlessness and the murder of innocents in *El Zarco* (*El Zarco the Blue-Eyed Bandit*, 1901). He based the character on Salomé Plasencia, an outlaw chief of the Plateados band who turned a kidnapped 16-year-old named Homobona Merelo into a *soldadera* (woman soldier), an amazon warrior and tender of the wounded. The fictional Zarco, a conceited glory hound known for sullen hostility and crude language, revels in womanizing and horsemanship, which he equates with a caballero's necessary skills. The rivalry of rich males—merchants, ranchers, officials, and gentry—sparks jealousy "complicated by a powerless, abject envy that led to his singular hatred and frenetic longing to snatch all such things at any cost" (Altamirano 2006, 93). For realism, the author spices the love story with troops swearing, tawdry marching and drinking songs, and bar frays arising from drunkenness and tedium. Justification for brigandage arises from widespread persecution of the vulnerable in Yautepec in southern Mexico and the formation of ad hoc police forces and vigilantes, some of them mestizos (of mixed parentage). The outcome is standard CORRIDO melodrama: Zarco's woman swoons and dies at the sight of her champion riddled with bullets and swinging from a tree.

Exposés and Protests

In an attempt to stem world mayhem, many authors produced antityranny works—for example, JOSEPH CONRAD's *Heart of Darkness* (1902); Anatoly Kuznetsov's antifascism novel *Babi Yar* (1967); and *The Underdogs* (1915), a battlefield threnody written by Mariano Azuela, a Mexican field surgeon under Pancho Villa. During the decline of the Russian Empire, LEO TOLSTOY, an aristocratic novelist turned Christian anarchist, observed the parallelism between empires and wars. In *Sevastopol Sketches* (1855), he reflects on the inevitable battlefield surgery and hasty amputations with crisp detail: "You see the sharp, curved knife enter the healthy, white body, you see the wounded man suddenly regain consciousness

with a piercing cry and curses, you see the army surgeon fling the amputated arm into a corner" (Tolstoy 1888, 17).

Tolstoy advanced from eyewitness vignettes to PROTEST LITERATURE in the treatise *The Kingdom of God Is within You* (1894). In this work, he observes that "the sense of the uselessness and even injurious effects of state violence is more and more penetrating into men's consciousness" (Tolstoy 1894, 245). He denounces brutal punishments—"prisons, galleys, gibbets, and guillotines" (256)—for failure to civilize Russians and charges that cruelty is more likely "to increase than diminish the number of malefactors" (256), a PROPHECY that violence begets violence. Because of his forthright condemnation of despotism, czarist censors suppressed the treatise for the next 23 years.

Still hammering at Russian imperial expansionism, Tolstoy promoted pacifism with his HERO novel *Hadji Murad* (1904), an antiwar book dramatizing the incursion of the Cossack troops of Czar Alexander I into Muslim territory between the Black and Caspian seas. Tolstoy's first chapter opens on a self-evident status quo: "Ah, what a destructive creature is man" (Tolstoy 1996, 22). Murad, reflecting on an agrarian culture, regrets the destruction of croplands and forests more than the waste of human life in battle. In a hospital scene, the probing of a stomach wound for a rifle bullet leaves the wounded soldier Peter Avdéev in a moribund state before he succumbs to trauma and hemorrhage. For its revelation of the imperial army's savagery to Chechen villagers and the brutality of Russian troops through the beheading of the Tartar mountaineer Murad, censors under the Romanovs suppressed the novel until the Bolshevik Revolution in 1917.

Atomic Age Threats

The presentation of violence in literature changed little after two world wars. In 1956, Anne Bodart (b. 1939), a Brussels-born fabulist, wrote *The Blue Dog and Other Fables for the French*, an atomic-age reflection on human cruelty and the frailty of hope. Translated by Alice B. Toklas and set during the brutal reign of Leopold II over the Belgian Congo, the collection of 17 moody tales dramatizes existentialism in a milieu occupied by an ant that poisons rats, a poodle in a dinner jacket, feline stalkers, a canine diarist, and a blue dog expiring in snow. The post–World War II apprehensions and secret fears take the symbolic form of a terrified magpie that cannot see its reflection and of Feverish Paw, a dog suffering from anxiety attacks. More historical is a stagy reprise of the assassination of Julius Caesar in "A London Night," which Bodart sets in a vermin-ridden sewer. Her perusal of the Roman underworld is a place where animals howl with glee at the River Styx sweeping over the corrupt skulls of humankind.

In the postcolonial angst in Palestine, the collapse of empires left unsettled issues that still fester into war and terrorism. The Galilean poet Mahmoud Darwish (1941–2008) expressed the ongoing misery of Arab-Israeli tensions and threats of factional reprisal by Fatah and Hamas following the partitioning of the former territory of the British Empire. In his poem "A State of Siege" (2002), he compares himself to a frustrated inmate: "We do what the prisoners do, . . . we nurture hope" (Darwish 2007, 121). His verse pictures artillery glistening in the night on guard against a sleepless enemy. He depicts the protracted state of siege as a wretchedness devoid of Homeric valor and triumph. He describes each loss as a "first death" (127) and urges Jewish soldiers to recall relatives in Nazi gas chambers and to abandon rifles for peaceful coexistence.

Sources

Altamirano, Ignacio Manuel. *El Zarco the Blue-eyed Bandit*. Translated by Ronald Christ. Santa Fe, N.M.: Lumen, 2006.

Bodart, Anne. *The Blue Dog and Other Fables for the French*. Translated by Alice B. Toklas. Boston: Houghton Mifflin, 1956.

Buck, Pearl. *The Good Earth*. New York: Pocket Books, 1931.

Dabove, Juan Pablo. *Nightmares of the Lettered City: Banditry and Literature in Latin America, 1816–1929*. Pittsburgh: University of Pittsburgh Press, 2007.

Darwish, Mahmoud. *The Butterfly's Burden*. Translated by Fady Joudah. Port Townsend, Wash.: Copper Canyon, 2007.

Judges. In the Holy Bible. Iowa Falls, Iowa: World Bible Publishers, 1986, 381–420.

Las Casas, Bartolomé de. *History of the Indies*. Translated by Andrée Collard. New York: Harper & Row, 1971.

Sturluson, Snorri. *The Prose Edda*. Translated by Arthur Gilchrist Brodeur. New York: American-Scandinavian Foundation, 1916.

The Tibetan Book of the Dead. Translated by W. Y. Evans-Wentz. Oxford: Oxford University Press, 2000.

Tolstoy, Leo. *Hadji Murád*. Translated by Aylmer Maude. Alexandria, Va.: Orchises Press, 1996.

———. *The Kingdom of God Is within You*. Translated by Constance Garnett. London: Heinemann, 1894.

———. *Sevastopol*, Isabel Florence Hapgood. New York: Thomas Y. Crowell, 1888.

Yee, Gale A. *Judges and Method: New Approaches in Biblical Studies*. Minneapolis: Fortress Press, 1995.

Virgil (Publius Vergilius Maro) (70–19 B.C.)
Roman poet

The father of the literary epic, Virgil composed classic verse as propaganda promoting the newly formed Roman Empire. Perhaps of Celto-Etrurian ancestry, he was born on October 15, 70 B.C., a contemporary of Rome's first emperor, Octavian, later known as Caesar Augustus. Tall and shy, he was the son of Polla Magia, a daughter of the bailiff Magus, and lived in Andes, a hamlet outside Mantua on the Mincio River in north-central Italy. Virgil learned country ways in his father Maro's pottery shop and from animal husbandry, beekeeping, and lumbering. Groomed for the law courts, he survived his brothers Flaccus and Silo and came to love a half brother, Valerius Proculus, who later inherited half of Virgil's estate.

After homeschooling at a young age, Virgil studied astronomy, math, medicine, and rhetoric in Cremona and Milan and specialized in philosophy. At age 17, he enrolled in oratory and law at Marcus Epidius's school in Rome, where the young Octavian and Mark Antony had studied. After Julius Caesar violated Roman law by bringing his army into Roman territory across the Rubicon River in 49 B.C., Virgil withdrew to Naples. At the Campanian villa in Herculaneum of the philosopher and mentor Siro the Epicurean, he wrote his first verses. His eclectic readings included Hesiod's *Works and Days* (ca. 700 B.C.); Theocritus's *Idylls* (ca. 200 B.C.), Lucretius's *De rerum natura* (*On the*

Nature of Things, ca. 60 B.C.), and the epigrams, elegies, and short epic in verse of Catullus, a late republican experimenter.

A Toppled Nation

The assassination of Julius Caesar in 44 B.C. and the resultant 17 years of civil war shattered loyalties and traditional beliefs. In 42 B.C., two years into Rome's difficult shift from a republic to a benevolent despotism and ultimately to an empire, Virgil lived with his parents and brother Flaccus in Mantua. He lost the Maro family estate as a result of state confiscation when the land was awarded to demobilized legionaries under Octavian who had won the Battle of Philippi in Macedonia on October 23, 42 B.C. In his *Eclogues* (Selections, ca. 35 B.C.), Virgil reflects on the vicissitudes of war and the arbitrary seizure of family holdings. In the 10th eclogue, as a token of a former idealistic period, he includes the sweeping epigram "Omnia vincit amor!" (Love conquers all) (Virgil 1984, 105).

Although he practiced law briefly, Virgil was determined to make his name as a poet. Perhaps because of ill health, he absented himself from the public forum to pursue literature and philosophy at his town house on the Esquiline Hill in Rome and at his rural retreats near Nola in Campania and in the lower Alps in Cisalpine Gaul. He ordered his days around morning dictation and afternoon polishings of highly distilled verses that he read aloud to friends. In his fourth eclogue, he foresaw a golden era of peace initiated by à divine birth, a messianic PROPHECY intended to elevate the emperor to the divine, the prediction of the Judaean seer Isaiah and an element of Elias Lönnrot's Finnish epic KALEVALA (1836). Critics connect Virgil's mystic poem to the Pax Romana, 27 B.C.–A.D. 180, a period of prosperity and comparative peace fostered by Augustus and his successors.

Augustus curried favor with Romans by discrediting his rival, Mark Antony. Along with the lyric poet HORACE and the epic poet Lucius Varius Rufus, Virgil became a propagandist under the direction of Gaius Maecenas, Augustus's court minister. According to the Roman historian SUETONIUS's *De vita Caesarum* (*Lives of the Caesars,* ca. A.D. 121), after Virgil completed the *Georgics* (On farming, 29 B.C.), he read them aloud to Augustus (then still Octavian) for four days in honor of Augustus's victory at Actium in the Ionian Sea off the shores of Greece on September 2, 31 B.C. Two years later, Virgil agreed to provide Augustus with a literary epic in Homeric style praising Rome's power.

Until his death at age 51, Virgil labored on the AENEID (17 B.C.), a nationalistic paean to the Trojan prince Aeneas and to Rome's foundations. In anticipation of a monumental work, the elegaic poet SEXTUS PROPERTIUS heralded the epic as a rival to Homer's *Iliad* (ca. 800 B.C.). Virgil was still refining the concluding books when he joined the imperial entourage across Italy to Greece. At the embarkation point at Brundisium (today's Brindisi) on September 21, 19 B.C., he succumbed to fever. Before his death, he dictated an epitaph describing himself as a singer of pastures, farmland, and rulers. Still marked by a tripod burner, a tribute to Apollo, Virgil's tomb at Piedigrotta outside Naples became a place of pilgrimage for centuries.

Shaping the *Aeneid*

Not to be cheated of his empire-boosting epic, Augustus countermanded Virgil's order to burn his unfinished manuscript. The emperor appointed two literary executors—Virgil's colleagues Lucius Varius Rufus and Plotius Tucca—to the task of completing the *Aeneid,* a cohesive work of prophecy and glory that lauds the first kings of Rome and the alleged beginnings of the illustrious Julio-Claudian line. A critical masterwork, the complicated story praises the Roman Empire and extols its leaders for vision and enterprise. To balance imperial expansionism, Virgil credits the protagonist Aeneas with organizational skills and *pietas* (moral duty), a pre-Christian concept of piety based on obligations to God, nation, home, and family. Like the Hebrew defender Moses in the biblical book of EXODUS (ca. 450 B.C.) and the mighty archer Arjuna, a hero of the Mauryan empire in the BHAGAVAD GITA (ca. 200 B.C.), Aeneas stands above lesser men as the self-controlled warrior who limits any VIOLENCE to actions necessary to the establishment in Italy of a new Troy.

Partly through the adulation for the *Aeneid* of Horace and the satirist Gaius Petronius Arbiter, Virgil quickly became recognized as Rome's national poet. Following the fall of Rome in A.D. 476 and the consequent rise of the Eastern Roman Empire, the *Aeneid* maintained its literary primacy among Christian apologists, notably the French historian Gregory of Tours and the Florentine poet Dante Alighieri. The latter chose Virgil as a fictional guide through hell and purgatory in the *Divine Comedy* (1321), in which Dante venerates his predecessor as a literary light for all ages. The Portuguese poet LUIZ DE CAMÕES mimicked the *Aeneid*'s grandeur and cadence in his composition of *Os Lusíadas* (*The Lusiads*, 1572). The writers Geoffrey Chaucer, Edmund Spenser, Christopher Marlowe, WILLIAM SHAKESPEARE, John Milton, John Dryden, JEAN DE LA FONTAINE, Tennyson, Elizabeth Barrett Browning, T. S. Eliot, and Walt Whitman all incorporated Virgil's graceful prosody and attention to detail in their own works.

Sources

Horsfall, Nicholas. *A Companion to the Study of Virgil.* Rev. ed. Leiden: Brill, 2001.

Virgil. *The Eclogues.* Translated by Arthur Guy Lee. New York: Penguin, 1984.

visionary literature

An element of PROPHECY, visionary literature provides an ecstatic glimpse of a future time, whether laden with VIOLENCE or blessed with prosperity and salvation. The conceptualization of the future suits a variety of genres, including Dante Alighieri's punishment of corrupt papal empire builders in his *Divine Comedy* (1321), Samuel Taylor Coleridge's ideal of the Mongolian Empire in the poem "Kubla Khan" (1816), H. RIDER HAGGARD's "lost world" novels, the Canadian Jules-Paul Tardivel's apocalyptic separatist novel *Pour la patrie* (*For My Country,* 1895), and AMOS TUTUOLA's abduction dreamscape in the Nigerian novel *My Life in the Bush of Ghosts* (1952). Writers like the apostle PAUL (ca. A.D. 3–ca. 67) of Tarsus, Cilicia, spoke directly to the issues of imperial power. He foretold a Christian overturn of Roman hegemony throughout the Mediterranean world with the second coming of Jesus and an unending haven for the righteous.

Previous to Paul's futurism, a dream narrative, the biblical book of Daniel (ca. 150 B.C.), connects revelation interpreters and seers with empire builders. Compiled in Aramaic and Hebrew from multiple sources, the HERO cycle characterizes a Judean exile to Babylon early in the Achaemenid-Persian Empire, which began around 550 B.C. Like the pharaonic adviser Joseph in Egypt in the book of EXODUS, Daniel is a captive, a banished Jew in the court of a Babylonian emperor who suffers premonitions of doom. Daniel is still a youth when he interprets the dreams of Nebuchadnezzar (605–562 B.C.) about a gold, silver, and bronze statue with feet of clay and iron. The dream reader foresees the succession of empires from Babylon to Persia, Greece, and Rome before the establishment of a divine kingdom on earth. The prophecy satisfies the king after the failed advice of "the magicians, and the astrologers, and the sorcerers, and the Chaldeans" (Daniel 2:2), the customary abasement of the pompous in hero tales.

A second explanation of the king's visions bears a tinge of gothicism. Courtiers view the disembodied "handwriting on the wall," a spectral portent that "thy kingdom is divided, and given to the Medes and Persians" (Daniel 5:28). The young visionary—who is featured in eight of the DEAD SEA SCROLLS—becomes a court seer and counselor to Belshazzar (fl. 553 B.C.) and remains in imperial service under Darius and Cyrus the Great. The final chapters, which Daniel writes in first person, take on a sobering tone, dividing the evil from the righteous. He predicts, "None of the wicked shall understand; but the wise shall understand" (Daniel 12:10). His commentary on wicked behavior and recompense through conquest recurs in Pseudo-Daniel, a three-book fragment from writings by semimonastic Jewish ascetics dating to 200 B.C.

A Future Determined by Cataclysm

During the Italian Empire (1885–1943), the radical polemist and poet Filippo Tommaso Marinetti (1876–1944) of Alexandria, Egypt, foresaw the value of anarchy as a jolt to imagination. In high school, he outraged Jesuit teachers by reading in class the overtly sexual fiction of French novelist Émile Zola. In 1904, Marinetti published *Destruction*, a vigorous verse cycle in French extolling chaos. On February 20, 1909, in the Paris journal *Le Figaro*, he issued the *Manifeste de futurisme*

(Futurist manifesto, 1908), a vision of art as an amalgam of creativity, speed, technology, and violence. To save art from complacency, he supported the dictator Benito Mussolini's nationalism and the colonizing of northeast Africa to satisfy Italian infatuation with the Roman Empire and the Italian Renaissance and to end the stagnation of ideas. In 1911, he covered the Libyan front as a combat reporter for the French and observed the siege of Adrianopolis, Turkey, during the Balkan War of 1912. The battle was the source of Marinetti's mimetic word sculpture *Zang Tumb Tumb* (1914), which used symbols and changes of font to produce a surreal orchestration of combat din and chaos: "long beard filth wildness fierceness skin tanned by explosive blasts shrapnel + danger **MASS EXECUTIONS** 500 prisoners off with the fez" (Marinetti 2002, 66).

While painters, sculptors, musicians, and architects realized the concept of futurism on canvas, in bronze, and through mechanized sound and youthful design, Marinetti composed anarchic works in French and Italian celebrating peril and brashness. He began with the play *Le roi bombance* (The feasting king, 1909); an erotic novel, *Mafarka le futuriste* (*Mafarka the Futurist*, 1910); and the satiric play *Anti-neutralità* (Anti-neutrality, 1912). A verse anthology, *Guerra sola igiene del mundo* (War the only hygiene of the world, 1915), echoed the beliefs of the Italian author GABRIEL D'ANNUNZIO, who championed the European war and Italy's military invasion of Libya. Marinetti supported Mussolini for creating a form of fascism that could spur the stagnant populace to active nationalism through mechanized warfare and mass cultural redirection. In 1932, he coauthored a revolution in Italian nutrition in *La cucina futurista* (*The Futurist Cookbook*), which denounced the national dish of *pastasciutta* (dry pasta) for its lack of nutrients and fiber. In place of nostalgic Italian fare, Marinetti proposed a two-day orgy he dubbed an "extremist banquet," a "tactile dinner party," a "soldier's dinner," and a "nocturnal love feast."

Sources

Daniel. In the Holy Bible. Iowa Falls, Iowa: World Bible Publishers, 1986, 1,227–1,251.

Marinetti, Filippo Tommaso. *The Futurist Cookbook.* Translated by Suzanne Brill. San Francisco: Bedford Arts, 1989.

———. *Selected Poems and Related Prose.* Translated by Elizabeth R. Napier. New Haven, Conn.: Yale University Press, 2002.

Segal, Alan F. *Two Powers in Heaven: Early Rabbinic Reports about Christianity and Gnosticism.* Amsterdam: Brill, 2002.

Voltaire (François-Marie Arouet) (1694–1778)
French poet, playwright, and satirist

A complex critic and writer, Voltaire turned the weapons of SATIRE against barbarity and tyranny in his masterwork *Candide* (1759). An aristocrat born François-Marie Arouet, he was educated by Jesuits and profited from training in Greek, Latin, and modern languages, but he rejected religion for its hypocrisy and lip service to human suffering. From reading the enlightened writers of his time, including the satires of JONATHAN SWIFT, Voltaire developed libertarian ideals. He traveled Europe, served the French foreign office in Holland, and crusaded for civil rights under the slogan *Ecrasez i'infame* (Crush infamy). His biographical play *Mahomet* (1736) expressed his distaste for religious fanaticism.

Early in his career, Voltaire's lampoons of the French monarchy cost him nearly a year in the Bastille (1717–18), two years of exile in England, and the confiscation of his library and private correspondence. At the Prussian court of Frederick the Great in Potsdam, the satirist enjoyed a handsome stipend and three years of leisure to write verse and drama (1750–53). The respite ended after Frederick disapproved of Voltaire's political satires. The author exiled himself to Ferney, on the French border with Switzerland, and from there he continued to fight injustice, ignorance, and tyranny. After his death in Paris in 1778, fans lionized him during the French Revolution.

Civility and the subjugation of nations dominated Voltaire's stage drama and nonfiction. In 1736, he produced a tragedy, *Alzire*, popular with Paris playgoers for its triangulation of the Peruvian governor Gusman, the Inca princess Alzire, and her lover, the Inca sovereign Zamore of Potosí. The retrospect on the Spanish conquest of the Incan empire and the religious conversion and enslavement of Peruvians in Lima idealizes the Incan empire as a model government. The text advocates tolerance and political alliance rather than violent seizure of the South American natives and the extermination of indigenous worship. In 1756, Voltaire published the first of 27 versions of *Essai sur les moeurs et l'esprit des nations* (Essay on customs and the spirit of nations), an ambitious survey of world history that literary historians call the first work on comparative civilization. His topics ranged from the Chinese and Roman empires to European expansionism. Of imperialism in Peru, he condemned the dehumanization of first peoples and the transportation of African slaves, who worked Spanish mines. He declared, "Neither these Negroes nor the inhabitants of the New World were treated like a human species" (as quoted by Miller, 2008, 73).

The amalgamation of absurdity, cliff-hangers, didacticism, invective, and parody energized Voltaire's picaresque novel *Candide,* which won an immediate wide readership after the City Council of Geneva condemned it for vulgarity. By word of mouth, readers spread the fame of the title figure, a naïf from Westphalia educated in the philosophy of optimism. Ousted by the priggish Baron of Thunder-ten-tronckh, Candide travels about Europe, from Holland to Portugal, in search of his adored Cunégonde, later the love object of the lustful governor of Buenos Aires. In Lisbon, he witnesses an auto-da-fé (burning of a heretic), strangulation, and hanging, and he suffers a flogging before traveling to Paraguay. The narrative pities victims of the Inquisition, including "a Basque, convicted of marrying his godmother, and two Portuguese Jews who had refused to eat bacon" (Voltaire 1981, 36), a test of their adherence to Levitican dietary laws. In addition to demonizing Catholic methods of tormenting Jews, Voltaire tweaks the papacy for hypocrisy by adding to his cast "the daughter of Pope Urban X and the Princess of Palestrina" (49). To avoid a Vatican lawsuit, the author defames a nonexistent pope for violating vows of celibacy.

Candide's harrowing adventures include a false charge of murder and threats by South American cannibals. He enjoys the bliss of Eldorado, Peru, an Incan utopia, and witnesses a contrast to the good life in the black slavery of Suriname. The extremes of VIOLENCE force his valet Cacambo to confide that "The new world, you see, is no better than the old" (52). In Italy, the hero encounters Pococurante, a Venetian sybarite who attains to artistic merit without appreciating books or music. The odyssey concludes in the Ottoman Empire at Constantinople, where the wanderer reflects on vice and suffering committed by men who "were not born wolves, yet they have become wolves" (24). He chooses to withdraw from religious wars and imperialism on the advice of an old Turk, who asserts, "Work keeps away three great evils: boredom, vice, and need" (100). Candide retires to personal serenity by cultivating his garden, which becomes the best of all possible worlds.

Sources

Fleming, Thomas. *The Morality of Everyday Life: Rediscovering an Ancient Alternative to the Liberal Tradition.* Columbia: University of Missouri Press, 2004.

Miller, Christopher L. *The French Atlantic Triangle.* Durham, N.C.: Duke University Press, 2008.

Poole, Deborah. *Vision, Race, and Modernity: A Visual Economy of the Andean Image World.* Princeton: Princeton University Press, 1997.

Voltaire. *Candide, Zadig, and Selected Stories.* Translated by Donald M. Frame. New York: New American Library, 1981.

W

War and Peace Leo Tolstoy (1869)

More epic than novel, the Russian author LEO TOLSTOY's *Voyna i mir* (War and Peace), a classic of world literature, dramatizes the human destruction following a clash of despots that threatens homes and families. The opening lines "The Invasion" in Volume II, Book I, chapter 1 declare Czar Alexander I of Russia and Napoleon I of France "the arbitrators of the world's fate" (Tolstoy 1915, 1), who control millions of lives and fortunes and a vast expanse of farmland, forests, waterways, and villages. To the detriment of health, rest, and passion plotted four years earlier, the battle of Borodino takes place on September 7, 1812. As though on a crusade, Napoleon Bonaparte, mounted on a thoroughbred Arabian, advances his troops from Dresden, Germany, against a Cossack force and marches toward Moscow, "the Holy City, the capital of an empire which reminded him of that of Alexander the Great" (200). The outsized fantasies of the French self-promoter conclude Volume II, Book I, chapter 24 with a Roman restatement of a Sophoclean PROPHECY, "Quos vult perdere Jupiter, dementat prius" (Whom Jupiter wishes to destroy, he first makes mad) (202).

Tolstoy is evenhanded in his blame of emperors for a national disaster, immense loss of life, and destruction of homes and crops. He emphasizes the vainglory of Czar Alexander I, who hopes to expand Russia from the Bosnian Gulf to the Danube. In a self-ennobling speech, the czar chooses the editorial "we" in directing an "ocean of soldiery" (351) toward a continental triumph: "We shall hasten to place our person in the midst of our people. . . . May the woes with which [Napoleon] hopes to crush us be visited on him alone, and may Europe, freed from the yoke, glorify Russia!" (265–266). The author accuses both French and Russian soldiers of battlefield bombast and jubilance. Men leave female characters with hopes of escape, trivial amusements, and feeble prayers that life can return to its former contentment, a major motif in William Makepeace Thackeray's epic novel *Vanity Fair* (1848). Boris Drubetskoy, an immature officer who leaves his wife Julie in Moscow, perpetuates the stereotype of the shallow female by "accusing all women of frivolity, inconstancy and caprice, according to the humour they were in and their fancy for accepting the homage of the latest favourite" (142). Tolstoy's aristocratic attitude also belittles peasants for fearing they will be enlisted among the Cossacks to ward off the anti-Christ and the APOCALYPSE.

Despite the thin narrative strand and miniaturization of characters, the social panorama of *War and Peace* has intrigued makers of epic cinema more than similar scenarios in the Napoleonic social satire of Thackeray's *Vanity Fair*. In 1956, King Vidor's film version of *War and Peace* featured Henry Fonda and Mel Ferrer as contrasting suitors for Audrey Hepburn. The actress won a BAFTA and a Golden Globe for the elevation of her girlish character, Natasha Rostova, to a combat nurse who opens her home as a makeshift hospital. In 1968, a Russian remake of the novel won an Academy Award for best foreign language cinema. A BBC miniseries in 1972 starred Anthony Hopkins as the HERO Pierre Bezukhov.

See also NAPOLEONIC LITERATURE.

Sources

Layton, Susan. *Russian Literature and Empire: Conquest of the Caucasus from Pushkin to Tolstoy.* Cambridge: Cambridge University Press, 1994.

Tolstoy, Leo. *War and Peace.* London: J. M. Dent & Sons, 1915.

Warren, Mercy Otis   See PROTEST LITERATURE.

White Roots of Peace, The   Paul A. W. Wallace (1946)

The alliance of the Cayuga, Mohawk, Oneida, Onondaga, Seneca, and Tuscarora in an Iroquois league known as the Six Nations, or the People of the Longhouse, was founded in the mid-16th century. A loose association of tribes reputedly formed as far back as 1150. About 1570, the Huron prophet and mystic Deganawida of Kingston, Ontario, preached a gospel of peace that civilized and brought together the first five nations, the Tuscarora joined the confederacy after migrating north in the early 18th century. The epic story of Deganawida was written by Paul A. W. Wallace as *The White Roots of Peace* (1946). Drawing on previously written English version of Iroquois oral tradition, Wallace recounts social and political reform among Indian peoples. Set on the Canadian shore of Lake Ontario, the epic turns legend into a national saga. Themes of coexistence with nature accompany motifs of negotiation and social order. The Indians' embrace of pacifism proved crucial to tribal coexistence during the years preceding the settlement of the Canadian frontier and the separation of American colonies from the British Empire.

The history of the Iroquois confederacy, as it is best known, coincided with a period of European struggle for sovereignty in North America. The alliance resisted attacks from, amongst others, the Huron of Canada and the Mohican of the Hudson Valley. Wallace's narrative depicts the peacemaker Deganawida as an incarnation of the Great Spirit, a suppressor of sorcery and cannibalism and an advocate of deer hunting and tree planting. Magical episodes featuring his navigation aboard a stone canoe, a symbol of permanence, and subsequent tests of strength and divination advance the prophet to semi-divinity. The text, like the Mesopotamian *Epic of* GILGAMESH (ca. 1800 B.C.) and the Solomonic book of Proverbs (ca. 180 B.C.), expresses a high level of rationality: "Peace was not . . . a negative thing, the mere absence of war or an interval between wars, to be recognized only as the stepchild of the law; to the Iroquois, peace was law" (Wallace 1994, 6).

As a sign of his righteousness, Deganawida, like the protagonist of VIRGIL's AENEID (17 B.C.) and like Arjuna, hero of the BHAGAVAD GITA (ca. 200 B.C.), accepts supernatural guidance. He obeys a prophetic dream and begins converting woodland Indians to nonviolence and brotherhood. To settle primacy among chiefs, he crowns each with antlers, a primitive symbol of power similar to the horns of the altar that Moses had made. For assistance, Deganawida allied with Yegowaneh, the Mother of Nations and descendant of the first woman; and with the Mohawk medicine man Hiawatha, whom Henry Wordsworth Longfellow immortalized in *The Song of Hiawatha* (1855), America's first literary epic. That poem, like *The White Roots of Peace,* commemorates an Indian HERO and is a striking reminder of an effective democratic alliance of nations.

Sources

Johansen, Bruce Elliott, and Barbara A. Mann. *Encyclopedia of the Haudenosaunee.* Westport, Conn.: Greenwood, 2000.

Waldman, Carl. *Encyclopedia of Native American Tribes.* Rev. ed. New York: Checkmark Books, 1999.

Wallace, Paul A. W. *The White Roots of Peace: The Iroquois Book of Life.* Santa Fe, N.M.: Clear Light, 1994.

Wiesel, Elie (Eliezer Wiesel) (1928–)
Romanian-born American journalist and autobiographer

Through grim realism, the ethicist Elie Wiesel vilifies tyranny and barbarity in speeches and memoirs about his survival of Nazi hellholes at Auschwitz, Birkenau, Buna, and Buchenwald. Born Eliezer Wiesel in Sighet, Transylvania, in the Carpathian Mountains, he studied Torah Hebrew, Kabbala, and biblical commentaries as well as astronomy, contemporary Hebrew, literature, and Freudian psychology. At age 12, as Nazism loomed, he heard rumors of lethal anti-Semitism, deportations, and mass murder by the Gestapo. While the Third Reich advanced as far as Budapest, he refused to accept the possibility of a Jewish GENOCIDE.

Wiesel's slim study of death, *La nuit* (*Night*, 1960) reprises his family's roundup by Nazis on Passover week, April 20, 1944, when police loot and shutter synagogues and jail ghetto leaders. By cattle car, the Gestapo deports citizens, 80 per car, ostensibly to crews in brick factories at Auschwitz-Birkenau, Poland. Wiesel's text pities refugees as "fallen, dragging their packs, dragging their lives, deserting their homes, the years of their childhood, cringing like beaten dogs" (Wiesel 1986, 15). At midnight, they view the gas crematoria that wipe out evidence of Central European Semites. He personalizes his narrative with memories of his mother and seven-year-old sister Tzipora, who vanish among the doomed, as do his maternal grandparents and nameless infants burned in a pit.

Wiesel endorses pacifism by depicting the work-or-die style of concentration camp life. He and his father survive as long as they elude the selection process of Dr. Josef Mengele, an SS officer who culls the feeble and sick. Camp dehumanization begins with head shaving, delousing, and tattooing before herding inside electric wires at Auschwitz and assignment to the electrical warehouse at Buna Werke. In the last days of World War II, Wiesel trudges 400 miles to Buchenwald, Germany, to drag stone blocks alongside criminals, gypsies, homosexuals, Jehovah's Witnesses, Jews, pacifists, and spies. Inmates take fleeting refuge in dreams of the diaspora to Haifa, Palestine. In January 1945, the SS flees the Red Army of the Russians and evacuates prisoners through snow to a subcamp at Gleiwitz.

Orphaned in the final days, Wiesel fears a pervasive PROPHECY: "This was the End! Hitler was going to keep his promise" (107). He chews potato peelings and grass until his rescue on April 10 by the U.S. Third Army.

Stateless and homeless, Wiesel sheltered in Normandy, France, and then, at the Sorbonne, studied Jewish mysticism and the works of FYODOR DOSTOYEVSKY, Franz Kafka, and Thomas Mann. From newspaper work and translation jobs, he advanced to postwar treatises that popularized the term *Holocaust* as a historical entity produced by Hitler's search for a "final solution" for unwanted non-Aryans. After the slow success of *Night*, Wiesel created a trilogy with his publication of *L'aube* (*Dawn*, 1961) and *Le jour* (*The Accident*, 1962), works that established his authority on Nazism and genocide. His public appearances, classroom teaching, and writings earned him the 1986 Nobel Peace Prize. The author of 58 books, he became a U.S. citizen in 1955 and, with his wife, formed the Elie Wiesel Foundation for humanity. He continues to write and lecture, keeping the horrors of the Holocaust fresh in the public memory in his most recent work, *A Mad Desire to Dance* (2009), a retrospect on psychological trauma.

Sources
Chmiel, Mark. *Elie Wiesel and the Politics of Moral Leadership.* New York: Temple University Press, 2001.

Houghton, Sarah. *Elie Wiesel: A Holocaust Survivor Cries Out for Peace.* New York: Red Brick Learning, 2003.

Wiesel, Elie. *Night.* New York: Bantam, 1986.

wisdom literature

From Muhammad and Siddhartha Gautama to Mohandas Gandhi and Constantine Cavafy, the acquisition and dissemination of wisdom has obsessed the authors of world literature. Among the treasures of empires, aphorisms, or wise sayings, accrued during the rise of powers and the inevitable corruption and grandiosity of ruling families, exemplified in such works as JEAN DE LA FONTAINE'S FABLES about the profligacy of Louis XIV of France. The range of wisdom literature encompasses ancient and modern languages from global empires, as demonstrated in the table.

TEXT, AUTHOR	DATE	LANGUAGE	EMPIRE
VEDAS, anonymous	ca. 1700–1400 B.C.	Sanskrit	Harappan; Indo-Gangetic
I CHING, anonymous	1144–206 B.C.	Chinese	Ancient Chinese
Aesop's Fables	ca. 550 B.C.	Greek	Greek
Proverbs, Ahiqar	ca. 670 B.C.	Aramaic	Assyrian
DAODEJING, Laozi	ca. 300 B.C.	Chinese	Chou dynasty
Proverbs, Callimachus	ca. 270 B.C.	Greek	Greco-Ptolemaic
ANALECTS, Confucius	ca. 210 B.C.	Chinese	Chinese
BHAGAVAD GITA, anonymous	ca. 200 B.C.	Sanskrit	Mauryan
PANCHATANTRA, Vishnu Sarma	ca. 200 B.C.	Sanskrit	Mauryan
Proverbs, Solomon et al.	ca. 180 B.C.	Hebrew	Seleucid
Ecclesiasticus, Sirach	ca. 180 B.C.	Hebrew	Seleucid
Wisdom of Solomon, anonymous	ca. 150 B.C.	Greek	Seleucid
DHAMMAPADA, Siddhartha Gautama	ca. 50 B.C.	Sanskrit	Mauryan
PAUL's epistles	A.D. 53–67	Greek	Roman
"The Pumpkinification of the Divine Claudius," SENECA	A.D. 54	Latin	Roman
Mishna, Rabbi Akiba ben Joseph and Rabbi Meir	ca. 135	Hebrew	Roman
Meditations, MARCUS AURELIUS	ca. 180	Greek	Roman
Garland of Birth Stories, Aryasura	ca. 350	Sanskrit	Gupta
KOANS of Bodhidharma	520	Sanskrit	Gupta
Kalilah and Dimnah, Burzoe	570	Persian	Sassanian
KORAN, Muhammad	633	Arabic	Islamic
Kalilah and Dimnah, Ibn al-Muqaffa	750	Arabic	Umayyid
The THOUSAND AND ONE NIGHTS, anonymous	ca. 942	Persian	Abbasid
The Ocean of the Stream of Stories, Somadeva	1070	Sanskrit	Ghaznavid
Blue Cliff Record, Yuanwu Keqin	1125	Chinese; Japanese	Khitan; Heian
Fables, MARIE DE FRANCE	ca. 1189	French	Angevin
The Proverbs of Alfred, ALFRED THE GREAT	ca. 1251	Anglo-Saxon	Viking
Rose Garden, Saadi	1258	Persian	Persian
GRANTH, Arjan	1604	Punjabi	Mughal
Selected Fables, Jean de La Fontaine	1668, 1678	French	French
Book of Fables, Rabbi Moses ben Eliezer Wallich	1697	Hebrew	Holy Roman
Fables, Gotthold Ephraim Lessing	1759	German	Holy Roman
Literary Fables, TOMÁS DE IRIARTE	1782	Spanish	Spanish
Fables, IVAN ANDREYEVICH KRYLOV	1809	Russian	Russian
aphorisms of JOSÉ MARTÍ	1880–95	Spanish	American; Spanish
Poems by Constantine Cavafy	Early 20th century	Greek	Ottoman
An Autobiography, or the Story of My Experiments with Truth, Mohandas Gandhi	1927–29	Gujarati	British
A Woman as Great as the World and Other Fables, Jacquetta Hopkins Hawkes	1953	English	Soviet

Each work or collection offers advice and insight into probity or moral judgment, such as the sage Ahiqar's advice on revenge to Sennacherib and Esarhaddon, Assyrian kings in the seventh century B.C., and the interpretations of the Torah by Rabbi Akiba ben Joseph and his pupil Rabbi Meir during the Roman rule of Jerusalem. In China, the antiquarian Laozi honored the sage for putting the self last and becoming a leader. In stave 15 of the Daodejing (*Tao-Te Ching*, Classic of the way of power, 300 B.C.), the philosopher pictures the thinker picking his way over thoughts like a pedestrian crossing a brook on stones in winter. In stave seven, he describes the advice of the sage, like the dao itself, as universal and never ending.

Scriptural Wisdom

A prized collection of maxims for the Judaeo-Christian world, the biblical book of 900 Proverbs (ca. 180 B.C.) alerts the wise to the pitfalls of life and to the need for character building, a theme reprised in AESOP's FABLEs and those of Ivan Andreyevich Krylov, a satirist of the Russian Empire. Credited to David's son Solomon (ca. 1000–931 B.C.), the judge-king of Jerusalem, the anthology of proverbs exemplifies Hebraic and Arabic culture ranging some 800 years up to the second century B.C. The accretion of aphorisms attests to the steady rise of civilization. The tone is heavily patriarchal, that of a father imparting pearls of right thinking to an untried youth, perhaps a ruler in training. In Proverbs 10:1–22:16, the ordering of 375 maxims of Solomon suit the needs of petitioners at the royal court at Jerusalem; Proverbs 25:1–29:27 provide similar guidance for petitioners at the court of the Judean king Hezekiah (ca. 752–ca. 698 B.C.). Like the Davidic PSALMS (ca. 900 B.C.), the proverbs exhort the wise to embrace Yahweh (God) as the source of moral perspective and justice. To the wielder of power, the maxims advise sobriety, humility, and respect. Like the Greek philosophers, the text warns of hubris by observing that "Pride goeth before destruction and an haughty spirit before a fall" (Proverbs 16:18). The sage reassures subjects that wisdom is the foundation of empire: "The king by judgment establisheth the land" (Proverbs 29:4). An earlier axiom reminds the ruler that moderation should prevail over hasty anger: "The king's wrath is as the roaring of a lion; but his favour is as dew upon the grass" (Proverbs 19:12).

During the Seleucid Empire, which began in 323 B.C. and spread from Turkey to the Indus Valley, a Hebrew scribe, Yeshua ben Sirach of Jerusalem, compiled an apocryphal text, Ecclesiasticus (The preacher, ca. 180 B.C.), a two-volume liturgical work that varies from verse stanzas to individual proverbs, injunctions, and rhetorical questions. Sirach's grandson, the Torah specialist Yeshua ben Eleazar, translated the book into Greek around 132 B.C. The pious Sirach, who claims God as the touchstone of wisdom, elaborates on the Mosaic law with praise for sobriety, charity, forgiveness, and compassion and warnings about envy, foolishness, greed, lust, pride, sin against God, and VIOLENCE. He glories in his residence in Zion and states that "in the beloved city [the Creator] gave me rest, and in Jeusalem was my power. And I took root in an honorable people" (Ecclesiasticus 24:11–12).

Unimpressed by political power, Sirach based his collection on the ethics of everyday life, including a pure conscience, respect for priests, and pity for the oppressed. The maxims in chapter 25 warn males of sexual license; in chapter 26:13–18, the preacher summarizes the best in womanhood by picturing the devoted family woman and housekeeper. As counsel to empire builders, chapter 10 values a prudent king, such as David of Judah; chapter 32 describes a good relationship between rulers and subjects as a necessary element in wise reigns. Chapter 38 salutes farmers and artisans as the power that drives the world. Chapter 49 includes a caution that Judah's impious kings forsook God and lost their empires to invaders, the source of the Babylonian captivity of the Jews from Judah in 586 B.C. For its probity, Ecclesiasticus is part of the biblical Apocrypha.

Scriptural Collections

In this same period, the anonymous apocryphal book the Wisdom of Solomon (ca. 150 B.C.), probably composed in Greek in Alexandria, Egypt, recycled Hebrew poetic techniques. A more pointed commentary on the responsibilities of judge and ruler, the text, written under Roman influence, reflects the ethics of the Hellenes and

Alexandrians, the most educated communities of the Mediterranean world. Like Ecclesiasticus, the Wisdom of Solomon praises understanding, "For in her is an understanding spirit, holy, one only, manifold, subtle, lively, clear, undefiled, plain, not subject to hurt, loving the thing that is good, . . . kind to man, steadfast, sure, free from care, having all power" (Wisdom of Solomon 7:22–23). In an era of unstable governments, the author credits wisdom for rescuing the Israelites from Egypt and for punishing unrighteous idolators.

The prophet Muhammad, author of the Koran (A.D. 633), regards wisdom as the reward of devotees of Islamic scripture. As in the Pauline epistles from the early Roman Empire, the responsibility of individuals for their own salvation echoes through Koranic passages. Muhammad accounts for the heroic traits of Abraham, Noah, Moses, Jonah, and Job. Surah six declares, "Thus do We make plain Our revelations, that they may say: 'You have studied deep' and that this may become clear to men of knowledge" (Koran 6:105). In a rebuttal of Christian New Testament doctrine, the prophet asserts, "Praise be to God who has never begotten a son; who has no partner in His Kingdom; who needs none to defend Him from humiliation" (Koran 17:111). The implications deny Jesus and the Holy Spirit the powers with which Christian scripture invests them.

Wisdom in the Second Millennium

A Persian sage and poet admired for his wise advice, Sheikh Saadi (1184–ca. 1291) of Shiraz, a disciple of FIRDAWSI's *Shahnameh* (*The Book of Kings*, ca. 1010), traveled Egypt, Iraq, Syria, and Turkey and wrote consistently on the commonalities of human life. One prevalent theme, the abuse of power, dominates stories involving the interaction of Islamic rulers and their subjects. In one of the parables of Saadi's *Gulistan* (*Rose Garden*, 1258) in which a king seeks wisdom from a vizier, an aphorism summarizes the weakness of despotism. In the didactic style of Aesop's beast fables, the vizier insists, "A tyrant cannot govern a kingdom, as a wolf cannot perform the office of shepherd. The tyrannic prince saps the foundation of his own empire" (Saadi 2003, 123). From the perspective of political strength, the poet explains

that a ruler who protects the peasantry wins allies to ward off enemies.

With similar emphasis on reason, the Norse bard SNORRI STURLUSON's *Prose Edda* (1225) draws on the vernacular statecraft of Ari the Wise, the father of Icelandic historiography. The text differentiates types of speech and the value of sage admonition. Of one court adviser to the Allfather, the narrative lauds an archangel: "Michael, wise of understanding, weighs what seems done ill, and good things" (Sturluson 1916, 136). Of prudence, he notes: "Understanding is called wisdom, counsel, discernment . . . far sight, craft, word-wit, pre-eminence" (240). A second sentence warns of the down side of empty oratory, which he labels "subtlety, wiliness, falsehood, fickleness" (240), a general dismissal of fatuous speech. The distinction drawn between different types of counsel derives from Sturluson's lengthy experience as the lawspeaker of Iceland's assembly during a period of uncertainty between the collapse of the Viking threat and the rise of the Norwegian empire.

Modern Wisdom

Disseminators of healing and spiritual renewal have frequently provided solace and encouragement to refugees and victims of the collapse of empires. During World War I, the Egyptian poet Constantine Cavafy (1863–1933), composing in Greek, wrote "But the Wise Perceive Things about to Happen" (1915), in which he advocates respect for the poet-seer, who hears about chaos in the streets "the hidden sound of things approaching" (Cavafy 1992, 53). In "Envoys from Alexandria" (1918), the poet names the "things" that the peasants must expect, the postwar partitioning of conquered lands. In a dire reliving of Julius Caesar's assassination, "The Ides of March" (1915) offers a prayer for restraint and protection of the soul from self-adulation. To conquerors in general, the poem "Theodotos" (1915) states a universal truth: "Whatever honors / your admirers decree for you in Rome, / Your elation, your triumph will not last, / nor will you feel yourself superior" (54).

At the approach of World War II, the world was in even greater need of pacifist wisdom. The Lutheran evangelist DIETRICH BONHOEFFER (1906–45) wrote sermons and essays encouraging Christians to reject Adolf Hitler's persecution of non-Aryans. A contemporary, Mohandas Karamchand Gandhi (1869–1948), a proponent of passive resistance through civil disobedience, encouraged third-world nations in *An Autobiography, or the Story of My Experiments with Truth* (1927–29). Composed in Gujarati, the two-volume apologia recounts events from Gandhi's youth and young manhood that shaped his humanism. For his own day-to-day peace of mind, he reread the Bhagavad Gita and debated truth with the poet RABINDRANATH TAGORE (1861–1941). Rather than cast blame for India's poverty on British imperialism, the philosopher placed guilt on Hinduism, which created the untouchable class. He believed that "every man or woman, however weak in body, is the guardian of his or her self-respect" (Gandhi 2002, 274), but he alerted the affluent to a political truth: that the poor and hungry are likely to cede all hope of liberty in exchange for food, especially for their children. At a less charitable point, he reminded fellow Indians that all despots are temporary: "No empire intoxicated with the red wine of power and plunder of weaker races has yet lived long in this world" (151).

The juggling of class and religious differences brought out the best in Gandhi's egalitarian speeches and essays, which he aimed at oppression in South Africa as well as the British Raj on the Indian subcontinent. One of his most repeated maxims, "An eye for an eye makes the whole world blind," found its way into the writings of the American civil rights leader Martin Luther King, Jr. Other memorable aphorisms influenced the anticolonialism of the South African martyrs Nelson Mandela and Steve Biko and the Burmese freedom fighter Aung San Suu Kyi. Gandhi tempered his anticipation of liberty and democracy with a call to men to accept the help of women and to Christians, Hindus, Jews, Muslims, Parsis, and Sikhs to rely on stoicism and brotherhood in the face of change. He defined courage as "freedom from all external fear—fear of disease, bodily injury and death" (299) and a reliance on the peace-loving peasantry rather than on police and the military. Among his responses to British racism and domination were refusals to accept military and civil service appointments and retreats to vegetarianism, drying salt from seawa-

ter, home laundry, and spinning yarn and weaving homespun cloth for garments. He issued a warning to the impatient: "Without suffering it is not possible to attain freedom" (135). As he predicted, after a three-decade crusade from 1916 to 1945, he saw the freeing of India from British control and the growth of respect and amity between Indians and their former masters.

Sources

The Apocrypha of the Old Testament. King James Version. New York: American Bible Society, 1972.

Cavafy, Constantine. *Collected Poems.* Translated by Edmund Keeley and Philip Sherrard. Princeton, N.J.: Princeton University Press, 1992.

Gandhi, Mohandas. *An Autobiography, or the Story of My Experiments with Truth.* Translated by Mahadev Desai. Ahmedabad, India: Navajvan Publishing, 1940.

———. *The Essential Gandhi: An Anthology of His Writings on His Life, Work, and Ideas.* New York: Vintage: 2002.

The Koran. Translated by N. J. Dawood. London: Penguin Classics, 2004.

Proverbs. In the Holy Bible. Iowa Falls, Iowa: World Bible Publishers, 1986, 920–954.

Proverbs of Ahiqar. Translated by James M. Lindenberger. Baltimore: Johns Hopkins University Press, 1983.

Saadi, Musle-Huddeen Sheik. *Gulistan, or Rose Garden.* Translated by George Gentius. Whitefish, Mont.: Kessinger, 2003.

Sturluson, Snorri. *The Prose Edda.* Translated by Arthur Gilchrist Brodeur. New York: American-Scandinavian Foundation, 1916.

women's journals, diaries, and letters

Eyewitness accounts in women's diaries, letters, and journals provide details of empire building crucial to history. The four-year visit of Lady Anne Lindsay Barnard (1750–1825) among the Hottentots of Cape Hope, South Africa, introduced a privileged Scot to the downside of empire. In *South Africa a Century Ago: Letters Written from the Cape of Good Hope* (written 1797–1801; published 1901), she muses on the slave quarters at the manor of a British planter: "His house has generally a slave-house belonging to it, which, alas!, is in place of that happier cottage at home where each Englishman has his wife, his child, his pig, and his cat or dog, as great within its four walls as any emperor within his palace. . . . At present unwilling drudgery toils, unthanked, for indolent apathy" (Barnard, 1901, 119). Like the later writer RUDYARD KIPLING, Barnard regretted the miscegenation of Europeans and people of color.

About this time, Anna Maria Norwood Falconbridge (1769–after 1794) of Bristol, England, traveled with her husband to the colony of Sierra Leone in an attempt to settle freed slaves in Freetown. At first, she abhorred SLAVERY as "a blemish on every civilized nation that countenanced or supported it" (Falconbridge 1794, 235). A journey to Jamaica, where she met Christian slavemasters, changed her opinion to relief that those blacks borne over the Middle Passage escaped "murdering, despotic chieftains" (236). The shift in attitude illustrates the naïveté of travelers who based their thinking on superficial observation of slavery. Falconbridge described her experiences in a series of letters published in 1794 as *Narrative of Two Voyages to the River Sierra Leone, During the years 1791–1792–1793*.

Though often lacking entrée into upper economic and court circles, female travelers unearthed details of colonial intrigues and shortcomings. In 1841, Florentia Wynch Sale (1790–1853) compiled *A Journal of the Disasters in Affghanistan, 1841–1842* (1843), a frontline commentary on the brutality of the First Anglo-Afghan War (1839–42), the first British attempt to win Afghanistan for the British Empire. Sale's narrative bristles at the barbarity of chiefs in Peshawar, who intend to seize women as war prizes. Terrorism reaches melodramatic heights with the plan to murder all men "except one, who is to have his hands and legs cut off, and is to be placed with a letter *in terrorem* at the entrance of the Khyber passes" (Sale 1843, 204).

Russians and Turks

To the north, the British traveler Lucy Sherrand Finley Atkinson (ca. 1820–63) delved into Russian political issues for *Recollections of Tartar Steppes and Their Inhabitants* (1863). In February 13, 1848, she joined her husband, the architect and painter Thomas Witlam Atkinson, on a six-year sledge journey across Siberia, Mongolia, the Kirchis

(now Kirghiz) steppes, and the region known as Chinese Tartary. They traveled under Cossack guard with a border pass issued by Czar Nicholas I. Atkinson interviewed P. I. Falenberg in Shush and M. I. Muravyov-Apostol and I. D. Yakushkin in Yalutorovsk, survivors of the Decembrist revolt of 1825, whom Czar Alexander II pardoned in 1856. Another Decembrist, V. L. Davydov of Krasnoyarsk, regretted "that we were betrayed by an Englishman . . . acting the ignoble part of a spy and a traitor" (Atkinson 1863, 319–320).

Islamic territory displayed its own perils. When Georgina Mary Muir Mackenzie (1833–74) traveled through Turkey with Adeline Paulina Irby (1831–1911) in the 1860s and early 1870s, they formed a poor impression of the Ottoman Empire that they reported in *Travels in the Slavonic Provinces of Turkey-in-Europe* (1877). At Scutari, Albania, they found "the same lamentable description— natural advantages unimproved, trade hampered, streets ill-built, and inhabitants ignorant and misruled" (Mackenzie and Irby 1877, 164). The two travelers departed the area in 1876, when the Serbs of Bosnia and Herzegovina began moves toward joining the Austro-Hungarian Empire.

Traveling Feminists

Feminist issues appear often in the texts of women's diaries and journals. Anna Brownell Murphy Jameson (1794–1860), a Dubliner heading to Ontario, denounced white occupiers of Indian land for debauching the Chippewa and Menominee of the Great Lakes and blamed native men as well for using their wives as beasts of burden. In *Winter Studies and Summer Rambles in Canada* (1838), she charges "the refuse of the white population" with denigrating and cheating natives, introducing them to drunkenness, and corrupting females (Jameson 1838, 45). Of the maltreatment of women by their own people, she proclaims: "*Barbarism!*—the heartless brutality on one side, and the shameless indifference on the other, may well make a woman's heart shrink within her" (306).

The Irish feminist Mabel Sharman Crawford (1820–68) viewed the difficulties of Islamic women in *Through Algeria* (1863), a land that the French had conquered in 1848. Of inequities among Muslims, she comments that "The Koran does hold out the hope of a paradise to women … whilst entering into minute details as to the blessings reserved for the pious Mussulman" (Crawford 1863, 54). With stronger criticism of Great Britain, she denounced manhandling in "Maltreatment of Wives" (1893), a diatribe published posthumously in the *Westminster Review* against wife beating in a Christian land that winked at extremes of VIOLENCE against women, some of them pregnant.

While popular GOTHIC LITERATURE was full of titillating female abduction stories, sexual sadism infuriated feminist nonfiction writers. On a journey to Egypt and Syria in 1858, the diarist Emily Anne Beaufort (1826–87), author of *Egyptian Sepulchres and Syrian Shrines* (1861), draws feminist conclusions about the "barbarous" nature of concubinage and harems in the Ottoman Empire. She charges the theocratic state, Muhammad, the KORAN, and a male Islamic hierarchy with tyranny: "What source more direct, and what original nobler, than revelations, prophecies, and miracles" (Beaufort 1861, 233). She vilifies Muslims for "[consigning woman] to the rank of an instrument of vice and debauchery" (236). The text decries the absence of romance: "Wherever conjugal love does not exist, paternal love exercises but a feeble influence; family ties thus become an illusion" (236).

Mary Henrietta Kingsley (1862–1900), a British diarist and explorer, spent time among the Bantu and Fan of the French Congo. Her book, *Travels in West Africa: Congo Français, Corisco and Cameroons* (1897), looks beyond marriage by bride purchase in the Cameroons to widowhood. Because surviving elder brothers control the settling of estates, women and minor children have no voice in the distribution of goods. Kingsley implies that such patriarchy is the root cause of homelessness, child mortality, and poverty.

Direct commentary on imperialism among female authors is often forthright. Isabella Lucy Bird (1831–1904) of Tattenhall, Cheshire, became one of the 19th century's most respected travel writers. Surveying the indigenous Ainu of Japan in *Unbeaten Tracks in Japan* (1880), Bird declares the Japanese imperial concept a success story of "almost miraculous progress within ten years" because of the spread of civilization creating "freeholders out of a nation of serfs" (Bird 1880, 160). In an over-

view of the island chain, she lauds the educational system and the Japanese postal department, which compiled a directory to the empire, and she ranks samurai warriors as the best educated and most public-spirited of citizens. Her optimism, a hallmark of Victorian England, anticipates ongoing cordiality and cooperation as a result of "friendly criticism" and predicts a time when Japan will not need British services to maintain progress (314). Bird's brisk survey reveals the eurocentrism of visitors from Britain. She warns that the future depends on overcoming "a vast mass of ignorance and superstition" and a "superficial exotic culture" (336). Her judgmental prose included views of Kurdistan and Persia in *Journeys in Persia and Kurdistan* (1891), the Himalayas in *Among the Tibetans* (1894), Korea and Russia in *Korea and Her Neighbours* (1898), and the Qing dynasty of China in *The Yangtze Valley and Beyond* (1899).

Similar to Bird, Constance Frederica Gordon Cumming (1837–1924), championed the association of imperialism with proselytizing. After the British colonized Fiji, Gordon Cumming's *At Home in Fiji* (1881) reports, "The position of Women in these isles has hitherto been as low, and their lot as hard, as in other uncivilised lands; but Christian teachers are now doing their utmost to raise them in the social scale" (Gordon Cumming 1881, 99). The narrative equates imperial governance with Christian education and moral inculcation as the most promising methods of turning imperial conquests into mirror images of Victorian England.

Imperial Pride

Female subjects of the British Empire honored Queen Victoria for her administrative skill and humanitarianism. Baroness Annie Allnutt Brassey (1839–87), author of the posthumously published *The Last Voyage* (1889), reported that the British felt affection and pride in their colonies. In a speech to the Royal Geographical Society of Australasia, she declared, "National sentiment and enlightened self-interest will bind and keep us together, so that not one limb of the great British Empire shall be severed" (Brassey 1889, 467). In September 1890, another pro-imperial writer, Kate Marsden (1859–1931), a London-born volunteer with the Red Cross and veteran of combat nursing at age 18 in Bulgaria during the Russo-Turkish War, traveled over 11,000 miles under the queen's sanction to eastern Siberia. As she explains in *On Sledge and Horseback to the Outcast Siberian Lepers* (1891), the isolation of the sick posed a duty to the civilized world: "But the lepers in the far-off uncivilised regions of the world—who cared for them? . . . Cut off from their fellow creatures, avoided, despised, and doomed to a living death" (Marsden 1877, 304). Influenced by the Christian piety of 19th-century England, she took on the 11-month journey to look for a curative herb and to study the feasibility of a leper colony at Yakutsk in Siberia above the Arctic Circle, where temperatures fell annually to -92° Fahrenheit. Through the cooperation of the empress of Russia, Maria Alexandrovna, Marsden created a working partnership to fight a disease her text describes in social, economic, and physical detail. To scientists and general readers, her book marked an era of colonial benevolence and health care.

A common strand among female diarists and journalists was compassion for the underdog, an element of the writings of the Bermuda-born slave MARY PRINCE, the American evangelist NANCY GARDNER PRINCE, and the Jamaican herbalist-nurse MARY JANE SEACOLE. In 1891, on a three-month safari taken by the American explorer May French Sheldon (1847–1936) through British territory from Zanzibar through Kenya to study the lives of East African women, she relied on 200 porters and soldiers, who revered Sheldon as BeBe Bwana (woman leader). As reported in *Sultan to Sultan: Adventures among the Masai and Other Tribes of East Africa* (1892), the bearers "proved faithful, uncomplaining, chivalrous, and marvels of patience, endurance, and consistent marching day after day" (Sheldon 1892, 131). A visionary suffragist, after a return trip in 1903 to the Belgian Congo, she repudiated reports of African savagery and told the press that the hope of the world required lifting women's status from drudge to first-class citizenry.

The Swiss-Algerian diarist Isabelle Eberhardt (1877–1904), dressed as a male Muslim in 1897 during a tour of Algeria, the Sahara, and French Tunisia. In *The Passionate Nomad: The Diary of Isabelle Eberhardt* (published posthumously in 1988),

she admires the beauty of Arab women, but mourns the constant whine of beggars: "Songs that sound infinitely sad, refrains turn into a curiously gripping obsession" (Eberhardt 1988, 28). The lyric survey of poverty echoes the comments of other female diarists who express altruism toward women, children, and the poor and handicapped.

With an eye toward the underclass, Gertrude Lowthian Bell (1868–1926) regretted the social and economic realities of the era of progress. A student of history at Oxford University and supporter of the Arabs, she produced 10 superb commentaries on travel, architecture, archeology, politics, and culture. In *The Desert and the Sown* (1907), her social survey preceding the birth of modern Iraq from the failing Ottoman Empire, she pities the Bedouin, who "live by bread alone . . . and for the whole length of their days they wander among the stones in fear of their lives" (Bell 1907, 120). She concludes her text with a native aphorism: "Men are short of vision, and they see but that for which they look. Some look for evil and they find evil; some look for good and it is good that they find, and moreover, some are fortunate and these find always what they want" (340). The statement leaves unsaid the destiny of the unlucky.

In 1871, a Hungarian expeditioner, Florence von Sass Baker (1841–1916), joined her husband, Sir Samuel White Baker (1821–93), on a journey through the Ottoman Empire to the source of the White Nile, a region that enriched the Arabs with sale of cattle, ivory, and slaves. At a slave market at Khartoum, she viewed the lewd groping of females by purchasers, the outcome of treating women as commodities. Ironically, Sir Samuel Baker had purchased her from an Ottoman slave market to save her from a similar fate. In a diary entry on August 24, she compares native Sudanese to dogs: "One tribe preying upon the other, and selling them into slavery; no honesty even in name; but idleness, sin, debauching, rapine, and murder . . . while every black revels in mischief up to his throat" (quoted in Shipman 2005, 118). She vilifies slave traders and pities bondsmen, including the Bakers' Abyssinian houseboy Amarn. Her diary, *Morning Star: Florence Baker's Diary of the Expedition to Put Down the Slave Trade on the Nile,*

1870–1873 (1972), reported on her husband's leadership of a military expedition to abolish slavery in Sudan in 1869–72, a journey in which she shared the difficulties. British imperial authorities suspected the Bakers of supporting enforcement of antislavery laws.

Sources

Anderson, Monica. *Women and the Politics of Travel, 1870–1914.* Teaneck, N.J.: Fairleigh Dickinson University Press, 2006.

Atkinson, Lucy Sherrand Finley. *Recollections of Tartar Steppes and Their Inhabitants.* London: John Murray, 1863.

Baker, Florence von Sass. *Morning Star: Florence Baker's Diary of the Expedition to Put Down the Slave Trade on the Nile, 1870–1873.* London: William Kimber, 1972.

Barnard, Lady Anne. *South Africa a Century Ago: Letters Written from the Cape of Good Hope (1797–1801).* London: Smith, Elder, 1901.

Beaufort, Emily Anne. *Egyptian Sepulchres and Syrian Shrines.* London: Longman, Green, Longman and Roberts, 1861.

Bell, Gertrude Lowthian. *The Desert and the Sown.* New York: Dutton, 1907.

Bird, Isabella Lucy. *Among the Tibetans.* London: Religious Tract Society, 1894.

———. *Journeys in Persia and Kurdistan.* London: John Murray, 1891.

———. *Korea and Her Neighbours.* London: John Murray, 1898.

———. *Unbeaten Tracks in Japan.* London: John Murray, 1880.

———. *The Yangtze Valley and Beyond.* London: John Murray, 1899.

Brassey, Anne. *The Last Voyage.* London: Longman, 1889.

Crawford, Mabel Sharman. *Through Algeria.* London: Bentley, 1863.

Eberhardt, Isabelle. *The Passionate Nomad: The Diary of Isabelle Eberhardt.* Boston: Beacon, 1988.

Falconbridge, Anna Maria. *Two Voyages to the Sierra Leone During the Years 1791–2–3.* London: privately published, 1794.

Gordon Cumming, Constance Frederica. *At Home in Fiji.* Edinburgh: Blackwood, 1881.

Jameson, Anna. *Winter Studies and Summer Rambles in Canada.* London: Saunders & Otley, 1838.

Kingsley, Mary. *Travels in West Africa: Congo Français, Corisco and Cameroons.* London: Macmillan, 1897.

Mackenzie, G. Muir, and A. P. Irby. *Travels in the Slavonic Provinces of Turkey-in-Europe.* London: Daldy, Isbister & Co., 1877.

Marsden, Kate. *On Sledge and Horseback to the Outcast Siberian Lepers.* New York: Cassell, 1877.

Newman, Louise Michele. *White Women's Rights: The Racial Origins of Feminism in the United States.* New York: Oxford University Press, 1999.

Sale, Florentia Wynch. *A Journal of the Disasters in Affghanistan, 1841–1842.* London: John Murray, 1843.

Sheldon, May French. *Sultan to Sultan: Adventures among the Masai and Other Tribes of East Africa.* Boston: Arena, 1892.

Shipman, Pat. *To the Heart of the Nile: Lady Florence Baker and the Exploration of Central Africa.* New York: HarperCollins, 2005.

X

Xenophon (ca. 431–354 B.C.) *Greek historian, essayist, and biographer*

An Athenian cavalryman as well as a writer and historian, Xenophon wrote eyewitness accounts of imperial conflicts. The son of Gryllus of Erchia, he studied under the philosopher Socrates and took part in the last years of the Peloponnesian War (431–404 B.C.) between Athens and Sparta. In 401, he hired out as a hoplite, or heavy infantry mercenary, under the Persian Cyrus the Younger, son of Darius II, during a civil uprising against Cyrus's brother Artaxerxes II. In his combat memoir *Anabasis* (*The Expedition of Cyrus,* or *The March Up Country,* 354 B.C.), Xenophon describes himself as the youngest regimental commander and typifies Cyrus as the most worthy of all to rule. After Artaxerxes had treacherously killed many of the Greek generals, Xenophon led the remainder of the Ten Thousand on a 1,000-mile journey north from Babylonia through the territories of hostile Armenians, Kurds, and Persians to Trapezus, a port on the Black Sea. Before turning west toward home, the Greek irregulars assisted Seuthes II to become ruler of Thrace.

On his return to Greece, Xenophon supported Agesilaus II of Sparta against Athens at the battle of Coronea, in 394 B.C. Athenians stripped him of his property and banished him, whereupon he moved to the western Spartan city of Scillus in Elis, two miles from Olympia. With his wife Philesia and their sons Gryllus and Diodorus, Xenophon spent his time writing. He set up a temple and grove to Diana the huntress, his patron goddess, and held annual feasts and games in her honor. Apparently the orator Eubulus recalled him to Athens in 355 B.C., but the chronicler was past his mid-70s and did not do so. History suggests that Xenophon received state honor as the father of the hero Gryllus, who was slain at the battle of Mantinea in 362 B.C. after killing the Theban general Epaminondas. Ironically, Xenophon died at Corinth, halfway between Athens and Sparta. As models of unembellished soldierly writing akin to Julius Caesar's *The Gallic Wars,* Xenophon's histories have survived for centuries as textbooks for students learning Greek

The Histories

After the Athenian historiographer THUCYDIDES died, leaving unfinished *The History of the Peloponnesian War* (ca. 400 B.C.), Xenophon appended the seven-book *Hellenica* (ca. 354 B.C.), an account of events from 411 to 362 B.C. Though he lacked Thucydides's astute reasoning, he earned regard for straightforward reportage of a half-century of events. In book 5, he noted the selfish logic that perpetuated expansionism in Attica: "The Athenians . . were none the less eager for the war being of the opinion that empire was theirs by right" (Xenophon *Hellenica,* 2007, 198). His commentary on imperial rationalization displays an unbiased view of his own empire's wrongheadedness.

Xenophon also wrote *Cyropaedia* (*The Education of Cyrus,* ca. 354 B.C.), a fictional biography of the Persian ruler Cyrus the Great that became a popular form of classic literature. The eight-book romance included genealogy, court tales, and monarchic chronicles. Hero worship robs the narrative of objectivity. Some historians believe it may be an attack on the teachings of Plato. During the didactic interaction between young Cyrus and his father, Cambyses I, the elder established the grounds of leadership: "Observe the sacrifices and pay heed to the omens; when they are against you, never risk your army or yourself" (Xenophon 2000, 33). Refuting the ideals of Greek individualism and democracy, Xenophon insists that the concept of empire is conducive to social order and serenity. The text influenced later statesmen, including Scipio Africanus, the Roman general during the Punic Wars; the English poet Edmund Spenser; and Thomas Jefferson, who valued the work equally with NICCOLÒ MACHIAVELLI's Renaissance statecraft handbook *The Prince* (1513).

An Imperial Error in Judgment

More memorable in the literature of empire, Xenophon's seven-book *Anabasis* chronicles a lengthy southeastern march from the Aegean Sea to the Euphrates and Tigris Rivers in Mesopotamia, a march that ended with the battle of Cunaxa (401 B.C.). In his account of soldiers of fortune from many tribes and nations, Xenophon emulates the epic lists of Homer's *Iliad* (ca. 850 B.C.) by numbering light-armed infantry, hoplites, archers, slingers, javelin throwers, and horsemen. The 10,400 Greek hoplites, extolled as the "Ten Thousand," triumph at Cunaxa, but Cyrus dies of a javelin wound to the eye, stranding the Greeks without a patron. Xenophon mourns the Persian leader, who fell alongside eight of his companions of the *suskenia* (mess table), despite a "bodyguard of cavalry about 600 strong, all armed with corselets" (Xenophon *Anabasis*, 2007, 57). A senseless vengeance takes place in the mutilation of his remains by Cyrus's enemies, who lop off his head and right hand, a meaningless posthumous insult.

After Cyrus's demise, the *Anabasis* summarizes the rapid overturn of fortunes. Xenophon describes the unstable fortunes of war: "We were not a whit more able to injure the enemy, while we had considerable difficulty in beating a retreat

ourselves" (175). He portrays hireling soldiers foraging and battling their way out of a no-win situation in Babylonia along a more than 4,000-mile retreat to northern Armenia. The overland journey requires constant pragmatic strategy and ad hoc decisions, the kind of spur-of-the-moment policy making necessary in adversity. Xenophon urges every man to take responsibility for group safety: "Whoever has a better play, let him speak" (175). The journey took eight months of marching, skirmishing, fighting, and negotiating, with frequent starvation, exhaustion, and frostbite. Xenophon regrets that more than 5,000 Greeks died on the route home.

Xenophon's *Anabasis* reveals exemplary standards of leadership. He, like conqueror Alexander I the Great, believed that no man could be "a good officer who does not undergo more than those he commands" (175). The historian dramatizes matters of loyalty and courage in a soldier's words: "If any man fail in aught of this, the goddess herself will look to it that the matter shall not sleep" (298). Until the great day when the Hellenes at last reach the sea, they live off the land, peacefully when they can but fighting when they have to do so.

Xenophon included such valuable data and advice on camping, ethnic relations, eating, sanitation, and health care that Alexander the Great carried the *Anabasis* along on his first foray against the Persians in 334 B.C. The events of the narrative influenced Machiavelli's *The Prince* as well as the Guadeloupian poet SAINT-JOHN PERSE's *Anabase* (*Anabasis*, 1924) and Sol Yurick's novel *The Warriors*, filmed in 1979 and reset as a gang war in Brooklyn, New York.

Sources

Lee, John W. I. *A Greek Army on the March: Soldiers and Survival in Xenophon's Anabasis.* Cambridge: Cambridge University Press, 2007.

Xenophon. *Anabasis.* Translated by H. G. Dakyns. New York: BiblioBazaar, 2007.

———. *Cyropaedia: The Education of Cyrus.* Translated by H. G. Dakyns. London: Macmillan, 2000.

———. *Hellenica.* Translated by H. G. Dakyns. New York: BiblioBazaar, 2007.

Y

Yamanoue no Okura (ca. 660–ca. 733)
Korean-born Japanese poet and aphorist

During Japan's Nara era, the experimental writer Yamanoue no Okura pictured in humanistic poems the lives of poor peasants and grief-stricken mortals. According to scraps of fact, he was born in Korea to an intellectual father and emigrated at age three from Paekche to Japan following the Sino-Korean victory over the Japanese army at Hakusukinoe. A loyalist aristocrat and family man, he settled at the royal compound in the Yamato province, which his verse exalts as a long-term imperial enclave since the reign of the mythic Emperor Kami as well as a seat of literature. The poet advanced at court through a series of appointments, but, as stated in "Upon Excusing Himself from a Banquet" (ca. 733), he valued husbandly and paternal responsibilities over displays of court courtesy.

As a scribe, at age 41, Okura received the honor of accompanying a Japanese embassy to the Tang court at China's capital at Chang-an (today's Xian). He traveled with some 5,000 men in a four-ship convoy and spent possibly six years absorbing Chinese culture, a sojourn that appears to have shaped his life and canon. One of his cryptic poems, "Soaring Like a Bird" (ca. 701), appears to compare the bird to the ghost of the eldest son of Emperor Kotoku, the rebel prince Arima, a traitor strangled by an executioner in 658 for plotting against the Empress Saimei. By 716, Okura had advanced to the rank of governor of Hoku. Five years later, Emperor Mommic hired the poet to teach the crown prince Shomu. Among Okura's court duties was the writing of occasional verse, for example, "Wishing Godspeed to the Ambassador to China" (ca. 733), a farewell to a courtier on a major imperial mission.

Okura broadened his nation's body of literature by applying imagination and pure emotion to poems. His canon showcases sardonic humor, earnest emotion, subtle detail, but plainspoken, often inelegant diction in both Chinese and Japanese. As a student of Sui and Tang texts, he centered his social criticism on the moral philosophy of the ANALECTS of Confucius (ca. 210 B.C.) and softened didacticism with a graceful Buddhist acceptance of destiny and belief in an afterlife. Although Okura's *Ruiju Karin* (Forest of classical poetry, ca. 721) did not survive intact, Otomo Yakamochi, an admirer, collected 78 of Okura's *choka* (long official verse) in MANYOSHU (*Ten Thousand Leaves*, ca. 759), Japan's oldest anthology. In his last years, Okura governed Chikuzen Province in northern Kyushu under his dicta of caring for the aged and valuing peasant culture as the glue of the empire. At age 73, he wrote a brief stanza thanking the ambassador to China for visiting the ailing author at home.

In an early form of existentialism, Okura surveyed the constant shift in human fate to disappointment and loss. In "What We Must Accept" (ca. 733), he follows the young warriors, who "girded at their waists sharp swords, keen-bladed weapons, into tottery old age" (quoted in Carter 1991, 45). His most famous *choka*, "Hinkyu mondo" (Dialogue on poverty, ca. 733), is a startling venture from staid court ritual featuring nobles. The conversation between two speakers discloses the alienation of the underclass because of hunger, cold, tattered clothing, and social injustice. He dramatizes the dilemma of the male householder surrounded by relatives "complaining and groaning" at slow starvation (47). The speaker wails, "Must it be like this, / so utterly without hope" (48). On a personal level, "What Value to Me the Seven Kinds of Treasures" (ca. 733) mourns the death in childhood of Okura's son Furuhi. The father tries to ease the passage into the afterlife by bribing death to "carry him on your back / messenger from the netherworld" (50). Another plaint, "Thinking of Children" (ca. 733), names chestnuts and melon as reminders of his children, whose deaths keep the poet awake at night. In "Seventh of the Seventh Month, 729" (ca. 729), he expressed a longing to reunite with his dead wife in heaven.

Sources

Carter, Steven D. *Traditional Japanese Poetry*. Palo Alto, Calif.: Stanford University Press, 1991.

Shirane, Haruo, and Sonja Amtzen. *Traditional Japanese Literature: An Anthology, Beginnings to 1600*. New York: Columbia University Press, 2007.

Yevtushenko, Yevgeny Aleksandrovich (Yevgeni Aleksandrovich Gangnus) (1933–)
Russian poet

A warrior on behalf of artistic freedom during the cold war, Yevgeny Yevtushenko used verse as a weapon against Stalinism and Soviet atrocities. His heritage includes maternal and paternal grandfathers seized in 1937 during a state purge of some 170,000 dissidents. Born Yevgeni Aleksandrovich Gangnus (he later took his mother's surname), he was born of Russian, Tartar, and Ukrainian blood among exiles living at Zima Junction in Irkutsk in southeastern Siberia. After three years at the Gorky Institute of Literature in Moscow, the poet was expelled for defending a censored novel. He published antistate verse that championed individualism while deriding bureaucratic bumblers and obfuscators, the distorters of history that GEORGE ORWELL denounced in the dystopic PROPHECY novel *1984* (1949). The poet gained an international audience with his autobiographical poem *Zima Junction* (1956), named after the town where he

was born. He counted among his contemporary admirers the novelists Norman Mailer, Gabriel Garcia Marquez, and John Steinbeck and the poets Robert Frost, Allen Ginsberg, Pablo Neruda, BORIS PASTERNAK, and Carl Sandburg. The anti-Soviet novelist Aleksandr Solzhenitsyn (see PRISON LITERATURE) esteemed Yevtushenko for his energy and resilience under Community Party criticism.

Yevtushenko gained credence through the underground press. In 1961, he resisted Stalinist propaganda and, in *Pravda*, published "Babi Yar," a poetic exposé of the Nazi SS's slaughter of 33,771 Ukrainian Jews in a ravine at Kiev on September 29 and 30, 1941. The extermination, conducted by machine gunning 10 victims at a time, continued at Babi Yar, boosting the mass murder to more than 200,000 Jews, gypsies, Ukrainian nationalists, prisoners of war, and psychiatric patients. In fall 1961, when Yevtushenko visited the unadorned common grave, the city was recovering from a flood that brought bones to the surface. The official Soviet position claimed that the victims had been Russians and had hidden the fact that they were Jewish.

Within days, the poet committed his outrage to paper and urged the Kiev-born writer Anatoly Kuznetsov to write *Babi Yar* (1967), a documentary novel describing the massacre. In addition to marking the largest slaughter of the Holocaust, Yevtushenko's poem castigates Soviet authorities for anti-Semitism and for rewriting genocidal history to exonerate and glorify the Soviet Union. Grotesque sense impressions—the sound of slander, the fly of spittle, a coarse gash in the earth, the stench of onions and vodka—precede the assault by Nazi soldiers. The speaker, identifying with the "thousand thousand" (Yevtushenko 1962, 83) child and adult victims of the pogrom, envisions himself as the Dutch teen diarist Anne Frank and calls ironically for the singing of the Russian version of "The Internationale" (1918), the Communist Party anthem.

Yevtushenko took his fictional role as witness seriously. After his recitation of "Babi Yar" to 1,200 Moscow students on September 16, 1961, the response to the lament and to the vampire poem "The Heirs of Stalin" (1962) ranged to extremes. On December 17, 1962, Premier Nikita

S. Khrushchev halted the poet's recitation of "Babi Yar" at a Communist Party gathering in Moscow; two days later, *Literaturnaya Gazeta* (Literary newspaper), the cultural journal of the Soviet Writers' Union, impugned the poet's patriotism and denounced his disrespect for Russian war veterans. A conservative-led smear campaign labeled Yevtushenko an elitist Gentile who grandstanded on behalf of Jews. The day after Khrushchev's action, the composer Dmitry Shostakovich performed "Babi Yar" to an adagio movement of his Symphony No. 13 in B Flat Minor (1962). Four subsequent movements in the piece decried the suppression of wit and whimsy depicted in the poem "Humor," famine in "At the Store," terrorism in "Fears," and suppression of Russian creativity in "Careers." Soviet officialdom banned performances of Shostakovich's symphony and forced the poet to tone down his denunciations. On April 2, 1963, an arts critic for a Minsk newspaper dismissed the episode of Jewish martyrdom at Babi Yar as a petty footnote of World War II.

To rouse interest in the full disclosure of Russian history, Yevtushenko evolved a flamboyant public presence. His lyrics spoke directly to Russia's miseries and sacrifices. With the skill of an aphorist, he warns in "Lies" (1962): "Who never knew the price of happiness will not be happy" (52). His public readings drew thousands. In 1963, he came under KGB scrutiny for accusing the Soviets of "Judeo-phobia." After publication of the allegorical "Ballad of False Beacons" (1964), Communist authorities recalled the poet, revoked his passport, and, until 1965, denied him travel privileges. He supported the cause of liberation through "The Torments of Conscience" and "The Execution of Stenka Razin," published in the collection *Bratsk Station* (1966), an emblematic text depicting Siberia as the Soviet Union's official gulag.

Yevtushenko became the epitome of the modern PROTEST poet. In 1968, he lambasted the Soviet invasion of Czechoslovakia with the poem "Russian Tanks in Prague," which the government withheld from readers for 22 years. In 1974, he demanded that Premier Leonid Brezhnev and KGB chief Yuri Andropov halt the harassment and censorship of Solzhenitsyn, whom officials had banished after the novelist won the Nobel Prize

in literature for his searing depictions of Stalin's concentration camps. In another confrontation with Soviet intransigence, Yevtushenko insisted that the government restore Boris Pasternak's reputation as a premier Russian author and allow Pasternak's son to claim the late writer's Nobel Prize won in 1958. The Soviet invasion of Afghanistan in 1979 elicited a new outburst from the poet. In March 1986, he enjoyed hearing the actor Robert De Niro read "Babi Yar" at the Cathedral of St. John the Divine in New York City. Another verbal salvo, Yevtushenko's "Half Measures" (1989), accused Premier Mikhail Gorbachev of only halfhearted support for civil liberties. While serving in the first freely elected Russian parliament in 1991, the poet resisted an attempted coup by reciting libertarian verses from a balcony to 200,000 marchers in the street. At age 60, the anti-imperialist author received a medal declaring him a Defender of Free Russia. In October 2007, as artist in residence at the University of Maryland, he performed "Babi Yar" to music played by the university symphony.

Sources

Kremer, S. Lillian. *Holocaust Literature: An Encyclopedia of Writers and Their Work.* New York: Routledge, 2003.

Specter, Robert Melvin. *World without Civilization: Mass Murder and the Holocaust, History and Analysis.* Lanham, Md.: University of America Press, 2005.

Yevtushenko, Yevgeny. *Early Poems.* London: Marion Boyars, 1989.

———. *Selected Poems.* Harmondsworth, Eng.: Penguin, 1962.

Yezierska, Anzia (ca. 1880–1970)
Polish-born American critic and writer

The Slavic memoirist Anzia Yezierska recreated stories, novels, and articles filled with the peasant customs that eastern European immigrants transported to the New World. Born to a downtrodden mother and an orthodox Jewish scholar in Plinsk, then within the Polish-Russian territory near present-day Belarus, she lived in a mud hut and grew up amid the pogroms, military conscription, and cruelties of the Russian Empire that the

Russian-American author Mary Antin (1881–1949) described in her immigrant autobiography *The Promised Land* (1912). At age 10, Yezierska's family reached Hester Street in New York City's Lower East Side, a Jewish microcosm that the Danish-American chronicler-photographer Jacob Riis (1849–1914) described in *How the Other Half Lives: Studies among the Tenements of New York* (1890). In "How I Found America" (1920), Yezierska reported that in Plinsk, every footstep had sounded like Cossack boots coming to enforce the czar's edict with a whiplash.

The Yezierskas pawned their possessions for 100 rubles to pay the way to America in steerage. In fealty to shtetl (ghetto) customs, her parents, Pearl and Reb Bernard Yezierska, continued allotting the gendered privileges that sent Anzia's three brothers to school and relegated the author and her three sisters to domestic drudgery. Anzia learned English in night school while operating a sweatshop sewing machine by day. The long days were the beginning of her transformation into a tenement Cinderella. At age 23, she enrolled in home economics at Columbia University and supported herself by doing laundry until she could locate teaching jobs.

In 1910, she married Jacob Gordon, an attorney, but the marriage was annulled after six months. Soon after, she married Arnold Levitas but subsequently left him because of his patriarchal views. She moved to San Francisco with their daughter, whom she eventually sent to live with Levitas. She then moved back to New York City. Yezierska developed her writing career with Yiddish-English essays, book reviews for the *New York Times*, and Yiddish-English dialect anecdotes and short stories issued in *Bookman, Century, Cosmopolitan, Forum, Good Housekeeping, Harper's,* and *Scribner's.* She gained notoriety for "The Fat of the Land," an immigrant domestic tale published in *The Best Short Stories of 1919.* In *Hungry Hearts and Other Stories* (1920), she expanded on the ethnic isolation of American Jews and on women demoralized by Old World patriarchy. The work found favor with the Hollywood producer Samuel Goldwyn, who hired her to coauthor a screenplay based on the collection. Yezierska abandoned

Hollywood and returned to New York and the people she loved and understood. In the feminist novel *Salome of the Tenements* (1923), she focused her creative vision on a fictional hero, Sonya Vrunsky, a relentless social climber. Sonya's future husband, Protestant philanthropist John Manning, commissions her to rescue Polish Russians like herself from the underclass: "You have the burning fire of the Russian Jew in you. . . . The real liberation of your people must come from within—from such as you" (Yezierska 1995, 3).

Yezierska's classic dialect novel *Bread Givers* (1925) expresses the need of first-generation American women to throw off household patriarchy and to assimilate into post-suffrage freedoms. The semiautobiographical protagonist, Sara Smolinsky, longs to seize the liberty that females enjoy in the United States, particularly control of courtship, marriage, motherhood, and career. She acknowledges the burden of an androcentric Russian tradition derived from the tyranny of Czar Alexander III and his predecessor: "It wasn't just my father, but the generations who made my father whose weight was still upon me" (297). In 1950, Yezierska contrasted Polish-Russian values with the materialism of New York City and Hollywood in a fictional AUTOBIOGRAPHY, *Red Ribbon on a White Horse: My Story.* The narrative features the low self-respect that dwellers of the ghetto conceal along with their disillusion in America, which they fantasize as their refuge from Russian czardom. Anzia Yezierska died in Ontario, California, on November 21, 1970.

Sources

Yezierska, Anzia. *Bread Givers.* New York: Persea Books, 2003.

———. *How I Found America: Collected Stories.* New York: Persea Books, 2003.

———. *Hungry Hearts.* Boston: Houghton Mifflin, 1920.

———. *Red Ribbon on a White Horse: My Story.* New York: Persea Books, 2004.

———. *Salome of the Tenements.* Champaign: University of Illinois Press, 1995.

Zipperstein, Steven J. *Imagining Russian Jewry: Memory History, Identity.* Seattle: University of Washington Press, 1999.

Yi Kwangsu (1892–ca. 1950) *Korean modernist fiction writer, and poet*

A suspect figure during the Japanese colonization of Korea, Yi Kwangsu teetered on the edge of betraying his country. Born in Pyongan Pukdo, in the northwestern area of today's North Korea, he studied Chinese literature until his parents died when he was 10 years old. He lived with various relatives and developed a liking for travel at an early age. In 1903, he joined the Tonghak (or Donghak) resistance group, a subversive organization countering the Japanese authorities in Korea. In 1904, when the Tonghak crumbled, he fled to Seoul.

In 1907, Yi attended the Meiji Gakuin academy in Tokyo, a Presbyterian mission school where he learned Japanese and English. He heard Christian teachings and read Lord Byron and LEO TOLSTOY, whom he greatly admired. He abandoned Confucianism and developed an admiration for the Japanese and their adoption of progressive Western methods. Toward the end of his school days, he published his first short story, "Sarangin' ga" ("Is It Love?," 1909), an allegorical tale of a Korean student yearning for a handsome Japanese boy. For a Korean magazine, he wrote a narrative poem about a caged owl, a reflection of his views on being oppressed by an occupying power.

In 1910, the year that Japan formally annexed and occupied Korea, Yi returned home and took up a teaching post at a school in Osan, where he also married. In 1913, he superintended the school but soon realized it was beyond his capabilities. He left Osan to travel Shanghai and Manchuria. He went back to Osan in 1914 but left in 1915 to return to Tokyo, where he attended Waseda University. In 1917, he wrote the novel for which he is best remembered: *Mujong* (The heartless).

The first modern novel by a Korean, *Mujong* was serialized in *Maeil sinbo* (Daily news) and became a best seller. The book examines free love from the perspective of Yi Hyong-sik, a teacher of English in a Seoul middle school, who adores two women: Sonhyong, an obedient traditionalist girl, and Pyonguk, a modern woman influenced by Western feminist ideals. An attack on traditional betrothal arrangements, the novel reprises the idea of the caged owl of Yi's earlier poem by criticizing androcentric standards of chastity and marriage customs ignoring a young couple's true feelings. The text poses a Western view: "Was it not inhumane to knowingly sacrifice another's life just to satisfy one's own selfish desires?" (Yi 1990, 3).

Yi fell in love with another Korean student in Tokyo, Ho Yongsuk, later to become Korea's first female doctor. She nursed him through a bout of tuberculosis, which infected him for the rest of his life. Having divorced his wife, Yi followed Ho to Seoul and persuaded her to elope with him to Beijing in 1918. The elopement, then considered a major scandal by both families and the public, led to a major drop in his popularity as a writer, which worsened after he left his bride after three months and returned to Tokyo.

In Tokyo, Yi involved himself in politics and drafted a Korean declaration of independence by Korean students in February 1919. Before its public announcement, however, he traveled to Shanghai, the center for Korean exiles. In 1921, Ho Yongsuk joined him.

Yi earned regard as a Korean nationalist striving for his country's independence from Japan. His sudden return to Korea in 1921, however, raised suspicion of collaboration with the Japanese. Some believe the Japanese authorities admitted him to create a positive image; others believe he made a secret agreement with them. Whatever the reason, his writing assumed a pro-Japanese tone and, on occasion, was openly derogatory toward Korea, as expressed in his 1922 poem "Reform of the Korean People," urging them to learn from more advanced nations.

From 1922 to 1931, though still in poor health from tuberculosis, Yi wrote stories and poems and became a convert to Buddhism. In 1929, he wrote *The Tragic History of King Tanjong,* a monarch who had died in 1457 at age 17, and in 1932, he published *Yi Sun-sin,* a biography of a heroic 16th-century Korean naval commander who helped defeat a Japanese invasion. In 1937, authorities imprisoned Yi but released him because of his deteriorating health.

In 1938, Yi became an even stronger apologist for the Japanese. He believed that the education of all Koreans was necessary before they could achieve parity with Japan. He embraced Japanese ideas, including the adoption of Japanese-style names. He wrote of Koreans: "They must become Japanese in flesh and blood" (quoted in Yu 1992, 98).

Yi supported the Japanese during World War II, although his novel *Great Master Wonyo* (1942) praised Korean spirit and victories. After the war, he and his wife divorced in order to save their property from confiscation. He retreated to a temple and wrote the poem "Stone Pillow," a symbol of his desolation. He returned to Seoul, which he refused to leave when the North Korean army invaded. Arrested by the North Korean authorities, he for refusing to confess to sedition, he disappeared in prison.

A complex character, Yi left many volumes of writing. His novel *Mujong* is regarded as a premier work. Critics honor him as modern Korea's first humanist.

Sources

Chung, Chong-wha. *Modern Korean Literature: An Anthology, 1908–65.* New York: Columbia University Press, 1995.

Lee, Ann Sung-Hi. *Yi Kwang-su and Modern Korean Literature.* New York: Columbia University East Asia Program, 2005.

Yi Kwangsu. *Modern Korean Literature: An Anthology.* Translated by Peter H. Lee. Honolulu: University of Hawaii Press, 1990.

———. *Modern Korean Short Stories and Plays.* Seoul: Korean Centre, 1970.

———. *The Silence of Love: Twentieth-Century Korean Poetry.* Honolulu: University Press of Hawaii, 1981.

Yu, Beongcheon. *Han Yong-un & Yi Kwang-Su: Two Pioneers of Modern Korean Literature.* Detroit: Wayne University Press, 1992.

APPENDIXES

I. MAJOR WORKS OF THE LITERATURE OF EMPIRE

Abdelazar; or, The Moor's Revenge (1671), Aphra Behn	Spanish Empire, 1492–1975
"The Absent-Minded Beggar" (1899), Rudyard Kipling	British Empire, 1583–
The Accident (1962), Elie Wiesel	Nazi Empire, 1933–1945
The Acharnians (425 B.C.), Aristophanes	Athenian Empire, 477–431 B.C.
The Adulateur (1772), Mercy Otis Warren	British Empire, 1583–
"The Adventure of the Speckled Band" (1892), Sir Arthur Conan Doyle	British Empire, 1583–
"The Adventure of the Sussex Vampire" (1924), Sir Arthur Conan Doyle	British Empire, 1583–
Aegyptiaca (ca. A.D. 40), Apion	Roman Empire, 27 B.C.–A.D. 476
Aeneid (17 B.C.), Virgil	Roman Empire, 27 B.C.–A.D. 476
Aesopic Fables (ca. A.D. 31), Phaedrus	Roman Empire, 27 B.C.–A.D. 476
Ahalya Baee (1849), Joanna Baillie	British Empire, 1583–
The Alchemy of Happiness (1097), al-Ghazali	Turco-Persian Empire, 1037–1307
Alexiad (1148), Anna Comnena	Byzantine Empire, 330–1453
	Crusades, 1096–1221
All Aboard for Freedom (1954), Marie McSwigan	Soviet Empire, 1922–1991
Allan Quartermain (1887), H. Rider Haggard	British Empire, 1583–
Allan's Wife (1889), H. Rider Haggard	British Empire, 1583–
"Al-Mamun" (1835), Nikolay Gogol	Islamic Empire, 632–1258
Almayer's Folly (1895), Joseph Conrad	Dutch Empire, 1620–
Almoran and Hamet (1761), John Hawkesworth	Turco-Persian Empire, 1037–1307
The Altar Stairs (1908), G. B. Lancaster	British Empire, 1583–
Amadis of Gaul (1508), Garci Rodríguez de Montalvo	Byzantine Empire, 330–1453
	Crusades, 1096–1221
	Portuguese Empire, 1415–1999
	Spanish Empire, 1492–1975
The Amateur Emigrant from Clyde to Sandy Hook (1895), Robert Louis Stevenson	British Empire, 1583–
Ambrosio, or the Monk (1796), Matthew Gregory Lewis	Spanish Empire, 1492–1975
American Notes (1842), Charles Dickens	American Empire, 1898–
Among the Believers: An Islamic Journey (1981), V. S. Naipaul	Dutch Empire, 1620–
	Qajar Dynasty, 1794–1925

Among the Tibetans (1894), Isabella Lucy Bird — Qing Empire, 1644–1912
Anabasis (ca. 354 B.C.), Xenophon — Athenian, 477–431 B.C.
Anabasis (1924), Saint-John Perse — French Empire, 1499–1513, 1605
"The Anaconda" (1808), Matthew Gregory Lewis — British Empire, 1583–
Analects of Confucius (ca. 210 B.C.), Confucius — Chu Empire, 770–221 B.C.
Anarchism and Other Essays (1910), Emma Goldman — American Empire, 1898–

German Empire, 1871–1918
Joseon Dynasty, 1392–1910
Russian Empire, 1547–1917

"And No One Knows Where to Go" (1957), Nelly Sachs — Nazi Empire, 1933–1945
Androcles and the Lion (ca. A.D. 40), Apion — Roman Empire, 27 B.C.–A.D. 476
Andromache (ca. 425 B.C.), Euripides — Athenian Empire, 477–431 B.C., 415–403 B.C.
The Angelic Avengers (1944), Isak Dinesen — German Empire, 1871–1918
Anglo-Saxon Chronicle (1154), Alfred the Great — Viking Conquests, 775–1100
Animal Farm: A Fairy Story (1946), George Orwell — British Empire, 1583–
Anna and the King of Siam (1944),
  Margaret Dorothea Landon — Siamese Empire, 1350–1909
Annals (A.D. 116), Tacitus — Roman Empire, 27 B.C.–A.D. 476
Annals of Tlatelolco (1528), anonymous — Aztec Empire, 1375–1521
Annie John (1983), Jamaica Kincaid — British Empire, 1583–
Anowa (1970), Ama Ata Aidoo — Ashanti Empire, 1670–1957

British Empire, 1583–

Anthills of the Savannah (1988), Chinua Achebe — British Empire, 1583–
"Antidote for the Scorpion's Sting" (ca. A.D. 211), Tertullian — Roman Empire, 27 B.C.–A.D. 476
Anti-Neutrality (1912), Filippo Tommaso Marinetti — Italian Empire, 1885–1943
Antony and Cleopatra (ca. 1605), William Shakespeare — Roman Empire, 27 B.C.–A.D. 476
The Apology (ca. A.D. 198), Tertullian — Roman Empire, 27 B.C.–A.D. 476
Aranyakas (600 B.C.), anonymous — Indo-Gangetic Empire, 1200–300 B.C.
"The Arctic Indian's Faith" (1869), Thomas D'Arcy McGee — British Empire, 1583–
An Area of Darkness (1964), V. S. Naipaul — British Empire, 1583–
Arrow of God (1964), Chinua Achebe — British Empire, 1583–
The Art of War (ca. 1520), Niccolò Machiavelli — Florentine Empire, 1406–1494, 1509

Papal Empire, 752–1798
Venetian Empire, 800–1797

"Asking of Wu Lang Again" (ca. A.D. 768), Du Fu — Tang Dynasty, 618–907
Aspects of a Novel (1927), E. M. Forster — British Empire, 1583–
Atharva Veda (800 B.C.), Dhanvantari — Indo-Gangetic Empire, 1200–300 B.C.
At Home in Fiji (1881), Constance Cumming — British Empire, 1583–
At the Edge of the Sea (1915), Anna Akhmatova — Russian Empire, 1547–1917
Attic Nights (ca. A.D. 180), Aulus Gellius — Roman Empire, 27 B.C.–A.D. 476
Aubin Codex (1576), Diego Durán — Aztec Empire, 1375–1521
Autobiographical Sketches (1886), Emilia Pardo Bazán — Ottoman Empire, 1300–1922
*An Autobiography, or the Story of My Experiments
  with Truth* (1927–29), Mohandas Gandhi — British Empire, 1583–
Avesta (ca. A.D. 530), anonymous — Spanish Empire, 1492–1975
Babette's Feast (1959), Isak Dinesen — Sassanid Dynasty, A.D. 226–651

Napoleonic Empire, 1852–1870
Swedish Union, 1814–1905

Book of Dithyramb of Maids and Valets (ca. 825), al-Jahiz	Islamic Empire, 632–1258
Book of Eloquence and Exposition (ca. 825), al-Jahiz	Islamic Empire, 632–1258
Book of Equanimity (ca. 1240), Hongzhi Zhengjue	Song Dynasty, 960–1279
Book of Fables (1697), Moses ben Eliezer Wallich	Holy Roman Empire, 962–1806
Book of Hours (1903), Rainer Maria Rilke	Austro-Hungarian Empire, 1867–1918
Book of Kings (ca. 1010), Firdawsi	Ghaznavid Empire, 975–1187
Book of Margery Kempe (1436), Margery Kempe	Holy Roman Empire, 962–1806
	Jagiellon Dynasty, 1377–1572
	Mamluk Dynasty, 1260–1517
Book of Misers (ca. 825), al-Jahiz	Islamic Empire, 632–1258
The Book of Songs (ca. 480 B.C.), Confucius	Chu Empire, 770 B.C.–A.D. 221
Book of the City of Ladies (ca. 1405), Christine de Pisan	French Empire, 1499–1513, 1605–
	Venetian Empire, 800–1797
Book of the Dead (ca. 1240 B.C.), anonymous	Egyptian Empire, 1550–1070 B.C.
The Book of the Three Virtues (1406), Christine de Pisan	French Empire, 1499–1513, 1605–
	Venetian Empire, 800–1797
Book of the 'Uthmaniyya (ca. 825), al-Jahiz	Islamic Empire, 632–1258
Book of What Is in the Netherworld (ca. 1554 B.C.), anonymous	Egyptian Empire, 1550–1070 B.C.
Boris Godunov (1825), Aleksandr Pushkin	Russian Empire, 1547–1917
Boy in Darkness (1956), Mervyn Peake	Nazi Empire, 1933–1945
Brahmanas (1000–600 B.C.), anonymous	Indo-Gangetic Empire, 1200–300 B.C.
Bratsk Station (1966), Yevgeny Yevtushenko	Soviet Empire, 1922–1991
Bread Givers (1925), Anzia Yezierska	Russian Empire, 1547–1917
The Bridal Wreath (1920), Sigrid Undset	Danish-Norwegian Empire, 1200–1979
The Bride Price (1976), Buchi Emecheta	British Empire, 1583–
The Bridge over the River Kwai (1952), Pierre Boulle	British Empire, 1583–
	Japanese Empire, 1871–1945
A Brief Report of the Devastation of the Indies (1552), Bartolomé de Las Casas	Spanish Empire, 1492–1975
Brighton Rock (1938), Graham Greene	British Empire, 1583–
The Bronze Horseman (1833), Aleksandr Pushkin	Russian Empire, 1547–1917
The Brothers Karamazov (1881), Fyodor Dostoyevsky	Russian Empire, 1547–1917
"The Brown Man's Servant" (1897), W. W. Jacobs	British Empire, 1583–
Bug-Jargal (1826), Victor Hugo	French Empire, 1499–1513, 1605–
The Burden of Memory, the Muse of Forgiveness (1998), Wole Soyinka	British Empire, 1583–
Burger's Daughter (1979), Nadine Gordimer	British Empire, 1583–
Buried Alive; or, Ten Years of Penal Servitude in Siberia (1881), Fyodor Dostoyevsky	Russian Empire, 1547–1917
Burmese Days (1934), George Orwell	British Empire, 1583–
A Burnt-Out Case (1960), Graham Greene	Belgian Empire, 1877–1962
Calendar of Holidays (A.D. 17), Ovid	Roman Empire, 27 B.C.–A.D. 476
The Call (1985), John Hersey	Qing Dynasty, 1644–1912
Canadian Born (1903), Pauline Johnson	British Empire, 1583–

The Canadian Brothers (1840), John Richardson	British Empire, 1583–
Canadian Crusoes: A Tale of the Rice Lake Plains (1852), Catharine Parr Traill	British Empire, 1583–
Canadian Wildflowers (1868), Catharine Parr Traill	British Empire, 1583–
Candide (1759), Voltaire	Holy Roman Empire, 962–1806
	Incan Empire, 1438–1533
	Ottoman Empire, 1300–1922
	Papal Empire, 752–1798
	Venetian Empire, 800–1797
Canopus in Argos (1979–1983), Doris Lessing	British Empire, 1583–
Capricornia (1938), Xavier Herbert	British Empire, 1583–
	Dutch Empire, 1620–
Captains Courageous: A Story of the Grand Banks (1897), Rudyard Kipling	British Empire, 1583–
Caramuru (1781), Santa Rita Durao	Brazilian Empire, 1822–1889
The Castle (1926), Franz Kafka	Austro-Hungarian Empire, 1867–1918
Castle Rackrent (1800), Maria Edgeworth	British Empire, 1583–
Changes: A Love Story (1991), Ama Ata Aidoo	British Empire, 1583–
"Chen-Tao Lament" (ca. A.D. 759), Du Fu	Tang Dynasty, 618–907
Childe Harold's Pilgrimage (1818), Lord Byron	Ottoman Empire, 1300–1922
	Russian Empire, 1547–1917
	First Napoleonic Empire, 1804–1815
Children's and Household Tales (1812, 1815, 1822), Jacob and Wilhelm Grimm	
China Sky (1941), Pearl S. Buck	Japanese Empire, 1871–1945
	Qing Dynasty, 1644–1912
Chinese Cinderella (1999), Adeline Yen Mah	Chinese Empire, 221 B.C.–
	Japanese Empire, 1871–1945
Chinese Cinderella and the Secret Dragon Society (2005), Adeline Yen Mah	Chinese Empire, 221 B.C.–
	Japanese Empire, 1871–1945
Christine's Vision (1405), Christine de Pisan	French Empire, 1499–1513, 1605–
	Venetian Empire, 800–1797
"Christmas in the Mountains" (1871), Ignacio Manuel Altamirano	Austrian Empire, 1804–1867
	Mexican Empire, 1822–1823, 1864–1867
Chronicle of Japan (A.D. 720), Sodoujinkei	Nara Period, 710–794
Chronicles (400 B.C.), anonymous	Assyrian Empire, 900–612 B.C.
El Cid (ca. 1150), anonymous	Abbasid Empire, 750–1258
	Almoravid Empire, 1040–1147
"The City Mouse and the Country Mouse" (30 B.C.), Horace	Roman Empire, 27 B.C.–A.D. 476
The City of God against the Pagans (A.D. 426), Augustine	Roman Empire, 27 B.C.–A.D. 476
"Civil Peace" (1971), Chinua Achebe	British Empire, 1583–
"Cleopatra" (1940), Anna Akhmatova	Nazi Empire, 1933–1945
	Soviet Empire, 1922–1991
Cligès (ca. 1176), Chrétien de Troyes	Crusades, 1096–1221
Collected Poems (1992), Constantine Cavafy	Ottoman Empire, 1300–1922

The Defeat (1773), Mercy Otis Warren	British Empire, 1583–
Deliverance from Error (ca. 1108), al-Ghazali	Turco-Persian Empire, 1037–1307
Departmental Ditties and Other Verses (1886), Rudyard Kipling	British Empire, 1583–
The Desert and the Sown (1907), Gertrude Lowthian Bell	Ottoman Empire, 1300–1922
Destruction (1904), Filippo Tommaso Marinetti	Italian Empire, 1885–1943
"The Destruction of Kreshev" (1942), Isaac Bashevis Singer	Russian Empire, 1547–1917
"The Destruction of Sennacherib" (1815), George Gordon, Lord Byron	Assyrian Empire, 900–612 B.C.
Dhammapada (ca. 50 B.C.), Siddhartha Gautama	Maurya Empire, A.D. 321–185
Dialogue on Orators (A.D. 105), Tacitus	Roman Empire, 27 B.C.–A.D. 476
"Dialogue on Poverty" (ca. 733), Yamanoue no Okura	Nara Period, 710–794
Diary of an African Journey (1914), H. Rider Haggard	British Empire, 1583–
The Diary of a Young Girl (1947), Anne Frank	Nazi Empire, 1933–1945
The Diary of Lady Murasaki (ca. 1010), Murasaki Shikibu	Heian Period, 794–1185
"Digging a Trench" (1945), Mervyn Peake	Nazi Empire, 1933–1945
The Dilemma of a Ghost (1965), Ama Ata Aidoo	British Empire, 1583–
"A Discovery of the Bermudas" (1610), Sylvester Jourdain	British Empire, 1583–
A Diversity of Creatures (1917), Rudyard Kipling	British Empire, 1583–
Divine Comedy (1308), Dante Alighieri	Papal Empire, 752–1798
Doctor Zhivago (1956), Boris Pasternak	Soviet Empire, 1922–1991
Dohakosha (ca. A.D. 790), Saraha	Pala Empire, 750–1174
Dombey and Son (1848), Charles Dickens	British Empire, 1583–
Don Juan (1824), Lord Byron	Ottoman Empire, 1300–1922
Don Quixote of La Mancha (1605), Miguel de Cervantes	Ottoman Empire, 1300–1922
	Spanish Empire, 1492–1975
Doom Book (ca. 900), Alfred the Great	Viking Conquests, 775–1100
Dream of the Red Chamber (1791), Cao Xueqin	Qing Dynasty, 1644–1912
Dreams of the Seasons (1898), Gabriele D'Annunzio	Italian Empire, 1885–1943
The Drover's Wife (ca. 1885), Henry Lawson	British Empire, 1583–
Dubliners (1914), James Joyce	British Empire, 1583–
Duke Rowlande and Sir Ottuell of Spayne (ca. 1390s), anonymous	Frankish Empire, 509–843
"The Dying Detective" (1894), Sir Arthur Conan Doyle	British Empire, 1583–
East of Home (1950), Santha Rama Rau	British Empire, 1583–
The Ebb-Tide (1894), Robert Louis Stevenson and Lloyd Osbourne	British Empire, 1583–
Ecclesiasticus (ca. 180 B.C.), Sirach of Jerusalem	French Empire, 1499–1513, 1605–
Eclogues (ca. 35 B.C.), Virgil	Seleucid Empire, 323–60 B.C.
Egyptian Sepulchres and Syrian Shrines (1861), Emily Anne Beaufort	Roman Empire, 27 B.C.–A.D. 476
	Ottoman Empire, 1300–1922
Elegies (15 B.C.), Propertius	Roman Empire, 27 B.C.–A.D. 476
Elegies (19 B.C.), Albius Tibullus	Roman Empire, 27 B.C.–A.D. 476
Eli: A Mystery of the Sorrows of Israel (1951), Nelly Sachs	Nazi Empire, 1933–1945
"The Emperor's New Clothes" (1837), Hans Christian Andersen	Danish-Norwegian Empire, 1200–1979

Fables of Lokman (ca. 1100 B.C.), Lokman	Sabaean Empire, 1700–115 B.C.
"Facing Night" (ca. A.D. 768), Du Fu	Tang Dynasty, 618–907
"Facing Snow" (ca. A.D. 757), Du Fu	Tang Dynasty, 618–907
Falling Leaves (1997), Adeline Yen Mah	Chinese Empire, 221 B.C.–
	Japanese Empire, 1871–1945
The Fall of Samaria (721 B.C.), Sargon II	Assyrian Empire, 900–612 B.C.
	Greek Colonies, 825–400 B.C.
	Sabaean Empire, 1700–115 B.C.
The Family Moskat (1950), Isaac Bashevis Singer	Nazi Empire, 1933–1945
	Soviet Empire, 1922–1991
The Fashion Shop (1807), Ivan Andreyevich Krylov	Russian Empire, 1547–1917
Fathers and Sons (1862), Ivan Turgenev	Russian Empire, 1547–1917
Faust (1826, 1831), Johann Wolfgang von Goethe	First Napoleonic Empire, 1804–1815
The Feasting King (1909), Filippo Tommaso Marinetti	Italian Empire, 1885–1943
The Fencing Master (1840), Alexandre Dumas (père)	Russian Empire, 1547–1917
"Feng-Hsien Return Chant" (ca. A.D. 755), Du Fu	Tang Dynasty, 618–907
Fire on the Mountain (1977), Anita Desai	British Empire, 1583–
The First Circle (1968), Aleksandr Solzhenitsyn	Soviet Empire, 1922–1991
The Flame of Life (1900), Gabriele D'Annunzio	Italian Empire, 1885–1943
Flint and Feather (1912), Pauline Johnson	British Empire, 1583–
Florentine Codex (1585), Bernardino de Sahagún	Aztec Empire, 1375–1521
The Florida of the Inca (1599), Garcilaso de la Vega	Holy Roman Empire, 962–1806
	Incan Empire, 1438–1533
	Spanish Empire, 1492–1975
"Flowers Have Come" (ca. 1460), Nezahualcoyotl	Aztec Empire, 1375–1521
Fool Divine (1917), G. B. Lancaster	American Empire, 1898–
For My Country (1895), Jules-Paul Tardivel	French Empire, 1499–1513, 1605–
"The Fox and Hedgehog" (650 B.C.), Archilochus	Greek Colonies, 825–400 B.C.
Francesca da Rimini (1901), Gabriele D'Annunzio	Italian Empire, 1885–1943
The Freedom Movement in India (1970), Nayantara Sahgal	British Empire, 1583–
From Fear Set Free (1962), Nayantara Sahgal	British Empire, 1583–
From the City's Founding (A.D. 14), Livy	Carthaginian Empire, 814 B.C.–A.D. 695
	Roman Empire, 27 B.C.–A.D. 476
The Futurist Cookbook (1932), Filippo Tommaso Marinetti	Italian Empire, 1885–1943
"Futurist Manifesto" (1908), Filippo Tommaso Marinetti	Italian Empire, 1885–1943
The Gallic Wars (ca. 50 B.C.), Julius Caesar	Roman Empire, 27 B.C.–A.D. 476
Garland of Birth Stories (ca. A.D. 350), Aryasura	Guptan Empire, 280–550
The Gateless Gate (1228), Wumen Ituikai	Song Dynasty, 960–1279
"Gazing at the Sacred Peak" (ca. A.D. 747), Du Fu	Tang Dynasty, 618–907
"Gazing into Antiquity at Su Terrace" (ca. A.D. 742), Li Bo	Tang Dynasty, 618–907
"Gazing into Antiquity in Yüeh" (ca. A.D. 742), Li Bo	Tang Dynasty, 618–907
Genesis (ca. 500 B.C.), anonymous	Ur Empire, 2100–2000 B.C.
	Achaemenid-Persian Empire, 550–330 B.C.
German Legends (1816, 1818), Jacob and Wilhelm Grimm	German Confederation, 1814–1871
The Giaour (1813), Lord Byron	Ottoman Empire, 1300–1922
Gifts of Passage (1961), Santha Rama Rau	British Empire, 1583–

La Gioconda (1899), Gabriele D'Annunzio	Italian Empire, 1885–1943
Glimpses of Unfamiliar Japan (1894), Lafcadio Hearn	Japanese Empire, 1871–1945
"The 'Gloria Scott'" (1894), Sir Arthur Conan Doyle	British Empire, 1583–
Going Home (1957), Doris Lessing	British Empire, 1583–
The Golden Ass (A.D. 158), Apuleius	Roman Empire, 27 B.C.–A.D. 476
"The Golden Mean" (23 B.C.), Horace	Roman Empire, 27 B.C.–A.D. 476
The Golden Notebook (1962), Doris Lessing	British Empire, 1583–
The Good Earth (1931), Pearl S. Buck	Qing Dynasty, 1644–1912
Gormenghast (1950), Mervyn Peake	Nazi Empire, 1933–1945
Götz von Berlichingen (1773), Johann Wolfgang von Goethe	Holy Roman Empire, 962–1806
The Government Inspector (1836), Nikolay Gogol	Russian Empire, 1547–1917
Grand Parade (1944), G. B. Lancaster	British Empire, 1583–
Granth (1604), ArjanDev	Mughal Empire, 1526–1857
The Grass Is Singing (1950), Doris Lessing	British Empire, 1583–
"The Grateful Negro" (1804), Maria Edgeworth	British Empire, 1583–
The Great Divan (ca. 1240), Rumi	Turco-Persian Empire, 1037–1307
Great Expectations (1861), Charles Dickens	British Empire, 1583–
Great Master Wonhyo (1942), Yi Kwangsu	Japanese Empire, 1871–1945
	Joseon Dynasty, 1392–1910
Gregorius (1195), Hartmann von Aue	Crusades, 1096–1221
The Group (1775), Mercy Otis Warren	British Empire, 1583–
Guantanamera (1891), José Martí	Spanish Empire, 1492–1975
Guerrillas (1975), V. S. Naipaul	British Empire, 1583–
Guhyasamaja Tantra (A.D. 350), Asanga	Guptan Empire, 280–550
The Gulag Archipelago (1973), Aleksandr Solzhenitsyn	Soviet Empire, 1922–1991
Gulliver's Travels (1726), Jonathan Swift	British Empire, 1583–
Gunnar's Daughter (1909), Sigrid Undset	Danish-Norwegian Empire, 1200–1979
Guru Granth Sahib (1708), Gobind Singh	Mughal Empire, 1526–1857
Hadji Murád (1904), Leo Tolstoy	Ottoman Empire, 1300–1922
	Russian Empire, 1547–1917
Half a Life (2001), V. S. Naipaul	Portuguese Empire, 1415–1999
"Half Measures" (1989), Yevgeny Yevtushenko	Soviet Empire, 1922–1991
Hamasa (ca. 845), Abu Tammam	Abbasid Empire, 750–1258
Hamlet (ca. 1599–1600), William Shakespeare	Danish-Norwegian Empire, 1200–1979
Happy Times in Norway (1943), Sigrid Undset	Danish-Norwegian Empire, 1200–1979
	Nazi Empire, 1933–1945
Hawaii's Story by Hawaii's Queen, Liliuokalani (1898), Liliuokalani	Hawaiian Kingdom, 1810–1893
Head above Water (1986), Buchi Emecheta	British Empire, 1583–
The Heartless (1917), Yi Kwangsu	Japanese Empire, 1871–1945
	Joseon Dynasty, 1392–1910
Heart of Darkness (1899), Joseph Conrad	Belgian Empire, 1877–1962
The Heart of the Matter (1948), Graham Greene	British Empire, 1583–
Heat and Dust (1975), Ruth Prawer Jhabvala	British Empire, 1583–
Hecuba (ca. 424 B.C.), Euripides	Athenian Empire, 477–431 B.C., 415–403 B.C.

"Ireland at the Bar" (1907), James Joyce	British Empire, 1583–
"Is It Love?" (1906), Yi Kwangsu	Japanese Empire, 1871–1945
	Joseon Dynasty, 1392–1910
Island Nights' Entertainments (1893), Robert Louis Stevenson	British Empire, 1583–
The Island of Dr. Moreau (1896), H. G. Wells	British Empire, 1583–
It's a Battlefield (1934), Graham Greene	British Empire, 1583–
I Want to Live (2006), Nina Lugovskaya	Soviet Empire, 1922–1991
Iwein (1203), Hartmann von Aue	Crusades, 1096–1221
Izumi Shikibu Diary (ca. 1008), Izumi Shikibu	Heian Period, 794–1185
Jane Eyre (1847), Charlotte Brontë	British Empire, 1583–
Japanese Fairy Tales (1898), Lafcadio Hearn	Japanese Empire, 1871–1945
The Jerusalem Tract (1097), al-Ghazali	Turco-Persian Empire, 1037–1307
Jewish Antiquities (A.D. 93), Flavius Josephus	Roman Empire, 27 B.C.–A.D. 476
"Jolly Is the Gypsy's Life" (ca. 1900), anonymous	German Empire, 1871–1918
Joshua (ca. 1050 B.C.), anonymous	Israelite Empire, 1050–920 B.C.
Journal of a West India Proprietor (1834), Matthew Gregory Lewis	British Empire, 1583–
A Journal of the Disasters in Affghanistan, 1841–1842 (1843), Florentia Wynch Sale	British Empire, 1583–
Journeys in Persia and Kurdistan (1891), Isabella Lucy Bird	Ottoman Empire, 1300–1922
Journey without Maps (1936), Graham Greene	British Empire, 1583–
	French Empire, 1499–1513, 1605–
	Qing Dynasty, 1644–1912
The Joy Luck Club (1989), Amy Tan	Chinese Empire, 221 B.C.–
The Joys of Motherhood (1979), Buchi Emecheta	British Empire, 1583–
Juan of Manila (1947), Marie McSwigan	Japanese Empire, 1871–1945
Judges (ca. 1040 B.C.), anonymous	Israelite Empire, 1050–920 B.C.
Judith (ca. 150 B.C.), anonymous	Assyrian Empire, 900–612 B.C.
Juju Shinron (A.D. 830), Kukai	Nara Period, 710–794
Julius Caesar (1599), William Shakespeare	Roman Empire, 27 B.C.–A.D. 476
July's People (1981), Nadine Gordimer	British Empire, 1583–
The Jungle Book (1894), Rudyard Kipling	British Empire, 1583–
Just So Stories for Little Children (1902), Rudyard Kipling	British Empire, 1583–
The Kadaitcha Sung (1990), Sam Watson	British Empire, 1583–
"Kaib: An Eastern Tale" (1792), Ivan Andreyevich Krylov	Russian Empire, 1547–1917
Kalachakra Tantra (A.D. 966), anonymous	Pala Empire, 750–1174
Kalevala (1836), Elias Lönnrot	Russian Empire, 1547–1917
Kalev's Son (1853), Friedrich Reinhold Kreutzwald	Russian Empire, 1547–1917
Kalilah and Dimnah (A.D. 570), Burzoe	Sassanid Empire, A.D. 226–651
Kalilah and Dimnah (ca. A.D. 750), Ibn al-Muqaffa	Umayyad Empire, 660–750
Kama Sutra (ca. A.D. 500), Vatsyayana	Guptan Empire, A.D. 280–550
Khurda Avesta (A.D. 232), anonymous	Sassanid Dynasty, A.D. 226–651
Kidnapped (1886), Robert Louis Stevenson	British Empire, 1583–
Kim (1901), Rudyard Kipling	British Empire, 1583–
	Russian Empire, 1547–1917
"The King of Apemama" (1896), Robert Louis Stevenson	British Empire, 1583–

King Rother (ca. 1150), anonymous	Crusades, 1096–1221
Kings (ca. 535 B.C.), anonymous	Assyrian Empire, 900–612 B.C.
King Solomon's Mines (1885), H. Rider Haggard	British Empire, 1583–
The Kitchen God's Wife (1991), Amy Tan	Chinese Empire, 221 B.C.–
The Knights (424 B.C.), Aristophanes	Athenian Empire, 477–431 B.C.
koans (A.D. 520), Bodhidharma	Gupta Empire, A.D. 280–550
koans (A.D. 920), Nanyuan Huiyung	Khitan Empire, 907–1125
Kojiki (A.D. 712), O no Yasumaro	Nara Period, 710–794
Konjaku Monogatari (1075), Minamoto Takakuni	Heian Period, 794–1185
Koran (A.D. 633), Muhammad	Islamic Empire, 622–1258
Korea and Her Neighbours (1898), Isabella Lucy Bird	Joseon Dynasty, 1392–1910
	Russian Empire, 1547–1917
"Kubla Khan" (1816), Samuel Taylor Coleridge	Mongolian Empire, 1206–1405
Kularnava Tantra (ca. 1000), anonymous	Pala Empire, 750–1174
Kuzari (ca. 1140), Yehuda Halevi	Abbasid Empire, 750–1258
Kwaidan (1904), Lafcadio Hearn	Japanese Empire, 1871–1945
The Ladies of Castile (1790), Mercy Otis Warren	Holy Roman Empire, 962–1806
Lady Mary and Her Nurse: or, a Peep into the Canadian Forest (1856), Catharine Parr Traill	British Empire, 1583–
"The Lagoon" (1897), Joseph Conrad	British Empire, 1583–
Laieikawai (1863), anonymous	Hawaiian Kingdom, 1810–1893
Lais (ca. 1175), Marie de France	Angevin Empire, 1135–1217
Lakshmi Tantra (ca. A.D. 950), anonymous	Pala Empire, 750–1174
Lancelot, or the Knight of the Cart (ca. 1181), Chrétien de Troyes	Crusades, 1096–1221
The Last Cavalier (2005), Alexandre Dumas (père)	First Napoleonic Empire, 1804–1815
	Ottoman Empire, 1300–1922
The Last Journals of David Livingstone in Central Africa (1874), David Livingstone	British Empire, 1583–
The Last Voyage (1889) Anne Brassey	British Empire, 1583–
"The Last Words of David" (ca. 900 B.C.), David, et al.	Israelite Empire, 1050–920 B.C.
The Law-Bringers (1913), G. B. Lancaster	British Empire, 1583–
The Left Bank and Other Stories (1927), Jean Rhys	French Empire, 1499–1513, 1605–
Legend of the Great Rama (ca. 1500), anonymous	Majapahit Empire, 1293–1500
The Legends and Myths of Hawaii (1888), David Kalakaua	Hawaiian Kingdom, 1810–1893
Legends of Vancouver (1911), Pauline Johnson	British Empire, 1583–
Lesson for Daughters (1807), Ivan Andreyevich Krylov	Russian Empire, 1547–1917
Less Than One (1986), Joseph Brodsky	Soviet Empire, 1922–1991
Letters (A.D. 97–113), Pliny the Younger	Roman Empire, 27 B.C.–A.D. 476
Letters from Pontus (A.D. 10), Ovid	Roman Empire, 27 B.C.–A.D. 476
The Letters of the Late Ignatius Sancho, an African (1782), Ignatius Sancho	Portuguese Empire, 1415–1999
	Spanish Empire, 1492–1975
"A Letter to a Hindu" (1908), Leo Tolstoy	British Empire, 1583–
	Russian Empire, 1547–1917
Letter to the God of Love (1399), Christine de Pisan	French Empire, 1499–1513, 1605–
	Venetian Empire, 800–1797

Lieutenant Schmidt (1927), Boris Pasternak	Soviet Empire, 1922–1991
The Life and Character of Julius Agricola (A.D. 98), Tacitus	Roman Empire, 27 B.C.–A.D. 476
Life and Travel in India (1884), Anna Leonowens	British Empire, 1583–
Life in the Clearings (1853), Susanna Strickland Moodie	British Empire, 1583–
Life of Alfred (893), Bishop Asser	Viking Conquests, 775–1100
The Life of Charlemagne (A.D. 830), Einhard	Frankish Empire, 509–843
The Life of Flavius Josephus (ca. A.D. 99), Flavius Josephus	Roman Empire, 27 B.C.–A.D. 476
The Life of Nelson (1813), Robert Southey	First Napoleonic Empire, 1804–1815
The Life of the Buddha (ca. A.D. 100), Ashvaghosa	Kushan Empire, A.D. 60–375
Life's Handicap: Being Stories of Mine Own People (1891), Rudyard Kipling	British Empire, 1583–
Life Together (1939), Dietrich Bonhoeffer	Nazi Empire, 1933–1945
The Light That Failed (1890), Rudyard Kipling	British Empire, 1583–
"The Lion and the Shepherd" (ca. A.D. 950), Romulus	Roman Empire, 27 B.C.–A.D. 476
"The Lion and the Unicorn" (1941), George Orwell	British Empire, 1583–
Literary Fables (1782), Tomás de Iriarte	Spanish Empire, 1492–1975
"The Little Shoemakers" (1982), Isaac Bashevis Singer	Nazi Empire, 1933–1945
	Soviet Empire, 1922–1991
Lives of the Caesars (ca. A.D. 121), Suetonius	Roman Empire, 27 B.C.–A.D. 476
The Living Corpse (1900), Leo Tolstoy	Russian Empire, 1547–1917
Living My Life (1931), Emma Goldman	American Empire, 1898–
	German Empire, 1871–1918
	Joseon Dynasty, 1392–1910
	Russian Empire, 1547–1917
	Japanese Empire, 1871–1945
	Joseon Dynasty, 1392–1910
The Living Reed (1963), Pearl S. Buck	Aztec Empire, 1375–1521
	British Empire, 1583–
"La Llorona" (ca. 1525), anonymous	British Empire, 1583–
Lord Jim (1900), Joseph Conrad	Spanish Empire, 1492–1975
"Lord Lorne in the Northwest" (1881), William Kirby	Dutch Empire, 1620–
The Loss of El Dorado (1969), V. S. Naipaul	Roman Empire, 27 B.C.–A.D. 476
Love Letters (1861), Eduard Douwes Dekker	Japanese Empire, 1871–1945
Lover of Lies (ca. A.D. 175), Lucian of Samosata	Joseon Dynasty, 1392–1910
Love's Silence (1926), Han Yong-un	Roman Empire, 27 B.C.–A.D. 476
Luke (ca. A.D. 90), Luke	Soviet Empire, 1922–1991
"Lullaby of Cape Cod" (1975), Joseph Brodsky	French Empire, 1499–1513, 1605–
Lures and Glimmers (1960), Birago Diop	Portuguese Empire, 1415–1999
The Lusiads (1572), Luís Vaz de Camões	Chinese Empire, 221 B.C.–
Luxuriant Gems of the Spring and Autumn Annals (ca. 100 B.C.), Zong Zongshu	British Empire, 1583–
The Lying Days (1953), Nadine Gordimer	Athenian Empire, 477–431 B.C.
Lysistrata (411 B.C.), Aristophanes	Seleucid Empire, 323–60 B.C.
Maccabees (ca. 125 B.C.), anonymous	Italian Empire, 1885–1943
Mafarka the Futurist (1910), Filippo Tommaso Marinetti	Guptan Empire, A.D. 280–550
Mahabharata (ca. A.D. 350), Vyasa	Pala Empire, 750–1174
Mahanirvana Tantra (1295), anonymous	

Mandela's Earth and Other Poems (1988), Wole Soyinka	British Empire, 1583–
The Man Died (1973), Wole Soyinka	British Empire, 1583–
"The Man from Snowy River" (ca. 1888), A. B. Paterson	British Empire, 1583–
A Man of the People (1966), Chinua Achebe	British Empire, 1583–
"The Man Who Liked Dickens" (1933), Evelyn Waugh	Brazilian Empire, 1822–1889
"The Man Who Was" (1890), Rudyard Kipling	British Empire, 1583–
	Russian Empire, 1547–1917
"The Man Who Would Be King" (1888), Rudyard Kipling	British Empire, 1583–
Manyoshu (Ten Thousand Leaves) (ca. 759), Otomo Yakamochi (comp.)	Nara Period, 710–794
Mark (ca. A.D. 70), John Mark	Roman Empire, 27 B.C.–A.D. 476
Martin Chuzzlewit (1844), Charles Dickens	British Empire, 1583–
Maru (1971), Bessie Head	British Empire, 1583–
"Mary Postgate" (1915), Rudyard Kipling	German Empire, 1871–1918
The Master of Ballantrae (1889), Robert Louis Stevenson	British Empire, 1583–
The Master of Hestviken (1925–27), Sigrid Undset	Danish-Norwegian Empire, 1200–1979
Mathnawi (ca. 1270), Rumi	Turco-Persian Empire, 1037–1307
Matthew (ca. A.D. 80), Matthew	Roman Empire, 27 B.C.–A.D. 476
Max Havelaar (1860), Eduard Douwes Dekker	Dutch Empire, 1620–
"May 1940" (1940), Mervyn Peake	Nazi Empire, 1933–1945
Meditations (ca. A.D. 180), Marcus Aurelius	Roman Empire, 27 B.C.–A.D. 476
Mein Kampf (1925–26), Adolf Hitler	Nazi Empire, 1933–1945
Memoirs of the Lord of Joinville (1309), Jean de Joinville	Crusades, 1096–1221
Mem-u Zin (1692), Ahmed-i Hani	Ottoman Empire, 1300–1922
	Safavid Empire, 1501–1722
The Men of the Last Frontier (1931), Grey Owl	British Empire, 1583–
Men on Bataan (1942), John Hersey	American Empire, 1898–
	Japanese Empire, 1871–1945
The Merchant of Venice (ca. 1596–98), William Shakespeare	Ottoman Empire, 1300–1922
	Venetian Empire, 800–1797
Mercy (1869), Ignacio Manuel Altamirano	Austrian Empire, 1804–1867
	Mexican Empire, 1822–1823, 1864–1867
Meshugah (1994), Isaac Bashevis Singer	Nazi Empire, 1933–1945
	Soviet Empire, 1922–1991
Metamorphoses (A.D. 8), Ovid	Roman Empire, 27 B.C.–A.D. 476
The Metamorphosis (1915), Franz Kafka	Austro-Hungarian Empire, 1867–1918
Meteorologica (ca. 335 B.C.), Aristotle	Macedonian Empire, 338–309 B.C.
Metrical Legends of Exalted Characters (1821), Joanna Baillie	Spanish Empire, 1492–1975
Mexican Songs (ca. 1590), anonymous	Aztec Empire, 1375–1521
The Middle Passage (1962), V. S. Naipaul	British Empire, 1583–
	French Empire, 1499–1513, 1605–
The Mikado (1885), W. S. Gilbert	British Empire, 1583–
	Japanese Empire, 1871–1945
The Mimic Men (1967), V. S. Naipaul	British Empire, 1583–
The Mint (1955), Thomas Edward Lawrence	British Empire, 1583–
Mishna (ca. A.D. 135), Akiba ben Joseph and Rabbi Meir	Roman Empire, 27 B.C.–A.D. 476

Miss Julie (1888), August Strindberg	Swedish Union, 1814–1905
Mistaken Identity (1988), Nayantara Sahgal	British Empire, 1583–
Mister Johnson (1939), Joyce Cary	British Empire, 1583–
The Moccasin Maker (1913), Pauline Johnson	British Empire, 1583–
A Modest Proposal (1729), Jonathan Swift	British Empire, 1583–
"The Monkey's Paw" (1902), W. W. Jacobs	British Empire, 1583–
"Moonlit Night" (ca. A.D. 757), Du Fu	Tang Dynasty, 618–907
The Moonstone (1868), Wilkie Collins	British Empire, 1583–
More Than Love (1906), Gabriele D'Annunzio	Italian Empire, 1885–1943
Morning Star (1873), Florence Baker	British Empire, 1583–
The Mother (1934), Pearl Buck	Qing Dynasty, 1644–1912
Mother Crocodile (1981), Birago Diop	French Empire, 1499–1513, 1605–
The Motley Assembly (1779), Mercy Otis Warren	British Empire, 1583–
"Mourning Chao" (ca. A.D. 755), Li Bo	Tang Dynasty, 618–907
"Mumu" (1852), Ivan Turgenev	Russian Empire, 1547–1917
Myazedi Inscription (1113), Rajakumar	Bagan Empire, 874–1369
My Disillusionment in Russia (1923), Emma Goldman	Russian Empire, 1547–1917
My Further Disillusionment in Russia (1924), Emma Goldman	Russian Empire, 1547–1917
My Life in the Bush of Ghosts (1954), Amos Tutuola	British Empire, 1583–
Myrmidons (ca. 470 B.C.), Aeschylus	Athenian Empire, 477–431 B.C., 415–403 B.C.
My Sister—Life (1921), Boris Pasternak	Soviet Empire, 1922–1991
The Mystery of Cloomber (1889), Sir Arthur Conan Doyle	British Empire, 1583–
The Mystery of Edwin Drood (1870), Charles Dickens	British Empire, 1583–
The Mystic Masseur (1957), V. S. Naipaul	British Empire, 1583–
Napoleon (1855), Alexandre Dumas (père)	Austrian Empire, 1804–1867
	First Napoleonic Empire, 1804–1815
"The Napoleon of the People" (1833), Honoré de Balzac	First Napoleonic Empire, 1804–1815
A Narrative of the Life and Travels of Mrs. Nancy Prince (1850), Nancy Gardner Prince	British Empire, 1583–
Nellie Bly's Book: Around the World in 72 Days (1890), Nellie Bly	British Empire, 1583–
	Japanese Empire, 1871–1945
	Ottoman Empire, 1300–1922
New Tales of Amadou Koumba (1958), Birago Diop	French Empire, 1499–1513, 1605–
The Nibbler (1804), Ivan Andreyevich Krylov	Russian Empire, 1547–1917
The Niche of Lights (ca. 1105), al-Ghazali	Turco-Persian Empire, 1037–1307
Night (1960), Elie Wiesel	Nazi Empire, 1933–1945
Nineteen Eighty-Four (1949), George Orwell	British Empire, 1583–
"Nisaba and Wheat" (ca. 1900 B.C.), anonymous	Babylonian Empire, 1900–1600 B.C.
"Nobel Prize" (1958), Boris Pasternak	Soviet Empire, 1922–1991
No Longer at Ease (1960), Chinua Achebe	British Empire, 1583–
Nostromo (1904), Joseph Conrad	Spanish Empire, 1492–1975
No Sweetness Here (1970), Ama Ata Aidoo	British Empire, 1583–
Notes from the Underground (1864), Fyodor Dostoyevsky	Russian Empire, 1547–1917
"Now Turn Me Back" (1893), Rabindranath Tagore	British Empire, 1583–
Observations on the New Constitution, and on the Federal and State Conventions (1788), Mercy Otis Warren	British Empire, 1583–

Occasion for Loving (1963), Nadine Gordimer	British Empire, 1583–
The Ocean of the Stream of Stories (1070), Somadeva	Ghaznavid Empire, 975–1187
Odes (23–13 B.C.), Horace	Roman Empire, 27 B.C.–A.D. 476
"Ode to Napoleon Buonaparte" (1814), George Gordon, Lord Byron	First Napoleonic Empire, 1804–1815
"Of Cannibals" (1580), Michel de Montaigne	French Empire, 1499–1513, 1605–
Offerings to the Lares (1895), Rainer Maria Rilke	Austro-Hungarian Empire, 1867–1918
"Of Idolatry" (A.D. 198), Tertullian	Roman Empire, 27 B.C.–A.D. 476
"Of Public Shows" (ca. A.D. 201), Tertullian	Roman Empire, 27 B.C.–A.D. 476
"Of the Crown" (A.D. 201), Tertullian	Roman Empire, 27 B.C.–A.D. 476
"Old Australian Ways" (1902), A. B. Paterson	British Empire, 1583–
"Old Tar" (1913), Katherine Mansfield	British Empire, 1583–
"On Benefits" (A.D. 56), Seneca	Roman Empire, 27 B.C.–A.D. 476
On Buildings (A.D. 561), Procopius	Byzantine Empire, 330–1453
The Once and Future King (1958), T. H. White	Crusades, 1096–1221
"On Clemency" (A.D. 56), Seneca	Roman Empire, 27 B.C.–A.D. 476
One Day in the Life of Ivan Denisovich (1962), Alexander Solzhenitsyn	Soviet Empire, 1922–1991
On Early Trains (1943), Boris Pasternak	Soviet Empire, 1922–1991
1 Samuel (ca. 920 B.C.), anonymous	Israelite Empire, 1050–920 B.C.
On Germany (1810), Anne-Louise-Germaine de Staël	First Napoleonic Empire, 1804–1815
On Grief and Reason (1995), Joseph Brodsky	Soviet Empire, 1922–1991
"On Passing the Ruined Capital at Omi" (ca. 700), Kakinomoto no Hitomaro	Nara Period, 710–794
"On Providence" (A.D. 64), Seneca	Roman Empire, 27 B.C.–A.D. 476
"On Seeing England for the First Time" (1991), Jamaica Kincaid	British Empire, 1583–
On Sledge and Horseback to the Outcast Siberian Lepers (1877), Kate Marsden	Russian Empire, 1547–1917
"On the Burning of the City" (A.D. 64), Lucan	Roman Empire, 27 B.C.–A.D. 476
On the Curiosities of Cities and the Wonders of Travel (1354), Ibn Battuta	Abyssinian Empire, 1270–1974
	Bagan Empire, 849–1287
	Byzantine Empire, 330–1453
	Kanem Empire, 700–1376
	Khmer Empire, 802–1462
	Majapahitan Empire, 1200–1500
	Malian Empire, 1200–1500
	Mamluk Dynasty, 1260–1517
	Mongolian Empire, 1206–1405
	Ottoman Empire, 1300–1922
	Songhai Empire, 1340–1591
	Yuan Dynasty, 1279–1368
"On the Death of Zhukov" (1974), Joseph Brodsky	Soviet Empire, 1922–1991
"On the Enshrinement of Takechi" (ca. 700), Kakinomoto no Hitomaro	Nara Period, 710–794
"On the Happy Life" (A.D. 58), Seneca	Roman Empire, 27 B.C.–A.D. 476

"On the Movement of Nations at the End of
   the Fifth Century" (1835), Nikolay Gogol
"On the Nature of Animals" (ca. A.D. 230),
   Claudius Aelian
On the Origin and Situation of the Germans (A.D. 98), Tacitus
"On the Road of Ambition" (ca. A.D. 745), Li Bo
"On the Sovereign's Visit to the Palace in Yoshinu"
   (ca. A.D. 700), Kakinomoto no Hitomaro
"On the Teaching of World History" (1835), Nikolay Gogol

On the Wars (A.D. 552), Procopius
On Treasure in Peru (1562), Bartolomé de Las Casas
"Onward, Christian Soldiers" (1864), Sabine Baring-Gould
The Open Sore of a Continent (1996), Wole Soyinka
Oresteia (458 B.C.), Aeschylus
Oroonoko, or The Royal Slave (1688), Aphra Behn

Oscar and Lucinda (1988), Peter Carey
"O the Chimneys" (1947), Nelly Sachs
Othello (ca. 1603–04), William Shakespeare

Otuel (ca. 1325), anonymous
O Uraguai (1769), Basílio da Gama

Our Man in Havana (1958), Graham Greene
Our Sister Killjoy (1977), Ama Ata Aidoo
Out of Africa (1937), Isak Dinesen

"An Outpost of Progress" (1896), Joseph Conrad
"Ovando" (1989), Jamaica Kincaid
Pageant (1933), G. B. Lancaster
Pages from the Journal of an Author (1864),
   Fyodor Dostoyevsky
The Painted Bird (1965), Jerzy Kosinski
The Palm-Wine Drinkard (1952), Amos Tutuola
Panchatantra (ca. 200 B.C.), Vishnu Sarma
Parallel Lives (ca. A.D. 110), Plutarch
Parsifal (1882), Richard Wagner
Parzival (ca. 1210), Wolfram von Eschenbach
A Passage to India (1924), E. M. Forster
The Passing of the Aborigines (1938), Daisy Bates
The Passionate Nomad (1988), Isabelle Eberhardt
"Passion in the Desert" (1850), Honoré de Balzac

Hunnic Empire, 370–469
Roman Empire, 27 B.C.–A.D. 476
Roman Empire, 27 B.C.–A.D. 476

Roman Empire, 27 B.C.–A.D. 476
Tang Dynasty, 618–907
Nara Period, 710–794

Hunnic Empire, 370–469
Roman Empire, 27 B.C.–A.D. 476
Papal Empire, 752–1798
Byzantine Empire, 330–1453
Incan Empire, 1438–1533
British Empire, 1583–
British Empire, 1583–
Athenian Empire, 477–431 B.C., 415–403 B.C.
British Empire, 1583–
Dutch Empire, 1620–
British Empire, 1583–
Nazi Empire, 1933–1945
Ottoman Empire, 1300–1922
Venetian Empire, 800–1797
Frankish Empire, 509–843
Brazilian Empire, 1822–1889
Papal Empire, 752–1798
Portuguese Empire, 1415–1999
Spanish Empire, 1492–1975
American Empire, 1898–
British Empire, 1583–
British Empire, 1583–
German Empire, 1871–1918
Belgian Empire, 1877–1962
Spanish Empire, 1492–1975
British Empire, 1583–
Russian Empire, 1547–1917

Nazi Empire, 1933–1945
British Empire, 1583–
Maurya Empire, 321–185 B.C.
Roman Empire, 27 B.C.–A.D. 476
Crusades, 1096–1221
Crusades, 1096–1221
British Empire, 1583–
British Empire, 1583–
French Empire, 1499–1513, 1605–
First Napoleonic Empire, 1804–1815

Peace (421 B.C.), Aristophanes	Athenian Empire, 477–431 B.C.
Pearls and Pebbles (1894), Catharine Parr Traill	British Empire, 1583–
Penguin Island (1908), France, Anatole	French Empire, 1499–1513, 1605–
"Peng-Ya Song" (ca. A.D. 757), Du Fu	Tang Dynasty, 618–907
Perceval, or the Account of the Grail (ca. 1182), Chrétien de Troyes	Crusades, 1096–1221
Persae (472 B.C.), Aeschylus	Athenian Empire, 477–431 B.C., 415–403 B.C.
Persepolis (2002), Marjane Satrapi	Qajar Dynasty, 1794–1925
	Soviet Empire, 1922–1991
Persuasion (1817), Jane Austen	British Empire, 1583–
Phaedo (ca. 345 B.C.), Plato	Spartan Empire, 404–371 B.C.
The Phantom Rickshaw and Other Ghost Tales (1888), Rudyard Kipling	British Empire, 1583–
Pharsalia (A.D. 63), Lucan	Roman Empire, 27 B.C.–A.D. 476
The Piano (1993), Jane Campion	British Empire, 1583–
The Pickup (2002), Nadine Gordimer	British Empire, 1583–
The Pickwick Papers (1837), Charles Dickens	British Empire, 1583–
The Pilgrimage of Charlemagne (ca. 1140), anonymous	Frankish Empire, 509–843
Pilgrims of the Wild (1934), Grey Owl	British Empire, 1583–
"The Pit and the Pendulum" (1843), Edgar Allan Poe	French Empire, 1499–1513, 1605–
Plain Tales from the Hills (1888), Rudyard Kipling	British Empire, 1583–
The Playboy of the Western World (1907), John Millington Synge	British Empire, 1583–
Poems (ca. A.D. 420), Tao Qian	Jin Dynasty, 265–420
Poems (ca. 1180s), Friedrich von Hausen	Crusades, 1096–1221
Poems, Dramatic and Miscellaneous (1790), Mercy Otis Warren	British Empire, 1583–
Poems from Prison (1969), Wole Soyinka	British Empire, 1583–
Poems on Naval Deeds (1912), Gabriele D'Annunzio	Italian Empire, 1885–1943
	Ottoman Empire, 1300–1922
Poem without a Hero (1943), Anna Akhmatova	Soviet Empire, 1922–1991
Poetry and Truth (1811–33), Johann Wolfgang von Goethe	First Napoleonic Empire, 1804–1815
"The Poet's Pilgrimage to Waterloo" (1816), Robert Southey	First Napoleonic Empire, 1804–1815
Point of View (1997), Nayantara Sahgal	British Empire, 1583–
"Poison" (1953), Roald Dahl	British Empire, 1583–
The Poisonwood Bible (1998), Barbara Kingsolver	Belgian Empire, 1877–1962
Politica (ca. 335 B.C.), Aristotle	Macedonian Empire, 338–309 B.C.
Political Imprisonment in Cuba (1871), José Martí	Spanish Empire, 1492–1975
Poltava (1828), Aleksandr Pushkin	Russian Empire, 1547–1917
	Swedish Empire, 1638–1663, 1785–1878
Poor Folk (1846), Fyodor Dostoyevsky	Russian Empire, 1547–1917
Poor Henry (1195), Hartmann von Aue	Crusades, 1096–1221
Popol Vuh (1558), anonymous	Mayan Empire, 1500 B.C.–A.D. 1523
A Portrait of the Artist as a Young Man (1916), James Joyce	British Empire, 1583–
The Possessed (1872), Fyodor Dostoyevsky	Russian Empire, 1547–1917
"Prayer" (ca. 1425 B.C.), Kantuzzili	Hittite Empire, 1460–1180 B.C.

Prayer Book (ca. 940), Saadiah ben-Joseph	Abbasid Empire, 750–1258
"Prayer for Gassuliyawiya" (ca. 1295 B.C.), Mursili II	Hittite Empire, 1460–1180 B.C.
"Prayer to Lelwani" (ca. 1295 B.C.), Mursili II	Hittite Empire, 1460–1180 B.C.
The Prince (1514), Niccolò Machiavelli	Athenian Empire, 477–431 B.C.
	Florentine Empire, 1406–1494, 1509
	French Empire, 1499–1513, 1605–
	Greek Colonies, 825–400 B.C.
	Greco-Ptolemaic Empire, 332–30 B.C.
	Holy Roman Empire, 962–1806
	Ottoman Empire, 1300–1922
	Papal Empire, 752–1798
	Roman Empire, 27 B.C.–A.D. 476
	Spartan Empire, 404–371 B.C.
	Venetian Empire, 800–1797
"Prince Karu's Retreat to Remember His Father" (ca. 700) Kakinomoto no Hitomaro	Nara Period, 710–794
"The Princess and the Pea" (1835), Hans Christian Andersen	Danish-Norwegian Empire, 1200–1979
A Princess Remembers (1976), Santha Rama Rau	British Empire, 1583–
Princess Toto (1876), W. S. Gilbert	British Empire, 1583–
Prison and Chocolate Cake (1954), Nayantara Sahgal	British Empire, 1583–
"A Prisoner in the Caucasus" (1872), Leo Tolstoy	Ottoman Empire, 1300–1922
	Russian Empire, 1547–1917
Prisons We Choose to Live Inside (1987), Doris Lessing	British Empire, 1583–
Progymnasmata (ca. 1175), Nikephoros Basilakis	Early Russian Principalities, 1168–1362
Prologue: A Dream within a Dream (1942), Anna Akhmatova	Soviet Empire, 1922–1991
Promenade (1938), G. B. Lancaster	British Empire, 1583–
The Promised Land (1912), Mary Antin	Russian Empire, 1547–1917
Prose Edda (1225), Snorri Sturluson	Viking Conquests, 775–1100
Proverbs (ca. 670 B.C.), Ahiqar	Assyrian Empire, 900–612 B.C.
Proverbs (ca. 270 B.C.), Callimachus	Greco-Ptolemaic Empire, 332–30 B.C.
Proverbs (ca. 180 B.C.), Solomon, et al.	Israelite Empire, 1050–920 B.C.
The Proverbs of Alfred (ca. 1251), Alfred the Great	Viking Conquests, 775–1100
Psalms (ca. 900 B.C.), David, et al.	Israelite Empire, 1050–920 B.C.
Pseudo-Daniel (200 B.C.), anonymous	Achaemenid-Persian Empire, 550–330 B.C.
"The Pumpkinification of the Divine Claudius" (A.D. 54), Seneca	Roman Empire, 27 B.C.–A.D. 476
Puppet Plays (1774), Johann Wolfgang von Goethe	Holy Roman Empire, 962–1806
The Queen's Songbook (1973), Liliuokalani	Hawaiian Kingdom, 1810–1893
Quest for the Holy Grail (ca. 1400), anonymous	Portuguese Empire, 1415–1999
"A Question by a Poor Villager" (ca. 732), Yamanoue no Okura	Nara Period, 710–794
A Question of Power (1973), Bessie Head	British Empire, 1583–
The Quiet American (1955), Graham Greene	American Empire, 1898–
	French Empire, 1499–1513, 1605–
Ramakien (1797), Rama I	Siamese Empire, 1350–1909
Rama Thagyin (1775), U Aung Phyo	Konbaung Dynasty, 1752–1885

Ramayana (ca. 400 B.C.), anonymous	Indo-Gangetic Empire, 1200–300 B.C.
The Rape of Shavi (1985), Buchi Emecheta	British Empire, 1583–
Reamker (ca. 1550), anonymous	Khmer Empire, 802–1462
"Recessional" (1897), Rudyard Kipling	British Empire, 1583–
Recollections of Tartar Steppes and Their Inhabitants (1863), Lucy Sherrand Finley Atkinson	Russian Empire, 1547–1917
Red Ribbon on a White Horse: My Story (1950), Anzia Yezierska	Russian Empire, 1547–1917
Refutation of the Christians (ca. 825), al-Jahiz	Islamic Empire, 632–1258
"The Reigate Puzzle" (1894), Sir Arthur Conan Doyle	British Empire, 1583–
"A Reply by a Man in Destitute Poverty" (ca. 732), Yamanoue no Okura	Nara Period, 710–794
The Reply to Sister Filotea of the Cross (1691), Sor Juana de la Cruz	Spanish Empire, 1492–1975
Requiem (1940), Anna Akhmatova	Soviet Empire, 1922–1991
The Restoration of Korean Buddhism (1910), Han Yong-un	Japanese Empire, 1871–1945
	Joseon Dynasty, 1892–1910
Return to the Future (1942), Sigrid Undset	Danish-Norwegian Empire, 1200–1979
	Nazi Empire, 1933–1945
	Soviet Empire, 1922–1991
Revelation (A.D. 95), John the Divine	Roman Empire, 27 B.C.–A.D. 476
Reynard the Fox (1794), Johann Wolfgang von Goethe	Holy Roman Empire, 962–1806
Reynard the Fox (1834), Jacob and Wilhelm Grimm	First Napoleonic Empire, 1804–1815
"The Rich Man and the Poor Man's Lamb" (ca. 950 B.C.), Nathan	Israelite Empire, 1050–920 B.C.
Rig Veda (ca. 1200 B.C.), anonymous	Harappan Empire, 2600–1300 B.C.
Roderick, Last of the Goths (1814), Robert Southey	First Napoleonic Empire, 1804–1815
Roland and Vernagu (ca. 1325), anonymous	Frankish Empire, A.D. 509–843
The Romance of the Harem (1872), Anna Leonowens	Siamese Empire, 1350–1909
The Rose Garden (1258), Saadi	Turco-Persian Empire, 1037–1307
Roughing It in the Bush (1852), Susanna Strickland Moodie	British Empire, 1583–
Royal Commentaries of the Incas and General History of Peru (1617), Garcilaso de la Vega	Holy Roman Empire, 962–1806
	Incan Empire, 1438–1533
	Spanish Empire, 1492–1975
Rubáiyát (ca. 1130), Omar Khayyám	Turco-Persian Empire, 1037–1307
Rudin (1855), Ivan Turgenev	Russian Empire, 1547–1917
Russia: Its People and Its Literature (1887), Emilia Pardo Bazán	Soviet Empire, 1922–1991
"Russian Tanks in Prague" (1968), Yevgeny Yevtushenko	Soviet Empire, 1922–1991
Ruth (ca. 900 B.C.), anonymous	Assyrian Empire, 900–612 B.C.
Sab (1841), Gertrudis Gómez de Avellaneda	Spanish Empire, 1492–1975
Sacred History (A.D. 400), Sulpicius Severus	Roman Empire, 27 B.C.–A.D. 476
Sadhana: The Realisation of Life (1913), Rabindranath Tagore	British Empire, 1583–
Sajo and the Beaver People (1935), Grey Owl	British Empire, 1583–
Saktisamagama Tantra (ca. 1000), anonymous	Pala Empire, 750–1174
Salathiel (1828), George Croly	Roman Empire, 27 B.C.–A.D. 476
Salomé (1893), Oscar Wilde	Roman Empire, 27 B.C.–A.D. 476

"A Study in Scarlet" (1887), Sir Arthur Conan Doyle — British Empire, 1583–

Sublime Malady (1925), Boris Pasternak — Soviet Empire, 1922–1991

"Such, Such Were the Joys" (1949), George Orwell — British Empire, 1583–

The Sultan of Babylon (ca. 1250), anonymous — Frankish Empire, 509–843

Sultan to Sultan: Adventures among the Masai and Other Tribes of East Africa (1892), May French Sheldon — British Empire, 1583–

Belgian Empire, 1877–1962

Sundiata: An Epic of Old Mali (ca. 1255), anonymous — Malian Empire, 1200–1500

Superiority of Blacks to Whites (ca. 825), al-Jahiz — Aksumite Empire, 100 B.C.–A.D. 1000

Islamic Empire, 632–1258

Sutras (800–350 B.C.), anonymous — Indo-Gangetic Empire, 1200–300 B.C.

The Tale of Genji (1008), Murasaki Shikibu — Heian Period, 794–1185

The Tale of Ralph the Collier (ca. 1475), anonymous — Frankish Empire, 509–843

A Tale of Two Cities (1859), Charles Dickens — British Empire, 1583–

The Tales of Amadou Koumba (1947), Birago Diop — French Empire, 1499–1513, 1605–

Nazi Empire, 1933–1945

Tales of an Empty Cabin (1936), Grey Owl — British Empire, 1583–

Tales of Fashionable Life (1809), Maria Edgeworth — British Empire, 1583–

"The Tamarisk and the Palm" (ca. 2300 B.C.), anonymous — Akkadian-Sumerian Empire, 2350–2150 B.C.

Taras Bulba (1842), Nikolay Gogol — Jagiellon Dynasty, 1377–1572

Russian Empire, 1547–1917

Tecumseh (1886), Charles Mair — British Empire, 1583–

A Tempest (1969), Aimé Césaire — British Empire, 1583–

Oyo Empire, 1400–1835

The Tempest (ca. 1610–11), William Shakespeare — British Empire, 1583–

Holy Roman Empire, 962–1806

Spanish Empire, 1492–1975

Ten Days That Shook the World (1919), John Reed — Russian Empire, 1547–1917

Soviet Empire, 1922–1991

Ten Years' Exile (1820), Anne-Louise-Germaine de Staël — First Napoleonic Empire, 1804–1815

Themes and Variations (1923), Boris Pasternak — Soviet Empire, 1922–1991

They Who Knock at Our Gates (1914), Mary Antin — Russian Empire, 1547–1917

Things Fall Apart (1958), Chinua Achebe — British Empire, 1583–

"Thinking of Children" (ca. 733), Yamanoue no Okura — Nara Period, 710–794

"Those Who Are Dead Are Never Gone" (1985), Birago Diop — French Empire, 1499–1513, 1605–

"Those Who Struck Him Once" (1939), Rabindranath Tagore — Nazi Empire, 1933–1945

Thoughts on South Africa (1923), Olive Schreiner — British Empire, 1583–

Dutch Empire, 1620–

The Thousand and One Nights (ca. A.D. 942), anonymous — Abbasid Empire, 750–1258

A Thousand Pieces of Gold (2002), Adeline Yen Mah — Chinese Empire, 221 B.C.–

Japanese Empire, 1871–1945

Through Algeria (1863), Mabel Sharman Crawford — French Empire, 1499–1513, 1605–

"Thunder-Storm in August" (ca. 1876), William Kirby — British Empire, 1583–

Thus Spoke Zarathustra (1883–85), Friedrich Nietzsche — Austro-Hungarian Empire, 1867–1918

German Empire, 1871–1918

Tibetan Book of the Dead (ca. A.D. 775), Padmasambhava — Tibetan Empire, 127 B.C.–A.D. 842

Titus Alone (1959), Mervyn Peake	Nazi Empire, 1933–1945
Titus Groan (1946), Mervyn Peake	Nazi Empire, 1933–1945
"To Celebrate Myself" (1897), Rainer Maria Rilke	Austro-Hungarian Empire, 1867–1918
"To His Friend Departing for Shuh" (ca. A.D. 745), Li Bo	Tang Dynasty, 618–907
"To My Mother Helvia" (A.D. 42), Seneca	Roman Empire, 27 B.C.–A.D. 476
"To Nations" (ca. A.D. 200), Tertullian	Roman Empire, 27 B.C.–A.D. 476
"To Polybius on Consolation" (A.D. 44), Seneca	Roman Empire, 27 B.C.–A.D. 476
"To Scapula" (A.D. 214), Tertullian	Roman Empire, 27 B.C.–A.D. 476
"To the Martyrs" (A.D. 197), Tertullian	Roman Empire, 27 B.C.–A.D. 476
A Town Like Alice (1950), Nevil Shute	British Empire, 1583–
	Dutch Empire, 1620–
	Japanese Empire, 1871–1945
"To Zaragoza" (1867), Onofre Cárdenas	Mexican Empire, 1822–1823, 1864–1867
The Tracks We Tread (1907), G. B. Lancaster	British Empire, 1583–
The Tragic History of King Tanjong (1929), Yi Kwangsu	Japanese Empire, 1871–1945
	Joseon Dynasty, 1392–1910
Travels in the Interior Districts of Africa (1799), Mungo Park	British Empire, 1583–
	French Empire, 1499–1513, 1605–
	Fulani Empire, 1790s–1890s
	Malian Empire, 1200–1500
Travels in the Slavonic Provinces of Turkey-in-Europe (1877), Georgina Mary Muir Mackenzie and Adeline Paulina Irby	Ottoman Empire, 1300–1922
Travels in West Africa: Congo Français, Corisco and Cameroons (1897), Mary Kingsley	French Empire, 1499–1513, 1605–
Travels of Marco Polo (1298), Marco Polo	Abyssinian Empire, 1270–1974
	Bagan Empire, 849–1287
	Islamic Empire, 632–1258
	Majapahitan Empire, 1200–1500
	Mamluk Dynasty, 1260–1517
	Mongolian Empire, 1206–1405
	Papal Empire, 752–1798
	Song Dynasty, 960–1279
	Turco-Persian Empire, 1037–1307
	Venetian Empire, 800–1797
	Yuan Dynasty, 1279–1368
Treasure Island (1883), Robert Louis Stevenson	British Empire, 1583–
	Spanish Empire, 1492–1975
The Trial (1925), Franz Kafka	Austro-Hungarian Empire, 1867–1918
"The Trial of Jomo Kenyatta" (1976), Santha Rama Rau	British Empire, 1583–
The Triumph of Death (1894), Gabriele D'Annunzio	Italian Empire, 1885–1943
The Trojan Women (415 B.C.), Euripides	Athenian Empire, 477–431 B.C., 415–403 B.C.
Trooper Peter Halket of Mashonaland (1897), Olive Schreiner	British Empire, 1583–
The Trouble with Nigeria (1998), Chinua Achebe	British Empire, 1583–
The Truce (1963), Primo Levi	Italian Empire, 1885–1943
	Nazi Empire, 1933–1945
"The Truce of the Bear" (1898), Rudyard Kipling	British Empire, 1583–
	Russian Empire, 1547–1917

True Country (1993), Kim Scott	British Empire, 1583–
A *True Declaration of the Estate of the Colonie in Virginia* (1610), anonymous	British Empire, 1583–
The True History of the Conquest of New Spain (1568), Bernal Díaz	Spanish Empire, 1492–1975
True History of the Kelly Gang (2000), Peter Carey	British Empire, 1583–
Tun-huang manuscripts (ca. 787), Fa-hai	Tang Dynasty, 618–907
Two Voyages to the Sierra Leone During the Years 1791–1792–1793 (1794), Anna Maria Falconbridge	British Empire, 1583–
Ulysses (1922), James Joyce	British Empire, 1583–
Unbeaten Tracks in Japan (1880), Isabella Lucy Bird	Japanese Empire, 1871–1945
Under My Skin (1994), Doris Lessing	British Empire, 1583–
Under Western Eyes (1911), Joseph Conrad	Russian Empire, 1547–1917
A *Universal History of Infamy* (1935), Jorge Luis Borges	Chinese Empire, 221 B.C.– Umayyad Empire, 660–750 Nara Period, 710–794
Upanishads (1000–600 B.C.), anonymous	Indo-Gangetic Empire, 1200–300 B.C.
"Upon Excusing Himself from a Banquet" (ca. 733), Yamanoue no Okura	Nara Period, 710–794
The Upstairs Room (1990), Johanna Reiss	Nazi Empire, 1933–1945
The Urewera Notebook (1933), Katherine Mansfield	British Empire, 1583–
Utopia, Limited (1893), W. S. Gilbert	British Empire, 1583–
Vanity Fair (1848), William Makepeace Thackeray	British Empire, 1583–
Vathek, an Arabian Tale (1782), William Beckford	First Napoleonic Empire, 1804–1815
"The Vendetta" (1850), Honoré de Balzac	Turco-Persian Empire, 1037–1307
"Victims" (1945), Mervyn Peake	First Napoleonic Empire, 1804–1815
"A View of the Formation of Little Russia" (1835), Nikolay Gogol	Nazi Empire, 1933–1945 Hunnic Empire, 370–469
Virgin Soil (1877), Ivan Turgenev	Russian Empire, 1547–1917
A *Voice for Freedom* (1977), Nayantara Sahgal	British Empire, 1583–
Voices in the City (1965), Anita Desai	British Empire, 1583–
Voyage of the Eyes (1348), al-Umari	Malian Empire, 1200–1500
Wacousta (1832), John Richardson	British Empire, 1583–
Waiting for the Barbarians (1980), J. M. Coetzee	British Empire, 1583–
Walking in the Shade (1997), Doris Lessing	British Empire, 1583–
The Wall (1950), John Hersey	Nazi Empire, 1933–1945
"Waltzing Matilda" (1895), A. B. Paterson	British Empire, 1583–
War and Peace (1869), Leo Tolstoy	First Napoleonic Empire, 1804–1815 Russian Empire, 1547–1917
The War in South Africa (1902), Sir Arthur Conan Doyle	British Empire, 1583–
War the Only Hygiene of the World (1915), Filippo Tommaso Marinetti	Italian Empire, 1885–1943
Wartime Writings (1938–44), Antoine de Saint-Exupéry	French Empire, 1499–1513, 1605– Nazi Empire, 1933–1945
The Waste Land (1922), T. S. Eliot	British Empire, 1583–

Watching the Tree (2000), Adeline Yen Mah

Ways of Escape (1980), Graham Greene
"We Live in a Rickety House" (1900),
  Alexander MacLachlan
West with the Night (1942), Beryl Markham
"What Value to Me the Seven Kinds of Treasures" (ca. 733),
  Yamanoue no Okura
"What We Must Accept" (ca. 733), Yamanoue no Okura
When My Name Was Keoko (2002), Linda Sue Park
When Rain Clouds Gather (1969), Bessie Head
"While the Billy Boils" (ca. 1885), Henry Lawson
White Flock (1917), Anna Akhmatova
"The White Man's Burden" (1899), Rudyard Kipling
The White Roots of Peace (1946), Paul A. W. Wallace

The White Wampum (1895), Pauline Johnson
"Why I Write" (1946), George Orwell
"Why Noah Chose the Dove" (1974), Isaac Bashevis Singer

Wide Sargasso Sea (1966), Jean Rhys
The Wife (1921), Sigrid Undset
"The Wild Colonial Boy" (1830), anonymous
Willehalm (ca. 1217), Wolfram von Eschenbach
Wind, Sand, and Stars (1939), Antoine de Saint-Exupéry

Winds (1946), Saint-John Perse

Winds of War (1946), Anna Akhmatova
Windward Heights (1995), Maryse Condé
Winter Studies and Summer Rambles in Canada (1838),
  Anna Jameson
Wisdom of Solomon (ca. 150 B.C.), anonymous
"Wishing Godspeed to the Ambassador to China" (ca. 733),
  Yamanoue no Okura
With His Pistol in His Hand (1958), Américo Paredes
"The Wolf and the Shepherd" (ca. 336 B.C.),
  Demosthenes of Athens
A Woman Alone (1990), Bessie Head
A Woman as Great as the World and Other Fables (1953),
  Jacquetta Hopkins Hawkes
The Woman Warrior (1975), Maxine Hong Kingston

Wonderful Adventures of Mrs. Seacole in Many Lands (1857),
  Mary Jane Seacole

Chinese Empire, 221 B.C.–
Japanese Empire, 1871–1945
British Empire, 1583–
British Empire, 1583–

British Empire, 1583–
Nara Period, 710–794

Nara Period, 710–794
Japanese Empire, 1871–1945
British Empire, 1583–
British Empire, 1583–
Russian Empire, 1547–1917
American Empire, 1898–
American Empire, 1898–
British Empire, 1583–
Iroquois Confederacy, 1150–
British Empire, 1583–
British Empire, 1583–
Nazi Empire, 1933–1945
Soviet Empire, 1922–1991
British Empire, 1583–
Danish-Norwegian Empire, 1200–1979
British Empire, 1583–
Crusades, 1096–1221
French Empire, 1499–1513, 1605–
Nazi Empire, 1933–1945
French Empire, 1499–1513, 1605–
Nazi Empire, 1933–1945
Soviet Empire, 1922–1991
French Empire, 1499–1513, 1605–
British Empire, 1583–

Greco-Ptolemaic Empire, 332–30 B.C.
Nara Period, 710–794

Mexican Empire, 1822–1823, 1864–1867
Macedonian Empire, 338–309 B.C.

British Empire, 1583–
Soviet Empire, 1922–1991

Chinese Empire, 221 B.C.–
Japanese Empire, 1871–1945
British Empire, 1583–
Colombian Empire 1830–1903
Russian Empire, 1547–1917

The Wonderful Adventures of Nils (1906–07), Selma Lagerlöf — Swedish Union, 1814–1905
Works and Days (ca. 700 B.C.), Hesiod — Greek Colonies, 825–400 B.C.
The World Is Yours (1934), G. B. Lancaster — British Empire, 1583–
World Travels (ca. 500 B.C.), Hecataeus of Miletus — Achaemenid-Persian Empire, 550–330 B.C.
Yajur Veda (1000–600 B.C.), anonymous — Indo-Gangetic Empire, 1200–300 B.C.
The Yangtze Valley and Beyond (1899), Isabella Lucy Bird — Qing Dynasty, 1644–1912
The Year 1905 (1927), Boris Pasternak — Soviet Empire, 1922–1991
Yi Sun-sin (1932), Yi Kwangsu — Japanese Empire, 1871–1945
— Joseon Dynasty, 1392–1910
Yogacara Bhumi Sutra (A.D. 284), anonymous — Guptan Empire, 280–550
Yvain, the Knight of the Lion (ca. 1177), Chrétien de Troyes — Crusades, 1096–1221
Zang Tumb Tumb (1914), Filippo Tommaso Marinetti — Italian Empire, 1885–1943
— Ottoman Empire, 1300–1922
El Zarco (1901), Ignacio Manuel Altamirano — Mexican Empire, 1822–1823, 1864–1867
Zhou Yi (Chou I) (1144 B.C.), Wen Wang — Zhou (Chou) Dynasty, 1122–256 B.C.
Zima Junction (1956), Yevgeny Yevtushenko — Soviet Empire, 1922–1991

II. MAJOR AUTHORS OF THE LITERATURE OF EMPIRE AND THEIR WORKS

Abu Bakr
    "Strike on This Spot" (A.D. 630)   Islamic Empire, 622–1258
Abu Tammam
    Hamasa (ca. 845)   Abbasid Empire, 750–1258
Achebe, Chinua
    Anthills of the Savannah (1988)   British Empire, 1583–
    Arrow of God (1964)   British Empire, 1583–
    Beware, Soul Brother (1971)   British Empire, 1583–
    "Civil Peace" (1971)   British Empire, 1583–
    Home and Exile (2000)   British Empire, 1583–
    "An Image of Africa: Racism in Conrad's 'Heart
        of Darkness'" (1975)   British Empire, 1583–
    A Man of the People (1966)   British Empire, 1583–
    No Longer at Ease (1960)   British Empire, 1583–
    Things Fall Apart (1958)   British Empire, 1583–
    The Trouble with Nigeria (1998)   British Empire, 1583–
Aelian, Claudius
    "On the Nature of Animals" (ca. A.D. 230)   Roman Empire, 27 B.C.–A.D. 476
Aeschylus
    Myrmidons (ca. 470 B.C.)   Athenian Empire, 477–431 B.C., 415–403 B.C.
    Oresteia (458 B.C.)   Athenian Empire, 477–431 B.C., 415–403 B.C.
    Persae (472 B.C.)   Athenian Empire, 477–431 B.C., 415–403 B.C.
Aesop
    Fables (ca. 550 B.C.)   Greek Colonies, 825–400 B.C.
Ahiqar
    Proverbs (ca. 670 B.C.)   Assyrian Empire, 900–612 B.C.
Ahmed-i Hani
    Mem-u Zin (1692)   Ottoman Empire, 1300–1922
                               Safavid Empire, 1501–1722
Aidoo, Ama Ata
    Anowa (1970)   Ashanti Empire, 1670–1957
                               British Empire, 1583–
    Changes: A Love Story (1991)   British Empire, 1583–

Maccabees (ca. 125 B.C.)	Seleucid Empire, 323–60 B.C.
Mahanirvana Tantra (1295)	Pala Empire, 750–1174
Mexican Songs (ca. 1590)	Aztec Empire, 1375–1521
"Nisaba and Wheat" (ca. 1900 B.C.)	Babylonian Empire, 1900–1600 B.C.
1 Samuel (ca. 920 B.C.)	Israelite Empire, 1050–920 B.C.
Otuel (ca. 1325)	Frankish Empire, 509–843
The Pilgrimage of Charlemagne (ca. 1140)	Frankish Empire, 509–843
Popol Vuh (1558)	Mayan Empire, 1500 B.C.–A.D. 1523
Pseudo-Daniel (200 B.C.)	Achaemenid-Persian Empire, 550–330 B.C.
Quest for the Holy Grail (ca. 1400)	Portuguese Empire, 1415–1999
Ramayana (ca. 400 B.C.)	Indo-Gangetic Empire, 1200–300 B.C.
Reamker (ca. 1550)	Khmer Empire, 802–1462
Rig Veda (ca. 1200 B.C.)	Harappan Empire, 2600–1300 B.C.
Roland and Vernagu (ca. 1325)	Frankish Empire, 509–843
Ruth (ca. 900 B.C.)	Assyrian Empire, 900–612 B.C.
Saktisamagama Tantra (ca. 1000)	Pala Empire, 750–1174
Sama Veda (1000 B.C.)	Indo-Gangetic Empire, 1200–300 B.C.
Seventy Tales of a Parrot (ca. 1100)	Srivijayan Empire, 600–1200
Sharada Tilaka Tantra (ca. 1000)	Pala Empire, 750–1174
The Siege of Milan (ca. 1350)	Frankish Empire, 509–843
Sir Ferumbras (ca. 1375)	Frankish Empire, 509–843
Song of Jerusalem (ca. 1150)	Latin Empire, 1204–1261
Song of Roland (ca. 1080)	Abbasid Empire, 750–1258
Song of the Captives (ca. 1150)	Latin Empire, 1204–1261
The Sultan of Babylon (ca. 1250)	Frankish Empire, 509–843
Sundiata: An Epic of Old Mali (ca. 1255)	Malian Empire, 1200–1500
Sutras (800–350 B.C.)	Indo-Gangetic Empire, 1200–300 B.C.
The Tale of Ralph the Collier (ca. 1475)	Frankish Empire, 509–843
"The Tamarisk and the Palm" (ca. 2300 B.C.)	Akkadian-Sumerian Empire, 2350–2150 B.C.
The Thousand and One Nights (ca. A.D. 942)	Abbasid Empire, 750–1258
A True Declaration of the Estate of the Colonie in Virginia (1610)	British Empire, 1583–
Upanishads (1000–600 B.C.)	Indo-Gangetic Empire, 1200–300 B.C.
"The Wild Colonial Boy" (1830)	British Empire, 1583–
Wisdom of Solomon (ca. 150 B.C.)	Greco-Ptolemaic Empire, 332–30 B.C.
Yajur Veda (1000–600 B.C.)	Indo-Gangetic Empire, 1200–300 B.C.
Yogacara Bhumi Sutra (A.D. 284)	Guptan Empire, 280–550

Antin, Mary

The Promised Land (1912)	Russian Empire, 1547–1917
They Who Knock at Our Gates (1914)	Russian Empire, 1547–1917

Apion

Aegyptiaca (ca. A.D. 40)	Roman Empire, 27 B.C.–A.D. 476
Androcles and the Lion (ca. A.D. 40)	Roman Empire, 27 B.C.–A.D. 476

Apuleius

The Golden Ass (A.D. 158)	Roman Empire, 27 B.C.–A.D. 476

Archilochus

"The Fox and Hedgehog" (650 B.C.)	Greek Colonies, 825–400 B.C.

Aristides, Aelius	
Fables (ca. 150 B.C.)	Roman Empire, 27 B.C.–A.D. 476
Aristophanes	
The Acharnians (425 B.C.)	Athenian Empire, 477–431 B.C., 415–403 B.C.
The Birds (414 B.C.)	Athenian Empire, 477–431 B.C., 415–403 B.C.
The Knights (424 B.C.)	Athenian Empire, 477–431 B.C., 415–403 B.C.
Lysistrata (411 B.C.)	Athenian Empire, 477–431 B.C., 415–403 B.C.
Peace (421 B.C.)	Athenian Empire, 477–431 B.C., 415–403 B.C.
Aristotle	
Meteorologica (ca. 335 B.C.)	Macedonian Empire, 338–309 B.C.
Politica (ca. 335 B.C.)	Macedonian Empire, 338–309 B.C.
Arjan Dev	
Granth (1604)	Mughal Empire, 1526–1857
Arnold, Matthew	
Sohrab and Rustum (1853)	Ghaznavid Empire, 975–1187
Aryasura	
Garland of Birth Stories (ca. A.D. 350)	Guptan Empire, 280–550
Asanga	
Guhyasamaja Tantra (A.D. 350)	Guptan Empire, 280–550
Ashvaghosa	
The Life of the Buddha (ca. A.D. 100)	Kushan Empire, A.D. 60–375
Asser, Bishop	
Life of Alfred (893)	Viking Conquests, 775–1100
Atkinson, Lucy Sherrand Finley	
Recollections of Tartar Steppes and Their Inhabitants (1863)	Russian Empire, 1547–1917
Augustine	
The City of God against the Pagans (A.D. 426)	Roman Empire, 27 B.C.–A.D. 476
Confessions (A.D. 398)	Roman Empire, 27 B.C.–A.D. 476
Aulus Gellius	
Attic Nights (ca. a.d. 180)	Roman Empire, 27 b.c.–a.d. 476
Austen, Jane	
Persuasion (1817)	British Empire, 1583–
Avianus, Flavius	
Fables (A.D. 400)	Roman Empire, 27 B.C.–A.D. 476
Bâ, Mariama	
Scarlet Song (1981)	French Empire, 1499–1513, 1605–
So Long a Letter (1979)	French Empire, 1499–1513, 1605–
Babrius, Valerius	
Fables (A.D. 235)	Roman Empire, 27 B.C.–A.D. 476
Baillie, Joanna	
Ahalya Baee (1849)	British Empire, 1583–
Metrical Legends of Exalted Characters (1821)	Spanish Empire, 1492–1975
Baker, Florence	
Morning Star: Florence Baker's Diary of the Expedition to Put Down the Slave Trade on the Nile, 1870–1873	British Empire, 1583–

Balzac, Honoré de
    "The Napoleon of the People" (1833)   First Napoleonic Empire, 1804–1815
    "Passion in the Desert" (1850)   First Napoleonic Empire, 1804–1815
    "A Shadowy Affair" (1850)   First Napoleonic Empire, 1804–1815
    "The Vendetta" (1850)   First Napoleonic Empire, 1804–1815
Baring-Gould, Sabine
    "Onward, Christian Soldiers" (1864)   British Empire, 1583–
Barnard, Lady Anne
    South Africa a Century Ago: Letters Written
        from the Cape of Good Hope (1797–1801)   Dutch Empire, 1620–
Basilakis, Nikephoros
    Progymnasmata (ca. 1175)   Early Russian Principalities, 1168–1362
Bates, Daisy
    The Passing of the Aborigines (1938)   British Empire, 1583–
Baylis, Samuel Mathewson
    "The Coureur-de-Bois" (1919)   British Empire, 1583–
Beaufort, Emily Anne
    Egyptian Sepulchres and Syrian Shrines (1861)   Ottoman Empire, 1300–1922
Beckford, William
    Vathek, an Arabian Tale (1782)   Turco-Persian Empire, 1037–1307
Behn, Aphra
    Abdelazar; or, The Moor's Revenge (1671)   Spanish Empire, 1492–1975
    Oroonoko, or The Royal Slave (1688)   British Empire, 1583–
                                 Dutch Empire, 1620–
Bell, Gertrude Lowthian
    The Desert and the Sown (1907)   Ottoman Empire, 1300–1922
Berryhill, Elizabeth
    The Cup of Trembling (1962)   Nazi Empire, 1933–1945
Bird, Isabella Lucy
    Among the Tibetans (1894)   Qing Dynasty, 1644–1912
    Journeys in Persia and Kurdistan (1891)   Ottoman Empire, 1300–1922
    Korea and Her Neighbours (1898)   Joseon Dynasty, 1392–1910
                                 Russian Empire, 1547–1917
    Unbeaten Tracks in Japan (1880)   Japanese Empire, 1871–1945
    The Yangtze Valley and Beyond (1899)   ´Qing Dynasty, 1644–1912
Bly, Nellie
    Nellie Bly's Book: Around the World in 72 Days (1890)   British Empire, 1583–
                                  Japanese Empire, 1871–1945
                                  Ottoman Empire, 1300–1922
    Six Months in Mexico (1888)   Mexican Empire, 1822–1823, 1864–1867
Bodart, Anne
    The Blue Dog and Other Fables for the French (1956)   Belgian Empire, 1877–1962
Bodhidharma
    koans (520)   Guptan Empire, 280–550
Bonhoeffer, Dietrich
    The Cost of Discipleship (1937)   Nazi Empire, 1933–1945

Creation and Fall (1933)	Nazi Empire, 1933–1945
Life Together (1939)	Nazi Empire, 1933–1945
Borges, Jorge Luis	
A Universal History of Infamy (1935)	Chinese Empire, 221 B.C.–
	Umayyad Empire, 660–750
	Nara Period, 710–794
Boulle, Pierre	
The Bridge over the River Kwai (1952)	British Empire, 1583–
	Japanese Empire, 1871–1945
Brassey, Anne	
The Last Voyage (1889)	British Empire, 1583–
Brodsky, Joseph	
"Infinitive" (1996)	Soviet Empire, 1922–1991
Less Than One (1986)	Soviet Empire, 1922–1991
"Lullaby of Cape Cod" (1975)	Soviet Empire, 1922–1991
On Grief and Reason (1995)	Soviet Empire, 1922–1991
"On the Death of Zhukov" (1974)	Soviet Empire, 1922–1991
So Forth (1996)	Soviet Empire, 1922–1991
Brontë, Charlotte	
Jane Eyre (1847)	British Empire, 1583–
Brown, Dan	
The Da Vinci Code (2003)	Crusades, 1096–1221
Bryant, Louise	
"How the Revolution Began in America" (1919)	Austro-Hungarian Empire, 1867–1918
	Russian Empire, 1547–1917
Buck, Pearl S.	
China Sky (1941)	Japanese Empire, 1871–1945
	Qing Dynasty, 1644–1912
The Good Earth (1931)	Qing Dynasty, 1644–1912
A House Divided (1935)	Qing Dynasty, 1644–1912
Imperial Woman (1956)	Qing Dynasty, 1644–1912
The Living Reed (1963)	Japanese Empire, 1871–1945
	Joseon Dynasty, 1392–1910
The Mother (1934)	Qing Dynasty, 1644–1912
Sons (1932)	Qing Dynasty, 1644–1912
Burzoe	
Kalilah and Dimnah (A.D. 570)	Sassanid Empire, A.D. 226–651
Byron, George Gordon Byron, Lord	
Childe Harold's Pilgrimage (1818)	British Empire, 1583–
	Ottoman Empire, 1300–1922
	Russian Empire, 1547–1917
"The Destruction of Sennacherib" (1815)	Assyrian Empire, 900–612 B.C.
Don Juan (1824)	Ottoman Empire, 1300–1922
"The Eve of Waterloo" (1818)	First Napoleonic Empire, 1804–1815
The Giaour (1813)	Ottoman Empire, 1300–1922
"Ode to Napoleon Buonaparte" (1814)	First Napoleonic Empire, 1804–1815

Caesar, Gaius Julius *Gallic Wars* (ca. 50 B.C.)	Roman Empire, 27 B.C.–A.D. 476
Callimachus *Proverbs* (ca. 270 B.C.)	Greco-Ptolemaic Empire, 332–30 B.C.
Camões, Luís Vaz de *The Lusiads* (1572)	Portuguese Empire, 1415–1999
Campion, Jane *The Piano* (1993)	British Empire, 1583–
Cao Xueqin *Dream of the Red Chamber* (1791)	Qing Dynasty, 1644–1912
Cárdenas, Onofre "To Zaragoza" (1867)	Mexican Empire, 1822–1823, 1864–1867

Carey, Peter
    Oscar and Lucinda (1988)
    True History of the Kelly Gang (2000)
	British Empire, 1583–
	British Empire, 1583–

Carlyle, Thomas "The Hero as Poet" (1840)	British Empire, 1583–
Cary, Joyce *Mister Johnson* (1939)	British Empire, 1583–
Cavafy, Constantine *Collected Poems* (1992)	Ottoman Empire, 1300–1922
Cervantes, Miguel de *Don Quixote of La Mancha* (1605)	Ottoman Empire, 1300–1922 Spanish Empire, 1492–1975
Césaire, Aimé *A Tempest* (1969)	British Empire, 1583– Oyo Empire, 1400–1835

Chrétien de Troyes
    Cligès (ca. 1176)
    Erec and Enide (ca. 1170)
    Lancelot, or the Knight of the Cart (ca. 1181)
    Perceval, or the Account of the Grail (ca. 1182)
    Yvain, the Knight of the Lion (ca. 1177)
	Crusades, 1096–1221
	Crusades, 1096–1221
	Crusades, 1096–1221
	Crusades, 1096–1221
	Crusades, 1096–1221

Christine de Pisan
    Book of Deeds of Arms and of Chivalry (1410)
 	
    Book of the City of Ladies (ca. 1405)
 	
    Book of the Three Virtues (1406)
 	
    Christine's Vision (1405)
 	
    Hymn to Joan of Arc (1429)
 	
    Letter to the God of Love (1399)
	French Empire, 1499–1513, 1605–
	Venetian Empire, 800–1797
	French Empire, 1499–1513, 1605–
	Venetian Empire, 800–1797
	French Empire, 1499–1513, 1605–
	Venetian Empire, 800–1797
	French Empire, 1499–1513, 1605–
	Venetian Empire, 800–1797
	French Empire, 1499–1513, 1605–
	Venetian Empire, 800–1797
	French Empire, 1499–1513, 1605–
	Venetian Empire, 800–1797

Clarke, Marcus
    His Natural Life (1874) — British Empire, 1583–

Coetzee, J. M.
    Waiting for the Barbarians (1980) — British Empire, 1583–

Coleridge, Samuel Taylor
    "Kubla Khan" (1816) — Mongolian Empire, 1206–1405

Collins, Wilkie
    The Moonstone (1868) — British Empire, 1583–

Condé, Maryse
    I, Tituba, Black Witch of Salem (1986) — British Empire, 1583–
    Segu: The Children of Segu (1984) — Bambara Empire, 1600–1861
    Segu: The Earth in Pieces (1985) — Bambara Empire, 1600–1861
    Windward Heights (1995) — French Empire, 1499–1513, 1605–

Confucius
    Analects of Confucius (ca. 210 B.C.) — Chu Empire, 770–221 B.C.
    The Book of Songs (ca. 480 B.C.) — Chu Empire, 770–221 B.C.

Conrad, Joseph
    Almayer's Folly (1895) — Dutch Empire, 1620–
    Heart of Darkness (1899) — Belgian Empire, 1877
    "The Lagoon" (1897) — British Empire, 1583—1962
    Lord Jim (1900) — British Empire, 1583–
    Nostromo, a Tale of the Seaboard (1904) — Spanish Empire, 1492–1975
    "An Outpost of Progress" (1896) — Belgian Empire, 1877–1962
    Under Western Eyes (1911) — Russian Empire, 1547–1917

Crawford, Mabel Sharman
    Through Algeria (1863) — French Empire, 1499–1513, 1605–

Croly, George
    Salathiel, the Wandering Jew (1828) — Roman Empire, 27 B.C.–A.D. 476

Cruickshank, Alfred Hamilton
    "The Convict Song" (1937) — British Empire, 1583–

Cruz, Sor Juana de la
    The Reply to Sister Filotea of the Cross (1691) — Spanish Empire, 1492–1975

Cumming, Constance
    At Home in Fiji (1881) — British Empire, 1583–

Dahl, Roald
    "Poison" (1953) — British Empire, 1583–

Daniel, et al.
    Daniel (ca. 150 B.C.) — Achaemenid-Persian Empire, 550–330 B.C.

D'Annunzio, Gabriele
    Dreams of the Seasons (1898) — Italian Empire, 1885–1943
    The Flame of Life (1900) — Italian Empire, 1885–1943
    Francesca da Rimini (1901) — Italian Empire, 1885–1943
    La Gioconda (1899) — Italian Empire, 1885–1943
    In Praise of Sky, Sea, Earth, and Heroes (1899) — Italian Empire, 1885–1943; Ottoman Empire, 1300–1922
    More Than Love (1906) — Italian Empire, 1885–1943

Poems on Naval Deeds (1912)	Italian Empire, 1885–1943
	Ottoman Empire, 1300–1922
The Triumph of Death (1894)	Italian Empire, 1885–1943
Dante Alighieri	
Divine Comedy (1308)	Papal Empire, 752–1798
Darwish, Mahmoud	
A State of Siege (2002)	British Empire, 1583–
David, et al.	
"The Last Words of David" (ca. 900 B.C.)	Israelite Empire, 1050–920 B.C.
Psalms (ca. 900 B.C.)	Israelite Empire, 1050–920 B.C.
Dekker, Eduard Douwes	
Love Letters (1861)	Dutch Empire, 1620–
Max Havelaar (1860)	Dutch Empire, 1620–
Demosthenes of Athens	
"The Wolf and the Shepherd" (ca. 336 B.C.)	Macedonian Empire, 338–309 B.C.
Desai, Anita	
Baumgartner's Bombay (1988)	British Empire, 1583–
Cry, the Peacock (1963)	British Empire, 1583–
Fire on the Mountain (1977)	British Empire, 1583–
In Custody (1984)	British Empire, 1583–
Voices in the City (1965)	British Empire, 1583–
Dhanvantari	
Atharva Veda (800 B.C.)	Indo-Gangetic Empire, 1200–300 B.C.
Díaz, Bernal	
The True History of the Conquest of New Spain (1568)	Spanish Empire, 1492–1975
Dickens, Charles	
American Notes (1842)	American Empire, 1898–
David Copperfield (1850)	British Empire, 1583–
Dombey and Son (1848)	British Empire, 1583–
Great Expectations (1861)	British Empire, 1583–
Martin Chuzzlewit (1844)	British Empire, 1583–
The Mystery of Edwin Drood (1870)	British Empire, 1583–
The Pickwick Papers (1837)	British Empire, 1583–
A Tale of Two Cities (1859)	British Empire, 1583–
Dinesen, Isak	
The Angelic Avengers (1944)	German Empire, 1871–1918
Babette's Feast (1959)	Napoleonic Empire, 1852–1870
	Swedish Union, 1814–1905
Daguerreotypes and Other Essays (1984)	Austro-Hungarian Empire, 1867–1918
	British Empire, 1583–
	German Empire, 1871–1918
Out of Africa (1937)	British Empire, 1583–
	German Empire, 1871–1918
Shadows on the Grass (1960)	British Empire, 1583–
Diop, Birago	
Lures and Glimmers (1960)	French Empire, 1499–1513, 1605–

Mother Crocodile (1981)	French Empire, 1499–1513, 1605–
New Tales of Amadou Koumba (1958)	French Empire, 1499–1513, 1605–
Stories and Commentaries (1963)	French Empire, 1499–1513, 1605–
The Tales of Amadou Koumba (1947)	French Empire, 1499–1513, 1605–
	Nazi Empire, 1933–1945
"Those Who Are Dead Are Never Gone" (1985)	French Empire, 1499–1513, 1605–
Dostoyevsky, Fyodor Mikhaylovich	
The Brothers Karamazov (1881)	Russian Empire, 1547–1917
Buried Alive; or, Ten Years of Penal Servitude in Siberia (1881)	Russian Empire, 1547–1917
Crime and Punishment (1866)	Russian Empire, 1547–1917
The House of the Dead (1862)	Russian Empire, 1547–1917
Notes from the Underground (1864)	Russian Empire, 1547–1917
Pages from the Journal of an Author (1864)	Russian Empire, 1547–1917
Poor Folk (1846)	Russian Empire, 1547–1917
The Possessed (1872)	Russian Empire, 1547–1917
Doyle, Sir Arthur Conan	
"The Adventure of the Speckled Band" (1892)	British Empire, 1583–
"The Adventure of the Sussex Vampire" (1924)	British Empire, 1583–
"The Bascombe Valley Mystery" (1891)	British Empire, 1583–
The Crime of the Congo (1909)	Belgian Empire, 1877–1962
"The Dying Detective" (1894)	British Empire, 1583–
"The 'Gloria Scott'" (1894)	British Empire, 1583–
"His Last Bow" (1894)	British Empire, 1583–
The Hound of the Baskervilles (1902)	British Empire, 1583–
The Mystery of Cloomber (1889)	British Empire, 1583–
"The Reigate Puzzle" (1894)	British Empire, 1583–
The Sign of the Four (1890)	British Empire, 1583–
A Study in Scarlet (1887)	British Empire, 1583–
The War in South Africa (1902)	British Empire, 1583–
Du Fu	
"Asking of Wu Lang Again" (ca. A.D. 768)	Tang Dynasty, 618–907
"Chen-Tao Lament" (ca. A.D. 759)	Tang Dynasty, 618–907
"Facing Night" (ca. A.D. 768)	Tang Dynasty, 618–907
Facing Snow" (ca. A.D. 757)	Tang Dynasty, 618–907
"Feng-Hsien Return Chant" (ca. A.D. 755)	Tang Dynasty, 618–907
"Gazing at the Sacred Peak" (ca. A.D. 747)	Tang Dynasty, 618–907
"Moonlit Night" (ca. A.D. 757)	Tang Dynasty, 618–907
"Peng-Ya Song" (ca. A.D. 757)	Tang Dynasty, 618–907
"The Song of the Wagons" (ca. A.D. 750)	Tang Dynasty, 618–907
Dumas, Alexandre (père)	
The Corsican Brothers (1844)	First Napoleonic Empire, 1804–1815
	Ottoman Empire, 1300–1922
The Count of Monte Cristo (1844)	First Napoleonic Empire, 1804–1815
	Ottoman Empire, 1300–1922
The Fencing Master (1840)	Russian Empire, 1547–1917

The Last Cavalier (2005)	First Napoleonic Empire, 1804–1815
	Ottoman Empire, 1300–1922
Napoleon (1855)	Austrian Empire, 1804–1867
	First Napoleonic Empire, 1804–1815
Durán, Diego	
Aubin Codex (1576)	Aztec Empire, 1375–1521
Durao, Santa Rita	
Caramuru (1781)	Brazilian Empire, 1822–1889
Eberhardt, Isabelle	
The Nomad (1988)	French Empire, 1499–1513, 1605–
Edgeworth, Maria	
Castle Rackrent (1800)	British Empire, 1583–
"The Grateful Negro" (1804)	British Empire, 1583–
Tales of Fashionable Life (1809)	British Empire, 1583–
Edgeworth, Maria, and	
Edgeworth, Richard Lovell	
Essay on Irish Bulls (1801)	British Empire, 1583–
Einhard	
The Life of Charlemagne (A.D. 830)	Frankish Empire, 509–843
Eliot, T. S.	
The Waste Land (1922)	British Empire, 1583–
Emecheta, Buchi	
The Bride Price (1976)	British Empire, 1583–
Head above Water (1986)	British Empire, 1583–
In the Ditch (1972)	British Empire, 1583–
The Joys of Motherhood (1979)	British Empire, 1583–
The Rape of Shavi (1985)	British Empire, 1583–
Second-Class Citizen (1974)	British Empire, 1583–
Equiano, Olaudah	
The Interesting Narrative of the Life of Olaudah Equiano (1789)	British Empire, 1583– Oyo Empire, 1400–1835
Eschenbach, Wolfram von	
Parzival (ca. 1210)	Crusades, 1096–1221
Willehalm (ca. 1217)	Crusades, 1096–1221
Euripides	
Andromache (ca. 425 B.C.)	Athenian Empire, 477–431 B.C., 415–403 B.C.
Hecuba (ca. 424 B.C.)	Athenian Empire, 477–431 B.C., 415–403 B.C.
The Trojan Women (415 B.C.)	Athenian Empire, 477–431 B.C., 415–403 B.C.
Fa-hai	
Tun-huang manuscripts (ca. 787)	Chinese Empire, 221 B.C.–
Falconbridge, Anna Maria	
Two Voyages to the Sierra Leone During the Years 1791–1792–1793 (1794)	British Empire, 1583–
Fenton, James	
A History of Tasmania (1883)	British Empire, 1583–

Firdawsi
  Book of Kings (ca. 1010)

Ghaznavid Empire, 975–1187
Sassanid Empire, 226–651 A.D.
Umayyad Empire, 660–750

Florian, Jean-Pierre Claris de
  Fables (1792)

French Empire, 1499–1513, 1605–

Forster, E. M.
  Aspects of a Novel (1927)
  The Hill of Devi (1921)
  A Passage to India (1924)

British Empire, 1583–
British Empire, 1583–
British Empire, 1583–

France, Anatole
  Penguin Island (1908)

French Empire, 1499–1513, 1605–

Frank, Anne
  The Diary of a Young Girl (1947)

Nazi Empire, 1933–1945

Gama, Basílio da
  O Uraguai (1769)

Brazilian Empire, 1822–1889
Papal Empire, 752–1798
Portuguese Empire, 1415–1999
Spanish Empire, 1492–1975

Gandhi, Mohandas
  *An Autobiography, or the Story of My Experiments
    with Truth* (1927–29)

British Empire, 1583–

Garcilaso de la Vega
  The Florida of the Inca (1599)

Holy Roman Empire, 962–1806
Incan Empire, 1438–1533
Spanish Empire, 1492–1975

  *Royal Commentaries of the Incas and General History
    of Peru* (1617)

Holy Roman Empire, 962–1806
Incan Empire, 1438–1533
Spanish Empire, 1492–1975

Ghazali, al-
  The Alchemy of Happiness (1097)
  Deliverance from Error (ca. 1108)
  The Jerusalem Tract (1097)
  The Niche of Lights (ca. 1105)

Turco-Persian Empire, 1037–1307
Turco-Persian Empire, 1037–1307
Turco-Persian Empire, 1037–1307
Turco-Persian Empire, 1037–1307

Gibbon, Edward
  The History of the Decline and Fall of the Roman Empire
    (1776)

Roman Empire, 27 B.C.–A.D. 476

Gilbert, W. S.
  H.M.S. Pinafore (1878)
  The Mikado (1885)

British Empire, 1583–
British Empire, 1583–
Japanese Empire, 1871–1945

  Princess Toto (1876)
  Utopia, Limited (1893)

British Empire, 1583–
British Empire, 1583–

Gobind Singh
  Guru Granth Sahib (1708)

Mughal Empire, 1526–1857

Goethe, Johann Wolfgang von
    Faust (1826, 1831)   First Napoleonic Empire, 1804–1815
    Götz von Berlichingen (1773)   Holy Roman Empire, 962–1806
    Poetry and Truth (1811–33)   Holy Roman Empire, 962–1806
    Puppet Plays (1774)   Holy Roman Empire, 962–1806
    Reynard the Fox (1794)   Holy Roman Empire, 962–1806
    The Sorceror's Apprentice (1797)   Holy Roman Empire, 962–1806
Gogol, Nikolay Vasilyevich
    "Al-Mamun" (1835)   Islamic Empire, 632–1258
    Dead Souls (1842)   Russian Empire, 1547–1917
    The Government Inspector (1836)   Russian Empire, 1547–1917
    "A History of Little Russia" (1835)   Polish-Lithuanian Commonwealth, 1569–1795
    "On the Movement of Nations at the End
       of the Fifth Century" (1835)   Hunnic Empire, 370–469
                                           Roman Empire, 27 B.C.–A.D. 476
    "On the Teaching of World History" (1835)   Hunnic Empire, 370–469
                                           Roman Empire, 27 B.C.–A.D. 476
                                           Papal Empire, 752–1798
    "The Songs of the Ukraine" (1834)   Russian Empire, 1547–1917
    Taras Bulba (1842)   Jagiellon Dynasty, 1377–1572
                                           Russian Empire, 1547–1917
    "A View of the Formation of Little Russia" (1835)   Hunnic Empire, 370–469
Goldman, Emma
    Anarchism and Other Essays (1910)   American Empire, 1898–
                                           German Empire, 1871–1918
                                         Joseon Dynasty, 1392–1910
                                         Russian Empire, 1547–1917
    Living My Life (1931)   Russian Empire, 1547–1917
    My Disillusionment in Russia (1923)   Russian Empire, 1547–1917
    My Further Disillusionment in Russia (1924)   Russian Empire, 1547–1917
Gómez de Avellaneda y Arteaga, Gertrudis
    Sab (1841)   Spanish Empire, 1492–1975
Gordimer, Nadine
    Burger's Daughter (1979)   British Empire, 1583–
    The Conservationist (1974)   British Empire, 1583–
    July's People (1981)   British Empire, 1583–
    The Lying Days (1953)   British Empire, 1583–
    Occasion for Loving (1963)   British Empire, 1583–
    The Pickup (2002)   British Empire, 1583–
Graindor de Douai
    Song of Antioch (ca. 1130)   Crusades, 1096–1221
Graves, Robert
    I, Claudius (1934)   Roman Empire, 27 B.C.–A.D. 476
Greene, Graham
    Brighton Rock (1938)   British Empire, 1583–
    A Burnt-Out Case (1960)   Belgian Empire, 1877–1962

The Heart of the Matter (1948)	British Empire, 1583–
The Human Factor (1978)	British Empire, 1583–
It's a Battlefield (1934)	British Empire, 1583–
Journey without Maps (1936)	British Empire, 1583–
	French Empire, 1499–1513, 1605–
Our Man in Havana (1958)	American Empire, 1898–
The Quiet American (1955)	American Empire, 1898–
	French Empire, 1499–1513, 1605–
Ways of Escape (1980)	British Empire, 1583–
Grey Owl	
The Men of the Last Frontier (1931)	British Empire, 1583–
Pilgrims of the Wild (1934)	British Empire, 1583–
Sajo and the Beaver People (1935)	British Empire, 1583–
Tales of an Empty Cabin (1936)	British Empire, 1583–
Grimm, Jacob, and Grimm, Wilhelm	
Children's and Household Tales (1812, 1815, 1822)	First Napoleonic Empire, 1804–1815
German Legends (1816, 1818)	First Napoleonic Empire, 1804–1815
Reynard the Fox (1834)	German Confederation, 1814–1871
Haggard, H. Rider	
Allan Quartermain (1887)	British Empire, 1583–
Allan's Wife (1889)	British Empire, 1583–
Black Heart and White Heart (1900)	British Empire, 1583–
Diary of an African Journey (1914)	British Empire, 1583–
King Solomon's Mines (1885)	British Empire, 1583–
Halevi, Yehuda	
Kuzari (ca. 1140)	Abbasid Empire, 750–1258
Han Yong-un	
The Restoration of Korean Buddhism (1910)	Japanese Empire, 1871–1945
Love's Silence (1926)	Joseon Dynasty, 1392–1910
Hartmann von Aue	
Erec (ca. 1190s)	Crusades, 1096–1221
Gregorius (1195)	Crusades, 1096–1221
Iwein (1203)	Crusades, 1096–1221
Poor Henry (1195)	Crusades, 1096–1221
Songs (1198)	Crusades, 1096–1221
Hausen, Friedrich von *Poems* (ca. 1180s)	Crusades, 1096–1221
Hawkes, Jacquetta Hopkins	
A Woman as Great as the World and Other Fables (1953)	Soviet Empire, 1922–1991
Hawkesworth, John	
Almoran and Hamet (1761)	Turco-Persian Empire, 1037–1307
Hawthorne, Nathaniel	
The Scarlet Letter (1850)	British Empire, 1583–
Head, Bessie	
Maru (1971)	British Empire, 1583–
A Question of Power (1973)	British Empire, 1583–

When Rain Clouds Gather (1969)	British Empire, 1583–
A Woman Alone (1990)	
Hearn, Lafcadio	
Glimpses of Unfamiliar Japan (1894)	Japanese Empire, 1871–1945
In Ghostly Japan (1899)	Japanese Empire, 1871–1945
Japanese Fairy Tales (1898)	Japanese Empire, 1871–1945
Kwaidan (1904)	Japanese Empire, 1871–1945
Hecataeus of Miletus	
World Travels (ca. 500 B.C.)	Achaemenid-Persian Empire, 550–330 B.C.
Heinrich von Veldeke	
Eneit (ca. 1186)	Crusades, 1096–1221
Herbert, Xavier	
Capricornia (1938)	British Empire, 1583–
	Dutch Empire, 1620–
Herodotus	
Histories (440 B.C.)	Athenian Empire, 477–431 B.C., 415–403 B.C.
Hersey, John Richard	
A Bell for Adano (1944)	Italian Empire, 1885–1943
The Call (1985)	Qing Dynasty, 1644–1912
Hiroshima (1946)	Japanese Empire, 1871–1945
Into the Valley (1943)	Japanese Empire, 1871–1945
Men on Bataan (1942)	American Empire, 1898–
	Japanese Empire, 1871–1945
The Wall (1950)	Nazi Empire, 1933–1945
Hesiod	
Works and Days (ca. 700 B.C.)	Greek Colonies, 825–400 B.C.
Hitler, Adolf	
Mein Kampf (1925—26)	Nazi Empire, 1933–1945
Second Book (1961)	Nazi Empire, 1933–1945
Hongzhi Zhengjue	
Book of Equanimity (ca. 1240)	Song Dynasty, 960–1279
Horace	
"The City Mouse and the Country Mouse" (30 B.C.)	Roman Empire, 27 B.C.–A.D. 476
"The Golden Mean" (23 B.C.)	Roman Empire, 27 B.C.–A.D. 476
Odes (23–13 B.C.)	Roman Empire, 27 B.C.–A.D. 476
Satires (35–30 B.C.)	Roman Empire, 27 B.C.–A.D. 476
Secular Hymn (17 B.C.)	Roman Empire, 27 B.C.–A.D. 476
Howe, Joseph	
"The Song of the Micmac" (1874)	British Empire, 1583–
Hugo, Victor	
Bug-Jargal (1826)	French Empire, 1499–1513, 1605–
Ibn Battuta	
On the Curiosities of Cities and the Wonders of Travel (1354)	Abyssinian Empire, 1270–1974
	Bagan Empire, 849–1287
	Byzantine Empire, 330–1453

Josephus, Flavius
    History of the Jewish War (A.D. 75)   Roman Empire, 27 B.C.–A.D. 476
    Jewish Antiquities (A.D. 93)   Roman Empire, 27 B.C.–A.D. 476
    The Life of Josephus (ca. A.D. 99)   Roman Empire, 27 B.C.–A.D. 476
Joshua ben Hananiah
    "The Crane and Lion" (ca. A.D. 120)   Roman Empire, 27 B.C.–A.D. 476
Jourdain, Sylvester
    "A Discovery of the Bermudas" (1610)   British Empire, 1583–
Joyce, James
    Dubliners (1914)   British Empire, 1583–
    "Ireland at the Bar" (1907)   British Empire, 1583–
    A Portrait of the Artist as a Young Man (1916)   British Empire, 1583–
    Ulysses (1922)   British Empire, 1583–
Juvenal
    Satires (ca. A.D. 127)   Roman Empire, 27 B.C.–A.D. 476
Kafka, Franz
    The Castle (1926)   Austro-Hungarian Empire, 1867–1918
    In the Penal Colony (1919)   Austro-Hungarian Empire, 1867–1918
    The Metamorphosis (1915)   Austro-Hungarian Empire, 1867–1918
    The Trial (1925)   Austro-Hungarian Empire, 1867–1918
Kakinomoto no Hitomaro
    "On Passing the Ruined Capital at Omi" (ca. 700) Nara Period, A.D. 710–794
    "On the Enshrinement of Takechi" (ca. 700)   Nara Period, A.D. 710–794
    "On the Sovereign's Visit to the Palace in Yoshinu"   Nara Period, A.D. 710–794
        (ca. 700)
    "Prince Karu's Retreat to Remember His Father"   Nara Period, A.D. 710–794
        (ca. 700)
Kalakaua, David
    The Legends and Myths of Hawaii (1888)   Hawaiian Kingdom, 1810–1893
Kantuzzili
    "Prayer" (ca. 1425 B.C.)   Hittite Empire, 1460–1180 B.C.
Kempe, Margery
    Book of Margery Kempe (1436)   Holy Roman Empire, 962–1806
                                Jagiellon Dynasty, 1377–1572
                                Mamluk Dynasty, 1260–1517

Keneally, Thomas
    Schindler's Ark (1982)   Nazi Empire, 1933–1945
Khani, Ahmed
    Mem-u Zin (1695)   Ottoman Empire, 1300–1922
                                Safavid Empire, 1501–1722
Kidd, Adam
    The Huron Chief (1830)   British Empire, 1583–
Kincaid, Jamaica
    Annie John (1983)   British Empire, 1583–
    "On Seeing England for the First Time" (1991)   British Empire, 1583–
    "Ovando" (1989)   Spanish Empire, 1492–1975
    A Small Place (1988)   British Empire, 1583–

"Sowers and Reapers: The Unquiet World of a
Flower Bed" (2001)

British Empire, 1583–

Kingsley, Mary

*Travels in West Africa: Congo Français, Corisco and
Cameroons* (1897)

French Empire, 1499–1513, 1605–

Kingsolver, Barbara

The Poisonwood Bible (1998)

Belgian Empire, 1877–1962

Kingston, Maxine Hong

The Woman Warrior (1975)

Chinese Empire, 221 B.C.
Japanese Empire, 1871–1945

Kipling, Rudyard

"The Absent-Minded Beggar" (1899)

British Empire, 1583–

"The Ballad of the King's Jest" (1890)

British Empire, 1583–
Russian Empire, 1547–1917

Barrack-Room Ballads and Other Verses (1892)

British Empire, 1583–

Captains Courageous: A Story of the Grand Banks (1897)

British Empire, 1583–

Departmental Ditties and Other Verses (1886)

British Empire, 1583–

A Diversity of Creatures (1917)

British Empire, 1583–

The Jungle Book (1894)

British Empire, 1583–

Just So Stories for Little Children (1902)

British Empire, 1583–

Kim (1901)

British Empire, 1583–
Russian Empire, 1547–1917

Life's Handicap: Being Stories of Mine Own People (1891)

British Empire, 1583–

The Light That Failed (1891)

British Empire, 1583–

"The Man Who Was" (1890)

British Empire, 1583–
Russian Empire, 1547–1917

"The Man Who Would Be King" (1888)

British Empire, 1583–

"Mary Postgate" (1915)

German Empire, 1871–1918

The Phantom Rickshaw and Other Ghost Tales (1888)

British Empire, 1583–

Plain Tales from the Hills (1888)

British Empire, 1583–

"Recessional" (1897)

British Empire, 1583–

Sea Warfare (1916)

German Empire, 1871–1918

The Second Jungle Book (1895)

British Empire, 1583–

*Something of Myself, For My Friends Known and
Unknown* (1937)

British Empire, 1583–

"The Truce of the Bear" (1898)

British Empire, 1583–
Russian Empire, 1547–1917

"The White Man's Burden" (1899)

American Empire, 1898–

Kirby, William

"Lord Lorne in the Northwest" (1881)

British Empire, 1583–

"Thunder-Storm in August" (ca. 1876)

British Empire, 1583–

Kosinski, Jerzy

The Painted Bird (1965)

Nazi Empire, 1933–1945
Russian Empire, 1547–1917

Kreutzwald, Friedrich Reinhold

Kalev's Son (1853)

Russian Empire, 1547–1917

Krylov, Ivan Andreyevich
    "Eulogy to the Memory of My Grandfather" (1792)   Russian Empire, 1547–1917
    Fables (1809)   Russian Empire, 1547–1917
    The Fashion Shop (1807)   Russian Empire, 1547–1917
    "Kaib: An Eastern Tale" (1792)   Russian Empire, 1547–1917
    Lesson for Daughters (1807)   Russian Empire, 1547–1917
    The Nibbler (1804)   Russian Empire, 1547–1917
Kukai
    Juju Shinron (A.D. 830)   Nara Period, 710–794
Kuznetsov, Anatoly
    Babi Yar (1967)   Nazi Empire, 1933–1945
        Soviet Empire, 1922–1991

La Fontaine, Jean de
    Selected Fables (1668, 1678)   French Empire, 1499–1513, 1605–
Lagerlöf, Selma
    The Wonderful Adventures of Nils (1906–07)   Swedish Union, 1814–1905
Lancaster, G. B.
    The Altar Stairs (1908)   British Empire, 1583–
    Fool Divine (1917)   American Empire, 1898–
    Grand Parade (1944)   British Empire, 1583–
    The Law-Bringers (1913)   British Empire, 1583–
    Pageant (1933)   British Empire, 1583–
    Promenade (1938)   British Empire, 1583–
    A Spur to Smite (1906)   British Empire, 1583–
    The Tracks We Tread (1907)   British Empire, 1583–
    The World Is Yours (1934)   British Empire, 1583–
Landon, Margaret Dorothea
    Anna and the King of Siam (1944)   Siamese Empire, 1350–1909
    Langhorne, John *Solyman and Almena* (1762)   Akkadian-Sumerian Empire, 2350–2150 B.C.
Laozi
    Daodejing (300 B.C.)   Zhou (Chou) Dynasty, 1122–256 B.C.
Las Casas, Bartolomé de
    A Brief Report of the Devastation of the Indies (1542)   Spanish Empire, 1492–1975
    Confessionario (1545)   Spanish Empire, 1492–1975
    History of the Indies (1875)   Spanish Empire, 1492–1975
    On Treasure in Peru (1562)   Incan Empire, 1438–1533
Lawrence, Thomas Edward
    The Mint (1955)   British Empire, 1583–
    Seven Pillars of Wisdom (1922)   British Empire, 1583–
        German Empire, 1871–1918
        Ottoman Empire, 1300–1922

Lawson, Henry
    The Drover's Wife (ca. 1885)   British Empire, 1583–
    "The Song of Australia" (1887)   British Empire, 1583–
    "While the Billy Boils" (ca. 1885)   British Empire, 1583–

Mansfield, Katherine
   "How Pearl Button Was Kidnapped" (1912)   British Empire, 1583–
   "Old Tar" (1913)   British Empire, 1583–
   The Urewera Notebook (1933)   British Empire, 1583–
Marcus Aurelius
   Meditations (ca. A.D. 180)   Roman Empire, 27 B.C.–A.D. 476)
Marie de France
   Fables (ca. 1189)   Angevin Empire, 1135–1217
   Lais (ca. 1175)   Angevin Empire, 1135–1217
Marinetti, Filippo Tommaso
   Anti-Neutrality (1912)   Italian Empire, 1885–1943
   Destruction (1904)   Italian Empire, 1885–1943
   The Feasting King (1909)   Italian Empire, 1885–1943
   The Futurist Cookbook (1932)   Italian Empire, 1885–1943
   "Futurist Manifesto" (1908)   Italian Empire, 1885–1943
   Mafarka le Futuriste (1910)   Italian Empire, 1885–1943
   War the Only Hygiene of the World (1915)   Italian Empire, 1885–1943
   Zang Tumb Tumb (1914)   Italian Empire, 1885–1943
      Ottoman Empire, 1300–1922

Mark, John
   Mark (ca. A.D. 70)   Roman Empire, 27 B.C.–A.D. 476
Marsden, Kate
   On Sledge and Horseback to the Outcast Siberian Lepers   Russian Empire, 1547–1917
     (1877)
Martí, José
   Guantanamera (1891)   Spanish Empire, 1492–1975
   Political Imprisonment in Cuba (1871)   Spanish Empire, 1492–1975
   Simple Verses (1891)
Matthew
   Matthew (ca. A.D. 80)   Roman Empire, 27 B.C.–A.D. 476
McGee, Thomas D'Arcy
   "The Arctic Indian's Faith" (1869)   British Empire, 1583–
McGowan, Kathleen
   The Expected One (2006)   Crusades, 1096–1221
McSwigan, Marie
   All Aboard for Freedom (1954)   Soviet Empire, 1922–1991
   Juan of Manila (1947)   Japanese Empire, 1871–1945
   Snow Treasure (1942)   Nazi Empire, 1933–1945
Meir, Rabbi
   Mishna (ca. A.D. 135)   Roman Empire, 27 B.C.–A.D. 476
Melville, Herman
   Benito Cereno (1855)   Spanish Empire, 1492–1975
Minamoto Takakuni
   Konjaku Monogatari (1075)   Heian Period, 794–1185
Montaigne, Michel de
   "Of Cannibals" (1580)   French Empire, 1499–1513, 1605–

Montalvo, Garci Rodríguez de
    Amadis of Gaul (1508)

                                        Byzantine Empire, 330–1453
                                        Crusades, 1096–1221
                                        Portuguese Empire, 1415–1999
                                        Spanish Empire, 1492–1975

Montejo, Victor
    Popol Vuh: A Sacred Book of the Maya (1999)   Mayan Empire, 1500 B.C.–A.D. 1523

Moodie, Susanna Strickland
    Life in the Clearings (1853)   British Empire, 1583–
    Roughing It in the Bush (1852)

Moreno, José Rosas
    Fables (1891)   Mexican Empire, 1822–1823, 1864–1867

Muhammad
    Koran (A.D. 633)   Islamic Empire, 622–1258

Muqaffa, al-
    Kalilah and Dimnah (ca. a.d. 750)   Umayyad Empire, 661–750

Murasaki Shikibu
    The Diary of Lady Murasaki (ca. 1010)   Heian Period, 794–1185
    The Tale of Genji (1008)

Mursili II
    "Prayer for Gassuliyawiya" (ca. 1295 B.C.)   Hittite Empire, 1460–1180 B.C.
    "Prayer to Lelwani" (ca. 1295 B.C.)   Hittite Empire, 1460–1180 B.C.

Naipaul, V(iadiadhar) S(urajprasad)
    Among the Believers: An Islamic Journey (1981)   Dutch Empire, 1620–
                                       Qajar Dynasty, 1794–1925
    An Area of Darkness (1964)   British Empire, 1583–
    A Bend in the River (1979)   Belgian Empire, 1877–1962
    Guerrillas (1975)   British Empire, 1583–
    Half a Life (2001)   Portuguese Empire, 1415–1999
    In a Free State (1971)   British Empire, 1583–
    India: A Million Mutinies Now (1990)   British Empire, 1583–
    India: A Wounded Civilization (1977)   British Empire, 1583–
    The Loss of El Dorado (1969)   Spanish Empire, 1492–1975
    The Middle Passage (1962)   British Empire, 1583–
                                       French Empire, 1499–1513, 1605–
    The Mimic Men (1967)   British Empire, 1583–
    The Mystic Masseur (1957)   British Empire, 1583–

Nanyuan Huiyung
    koans (A.D. 920)   Khitan Empire, 907–1125

Nathan
    "The Rich Man and the Poor Man's Lamb"   Israelite Empire, 1050–920 B.C.
      (ca. 950 B.C.)

Nezahualcoyotl
    "Flowers Have Come" (ca. 1460)   Aztec Empire, 1375–1521

Nietzsche, Friedrich
    Thus Spoke Zarathustra (1883–85)   Austro Hungarian Empire, 1867–1918

Pasternak, Boris
    Doctor Zhivago (1956)   Soviet Empire, 1922—1991
    In Early Trains (1943)   Soviet Empire, 1922—1991
    Lieutenant Schmidt (1927)   Soviet Empire, 1922—1991
    My Sister—Life (1921)   Soviet Empire, 1922—1991
    "Nobel Prize" (1958)   Soviet Empire, 1922—1991
    The Second Birth (1932)   Soviet Empire, 1922—1991
    Sublime Malady (1925)   Soviet Empire, 1922—1991
    Themes and Variations (1923)   Soviet Empire, 1922—1991
    The Year 1905 (1927)   Soviet Empire, 1922—1991
Paterson, A. B.
    "The Man from Snowy River" (ca. 1888)   British Empire, 1583–
    "Old Australian Ways" (1902)   British Empire, 1583–
    "Song of the Pen" (ca. 1885)   British Empire, 1583–
    "Waltzing Matilda" (1895)   British Empire, 1583–
Paul
    Epistles (A.D. 53–67)   Roman Empire, 27 B.C.–A.D. 476
Peake, Mervyn
    Boy in Darkness (1956)   Nazi Empire, 1933—1945
    "The Consumptive, Belsen 1945" (1945)   Nazi Empire, 1933—1945
    "Digging a Trench" (1945)   Nazi Empire, 1933—1945
    Gormenghast (1950)   Nazi Empire, 1933—1945
    "May 1940" (1940)   Nazi Empire, 1933—1945
    Titus Alone (1959)   Nazi Empire, 1933—1945
    Titus Groan (1946)   Nazi Empire, 1933—1945
    "Victims" (1945)   Nazi Empire, 1933—1945
Perse, Saint-John
    Anabasis (1924)   French Empire, 1499–1513, 1605–
    Exile (1942)   Nazi Empire, 1933—1945
    Seamarks (1957)   French Empire, 1499–1513, 1605–
    Winds (1946)   French Empire, 1499–1513, 1605–
                                Nazi Empire, 1933—1945

Phaedrus
    Aesopic Fables (ca. A.D. 31)   Roman Empire, 27 B.C.–A.D. 476
Phyo, U Aung
    Rama Thagyin (1775)   Konbaung Dynasty, 1752–1885
Planudes, Maximus
    Fables (ca. 1290)   Byzantine Empire, 330–1453
Plato
    Phaedo (ca. 345 b.c.)   Spartan Empire, 404–371 b.c.
Pliny the Younger
    Encomium to Trajan (A.D. 100)   Roman Empire, 27 B.C.–A.D. 476
    Letters (A.D. 97–113)   Roman Empire, 27 B.C.–A.D. 476
Plutarch
    Customs (ca. A.D. 110)   Roman Empire, 27 B.C.–A.D. 476
    Parallel Lives (ca. A.D. 110)   Roman Empire, 27 B.C.–A.D. 476

Poe, Edgar Allan
   "The Pit and the Pendulum" (1843)   French Empire, 1499–1513, 1605–
Polo, Marco
   Travels of Marco Polo (1298)   Abyssinian Empire, 1270—1974
                                      Bagan Empire, 849–1287
                                      Islamic Empire, 632–1258
                                      Majapahitan Empire, 1200–1500
                                      Mamluk Dynasty, 1260–1517
                                      Mongolian Empire, 1206–1405
                                      Papal Empire, 752–1798
                                      Song Dynasty, 960–1279
                                      Turco-Persian Empire, 1037–1307
                                      Venetian Empire, 800–1797
                                      Yuan Dynasty, 1279–1368

Polybius
   Histories (ca. 145 B.C.)   Carthaginian Empire, 814 B.C.–A.D. 695
Pomar, Juan Bautista
   Ballads of the Lords of New Spain (1582)   Aztec Empire, 1375–1521
Prescott, William H.
   History of the Conquest of Mexico (1843)   Aztec Empire, 1375–1521
                                        Spanish Empire, 1492—1975
                                      Holy Roman Empire, 962–1806
                                      Incan Empire, 1438–1533
   History of the Conquest of Peru (1847)   Spanish Empire, 1492—1975
Prince, Mary
   The History of Mary Prince, a West Indian Slave (1831)   British Empire, 1583–
Prince, Nancy Gardner
   A Narrative of the Life and Travels of Mrs. Nancy Prince (1850)   British Empire, 1583–
                                        Russian Empire, 1547—1917
Procopius
   On Buildings (A.D. 561)   Byzantine Empire, 330–1453
   On the Wars (A.D. 552)   Byzantine Empire, 330–1453
   Secret History (ca. A.D. 550)   Byzantine Empire, 330–1453
Propertius
   Elegies (15 B.C.)   Roman Empire, 27 B.C.–A.D. 476
Pushkin, Aleksandr Sergeyevich
   Boris Godunov (1825)   Russian Empire, 1547—1917
   The Bronze Horseman (1833)   Russian Empire, 1547—1917
   Eugene Onegin (1832)   Russian Empire, 1547—1917
   Poltava (1828)   Swedish Empire, 1638–1663, 1785–1878
   "The Shot" (1830)   First Napoleonic Empire, 1804–1815
Rajakumar
   Myazedi Inscription (1113)   Bagan Empire, 849–1287
Rama I
   Ramakien (1797)   Siamese Empire, 1350—1909

Rau, Santha Rama
    East of Home (1950)   British Empire, 1583–
    Gifts of Passage (1961)   British Empire, 1583–
    Home to India (1944)   British Empire, 1583–
    A Princess Remembers (1976)   British Empire, 1583–
    "The Trial of Jomo Kenyatta" (1976)   British Empire, 1583–
Reed, John
    Ten Days That Shook the World (1919)   Russian Empire, 1547—1917
                                         Soviet Empire, 1922—1991

Reiss, Johanna
    The Upstairs Room (1990)   Nazi Empire, 1933—1945
Rhys, Jean
    The Left Bank and Other Stories (1927)   French Empire, 1499–1513, 1605–
    Wide Sargasso Sea (1966)   British Empire, 1583–
Richardson, John
    The Canadian Brothers (1840)   British Empire, 1583–
    Wacousta (1832)   British Empire, 1583–
Rilke, Rainer Maria
    Book of Hours (1903)   Austro-Hungarian Empire, 1867—1918
    The Cornet (1899)   Austro-Hungarian Empire, 1867—1918
    Offerings to the Lares (1895)   Austro-Hungarian Empire, 1867—1918
    To Celebrate Myself (1897)   Austro-Hungarian Empire, 1867—1918
Romulus
    "The Lion and the Shepherd" (ca. A.D. 950)   Roman Empire, 27 B.C.–A.D. 476
Rumi
    "The Blind Man and the Elephant" (ca. 1270)   Turco-Persian Empire, 1037–1307
    The Great Divan (ca. 1240)   Turco-Persian Empire, 1037–1307
    Mathnawi (ca. 1270)   Turco-Persian Empire, 1037–1307
Saadi
    The Rose Garden (1258)   Turco-Persian Empire, 1037–1307
Saadiah ben-Joseph
    Prayer Book (ca. 940)   Abbasid Empire, 750–1258
Sachs, Nelly
    "And No One Knows Where to Go" (1957)   Nazi Empire, 1933—1945
    Eli: A Mystery of the Sorrows of Israel (1951) Nazi Empire, 1933—1945
    In the Habitations of Death (1947)   Nazi Empire, 1933—1945
    "O the Chimneys" (1947)   Nazi Empire, 1933—1945
Sahagún, Bernardino de
    Florentine Codex (1585)   Aztec Empire, 1375–1521
Sahgal, Nayantara
    The Freedom Movement in India (1970)   British Empire, 1583–
    From Fear Set Free (1962)   British Empire, 1583–
    Indira Gandhi: Her Road to Power (1982)   British Empire, 1583–
    Mistaken Identity (1988)   British Empire, 1583–
    Point of View (1997)   British Empire, 1583–

Prison and Chocolate Cake (1954)	British Empire, 1583–
A Voice for Freedom (1977)	British Empire, 1583–
Saint-Exupéry, Antoine de	
Wartime Writings (1938—1944)	French Empire, 1499–1513, 1605–
	Nazi Empire, 1933—1945
Wind, Sand, and Stars (1939)	French Empire, 1499–1513, 1605–
	Nazi Empire, 1933—1945
Sale, Florentia Wynch	
A Journal of the Disasters in Afghanistan, 1841–1842 (1843)	British Empire, 1583–
Sancho, Ignatius	
The Letters of the Late Ignatius Sancho, an African (1782)	Portuguese Empire, 1415—1999
	Spanish Empire, 1492—1975
Sand, George	
Story of My Life (1855)	Second Napoleonic Empire, 1852–1870
Saraha	
Dohakosha (ca. A.D. 790)	Pala Empire, 750–1174
Sargon II	
The Fall of Samaria (721 B.C.)	Assyrian Empire, 900–612 B.C.
	Greek Colonies, 825–400 B.C.
	Sabaean Empire, 1700–115 B.C.
Sarma, Vishnu	
Panchatantra (ca. 200 B.C.)	Maurya Empire, 321–185 B.C.
	Qajar Dynasty, 1794—1925
	Soviet Empire, 1922—1991
Satrapi, Marjane	
Persipolis (2002)	Qajar Dynasty, 1794—1925
	Soviet Empire, 1922—1991
Schreiner, Olive	
The South African Question (1899)	British Empire, 1583–
	Dutch Empire, 1620–
The Story of an African Farm (1883)	British Empire, 1583–
Thoughts on South Africa (1923)	Dutch Empire, 1620–
Trooper Peter Halket of Mashonaland (1897)	British Empire, 1583–
Scott, Kim	
Benang: From the Heart (1999)	British Empire, 1583–
True Country (1993)	British Empire, 1583–
Seacole, Mary Jane	
Wonderful Adventures of Mrs. Seacole in Many Lands (1857)	British Empire, 1583–
	Colombian Empire, 1830—1903
	Russian Empire, 1547—1917
Seneca	
"On Benefits" (A.D. 56)	Roman Empire, 27 B.C.–A.D. 476
"On Clemency" (A.D. 56)	
"On Providence" (A.D. 64)	
"On the Happy Life" (A.D. 58)	

"The Pumpkinification of the Divine Claudius" (A.D. 54)
"To My Mother Helvia" (A.D. 42)
"To Polybius on Consolation" (A.D. 44)
Shakespeare, William
    Antony and Cleopatra (ca. 1605)   Roman Empire, 27 B.C.–A.D. 476
    Coriolanus (ca. 1605–09)   Roman Empire, 27 b.c.–a.d. 476
    Hamlet (ca. 1599–1600)   Danish-Norwegian Empire, 1200—1979
    Julius Caesar (1599)   Roman Empire, 27 B.C.–A.D. 476
    The Merchant of Venice (ca. 1596–98)   Ottoman Empire, 1300—1922
    Venetian Empire, 800–1797
    Othello (ca. 1603–04)   Ottoman Empire, 1300—1922
    Venetian Empire, 800–1797
    The Tempest (ca. 1610–11)   British Empire, 1583–
    Holy Roman Empire, 962–1806
    Spanish Empire, 1492—1975

Sheldon, May French
    Sultan to Sultan: Adventures among the Masai and Other   British Empire, 1583–
      Tribes of East Africa (1892)   Belgian Empire, 1877—1962
Sheridan, Frances Chamberlaine
    The History of Nourjahad (1767)   Turco-Persian Empire, 1037–1307
Shute, Nevil
    A Town Like Alice (1950)   British Empire, 1583–
    Dutch Empire, 1620–
    Japanese Empire, 1871—1945

Siddhartha Gautama
    Dhammapada (ca. 50 B.C.)   Maurya Empire, 321–185 B.C.
Singer, Isaac Bashevis
    "The Destruction of Kreshev" (1942)   Russian Empire, 1547—1917
    Enemies, a Love Story (1972)   Nazi Empire, 1933—1945
    Soviet Empire, 1922—1991
    The Family Moskat (1950)   Nazi Empire, 1933—1945
    Soviet Empire, 1922—1991
    "The Little Shoemakers" (1982)   Nazi Empire, 1933—1945
    Soviet Empire, 1922—1991
    Meshugah (1994)   Nazi Empire, 1933—1945
    Soviet Empire, 1922—1991
    Satan in Goray (1932)   Nazi Empire, 1933—1945
    Soviet Empire, 1922—1991
    Short Friday (1964)   Nazi Empire, 1933—1945
    Soviet Empire, 1922—1991
    Shosha (1978)   Russian Empire, 1547—1917
    Nazi Empire, 1933—1945
    Soviet Empire, 1922—1991
    The Slave (1962)   Russian Empire, 1547—1917
    "Why Noah Chose the Dove" (1974)   Nazi Empire, 1933—1945
    Soviet Empire, 1922—1991

Strindberg, August
    Miss Julie (1888)   Swedish Union, 1814—1905
    The Red Room (1879)   Swedish Union, 1814—1905

Sturluson, Snorri
    Orb of the World (1220)   Viking Conquests, 775–1100
    Prose Edda (1225)

Suetonius
    Lives of the Caesars (ca. A.D. 121)   Roman Empire, 27 B.C.–A.D. 476

Sulpicius Severus
    Sacred History (A.D. 400)   Roman Empire, 27 B.C.–A.D. 476

Swift, Jonathan
    Gulliver's Travels (1726)   British Empire, 1583–
    A Modest Proposal (1729)   British Empire, 1583–

Synge, John Millington
    The Playboy of the Western World (1907)   British Empire, 1583–

Tacitus
    Annals (A.D. 116)   Roman Empire, 27 B.C.–A.D. 476
    Dialogue on Orators (A.D. 105)   Roman Empire, 27 B.C.–A.D. 476
    Histories (A.D. 107)   Roman Empire, 27 B.C.–A.D. 476
    The Life and Character of Julius Agricola (A.D. 98)   Roman Empire, 27 B.C.–A.D. 476
    On the Origin and Situation of the Germans (A.D. 98)   Roman Empire, 27 B.C.–A.D. 476

Tagore, Rabindranath
    The Home and the World (1916)   British Empire, 1583–
    Sadhana: The Realisation of Life (1913)   British Empire, 1583–
    "Shah-Jahan" (1916)   British Empire, 1583–
    Sidhana (1912)   British Empire, 1583–
    Song Offerings (1912)   British Empire, 1583–
    "Those Who Struck Him Once" (1939)   Nazi Empire, 1933—1945
    "Now Turn Me Back" (1893)   British Empire, 1583–

Taira no Yasuyori
    Collection of Jewels (ca. 1100)   Heian Period, 794–1185

Tan, Amy
    The Bonesetter's Daughter (2001)   Chinese Empire, 221 B.C.–
    The Hundred Secret Senses (1995)   Chinese Empire, 221 B.C.–
    The Joy Luck Club (1989)   Chinese Empire, 221 B.C.–
    The Kitchen God's Wife (1991)   Chinese Empire, 221 B.C.–

Tao Qian
    Poems (ca. A.D. 420)   Jin Dynasty, 265–420

Tardivel, Jules-Paul
    For My Country (1895)   French Empire, 1499–1513, 1605–

ten Boom, Corrie
    The Hiding Place (1971)   Nazi Empire, 1933—1945

Tennyson, Alfred, Lord
    Idylls of the King (1869)   Crusades, 1096–1221

Tertullian
    "Antidote for the Scorpion's Sting" (ca. A.D. 211)   Roman Empire, 27 B.C.–A.D. 476

The Apology (ca. A.D. 198)	Roman Empire, 27 B.C.–A.D. 476
"Of Idolatry" (A.D. 198)	Roman Empire, 27 B.C.–A.D. 476
"Of Public Shows" (ca. A.D. 201)	Roman Empire, 27 B.C.–A.D. 476
"Of the Crown" (A.D. 201)	
"To Nations" (ca. A.D. 200)	
"To Scapula" (a.d. 214) "To the Martyrs" (A.D. 197)	
Thackeray, William Makepeace	
Barry Lyndon (1844)	British Empire, 1583–
	First Napoleonic Empire, 1804–1815
Vanity Fair (1848)	British Empire, 1583–
	First Napoleonic Empire, 1804–1815
Thucydides	
The History of the Peloponnesian War (ca. 400 B.C.)	Athenian Empire, 477–431 B.C., 415–403 B.C.
Tibullus, Albius	
Elegies (19 B.C.)	Roman Empire, 27 B.C.–A.D. 476
Tolstoy	
The Cossacks: A Caucasian	Russian Empire, 1547—1917
Story of 1852 (1863)	Ottoman Empire, 1300—1922
Hadji Murád (1904)	Ottoman Empire, 1300—1922
"A Letter to a Hindu" (1908)	British Empire, 1583–
The Living Corpse (1900)	Russian Empire, 1547—1917
"A Prisoner in the Caucasus" (1872)	Ottoman Empire, 1300—1922
Sevastopol Sketches (1855)	British Empire, 1583–
	French Empire, 1499–1513, 1605–
	Ottoman Empire, 1300—1922
War and Peace (1869)	First Napoleonic Empire, 1804–1815
Traill, Catharine Parr	
The Backwoods of Canada (1836)	British Empire, 1583–
Canadian Crusoes: A Tale of the Rice Lake Plains (1852)	British Empire, 1583–
Canadian Wildflowers (1868)	British Empire, 1583–
Lady Mary and Her Nurse: or, a Peep into the Canadian Forest (1856)	British Empire, 1583–
Pearls and Pebbles (1894)	British Empire, 1583–
Studies of Plant Life in Canada (1885)	British Empire, 1583–
Turgenev, Ivan Sergeyevich	
Fables (1878)	Russian Empire, 1547—1917
Fathers and Sons (1862)	Russian Empire, 1547—1917
"Mumu" (1852)	Russian Empire, 1547—1917
Rudin (1855)	Russian Empire, 1547—1917
A Sportsman's Sketches (1852)	Russian Empire, 1547—1917
Virgin Soil (1877)	Russian Empire, 1547—1917
Tutuola, Amos	
My Life in the Bush of Ghosts (1954)	British Empire, 1583–
The Palm-Wine Drinkard (1952)	British Empire, 1583–
Umari, al-	
Voyage of the Eyes (1348)	Malian Empire, 1200–1500

Undset, Sigrid
    The Bridal Wreath (1920)   Danish-Norwegian Empire, 1200–1979
    The Cross (1922)   Danish-Norwegian Empire, 1200–1979
    Gunnar's Daughter (1909)   Danish-Norwegian Empire, 1200–1979
    Happy Times in Norway (1943)   Danish-Norwegian Empire, 1200–1979
     Nazi Empire, 1933—1945
    The Master of Hestviken (1925–27)   Danish-Norwegian Empire, 1200–1979
    Return to the Future (1942)   Danish-Norwegian Empire, 1200–1979
     Nazi Empire, 1933—1945
     Soviet Empire, 1922—1991
    The Wife (1921)   Danish-Norwegian Empire, 1200–1979

Vatsyayana
    Kama Sutra (ca. A.D. 500)   Guptan Empire, A.D. 280–550

Villehardoin, Geoffroy de
    The Conquest of   Crusades, 1096–1221
    Constantinople (1207)

Virgil
    Aeneid (17 B.C.)   Roman Empire, 27 B.C.–A.D. 476
    Catalepton (ca. 47 B.C.)
    Eclogues (ca. 35 B.C.

Voltaire
    Candide (1759)   Holy Roman Empire, 962–1806
     Incan Empire, 1438–1533
     Ottoman Empire, 1300—1922
     Papal Empire, 752–1798
     Venetian Empire, 800–1797
    The Maid of Orleans (1778)   French Empire, 1499–1513, 1605–

Vyasa
    Mahabharata (ca. A.D. 350)   Guptan Empire, A.D. 280–550

Wagner, Richard
    Parsifal (1882)   Crusades, 1096–1221

Wallace, Paul A. W.
    The White Roots of Peace (1946)   American Empire, 1898–
     British Empire, 1583–
     Iroquois Confederacy, 1150–

Wallich, Moses ben Eliezer
    Book of Fables (1697)   Holy Roman Empire, 962–1806

Warren, Mercy Otis
    The Adulateur (1772)   British Empire, 1583–
    The Blockheads: or, The Affrighted Officers (1774)   British Empire, 1583–
    The Defeat (1773)   British Empire, 1583–
    The Group (1775)   British Empire, 1583–
    History of the Rise, Progress, and Termination of the   British Empire, 1583–
      American Revolution (1805)
    The Ladies of Castile (1790)   Holy Roman Empire, 962–1806
    The Motley Assembly (1779)   British Empire, 1583–

"Seventh of the Seventh Month, 729" (ca. 729)   Nara Period, 710–794
"Soaring Like a Bird" (ca. 701)   Nara Period, 710–794
"Thinking of Children" (ca. 733)   Nara Period, 710–794
"Upon Excusing Himself from a Banquet" (ca. 733)   Nara Period, 710–794
"What Value to Me the Seven Kinds of Treasures"   Nara Period, 710–794
     (ca. 733)
"What We Must Accept" (ca. 733)   Nara Period, 710–794
"Wishing Godspeed to the Ambassador to China"   Nara Period, 710–794
     (ca. 733)

Yevtushenko, Yevgeny Aleksandrovich
  "Babi Yar" (1961)   Soviet Empire, 1922—1991
  Bratsk Station (1966)   Soviet Empire, 1922—1991
  "Half Measures" (1989)   Soviet Empire, 1922—1991
  "The Heirs of Stalin" (1962)   Soviet Empire, 1922—1991
  "Russian Tanks in Prague" (1968)   Soviet Empire, 1922—1991
  Zima Junction (1956)   Soviet Empire, 1922—1991

Yezierska, Anzia
  Bread Givers (1925)   Russian Empire, 1547—1917
  "How I Found America" (1920)   Russian Empire, 1547—1917
  Hungry Hearts and Other Stories (1920)   Russian Empire, 1547—1917
  Red Ribbon on a White Horse: My Story (1950)   Russian Empire, 1547—1917
  Salome of the Tenements (1923)   Russian Empire, 1547—1917

Yi Kwangsu
  Great Master Wonhyo (1942)   Japanese Empire, 1871—1945
                                                    Joseon Dynasty, 1392—1910
  The Heartless (1917)   Japanese Empire, 1871—1945
                                                    Joseon Dynasty, 1392—1910
  "Is It Love?" (1906)   Japanese Empire, 1871—1945
                                                    Joseon Dynasty, 1392—1910
  "Stone Pillow" (1948)   Japanese Empire, 1871—1945
                                                    Joseon Dynasty, 1392—1910
  The Tragic History of King Tanjong (1929)   Japanese Empire, 1871—1945
                                                    Joseon Dynasty, 1392—1910
  Yi Sun-sin (1932)   Japanese Empire, 1871—1945
                                                    Joseon Dynasty, 1392—1910

Yuanwu Keqin
  Blue Cliff Record (1125)   Khitan Empire, 907–1125
Zafar al-Siqilli
  Consolation for the Ruler (1154)   Islamic Empire, 632–1258
Zong Zhongshu
  Luxuriant Gems of the Spring and Autumn Annals Chinese Empire, 221 B.C.–
     (ca. 100 B.C.)

III. TIME LINE OF EMPIRES

Ancient Chinese Empire, 2800–2100 B.C.
China
I Ching (1144–206 B.C.), anonymous

Harappan Empire, 2600–1300 B.C.
India
Rig Veda (1700–1400 B.C.), anonymous
Akkadian-Sumerian Empire, 2350–2150 B.C.
Babylon
Histories (440 B.C.), Herodotus
Mesopotamia
"The Courtship of Inanna and Dumuzi"
   (ca. 2800 B.C.), anonymous
Creation Myth (2000 B.C.), anonymous
Epic of Gilgamesh (ca. 1800 B.C.), anonymous
Solyman and Almena (1762), John Langhorne
"The Tamarisk and the Palm" (ca. 2300 B.C.),
   anonymous

Ur Empire, 2100–2000 B.C.
Mesopotamia
Genesis (ca. 500 B.C.), anonymous

Babylonian Empire, 1900–1600 B.C.
Babylonia
Enuma Elish (ca. 1700 B.C.), anonymous
"Nisaba and Wheat" (ca. 1900 B.C.), anonymous

Sabaean Empire, 1700–115 B.C.
Yemen
Fables (ca. 1100 B.C.), Lokman
The Fall of Samaria (721 B.C.), Sargon II

Egyptian Empire, 1550–1070 B.C.
Egypt
Book of the Dead (ca. 1240 B.C.), anonymous
Book of What Is in the Netherworld
   (ca. 1554 B.C.), anonymous
Creating the World and Defeating Apophis
   (2000 B.C.), anonymous
Exodus (ca. 450 B.C.), anonymous

Mayan Empire, 1500 B.C.–A.D. 1523
Guatemala and Mexico
"Hymn to the All-Mother" (ca. 1500 B.C.),
   anonymous
Popul Vuh (1558), anonymous

Hittite Empire, 1460–1180 B.C.
Anatolia "Prayer" (ca. 1425 B.C.), Kantuzzili
"Prayer for Gassuliyawiya" (ca. 1295 B.C.),
   Mursili II
"Prayer to Lelwani" (ca. 1295 B.C.), Mursili II

Indo-Gangetic Empire, 1200–300 B.C.
India
Aranyakas (600 B.C.), anonymous
Atharva Veda (800 B.C.), Dhanvantari
Brahmanas (1000–600 B.C.), anonymous
Ramayana (400 B.C.), anonymous
Sama Veda (1000 B.C.), anonymous
Sutras (800–350 B.C.), anonymous
Upanishads (1000–600 B.C.), anonymous
Yajur Veda (1000–600 B.C.), anonymous

Zhou (Chou) Dynasty, 1122–256 B.C.
China
Chou I (1144 B.C.), Wen Wang
Daodejing (300 B.C.), Laozi

Israelite Empire, 1050–920 B.C.
Palestine
Joshua (ca. 1050 B.C.), anonymous
Judges (ca. 1040 B.C.), anonymous
"The Last Words of David" (ca. 900 B.C.), David
1 Samuel (ca. 920 B.C.), anonymous
Proverbs (ca. 180 B.C.), Solomon, et al.
Psalms (ca. 900 B.C.), David, et al.
"The Rich Man and the Poor Man's Lamb"
    (ca. 950 B.C.), Nathan
Song of Solomon (ca. 950 B.C.), Solomon

Assyrian Empire, 900–612 B.C.
Egypt
Histories (440 B.C.), Herodotus
Judah
Chronicles (400 B.C.), anonymous
"The Destruction of Sennacherib" (1815),
    Lord Byron
Judith (ca. 150 B.C.), anonymous
Kings (ca. 535 B.C.), anonymous
Proverbs (ca. 670 B.C.), Ahiqar
Ruth (ca. 900 B.C.), anonymous

Colonies of Greek Empire, 825–400 B.C.
Greece
Fables (ca. 550 B.C.), Aesop
"The Fox and Hedgehog" (650 B.C.), Archilochus
Works and Days (ca. 700 B.C.), Hesiod
Ionia
The Fall of Samaria (721 B.C.), Sargon II
Syracusa
The Prince (1514), Niccolò Machiavelli

Carthaginian Empire, 814 B.C.–A.D. 695
Libya
From the Foundation of the City (ca. A.D. 14), Livy
Histories (ca. 145 B.C.), Polybius

Chu Empire, 770–221 B.C.
China
Analects of Confucius (ca. 210 B.C.), Confucius
The Book of Songs (ca. 480 B.C.), Confucius

Achaemenid-Persian Empire, 550–330 B.C.
Egypt
Histories (440 B.C.), Herodotus
Lydia
Histories (440 B.C.), Herodotus
Persia
Daniel (ca. 150 B.C.), Daniel, et al.
Esther (ca. 175 B.C.), anonymous
Genesis (ca. 500 B.C.), anonymous
The Prince (1514), Niccolò Machiavelli
Pseudo-Daniel (200 B.C.), anonymous
World Travels (ca. 500 B.C.), Hecataeus of Miletus
Thrace
Histories (440 B.C.), Herodotus

Athenian Empire, 477–431 B.C., 415–403 B.C.
Athens
The Acharnians (425 B.C.), Aristophanes
Anabasis (ca. 354 B.C.), Xenophon
The Birds (414 B.C.), Aristophanes
Hellenica (ca. 354 B.C.), Xenophon
Histories (440 B.C.), Herodotus
The History of the Peloponnesian War
    (ca. 400 B.C.), Thucydides
The Knights (424 B.C.), Aristophanes
Lysistrata (411 B.C.), Aristophanes
Peace (421 B.C.), Aristophanes
The Prince (1514), Niccolò Machiavelli
Persia
Cyropaedia (ca. 354 B.C.), Xenophon
Histories (440 B.C.), Herodotus
Persae (472 B.C.), Aeschylus
The Prince (1514), Niccolò Machiavelli
Sicily
Histories (440 B.C.), Herodotus
Troy
Andromache (ca. 425 B.C.), Euripides
Hecuba (ca. 424 B.C.), Euripides

Myrmidons (ca. 470 B.C.), Aeschylus
Oresteia (458 B.C.), Aeschylus
The Trojan Women (415 B.C.), Euripides

Spartan Empire, 404–371 B.C.
Sparta
Phaedo (ca. 345 B.C.), Plato
The Prince (1514), Niccolò Machiavelli

Macedonian Empire, 338–309 B.C.
Macedonia
Meteorologica (ca. 335 B.C.), Aristotle
Politica (ca. 335 B.C.), Aristotle
"The Wolf and the Shepherd" (ca. 336 B.C.),
  Demosthenes of Athens

Greco-Ptolemaic Empire, 332–30 B.C.
Alexandria
Proverbs (ca. 270 B.C.), Callimachus
Wisdom of Solomon (ca. 150 B.C.), anonymous
Italy
The Prince (1514), Niccolò Machiavelli

Seleucid Empire, 323–60 B.C.
Anatolia
Ecclesiasticus (ca. 180 B.C.), Sirach of Jerusalem
Israel
Maccabees (ca. 125 B.C.)

Maurya Empire, 321–185 B.C.
India
Bhagavad Gita (ca. 200 B.C.), anonymous
Dhammapada (ca. 50 B.C.), Siddhartha Gautama
Panchatantra (ca. 200 B.C.), Vishnu Sarma

Chinese Empire, 221 B.C.–1912
China
The Bonesetter's Daughter (2001), Amy Tan
The Hundred Secret Senses (1995), Amy Tan
The Joy Luck Club (1989), Amy Tan
A Thousand Pieces of Gold (2002), Adeline
  Yen Mah
A Universal History of Infamy (1935), Jorge
  Luis Borges
Watching the Tree (2000), Adeline Yen Mah
The Woman Warrior (1975), Maxine Hong
  Kingston

Shanghai
Chinese Cinderella (1999), Adeline Yen Mah
Chinese Cinderella and the Secret Dragon Society
  (2005), Adeline Yen Mah
Falling Leaves (1997), Adeline Yen Mah
United States
The Joy Luck Club (1989), Amy Tan
The Kitchen God's Wife (1991), Amy Tan

Early Han Dynasty, 206 B.C.–A.D. 9
China
*Luxuriant Gems of the Spring and Autumn
  Annals* (ca. 100 B.C.), Zong Zhongshu

Tibetan Empire, 127 B.C.–A.D. 842
Tibet
Tibetan Book of the Dead (ca. A.D. 775),
  Padmasambhava

Aksumite Empire, 100 B.C.–A.D. 1000
Ethiopia
Ethiopian Book of the Dead (A.D. 400),
  anonymous
Superiority of Blacks to Whites (ca. 825), al-Jahiz

Roman Empire, 27 B.C.–A.D. 476
Aquitania
Sacred History (A.D. 400), Sulpicius Severus
Assyria
Lover of Lies (ca. A.D. 175), Lucian of Samosata
Carthage
"Antidote for the Scorpion's Sting"
  (ca. A.D. 211), Tertullian
The Apology (ca. A.D. 198), Tertullian
"Of Idolatry" (A.D. 198), Tertullian
"Of Public Shows" (ca. A.D. 201), Tertullian
"Of the Crown" (A.D. 201), Tertullian
"To Nations" (ca. A.D. 200), Tertullian
"To Scapula" (A.D. 214), Tertullian
"To the Martyrs" (A.D. 197), Tertullian
Cilicia
Epistles (A.D. 53–67), Paul
Egypt
Aegyptiaca (ca. A.D. 40), Apion
Androcles and the Lion (ca. A.D. 40), Apion
Antony and Cleopatra (ca. 1605), William
  Shakespeare

Greece
Dissertations (ca. A.D. 150), Maximus of Tyre
Pharsalia (A.D. 63), Lucan

Jerusalem
"The Crane and Lion" (ca. A.D. 120), Joshua
    ben Hananiah
Salathiel, the Wandering Jew (1828), George Croly
The Smaller Book of Celestial Palaces
    (ca. A.D. 100), Akiba ben Joseph

Mysia
Fables (ca. 150 B.C.), Aelius Aristides

Numidia
The City of God against the Pagans (A.D. 426),
    Augustine
Confessions (A.D. 398), Augustine
The Golden Ass (A.D. 158), Apuleius

Palestine
Book of Creation (A.D. 200–500), anonymous
Dead Sea Scrolls (150 B.C.–A.D. 70), anonymous
History of the Jewish War (A.D. 75), Flavius
    Josephus
Jewish Antiquities (A.D. 93), Flavius Josephus
The Life of Josephus (ca. A.D. 99), Flavius Josephus
Luke (ca. A.D. 90), Luke
Mark (ca. A.D. 70), John Mark
Matthew (ca. A.D. 80), Matthew
Mishna (ca. A.D. 135), Rabbi Akiba ben Joseph
    and Rabbi Meir
Salomé (1893), Oscar Wilde

Patmos
Revelation (A.D. 95), John the Divine

Rome
Aeneid (17 B.C.), Virgil
Aesopic Fables (ca. A.D. 31), Phaedrus
Amores (15 B.C.), Ovid
Annals (A.D. 116), Tacitus
The Art of Love (ca. 3 B.C.), Ovid
Attic Nights (ca. A.D. 180), Aulus Gellius
Calendar of Holidays (A.D. 17), Ovid
Catalepton (ca. 47 B.C.), Virgil
"The City Mouse and the Country Mouse"
    (30 B.C.), Horace
The City of God against the Pagans (A.D. 426),
    Augustine
Confessions (A.D. 398), Augustine
Customs (ca. A.D. 110), Plutarch
Dialogue on Orators (A.D. 105), Tacitus

Eclogues (ca. 35 B.C.), Virgil
Elegies (15 B.C.), Propertius
Elegies (19 B.C.), Tibullus
Encomium to Trajan (A.D. 100), Pliny the Younger
Fables (A.D. 400), Flavius Avianus
From the City's Founding (A.D. 14), Livy
The Gallic Wars (ca. 50 B.C.), Julius Caesar
"The Golden Mean" (23 B.C.), Horace
Histories (A.D. 107), Tacitus
*The History of the Decline and Fall of the Roman
    Empire* (1776), Edward Gibbon
I, Claudius (1934), Robert Graves
Julius Caesar (1599), William Shakespeare
Letters (A.D. 97–113), Pliny the Younger
The Life and Character of Julius Agricola
    (A.D. 98), Tacitus
"The Lion and the Shepherd" (ca. A.D. 950),
    Romulus
Lives of the Caesars (ca. A.D. 121), Suetonius
Meditations (ca. A.D. 180), Marcus Aurelius
Metamorphoses (A.D. 8), Ovid
Odes (23–13 B.C.), Horace
"On Benefits" (A.D. 56), Seneca
"On Clemency" (A.D. 56), Seneca
"On Providence" (A.D. 64), Seneca
"On the Burning of the City" (A.D. 64), Lucan
"On the Happy Life" (A.D. 58), Seneca
"On the Nature of Animals" (ca. A.D. 230),
    Claudius Aelian
On the Origin and Situation of the Germans
    (A.D. 98), Tacitus
"On the Teaching of World History" (1835),
    Nikolay Gogol
Parallel Lives (ca. A.D. 110), Plutarch
The Prince (1514), Niccolò Machiavelli
"The Pumpkinification of the Divine Claudius"
    (A.D. 54), Seneca
Satires (35–30 B.C.), Horace
Satires (ca. A.D. 127), Juvenal
Secular Hymn (17 B.C.), Horace
"To My Mother Helvia" (A.D. 42), Seneca
"To Polybius on Consolation" (A.D. 44), Seneca

Syria
Fables (ca. A.D. 235), Valerius Babrius

Thrace
Ibis (A.D. 11), Ovid
Letters from Pontus (A.D. 10), Ovid
Sorrows (A.D. 10), Ovid

Ukraine
"On the Movement of Nations at the End of
the Fifth Century" (1835), Nikolay Gogol

Kushan Empire, A.D. 60–375
Afghanistan
The Life of the Buddha (ca. A.D. 100),
Ashvaghosa

Sassanid Empire, A.D. 226–651
Persia
Avesta (ca. A.D. 530), anonymous
The Book of Kings (ca. 1010), Firdawsi
Kalilah and Dimnah (A.D. 570), Burzoe
Khurda Avesta (A.D. 232), anonymous

Jin Dynasty, A.D. 265–420
China
Poems (ca. A.D. 420), Tao Qian

Guptan Empire, A.D. 280–550
India
Garland of Birth Stories (ca. A.D. 350),
Aryasura
Guhyasamaja Tantra (A.D. 350), Asanga
Kama Sutra (ca. A.D. 500), Vatsyayana
koans (A.D. 520), Bodhidharma
Mahabharata (ca. A.D. 350), Vyasa
Yogacara Bhumi Sutra (A.D. 284), anonymous

Byzantine Empire, A.D. 330–1453
Greece
The Prince (1514), Niccolò Machiavelli
Turkey
Alexiad (1148), Anna Comnena
Amadis of Gaul (1508), Garci Rodríguez de
Montalvo
Fables (ca. 1290), Maximus Planudes
On Buildings (A.D. 561), Procopius
On the Curiosities of Cities and the Wonders of
Travel (1354), Ibn Battuta
On the Wars (A.D. 552), Procopius
Secret History (ca. A.D. 550), Procopius

Hunnic Empire, 370–469
Rome
"On the Teaching of World History" (1835),
Nikolay Gogol

Ukraine
"On the Movement of Nations at the End of
the Fifth Century" (1835), Nikolay Gogol
"A View of the Formation of Little Russia"
(1835), Nikolay Gogol

Frankish Empire, 509–843
Babylon
The Sultan of Babylon (ca. 1250), anonymous
Constantinople
Roland and Vernagu (ca. 1325), anonymous
France
The Life of Charlemagne (A.D. 830), Einhard
The Siege of Milan (ca. 1350), anonymous
The Tale of Ralph the Collier (ca. 1475),
anonymous
Holy Lands
The Pilgrimage of Charlemagne (ca. 1140),
anonymous
Spain
Duke Rowlande and Sir Ottuell of Spayne
(ca. 1390s), anonymous
Otuel (ca. 1325), anonymous
Roland and Vernagu (ca. 1325), anonymous
Sir Ferumbras (ca. 1375), anonymous

Ghanian Empire, 600–1200
Ghana
Epic of Wagadu (ca. A.D. 750), anonymous

Srivijayan Empire, 600–1200
Indonesia
Seventy Tales of a Parrot (ca. 1100), anonymous

Tang Dynasty, 618–907
China
"Asking of Wu Lang Again" (ca. A.D. 768),
Du Fu
"Ch'en-T'ao Lament" (ca. A.D. 759), Du Fu
"Facing Night" (ca. A.D. 768), Du Fu
"Facing Snow" (ca. A.D. 757), Du Fu
"Feng-Hsien Return Chant" (ca. A.D. 755),
Du Fu
"Gazing at the Sacred Peak" (ca. A.D. 747),
Du Fu
"Gazing into Antiquity at Su Terrace" (ca. A.D.
742), Li Bo

"Gazing into Antiquity in Yüeh" (ca. A.D. 742),
Li Bo
"Moonlit Night" (ca. A.D. 757), Du Fu
"Mourning Chao" (ca. A.D. 755), Li Bo
"On the Road of Ambition" (ca. A.D. 745), Li
Bo
"P'eng-Ya Song" (ca. A.D. 757), Du Fu
"The Song of the Wagons" (ca. A.D. 750), Du Fu
"To His Friend Departing for Shuh"
(ca. A.D. 745), Li Bo
Tun-huang manuscripts (ca. A.D. 787), Fa-hai

Islamic Empire, 632–1258. *See also specific Islamic empires; Abbasid Empire, Almoravid Empire, Ghaznavid Empire, Mamluk Dynasty, Ummayad Empire.*

India
Mahanirvana Tantra (1295), anonymous

Khurasan
"Al-Mamun" (1835), Nikolay Gogol

Mongolia
Travels of Marco Polo (1298), Marco Polo

Saudi Arabia
The Book of Animals (ca. A.D. 825), al-Jahiz
The Book of Dithyramb of Maids and Valets
(ca. A.D. 825), al-Jahiz
The Book of Eloquence and Exposition
(ca. A.D. 825), al-Jahiz
The Book of Misers (ca. A.D. 825), al-Jahiz
The Book of the Uthmaniyya (ca. A.D. 825), al-
Jahiz
Exploits of the Turks (ca. A.D. 825), al-Jahiz
Koran (A.D. 633), Muhammad
Refutation of the Christians (ca. A.D. 825), al-
Jahiz
"Strike on This Spot" (A.D. 630), Abu Bakr
Superiority of Blacks to Whites (ca. A.D. 825),
al-Jahiz

Sicily
Consolation for the Ruler (1154), Zafar al-Siqilli

Umayyad Empire, 660–750
Persia
Kalilah and Dimnah (ca. A.D. 750), Ibn al-
Muqaffa
A Universal History of Infamy (1935), Jorge Luis
Borges

Kanem Empire, 700–1376
Nigeria
*On the Curiosities of Cities and the Wonders of
Travel* (1354), Ibn Battuta

Nara Imperial Period, 710–794
Japan
Chronicle of Japan (720), Sodoujinkei
"Dialogue on Poverty" (ca. 733), Yamanoue no
Okura
Juju Shinron (830), Kukai *Kojiki* (712), O no
Yasumaro
Kojiki (712), O no Yasumoro
Manyoshu (*Ten Thousand Leaves*) (ca. 759),
Otomo Yakamochi
"On Passing the Ruined Capital at Omi"
(ca. 700), Kakinomoto no Hitomaro
"On the Enshrinement of Takechi" (ca. 700),
Kakinomoto no Hitomaro
"On the Sovereign's Visit to the Palace in
Yoshinu" (ca. 700), Kakinomoto no
Hitomaro
"Prince Karu's Retreat to Remember His Father"
(ca. 700), Kakinomoto no Hitomaro
"A Question by a Poor Villager" (ca. 732),
Yamanoue no Okura
"A Reply by a Man in Destitute Poverty"
(ca. 732), Yamanoue no Okura
"Seventh of the Seventh Month, 729" (ca. 729),
Yamanoue no Okura
"Soaring Like a Bird" (ca. 701), Yamanoue no
Okura
"Thinking of Children" (ca. 733), Yamanoue no
Okura
A Universal History of Infamy (1935), Jorge Luis
Borges
"Upon Excusing Himself from a Banquet"
(ca. 733), Yamanoue no Okura
"What Value to Me the Seven Kinds of
Treasures" (ca. 733), Yamanoue no Okura
"What We Must Accept" (ca. 733), Yamanoue
no Okura
"Wishing Godspeed to the Ambassador to
China" (ca. 733), Yamanoue no Okura

Pala Empire, 750–1174
India
Dohakosha (ca. 790), Saraha

Hevajra Tantra (ca. 790), anonymous
Kalachakra Tantra (966), anonymous
Kularnava Tantra (ca. 1000), anonymous
Lakshmi Tantra (ca. 950), anonymous
Mahanirvana Tantra (1295), anonymous
Saktisamagama Tantra (ca. 1000), anonymous
Sharada Tilaka Tantra (ca. 1000), anonymous

Abbasid Empire, 750–1258
Iraq
The Thousand and One Nights (ca. 942), anonymous

Spain
El Cid (ca. 1150), anonymous
Kuzari (ca. 1140), Yehuda Halevi
Song of Roland (ca. 1080), anonymous
Syria
Hamasa (ca. 845), Abu Tammam
Prayer Book (ca. 940), Saadiah ben-Joseph

Papal Empire (Papal States), 752–1798
Florence
The Art of War (ca. 1520), Niccolò Machiavelli
Divine Comedy (1308), Dante
The History of Florence (1521–25), Niccolò Machiavelli
Portugal
Candide (1759), Voltaire
Songs to the Virgin Mary (ca. 1283), Alfonso X
Paraguay
Candide (1759), Voltaire
O Uraguai (1769), Basílio da Gama
Vatican
"On the Teaching of World History" (1835), Nikolay Gogol
The Prince (1514), Niccolò Machiavelli
Travels of Marco Polo (1298), Marco Polo

Viking Conquests, 775–1100
England
Anglo-Saxon Chronicle (1154), Alfred the Great
Doom Book (ca. 900), Alfred the Great
Life of Alfred (893), Bishop Asser
The Proverbs of Alfred (ca. 1251), Alfred the Great
Iceland
Orb of the World (1220), Snorri Sturluson
Prose Edda (1225), Snorri Sturluson

Scandinavia
Beowulf (800), anonymous

Heian Period, 794–1185
Japan
Collection of Jewels (ca. 1100), Tairano Yasuyori
The Diary of Lady Murasaki (ca. 1010), Murasaki Shikibu
Izumi Shikibu's Diary (ca. 1008), Izumi Shikibu
Konjaku Monogatari (1075), Minamoto Takakuni
The Tale of Genji (1008), Murasaki Shikibu

Venetian Empire, 800–1797
Cyprus
Othello (ca. 1603–04), William Shakespeare
Ferrara
The Prince (1514), Niccolò Machiavelli
Florence
The Art of War (ca. 1520), Niccolò Machiavelli
The History of Florence (1521–25), Niccolò Machiavelli
France
Book of Deeds of Arms and of Chivalry (1410), Christine de Pisan
Book of the City of Ladies (ca. 1405), Christine de Pisan
Book of the Three Virtues (1406), Christine de Pisan
Christine's Vision (1405), Christine de Pisan
Hymn to Joan of Arc (1429), Christine de Pisan
Letter to the God of Love (1399), Christine de Pisan
Turkey
The Giaour (1813), Lord Byron
Venice
Candide (1759), Voltaire
The Merchant of Venice (ca. 1596–98), William Shakespeare
The Prince (1514), Niccolò Machiavelli
Travels of Marco Polo (1298), Marco Polo

Khmer Empire, 802–1462
Cambodia
Reamker (ca. 1550), anonymous
Vietnam
On the Curiosities of Cities and the Wonders of Travel (1354), Ibn Battuta

Bagan Empire, 849–1287
Burma
Myazedi Inscription (1113), Rajakumar
*On the Curiosities of Cities and the Wonders of
    Travel* (1354), Ibn Battuta
Travels of Marco Polo (1298), Marco Polo

Khitan Empire, 907–1125
China
Blue Cliff Record (1125), Yuanwu Keqin
koans (920), Nanyuan Huiyung

Song Dynasty, 960–1279
China
Book of Equanimity (ca. 1240), Hongzhi
    Zhengjue
The Gateless Gate (1228), Wumenguan
Travels of Marco Polo (1298), Marco Polo

Holy Roman Empire, 962–1806
Florence
The Prince (1514), Niccolò Machiavelli
Germany
Book of Fables (1697), Moses ben Eliezer
    Wallich
The Book of Margery Kempe (1436), Margery
    Kempe
Fables (1759), Gotthold Ephraim Lessing
Götz von Berlichingen (1773), Johann Wolfgang
    von Goethe
Puppet Plays (1774), Johann Wolfgang von
    Goethe
Reynard the Fox (1794), Johann Wolfgang von
    Goethe
The Sorceror's Apprentice (1797), Johann
    Wolfgang von Goethe
Milan
The Tempest (ca. 1610–11), William Shakespeare
Peru
History of the Conquest of Peru (1847), William
    H. Prescott
*Royal Commentaries of the Incas and General
    History of Peru* (1617), Garcilaso de la Vega
Prussia
Candide (1759), Voltaire
Spain
The Ladies of Castile (1790), Mercy Otis Warren

Ghaznavid Empire, 975–1187
Kashmir
The Ocean of the Stream of Stories (1070),
    Somadeva
Persia
The Book of Kings (ca. 1010), Firdawsi
Sohrab and Rustum (1853), Matthew Arnold

Turco-Persian Empire, 1037–1307
India
The History of Nourjahad (1767), Frances
    Chamberlaine Sheridan
Travels of Marco Polo (1298), Marco Polo
Persia
The Alchemy of Happiness (1097), al-Ghazali
Almoran and Hamet (1761), John Hawkesworth
"The Blind Man and the Elephant" (ca. 1270),
    Rumi
Deliverance from Error (ca. 1108), al-Ghazali
The Great Divan (ca. 1240), Rumi
The History of Nourjahad (1767), Frances
    Chamberlaine Sheridan
The Jerusalem Tract (1097), al-Ghazali
Mathnawi (ca. 1270), Rumi
The Niche of Lights (ca. 1105), al-Ghazali
The Rose Garden (1258), Saadi
Rubáiyát (ca. 1130), Omar Khayyám
Travels of Marco Polo (1298), Marco Polo
Vathek, an Arabian Tale (1782), William Beckford

Almoravid Empire, 1040–1147
Spain
El Cid (ca. 1150), anonymous

Crusades, 1096–1221
Constantinople
Alexiad (1148), Anna Comnena
Amadis of Gaul (1508), Garci Rodríguez de
    Montalvo
Cligès (ca. 1176), Chrétien de Troyes
The Conquest of Constantinople (1207), Geoffroy
    de Villehardoin
Eneit (ca. 1186), Heinrich von Veldeke
King Rother (ca. 1150), anonymous
Memoirs of the Lord of Joinville (1309), Jean de
    Joinville
Parsifal (1882), Richard Wagner
Parzival (ca. 1210), Wolfram von Eschenbach

Perceval, or the Account of the Grail (ca. 1182), Chrétien de Troyes
Poems (ca. 1180s), Friedrich von Hausen
Poor Henry (1195), Hartmann von Aue
Songs (1198), Hartmann von Aue
Willehalm (ca. 1217), Wolfram von Eschenbach

England
Erec et Enide (ca. 1170), Chrétien de Troyes
Erec (ca. 1190s), Hartmann von Aue
Iwein (1203), Hartmann von Aue
Idylls of the King (1869), Alfred, Lord Tennyson
Lancelot, or the Knight of the Cart (ca. 1181), Chrétien de Troyes
The Once and Future King (1958), T. H. White
The Waste Land (1922), T. S. Eliot
Yvain, the Knight of the Lion (ca. 1177), Chrétien de Troyes

France
Gregorius (1195), Hartmann von Aue
Song of the Albigensian Crusade (1213), William of Tudela

Palestine
Song of Antioch (ca. 1130), Graindor de Douai

Angevin Empire, 1135–1217
France
Fables (ca. 1189), Marie de France
Lais (ca. 1175), Marie de France

Iroquois Confederacy, 1150–
North America
The White Roots of Peace (1946), Paul A. W. Wallace

Early Russian Principalities, 1168–1362
Russia
Progymnasmata (ca. 1175), Nikephoros Basilakis

Majapahitan Empire, 1200–1500
Malaya
Legend of the Great Rama (ca. 1500), anonymous
Sumatra
On the Curiosities of Cities and the Wonders of Travel (1354), Ibn Battuta
Travels of Marco Polo (1298), Marco Polo

Malian Empire, 1200–1500
Mali
History of the Arabs (1375), Ibn Khaldun
On the Curiosities of Cities and the Wonders of Travel (1354), Ibn Battuta
Sundiata: An Epic of Old Mali (ca. 1255), anonymous
Travels in the Interior Districts of Africa (1799), Mungo Park
Voyage of the Eyes (1348), al-Umari

Danish-Norwegian Empire, 1200–1979
Denmark
"The Emperor's New Clothes" (1837), Hans Christian Andersen
Hamlet (ca. 1599–1600), William Shakespeare
"The Princess and the Pea" (1835), Hans Christian Andersen
Iceland
Gunnar's Daughter (1909), Sigrid Undset
Norway
The Bridal Wreath (1920), Sigrid Undset
The Cross (1922), Sigrid Undset
Gunnar's Daughter (1909), Sigrid Undset
Happy Times in Norway (1943), Sigrid Undset
The Master of Hestviken (1925–1927), Sigrid Undset
Return to the Future (1942), Sigrid Undset
The Wife (1921), Sigrid Undset

Latin Empire, 1204–1261
Palestine
Song of Jerusalem (ca. 1150), anonymous
Song of the Captives (ca. 1150), anonymous

Mongolian Empire, 1206–1405
Mongolia
"Kubla Khan" (1816), Samuel Taylor Coleridge
On the Curiosities of Cities and the Wonders of Travel (1354), Ibn Battuta
Travels of Marco Polo (1298), Marco Polo

Mamluk Dynasty, 1260–1517
Jerusalem
The Book of Margery Kempe (1436), Margery Kempe

On the Curiosities of Cities and the Wonders of Travel (1354), Ibn Battuta
Travels of Marco Polo (1298), Marco Polo

Abyssinian Empire, 1270–1974
Ethiopia
Black Mischief (1932), Evelyn Waugh
The History of Rasselas, Prince of Abissinia (1759), Samuel Johnson
On the Curiosities of Cities and the Wonders of Travel (1354), Ibn Battuta
Travels of Marco Polo (1298), Marco Polo

Yuan Dynasty, 1279–1368
China
On the Curiosities of Cities and the Wonders of Travel (1354), Ibn Battuta
Travels of Marco Polo (1298), Marco Polo

Ottoman Empire, 1300–1922
Albania
Travels in the Slavonic Provinces of Turkey-in-Europe (1877), Georgina Mary Muir Mackenzie and Adeline Paulina Irby

Chechnya
The Cossacks: A Caucasian Story of 1852 (1863), Leo Tolstoy
Hadji Murád (1904), Leo Tolstoy
"A Prisoner in the Caucasus" (1872), Leo Tolstoy

Crimea
On the Curiosities of Cities and the Wonders of Travel (1354), Ibn Battuta
Sevastopol Sketches (1855), Leo Tolstoy
War and Peace (1869), Leo Tolstoy

Cyprus
Othello (ca. 1603–04), William Shakespeare

Egypt
Collected Poems (1992), Constantine Cavafy

France
The Last Cavalier (first serialized 1869; reissued 2005), Alexandre Dumas

Greece
Don Juan (1824), Lord Byron

Jordan
Seven Pillars of Wisdom (1922), T. E. Lawrence

Kurdistan
Journeys in Persia and Kurdistan (1891), Isabella Lucy Bird
Mem-u Zin (1692), Ahmed-i Hani

Libya
More Than Love (1906), Gabriele D'Annunzio
Poems on Naval Deeds (1912), Gabriele D'Annunzio

Maldives
On the Curiosities of Cities and the Wonders of Travel (1354), Ibn Battuta

Morocco
Autobiographical Sketches (1886), Emilia Pardo Bazán
The Merchant of Venice (ca. 1596–98), William Shakespeare
On the Curiosities of Cities and the Wonders of Travel (1354), Ibn Battuta

Persia
Journeys in Persia and Kurdistan (1891), Isabella Lucy Bird
On the Curiosities of Cities and the Wonders of Travel (1354), Ibn Battuta

Spain
Don Quixote of La Mancha (1605), Miguel de Cervantes

Sudan
Morning Star (1972), Florence Baker
On the Curiosities of Cities and the Wonders of Travel (1354), Ibn Battuta

Syria
The Desert and the Sown (1907), Gertrude Lowthian Bell
Egyptian Sepulchres and Syrian Shrines (1861), Emily Anne Beaufort
On the Curiosities of Cities and the Wonders of Travel (1354), Ibn Battuta

Turkey
Candide (1759), Voltaire
Childe Harold's Pilgrimage (1818), Lord Byron
The Count of Monte Cristo (1844), Alexandre Dumas (père)
On the Curiosities of Cities and the Wonders of Travel (1354), Ibn Battuta
The Prince (1514), Niccolò Machiavelli

Zang Tumb Tumb (1914), Filippo Tommaso
Marinetti
Yemen
Nellie Bly's Book: Around the World in 72 Days
(1890), Nellie Bly

Songhai Empire, 1340–1591
Gao and Timbuktu
*On the Curiosities of Cities and the Wonders of
Travel* (1354), Ibn Battuta

Siamese Empire, 1350–1909
Siam
Anna and the King of Siam (1944), Margaret
Dorothea Landon
The English Governess at the Siamese Court
(1870), Anna Leonowens
Ramakien (1797), King Rama I
The Romance of the Harem (1872), Anna
Leonowens

Lan Xang Empire, 1354–1707
Laos
Beloved Lakshma and Beloved Rama (ca. 1600),
anonymous

Ming Dynasty, 1368–1644
Korea
Yi Sun-sin (1932), Yi Kwangsu

Aztec Empire, 1375–1521
Mexico
Annals of Tlatelolco (1528), anonymous
Aubin Codex (1576), Diego Durán
Ballads of the Lords of New Spain (1582), Juan
Bautista Pomar
Florentine Codex (1585), Bernardino de
Sahagún
"Flowers Have Come" (ca. 1460),
Nezahualcoyotl
History of the Conquest of Mexico (1843),
William H. Prescott
"La Llorona" (ca. 1525), anonymous
Mexican Songs (ca. 1590), anonymous
The True History of the Conquest of New Spain
(1568), Bernal Díaz

Jagiellon Dynasty, 1377–1572
Danzig
The Book of Margery Kempe (1436), Margery
Kempe
Ukraine
Taras Bulba (1842), Nikolay Gogol

Joseon Dynasty, 1392–1910
Korea
Anarchism and Other Essays (1911), Emma
Goldman
Great Master Wonhyo (1942), Yi Kwangsu
The Heartless (1917), Yi Kwangsu
"Is It Love?" (1906), Yi Kwangsu
Korea and Her Neighbours (1898), Isabella Lucy
Bird
The Living Reed (1963), Pearl Buck
The Restoration of Korean Buddhism (1910), Han
Yong-un
Love's Silence (1926), Han Yong-un
"Stone Pillow" (1948), Yi Kwangsu
The Tragic History of King Tanjong (1929), Yi
Kwangsu *Yi Sun-sin* (1932), Yi Kwangsu

Oyo Empire, 1400–1835
Benin
*The Interesting Narrative of the Life of Olaudah
Equiano* (1789), Olaudah Equiano
Nigeria
A Tempest (1969), Aimé Césaire

Florentine Empire, 1406–1494, 1509
Florence
The Art of War (ca. 1520), Niccolò Machiavelli
The History of Florence (1521–25), Niccolò
Machiavelli
The Prince (1514), Niccolò Machiavelli
Pisa
The Prince (1514), Niccolò Machiavelli

Portuguese Empire, 1415–1999
Brazil
Caramuru (1781), Santa Rita Durao
Guinea
*The Letters of the Late Ignatius Sancho, an
African* (1782)

Mozambique
Half a Life (2001), V. S. Naipaul
Paraguay
O Uraguai (1769), Basílio da Gama
Portugal
Amadis of Gaul (1508), Garci Rodríguez de
   Montalvo
The Lusiads (1572), Luís Vaz de Camões
Quest for the Holy Grail (ca. 1400), anonymous
Songs to the Virgin Mary (ca. 1283), Alfonso X

Incan Empire, 1438–1533

Peru
Candide (1759), Voltaire
History of the Conquest of Peru (1847), William
   H. Prescott
On Treasure in Peru (1564), Bartolomé de Las
   Casas
*Royal Commentaries of the Incas and General
   History of Peru* (1617), Garcilaso de la Vega

Spanish Empire, 1492–1975

Caribbean
A Brief Report of the Devastation of the Indies
   (1552), Bartolomé de Las Casas
Confessionario (1545), Bartolomé de Las Casas
History of the Indies (1875), Bartolomé de Las
   Casas
Treasure Island (1883), Robert Louis Stevenson

Chile
Benito Cereno (1855), Herman Melville
The House of the Spirits (1981), Isabel Allende

Cuba
Guantanamera (1891), José Martí
Political Imprisonment in Cuba (1871), José Martí
Sab (1841), Gertrudis Gómez de Avellaneda y
   Arteaga
Simple Verses (1891), José Martí

Florida
The Florida of the Inca (1599), Garcilaso de la
   Vega

Hispaniola
"Ovando" (1989), Jamaica Kincaid

Mexico
History of the Conquest of Mexico (1843),
   William H. Prescott

The Reply to Sister Filotea of the Cross (1691),
   Sor Juana de la Cruz
The True History of the Conquest of New Spain
   (1568), Bernal Díaz

Morocco
Autobiographical Sketches (1886), Emilia Pardo
   Bazán

Naples
The Tempest (ca. 1610–11), William Shakespeare
The Prince (1514), Niccolò Machiavelli

New Granada
The Letters of the Late Ignatius Sancho, an African
   (1782)

Paraguay
O Uraguai (1769), Basílio da Gama

Peru
History of the Conquest of Peru (1847), William
   H. Prescott
On Treasure in Peru (1562), Bartolomé de Las
   Casas
*Royal Commentaries of the Incas and General
   History of Peru* (1617), Garcilaso de la Vega

South America
Nostromo, a Tale of the Seaboard (1904), Joseph
   Conrad

Spain
Abdelazar; or, The Moor's Revenge (1671),
   Aphra Behn
Amadis of Gaul (1508), Garci Rodríguez de
   Montalvo *Ambrosio, or the Monk* (1796),
   Matthew Gregory Lewis
Don Quixote of La Mancha (1605), Miguel de
   Cervantes
The House of Ulloa (1886), Emilia Pardo Bazán
Literary Fables (1782), Tomás de Iriarte
Metrical Legends of Exalted Characters (1821),
   Joanna Baillie

Venezuela
The Loss of El Dorado (1969), V. S. Naipaul

French Empire, 1499–1513, 1605–

Algeria
Through Algeria (1863), Mabel Sharman
   Crawford
Antilles
The Left Bank and Other Stories (1927), Jean Rhys

Brazil
"Of Cannibals" (1580), Michel de Montaigne

Cameroons
Travels in West Africa: Congo Français, Corisco and Cameroons (1897), Mary Kingsley

Canada
Song of Hiawatha (1855), Henry Wadsworth Longfellow

China
Anabasis (1924), Saint-John Perse

Crimea
Sevastopol Sketches (1855), Leo Tolstoy

France
Book of Deeds of Arms and of Chivalry (1410), Christine de Pisan
Book of the City of Ladies (ca. 1405), Christine de Pisan
The Book of the Three Virtues (1406), Christine de Pisan
Christine's Vision (1405), Christine de Pisan
Fables (1792), Jean-Pierre Claris de Florian
Hymn to Joan of Arc (1429), Christine de Pisan
Letter to the God of Love (1399), Christine de Pisan
The Maid of Orleans (1778), Voltaire
Penguin Island (1908), Anatole France
Selected Fables (1668, 1678), Jean de La Fontaine
A Tale of Two Cities (1859), Charles Dickens
Wartime Writings (1938–44), Antoine de Saint-Exupéry *Wind, Sand, and Stars* (1939), Antoine de Saint-Exupéry

Guadeloupe
Seamarks (1957), Saint-John Perse
Winds (1946), Saint-John Perse
Windward Heights (1995), Maryse Condé

Guinea
Epic of Almami Samori Ture (ca. 1900)

Haiti
Bug-Jargal (1826), Victor Hugo

Martinique
The Middle Passage (1962), V. S. Naipaul

Milan
The Prince (1514), Niccolò Machiavelli

Quebec
For My Country (1895), Jules-Paul Tardivel

Senegal
Lures and Glimmers (1960), Birago Diop
Mother Crocodile (1981), Birago Diop
New Tales of Amadou Koumba (1958), Birago Diop
Scarlet Song (1981), Mariama Bâ
So Long a Letter (1979), Mariama Bâ
Stories and Commentaries (1963), Birago Diop
The Tales of Amadou Koumba (1947), Birago Diop
"Those Who Are Dead Are Never Gone" (1985), Birago Diop
Travels in the Interior Districts of Africa (1799), Mungo Park

Spain
"The Pit and the Pendulum" (1843), Edgar Allan Poe

Tahiti
The Ebb-Tide (1894), Robert Louis Stevenson and Lloyd Osbourne

Tunisia
The Nomad (1988), Isabella Eberhardt

Vietnam
The Quiet American (1955), Graham Greene

West Africa
Journey without Maps (1936), Graham Greene

Safavid Empire, 1501–1722

Kurdistan
Mem-u Zin (1695), Ahmed-i Hani

Mughal Empire, 1526–1857

Punjab
Granth (1604), Arjan Dev
Guru Granth Sahib (1708), Gobind Singh

Russian Empire, 1547–1917

Belarus
Bread Givers (1925), Anzia Yezierska
"How I Found America" (1920), Anzia Yezierska
Hungry Hearts and Other Stories (1920), Anzia Yezierska
The Promised Land (1912), Mary Antin
Red Ribbon on a White Horse: My Story (1950), Anzia Yezierska
Salome of the Tenements (1923), Anzia Yezierska

They Who Knock at Our Gates (1914), Mary Antin

Chechnya

The Cossacks: A Caucasian Story of 1852 (1863), Leo Tolstoy

Hadji Murád (1904), Leo Tolstoy

"A Prisoner in the Caucasus" (1872), Leo Tolstoy

Crimea

Sevastopol Sketches (1855), Leo Tolstoy

Wonderful Adventures of Mrs. Seacole in Many Lands (1857), Mary Jane Seacole

Estonia

Kalev's Son (1853), Friedrich Reinhold Kreutzwald

Finland

Anarchism and Other Essays (1911), Emma Goldman

Kalevala (1836), Elias Lönnrot

India

"The Ballad of the King's Jest" (1890), Rudyard Kipling

"The Man Who Was" (1890), Rudyard Kipling

"The Truce of the Bear" (1898), Rudyard Kipling

Poland

"The Destruction of Kreshev" (1942), Isaac Bashevis Singer

The Painted Bird (1965), Jerzy Kosinski

The Slave (1962), Isaac Bashevis Singer

"Why Noah Chose the Dove" (1974), Isaac Bashevis Singer

Russia

Anarchism and Other Essays (1911), Emma Goldman

Animal Farm: A Fairy Story (1946), George Orwell

At the Edge of the Sea (1915), Anna Akhmatova

Boris Godunov (1825), Aleksandr Pushkin

The Bronze Horseman (1833), Aleksandr Pushkin

The Brothers Karamazov (1881), Fyodor Dostoyevsky

Crime and Punishment (1866), Fyodor Dostoyevsky

Eugene Onegin (1832), Aleksandr Pushkin

"Eulogy to the Memory of My Grandfather" (1792), Ivan Andreyevich Krylov

Evening (1912), Anna Akhmatova

Fables (1878), Ivan Turgenev

Fables (1809), Ivan Andreyevich Krylov

The Fashion Shop (1807), Ivan Andreyevich Krylov

Fathers and Sons (1862), Ivan Turgenev

The Fencing Master (1840), Alexandre Dumas (père)

"How the Revolution Began in America" (1919), Louise Bryant

"The Internationale" (1918), various authors

"Kaib: An Eastern Tale" (1792), Ivan Andreyevich Krylov

The Kingdom of God Is Within You (1894), Leo Tolstoy

Lesson for Daughters (1807), Ivan Andreyevich Krylov

"A Letter to a Hindu" (1908), Leo Tolstoy

The Living Corpse (1900), Leo Tolstoy

Living My Life (1931), Emma Goldman

My Disillusionment in Russia (1923), Emma Goldman

My Further Disillusionment in Russia (1924), Emma Goldman

"Mumu" (1852), Ivan Turgenev

A Narrative of the Life and Travels of Mrs. Nancy Prince (1850), Nancy Gardner Prince

The Nibbler (1804), Ivan Andreyevich Krylov

Notes from the Underground (1864), Fyodor Dostoyevsky

Pages from the Journal of an Author (1864), Fyodor Dostoyevsky

Poor Folk (1846), Fyodor Dostoyevsky

The Possessed (1872), Fyodor Dostoyevsky

Rudin (1855), Ivan Turgenev

Russia: Its People and Its Literature (1887), Emilia Pardo Bazán

A Sportsman's Sketches (1852), Ivan Turgenev

Ten Days That Shook the World (1919), John Reed

Under Western Eyes (1911), Joseph Conrad

Virgin Soil (1877), Ivan Turgenev

War and Peace (1869), Leo Tolstoy

White Flock (1917), Anna Akhmatova

Siberia

Buried Alive; or, Ten Years of Penal Servitude in Siberia (1881), Fyodor Dostoyevsky

The House of the Dead (1862), Fyodor
  Dostoyevsky
Korea and Her Neighbours (1898), Isabella Lucy
  Bird
*On Sledge and Horseback to the Outcast Siberian
  Lepers* (1877), Kate Marsden
*Recollections of Tartar Steppes and Their
  Inhabitants* (1863), Lucy Sherrand Finley
  Atkinson

Sweden
Poltava (1828), Aleksandr Pushkin

Tibet
Kim (1901), Rudyard Kipling

Ukraine
Dead Souls (1842), Nikolay Gogol
The Government Inspector (1836), Nikolay Gogol
"A History of Little Russia" (1834), Nikolay
  Gogol
"On the Movement of Nations at the End of
  the Fifth Century" (1834), Nikolay Gogol
"On the Teaching of World History" (1834),
  Nikolay Gogol
"The Songs of the Ukraine" (1834), Nikolay
  Gogol
Taras Bulba (1842), Nikolay Gogol

Polish-Lithuanian Commonwealth, 1569–1795

Ukraine
"A History of Little Russia" (1835), Nikolay
  Gogol

British Empire, 1583–

Afghanistan
*A Journal of the Disasters in Affghanistan,
  1841–1842* (1843), Florentia Wynch Sale
"The Man Who Would Be King" (1888),
  Rudyard Kipling

Africa
Journey without Maps (1936), Graham Greene
Seven Pillars of Wisdom (1922), T. E. Lawrence

Antigua
Annie John (1983), Jamaica Kincaid
The History of Mary Prince, a West Indian Slave
  (1831), Mary Prince
"On Seeing England for the First Time" (1991),
  Jamaica Kincaid

A Small Place (1988), Jamaica Kincaid
"Sowers and Reapers: The Unquiet World of a
  Flower Bed" (2001), Jamaica Kincaid

Australia
Benang: From the Heart (1999), Kim Scott
Capricornia (1938), Xavier Herbert
The Drover's Wife (ca. 1885), Henry Lawson
The Kadaitcha Sung (1990), Sam Watson
The Last Voyage (1889), Anne Brassey
"The Man from Snowy River" (ca. 1888), A. B.
  Paterson
"Old Australian Ways" (1902), A. B. Paterson
Oscar and Lucinda (1988), Peter Carey
The Passing of the Aborigines (1938), Daisy Bates
"The Song of Australia" (1887), Henry Lawson
"Song of the Pen" (ca. 1885), A. B. Paterson
A Spur to Smite (1906), G. B. Lancaster
The Tracks We Tread (1907), G. B. Lancaster
True Country (1993), Kim Scott
True History of the Kelly Gang (2000), Peter Carey
"Waltzing Matilda" (1895), A. B. Paterson
"While the Billy Boils" (ca. 1885), Henry
  Lawson
"The Wild Colonial Boy" (1830), anonymous

Barbados
I, Tituba, Black Witch of Salem (1986), Maryse
  Condé

Benin
*The Interesting Narrative of the Life of Olaudah
  Equiano* (1789), Olaudah Equiano

Bermuda
"A Discovery of the Bermudas" (1610),
  Sylvester Jourdain
The History of Mary Prince, a West Indian Slave
  (1831), Mary Prince
A Tempest (1969), Aimé Césaire
The Tempest (ca. 1610–11), William Shakespeare

Botswana
Maru (1971), Bessie Head
A Question of Power (1973), Bessie Head
When Rain Clouds Gather (1969), Bessie Head
A Woman Alone (1990), Bessie Head

Burma
Barrack-Room Ballads and Other Verses (1892),
  Rudyard Kipling
"The Brown Man's Servant" (1897), W. W.
  Jacobs

Burmese Days (1934), George Orwell

"Shooting an Elephant" (1936), George Orwell

Burma and Thailand

The Bridge over the River Kwai (1952), Pierre Boulle Caicos Islands

The History of Mary Prince, a West Indian Slave (1831), Mary Prince

Canada

The Backwoods of Canada (1836), Catharine Parr Traill

Canadian Born (1903), Pauline Johnson

The Canadian Brothers (1840), John Richardson

Canadian Crusoes: A Tale of the Rice Lake Plains (1852), Catharine Parr Traill

Canadian Wildflowers (1868), Catharine Parr Traill

Flint and Feather (1912), Pauline Johnson

The Huron Chief (1830), Adam Kidd

"Indian Summer" (1900), Alexander MacLachlan

Lady Mary and Her Nurse: or, a Peep into the Canadian Forest (1856), Catharine Parr Traill

The Law-Bringers (1913), G. B. Lancaster

Legends of Vancouver (1911), Pauline Johnson

Life in the Clearings (1853), Susanna Strickland Moodie

"Lord Lorne in the Northwest" (1881), William Kirby

"Thunder-Storm in August" (ca. 1876), William Kirby

The Men of the Last Frontier (1931), Grey Owl

The Moccasin Maker (1913), Pauline Johnson

Pearls and Pebbles (1894), Catharine Parr Traill

Pilgrims of the Wild (1934), Grey Owl

Roughing It in the Bush (1852), Susanna Strickland Moodie

Sajo and the Beaver People (1935), Grey Owl

Studies of Plant Life in Canada (1885), Catharine Parr Traill

Tales of an Empty Cabin (1936), Grey Owl

Tecumseh (1886), Charles Mair

"Thunder-Storm in August" (ca. 1876), William Kirby

Wacousta (1832), John Richardson

"We Live in a Rickety House" (1900), Alexander MacLachlan

The White Roots of Peace (1946), Paul A. W. Wallace

The White Wampum (1895), Pauline Johnson

Caribbean

In a Free State (1971), V. S. Naipaul

Jane Eyre (1847), Charlotte Brontë

The Mimic Men (1967), V. S. Naipaul

Treasure Island (1883), Robert Louis Stevenson

Ceylon

"The Anaconda" (1808), Matthew Gregory Lewis

Comoro Islands

The Last Journals of David Livingstone in Central Africa (1874)

Crimea

Sevastopol Sketches (1855), Leo Tolstoy

Wonderful Adventures of Mrs. Seacole in Many Lands (1857), Mary Jane Seacole

Egypt

The English Patient (1992), Michael Ondaatje

Nellie Bly's Book: Around the World in 72 Days (1890), Nellie Bly

England

"The Adventure of the Speckled Band" (1892), Sir Arthur Conan Doyle

"The Adventure of the Sussex Vampire" (1924), Sir Arthur Conan Doyle

The Amateur Emigrant from Clyde to Sandy Hook (1895), Robert Louis Stevenson

Animal Farm: A Fairy Story (1946), George Orwell

Aspects of a Novel (1927), E. M. Forster

Barry Lyndon (1844), William Makepeace Thackeray

"The Bascombe Valley Mystery" (1891), Sir Arthur Conan Doyle

Brighton Rock (1938), Graham Greene

Canopus in Argos (1979–1983), Doris Lessing

Coriolanus (ca. 1605–1609), William Shakespeare

David Copperfield (1850), Charles Dickens

A Diversity of Creatures (1917), Rudyard Kipling

Dombey and Son (1848), Charles Dickens

"The Dying Detective" (1894), Sir Arthur Conan Doyle

"The Eve of Waterloo" (1818), George Gordon, Lord Byron

"The 'Gloria Scott'" (1894), Sir Arthur Conan Doyle

Great Expectations (1861), Charles Dickens

"The Hero as Poet" (1840), Thomas Carlyle
"His Last Bow" (1894), Sir Arthur Conan Doyle
H.M.S. Pinafore (1878), W. S. Gilbert *The Hound of the Baskervilles* (1902), Sir Arthur Conan Doyle
The Idler (1758–59), Samuel Johnson
It's a Battlefield (1934), Graham Greene
"The Lion and the Unicorn" (1941), George Orwell
Martin Chuzzlewit (1844), Charles Dickens
The Mikado (1885), W. S. Gilbert
The Mint (1955), T. E. Lawrence
The Mystery of Cloomber (1889), Sir Arthur Conan Doyle
The Mystery of Edwin Drood (1870), Charles Dickens
Nellie Bly's Book: Around the World in 72 Days (1890), Nellie Bly
Nineteen Eighty-Four (1949), George Orwell
"Onward, Christian Soldiers" (1864), Sabine Baring-Gould
Persuasion (1817), Jane Austen
The Pickwick Papers (1837), Charles Dickens
Princess Toto (1876), W. S. Gilbert
"Recessional" (1897), Rudyard Kipling
"The Reigate Puzzle" (1894), Sir Arthur Conan Doyle
The Sign of the Four (1890), Sir Arthur Conan Doyle
A Study in Scarlet (1887), Sir Arthur Conan Doyle
"Such, Such Were the Joys" (1949), George Orwell
A Tale of Two Cities (1859), Charles Dickens
Tales of Fashionable Life (1809), Maria Edgeworth
Utopia, Limited (1893), W. S. Gilbert
Vanity Fair (1848), William Makepeace Thackeray
"Why I Write" (1946), George Orwell

Fiji
At Home in Fiji (1881), Constance Cumming

Gambia
Travels in the Interior Districts of Africa (1799), Mungo Park

Ghana
Anowa (1970), Ama Ata Aidoo
Changes: A Love Story (1991), Ama Ata Aidoo

The Dilemma of a Ghost (1965), Ama Ata Aidoo
No Sweetness Here (1970), Ama Ata Aidoo
Our Sister Killjoy (1977), Ama Ata Aidoo

Gilbert Islands
"The King of Apemama" (1896), Robert Louis Stevenson

Guiana
The Middle Passage (1962), V. S. Naipaul

Hawaii
Island Nights' Entertainments (1893), Robert Louis Stevenson

Hong Kong
Nellie Bly's Book: Around the World in 72 Days (1890), Nellie Bly

India
Ahalya Baee (1849), Joanna Baillie
An Area of Darkness (1964), V. S. Naipaul
An Autobiography, or the Story of My Experiments with Truth (1927–29), Mohandas Gandhi
Barrack-Room Ballads and Other Verses (1892), Rudyard Kipling
Baumgartner's Bombay (1988), Anita Desai
Cry, the Peacock (1963), Anita Desai
Departmental Ditties and Other Verses (1886), Rudyard Kipling
East of Home (1950), Santha Rama Rau
Fire on the Mountain (1977), Anita Desai
The Freedom Movement in India (1970), Nayantara Sahgal
From Fear Set Free (1962), Nayantara Sahgal
Gifts of Passage (1961), Santha Rama Rau
Heat and Dust (1975), Ruth Prawer Jhabvala
The Hill of Devi (1921), E. M. Forster
The Home and the World (1916), Rabindranath Tagore
Home to India (1944), Santha Rama Rau
In Custody (1984), Anita Desai
India: A Million Mutinies Now (1990), V. S. Naipaul
India: A Wounded Civilization (1977), V. S. Naipaul
Indira Gandhi: Her Road to Power (1982), Nayantara Sahgal
The Jungle Book (1894), Rudyard Kipling
Kim (1901), Rudyard Kipling
"A Letter to a Hindu" (1908), Leo Tolstoy
Life and Travel in India (1884), Anna Leonowens

Life's Handicap (1891), Rudyard Kipling
Mistaken Identity (1988), Nayantara Sahgal
"The Monkey's Paw" (1902), W. W. Jacobs
The Moonstone (1868), Wilkie Collins
"Now Turn Me Back" (1893), Rabindranath
    Tagore
A Passage to India (1924), E. M. Forster
The Phantom Rickshaw and Other Ghost Tales
    (1888), Rudyard Kipling
Plain Tales from the Hills (1888), Rudyard Kipling
Point of View (1997), Nayantara Sahgal
"Poison" (1953), Roald Dahl
A Princess Remembers (1976), Santha Rama Rau
Prison and Chocolate Cake (1954), Nayantara
    Sahgal
Sadhana: The Realisation of Life (1913),
    Rabindranath Tagore
The Second Jungle Book (1895), Rudyard Kipling
"Shah-Jahan" (1916), Rabindranath Tagore
Sidhana (1912), Rabindranath Tagore
Something of Myself, For My Friends Known and
    Unknown (1937), Rudyard Kipling
Song Offerings (1912), Rabindranath Tagore
A Voice for Freedom (1977), Nayantara Sahgal
Voices in the City (1965), Anita Desai

Indonesia
"The Lagoon" (1897), Joseph Conrad
Lord Jim (1900), Joseph Conrad

Ireland
Castle Rackrent (1800), Maria Edgeworth
Dubliners (1914), James Joyce
Essay on Irish Bulls (1801), Maria Edgeworth
    and Richard Lovell Edgeworth
Gulliver's Travels (1726), Jonathan Swift
"Ireland at the Bar" (1907), James Joyce
A Modest Proposal (1729), Jonathan Swift
The Playboy of the Western World (1907), John
    Millington Synge
A Portrait of the Artist as a Young Man (1916),
    James Joyce
Ulysses (1922), James Joyce

Jamaica
"The Grateful Negro" (1804), Maria Edgeworth
Journal of a West India Proprietor (1834),
    Matthew Gregory Lewis
The Middle Passage (1962), V. S. Naipaul

A Narrative of the Life and Travels of Mrs. Nancy
    Prince (1850), Nancy Prince
Wide Sargasso Sea (1966), Jean Rhys
Wonderful Adventures of Mrs. Seacole in Many
    Lands (1857), Mary Jane Seacole

Jordan
Seven Pillars of Wisdom (1922), T. E. Lawrence

Kenya
Daguerreotypes and Other Essays (1984)
Journey without Maps (1936), Graham Greene
Out of Africa (1937), Isak Dinesen
Shadows on the Grass (1960), Isak Dinesen
Sultan to Sultan: Adventures among the Masai
    and Other Tribes of East Africa (1892), May
    French Sheldon
"The Trial of Jomo Kenyatta" (1976), Santha
    Rama Rau
West with the Night (1942), Beryl Markham

Malaya
Nellie Bly's Book: Around the World in 72 Days
    (1890), Nellie Bly
A Town Like Alice (1950), Nevil Shute
Ways of Escape (1980), Graham Greene

Massachusetts Bay Colony
The Adulateur (1772), Mercy Otis Warren
"The Crisis" (1776), Thomas Paine
The Defeat (1773), Mercy Otis Warren
The Blockheads: or, The Affrighted Officers
    (1774), Mercy Otis Warren
The Group (1775), Mercy Otis Warren
History of the Rise, Progress, and Termination of
    the American Revolution (1805), Mercy Otis
    Warren
I, Tituba, Black Witch of Salem (1986), Maryse
    Condé
The Motley Assembly (1779), Mercy Otis
    Warren
Observations on the New Constitution, and on
    the Federal and State Conventions (1788),
    Mercy Otis Warren
Poems, Dramatic and Miscellaneous (1790),
    Mercy Otis Warren
The Scarlet Letter (1850), Nathaniel
    Hawthorne

New Caledonia
The Altar Stairs (1908), G. B. Lancaster

Newfoundland
Captains Courageous: A Story of the Grand Banks (1897), Rudyard Kipling

New Zealand
"How Pearl Button Was Kidnapped" (1912), Katherine Mansfield
"Old Tar" (1913), Katherine Mansfield
The Piano (1993), Jane Campion
Promenade (1938), G. B. Lancaster
The Urewera Notebook (1933), Katherine Mansfield

Nigeria
Anthills of the Savannah (1988), Chinua Achebe
Arrow of God (1964), Chinua Achebe
Beware, Soul Brother (1971), Chinua Achebe
The Bride Price (1976), Buchi Emecheta
The Burden of Memory, the Muse of Forgiveness (1998), Wole Soyinka
"Civil Peace" (1971), Chinua Achebe
Head above Water (1986), Buchi Emecheta
Home and Exile (2000), Chinua Achebe
"An Image of Africa: Racism in Conrad's 'Heart of Darkness'" (1975), Chinua Achebe
In the Ditch (1972), Buchi Emecheta
The Joys of Motherhood (1979), Buchi Emecheta
Mandela's Earth and Other Poems (1988), Wole Soyinka
The Man Died (1973), Wole Soyinka
A Man of the People (1966), Chinua Achebe
Mister Johnson (1939), Joyce Cary
My Life in the Bush of Ghosts (1954), Amos Tutuola
No Longer at Ease (1960), Chinua Achebe
The Open Sore of a Continent (1996), Wole Soyinka
The Palm-Wine Drinkard (1952), Amos Tutuola
Poems from Prison (1969), Wole Soyinka
The Rape of Shavi (1985), Buchi Emecheta
Second-Class Citizen (1974), Buchi Emecheta
A Shuttle in the Crypt (1972), Wole Soyinka
Things Fall Apart (1958), Chinua Achebe
The Trouble with Nigeria (1998), Chinua Achebe

Nova Scotia
Grand Parade (1944), G. B. Lancaster
"The Song of the Micmac" (1874), Joseph Howe

Ontario
Winter Studies and Summer Rambles in Canada (1838), Anna Jameson

Pakistan
Among the Believers: An Islamic Journey (1981), V. S. Naipaul

Palestine
A State of Siege (2002), Mahmoud Darwish

Quebec
"The Arctic Indian's Faith" (1869), Thomas D'Arcy McGee
"The Coureur-de-Bois" (1919), Samuel Mathewson Baylis

Rhodesia
Diary of an African Journey (1914), H. Rider Haggard
Going Home (1957), Doris Lessing
The Golden Notebook (1962), Doris Lessing
The Grass Is Singing (1950), Doris Lessing
Journey without Maps (1936), Graham Greene
Trooper Peter Halket of Mashonaland (1897), Olive Schreiner
Under My Skin (1994), Doris Lessing

Samoa
The Beach of Falesá (1893), Robert Louis Stevenson
Fables (1888), Robert Louis Stevenson
An Inland Voyage (1878), Robert Louis Stevenson
In the South Seas (1891), Robert Louis Stevenson
The Island of Dr. Moreau (1896), H. G. Wells

Scotland
Kidnapped (1886), Robert Louis Stevenson
The Master of Ballantrae (1889), Robert Louis Stevenson
Metrical Legends of Exalted Characters (1821), Joanna Baillie

Sierra Leone
The Heart of the Matter (1948), Graham Greene
Journey without Maps (1936), Graham Greene
Two Voyages to the Sierra Leone During the Years 1791–1792–1793 (1794), Anna Maria Falconbridge

Singapore
Nellie Bly's Book: Around the World in 72 Days (1890), Nellie Bly

Solomon Islands
The Altar Stairs (1908), G. B. Lancaster

South Africa
"The Absent-Minded Beggar" (1899), Rudyard Kipling

Allan Quartermain (1887), H. Rider Haggard

Allan's Wife (1889), H. Rider Haggard

An Autobiography, or the Story of My Experiments with Truth (1940), Mohandas Gandhi

Black Heart and White Heart (1900), H. Rider Haggard

Burger's Daughter (1979), Nadine Gordimer

The Conservationist (1974), Nadine Gordimer

The Human Factor (1978), Graham Greene

Journey without Maps (1936), Graham Greene

July's People (1981), Nadine Gordimer

Just So Stories for Little Children (1902), Rudyard Kipling

King Solomon's Mines (1885), H. Rider Haggard

The Lying Days (1953), Nadine Gordimer

Occasion for Loving (1963), Nadine Gordimer

The Pickup (2002), Nadine Gordimer

The South African Question (1899), Olive Schreiner

The Story of an African Farm (1883), Olive Schreiner

Thoughts on South Africa (1923), Olive Schreiner

Waiting for the Barbarians (1980), J. M. Coetzee

The War in South Africa: Its Cause and Conduct (1902), Sir Arthur Conan Doyle

South Seas
Utopia, Limited (1893), W. S. Gilbert

Sudan
The Light That Failed (1891), Rudyard Kipling

Surinam
Oroonoko, or The Royal Slave (1688), Aphra Behn

Tahiti
The Ebb-Tide (1894), Robert Louis Stevenson and Lloyd Osbourne

Tasmania
Capricornia (1938), Xavier Herbert

A History of Tasmania (1883), James Fenton

The History of Tasmania (1852), John West

His Natural Life (1874), Marcus Clarke

Pageant (1933), G. B. Lancaster

Trinidad
"The Convict Song" (1937), Alfred Hamilton Cruickshank

Guerrillas (1975), V. S. Naipaul

The Mystic Masseur (1957), V. S. Naipaul

Virginia Colony
The Interesting Narrative of the Life of Olaudah Equiano (1789), Olaudah Equiano

A True Declaration of the Estate of the Colonie in Virginia (1610), anonymous

Yemen
Nellie Bly's Book: Around the World in 72 Days (1890), Nellie Bly

Yukon
The World Is Yours (1934), G. B. Lancaster

Zambia
The Last Journals of David Livingstone in Central Africa (1874)

Zanzibar
Sultan to Sultan: Adventures among the Masai and Other Tribes of East Africa (1892), May French Sheldon

Zimbabwe
Prisons We Choose to Live Inside (1987), Doris Lessing

Walking in the Shade (1997), Doris Lessing

Bambara Empire, 1600–1861
Mali
Epic of Bamana Segu (ca. 1850), anonymous

Segu: The Children of Segu (1984), Maryse Condé

Segu: The Earth in Pieces (1985), Maryse Condé

Dutch Empire, 1620–
Borneo
Almayer's Folly (1895), Joseph Conrad

Java
Love Letters (1861), Eduard Douwes Dekker

Max Havelaar (1860), Eduard Douwes Dekker

Malaysia
Among the Believers: An Islamic Journey (1981), V. S. Naipaul

A Town Like Alice (1950), Nevil Shute

South Africa
South Africa a Century Ago (1797–1801), Lady Anne Barnard

The South African Question (1899), Olive Schreiner

The Story of an African Farm (1883), Olive Schreiner

Thoughts on South Africa (1923), Olive Schreiner

Suriname
The Middle Passage (1962), V. S. Naipaul
Oroonoko, or The Royal Slave (1688), Aphra Behn

Swedish Empire, 1638–1663, 1785–1878
Sweden *Poltava* (1828), Aleksandr Pushkin

Qing Dynasty, 1644–1912
China
The Call (1985), John Hersey
China Sky (1941), Pearl S. Buck
Dream of the Red Chamber (1791), Cao Xueqin
The Good Earth (1931), Pearl S. Buck
A House Divided (1935), Pearl S. Buck
Imperial Woman (1956), Pearl S. Buck
The Mother (1934), Pearl S. Buck
Sons (1932), Pearl S. Buck
The Yangtze Valley and Beyond (1899), Isabella Lucy Bird
Tibet
Among the Tibetans (1894), Isabella Lucy Bird

Ashanti Empire, 1670–1957
Ghana
Anowa (1970), Ama Ata Aidoo

Konbaung Dynasty, 1752–1885
Burma
Rama Thagyin (1775), U Aung Phyo

Kaartan Empire, 1753–1854
Ghana
Epic of Sonsan of Kaarta (ca. 1850)

Fulani Empire, 1790s–1890s
Nigeria
Travels in the Interior Districts of Africa (1799), Mungo Park

Qajar Dynasty, 1794–1925
Persia
Among the Believers: An Islamic Journey (1981), V. S. Naipaul
Persepolis (2002), Marjane Satrapi

First Napoleonic Empire, 1804–1815
Belgium
"The Eve of Waterloo" (1818), Lord Byron
"The Poet's Pilgrimage to Waterloo" (1816), Robert Southey
Vanity Fair (1848), William Makepeace Thackeray
Corsica
The Corsican Brothers (1844), Alexandre Dumas (père)
Napoleon (1855), Alexandre Dumas (père)
Egypt
"Passion in the Desert" (1850), Honoré de Balzac
England
The Life of Nelson (1813), Robert Southey
"Ode to Napoleon Buonaparte" (1814), Lord Byron
France
Considerations on the French Revolution (1818), Anne-Louise-Germaine de Staël
The Count of Monte Cristo (1844), Alexandre Dumas
The Last Cavalier (2005), Alexandre Dumas
"The Napoleon of the People" (1833), Honoré de Balzac
"A Shadowy Affair" (1850), Honoré de Balzac
Ten Years' Exile (1820), Anne-Louise-Germaine de Staël
"The Vendetta" (1850), Honoré de Balzac
Germany
Children's and Household Tales (1812, 1815, 1822), Jacob and Wilhelm Grimm
Faust (1826, 1831), Johann Wolfgang von Goethe
German Legends (1816, 1818), Jacob and Wilhelm Grimm
On Germany (1810), Anne-Louise-Germaine de Staël
Poetry and Truth (1811–33), Johann Wolfgang von Goethe
Russia
"The Crow and the Hen," Ivan Andreyevich Krylov
"The Shot" (1830), Aleksandr Pushkin
War and Peace (1869), Leo Tolstoy
"The Wolf in the Kennel," Ivan Andreyevich Krylov

Spain

Roderick, Last of the Goths (1814), Robert
Southey

Austrian Empire, 1804–1867

Austria

Napoleon (1855), Alexandre Dumas

Mexico

"Christmas in the Mountains" (1871), Ignacio
Manuel Altamirano

Mercy (1869), Ignacio Manuel Altamirano

Hawaiian Kingdom, 1810–1893

The Beginning (1897), Liliuokalani

Hawaii's Story by Hawaii's Queen, Liliuokalani
(1898), Liliuokalani

Island Nights' Entertainments (1893), Robert
Louis Stevenson

The Legends and Myths of Hawaii (1888), David
Kalakaua

Laieikawai (1863), anonymous

The Queen's Songbook (1973), Liliuokalani

German Confederation, 1814–1871

Germany

Children's and Household Tales (1812, 1815,
1822), Jacob and Wilhelm Grimm

Faust (1826, 1831), Johann Wolfgang von
Goethe

German Legends (1816, 1818), Jacob and
Wilhelm Grimm

Poetry and Truth (1810), Johann Wolfgang von
Goethe

Reynard the Fox (1834), Jacob and Wilhelm
Grimm

Swedish Union, 1814–1905

Norway

Babette's Feast (1959), Isak Dinesen

Sweden

Miss Julie (1888), August Strindberg

The Red Room (1879), August Strindberg

Sara Videbeck (1839), Carl Almquist

The Wonderful Adventures of Nils (1906–07),
Selma Lagerlöf

Brazilian Empire, 1822–1889

Brazil

Caramuru (1781), Santa Rita Durao

"The Man Who Liked Dickens" (1933), Evelyn
Waugh

O Uraguai (1769), Basílio da Gama

Mexican Empire, 1822–1823, 1864–1867

Mexico

"Ballad of Gregorio Cortez" (ca. 1890),
anonymous

"Ballad of Ignacio Zaragoza" (1867), anonymous

"Ballad of Kansas" (ca. 1860), anonymous

"Ballad of the Coup de Grâce" (1867),
anonymous

"Ballad of the French" (1860s), anonymous

"Ballad of the Oppressed" (1821), anonymous

"Christmas in the Mountains" (1871), Ignacio
Manuel Altamirano

Fables (1891), José Rosas Moreno

Mercy (1869), Ignacio Manuel Altamirano

Six Months in Mexico (1888), Nellie Bly

"To Zaragoza" (1867), Onofre Cárdenas

With His Pistol in His Hand (1958), Américo
Paredes

El Zarco (1901), Ignacio Manuel Altamirano

Colombian Empire, 1830–1903

Panama

*Wonderful Adventures of Mrs. Seacole in Many
Lands* (1857), Mary Jane Seacole

Second Napoleonic Empire, 1852–1870

France

Story of My Life (1855), George Sand

Norway

Babette's Feast (1959), Isak Dinesen

Austro-Hungarian Empire, 1867–1918

Bohemia

The Book of Hours (1903), Rainer Maria Rilke

The Castle (1926), Franz Kafka

The Comet (1899), Rainer Maria Rilke

In the Penal Colony (1919), Franz Kafka

The Metamorphosis (1915), Franz Kafka

Offerings to the Lares (1895), Rainer Maria Rilke

To Celebrate Myself (1897), Rainer Maria Rilke
The Trial (1925), Franz Kafka

Russia
"How the Revolution Began in America" (1919), Louise Bryant
Ten Days That Shook the World (1919), John Reed

Germany
Thus Spoke Zarathustra (1883–85), Friedrich Nietzsche

Jutland
My Disillusionment in Russia (1923), Emma Goldman
Sea Warfare (1916), Rudyard Kipling

Russia
Ten Days That Shook the World (1919), John Reed

Samoa
An Inland Voyage (1878), Robert Louis Stevenson
The Island of Dr. Moreau (1896), H. G. Wells

Tanzania
Daguerreotypes and Other Essays (1984), Isak Dinesen
Out of Africa (1937), Isak Dinesen

German Empire, 1871–1918
Germany
Anarchism and Other Essays (1910), Emma Goldman
"Jolly Is the Gypsy's Life" (ca. 1900), anonymous
"Mary Postgate" (1915), Rudyard Kipling
Sea Warfare (1916), Rudyard Kipling
Thus Spoke Zarathustra (1883–85), Friedrich Nietzsche

Jordan
Seven Pillars of Wisdom (1922), T. E. Lawrence

Japanese Empire, 1871–1945
Burma and Thailand
The Bridge over the River Kwai (1952), Pierre Boulle

China
China Sky (1941), Pearl S. Buck
Chinese Cinderella (1999), Adeline Yen Mah
Chinese Cinderella and the Secret Dragon Society (2005), Adeline Yen Mah
Falling Leaves (1997), Adeline Yen Mah

A Thousand Pieces of Gold (2002), Adeline Yen Mah
Watching the Tree (2000), Adeline Yen Mah
The Woman Warrior (1975), Maxine Hong Kingston

Japan
Glimpses of Unfamiliar Japan (1894), Lafcadio Hearn
Hiroshima (1946), John Hersey
In Ghostly Japan (1899), Lafcadio Hearn
Japanese Fairy Tales (1898), Lafcadio Hearn
Kwaidan (1904), Lafcadio Hearn
The Mikado (1885), W. S. Gilbert
Nellie Bly's Book: Around the World in 72 Days (1890), Nellie Bly
Unbeaten Tracks in Japan (1880), Isabella Lucy Bird

Korea
Great Master Wonhyo (1942), Yi Kwangsu
The Heartless (1917), Yi Kwangsu
"Is It Love?" (1906), Yi Kwangsu
The Living Reed (1963), Pearl S. Buck
The Restoration of Korean Buddhism (1910), Han Yong-un
Love's Silence (1926), Han Yong-un
"Stone Pillow" (1948), Yi Kwangsu
The Tragic History of King Tanjong (1929), Yi Kwangsu
Yi Sun-sin (1932), Yi Kwangsu
When My Name Was Keoko (2002), Linda Sue Park

Malaya
A Town Like Alice (1950), Nevil Shute

Philippines
Juan of Manila (1947), Marie McSwigan
Men on Bataan (1942), John Hersey

Solomon Islands
Into the Valley: A Skirmish of the Marines (1943), John Hersey

Belgian Empire, 1877–1962
Belgium
The Blue Dog and Other Fables for the French (1956), Anne Bodart

Congo
A Bend in the River (1979), V. S. Naipaul
A Burnt-Out Case (1960), Graham Greene

The Crime of the Congo (1909), Sir Arthur
  Conan Doyle
Heart of Darkness (1899), Joseph Conrad
"An Outpost of Progress" (1896), Joseph Conrad
The Poisonwood Bible (1998), Barbara
  Kingsolver
*Sultan to Sultan: Adventures among the Masai
  and Other Tribes of East Africa* (1892), May
  French Sheldon

Wassoulou Empire, 1878–1898
Guinea
Epic of Almami Samori Ture (ca. 1900),
  anonymous

Italian Empire, 1885–1943
Italy
Anti-Neutrality (1912), Filippo Tommaso
  Marinetti
Destruction (1904), Filippo Tommaso Marinetti
Dreams of the Seasons (1898), Gabriele
  D'Annunzio
The English Patient (1992), Michael Ondaatje
The Feasting King (1909), Filippo Tommaso
  Marinetti
The Flame of Life (1900), Gabriele D'Annunzio
Francesca da Rimini (1901), Gabriele
  D'Annunzio
The Futurist Cookbook (1932), Filippo Tommaso
  Marinetti
"Futurist Manifesto" (1908), Filippo Tommaso
  Marinetti
La Gioconda (1899), Gabriele D'Annunzio
In Praise of Sky, Sea, Earth, and Heroes (1899),
  Gabriele D'Annunzio
Mafarka the Futurist (1910), Filippo Tommaso
  Marinetti
The Triumph of Death (1894), Gabriele
  D'Annunzio
War the Only Hygiene of the World (1915),
  Filippo Tommaso Marinetti

Libya
Poems on Naval Deeds (1912), Gabriele
  D'Annunzio

Poland
The Black Hole of Auschwitz (2005), Primo Levi
If Not Now, When? (1984), Primo Levi

If This Is a Man (1947), Primo Levi
The Truce (1963), Primo Levi

Sicily
A Bell for Adano (1944), John Hersey

American Empire, 1898–
Cuba
Anarchism and Other Essays (1911), Emma
  Goldman
Fool Divine (1917), G. B. Lancaster
Our Man in Havana (1958), Graham Greene
Simple Verses (1891), José Martí

Panama
Fool Divine (1917), G. B. Lancaster

Philippines
Anarchism and Other Essays (1910), Emma
  Goldman
Living My Life (1931), Emma Goldman
Men on Bataan (1942), John Hersey
"The White Man's Burden" (1899), Rudyard
  Kipling

United States
American Notes (1842), Charles Dickens
Anarchism and Other Essays (1910), Emma
  Goldman
Song of Hiawatha (1855), Henry Wadsworth
  Longfellow
The White Roots of Peace (1946), Paul A. W.
  Wallace

Vietnam
The Quiet American (1955), Graham Greene

Soviet Empire, 1922–1991
Azerbaijan
Persepolis (2002), Marjane Satrapi

Czechoslovakia
All Aboard for Freedom (1954), Marie
  McSwigan
"Russian Tanks in Prague" (1968), Yevgeny
  Yevtushenko

England
A Woman as Great as the World and Other Fables
  (1953), Jacquetta Hopkins Hawkes

Poland
"The Destruction of Kreshev" (1942), Isaac
  Bashevis Singer

Enemies, a Love Story (1972), Isaac Bashevis
  Singer
The Family Moskat (1950), Isaac Bashevis
  Singer
"The Little Shoemakers" (1982), Isaac Bashevis
  Singer
Meshugah (1994), Isaac Bashevis Singer
Satan in Goray (1932), Isaac Bashevis Singer
Short Friday (1964), Isaac Bashevis Singer
Shosha (1978), Isaac Bashevis Singer
"Why Noah Chose the Dove" (1974), Isaac
  Bashevis Singer

Russia (Soviet Union)

Animal Farm: A Fairy Story (1946), George
  Orwell
Babi Yar (1967), Anatoly Kuznetsov
"Babi Yar" (1961), Yevgeny Yevtushenko
Bratsk Station (1966), Yevgeny Yevtushenko
"Cleopatra" (1940), Anna Akhmatova
Doctor Zhivago (1956), Boris Pasternak
"Half Measures" (1989), Yevgeny Yevtushenko
"The Heirs of Stalin" (1962), Yevgeny
  Yevtushenko
In Early Trains (1943), Boris Pasternak
"Infinitive" (1996), Joseph Brodsky
"In 1940" (1940), Anna Akhmatova
I Want to Live (2006), Nina Lugovskaya
Less Than One (1986), Joseph Brodsky
Lieutenant Schmidt (1927), Boris Pasternak
"Lullaby of Cape Cod" (1975), Joseph Brodsky
My Sister—Life (1921), Boris Pasternak
"Nobel Prize" (1958), Boris Pasternak
On Grief and Reason (1995), Joseph Brodsky
"On the Death of Zhukov" (1974), Joseph
  Brodsky
Poem without a Hero (1943), Anna Akhmatova
Prologue: A Dream within a Dream (1942),
  Anna Akhmatova
Requiem (1940), Anna Akhmatova
Return to the Future (1942), Sigrid Undset
The Second Birth (1932), Boris Pasternak
So Forth (1996), Joseph Brodsky
Sublime Malady (1925), Boris Pasternak
Ten Days That Shook the World (1919), John
  Reed
Themes and Variations (1923), Boris Pasternak
Winds of War (1946), Anna Akhmatova
The Year 1905 (1927), Boris Pasternak

Zima Junction (1956), Yevgeny Yevtushenko

Siberia

The First Circle (1968), Aleksandr
  Solzhenitsyn
The Gulag Archipelago (1973), Aleksandr
  Solzhenitsyn
One Day in the Life of Ivan Denisovich (1962),
  Aleksandr Solzhenitsyn

Nazi Empire, 1933–1945

Denmark

The Angelic Avengers (1944), Isak Dinesen

England

Animal Farm: A Fairy Story (1946), George
  Orwell

France

Exile (1942), Saint-John Perse
The Stories of Amadou Koumba (1947), Birago
  Diop
Wartime Writings (1938–44), Antoine de Saint-
  Exupéry
Winds (1946), Saint-John Perse
Wind, Sand, and Stars (1939), Antoine de
  Saint-Exupéry

Germany

The Accident (1962), Elie Wiesel
Boy in Darkness (1956), Mervyn Peake
"Cleopatra" (1940), Anna Akhmatova
"The Consumptive, Belsen 1945" (1945),
  Mervyn Peake
The Cost of Discipleship (1937), Dietrich
  Bonhoeffer
Creation and Fall (1933), Dietrich Bonhoeffer
The Cup of Trembling (1962), Elizabeth
  Berryhill
Dawn (1961), Elie Wiesel
"Digging a Trench" (1945), Mervyn Peake
Gormenghast (1950), Mervyn Peake
Life Together (1939), Dietrich Bonhoeffer
"May 1940" (1940), Mervyn Peake
Mein Kampf (1925–26), Adolf Hitler
Night (1960), Elie Wiesel
Schindler's Ark (1982), Thomas Keneally
Titus Alone (1959), Mervyn Peake
Titus Groan (1946), Mervyn Peake
"Victims" (1945), Mervyn Peake
Zweites Buch (1961), Adolf Hitler

Holland
The Diary of a Young Girl (1947), Anne Frank
The Hiding Place (1971), Corrie ten Boom
The Upstairs Room (1990), Johanna Reiss

India
"Those Who Struck Him Once" (1939),
     Rabindranath Tagore

Italy
The English Patient (1992), Michael Ondaatje

Kenya
Shadows on the Grass (1960), Isak Dinesen

Norway
Happy Times in Norway (1943), Sigrid Undset
The Master of Hestviken (1925–1927), Sigrid
     Undset
Snow Treasure (1942), Marie McSwigan

Poland
The Black Hole of Auschwitz (2005), Primo Levi
"The Destruction of Kreshev" (1942), Isaac
     Bashevis Singer
Enemies, a Love Story (1972), Isaac Bashevis
     Singer
The Family Moskat (1950), Isaac Bashevis Singer
If Not Now, When? (1984), Primo Levi

If This Is a Man (1947), Primo Levi
"The Little Shoemakers" (1982), Isaac Bashevis
     Singer
Meshugah (1994), Isaac Bashevis Singer
The Painted Bird (1965), Jerzy Kosinski
Satan in Goray (1932), Isaac Bashevis Singer
Short Friday (1964), Isaac Bashevis Singer
Shosha (1978), Isaac Bashevis Singer
The Truce (1963), Primo Levi
The Wall (1950), John Hersey
"Why Noah Chose the Dove" (1974), Isaac
     Bashevis Singer

Russia
Babi Yar (1967), Anatoly Kuznetsov
"Babi Yar" (1961), Yevgeny Yevtushenko
"In 1940" (1940), Anna Akhmatova
Night (1960), Elie Wiesel
Return to the Future (1942), Sigrid Undset

Sweden
"And No One Knows Where to Go" (1957),
     Nelly Sachs
Eli: A Mystery of the Sorrows of Israel (1951),
     Nelly Sachs
In the Habitations of Death (1947), Nelly Sachs
"O the Chimneys" (1947), Nelly Sachs

IV. FILMOGRAPHY

Aladdin (1992)

Allan Quatermain and the Lost City of Gold (1987)

Androcles and the Lion (1952)

Animal Farm (1954)

Anna and the King (1999)

Anna and the King of Siam (1946)

Anne Frank Remembered (1995)

Antony and Cleopatra (1972, 1983)

Apocalypse Now (1979)

Arabian Nights (1942)

Babette's Feast (1988)

A Bell for Adano (1945)

Ben-Hur (1959)

Bonhoeffer (2005)

Bonhoeffer—Agent of Grace (2000)

Boy in Darkness (2000)

The Bridge on the River Kwai (1957)

The Brothers Grimm (2005)

The Brothers Karamazov (1958)

Byron (2003)

The Cafeteria (1984)

Camelot (1967)

Captains Courageous (1937,1977,1996)

Charlemagne (1995)

Cinderella (1950)

Cleopatra (1963)

The Count of Monte Cristo (1975, 2002)

Abbasid Empire, 750–1258

British Empire, 1583–

Roman Empire, 27 B.C.–A.D. 476

British Empire, 1583–

Siamese Empire, 1350–1909

Siamese Empire, 1350–1909

Nazi Empire, 1933–1945

Roman Empire, 27 B.C.–A.D. 476

American Empire, 1898–

Abbasid Empire, 750–1258

Second Napoleonic Empire, 1852–1870

Swedish Union, 1814–1905

Italian Empire, 1885–1943

Roman Empire, 27 B.C.–A.D. 476

Nazi Empire, 1933–1945

Nazi Empire, 1933–1945

Nazi Empire, 1933–1945

British Empire, 1583–

Japanese Empire, 1871–1945

First Napoleonic Empire, 1804–1815

Russian Empire, 1721–1917

Ottoman Empire, 1300–1922

Russian Empire, 1721–1917

Italian Empire, 1885–1943

Nazi Empire, 1933–1945

Soviet Empire, 1922–1991

The Crusades, 1096–1221

British Empire, 1583–

Frankish Empire, 509–843

First Napoleonic Empire, 1804–1815

Roman Empire, 27 B.C.–A.D. 476

First Napoleonic Empire, 1804–1815

Ottoman Empire, 1300–1922

Crime and Punishment (1998, 2002)	Russian Empire, 1721–1917
Daana Veera Shura Karna (1977)	Maurya Empire, 321–60 B.C.
A Dangerous Man: Lawrence after Arabia (1990)	British Empire, 1583–
	Ottoman Empire, 1300–1922
David (1997)	Israelite Empire, 1050–920 B.C.
David and Bathsheba (1951)	Israelite Empire, 1050–920 B.C.
David Copperfield (1969, 1999)	British Empire, 1583–
The Da Vinci Code (2006)	Crusades, 1096–1221
The Day the Earth Froze (1959)	Russian Empire, 1547–1917
The Dead (1987)	British Empire, 1583–
The Diary of Anne Frank (1959)	Nazi Empire, 1933–1945
Don Quixote (2000)	Ottoman Empire, 1300–1922
	Spanish Empire, 1492–1975
The Enchanted Boy (1955)	Swedish Union, 1814–1905
Enemies, a Love Story (1989)	Italian Empire, 1885–1943
	Nazi Empire, 1933–1945
	Soviet Empire, 1922–1991
The English Patient (1996)	British Empire, 1583–
	Italian Empire, 1885–1943
	Nazi Empire, 1933–1945
Esther (1999)	Achaemenid-Persian Empire, 550–330 B.C.
Esther and the King (1960)	Achaemenid-Persian Empire, 550–330 B.C.
The Fall of the Roman Empire (1964)	Roman Empire, 27 B.C.–A.D. 476
Fantasia (1940)	Roman Empire, 27 B.C.–A.D. 476
	Holy Roman Empire, 962–1806
First Circle (1973, 1991, 2007)	Soviet Empire, 1922–1991
First Knight (1995)	Crusades, 1096–1221
The Giant of Marathon (1959)	Athenian Empire, Battle of Marathon, 490 B.C.
Gladiator (2000)	Roman Empire, 27 B.C.–A.D. 476
The Good Earth (1937)	Qing Empire, 1644–1912
Gormenghast (1999)	Nazi Empire, 1933–1945
The Greatest Heroes of the Bible (1978)	Achaemenid-Persian Empire, 550–330 B.C.
The Greatest Story Ever Told (1965)	Roman Empire, 27 B.C.–A.D. 476
Great Expectations (1946, 1974, 1989, 1998)	British Empire, 1583–
Grey Owl (1999)	British Empire, 1583–
Gulliver's Travels (1992, 1996)	British Empire, 1583–
Gunga Din (1939)	British Empire, 1583–
Hamlet (1948, 1964, 1964, 1970, 1980, 1990, 1990, 1996, 2000)	Danish Empire, 1200–1953
Hanged on a Twisted Cross (1996)	Nazi Empire, 1933–1945
Hans Christian Andersen (1952)	Danish Empire, 1200–1953
The Home and the World (1916)	British Empire, 1583–
The House of the Spirits (1993)	Spanish Empire, 1492–1975
The Human Factor (1979)	British Empire, 1583–
I, Claudius (1976)	Roman Empire, 27 B.C.–A.D. 476
I, the Worst of All (1990)	Spanish Empire, 1492–1975

Masada (1981)
The Master of Ballantrae (1953, 1984)
Mem-u Zin (1991)

The Merchant of Venice (1973, 2004)

The Mission (1986)

Moses (1996)
The Mystic Masseur (2001)
The Nativity Story (2006)
1984 (1984)
Nora (2000)
Notes from the Underground (1995)
Onegin (1999)
One Night with the King (2006)

Oscar and Lucinda (1997)
Othello (1981, 1995)

Out of Africa (1985)

A Passage to India (1984)
The Passion of the Christ (2004)
Persepolis (2007)

Persuasion (1971, 1995, 2007)
The Piano (1993)
Poison (1980)
The Possessed (1970)
The Prince of Egypt (1998)
Prospero's Books (1991)
The Quiet American (1958, 2002)

Rabbit-Proof Fence (2002)
Rabindranath Tagore (1961)
Ramayan (1986)
Ramayana: The Legend of Prince Rama (1992)
Reds (1981)
The Restless Conscience (1991)
The Robe (1953)
Robin Hood: Prince of Thieves (1991)

Turco-Persian Empire, 1037–1307
Venetian Empire, 800–1797
Roman Empire, 27 B.C.–A.D. 476
British Empire, 1583–
Ottoman Empire, 1300–1922
Safavid Empire, 1501–1722
Venetian Empire, 800–1797
Ottoman Empire, 1300–1922
Brazilian Empire, 1822–1889
Papal Empire, 752–1798
Portuguese Empire, 1415–1999
Spanish Empire, 1492–1975
Egyptian Empire, 1550–1070 B.C.
British Empire, 1583–
Roman Empire, 27 B.C.–A.D. 476
British Empire, 1583–
British Empire, 1583–
Russian Empire, 1721–1917
Russian Empire, 1721–1917
Achaemenid-Persian Empire,
550–330 B.C.
British Empire, 1583–
Ottoman Empire, 1300–1922
Venetian Empire, 800–1797
British Empire, 1583–
German Empire, 1871–1917
British Empire, 1583–
Roman Empire, 27 B.C.–A.D. 476
Qajar Dynasty, 1794–1925
Soviet Empire, 1922–1991
British Empire, 1583–
British Empire, 1583–
British Empire, 1583–
Russian Empire, 1721–191
Egyptian Empire, 1550–1070 B.C.
British Empire, 1583–
American Empire, 1898–
French Empire, 1605–
British Empire, 1583–
British Empire, 1583–
Indo-Gangetic Empire, 1200–300 B.C.
Indo-Gangetic Empire, 1200–300 B.C.
Russian Empire, 1721–1917
Nazi Empire, 1933–1945
Roman Empire, 27 B.C.–A.D. 476
Crusades, 1096–1221

Rudyard Kipling's The Second Jungle Book: Mowgli and Baloo (1997)
Samson and Delilah (1949)
Sand of the Eye (2003)
The Scarlet Letter (1926, 1979 1995)
Schindler's List (1993)
Shadow on the Sun (1988)
Sinbad: Legend of the Seven Seas (2003)
Sleeping Beauty (1959)
Snow White and the Seven Dwarfs (1937)
Solomon and Sheba (1959)
A Story of David (1960, 1976)
The Story of Ruth (1960)
The Sword in the Stone (1963)
Taras Bulba (1962)

Tempest (1982)

The Ten Commandments (1956)
13th Warrior (1999)
300 (2006)
Topsy Turvy (1999)

A Town Like Alice (1950, 1981)
Treasure Island (1934, 1950, 1990)

Tristan & Isolde (2006)
The Trojan Woman (1971)
Vanity Fair (2004)
The Vikings (1958)
The Wall (1982)
War and Peace (1956, 1968, 1972)

The Warriors (1979)
Watusi: Guardians of King Solomon's Mines (1959)
Wee Willie Winkie (1937)
Wide Sargasso Sea (1993, 2006)
The Wonderful World of the Brothers Grimm (1962)
Yentl (1983)

British Empire, 1583–
Israelite Empire, 1050–920 B.C.
British Empire, 1583–
British Empire, 1583–
Nazi Empire, 1933–1945
British Empire, 1583–
Abbasid Empire, 750–1258
First Napoleonic Empire, 1804–1815
First Napoleonic Empire, 1804–1815
Israelite Empire, 1050–920 B.C.
Israelite Empire, 1050–920 B.C.
Assyrian Empire, 900–612 B.C.
Crusades, 1096–1221
Jagiellon Dynasty, 1377–1572
Russian Empire, 1721–1917
British Empire, 1583–
Holy Roman Empire, 962–1806
Spanish Empire, 1492–1975
Egyptian Empire, 1550–1070 B.C.
Viking Conquests, 775–1100
Persian Empire, Battle of Thermopylae, 480 B.C.
British Empire, 1583–
Japanese Empire, 1871–1945
Japanese Empire, 1871–1945
British Empire, 1583–
Spanish Empire, 1492–1975
Crusades, 1096–1221
Athenian Empire, 477–431 B.C.
First Napoleonic Empire, 1804–1815
Viking Conquests, 775–1100
Nazi Empire, 1933–1945
Russian Empire, 1721–1917
First Napoleonic Empire, 1804–1815
Persian Empire, Battle of Cunaxa, 401 B.C.
British Empire, 1583–
British Empire, 1583–
British Empire, 1583–
First Napoleonic Empire, 1804–1815
Italian Empire, 1885–1943
Nazi Empire, 1933–1945
Soviet Empire, 1922–1991

V. BIBLIOGRAPHY OF PRIMARY SOURCES

Abu Tammam. *The Hamasa of Abu Tammam.* Translated by Felix Klein-Franke. Leiden: E. J. Brill, 1972.

Achebe, Chinua. *Anthills of the Savannah.* New York: Heinemann, 1988.

———. "Beware, Soul Brother." In *Divine Inspiration: The Life of Jesus in World Poetry,* edited by Robert Atwan, George Dardess, Peggy Rosenthal, p. Oxford: Oxford University Press, 1997.

———. *Home and Exile.* Oxford: Oxford University Press, 2000.

———. "An Image of Africa: Racism in Conrad's 'Heart of Darkness.'" In *The Norton Anthology of Theory and Criticism,* edited by Vincent B. Leitch, et al., p. New York: Norton, 2001.

———. *A Man of the People.* New York: Anchor, 1988.

———. *Things Fall Apart.* New York: Macmillan, 2005.

———. *The Trouble with Nigeria.* New York: Heinemann, 1998.

———, and Bernth Lindfors. *Conversations with Chinua Achebe.* Jackson: University Press of Mississippi, 1997.

Addison, Joseph, and Richard Steele. *The Spectator.* Vol. 2. London: J. M. Dent & Sons, 1907.

The Adi Granth, or, The Holy Scriptures of the Sikhs. Translated by Ernst Trumpp. London: Great Britain India Office, 1877.

Aelian. *On the Characteristics of Animals.* Translated by Alwyn Faber Scholfield. Cambridge, Mass.: Harvard University Press, 1959.

Aeschylus. *Persians.* Translated by Janet Lembke and C. John Herington. Oxford: Oxford University Press, 1991.

Aesop. *Aesop's Fables with a Life of Aesop.* Translated by John E. Keller and L. Clark Keating. Lexington: University Press of Kentucky, 1993.

Aidoo, Ama Ata. *Changes: A Love Story.* New York: Feminist Press, 1993.

———. *The Dilemma of a Ghost and Anowa: Two Plays.* Harlow, U.K.: Longman, 1987.

———. *No Sweetness Here and Other Stories.* New York: Feminist Press, 1995.

Akhmatova, Anna. *The Complete Poems of Anna Akhmatova.* Brookline, Mass.: Zephyr Press, 1998.

———. *Selected Poems of Anna Akhmatova.* Brookline, Mass.: Zephyr Press, 2000.

Alfonso X. *Songs of Holy Mary of Alfonso X, the Wise: A Translation of the Cantigas de Santa María.* Translated by Kathleen Kulp-Hill. Tempe: Arizona Center for Medieval and Renaissance Studies, 2000.

Alfred the Great. *The Proverbs of Alfred.* Translated by Edvard Borgström. Stockholm: Hakan Ohlsson, 1908.

Allende, Isabel. *The House of the Spirits.* New York: Bantam Books, 1982.

Almquist, Carl. *Sara Videbeck.* Translated by Adolph Burnett Benson. New York: American-Scandinavian Foundation, 1839.

Altamirano, Ignacio Manuel. *El Zarco the Blue-eyed Bandit.* Translated by Ronald Christ. Santa Fe, N.Mex.: Lumen, 2006.

Anna Comnena. *The Alexiad of the Princess Anna Comnena: Being the history of the reign of her father, Alexius I, emperor of the Romans, 1081–1118 A.D.* Translated by Elizabeth A. S. Dawes. New York: Kegan Paul, 2003.

———. *Alexias.* Translated by E. R. A. Sewter. London: Penguin, 2004.

Antin, Mary. *The Promised Land.* Boston: Houghton Mifflin, 1912.

———. *They Who Knock at Our Gates: A Complete Gospel of Immigration.* Boston: Houghton Mifflin, 1914.

The Apocrypha of the Old Testament. The Holy Bible, King James version. New York: American Bible Society, 1972.

Apuleius. *The Golden Ass.* Translated by P. G. Walsh. Oxford: Oxford University Press, 1999.

The Arabian Nights: Tales from a Thousand and One Nights. Translated by Richard Francis Burton. New York: Modern Library, 2001.

Arbiter, Petronius, and Lucius Annaeus Seneca. *The Satyricon; The Apocolocyntosis.* Translated by John Patrick Sullivan. London: Penguin, 1986.

Archilochus. "The Fox and the Hedgehog." In *Early Greek Poetry.* Translated by David D. Mulroy, p. Ann Arbor: University of Michigan Press, 1992.

Aristophanes. *The Knights/Peace/The Birds/The Assemblywomen/Wealth.* Translated by Alan H. Sommerstein and David Barrett. New York: Penguin, 1978.

———. *Lysistrata.* Translated by Nicholas Rudall. Chicago: Ivan R. Dee, 2007.

Aryasura. *Once the Buddha Was a Monkey.* Translated by Peter Khoroche. Chicago: University of Chicago Press, 1989.

Ashvaghosa. *The Buddha-Karita of Asvaghosha* in *Buddhist Mahayana Texts.* Translated by E. B. Cowell. New York: Dover, 1969.

Atharva Veda Samhita. Translated by William Dwight Whitney. Edited by Charles Rockwell Lanman. Cambridge, Mass.: Harvard University, 1905.

Atkinson, Lucy Sherrand Finley. *Recollections of Tartar Steppes and Their Inhabitants.* London: John Murray, 1863.

Augustine. *Concerning the City of God against the Pagans.* Translated by Henry Bettenson. London: Penguin, 1984.

———. *The Confessions of St. Augustine.* Translated by Rex Warner. New York: Signet, 2001.

Aulus Gellius. *The Attic Nights of Aulus Gellius.* 3 vols. Translated by William Beloe. London: J. Johnson, 1795.

Austen, Jane. *Persuasion.* Ware, U.K.: Wordsworth Editions, 1995.

Avesta Khorda Avesta: Book of Common Prayer. Translated by James Darmesteter. Whitefish, Mont.: Kessenger, 2004.

Ba, Mariama. *Scarlet Song.* Translated by Dorothy S. Blair. London: Longman, 1985.

———. *So Long a Letter.* Translated by Modupé Bodé-Thomas. Heinemann, 1981.

Babrius. *Babrius and Phaedrus.* Translated by Ben Edwin Perry. Cambridge, Mass.: Loeb Classical Library, 1990.

Baillie, Joanna. *The Collected Letters of Joanna Baillie.* Edited by Judith Bailey Slagle. Cranbury, N.J.: Fairleigh Dickinson University Press, 1999.

———. *The Dramatic and Poetical Works of Joanna Baillie.* London: Longman, Brown, Green, and Longmans, 1851.

Baker, Florence von Sass. *Morning Star: Florence Baker's Diary of the Expedition to Put Down the Slave Trade on the Nile, 1870–1873.* London: William Kimber, 1972.

Balzac, Honoré de. *The Comédie Humaine.* Translated by Katharine Prescott Wormeley. Boston: Little, Brown, 1905.

———. *The Country Doctor.* Philadelphia: Gebbie Publishing, 1895.

The Bandlet of Righteousness: An Ethiopian Book of the Dead. Translated by E. A. Wallis Budge. London: Kegan Paul International, 2002.

Barnard, Lady Anne. *South Africa a Century Ago: Letters Written from the Cape of Good Hope (1797–1801).* London: Smith, Elder, 1901.

Bazán, Emilia Pardo. *The House of Ulloa.* Translated by Paul O'Prey and Lucia Graves. London: Penguin, 1990.

———. *Russia: Its People and Its Literature.* Translated by Fanny Hale Gardiner. Chicago: A. C. McClurg and Co., 1890.

Beaufort, Emily Anne. *Egyptian Sepulchres and Syrian Shrines.* London: Longman, Green, Longman and Roberts, 1861.

Beckford, William. *Vathek.* London: Oxford University Press, 1970.

Behn, Aphra. *Abdelazar; or, The Moor's Revenge.* Whitefish, Mont.: Kessinger, 2004.

———. *Oroonoko and Other Writings.* Oxford: Oxford University Press, 1994.

Bell, Gertrude Lowthian. *The Desert and the Sown.* New York: Dutton, 1907.

Beowulf: An Illustrated Edition. Translated by Seamus Heaney. New York: W. W. Norton, 2007.

Berryhill, Elizabeth. *The Cup of Trembling—A Play in Two Acts Derived from the Life of Dietrich Bonhoeffer.* New York: Seabury, 1962.

Bhagavad-Gita As It Is, The. Translated by A. C. Bhaktivedanta Swami Prabhupada. Los Angeles: Bhaktivedanta Book Trust, 1989.

Bird, Isabella Lucy. *Among the Tibetans.* London: Religious Tract Society, 1894.

———. *Journeys in Persia and Kurdistan.* London: John Murray, 1891.

———. *Korea and Her Neighbours.* London: John Murray, 1898.

———. *Unbeaten Tracks in Japan.* London: John Murray, 1880.

———. *The Yangtze Valley and Beyond.* London: John Murray, 1899.

Bly, Nellie. *Around the World in 72 Days.* Brookfield, Conn.: Twenty-First Century Books, 1998.

Bodart, Anne. *The Blue Dog and Other Fables for the French.* Translated by Alice B. Toklas. Boston: Houghton Mifflin, 1956.

Bonhoeffer, Dietrich. *Discipleship.* Translated by John D. Godsey. Minneapolis, Minn.: Fortress Press, 2003.

Boulle, Pierre. *The Bridge over the River Kwai.* Translated by Xan Fielding. New York: Bantam, 1954.

Brassey, Anne. *The Last Voyage.* London: Longman, 1889.

Brinton, Daniel Garrison. *Rig Veda Americanus: Sacred Songs of the Ancient Mexicans, with a Gloss in Nahuatl.* Philadelphia: D. G. Brinton, 1890.

Brodsky, Joseph. *Joseph Brodsky: Selected Poems.* Translated by George L. Kline. New York: Harper & Row, 1974.

———. *Less Than One.* New York: Farrar, Straus and Giroux, 1986.

———. *So Forth.* New York: Farrar, Straus and Giroux, 1998.

Brodsky, Joseph, and Cynthia L. Haven, eds. *Joseph Brodsky: Conversations.* Jackson: University Press of Mississippi, 2003.

Bryant, Louise. "How the Revolution Began in America." *Revolutionary Age* (January 25, 1919): 6.

Buck, Pearl. *The Good Earth.* New York: Pocket Books, 1931.

———. *A House Divided.* Berkeley, Calif.: Moyer Bell, 1984.

———. *The Mother.* New York: HarperCollins, 1971.

Byron, George Gordon Byron, Lord. *Childe Harold's Pilgrimage: A Romaunt.* Philadelphia: Henry Carey Baird, 1854.

———. *The Works of Lord Byron Complete in One Volume.* Frankfurt: H. L. Broenner, 1826.

Camões, Luís Vaz de. *The Lusiads.* Translated by Landeg White. Oxford: Oxford University Press, 2002.

Campion, Jane. *The Piano.* New York: Miramax Books, 1995.

Cantares Mexicanos: Songs of the Aztecs. Translated by John Bierhorst. Stanford, Calif.: Stanford University Press, 1985.

Cao Xueqin. *Dream of the Red Chamber.* Translated by Chi-Chen Wang. Garden City, N.Y.: Doubleday Anchor, 1958.

Carey, Peter. *Oscar and Lucinda.* Brisbane: University of Queensland Press, 1988.

———. *True History of the Kelly Gang: A Novel.* New York: Vintage, 2001.

Carlyle, Thomas. *Heroes, Hero-worship and the Heroic in History.* Philadelphia: Henry Altemus, 1895.

Cavafy, Constantine. *Collected Poems.* Translated by Edmund Keeley and Philip Sherrard. Princeton, N.J.: Princeton University Press, 1992.

Celan, Paul, and Nelly Sachs. *Correspondence.* Translated by Christopher Clark. Berlin: Sheep Meadow, 1995.

Cervantes, Miguel de. *Don Quixote of La Mancha.* Translated by Walter Starkie. New York: New American Library, 1957.

Césaire, Aimé. *A Tempest.* Translated by Richard Miller. New York: Borchardt, 1985.

Chrétien de Troyes. *Perceval: The Story of the Grail.* Translated by Burton Raffel. Hartford, Conn.: Yale University Press, 1999.

Christine de Pisan. *The Book of Deeds of Arms and of Chivalry.* Translated by Sumner Willard. Philadelphia: Pennsylvania State University Press, 1999.

———. *The Treasure of the City of Ladies: or, The Book of Three Virtues.* Translated by Sarah Lawson. London: Penguin, 1985.

Clarke, Marcus. *His Natural Life.* London: Adamant Media, 2006.

Coetzee, J. M. *Giving Offense: Essays on Censorship.* Chicago: University of Chicago Press, 1997.

Collins, Wilkie. *The Moonstone.* London: Penguin Books, 1998.

Condé, Maryse. *I, Tituba, Black Witch of Salem.* Translated by Richard Philcox. New York: Ballantine, 1994.

———. *Segu.* Translated by Barbara Bray. New York: Penguin, 1998.

———. *Windward Heights*. Translated by Richard Philcox. New York: Soho, 1998.

Confucius. *The Book of Songs: The Ancient Chinese Classic of Poetry*. Translated by Arthur Waley. New York: Grove, 1996.

———. *The Sayings of Confucius*. Translated by Lionel Giles. New York: E. P. Dutton, 1910.

Conrad, David. *A State of Intrigue: The Epic of Bamana Segu according to Tayiru Bambera*. Oxford: Oxford University Press, 1990.

Conrad, Joseph. *Almayer's Folly: A Story of an Eastern River*. London: Eveleigh Nash, 1904.

———. *Heart of Darkness and The Secret Sharer*. New York: Signet, 1983.

———. *Lord Jim*. Garden City, N.Y.: Doubleday, Doran, 1920.

Crawford, Mabel Sharman. *Through Algeria*. London: Bentley, 1863.

Croly, George. *Salathiel: A Story of the Past, the Present, and the Future*. London: Henry Colburn, 1828.

Cruz, Sor Juana Inés de la. *The Answer/La Respuesta: Including a selection of Poems*. Translated by Electa Arenal and Amanda Powell. New York: Feminist Press, 1994.

———. *A Sor Juana Anthology*. Translated by Alan S. Trueblood. Cambridge, Mass.: Harvard University Press, 1988.

Dahl, Roald. *The Collected Short Stories of Roald Dahl*. London: Penguin, 1992.

D'Annunzio, Gabriele. *The Flame of Life*. Translated by Kassandra Vivaria. Boston: L. C. Page, 1900.

———. *Francesca da Rimini*. Translated by Arthur Symons. Whitefish, Mont.: Kessinger, 2005.

———. *The Triumph of Death*. New York: George H. Richmond, 1896.

Dalai Lama XIV. *Kalachakra Tantra: Rite of Initiation*. Edited and translated by Jeffrey Hopkins. Somerville, Mass: Wisdom Publications, 1999.

Darwish, Mahmoud. *The Butterfly's Burden*. Translated by Fady Joudah. Port Townsend, Wash.: Copper Canyon, 2007.

The Dead Sea Scrolls: A New Translation. Rev. ed. Translated by Michael O. Wise, Martin G. Abegg, and Edward M. Cook. San Francisco: HarperSanFrancisco, 2005.

Desai, Anita. *Baumgartner's Bombay*. New York: Knopf, 1989.

———. *In Custody*. New York: Harper & Row, 1984.

———. *Voices in the City*. New Delhi: Orient Paperbacks, 1965.

The Dhammapada: The Buddha's Path to Freedom. Translated by Acharya Buddharakkhita. Kandy, Sri Lanka: Buddhist Publication Society, 1985.

Díaz del Castillo, Bernal. *The Memoirs of the Conquistador Bernal Díaz del Castillo: Containing a True and Full Account of the Discovery and Conquest of Mexico and New Spain*. Translated by John Ingram Lockhart. London: J. Hatchard and Son, 1844.

Dickens, Charles. *American Notes for General Circulation*. Boston: Ticknor and Fields, 1867.

———. *The Annotated Dickens*. 2 vols. Edited by Edward Guiliano and Philip Collins. New York: Clarkson N. Potter, 1986.

Dinesen, Isak. *Anecdotes of Destiny*. London: Michael Joseph, 1958.

———. *The Angelic Avengers*. London: Putnam, 1946.

———. *Babette's Feast and Other Anecdotes of Destiny*. New York: Vintage Books, 1953.

———. *Daguerreotypes and Other Essays*. Chicago: University of Chicago Press, 1984.

———. *Out of Africa and Shadows on the Grass*. New York: Vintage, 1985.

Diop, Birago. *Mother Crocodile*. Translated by Rosa Guy. New York: Delacorte, 1981.

Dostoyevsky, Fyodor. *Buried Alive; or, Ten Years of Penal Servitude in Siberia*. Translated by Marie von Thilo. London: Longmans, Green, & Co., 1881.

———. *Notes from the Underground*. Translated by Jane Kentish. Oxford: Oxford University Press, 1999.

———. *Pages from the Journal of an Author*. Translated by S. Koteliansky and J. Middleton Murry. Boston: John W. Luce, 1916.

———. *Poor Folk*. Translated by Lena Milman. London: Elkin Matthews and John Lane, 1894.

Doyle, Arthur Conan. *The Complete Sherlock Holmes*. New York: Bantam, 1960.

———. *The Crime of the Congo*. New York: Doubleday, Page & Co., 1909.

Du Fu. *The Selected Poems of Tu Fu*. Translated by David Hinton. New York: New Directions, 1989.

Dumas, Alexandre. *The Count of Monte Cristo*. 2 vols. Translated by Pier Angelo Fiorentino. Boston: Little, Brown, 1889.

————. *The Last Cavalier: Being the Adventures of Count Sainte-Hermine in the Age of Napoleon.* Translated by Lauren Wayne Yoder. New York: Pegasus, 2005.

Durán, Diego. *The History of the Indies of New Spain.* Translated by Doris Heyden. Norman: University of Oklahoma Press, 1994.

————. *The True History of the Conquest of New Spain.* 5 vols. Edited by Genaro García. Translated by Alfred Percival Maudslay. London: Hakluyt Society, 1908–16.

Dutta, Krishna, and Anita Desai. *Calcutta: A Cultural and Literary History.* Oxford: Signal Books, 2003.

Eberhardt, Isabelle. *The Passionate Nomad: The Diary of Isabelle Eberhardt.* Boston: Beacon, 1988.

Edgeworth, Maria. *Castle Rackrent.* Edited by Susan Kubica Howard. Indianapolis: Hackett Publishing, 2007.

————. *Tales of Fashionable Life.* London: Baldwin & Cradock, 1832.

Edgeworth, Richard Lovell, and Maria Edgeworth. *Essay on Irish Bulls.* New York: J. Swaine, 1803.

The Egyptian Book of the Dead: The Chapters of Coming Forth by Day. Translated by E. A. Wallis Budge. London: Kegan Paul, Trench, Trübner, & Co., 1898.

Einhard. *Two Lives of Charlemagne.* Translated by Lewis Thorpe. Harmondsworth, U.K.: Penguin, 1969.

Emecheta, Buchi. *The Joys of Motherhood.* New York: George Braziller, 1980.

————. *The Rape of Shavi.* New York: George Braziller, 1985.

————. *Second-Class Citizen.* New York: George Braziller, 1983.

The English Charlemagne Romances: Sir Ferumbras. Boston: Adamant Media, 2001.

Enuma Elish: The Epic of Creation. Translated by L. W. King. Whitefish, Mont.: Kessinger, 2004.

The Epic of Gilgamesh. Translated by Danny P. Jackson. Wauconda, Ill.: Bolchazy-Carducci, 1992.

Equiano, Olaudah. *The Life of Olaudah Equiano, or Gustavus Vassa, the African, Written by Himself.* Boston: Isaac Knapp, 1837.

Falconbridge, Anna Maria. *Two Voyages to the Sierra Leone During the Years 1791–1792–1793.* London: privately published, 1794.

Fenton, James. *A History of Tasmania.* Hobart, Tasmania: J. Welch and Sons, 1884.

Firdawsi. *Shahnameh: The Persian Book of Kings.* Translated by Dick Davis. New York: Viking, 2006.

Florian, Jean-Pierre Claris de. *Fables of Florian.* Translated by J. W. Phelps. New York: John B. Alden, 1888.

Forster, E. M. *Aspects of the Novel.* New York: Harvest Books, 1956.

————. *A Passage to India.* London: Macmillan, 2002.

France, Anatole. *Penguin Island.* Translated by A. W. Evans. London: John Lane, 1921.

Frank, Anne. *The Diary of a Young Girl: The Definitive Edition.* Edited by Otto H. Frank and Mirjam Pressler. Translated by Susan Massotty. New York: Bantam, 1997.

Gama, Basilio da. *The Uruguay: A Historical Romance of South America.* Translated by Sir Richard F. Burton. Berkeley: University of California Press, 1982.

Gandhi, Mohandas. *An Autobiography, or the Story of My Experiments with Truth.* Translated by Mahadev Desai. Ahmedabad, India: Navajvan Publishing, 1940.

Garcilaso de la Vega. *The Florida of the Inca.* Translated by John Grier Varner and Jeannette Johnson Varner. Austin: University of Texas Press, 1951.

————. *Royal Commentaries of the Incas and General History of Peru.* Translated by Harold Livermore. Norman: University of Oklahoma Press, 1966.

Ghazali, al-. *The Niche of Lights.* Translated and annotated by David Buchman. Salt Lake City, Utah: Brigham Young University, 1998.

Gilbert, William, and Arthur Sullivan. *The Complete Annotated Gilbert and Sullivan.* New York: W. W. Norton, 1996.

Goethe, Johann Wolfgang von. *Faust: A Tragedy.* Translated by Bayard Taylor. Boston: Houghton, Mifflin, 1898.

————. *Faust: A Tragedy, the Second Part.* Translated by Bayard Taylor. Boston: Houghton, Mifflin, 1899.

————. *Poems and Ballads of Goethe.* New York: Holt and Williams, 1871.

————. *The Story of Reynard the Fox.* New York: Heritage Press, 1954.

Gogol, Nikolay. *Arabesques.* Translated by Alexander Tulloch. Ann Arbor, Mich.: Ardis, 1982.

————. *Dead Souls.* Translated by Bernard Guilbert Guerney. New Haven, Conn.: Yale University Press, 1996.

————. *The Inspector General.* Translated by John Anderson. New York: Samuel French, 1931.

————. *Taras Bulba: A Story of the Dnieper Cossacks.* Translated by Beatrice C. Baskerville. London: Walter Scott, 1907.

Goldman, Emma. *Anarchism and Other Essays.* New York: Mother Earth Publishing, 1910.

————. *Living My Life.* New York: A. A. Knopf, 1931.

————. *My Disillusionment in Russia.* Garden City, N.Y.: Doubleday, 1923.

————. *My Further Disillusionment in Russia.* Garden City, N.Y.: Doubleday, 1924.

Gómez de Avellaneda y Arteaga, Gertrudis. *Sab and Autobiography.* Translated and edited by Nina M. Scott. Austin: University of Texas, 1993.

Gordimer, Nadine. *Burger's Daughter.* London: Penguin, 1980.

————. *July's People.* London: Penguin, 1982.

————. *The Pickup.* London: Penguin, 2002.

Gordon-Cumming, Constance Frederico. *At Home in Fiji.* Edinburgh: Blackwood, 1881.

Greaney, Michael. *Conrad, Language, and Narrative.* Cambridge: Cambridge University Press, 2002.

Greene, Graham. *A Burnt-Out Case.* New York: Viking, 1961.

————. *The Heart of the Matter.* London: Penguin, 2004.

————. *Journey without Maps.* London: Penguin, 1992.

————. *Our Man in Havana.* London: Penguin, 2007.

————. *The Quiet American.* London: Penguin, 2002.

Grey Owl. *The Men of the Last Frontier.* Toronto: Macmillan, 1931.

————. *Tales of an Empty Cabin.* Toronto: Macmillan, 1936.

Grimm, Jacob, and Wilhelm Grimm. *The Complete Grimm's Fairy Tales.* Introduction by Padraic Colum. New York: Pantheon Books, 2005.

Grimm, Jacob. *Teutonic Mythology.* 3 vols. Translated by James Steven Stallybrass. London: George Bell & Sons, 1882–83.

Haggard, H. Rider. *Allan Quatermain: The Zulu Trilogy, Marie, Child of Storm, and Finished.* New York: Wilder, 2007.

————. *Allan's Wife.* London: Spencer Blackett, 1889.

————. *Black Heart and White Heart.* London: Longmans, Green, 1900.

————. *Diary of an African Journey: The Return of Rider Haggard.* New York: New York University Press, 2001.

————. *King Solomon's Mines.* Whitefish, Mont.: Kessinger, 2004.

Halevi, Yehuda. *The Kuzari: In Defense of the Despised Faith.* Translated by Hartwig Hirschfeld. New York: E. P. Dutton, 1905.

————. *Ninety-Two Poems and Hymns of Yehuda Halevi.* Translated by Thomas Kovoch, Eva Jospe, and Gilya Gerda Schmidt. Edited by Richard A. Cohen. New York: State University of New York Press, 2000.

Han Yong-un. *Love's Silence & Other Poems.* Translated by Jaihiun Kim and Ronald B. Hatch. Vancouver: Ronsdale Press, 1999.

Hartmann von Aue. *Arthurian Romances, Tales, and Lyric Poetry: The Complete Works of Hartmann von Aue.* Translated by Frank Tobin, Kim Vivian, and Richard H. Lawson. Philadelphia: Pennsylvania State University Press, 2001.

Head, Bessie. *Maru.* London: Heinemann, 1997.

————. *A Question of Power.* London: Heinemann, 1974.

————. *When Rain Clouds Gather.* London: Heinemann, 1995.

————. *A Woman Alone: Autobiographical Writings.* London: Heinemann, 1990.

Heaney, Seamus. *Death of a Naturalist.* London: Faber & Faber, 1966.

————. *Opened Ground: Selected Poems 1966–1996.* New York: Farrar, Straus, and Giroux, 1998.

Hearn, Lafcadio. *Glimpses of Unfamiliar Japan.* Boston: Houghton, Mifflin, 1894.

————. *In Ghostly Japan.* Boston: Little, Brown, and Co., 1899.

————. *Kwaidan.* Boston: Houghton, Mifflin, 1904.

Herodotus. *The Histories.* Translated by Aubrey de Sélincourt. Baltimore, Md.: Penguin, 1961.

Hersey, John. *A Bell for Adano.* New York: Vintage, 1988.

————. *Hiroshima.* New York: Random House, 1946.

————. *Into the Valley: A Skirmish of the Marines.* New York: Alfred A. Knopf, 1943.

————. *The Wall.* New York: Alfred A. Knopf, 1950.

Hitler, Adolf. *Hitler's Second Book.* Translated by Krista Smith. Minneapolis, Minn.: Consortium books, 2006.

————. *Mein Kampf.* Translated by Edgar Dugdale. London: Hurst and Blackett, 1939.

Holy Bible. Iowa Falls: World Bible Publishers, 1986.

Horace. *Horace, the Odes: New Translations by Contemporary Poets.* Edited by J. D. McClatchy. Princeton, N.J.: Princeton University Press, 2002.

————. *Satires and Epistles of Horace*. Translated by Smith Palmer Bovie. Chicago: University of Chicago Press, 1959.

Hugo, Victor. *Bug-Jargal*. Translated by Chris Bongie. Buffalo, N.Y.: Broadview, 2004.

Ibn Battuta. *Travels in Asia and Africa, 1325–1354*. Translated by H. A. R. Gibb. New Delhi: Manohar, 2001.

Iriarte, Tomás de. *Literary Fables of Yriarte*. Translated by George H. Devereux. Boston: Ticknor and Fields, 1855.

Izumi Shikibu. *Diaries of Court Ladies of Old Japan*. Translated by Annie Shepley Omori and Kochi Doi. Boston: Houghton Mifflin, 1920.

Jacobs, W. W. *The Lady of the Barge and Others*. Whitefish, Mont.: Kessinger, 2004.

Jahiz, al-. *The Book of Misers: Al-Bukhala*. Translated by R. B. Serjeant. London: Garnet, 2000.

Jameson, Anna. *Winter Studies and Summer Rambles in Canada*. London: Saunders & Otley, 1838.

Jhabvala, Ruth Prawer. *Heat and Dust*. New York: Touchstone, 1975.

Johnson, Pauline. *Flint and Feathers*. Toronto: Musson Books, 1913.

————. *The Moccasin Maker*. Whitefish, Mont.: Kessinger, 2004.

Joinville, Jean de, and Geoffroy de Villehardouin. *Chronicles of the Crusades*. Translated by Margaret R. B. Shaw. London: Penguin, 1963.

Josephus, Flavius. *Josephus: Complete Works*. Translated by William Whiston. Grand Rapids, Mich.: Kregel, 1960.

Joyce, James. *Dubliners*. New York: Signet, 2007.

————. *Occasional, Critical, and Political Writing*. Oxford: Oxford University Press, 2000.

————. *A Portrait of the Artist as a Young Man*. London: Penguin, 2003.

————. *Ulysses*. New York: Vintage, 1990.

Juvenal. *The Satires*. Translated by Niall Rudd. Oxford: Oxford University Press, 1992.

Kafka, Franz. *The Castle*. Translated by Harmon. New York: Schocken, 1998.

————. *The Trial*. Translated by Breon Mitchell. New York: Schocken, 1999.

Kalakaua, David. *The Legends and Myths of Hawaii: The Fables and Folklore of a Strange People*. Rutland, Vt.: Charles E. Tuttle, 1972.

Kalilah and Dimnah: or, the Fables of Bidpai. Translated by Ion Grand Neville Keith-Falconer. Cambridge: Cambridge University Press, 1885.

Kempe, Margery. *The Book of Margery Kempe*. Translated by Barry Windeatt. Rochester, N.Y.: D. S. Brewer, 2006.

Kidd, Adam. *The Huron Chief and Other Poems*. Montreal: Herald and New Gazette, 1830.

Kincaid, Jamaica. *Annie John*. New York: Farrar, Straus and Giroux, 1985.

————. *The Autobiography of My Mother*. New York: Plume, 1996.

————. *My Garden*. New York: Farrar, Straus, Giroux, 1999.

————. "Ovando." *Conjunctions* 14, no. 10 (Fall 1989): 75–83.

————. *A Small Place*. New York: Farrar, Straus and Giroux, 1988.

————. "Sowers and Reapers: The Unquiet World of a Flower Bed." *New Yorker* 76, no. 43 (January 22, 2001): 41–45.

Kingsley, Mary. *Travels in West Africa: Congo Français, Corisco and Cameroons*. London: Macmillan, 1897.

Kipling, Rudyard. "The Absent-Minded Beggar," *Daily Mail* (London), 1899, n.p.

————. *Barrack-Room Ballads and Other Verses*. London: Methuen, 1892.

————. *Captains Courageous: A Story of the Grand Banks*. London: Macmillan, 1897.

————. *The Collected Poems of Rudyard Kipling*. London: Wordsworth Editions, 1999.

————. *Departmental Ditties and Other Verses*. Lahore: The Civil and Military Gazette Press, 1886.

————. *The Five Nations*. London: Methuen, 1903.

————. *The Jungle Book*. London: Macmillan, 1894.

————. *Just So Stories for Little Children*. London: Macmillan, 1902.

————. *Kim*. London: Macmillan, 1901.

————. *Life's Handicap: Being Stories of Mine Own People*. London: Macmillan, 1891.

————. *The Light That Failed*. Philadelphia: J. B. Lippincott, 1891.

————. *The Phantom Rickshaw and Other Tales*. Allahabad, India: A. H. Wheeler, 1888.

————. *Plain Tales from the Hills*. London: W. Thacker, 1888.

————. *Sea Warfare*. London: Macmillan, 1916.

————. *The Second Jungle Book*. London: Macmillan, 1895.

————. *Something of Myself and Other Autobiographical Writings*. Cambridge: Cambridge University Press, 1937.

————. *Stalky & Co.* London: Macmillan, 1899.

The Kojiki: Records of Ancient Matters. Translated by Basil Hall Chamberlain. North Clarendon, Vt.: Tuttle, 2005.

The Koran. Translated by Nessim Joseph Dawood. London: Penguin Classics, 2004.

Kosinski, Jerzy. *The Painted Bird*. New York: Grove, 1976.

Krylov, Ivan. *Krilof and His Fables*. Translated by W. R. S. Ralston. London: Cassell & Co., 1883.

Kuznetsov, Anatoly. *Babi Yar*. New York: Dell, 1966.

La Fontaine, Jean de. *Fables of La Fontaine*. Translated by Elizur Wright. New York: Derby & Jackson, 1860.

Laksmi Tantra: A Pancaratra Text. Translated by Sanjukta Gupta. Amsterdam: Brill, 1972.

Lancaster, G. B. *The Law-Bringers*. New York: Hodder & Stoughton, 1913.

————. *Pageant*. Victoria, Aust.: Penguin, 1933.

————. *Promenade*. Sydney: Angus & Robertson, 1938.

Laozi. *Tao Te Ching*. Translated by Aleister Crowley. Newburyport, Mass.: Weiser, 1997.

Las Casas, Bertolomé de. *History of the Indies*. Translated by Andrée Collard. New York: Harper & Row, 1971.

————. *A Short Account of the Destruction of the Indies*. Edited and translated by Nigel Griffin. London and New York: Penguin, 1992.

Lawrence, T. E. *The Mint*. New York: W. W. Norton, 1963.

————. *Seven Pillars of Wisdom*. London: Wordsworth Editions, 1997.

Lawson, Henry. *Henry Lawson: Twenty Stories and Seven Poems*. Perth, Aust.: Angus and Robertson, 1947.

Leonowens, Anna. *The English Governess at the Siamese Court: Being Recollections of Six Years in the Royal Palace at Bangkok*. London: Trubner, 1870.

————. *Life and Travel in India: Being Recollections of a Journey before the Days of Railroads*. Philadelphia: Porter & Coates, 1884.

————. *The Romance of the Harem*. Philadelphia: Porter & Coates, 1872.

Lessing, Doris. *Canopus in Argos: Archives*. New York: Vintage, 1992.

————. *Going Home*. New York: Harper Perennial, 1996.

————. *The Golden Notebook*. New York: HarperCollins, 1999.

————. *The Grass Is Singing*. New York: Heinemann, 1973.

————. *Prisons We Choose to Live Inside*. New York: Harper Perennial, 1987.

————. *Under My Skin: Volume One of My Autobiography, to 1959*. New York: Harper Perennial, 1995.

————. *Walking in the Shade: Volume Two of My Autobiography—1949–1962*. New York: Harper Perennial, 1998.

Levi, Primo. *The Black Hole of Auschwitz*. Translated by Marco Belpoliti and Sharon Wood. Cambridge, U.K.: Polity, 2005.

————. *If Not Now, When?* Translated by William Weaver. New York: Penguin, 1986.

————. *Survival in Auschwitz*. Translated by Giulio Einaudi. New York: Touchstone, 1996.

Lewis, Matthew Gregory. *Journal of a West India Proprietor*. London: John Murray, 1834.

————. *Romantic Tales*. London: Longman, Hurst, Rees, and Orme, 1808.

Liliuokalani. *Hawaii's Story by Hawaii's Queen, Liliuokalani*. Boston: Lothrop, Lee & Shepard, 1898.

————. *The Kumulipo: An Hawaiian Creation Myth*. Honolulu, Hawaii: Pueo Press, 1978.

————. *The Queen's Songbook*. Edited by Dorothy K. Gillett and Barbara B. Smith. Honolulu, Hawaii: Hui Hanai, 1999.

Li Bo. *The Works of Li Po, the Chinese Poet*. Translated by Shigeyoshi Obata. New York: E. P. Dutton, 1922.

Livingstone, David. *The Last Journals of David Livingstone in Central Africa*. London: John Murray, 1874.

Livy. *The History of Rome*. Translated by D. Spillan. London: Henry G. Bohn, 1853.

Lochhead, Douglas, and Raymond Souster, comps. *100 Poems of Nineteenth Century Canada*. Toronto: Macmillan, 1974.

Lönnrot, Elias. *The Kalevala: The Epic Poem of Finland*. Translated by John Martin Crawford. Cincinnati: Robert Clarke, 1904.

Love Songs from the Man'yoshu. Translated by Ian Hideo Levy. Tokyo: Kodansha International, 2000.

Lucan. *Pharsalia*. Translated by Jane Wilson Joyce. Ithaca, N.Y.: Cornell University Press, 1993.

Lugovskaya, Nina. *I Want to Live: The Diary of Young Girl in Stalin's Russia*. Translated by Andrew Bromfield. Boston: Houghton Mifflin, 2006.

Machiavelli, Niccolò. *The Art of War.* Translated by Christopher Lynch. Chicago: University of Chicago Press, 2003.

———. *The History of Florence.* Translated by Charles W. Colby. New York: Colonial Press, 1901.

———. *The Prince.* Translated by Luigi Ricci. New York: Mentor, 1952.

Mackenzie, G. Muir, and A. P. Irby. *Travels in the Slavonic Provinces of Turkey-in-Europe.* London: Daldy, Isbister & Co., 1877.

Mah, Adeline Yen. *Falling Leaves: The True Story of an Unwanted Chinese Daughter.* New York: John Riley and Sons, 1997.

Mair, Charles. *Tecumseh: A Drama.* Toronto: Hunter, Rose, 1886.

Mansfield, Katherine. *Katherine Mansfield's Selected Stories.* New York: W. W. Norton and Co., 2006.

———. *The Katherine Mansfield Notebooks.* Wellington, N.Z.: Lincoln University Press, 1997.

Marcus Aurelius. *The Emperor's Handbook.* Translated by C. Scot Hicks and David V. Hicks. New York: Scribner, 2002.

Marie de France. *Fables.* Translated by Harriet Spiegel. Toronto: University of Toronto Press, 1995.

———. *The Lais of Marie de France.* Translated by Glyn S. Burgess and Keith Busby. London: Penguin, 1999.

Marinetti, Filippo Tommaso. *The Futurist Cookbook.* Translated by Suzanne Brill. San Francisco: Bedford Arts, 1989.

———. *Selected Poems and Related Prose.* Translated by Elizabeth R. Napier. New Haven, Conn.: Yale University Press, 2002.

Markham, Beryl. *The Good Lion.* Boston: Houghton Mifflin, 1983.

———. *The Splendid Outcast: Beryl Markham's African Stories.* San Francisco, Calif.: North Point, 1987.

———. *West with the Night.* Berkeley, Calif.: North Point Press, 1942.

Marsden, Kate. *On Sledge and Horseback to the Outcast Siberian Lepers.* New York: Cassell, 1877.

Martí, José. *José Martí Reader: Writings on the Americas.* New York: Ocean Press, 1999.

———. *Selected Writings.* New York: Penguin, 2002.

———. *Versos Sencillos: Simple Verses.* Translated by Manuel A. Tellechea. Houston, Tex.: Arte Publico Press, 1997.

McSwigan, Marie. *Snow Treasure.* New York: E. P. Dutton, 1942.

Melville, Herman. *Piazza Tales.* New York: Dix & Edwards, 1856.

Montalvo, Garci Rodriguez de. *Amadis of Gaul, Books I & II.* Translated by Edwin Place and Herbert Behm. Lexington: University Press of Kentucky, 2003.

Moodie, Susanna. *Roughing It in the Bush; or, Life in Canada.* London: Richard Bentley, 1852.

Multatuli. *The Oyster and the Eagle: Selected Aphorisms & Parables of Multatuli.* Translated by E. M. Beekman. Amherst: University of Massachusetts Press, 1974.

Murasaki Shikibu. *The Diary of Lady Murasaki.* Translated by Richard Bowring. New York: Penguin, 1999.

———. *The Tale of Genji.* Translated by Royall Tyler. New York: Penguin, 2002.

Naipaul, V. S. *A Bend in the River.* New York: Random House, 1989.

———. *The Loss of El Dorado.* New York: Alfred A. Knopf, 1970.

———. *Miguel Street.* New York: Heinemann, 2000.

———. *The Return of Eva Perón and the Killings in Trinidad.* New York: Random House, 1980.

Nelson, Jan, ed. *La Chanson d'Antioche.* Tuscaloosa: University of Alabama Press, 2003.

Niane, D. T. *Sundiata: An Epic of Old Mali.* Translated by G. D. Pickett. Harlow, U.K.: Longman, 1965.

Nicholson, Frank Carr, trans. *Old German Love Songs.* Chicago: University of Chicago Press, 1907.

Nihongi: Chronicles of Japan from the Earliest Times to A.D. *697.* Translated by W. G. Aston. New York: Cosimo Classics, 2006.

Omar Khayyám. "Rubáiyát." In *Harvard Classics.* Translated by Frederick Lamar Sargent, p. Cambridge, Mass.: Harvard University Press, 1909.

Ondaatje, Michael. *The English Patient.* New York: Vintage, 1993.

Orwell, George. *Animal Farm.* New York: Signet, 1946.

———. *Burmese Days.* Fairfield, Iowa: 1st World Publishing, 2004.

———. *A Collection of Essays.* Fort Washington, Pa.: Harvest Books, 1970.

———. *My Country Right or Left 1940–1943: The Collected Essays, Journalism and Letters of George Orwell.* Edited by Sonia Orwell and Ian Angus. Boston: David R. Godine, 2000.

———. *1984.* New York: Signet, 1983.

———. *The Orwell Reader: Fiction, Essays, and Reportage.* Fort Washington, Pa.: Harvest Books, 1961.

————. *Shooting an Elephant and Other Essays*. New York: Harcourt, Brace, 1950.

————. *Why I Write*. New York: Penguin, 2005.

Ovid. *Metamorphoses*. 2 vols. Translated by Frank Justus Miller. Cambridge, Mass.: Harvard University Press, 1984.

————. *Sorrows of an Exile*. Translated by A. D. Melville. Oxford: Oxford University Press, 1995.

Pancatantra. Translated by Visnu Sarma. London: Penguin Classics, 2007.

Paredes, Américo. *With His Pistol in His Hand: A Border Ballad and Its Hero*. Austin: University of Texas Press, 1958.

Park, Linda Sue. *When My Name Was Keoko*. New York: Random House, 2002.

Park, Mungo. *Travels in the Interior Districts of Africa*. London: John Murray, 1816.

Pasternak, Boris. *Dr. Zhivago*. New York: Pantheon, 1958.

————. *My Sister—Life*. Translated by Mark Rudman and Bohdan Boychuk. Chicago: Northwestern University Press, 2002.

Paterson, Andrew Barton. *Banjo Paterson's Poems of the Bush*. London: J. M. Dent, 1987.

————. *Saltbush Bill, J. P., and Other Verses*. Whitefish, Mont.: Kessinger, 2004.

Peake, Mervyn. *Gormenghast*. Woodstock, N.Y.: Overlook, 2007.

————. *Peake's Progress*. Edited by Maeve Peake. Woodstock, N.Y.: Overlook, 1981.

Perse, Saint-John. *Selected Poems*. Edited by Mary Ann Caws. New York: New Directions, 1982.

Phaedrus. *Fabulae Aesopiae*. Translated by J. T. White. London: Spottiswoode & Co., 1876.

Plato. *Plato's Phaedo*. Translated by E. M. Cope. Cambridge: University Press, 1875.

Pliny. *Pliny's Letters*. Translated by Alfred Church and W. J. Brodribb. Edinburgh: William Blackwood and Sons, 1872.

Plutarch. *Moralia*. Translated by Frank Cole Babbitt. Whitefish, Mont.: Kessinger, 2005.

————. *Parallel Lives*. 11 vols. Translated by Bernadotte Perrin. Cambridge, Mass.: Harvard University Press, 1926.

The Poem of the Cid. Translated by W. S. Merwin. New York: New American Library 1959.

Polo, Marco. *The Travels of Marco Polo*. Translated by Aldo Ricci. London: George Routledge, 1931.

Popol Vuh: The Mayan Book of the Dawn of Life. Translated by Dennis Tedlock. New York: Touchstone Books, 1996.

Prince, Mary. *The History of Mary Prince, a West Indian Slave*. London: F. Westley and A. H. Davis, 1831.

Prince, Nancy. *A Narrative of the Life and Travels of Mrs. Nancy Prince*. Boston: Wm. A. Hall, 1850.

Procopius. *History of the Wars*. Translated by H. B. Dewing. London: Heinemann, 1914.

————. *Of the Buildings of Justinian*. Boston: Adament Media, 2004.

————. *The Secret History*. Translated by Geoffrey Arthur Williamson. London: Penguin, 1966.

Propertius, Sextus. *The Poems*. Translated by Guy Lee. Oxford: Oxford University Press, 1996.

Proverbs of Ahiqar. Translated by James M. Lindenberger. Baltimore: Johns Hopkins University Press, 1983.

Pushkin, Alexander. *Eugene Onegin*. Translated by Charles Johnston. London: Penguin, 2003.

————. *Poems*. Translated by Ivan Panin. Boston: Cupples and Hurd, 1888.

————. *The Queen of Spades and Other Stories: A New Translation*. Translated by Alan Myers. New York: Oxford University Press, 1999.

Ralph, Julian, A. Conan Doyle, and Rudyard Kipling. *War's Brighter Side: The Story of "The Friend" Newspaper Edited by the Correspondents with Lord Roberts's Forces, March–April, 1900*. New York: D. Appleton & Co., 1901.

Rau, Santha Rama. *The Adventuress*. New York: Dell, 1971.

————. *A Princess Remembers: The Memoirs of the Maharani of Jaipur*. Philadelphia: J. B. Lippincott, 1976.

————. "The Trial of Jomo Kenyatta." In *The Reporter Reader*, edited by Max Ascoli. New York: Doubleday, 1969.

Reed, John. *Ten Days That Shook the World*. New York: Boni and Liveright, 1919.

Rhys, Jean. *The Collected Short Stories*. Edited by Diana Athill. New York: W. W. Norton, 1992.

————. *Wide Sargasso Sea*. New York: Norton, 1967.

Richardson, John. *The Canadian Brothers; or, The Prophecy Fulfilled*. Montreal: A. H. Armour and H. Ramasay, 1840.

————. *Wacousta; or, The Prophecy: A Tale of the Canadas*. London: T. Cadell and W. Blackwood, 1832.

The Rig Veda. Translated and edited by Wendy Doniger. Harmondsworth, U.K.: Penguin Classics, 1981.

Rumi, Mevlana Jalaluddin. *Spiritual Verses*. Translated by Alan Williams. London: Penguin, 2007.

Saadi, Musle-Huddeen Sheik. *Gulistan, or Rose Garden*. Translated by George Gentius. Whitefish, Mont.: Kessinger, 2003.

Sachs, Nelly. *O the Chimneys: Selected Poems, Including the Verse Play, Eli*. Translated by Michael Hamburger, et al. New York: Farrar, Straus and Giroux, 1967.

Sahagún, Bernardino de. *Florentine Codex*. Translated by Charles E. Dibble and Arthur J. Anderson. Santa Fe: Monographs of the School of American Research and Museum of New Mexico, 1979.

Sahgal, Nayantara. *Mistaken Identity*. London: Heinemann, 1988.

Saktisamagama Tantra. Translated by Binaytosh Bhattacharya. Baroda: Gaekwad Oriental series, 1978.

Sale, Florentia Wynch. *A Journal of the Disasters in Affghanistan, 1841–1842*. London: John Murray, 1843.

Sama Veda. Translated by S. V. Ganapati. Delhi: Motilal Banarsidass, 1992.

Sancho, Ignatius. *Letters of the Late Ignatius Sancho, an African*. Translated by Joseph Jekyll. London: J. Nichols, 1782.

Sand, George. *Story of My Life: The Autobiography of George Sand*. Edited by Thelma Jurgrau. New York: State University of New York Press, 1991.

Satrapi, Marjane. *Persepolis: The Story of a Childhood*. Paris: L'Association, 2003.

Schreiner, Olive. *The South African Question*. Chicago: Charles H. Sergel, 1899.

———. *The Story of an African Farm*. Boston: Roberts Brothers, 1888.

———. *Trooper Peter Halket of Mashonaland*. Boston: Roberts Brothers, 1897.

Seacole, Mary. *Wonderful Adventures of Mrs. Seacole in Many Lands*. London: James Blackwood, 1857.

Seneca, Lucius Annaeus. *Seneca's Morals of a Happy Life, Benefits, Anger and Clemency*. Translated by Roger L'Estrange. Chicago: Belford, Clarke, 1882.

Shakespeare, William. *Antony and Cleopatra*. New York: Washington Square Press, 2004.

———. *Hamlet*. New York: Washington Square Press, 2003.

———. *Julius Caesar*. New York: Washington Square Press, 2004.

———. *The Merchant of Venice*. New York: Washington Square Press, 1995.

———. *Othello*. New York: Washington Square Press, 2004.

———. *The Tempest*. New York: Washington Square Press, 1961.

———. *Titus Andronicus*. New York: Washington Square Press, 2005.

Shaw, George Bernard. *Androcles and the Lion; Overruled; Pygmalion*. New York: Brentano's, 1916.

Sheldon, May French. *Sultan to Sultan: Adventures among the Masai and Other Tribes of East Africa*. Boston: Arena, 1892.

Sheridan, Frances Chamberlaine. *The History of Nourjahad*. Philadelphia: Hickman & Hazzard, 1822.

Shuka Saptati: Seventy Tales of the Parrot. Translated by Aditya Narayan Dhairyasheel Haksar. India: HarperCollins India, 2000.

Shute, Nevil. *A Town Like Alice*. Callington, U.K.: House of Stratus, 2002.

Singer, Isaac Bashevis. *Enemies, a Love Story*. New York: Farrar, Straus and Giroux, 1988.

———. *The Family Moskat*. New York: Farrar, Straus and Giroux, 2007.

———. *An Isaac Bashevis Singer Reader*. New York: Farrar, Straus, & Giroux, 1960.

———. *Meshugah*. New York: Farrar, Straus and Giroux, 1994.

———. *Shosha*. New York: Farrar, Straus and Giroux, 1982.

———. *Why Noah Chose the Dove*. New York: Trumpet Club, 1974.

Solzhenitsyn, Aleksandr. *One Day in the Life of Ivan Denisovich*. Translated by Max Hayward and Ronald Hingley. New York: Bantam, 1963.

Somadeva. *The Katha Sarit Sagara; or, Ocean of the Streams of Story*. Translated by C. H. Tawney. Calcutta: J. W. Thomas, 1884.

The Song of Roland. Translated by Glyn S. Burgess. London: Penguin, 1990.

Southey, Robert. *The Poet's Pilgrimage to Waterloo*. London: Longman, Hurst, Rees, Orme, and Brown, 1816.

Soyinka, Wole. *Mandela's Earth and Other Poems*. Ibadan, Nigeria: Fountain, 1989.

———. *The Man Died: The Prison Notes of Wole Soyinka*. New York: Noonday, 1988.

———. *A Shuttle in the Crypt*. London: Methuen, 1972.

Staël, Madame de. *Considerations of the Principal Events of the French Revolution*. Edited by Duke de Broglie and the Baron de Staël. London: Baldwin, Cradock & Joy, 1818.

———. *On Germany*. Translated by John Murray. London: John Murray, 1813.

———. *Ten Years' Exile*. Edited by Auguste Louis de Staël. London: BiblioBazaar, 2007.

Stevenson, Robert Louis. *The Amateur Emigrant from the Clyde to Sandy Hook*. Chicago: Stone and Kimball, 1895.

———. *An Inland Voyage*. New York: Charles Scribner's Sons, 1905.

———. *In the South Seas*. London: S. S. McClure, 1891.

———. *Island Nights' Entertainments*. New York: Charles Scribner's Sons, 1917.

———. *Kidnapped*. New York: Blue Ribbons Books, 1921.

———. *Selected Letters of Robert Louis Stevenson*. Edited by Ernest Mehew. New Haven, Conn.: Yale University Press, 1997.

———. *Treasure Island*. New York: Charles Scribner's Sons, 1918.

Stevenson, Robert Louis, and Lloyd Osbourne. *The Ebb-Tide: A Trio and Quartette*. New York: Charles Scribner's Sons, 1905.

Sturluson, Snorri. *The Heimskringla; or, Chronicle of the Kings of Norway*. Edited by Samuel Laing and Rasmus B. Anderson. London: Longman, Brown, Green, and Longmans, 1833.

———. *The Prose Edda*. Translated by Arthur Gilchrist Brodeur. New York: American-Scandinavian Foundation, 1916.

Suetonius. *Suetonius*. 2 vols. Translated by J. C. Rolfe. London: Heinemann, 1920.

Swift, Jonathan. *Gulliver's Travels and Other Writings*. New York: Modern Library, 1958.

Tacitus. *Annals of Tacitus*. Translated by Alfred John Church and William Jackson Brodribb. London: Macmillan, 1906.

———. *The History of Tacitus*. Translated by Alfred John Church. London: Macmillan, 1876.

Tagore, Rabindranath. *Gitanjali*. London: Branden, 1996.

———. *Sadhana: The Realization of Life*. New York: Three Leaves Press, 2004.

———. *Selected Letters of Rabindranath Tagore*. Edited by Krishna Dutta and Andrew Robinson. Cambridge: Cambridge University Press, 1997.

———. *Selected Poems*. Translated by William Radice. London: Penguin Classics, 2005.

———. *Selected Short Stories*. Translated by William Radice. London: Penguin Classics, 2005.

Tan, Amy. *The Joy Luck Club*. New York: Penguin, 1989.

———. *The Kitchen God's Wife*. New York: Penguin, 1991.

Tao Qian. *The Selected Poems of T'ao Ch'ien*. Translated by David Hinton. Port Townsend, Wash.: Copper Canyon Press, 2000.

Tardivel, Jules-Paul. *For My Country*. Translated by Sheila Fischman. Toronto: University of Toronto Press, 1975.

The Ten Thousand Leaves. Translated by Ian Hideo Levy. Princeton, N.J.: Princeton University Press, 1981.

Tertullian. *Tertullian: Apologetic and Practical Treatises*. Translated by C. Dodgson. Oxford: F. & J. Rivington, 1854.

Thackeray, William Makepeace. *Vanity Fair*. 3 vols. Leipzig: Bernhard Tauchnitz, 1848.

Thucydides. *The Peloponnesian Wars*. Translated by Benjamin Jowett. New York: Washington Square Press, 1963.

The Tibetan Book of the Dead. Translated by W. Y. Evans-Wentz. Oxford: Oxford University Press, 2000.

Tibullus, Albius. *Elegies*. Translated by James Cranstoun. Edinburgh: William Blackwood, 1872.

Tolstoy, Leo. *Hadji Murád*. Translated by Aylmer Maude. Alexandria, Va.: Orchises Press, 1996.

———. *The Kingdom of God Is Within You*. Translated by Constance Garnett. London: Heinemann, 1894.

———. *The Living Corpse*. Translated by Anna Monossowich Evarts. New York: Nicholas L. Brown, 1919.

———. *Sevastopol*. Translated by Isabel Florence Hapgood. New York: Thomas Y. Crowell, 1888.

———. *War and Peace*. London: J. M. Dent & Sons, 1915.

Traill, Catharine Parr. *The Backwoods of Canada: Being Letters from the Wife of an Emigrant Officer, Illustrative of the Domestic Economy of British America*. London: Charles Knight, 1836.

———. *Studies of Plant Life in Canada: Wild Flowers, Flowering Shrubs, and Grasses*. Toronto: William Briggs, 1906.

Turgenev, Ivan. *Fathers and Sons*. Translated by Rosemary Edmonds and Isaiah Berlin. London: Penguin, 1975.

———. *Rudin: A Romance*. Translated by Isabel F. Hapgood. Boston: Jefferson Press, 1908.

———. *A Sportsman's Sketches*. Translated by Constance Garnett. London: Heinemann, 1895.

———. *Virgin Soil*. Translated by Constance Garnett. London: Heinemann, 1920.

Tutuola, Amos. *The Palm-Wine Drinkard; and My Life in the Bush of Ghosts*. New York: Grove, 1994.

Undset, Sigrid. *Gunnar's Daughter*. Translated by Arthur G. Chater. New York: Penguin, 1998.

———. *Kristin Lavransdatter: The Cross*. Translated by Tiina Nunnally. New York: Penguin, 2001.

———. *Kristin Lavransdatter: The Wife*. Translated by Tiina Nunnally. New York: Penguin, 1999.

———. *Kristin Lavransdatter: The Wreath*. Translated by Tiina Nunnally. New York: Penguin, 1997.

———. *Return to the Future*. Translated by Henriette C. K. Naeseth. New York: A. A. Knopf, 1942.

The Upanishads. Translated by Friedrich Max Müller. Oxford: Oxford University Press, 1897.

Valmiki. *The Ramayana*. Translated and edited by Manmatha Nath Dutt. Calcutta: H. C. Das, 1894.

———. *Reamker: The Cambodian Version of the Ramayana*. Translated by Judith M. Jacob. New York: Routledge, 1986.

Virgil. *The Aeneid*. Translated by Patric Dickinson. New York: Mentor, 1961.

Voltaire. *Candide, Zadig, and Selected Stories*. Translated by Donald M. Frame. New York: New American Library, 1981.

Wallace, Paul A. W. *The White Roots of Peace: The Iroquois Book of Life*. Santa Fe, N.M.: Clear Light, 1994.

Walker, Brian Browne, trans. *The I Ching or Book of Changes: A Guide to Life's Turning Points*. New York: Macmillan, 1993.

Warren, Mercy Otis. *The Group*. Boston: Edes and Gill, 1775.

———. *History of the Rise, Progress, and Termination of the American Revolution*. Boston: E. Larkin, 1805.

———. *Poems, Dramatic and Miscellaneous*. Boston: I. Thomas and E. T. Andrews, 1790.

Wells, H. G. *The Island of Dr. Moreau*. New York: Modern Library, 1996.

West, John. *The History of Tasmania*. Launceston, Tas.: Henry Dowling, 1852.

Wiesel, Elie. *Night*. New York: Bantam, 1986.

Wolfram von Eschenbach. *Parzival and Titurel*. Translated by Cyril Edwards. Oxford: Oxford University Press, 2006.

Wolkstein, Diane, and Samuel Noah Kramer. *Inanna, Queen of Heaven and Earth: Her Stories and Hymns from Sumer*. New York: Harper & Row, 1983.

Wumen Hukai. *The Gateless Barrier: The Wu-Men Kuan (Mumonkan)*. Translated by Robert Aitken. New York: Macmillan, 1990.

Xenophon. *Anabasis*. Translated by H. G. Dakyns. New York: BiblioBazaar, 2007.

———. *Cyropaedia: The Education of Cyrus*. Translated by H. G. Dakyns. London: Macmillan, 2000.

———. *Hellenica*. Translated by H. G. Dakyns. New York: BiblioBazaar, 2007.

The Yajur Veda Taittiriya Sanhita. Whitefish, Mont.: Kessinger, 2004.

Yevtushenko, Yevgeny. *Early Poems*. Translated by George Reavey. London: Marion Boyars, 1989.

———. *Selected Poems*. Harmondsworth, U.K.: Penguin, 1962.

Yezierska, Anzia. *Bread Givers*. New York: Persea Books, 2003.

———. *How I Found America: Collected Stories*. New York: Persea Books, 2003.

———. *Hungry Hearts*. Boston: Houghton Mifflin, 1920.

———. *Red Ribbon on a White Horse: My Story*. New York: Persea Books, 2004.

———. *Salome of the Tenements*. Champaign: University of Illinois Press, 1995.

Yi Kwang-su. *Modern Korean Literature: An Anthology*. Translated by Peter H. Lee. Honolulu: University of Hawaii Press, 1990.

———. *Modern Korean Short Stories and Plays*. Seoul: Korean Centre, 1970.

———. *The Silence of Love: Twentieth-Century Korean Poetry*. Honolulu: University Press of Hawaii, 1981.

VI. BIBLIOGRAPHY OF SECONDARY SOURCES

Abrahamov, Binyamin. *Divine Love in Islamic Mysticism: The Teachings of al-Ghazali and al-Dabbagh.* London: Routledge, 2003.

Adler, Eve. *Vergil's Empire: Political Thought in the Aeneid.* Lanham, Md.: Rowman & Littlefield, 2003.

Adorno, Rolena. *The Polemics of Possession in Spanish American Narrative.* New Haven, Conn.: Yale University Press, 2008.

Allen, Brooke. "Imperialism Is the Mama of All Sorrows," *Wall Street Journal,* 2 February 1996, p. A8.

Ambrosini, Richard, and Richard Dury. *Robert Louis Stevenson: Writer of Boundaries.* Madison: University of Wisconsin Press, 2006.

Amert, Susan. *In a Shattered Mirror: The Later Poetry of Anna Akhmatova.* Palo Alto, Calif.: Stanford University Press, 1992.

Anderson, Graham. *Greek and Roman Folklore.* Westport, Conn.: Greenwood, 2006.

Anderson, Monica. *Women and the Politics of Travel, 1870–1914.* Teaneck, N.J.: Fairleigh Dickinson University Press, 2006.

Andrew, Joe, and Robert Reid. *Two Hundred Years of Pushkin.* Amsterdam: Rodopi, 2003.

Angier, Carole. *The Double Bond: Primo Levi, A Biography.* New York: Macmillan, 2002.

Arata, Stephen. *Fictions of Loss in the Victorian Fin de Siècle: Identity and Empire.* Cambridge: Cambridge University Press, 1996.

Arias, Santa, and Mariselle Meléndez. *Mapping Colonial Spanish America: Places and Commonplaces of Identity, Culture, and Experience.* Lewisburg, Pa.: Bucknell University Press, 2002.

Armitage, David. "Literature and Empire." In *The Oxford History of British Empire, Vol. 1: Origins of Empire,* edited by Nicholas Canny, 99–123. Oxford: Oxford University Press, 2001.

Ash, Beth Sharon. *Writing in Between: Modernity and Psychosocial Dilemma in the Novels of Joseph Conrad.* London: Macmillan, 1999.

Assmann, Jan. *Death and Salvation in Ancient Egypt.* Ithaca, N.Y.: Cornell University Press, 2005.

Baker, Peter. *Obdurate Brilliance: Exteriority and the Modern Long Poem.* Gainesville: University Press of Florida, 1991.

Balfour, Sebastian. *The End of the Spanish Empire, 1898–1923.* Oxford: Oxford University Press, 1997.

Baring, Maurice. *An Outline of Russian Literature.* New York: Nova, 2006.

Barnard, Rita. *Apartheid and Beyond: South African Writers and the Politics of Place.* Oxford: Oxford University Press, 2006.

Barnes, Christopher. *Boris Pasternak: A Literary Biography.* Cambridge: Cambridge University Press, 2004.

Barrett, Tracy. *Anna of Byzantium.* New York: Delacorte Press, 1999.

Barton, Simon, and Richard Fletcher, anno. and trans. *The World of El Cid: Chronicles of the Spanish Reconquest.* Manchester, U.K.: Manchester University Press, 2000.

Beal, Timothy Kandler. *The Book of Hiding: Gender, Ethnicity, Annihilation, and Esther.* New York: Routledge, 1997.

Beckwith, Martha Warren. *Hawaiian Mythology.* Honolulu: University of Hawaii Press, 1977.

Behn, Aphra. *Oroonoko and Other Writings.* Oxford: Oxford University Press, 1994.

Belcher, Stephen Paterson. *Epic Traditions of Africa.* Bloomington: Indiana University Press, 1999.

Bentley, D. M. R. *Mimic Fires*. Montreal: McGill-Queen's University Press, 1994.

Benton, Catherine. *God of Desire: Tales of Kamadeva in Sanskrit Story Literature*. New York: State University New York Press, 2005.

Bethge, Eberhard. *Dietrich Bonhoeffer: A Biography*. Minneapolis: Augsburg Fortress, 2000.

Bethge, Renate. *Dietrich Bonhoeffer: A Brief Life*. Translated by K. C. Hanson. Minneapolis: Augsburg Fortress, 2004.

Bialock, David T. *Eccentric Spaces, Hidden Histories: Narrative, Ritual, and Royal Authority from The Chronicles of Japan to The Tale of the Heike*. Palo Alto, Calif.: Stanford University Press, 2007.

Birley, Anthony Richard. *Marcus Aurelius*. New York: Routledge, 2000.

Bivona, Daniel. *British Imperial Literature, 1870–1940: Writing and the Administration of Empire*. Cambridge: Cambridge University Press, 1998.

Boatwright, Mary T., Daniel J. Gargola, and Richard J. A. Talbert. *The Romans: From Village to Empire*. New York: Oxford University Press, 2004.

Boehmer, Elleke. *Colonial and Postcolonial Literature*. 2nd ed. Oxford: Oxford University Press, 2005.

———, ed. *Empire Writing: An Anthology of Postcolonial Literature, 1870–1918*. Oxford and New York: Oxford University Press, 1998.

Boone, Elizabeth Hill. *Cycles of Time and Meaning in the Mexican Books of Fate*. Austin: University of Texas Press, 2007.

Booth, Howard J., and Nigel Rigby. *Modernism and Empire: Writing and British Coloniality 1890–1940*. Manchester, U.K.: Manchester University Press, 2000.

Bose, Mandakranta. *Faces of the Feminine in Ancient, Medieval, and Modern India*. Oxford: Oxford University Press, 2000.

———. *The Ramayana Revisited*. Oxford: Oxford University Press, 2004.

Bower, Kathrin M. *Ethics and Remembrance in the Poetry of Nelly Sachs and Rose Auslander*. Rochester, N.Y.: Boydell and Brewer, 2000.

Brantly, Susan. *Understanding Isak Dinesen*. Columbia: University of South Carolina Press, 2002.

Brown, Laura. *Ends of Empire: Women and Ideology in Early Eighteenth-Century English Literature*. Ithaca, N.Y.: Cornell University Press, 1993.

Brown, Richard Danson, and Suman Gupta. *Aestheticism and Modernism: Debating Twentieth-Century Literature 1900–1960*. New York: Routledge, 2005.

Brownlee, John S. *Political Thought in Japanese Historical Writing: From Kojiki (712) to Tokushi Yoron (1712)*. Waterloo, Ont.: Wilfrid Laurier University Press, 1991.

Bruce, F. F. *Paul, Apostle of the Heart Set Free*. Grand Rapids, Mich.: Eerdmans, 2000.

Bryce, Trevor. *Life and Society in the Hittite World*. Oxford: Oxford University Press, 2002.

Burdett, Carolyn. *Olive Schreiner and the Progress of Feminism: Evolution, Gender, Empire*. London: Palgrave Macmillan, 2001.

Burnett, Paula, ed. *The Penguin Book of Caribbean Verse*. Middlesex, U.K.: Viking Penguin, 1986.

Camara Sana. "Birago Diop's Poetic Contribution to the Ideology of Negritude." *Research in African Literatures* 33, no. 4 (January 2002): 101–123.

Cameron, Averil. *Procopius and the Sixth Century*. New York: Routledge, 1996.

Carter, Steven D. *Traditional Japanese Poetry*. Palo Alto, Calif.: Stanford University Press, 1991.

Castro, Daniel. *Another Face of Empire: Bartolomé de Las Casas, Indigenous Rights, and Ecclesiastical Imperialism*. Durham, N.C.: Duke University Press, 2007.

Chatfield-Taylor, Joan, "Cosmo Talks to Amy Tan: Dazzling New Literary Light." *Cosmopolitan*, November 1989, pp. 178–180.

Chatterjee, Suhas. Indian Civilization and Culture. New Delhi: M. D. Publications, 1998.

Childs, Peter. *Modernism and the Post-Colonial: Literature and Empire, 1885–1930*. London: Continuum, 2007.

Chilton, Lisa. *Agents of Empire: British Female Migration to Canada and Australia, 1860s–1930*. Toronto: University of Toronto Press, 2007.

Chmiel, Mark. *Elie Wiesel and the Politics of Moral Leadership*. New York: Temple University Press, 2001.

Chou, Eva Shan. *Reconsidering Tu Fu: Literary Greatness and Cultural Context*. Cambridge: Cambridge University Press, 2006.

Chung, Chong-wha. *Modern Korean Literature: An Anthology, 1908–65*. New York: Columbia University Press, 1995.

Chyet, Michael Lewisohn. *"And a Thornbush Sprang Up Between Them": Studies on "Mem u Zin," a Kurdish*

Romance. 2 vols. Berkeley: University of California at Berkeley, 1991.

Clements, Jonathan. *Confucius: A Biography.* Charleston, S.C.: History Press, 2005.

Cloy, John D. *Pensive Jester: The Literary Career of W. W. Jacobs.* Lanham, Md.: University Press of America, 1996.

Collingwood-Whittick, Sheila, and Germaine Greer. *The Pain of Unbelonging: Alienation and Identity in Australasian Literature.* Amsterdam: Rodopi, 2007.

Combs-Schilling, M. E. *Sacred Performances: Islam, Sexuality, and Sacrifice.* New York: Columbia University Press, 1989.

Compier, Don H., Pui-lan Kwok, and Joerg Rieger. *Empire and the Christian Tradition: New Readings of Classical Theologians.* Minneapolis: Fortress Press, 2007.

Conn, Peter. *Pearl S. Buck: A Cultural Biography.* Cambridge: Cambridge University Press, 1998.

Cook, Michael. *The Koran: A Very Short Introduction.* Oxford: Oxford University Press, 2000.

Courlander, Harold. *A Treasury of African Folklore: The Oral Literature, Traditions, Myths, Legends, Epics, Tales, Recollections, Wisdom, Sayings, and Humor of Africa.* New York: Marlowe & Co., 1996.

Crane, Gregory. *The Blinded Eye: Thucydides and the New Written Word.* Lanham, Md.: Rowman & Littlefield, 1996.

Cross, Frank Moore. *From Epic to Canon: History and Literature in Ancient Israel.* Baltimore: Johns Hopkins University Press, 1998.

Crowther, Andrew. *Contradiction Contradicted: The Plays of W. S. Gilbert.* Cranbury, N.J.: Fairleigh Dickinson University Press, 2000. ·

Curtis, John, and Nigel Tallis, eds. *Forgotten Empire: The World of Ancient Persia.* Berkeley: University of California Press, 2005.

Dabove, Juan Pablo. *Nightmares of the Lettered City: Banditry and Literature in Latin America, 1816–1929.* Pittsburgh: University of Pittsburgh Press, 2007.

Dagg, Anne Innis. *The Feminine Gaze: A Canadian Compendium of Non-Fiction Women Authors and Their Books, 1836–1945.* Waterloo, Ont.: Wilfred Laurier University Press, 2001.

Dass, Nirmal. *Songs of the Saints from the Adi Granth.* Albany: State University of New York Press, 2000.

Davé, Shilpa, et al., eds. *East Main Street: Asian American Popular Culture.* New York City: New York University Press, 2005.

Davies, Kate. *Catharine Macauley and Mercy Otis Warren: The Revolutionary Atlantic and the Politics of Gender.* Oxford: Oxford University Press, 2005.

De Bary, William Theodora, Donald Keene, George Tanabe, and Paul Varley. *Sources of Japanese Tradition from Earliest Times to 1600.* New York: Columbia University Press, 2001.

Dickson, Lovat. *Wilderness Man: The Strange Story of Grey Owl.* New York: Atheneum, 1973.

Dihle, Albrecht. *Greek and Latin Literature of the Roman Empire: From Augustus to Justinian.* Translated by Manfred Malzahn. London: Routledge, 1994.

Dijk, Gert-Jan van. *Ainoi, Logoi, Mythoi: Fables in Archaic, Classical, and Hellenistic Greek.* Amsterdam: Brill, 1997.

Dixon, Miriam. *The Real Matilda: Woman and Identity in Australia 1788 to 1975.* Middlesex, U.K.: Penguin, 1976.

Djangrang, Nimrod Bena. "Africa: The Breath of Life." *UNESCO Courier* 51, no. 3 (March 1998): 6–9.

Dooley, Gillian. *V. S. Naipaul, Man and Writer.* Columbia: University of South Carolina Press, 2006.

Driem, George von. *Languages of the Himalayas.* Amsterdam: Brill, 2001.

Duff, Timothy E. *Plutarch's Lives: Exploring Virtue and Vice.* Oxford: Oxford University Press, 2002.

Dumoulin, Heinrich, James W. Heisig, and Paul F. Knitter. *Zen Buddhism: A History.* Bloomington, Ind.: World Wisdom, 2005.

Dunn, Geoffrey D. *Tertullian.* New York: Routledge, 2004.

Dunn, Ross E. *The Adventures of Ibn Battuta: A Muslim Traveler of the 14th Century.* Berkeley: University of California Press, 2004.

Ebersole, Gary L. *Ritual Poetry and the Politics of Death in Early Japan.* Princeton, N.J.: Princeton University Press, 1989.

Edgington, Susan, and Sarah Lambert. *Gendering the Crusades.* New York: Columbia University Press, 2002.

Edmond, Rod. *Representing the South Pacific: Colonial Discourse from Cook to Gauguin.* Cambridge: Cambridge University Press, 2005.

Eisenstadt, Shmuel Noah, Michel Abitbol, and Naomi Chazan. *The Early State in African Perspective: Culture, Power, and Division of Labor.* Amsterdam: Brill, 1988.

El Saadawi, Nawal. *The Hidden Face of Eve: Women in the Arab World.* London: Zed Books, 2007.

Fairweather, Maria. *Madame de Staël.* New York: Carroll and Graf, 2005.

Feldman, Louis H., and Gōhei Hata. *Joseph, the Bible and History.* Tokyo: Yamamoto Shoten Publishing House, 1987.

Ferguson, Moira. "A Lot of Memory: An Interview with Jamaica Kincaid." *Kenyon Review* 16, no. 1 (Summer 1994): 163–188.

———. *Subject to Others: British Women Writers and Colonial Slavery, 1670–1834.* New York: Routledge, 1992.

Figes, Orlando. *Natasha's Dance: A Cultural History of Russia.* London: Macmillan, 2003.

Fischer, Barbara, and Thomas C. Fox, eds. *A Companion to the Works of Gotthold Ephraim Lessing.* Rochester, N.Y.: Boydell & Brewer, 2005.

Fisher, William Bayne. *The Cambridge History of Iran.* Cambridge: Cambridge University Press, 1993.

Fitzgerald, William. *Slavery and the Roman Literary Imagination.* Cambridge: Cambridge University Press, 2000.

Fleming, Thomas. *The Morality of Everyday Life: Rediscovering an Ancient Alternative to the Liberal Tradition.* Columbia: University of Missouri Press, 2004.

Forhan, Kate Langdon. *The Political Theory of Christine de Pizan.* Aldershot, U.K.: Ashgate, 2002.

Forrest, W. G. "Aristophanes *Lysistrata* 231." *Classical Quarterly* 45, no. 1 (January–June 1995): 240–241.

Frank, Joseph. *Dostoevsky: The Stir of Liberation, 1860–1865.* Princeton, N.J.: Princeton University Press, 1988.

Frazer, Chris. *Bandit Nation: A History of Outlaws and Cultural Struggle in Mexico, 1810–1920.* Lincoln: University of Nebraska Press, 2006.

French, Patrick. *The World Is What It Is.* New York: Knopf, 2008.

Frese, Mary Ann. *The Search for Modern Tragedy: Aesthetic Fascism in Italy and France.* Ithaca, N.Y.: Cornell University Press, 2001.

Friberg, Eino, George C. Schoolfield, and Björn Landström, eds. *The Kalevala.* Chicago: University of Illinois Press, 1988.

Gaile, Andreas. *Fabulating Beauty: Perspectives on the Fiction of Peter Carey.* Amsterdam: Rodopi, 2005.

Gérard, Albert S. *European-Language Writing in Sub-Saharan Africa.* Amsterdam: John Benjamins, 1986.

Gonadeo, Alfredo. *D'Annunzio and the Great War.* Madison, N.J.: Fairleigh Dickinson University Press, 1995.

Goonetilleke, D. C. R. A. *Images of the Raj: South Asia in the Literature of Empire.* London: Macmillan, 1998.

Gouma-Peterson, Thalia, ed. *Anna Komnene and Her Times.* New York: Routledge, 2000.

Grice, Helena. *Negotiating Identities: An Introduction to Asian American Women's Writing.* Manchester, U.K.: Manchester University Press, 2002.

Griffin, Miriam T. *Nero: The End of a Dynasty.* New York: Routledge, 2000.

Habinek, Thomas N. *The Politics of Latin Literature: Writing, Identity, and Empire in Ancient Rome.* Princeton, N.J.: Princeton University Press, 1998.

Hadda, Janet. *Isaac Bashevis Singer: A Life.* Madison: University of Wisconsin Press, 2003.

Hamilton, Edith. *The Greek Way.* New York: Mentor Books, 1962.

Hansen, Frantz Leander. *The Aristocratic University of Karen Blitzen: Destiny and the Denial of Fate.* Eastbourne, U.K.: Sussex Academic Press, 2003.

Hargreaves, Alec G. *Memory, Empire, and Postcolonialism: Legacies of French Colonialism.* Lanham, Md.: Lexington Books, 2005.

Harlow, Barbara, and Mia Carter, eds. *Archives of Empire: The Scramble for Africa.* Durham: Duke University Press, 2004.

Harvey, G. E. *History of Burma.* New Delhi: Asian Educational Services, 2000.

Haw, Stephen. *Marco Polo in China: A Venetian in the Realm of Khubilai Khan.* New York: Routledge, 2006.

Hawkins, Peter, and Lesleigh Cushing Stahlberg. *Scrolls of Love: Reading Ruth and the Song of Songs.* Bronx, N.Y.: Fordham University Press, 1999.

Haynes, Holly. *The History of Make-Believe: Tacitus on Imperial Rome.* Berkeley: University of California Press, 2003.

Hayward, Helen. *The Enigma of V. S. Naipaul.* Basingstoke, Hampshire, U.K.: Palgrave Macmillan, 2002.

Hayward, Jack Ernest Shalom. *Fragmented France: Two Centuries of Disputed Identity.* Oxford: Oxford University Press, 2007.

Heine, Steven, and Dale S. Wright. *The Koan: Texts and Contexts in Zen Buddhism.* Oxford: Oxford University Press, 2000.

Henderson, John. *Telling Tales on Caesar.* Oxford: Oxford University Press, 2001.

Herbert-Brown, Geraldine. *Ovid and the Fasti: An Historical Study.* Oxford: Oxford University Press, 1994.

Hessing, Melody, and Rebecca Sue Raglon. *This Elusive Land: Women and the Canadian Environment.* Vancouver: University of British Columbia Press, 2005.

Higuera, Henry. *Eros and Empire: Politics and Christianity in Don Quixote.* Lanham, Md.: Rowman & Littlefield, 1995.

Hindman, Sandra. *Sealed in Parchment: Rereadings of Knighthod in the Illuminated Manuscripts of Chrétien de Troyes.* Chicago: University of Chicago Press, 1994.

Hobbs, Anne Stevenson, ed. *Fables.* London: Victoria and Albert Museum, 1986. Hoffer, Stanley E. *The Anxieties of Pliny the Younger.* Philadelphia: American Philological Association, 1999.

Hogan, Patrick Colm. *Empire and Poetic Voice: Cognitive and Cultural Studies of Literary Tradition and Colonialism.* New York: State University of New York Press, 2004.

Holford-Strevens, Leofranc, and Amiel D. Vardi. *The Worlds of Aulus Gellius.* Oxford: Oxford University Press, 2004.

Holloway, Julia Bolton, Constance S. Wright, and Joan Bechtold. *Equally in God's Image: Women in the Middle Ages.* Florence, Italy: Aureo Anello, 1990.

Hooley, Daniel M. *Roman Satire.* Oxford: Blackwell, 2007.

Hopkins, Lisa. *Giants of the Past.* Lewisburg, Pa.: Bucknell University Press, 2004.

Hopkirk, Peter. *Quest for Kim.* Ann Arbor: University of Michigan Press, 1999.

Hörnqvist, Mikael. *Machiavelli and Empire.* Cambridge: Cambridge University Press, 2004.

Horsfall, Nicholas. *A Companion to the Study of Virgil.* Rev. ed. Leiden: Brill, 2001.

Houghton, Sarah. *Elie Wiesel: A Holocaust Survivor Cries Out for Peace.* New York: Red Brick Learning, 2003.

Hovannisian, Richard G., and Georges Sabagh. *The Thousand and One Nights in Arabic Literature and Society.* Cambridge: Cambridge University Press, 1997.

Howard, Jennifer. "Unraveling the Narrative." *Chronicle of Higher Education* 52, no. 1 (September 9, 2005): A11.

Huang, Guiyou. *Asian American Autobiographers: A Bio-Bibliographical Critical Sourcebook.* Westport, Conn.: Greenwood, 2001.

Hung, William. *Tu Fu, China's Greatest Poet.* New York: Textbook Publishers, 2003.

Ibnlfassi, Laila, and Nicki Hitchcott. *African Francophone Writing: A Critical Introduction.* Oxford: Berg, 1996.

Ingle, Stephen. "The Anti-Imperialism of George Orwell." In *Literature and the Political Imagination,* edited by John Horton and Andrea Baumeister. New York: Routledge, 1996.

Jackson, William E. *Ardent Complaints and Equivocal Pietry: The Portrayal of the Crusader in Medieval German Poetry.* Lanham, Md.: University Press of America, 2003.

Jay, Betty. *E. M. Forster.* London: Macmillan, 2003.

Jewell, Keala Jane. *Monsters in the Italian Literary Imagination.* Chicago: Wayne State University Press, 2001.

Jeyifo, Biodun, ed. *Perspectives on Wole Soyinka: Freedom and Complexity.* Jackson: University Press of Mississippi, 2001.

Johansen, Bruce Elliott, and Barbara A. Mann. *Encyclopedia of the Haudenosaunee.* Westport, Conn.: Greenwood, 2000.

Joseph, Gilbert Michael, and Timothy J. Henderson. *The Mexico Reader: History, Culture, Politics.* Durham, N.H.: Duke University Press, 2003.

Kassis, Riad Aziz. *The Book of Proverbs and Arabic Proverbial Works.* Amsterdam: Brill, 1999.

Kato, Megumi. "Typical Evil? The Japanese Represented in Australian War Writings." In *Beyond Good and Evil?: Essays on the Literature and Culture of the Asia-Pacific Region,* edited by Dennis Haskell, Megan McKinlay, and Pamina Rich. Claremont: University of West Australia Press, 2006.

Kaufmann, Wanda Ostrowska. *The Anthropology of Wisdom Literature.* Westport, Conn.: Greenwood, 1996.

Kelly, Christopher. *The Roman Empire.* Oxford: Oxford University Press, 2006.

Kennedy-Andrews, Elmer. *The Poetry of Seamus Heaney.* New York: Columbia University Press, 2000.

Kenny, Kevin. *Ireland and the British Empire.* Oxford: Oxford University Press, 2004.

Kershaw, Ian. *Hitler: 1889–1936: Hubris.* New York: W. W. Norton, 2000.

Ketterer, David. *Canadian Science Fiction and Fantasy.* Bloomington: Indiana University Press, 1992.

Killam, G. D. *Literature of Africa.* Westport, Conn.: Greenwood, 2004.

Klein, Carole. *Doris Lessing: a Biography.* New York: Carroll & Graf, 2000.

Klein, Christina. *Cold War Orientalism: Asia in the Middlebrow Imagination, 1945–1961.* Berkeley: University of California Press, 2003.

Kraus, Hans-Joachim. *Theology of the Psalms.* Minneapolis: Fortress Press, 1992.

Kremer, S. Lillian. *Holocaust Literature: An Encyclopedia of Writers and Their Work.* New York: Routledge, 2003.

Lamb, Jonathan, et al., eds. *Exploration and Exchange: A South Seas Anthology, 1680–1900.* Chicago: University of Chicago Press, 2000.

Lane, George. *Genghis Khan and Mongol Rule.* Westport, Conn.: Greenwood, 2004.

Langer, Lawrence L. *Art from the Ashes: A Holocaust Anthology.* Oxford: Oxford University Press, 1995.

Larsen, Anne R., and Colette H. Winn. *Writings by Pre-Revolutionary French Women.* New York: Routledge, 2000.

Layton, Susan. *Russian Literature and Empire: Conquest of the Caucasus from Pushkin to Tolstoy.* Cambridge: Cambridge University Press, 1994.

Lee, Ann Sung-Hi. *Yi Kwang-su and Modern Korean Literature.* New York: Columbia University East Asia Program, 2005.

Lee, John W. I. *A Greek Army on the March: Soldiers and Survival in Xenophon's Anabasis.* Cambridge: Cambridge University Press, 2007.

Lee-Stecum, Parshia. *Powerplay in Tibullus: Reading Elegies Book One.* Cambridge: Cambridge University Press, 1998.

Le Guin, Ursula K. *Dancing at the Edge of the World.* New York: Grove, 1989.

Leipoldt, C. Louis. "Multatuli and the 'Max Havelaar.'" *Westminster Review* 160, no. 10 (October 1903): 438–447.

Lesky, Albin. *A History of Greek Literature.* London: Gerald Duckworth, 1996.

Levy, Dore Jesse. *Ideal and Actual in the Story of the Stone.* New York: Columbia University Press, 1999.

Levy, Ian Hideo. *Hitomaro and the Birth of Japanese Lyricism.* Princeton, N.J.: Princeton University Press, 1984.

Lewis, Desiree. *Living on the Horizon: Bessie Head and the Politics of Imagining.* Lansing: University of Michigan Press, 2007.

Lincoln, Bruce. *Sunlight at Midnight: St. Petersburg and the Rise of Modern Russia.* New York: Basic Books, 2002.

Lorenz, Dagmar C. G. *Keepers of the Motherland; German Texts by Jewish Women Writers.* Lincoln: University of Nebraska Press, 1997.

Lupton, Julia Reinhard. *Citizen-Saints: Shakespeare and Political Theology.* Chicago: University of Chicago Press, 2005.

Ma, Sheng-mei. *The Deathly Embrace: Orientalism and Asian American Identity.* Minneapolis: University of Minnesota Press, 2000.

Mack, Douglas S. *Scottish Fiction and the British Empire.* Edinburgh: Edinburgh University Press, 2006.

Mair, Victor H. *The Columbia History of Chinese Literature.* New York: Columbia University Press, 2001.

Majumdar, A. K. Basu. *Rabindranath Tagore, the Poet of India.* New Delhi: Indus, 1993.

Maley, Willy. *Nation, State and Empire in English Renaissance Literature, Shakespeare to Milton.* London: Macmillan, 2003.

Mann, Gurinder Singh. *The Making of Sikh Scripture.* Oxford: Oxford University Press, 2001.

Masters, Jamie. *Poetry and Civil War in Lucan's Bellum Civile.* Cambridge: Cambridge University Press, 2007.

Maurois, Andre. *Alexandre Dumas—A Great Life in Brief.* Maurois Press, 2007.

May, Larry. *War Crimes and Just War.* Cambridge: Cambridge University Press, 2007.

McCay, Mary A. "Beyond Femaleness: Beryl Markham, Africa's Adopted Daughter in *West with the Wind.*" In *Nwanyibu: Womanbeing & African Literature,* edited by Phanuel Akubueze Egejuru and Ketu H. Katrak. New Orleans, La.: Africa World Press, 1997.

McLeod, Jacqueline. *Crossing Boundaries: Comparative History of Black People in Diaspora.* Bloomington: Indiana University Press, 2001.

McNeill, Randall L. B. *Horace: Image, Identity, and Audience.* Baltimore: Johns Hopkins University Press, 2001.

Mehrota, Arvind Krishna. *A History of Indian Literature in English.* New York: Columbia University Press, 2003.

Miles, Gary B. *Livy: Reconstructing Early Rome.* Ithaca, N.Y.: Cornell University Press, 1995.

Mitchell, Stephen. *A History of the Later Roman Empire, A.D. 284–641: The Transformation of the Ancient World.* London: Blackwell, 2006.

Mitha, Farouk. *Al-Ghazali and the Ismailis: A Debate on Reason and Authority in Medieval Islam.* London: I. B. Tauris, 2001.

Mobley, Gregory. *Samson and the Liminal Hero in the Ancient Near East.* London: Continuum, 2006.

Mohanty, Sachidananda, ed. *Travel Writing and the Empire.* New Delhi: Katha, 2003.

Moore, Grace. *Dickens and Empire: Discourses of Class, Race, and Colonialism in the Works of Charles Dickens.* Aldershot, U.K.: Ashgate, 2004.

Morgan, Philip D., and Sean Hawkins. *Black Experience and the Empire.* Oxford: Oxford University Press, 2004.

Moss, John. *Future Indicative: Literary Theory and Canadian Literature.* Ottawa: University of Ottawa Press, 1987.

Moulton, James Hope. *Early Religious Poetry of Persia.* Boston: Adamant Media, 2005.

Mulhern, Chieko Irie. *Japanese Women Writers: A Bio-critical Sourcebook.* Westport, Conn.: Greenwood, 1994.

Nash, Julie. *New Essays on Maria Edgeworth.* Aldershot, U.K.: Ashgate, 2006.

Nejmann, Daisy L. *A History of Icelandic Literature.* Lincoln: University of Nebraska Press, 2007.

Neptune, Harvey R. *Caliban and the Yankees: Trinidad and the United States Occupation.* Chapel Hill: University of North Carolina Press, 2007.

Newman, Louise Michele. *White Women's Rights: The Racial Origins of Feminism in the United States.* New York: Oxford University Press, 1999.

Nicolopulos, James. *The Poetics of Empire in the Indies: Prophecy and Imitation in La Araucana and Os Lusiadas.* Philadelphia: Pennsylvania State University Press, 2000.

Nutall, A. D. *Two Concepts of Allegory: A Study of Shakespeare's The Tempest and the Logic of Allegorical Expression.* New Haven, Conn.: Yale University Press, 2007.

Obejas, Achy. "Jamaica Bound: Imagining Lives of Those Never Let to Be," *Chicago Tribune,* 31 March 1996.

O'Callaghan, Joseph F. *Alfonso X and the Cantigas de Santa Maria: A Poetic Biography.* Amsterdam: Brill, 2000.

Oelsner, Herman. *History of Italian Literature to the Death of Dante.* Translated by Adolf Gaspary. London: George Bell & Sons, 1901.

Orique, David. "Bartolomé de las Casas: A Brief Outline of His Life and Labor." Available online. URL: http://www.lascasas.org/manissues.htm. Downloaded on January 9, 2009.

Osborne, Catherine. *Dumb Beasts and Dead Philosophers: Humanity and the Humane in Ancient Philosophy and Literature.* Oxford: Oxford University Press, 2007.

Ozoglu, Hakan. *Kurdish Notables and the Ottoman State.* New York: State University of New York Press, 2004.

Palumbo-Liu, David, ed. *The Ethnic Canon: Histories, Institutions, and Interventions.* Minneapolis: University of Minnesota Press, 1995.

Peake, Sebastian. *Mervyn Peake: The Man and His Art.* London: Peter Owen, 2006.

Peppard, Murray B. *Paths through the Forest: A Biography of the Brothers Grimm.* New York: Holt, Rinehart & Winston, 1971.

Peterson, Nancy M. *Walking in Two Worlds: Mixed-Blood Indian Women Seeking Their Path.* Caldwell, Idaho: Caxton Press, 2006.

Plutschow, Herbert E. *Chaos and Cosmos: Ritual in Early and Medieval Japanese Literature.* Amsterdam: Brill, 1990.

Portilla, Miguel León. *Bernardino de Sahagún, First Anthropologist.* Translated by Mauricio J. Mixco. Norman: University of Oklahoma Press, 2002.

———— and Earl Shorris. *In the Language of Kings: An Anthology of Mesoamercian Literature—Pre-Columbian to the Present.* New York: W. W. Norton, 2002.

Proudfoot, Lindsay J., and M. M. Roche. *(Dis)placing Empire: Renegotiating British Colonial Geographics.* Aldershot, U.K.: Ashgate, 2005.

Quayson, Ato. *Strategic Transformations in Nigerian Writing.* Bloomington: Indiana University Press, 1997.

Quint, David. *Epic and Empire: Politics and Generic Form from Virgil to Milton.* Princeton, N.J.: 1993.

Raser, Timothy Bell. *The Simplest of Signs: Victor Hugo and the Language of Images in France, 1850–1950.* Cranbury, N.J.: University of Delaware Press, 2004.

Rilke, Rainer Maria. *Sonnets to Orpheus.* Translated by David Young. Middletown, Conn.: Wesleyan University Press, 1987.

Ritsema, Rudolf, and Shantena Augusto Sabbadini. *The Original I Ching Oracle: The Pure and Complete Texts with Concordance.* New York: Sterling, 2005.

Roberts, Elizabeth, and Elias Amidon, eds. *Earth Prayers from Around the World.* San Francisco: HarperSanFrancisco, 1991.

Robinson, Jane. *Mary Seacole: The Black Who Invented Modern Nursing.* New York: Carroll & Graf, 2004.

Rotker, Susana. *The American Chronicles of José Martí: Journalism and Modernity in Spanish America.* Lebanon, N.H.: University Press of New England, 2000.

Saebo, Magne. *On the Way to Canon: Creative Tradition History in the Old Testament.* New York: Continuum International, 1998.

Sahlins, Marshall. *Apologies to Thucydides: Understanding History as Culture and Vice Versa.* Chicago: University of Chicago Press, 2004.

Said, Edward. *Culture and Imperialism.* New York: Knopf, 1993.

———. *Orientalism.* New York: Vintage, 1979.

Savory, Elaine. *Jean Rhys.* Cambridge: Cambridge University Press, 1998.

Schiwy, Marlene A. *Voice of Her Own: Women and the Journal Writing Journey.* New York: Fireside, 1996.

Schueller, Malini Johar. *U.S. Orientalisms: Race, Nation, and Gender in Literature, 1790–1890.* Ann Arbor: University of Michigan Press, 1998.

Scott, Jamie S., and Paul Simpson-Housley, eds. *Mapping the Sacred: Religion, Geography and Postcolonial Literature.* Amsterdam: Rodopi, 2001.

Segal, Alan F. *Two Powers in Heaven: Early Rabbinic Reports about Christianity and Gnosticism.* Amsterdam: Brill, 2002.

Shapiro, Michael, Daniel Shapiro, and Nancy Hartman. *The Jewish 100.* New York: Citadel, 1994.

Sherry, Norman. *The Life of Graham Greene: Volume II: 1939–1955.* London: Penguin, 2004.

Shields, David S. *Oracles of Empire: Poetry, Politics, and Commerce in British America, 1690–1750.* Chicago: University of Chicago Press, 1990.

Shipman, Pat. *To the Heart of the Nile: Lady Florence Baker and the Exploration of Central Africa.* New York: HarperCollins, 2005.

Shirane, Haruo, and Sonja Amtzen. *Traditional Japanese Literature: An Anthology, Beginnings to 1600.* New York: Columbia University Press, 2007.

Silva, Noenoe K. *Aloha Betrayed: Native Hawaiian Resistance to American Colonialism.* Durham, N.C.: Duke University Press, 2004.

Simmons, Diane. *The Narcissism of Empire: Loss, Rage and Revenge in Thomas De Quincey, Robert Louis Stevenson, Arthur Conan Doyle, Rudyard Kipling, and Isak Dinesen.* Eastbourne, U.K.: Sussex Academic Press, 2007.

Simmons, Ernest Joseph. *Tolstoy.* New York: Routledge, 1973.

Singer, Itamar. *Hittite Prayers.* Amsterdam: Brill, 2002.

Smith, Andrew, and William Hughes. *Empire and the Gothic: The Politics of Genre.* London: Palgrave Macmillan, 2003.

Smith, Angela. "Landscape and the Foreigner Within: Katherine Mansfield and Emily Carr." In *Landscape and Empire 1770–2000,* edited by Glenn Hopper. Aldershot, U.K.: Ashgate, 2005.

Smyth, Alfred P. *King Alfred the Great.* New York: Oxford University Press, 1996.

Snodgrass, Mary Ellen. *Encyclopedia of Satire.* Santa Barbara, Calif.: ABC-Clio, 1996.

———. *Encyclopedia of World Scripture.* Jefferson, N.C.: McFarland, 2001.

Sougou, Omar. *Writing Across Cultures: Gender Politics and Difference in the Fiction of Buchi Emecheta.* Amsterdam: Rodopi, 2002.

Specter, Robert Melvin. *World without Civilization: Mass Murder and the Holocaust, History and Analysis.* Lanham, Md.: University of America Press, 2005.

Stabler, Jane. *Byron, Poetics and History.* Cambridge: Cambridge University Press, 2002.

Stach, Reiner. *Kafka: The Decisive Years.* Translated by Shelley Frisch. New York: Harcourt, 2005.

Steenman-Marcusse, Cornelia Janneke. *Re-writing Pioneer Women in Anglo-Canadian Literature.* Amsterdam: Rodopi, 2001.

Stetkevych, Jaroslav. *The Zephyrs of Najd: The Poets of Nostalgia in the Classical Arabic Nasib.* Chicago: University of Chicago Press, 1993.

Stone, Harry. *Writing in the Shadow: Resistance Publications in Occupied Europe.* New York: Routledge, 1996.

Strongman, Luke. *The Booker Prize and the Legacy of Empire.* Amsterdam: Rodopi, 2002.

Sturm, Terry. *An Unsettled Spirit: The Life and Frontier Fiction of Edith Lyttleton.* Calgary, Alb.: University of Calgary Press, 2003.

Sugirtharajah, Rasiah S. *The Postcolonial Biblical Reader.* London: Blackwell, 2006.

Sullivan, Zohreh T. *Narratives of Empire: The Fictions of Rudyard Kipling.* Cambridge: Cambridge University Press, 1993.

Sundquist, Eric J. *Empire and Slavery in American Literature, 1820–1865.* Jackson: University Press of Mississippi, 2006.

Tennenhouse, Leonard. *Power on Display: The Politics of Shakespeare's Genres.* New York: Routledge, 1986.

Thiede, Carsten Peter. *The Dead Sea Scrolls and the Jewish Origins of Christianity.* New York: Macmillan, 2003.

Thomas, Sue. *The Worlding of Jean Rhys.* Westport, Conn.: Greenwood, 1999.

Thompson, Norma. *Herodotus and the Origins of the Political Community: Arion's Leap.* New Haven, Conn.: Yale University Press, 1996.

Todorov, Tzvetan. *The Morals of History.* Translated by Alyson Waters. Minneapolis: University of Minnesota Press, 1995.

Toews, John Edward. *Becoming Historical: Cultural Reformation and Public Memory in Early Nineteenth-Century Berlin.* Cambridge: Cambridge University Press, 2004.

Tosi, Alessandra. *Waiting for Pushkin: Russian Fiction in the Reign of Alexander I (1801–1825).* Amsterdam: Rodopi, 2006.

Travis, Anna A. *Rilke's Russia: A Cultural Encounter.* Chicago: Northwestern University Press, 1997.

Treece, Dave. *Exiles, Allies, Rebels: Brazil's Indianist Movement, Indigenist Politics.* Westport, Conn.: Greenwood, 2000.

Tsumara, David Toshio. *The First Book of Samuel.* Grand Rapids, Mich.: Eerdmans, 2007.

Turner, Martha A. *Mechanism and the Novel: Science in the Narrative Process.* Cambridge: Cambridge University Press, 1993.

Urban, Hugh B. *Tantra: Sex, Secrecy, Politics, and Power in the Study of Religion.* Berkeley: University of California Press, 2003.

Vice, Sue. *Holocaust Fiction.* Westport, Conn.: Routledge, 2000.

Waldman, Carl. *Encyclopedia of Native American Tribes.* Rev. ed. New York: Checkmark Books, 1999.

Welch, Tara S. *The Elegaic Cityscape: Propertius and the Meaning of Roman Monuments.* Columbus: Ohio State University Press, 2005.

Wertheimer, Eric. *Imagined Empires: Incas, Aztecs, and the New World of American Literature, 1771–1876.* Cambridge: Cambridge University Press, 1998.

Wheatley, Edward. *Mastering Aesop: Medieval Education, Chaucer and His Followers.* Gainesville: University Press of Florida, 2000.

Whitlock, Gillian. *The Intimate Empire: Reading Women's Autobiography.* New York: Continuum, 2000.

Williams, John R. *The Life of Goethe: A Critical Biography.* London: Blackwell, 2001.

Wolffe, John. *God and Greater Britain: Religion and National Life in Britain and Ireland.* New York: Routledge, 1994.

Woodbridge, Linda, ed. *Money and the Age of Shakespeare: Essays in New Economic Criticism.* London: Macmillan, 2003.

Woodcock, George. *The Crystal Spirit: A Study of George Orwell.* Toronto: Black Rose Books, 2005.

Woodhouse, John. *Gabriele d'Annunzio: Defiant Archangel.* Oxford: Oxford University Press, 2001.

Wright, Julia M. *Ireland, India, and Nationalism in Nineteenth-Century Literature.* Cambridge: Cambridge University Press, 2007.

Wynne, Catherine. *The Colonial Conan Doyle: British Imperialism, Irish Nationalism, and the Gothic.* Westport, Conn.: Greenwood, 2004.

Yee, Gale A. *Judges and Method: New Approaches in Biblical Studies.* Minneapolis: Fortress Press, 1995.

Yu, Beongcheon. *Han Yong-un & Yi Kwang-su: Two Pioneers of Modern Korean Literature.* Detroit: Wayne State University Press, 1992.

Zipperstein, Steven J. *Imagining Russian Jewry: Memory History, Identity.* Seattle: University of Washington Press, 1999.

Zongqi Cai, ed. *Chinese Aesthetics: The Ordering of Literature, the Arts, and the Universe in the Six Dynasties.* Honolulu: University of Hawaii Press, 2004.

Zornado, Joseph L. *Inventing the Child: Culture, Ideology, and the Story of Childhood.* New York: Routledge, 2001.

INDEX

Note: **Boldface** page numbers indicate main treatment of a topic.